# BASIC ECONOMICS
a natural law approach to economics

Also available from Boundary Stone

By Clarence B. Carson
- *Basic History of the United States, six volume set*
  - Vol. 1: *The Colonial Experience, 1607-1775*
  - Vol. 2: *The Beginning of the Republic, 1774-1825*
  - Vol. 3: *The Sections and the Civil War, 1826-1877*
  - Vol. 4: *The Growth of America, 1878-1928*
  - Vol. 5: *The Welfare State, 1929-1985*
  - Vol. 6: *America in Gridlock, 1985-2001*
- *Basic History of the United States, Teachers Guide*
- *Basic American Government*

By Paul A. Cleveland
- *Understanding the Modern Culture Wars*
- *Unmasking the Sacred Lies*

By Clarence B. Carson, Paul A. Cleveland, and L. Dwayne Barney
- *The Great Utopian Delusion*

# BASIC ECONOMICS

a natural law approach to economics

Clarence B. Carson &
Paul A. Cleveland

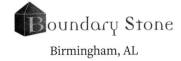

Boundary Stone
Birmingham, AL

*Basic Economics: A Natural Law Approach to Economics*, Fourth Edition
Clarence B. Carson and Paul A. Cleveland

Copyright © 1988, 2003 Clarence B. Carson; & 2010, 2018 Paul A. Cleveland

Fourth Edition: Second Printing, 2022

All rights reserved.

Scripture quotations are from *The Holy Bible, English Standard Version ® (ESV®)*, copyright ©2001 by Crossway, a publishing ministry of Good News Publishers. Used by permission. All rights reserved.

No part of this publication may be reproduced, stored in a retrieval system, or transmitted in any form by any means, electronic, mechanical, photocopy, recording, or otherwise, without prior written permission of Paul Cleveland, except for brief quotations in critical reviews or articles.

ISBN 978-0-9727401-4-2

Library of Congress Control Number: 2018938721

Cover Design: Katie Caloway Ward

*Printed in the United States of America*

For information about useful reference materials, additional reading lists, and other available resources from Boundary Stone, visit our web site:

boundarystone.org

Boundary Stone
P.O. Box 19515
Birmingham, AL 39219

# Brief Contents

## Section I  The Framework of Economics — 1
1. Why Basic Economics? — 3
2. In the Nature of Things — 11
3. Government — 23
4. Society and Morality — 39
5. Property — 49

## Section II  The Production and Distribution of Goods — 61
6. Scarcity and Economy — 63
7. How We Get What We Want — 73
8. A Medium of Exchange—Money — 87
9. The Age of Inflation — 107
10. The Market and Prices — 129
11. Failed Attempts to Control Prices — 145
12. Monopoly and Competition — 163
13. The Means of Production — 189
14. The Entrepreneur and Production — 205
15. The Distribution of Wealth — 225
16. International Trade — 241

## Section III  Politico-Economic Systems — 257
17. Manorial-Feudal System — 261
18. Mercantilism — 273
19. Free Enterprise — 289
20. Corporatism — 309
21. Welfarism — 331
22. Communism — 347

# Contents

## Section I
## The Framework of Economics — 1

### 1 Why Basic Economics? — 3
1.1 In the Beginning . . . — 3
1.2 Questions Addressed by Economics — 4
1.3 A Brief History of Economic Thought — 5
1.4 Broad Framework for Economics — 7
Study Guide — 9

### 2 In the Nature of Things — 11
2.1 The Effect of Evolutionary Ideas — 11
2.2 Three Levels of Reality — 12
2.3 The Metaphysical Level — 13
2.4 The Role of Reason — 14
2.5 Human Nature Described — 15
2.6 The Natural Order of the Universe — 15
2.7 The Natural Order and the Roots of Economics — 16
Budget Project — 20
Study Guide — 21

### 3 Government — 23
3.1 The Necessity for Government — 24
3.2 The Nature of Government — 25
3.3 How Government Impacts the Economy — 26
    3.3.1 Minimizing the Impact of Taxes — 27
    3.3.2 Describing Just Taxation — 29
    3.3.3 Taxes That Are Commonly Used — 31
3.4 Constitutional Limits on Government — 32
    3.4.1 Prohibiting Certain Actions — 33
    3.4.2 Separating Powers — 35
    3.4.3 Limiting Involvement in Economy — 36
Study Guide — 37

## 4 Society and Morality — 39
- 4.1 The Necessity of Morality — 39
- 4.2 Morality without Authority — 40
- 4.3 Imparting Morality — 41
- 4.4 Morality Outranks Economy — 42
- 4.5 Political Economy — 42
- 4.6 Morality in Government Policy — 43
- 4.7 Religion and Morality — 43
- 4.8 The Problem of Moral Positivism — 44
- 4.9 Jeremy Bentham and Utilitarianism — 45
- Study Guide — 47

## 5 Property — 49
- 5.1 Varieties of Property — 50
- 5.2 Origins of Property — 52
- 5.3 Legal Protection of Property — 55
- 5.4 Assault on Property — 56
- Study Guide — 59

# Section II
# The Production and Distribution of Goods — 61

## 6 Scarcity and Economy — 63
- 6.1 Economy — 63
- 6.2 Scarcity — 64
- 6.3 Allegations about Surpluses — 67
- 6.4 Fallacy of Abundance — 69
- Study Guide — 71

## 7 How We Get What We Want — 73
- 7.1 Acquisition by Gift — 74
- 7.2 Producing for Ourselves — 75
- 7.3 Acquisition by Exchange — 77
  - 7.3.1 Auction in the Market — 77
  - 7.3.2 Advantages of Market Exchange — 79
- 7.4 Theft by Government for Redistribution — 81
- Study Guide — 85

## 8 A Medium of Exchange—Money — 87
- 8.1 The Function of Money — 88
  - 8.1.1 As a Medium of Exchange — 88
  - 8.1.2 As a Standard of Calculation — 90
  - 8.1.3 As a Store of Wealth — 91
- 8.2 The Origin of Money — 93
  - 8.2.1 Gold and Silver as Money — 94
  - 8.2.2 Gresham's Law and Government Interference — 95
- 8.3 Government and Money — 96
- 8.4 Paper Money — 98
  - 8.4.1 Origins of Debt Money in Europe — 99
  - 8.4.2 Fractional Reserve Banking — 101
- Study Guide — 105

## 9 The Age of Inflation — 107
- 9.1 Eighteenth Century Inflationist Schemes — 108
  - 9.1.1 John Law's Mississippi Stock Inflation — 108
  - 9.1.2 The Continental Currency Inflation — 111
  - 9.1.3 The French Revolution Inflation — 113
  - 9.1.4 Lessons Learned — 115
- 9.2 The Twentieth Century Age of Credit and Inflation — 116
  - 9.2.1 Paving The Way for the Federal Reserve — 117
  - 9.2.2 The Federal Reserve Act — 119
- 9.3 Abandoning the Gold Standard — 120
  - 9.3.1 Boom–Bust Cycles — 121
  - 9.3.2 Living on Credit — 122
  - 9.3.3 Federal Reserve Notes as Money — 125
- Study Guide — 127

## 10 The Market and Prices — 129
- 10.1 Who or What Determines Price? — 130
- 10.2 Diversity of Products and Prices — 131
- 10.3 Going Prices — 132
- 10.4 Factors that Determine Prices — 133
  - 10.4.1 Supply — 133
  - 10.4.2 Demand — 134
  - 10.4.3 Elasticity — 137
  - 10.4.4 Taxes — 138
  - 10.4.5 Monetary Inflation — 138
  - 10.4.6 Competition — 139
- 10.5 Wages — 141
- Study Guide — 143

## 11 Failed Attempts to Control Prices — 145
- 11.1 Protective Tariffs — 146
- 11.2 Labor Unions — 149
  - 11.2.1 Government Support for Unions — 153
  - 11.2.2 The Impact of Wage Controls — 156
- 11.3 Consumer Prices — 157
- Study Guide — 161

## 12 Monopoly and Competition — 163
- 12.1 Monopoly — 164
  - 12.1.1 The United States Postal Service (USPS) — 165
  - 12.1.2 The Tennessee Valley Authority (TVA) — 166
  - 12.1.3 Government Grants of Monopoly — 167
  - 12.1.4 Private Monopolies — 169
- 12.2 Competition — 171
  - 12.2.1 First Class Mail Delivery — 172
  - 12.2.2 Organization of Petroleum Exporting Countries — 172
  - 12.2.3 Railroads — 173
  - 12.2.4 Business Strategies to Lessen Competition — 176
- 12.3 Government Regulation of Monopoly and Competition — 178
  - 12.3.1 The Sherman Antitrust Act — 179
  - 12.3.2 Rate Fixing the Railroads — 180
  - 12.3.3 Flood of Regulatory Legislation — 181
  - 12.3.4 Government Monopoly of Schooling — 184
- Study Guide — 187

## 13 The Means of Production — 189
- 13.1 Land — 190
  - 13.1.1 Natural Resources — 190
  - 13.1.2 Common Ownership of Land — 191
- 13.2 Labor — 192
  - 13.2.1 Labor as a Class of People — 194
  - 13.2.2 Clarifying the Meaning of Labor — 194
- 13.3 Capital — 195
  - 13.3.1 Fixed Capital — 195
  - 13.3.2 Circulating Capital — 196
  - 13.3.3 The Process of the Use of Capital — 197
  - 13.3.4 Saving and Investment — 198
  - 13.3.5 The Multiplier Effect of Capital — 199
  - 13.3.6 The Importance of Capital — 200
- Study Guide — 203

## 14 The Entrepreneur and Production — 205
- 14.1 The Role of the Entrepreneur — 206
- 14.2 Raising the Money — 208
  - 14.2.1 Partnerships — 208
  - 14.2.2 Corporations — 209
  - 14.2.3 The Stock Market — 211
  - 14.2.4 Lending Institutions — 213
- 14.3 Organizing to Produce — 214
  - 14.3.1 The Factory System — 214
  - 14.3.2 The Downside of the Factory System — 216
  - 14.3.3 Home Based Businesses — 217
  - 14.3.4 Segregating Commercial and Residential Areas — 219
  - 14.3.5 Economies of Scale and Specialization — 220
  - 14.3.6 Managers — 221
- Study Guide — 223

## 15 The Distribution of Wealth — 225
- 15.1 Rent — 228
- 15.2 Wages — 230
- 15.3 Interest — 231
  - 15.3.1 Time Preference — 233
  - 15.3.2 Impact of Government on Interest Rates — 234
- 15.4 Profit and Loss — 234
- 15.5 Inheritance — 237
- Study Guide — 239

## 16 International Trade — 241
- 16.1 Advantages of International Trade — 243
- 16.2 Money and Trade — 244
  - 16.2.1 Precious Metals — 244
  - 16.2.2 Fiat Money in Trade — 246
  - 16.2.3 The International Monetary Fund (IMF) — 248
  - 16.2.4 Government Obstacles to Trade — 248
  - 16.2.5 The Impact of Socialism on International Trade — 251
  - 16.2.6 Effects of Internal Redistributionist Policies — 252
- Study Guide — 255

# Section III
# Politico-Economic Systems                                                257

## 17 Manorial-Feudal System                                               261
- 17.1 Feudalism                                                          262
- 17.2 The Manor                                                          264
- 17.3 The Revival of Trade                                               266
- 17.4 The Growth of Towns                                                267
- 17.5 Medieval Guilds                                                    268
- 17.6 The Lasting Impact of Medieval Ways                                269
- Study Guide                                                             271

## 18 Mercantilism                                                         273
- 18.1 The Theory of Mercantilism                                         275
- 18.2 Mercantilism in England                                            276
  - 18.2.1 By Granting Monopolies                                         277
  - 18.2.2 By Passing Laws                                                278
- 18.3 Mercantilism in France                                             279
  - 18.3.1 Prior to Colbert                                               280
  - 18.3.2 Colbertism                                                     282
- 18.4 Mercantilism in Colonial America                                   283
- 18.5 The Consequences of Mercantilism                                   284
- Study Guide                                                             287

## 19 Free Enterprise                                                      289
- 19.1 Economic Freedom                                                   291
- 19.2 Free Enterprise in Britain                                         293
  - 19.2.1 The Industrial Surge                                           295
  - 19.2.2 The Workshop of the World                                      296
  - 19.2.3 How British Workers Fared                                      298
- 19.3 Free Enterprise in the United States                               300
  - 19.3.1 1789–1860                                                      302
  - 19.3.2 After the Civil War Through World War I                        303
- 19.4 Conclusions                                                        305
- Study Guide                                                             307

## 20 Corporatism                                                          309
- 20.1 The Meaning of Capitalism                                          309
- 20.2 Private Corporatism                                                312
  - 20.2.1 Corporatist Legacy of Alexander Hamilton                       312
  - 20.2.2 Federally Chartered Banks                                      313
  - 20.2.3 Corporatism of Early Republicans                               314
  - 20.2.4 Increasing Use of Regulation                                   316
  - 20.2.5 Corporatism of the New Deal                                    317
  - 20.2.6 Entanglement of Business with Politics                         318
  - 20.2.7 Corporatism in the Farm Industry                               320
  - 20.2.8 In Sweden                                                      324
- 20.3 State Corporatism                                                  325
- Study Guide                                                             329

## 21 Welfarism — 331
- 21.1 Socialism in Great Britain — 333
  - 21.1.1 The Labour Party in Power — 334
  - 21.1.2 The Failure of British Socialism — 337
  - 21.1.3 The Repercussions of the British Failure — 338
- 21.2 Welfarism in the United States — 339
  - 21.2.1 Social Security — 339
  - 21.2.2 Ever-Increasing Welfarist Programs — 341
  - 21.2.3 The Corporatism of Welfarism — 342
  - 21.2.4 Negative Consequences of Welfarism — 343
- Study Guide — 345

## 22 Communism — 347
- 22.1 Communist Ideology and Practice — 348
- 22.2 The Centrally Planned Economy — 351
- 22.3 The Production of Goods — 353
- 22.4 The Distribution of Goods — 357
- Study Guide — 361

## Glossary — 363

## Index — 373

# Section I
# The Framework of Economics

## Chapters

1. Why Basic Economics?   3
2. In the Nature of Things   11
3. Government   23
4. Society and Morality   39
5. Property   49

*There is only one difference between a bad economist and a good one: the bad economist confines himself to the visible effect; the good economist takes into account both the effect that can be seen and those effects that must be foreseen.*
**Frédéric Bastiat**

*The art of economics consists of looking not merely at the immediate but at the longer effects of any act or policy; it consists in tracing the consequences of that policy not merely for one group but for all groups.*
**Henry Hazlitt**

**CHAPTER CONTENT**

1.1 In the Beginning... 3
1.2 Questions Addressed by Economics 4
1.3 A Brief History of Economic Thought 5
1.4 Broad Framework for Economics 7

# 1 Why Basic Economics?

**The Dominion Mandate**
And God blessed them. And God said to them, "Be fruitful and multiply and fill the earth and subdue it, and have dominion over the fish of the sea and over the birds of the heavens and over every living thing that moves on the earth."

**Genesis 1:28**

"Why do we have to have money?" a five-year-old girl asked. It was clear both from her manner in asking the question and her surrounding remarks that she was not interested in learning about the function of money. That is, she was not interested in an account of the origin of money or a discussion of the great convenience of having a medium of exchange. She was concerned that there is a price to pay for the things she wants; that they cost money, and that she did not have enough. To put it another way, she was asking why she could not have whatever she wanted without any cost attached to it. No doubt, hers was an age-old question. Pushed to answer the question briefly, most of us would probably say, "Well, that's just the way it is." But there is more to this answer. It is in the nature of things. That is, economics is built into the nature of the very world we inhabit.

## 1.1 In the Beginning . . .

In terms of the origin of her problem, the Bible gives an answer in the book of Genesis. After God created Adam and Eve, He placed them in the Garden of Eden and gave them a mission. There are several observations to be noted in the description of life in its perfect state before the Fall. Eden was a garden, rather than a wilderness. Planning had gone into its design to provide fully for the needs of its inhabitants. All their material needs could be met by the numerous plants that grew there and the bountiful fruit they produced. Nevertheless, the man and woman still had to tend to the Garden to produce the things that they wanted. Beyond that in Genesis 1:28, in what is known as the **Dominion Mandate**, they were instructed to venture out beyond the Garden and to turn the whole earth into a garden by taking dominion over it. This project could only be accomplished by work. Thus, even in the condition of moral perfection, work was instituted to achieve a purpose. The reality that we must work to produce things and, thus, that there will always be a cost connected to

**Dominion Mandate**—as recorded in Genesis 1:28, after God created Adam and Eve and placed them in the Garden of Eden, he commanded them and their descendants to take dominion of the whole earth.

> **Getting the Point . . .**
>
> What are some differences between a garden and a wilderness?

**good (n.)**—a commodity or service that can be utilized to satisfy human wants and that has exchange value; in other words, the means that we use to achieve our ends.

There are four necessary conditions for something to be considered an economic good:

- the existence of a human desire
- the commodity or service must be useful to the satisfaction of that desire
- the causal connection (that it is useful to satisfy a desire) must be known
- humans must have command over the commodity or service to direct it to productive use.

Example: crude oil was not always thought of as a good, but was once thought of as merely a pollutant.

**public policy**—programs of action that proceed from legislation. Policy is set by government action; first by the legislature that passes laws, then by the executive branch that executes laws, and finally by the judicial branch that judges whether the law is upheld. The limits of what the government could do were explicitly restricted by the U.S. Constitution. The basic underlying assumptions about human nature and economic principles will determine the results of policy.

**economics**—the systematic study of the effective production of those goods that are most wanted with the least use of the scarce resources available.

**economic principles**—God's built-in features of well-functioning human interaction in the material world.

**universal principles**—principles that apply to all people, in all places, at all times.

the things we want, has always been a part of the human condition. Since humans are finite creatures and cannot do everything they might desire to do at once, they must choose their individual courses of action to accomplish their own unique parts of this grand project.

But something else happened. There was one tree in the Garden whose fruit they were warned not to eat lest they die. Eve disobeyed, ate the fruit, and also gave some of it to Adam to eat. As a result, God judged them and cast them out of the Garden. Moreover, He cursed the earth so that it would no longer fully cooperate with their efforts. "By the sweat of your face," He said, "you shall eat bread." In short, thereafter their labor would not be as effective as it otherwise would have been. That is, from this point forward mankind faced increasing difficulty in achieving their intended purpose since the creation would not respond as well as it was originally designed. Thus, the matter of work became more complicated. If we followed these ideas through to their many implications, it would lead us toward the answer of why we cannot have what we want without giving up something else we may also want.

## 1.2 Questions Addressed by Economics

Economics does not attempt to answer the question of why things are the way that they are. It does, however, give help in answering a whole range of other questions. It deals with an essential and pressing aspect of life. Its subject matter is the production and distribution of **goods** and all that is entailed in it. Economics deals with such questions as who gets what? How are prices determined? How do markets operate? What motivates people to produce? What goes into production? And even what makes certain things goods? Since this is its field, it also treats many matters that deal with **public policy**. Indeed, no single subject appears to occupy more attention in the issues that arise and tends to divide people more than economic questions. Nor is it too much to say that how governments deal with these questions is often a matter of life and death and can entail liberty or serfdom.

That is not to suggest that economists do, or should be the only ones to, make public policy decisions touching upon the economy. Rather, it is to suggest that all of us who participate in public policy decisions need to be versed to some degree in the subject of economics. That is not only the case concerning public policy but also in private matters that have to do with ourselves, our families, and our business concerns.

This work is intended as an introduction to economics, to the principles of economics, and to the issues and problems that economics touches. It is a basic work. It does not intend to deal with the complexities that arise at the more sophisticated levels of the discipline, to confound understanding with numerous charts, to present econometric models, nor to introduce accounting or statistics problems. These may all have their places, but they are not in a basic economics.

In the simplest terms, **economics** is a study of the thrifty use of scarce resources to satisfy human wants. God created an orderly universe, and there are discoverable principles that govern how systems operate. **Economic principles**, so far as they are valid, are **universal** in their application. That is, they apply to all peoples at all times: to Australians as well as to Americans, to Englishmen as well as to the Japanese, to those who live on the smallest most remote island as well as to the inhabitants of the largest cities. That is, they exist in the nature of things and have their foundations in human nature and the nature of human relationships. That is not to say that economic principles are well known to all peoples in all places at all times. Nor even to say that they are well known by people generally anywhere at any time, though the degree to which they are known certainly does vary. It is rather to say that in this respect the principles of economics resemble the laws of physics and chemistry, though lacking both the measurable precision and the widespread agreement that prevails for some of chemistry and physics.

Any given study of economics does have a cultural context. It must be written in some language or languages and thus will be colored by the usages of language. It is apt to be influenced by the prevailing popularity of ideas at any given time and place. Moreover, each individual has his own outlook, manner, prejudices, and assumptions that will have bearing on what he writes. Even so, the principles of economics, so far as they are valid, are universal, for they are derived from underlying conditions, which are themselves universals. These frameworks will be further developed as we proceed in the following chapters.

## 1.3 A Brief History of Economic Thought

Economics is a fairly new subject to make its appearance in schools and colleges. It did not become a full-fledged academic discipline until the last half of the nineteenth century, although a considerable body of thought on it had been developed over the three centuries preceding that. While economics is generally taught in many high schools today, many college students manage to evade the study of it. It is taught in most colleges and universities, although often as an elective course. It should be emphasized, however, that many people have grasped some of the principles of economics long before it was taught in the schools and colleges, much as people have known more or less of astronomy whether they learned it formally or not. The teaching of economics formally has been a mixed blessing. Teaching economics in schools just barely preceded two other developments: the development of sociology and the spread of socialist doctrines. For Europeans especially, the study of economics has been entangled with sociology, and socialist ideas have greatly altered what is often taught as economics. In American colleges and universities, there is great disagreement as to whether economics should be placed in schools of business, or social sciences.

Moreover, economists often differ heatedly with one another. There are a number of **"schools"** and persuasions of economics. There are Marxists, Fabians (gradualist socialists), Austrians, Keynesians, classicists, neoclassicists, institutionalists, mercantilists, syndicalists, and those who write of Christian economics. Besides which, in even less precise terms, there are interventionists, socialists, monetarists, free traders, nationalists, redistributionists, advocates of corporatism, and an assortment of other isms. Some are proud of their persuasion. Others do not avow any particular persuasion but may be tagged by others. In an important sense, there are probably as many or more varieties of economics in the world as there are ideologies.

The starting point for the study of economics is of fundamental importance in the identification of economic principles and their application. While there may be a tacit agreement among economists on certain principles, one's underlying starting assumptions can lead to a marked difference of opinion as to how we should act upon them. For example, some economists assume the law should be based on a cost/benefit basis without regard to ultimate moral principles. While they might affirm that a free economy is the best one, they do so for an entirely different reason from those who begin with a natural rights foundation. Usually, it is not

---

**Getting the Point...**

List a few universal principles you have learned from other subject areas.

What would be the consequences of acting in such a way that you are trying to deny or "break" them?

Can you think of any universal principle that a person could break?

---

**"schools" of economic thought**—general categories of ideas related to the application of economic principles. This book is based in the Austrian school of thought because it is based on the natural law premise. Other schools you may hear of during the course are Keynesian, monetarist, and Marxian.

**anarchists**—people who believe that there is no need for government.

**totalitarian**—state where government uses force to control any aspect of life that the leader might decree. In an economic sense, central planning would be used to determine the production and distribution of goods and would displace the market.

**theology**—the study of God.

**philosophy**—the study of God's creation..

that economists disagree on the economic principles themselves. It is typically disagreement on how important they are and what political application, if any, should be made of them. It may be easier to begin to grasp the lines of difference by describing the two extremes. At one extreme are those who believe in the autonomy of economics and who tend to be political **anarchists**, i.e., doubt that government is essential or think it can be replaced entirely by the market. At the other extreme are **totalitarian** economists (usually Marxists or communists but also including democratic socialists and some Keynesians). The totalitarians would have government control the production and distribution of goods, and would, therefore, displace the market with central planning. They seek to solve every problem by government-directed analysis to determine what laws and regulations should be put into place that would supposedly make things cheaper. In reality, this planning only results in shoddy goods and services that are unaffordable, and often simply unavailable.

To anyone who has ever become enthralled with the free market and theories of how it works, it is easy to see how they might proceed to become anarchists. This is made easier if they conceive of economics as autonomous, that is, as having no subordination to **theology** or **philosophy**. In short, they conceive of a science that can stand on its own philosophical feet, so to speak. The next step would be to contrive a philosophy for economics (which might, incidentally, be supposed to embrace other aspects of life as well). This was the tendency of the English utilitarians, Jeremy Bentham and John Stuart Mill, as well as the Austrians, notably Ludwig von Mises, though none of these was anarchistic. Having established the autonomy of economics as a science, it is easy enough by focusing on the working of the market to imagine that government is unnecessary, that people could provide for all their wants and needs in the market.

Totalitarian economics goes to the opposite extreme. It tends to vest all control over the economy in government, to have government control all productive property, command production, and determine how the product shall be distributed. Such a system is necessarily tyrannical since it denies people generally any but the most remote control over their own economic affairs. Moreover, it tends to be not only tyrannical in all economic matters, but in other spheres of life as well. Modern totalitarian governments have demonstrated well the thesis that where there is no economic freedom there is hardly any freedom at all.

This work should be placed somewhere between the anarchistic and totalitarian position. To say that it is simply in the middle would be to talk not only nonsense but to abandon principle as if it did not rely on other principles. That there are principles that are neither anarchistic nor totalitarian will be one of the theses of this work. These principles are not drawn from either anarchism or totalitarianism. They have a much sounder and longer established basis. They are principles rooted in the **Greco-Roman** and the **Judeo-Christian traditions**—that is, in Western Civilization. In this framework, economics is not an autonomous study or discipline. Rather, it is subordinate to moral and philosophical truths that do not simply exist to promote some version of economics. Government is not supposed to be omnipotent or omni-competent to direct all human affairs. One principle, among many others, looms out of that long experience. It is what may well be called the **doctrine of limits**. It is that humans are limited and fallible creatures, that all of their organizations, institutions, and structures are affected by these limitations; that the power and sway of anything must be limited by design; that government, above all, must be severely limited.

These are, of course, only the most general terms for moving toward setting out some principles of economics. They tell us little specifically

**Greco-Roman tradition**—Western Civilization draws its roots from Greece and Rome. Specifically, Greek and Roman philosophers used reason and observation to find universal principles, from which, they attempted to build their philosophy.

**Judeo-Christian tradition**—tradition pertaining to Jewish and Christian heritage. Specifically, that all humans are fallen, guilty of sin, and desperately in need of a Savior.

**doctrine of limits**—because all humans are fallible, all the organizations, institutions, and structures that we create will also be flawed.

about the sort of economics that is to follow and something more on that needs to be said as well. Perhaps the best way to describe it is to say that it is an Anglo-American economics. To call it Anglo-American (it is not much distinct from classical economics) is not meant to suggest that it is ethnic, nor that it excludes work done by those of other nationalities. Rather, it is to suggest that it came out of the English traditions that provided the foundation for the rapid economic growth and prosperity that began in the nineteenth century.

> **Doctrine of Limits**
> Humans are limited and fallible creatures, and every area of their being is impacted by the fall. Because of this, all organizations, institutions, and structures are also affected by these limitations, and the power and sway of all of them must be limited by design. Government above all must be severely limited because of its monopoly on the use of force.

That is, it is an economics written in that strain of thought that began to take shape in England in the late seventeenth century with John Locke, among others, and came to fruition in the eighteenth and nineteenth centuries with Adam Smith (who will be discussed more fully in the next chapter), Pelatiah Webster, David Ricardo, and was added to by many others. It is an economics nurtured by the natural law philosophy that recognizes the individual's natural rights of life, liberty, and property. It is an economics arising in the framework of the unfettered spread of Christianity. Anglo-American economics is obviously economics phrased in the English language and given form within that culture and tradition. Again, it must be said, economic principles are universal, so far as they are valid, but they can only be put into effect—indeed, they are apt only to be believed—in a cultural soil attuned to them. In any case, economic principles, when separated from their cultural, moral, and philosophical framework, wither and die.

## 1.4 Broad Framework for Economics

Why not a Christian Economics? Well, why not a Christian Political Science? Why not a Christian Biology? Why not a Christian Physics? Why not a Christian Chemistry—and so on through all academic disciplines and fields of study? We might as well ask, why not a Christian Science? In fact, there is a sect that goes by the name of Christian Science, which provides one of the clues why a Christian Economics might be a dubious proposition. The main reason is that Christianity is

> **John Locke (1632–1704)**
> English philosopher, with a Puritan background. He was much embroiled in controversy and sometimes in politics. His most famous philosophical work is an Essay Concerning Human Understanding. In this work, he argued that our knowledge is not innate but comes to us from sense impressions. He was an early (and late) advocate of religious toleration and wrote on such subjects as education, economics, political theory, and religion. Probably his greatest impact on the world was the natural rights doctrine.
>
> **Peletiah Webster (1726–1795)**
> American economist and political thinker. He was born in Connecticut, educated in New England, and became a Congregational minister. Later, Webster left the ministry to go into business. He emerged during the constitution making period as a spokesman and writer for free enterprise and free markets. As one encyclopedia says, "Webster's contributions to the Union were his cogent arguments for the Constitution, and his vigorously stated views on money, credit, taxation, and trade."

not primarily concerned with economics, or science, or physics, or with many other fields of learning or disciplines. Its concern is primarily with the eternal, the Revelation of God to man, the norms for man, and his redemption. In truth, the chief message of the Scriptures is the gospel. It is God's revelation of how people can be saved from their rebellion against God and against His natural order of creation. The study of economics deals with the mundane and the earthly. It is concerned with the production and distribution of goods, and with the discovery and setting forth of the principles that apply to this realm of human activity.

That is not to suggest that Christianity is irrelevant to economics, or any other aspect of life. Rather, Christianity, or any other transcendent religion, may best be thought of as the overarching framework within which the study of economics takes place. The Scriptures do not enumerate or explain the principles of economics. These must be discovered by reason and investigation in the same way we would study any other subject. Thus, we are proceeding here on the idea that God has revealed Himself in His Word (the Bible) and in His Work (Creation). Science is the study of Creation and economics is one of its subjects. Theology is the study of God, and the Scriptures are God's self-revelation to mankind. While some truths about economics can be derived from the Scriptures, that is not their primary purpose.

The main point here, however, is to demonstrate that economies and economics exist in contexts or broader frameworks. It is possible to discuss and study the market as if it has an existence all its own and is separate from other and sometimes higher considerations and determinations. But it is well that we keep in mind that such examinations are **abstractions** from the political, moral, and natural setting within which they always exist. When economics deals only with these abstractions, it can never be much more than a greenhouse plant, so to speak.

Having dealt with the framework broadly, it is time now to flesh it out with particulars.

---

**David Ricardo (1772–1823)**

English economist who made one of the earliest attempts to systematize economics. He was born in London and as a youth went to his father's business on the stock exchange there. By the time he had reached the age of 25 he had sufficient wealth to turn his attention to study and writing. Ricardo read and was greatly influenced by Adam Smith's *Wealth of Nations*. In consequence, he gave his attention to the systematic study of economics and is one of the main figures in the school of Classical Economics. Although he wrote treatises on a variety of aspects of economics, by far his most important work was *Principles of Economics*. He set economics on the path to become an academic discipline.

---

**abstractions**—an attempt to model or simplify some real world phenomenon to a general quality or characteristic, apart from concrete realities, specific objects, or actual instances in order to promote a better understanding.

---

*It is no crime to be ignorant of economics, which is, after all, a specialized discipline and one that most people consider to be a 'dismal science.' But it is totally irresponsible to have a loud and vociferous opinion on economic subjects while remaining in this state of ignorance.*

**Murray Rothbard**

# Study Guide for:

# 1 Why Basic Economics?

## Chapter Summary

Economics is a study of the thrifty use of scarce resources to satisfy human wants. Since these wants are unlimited while the resources available to satisfy them are scarce, choices must be made. Thus, economics involves the study of the production and distribution of goods and services, the operation of markets, an examination of prices, and an analysis of public policy. The aim of this study is the identification of underlying universal principles with which all people, regardless of cultural differences, must learn to live.

Though there is considerable agreement among economists about the basic principles of economics, there is widespread disagreement as to how these principles apply to public policy. When applied in political systems, the results range from totalitarian to anarchistic. One is therefore tempted to classify all economic schools of thought as lying somewhere along this spectrum. Yet such a classification is naive since it asserts that only the tension between these extremes informs the political debate, but this is not the case.

Economics is not an autonomous subject. It is subordinate to the principles of theology and philosophy. In the study of Western Civilization, the Judeo-Christian and Greco-Roman traditions provide the background within which the study of economics proceeds. These traditions include a natural law philosophy and an understanding of the natural rights of the individual. This understanding of life and the environment provides the informing framework within which it is possible to identify the principles of economics that promote growth and prosperity. It is also possible to compare the outcomes from this understanding of the world to those of competing theologies and philosophies to clarify sound economic principles.

## Points of Emphasis

1. The Creation, Dominion Mandate, and Fall all have implications in understanding economics. That a purposeful God intentionally created an orderly universe for His glory, that He created each human to bear His image as he takes dominion in creation, and that man through the Fall brought sin into the world all provide the foundation for our study.

2. Work was not a result of the Fall. It was part of God's perfect original Creation design. It was made more difficult by the Fall.

3. Valid economic principles are universal. That is, they apply to all people in all places at all times.

4. There are many "schools" of economic thought. They differ greatly in how economic principles should be applied politically. They all generally fall somewhere within two extremes: anarchists and totalitarians. Anarchists hold that government is unnecessary and should not intervene in human interactions. Totalitarians hold that government should always step into every supposed problem situation with central planning and regulation.

5. Because all humans are fallible creatures, all human organizations, institutions, and structures will have weaknesses and must be designed so as to limit their power and sway.

6. Economics must be understood within a broader philosophical context where it is subordinate to higher principles of theology and philosophy.

## Identification

1. Dominion Mandate
2. good (n.)
3. public policy
4. economics
5. economic principles
6. universal principles
7. "schools" of economic thought
8. anarchists
9. totalitarian
10. theology
11. philosophy
12. Greco-Roman tradition
13. Judeo-Christian tradition
14. doctrine of limits
15. abstraction

## Review Questions

1. In the Genesis creation account, when is human work mentioned? Why is this significant?
2. Describe some similarities and some differences in the nature of work before and after the fall. List some words used in Genesis 3 to describe the difference..
3. Why is discovering universal principles important?
4. What are the consequences of trying to "break," deny, or disobey these principles?
5. What are some practical reasons that it is important to discover principles of economics?
6. Briefly, describe where economists agree and disagree about the principles of economics.
7. Briefly, describe the two extremes of thought on the political application of economic principles.
8. Taking the doctrine of limits into account, what would you have to conclude about any legislative answers our Congress designs?
9. Why is a written constitution important to the functioning of a nation?

## Activity

"The worst thing that can happen to a good cause is, not to be skillfully attacked, but to be ineptly defended."
~ **Frédéric Bastiat**

1. In the study guide for many chapters you will be asked to prepare a case for or against a position on an issue. In preparation for that, do some research on writing a position paper, and work with your teacher to establish some guidelines.

## For Further Study

1. Hugh Welchel, "Are there Economic Implications in the Creation Story?," The Institute for Faith, Work & Economics, June 29, 2017, https://tifwe.org/are-there-economic-implications-in-the-creation-story/.

> **CHAPTER CONTENT**
>
> 2.1 The Effect of Evolutionary Ideas     11
> 2.2 Three Levels of Reality     12
> 2.3 The Metaphysical Level     13
> 2.4 The Role of Reason     14
> 2.5 Human Nature Described     15
> 2.6 The Natural Order of the Universe     15
> 2.7 The Natural Order and the Roots of Economics     16

# 2 IN THE NATURE OF THINGS

The phrase, "in the nature of things," is not heard very often any more. Yet at the time of the making of the United States Constitution, it was commonplace. That is so because we have been in an epoch in which we have shifted our focus and attention away from the nature of things. There are fashions in prevailing ideas and beliefs as there are fashions in clothing, though the former fashions do not change so rapidly as the latter. In the intellectual realm, and eventually among people more generally, over the past hundred years or so the focus has been upon the changing rather than the enduring. As a result, little attention is focused upon any enduring nature of things.

## 2.1 The Effect of Evolutionary Ideas

The focus upon the changing was given its greatest impetus by **evolutionary ideas**. Universal evolution, as described by Herbert Spencer, and biological evolution, as advanced by Charles Darwin, tended to the view that all was undergoing change. Change, such as was ascribed to the species, occurred over great spans of time, and the period of the existence of life on earth was pushed backward millions of years to allow for these exceedingly slow changes. Everything was supposed to be undergoing change. For societal reformers who bought the evolutionary hypothesis, everything could be changed, and in the popular mind, change became the focus of attention, without much regard to any great span of time in which changes might be imperceptible.

The tendency of this focus on change was to undercut the basis for any fixed principles of economics. Indeed, it is logical to conclude that if everything is changing there are no fixed principles or laws. According to this view, there is no such thing as human nature, natural laws or principles. There is no order except such as people temporarily impose on things. There are, to the case in point, no principles of economics.

The kindest thing that can be said of this view is that it is the result of a large oversight, the result of a nearly exclusive focus on the changing. It runs counter not only to the major conclusions of Western philosophy but also to insights that go back before any extensive philosophies were written. This view of flux, if

**evolutionary ideas**—view that everything is always undergoing change. Some changes take longer than others, but everything changes. These ideas undercut any fixed principles or absolutes because those principles would also be subject to change.

carried out to its logical conclusion, would undercut all science and most of the great body of learning that has accumulated through the centuries. Happily, most of us are not that logical in applying prevailing assumptions, and many people are not sheep enough to be herded into prevailing intellectual fashion. To put it another way, the view that all things are changing is a truncated and willfully blind view of reality. Most of us still believe that things have a nature, even though we might not be able to take the insight very far unaided.

In any case, this work proceeds upon the premise that there is a natural order in the universe, that things, including man, do indeed have a nature, and that all creation is informed by, and can be in tune with, that order. It will not do, however, merely to assert this premise. In view of the widespread explicit or implicit challenge to it today, it is necessary to make as clear as possible what is meant by a nature and how we gain knowledge of it. To do this, it is necessary to delve a little into philosophy, not to invent some philosophic concept but to set forth in an organized way the philosophical ground of our inquiry.

> **Natural Order**
> This work proceeds upon the premise that there is a natural order in the universe, that things, including man, do indeed have a nature, and that all creation is informed by, and can be in tune with, that order.

## 2.2 Three Levels of Reality

To go about this, let us populate the house of philosophy a little, so to speak. There are at least three levels of reality. Most of us acknowledge these in one way or another in our language, though a variety of words are used to apply to them. The three levels, in ascending order, are the physical, the **metaphysical**, and the spiritual. In human terms, these may be thought of, in ascending order, as having their expression as body, mind, and soul. Knowledge in each of these three levels comes in different ways. Again in ascending order, knowledge comes through the senses, through reason, and by revelation and faith, to which feeling and intuition may be adjuncts. In terms of duration, which is of considerable concern here, the three levels, in ascending order, belong to the realms of the changing, the enduring, and the eternal. They can be charted in this fashion:

**metaphysical**—metaphysical reality is discovered by reason and empirical observation. It is enduring, meaning it lasts over time. Metaphysical realities exist between the physical world that changes and the spiritual world that is eternal. This reality is where we find natural law, which gives an underlying order to the way things work.

| Levels of Reality | Human Expression | Knowledge Comes by | Duration |
|---|---|---|---|
| Spiritual | Soul | Revelation | Eternal |
| Metaphysical | Mind | Reason | Enduring |
| Physical | Body | Senses | Changing |

(Some may notice that the above formulation is Trinitarian and may suppose that it is derived from or related to the doctrine of the Trinity. The thought has occurred to others as well, but we will neither offer further clarification nor press the point, except perhaps to say that man's eternal standing is subject to his position with respect to the gospel message of

Jesus Christ. In other words, one's spiritual standing depends on a real ongoing relationship with God through salvation in Christ.)

## 2.3 The Metaphysical Level

Our main concern here is with the second level of reality, that is, with metaphysics. The term is not used much, if at all any longer. Indeed, it has become a term of derision, as a synonym for fuzzy, vague, or ethereal. A definition of the word in terms of its origins or roots does not help much either. It means, simply, after (or beyond) the physical, and was used in that way originally to refer to a category of writings by Aristotle. It is well enough, so far as it goes, to think of metaphysics as beyond the physical, but that is not very illuminating. One dictionary says that it "treats of first principles" and of "the structure of the universe." But the word is not being used here simply to refer to a branch of philosophy but rather to a level of reality. It refers to a level of reality between the spiritual and the physical that is at least an enduring realm that can be reached only by reason, not by the senses, for it cannot be seen, felt, tasted, smelled, nor heard. It is the level of underlying or **natural law**, of that which gives form and order to actual classes of physical beings, the structural part of reality, so to speak.

Let us begin with a fairly familiar idea, the law of gravity, to get at the meaning. The law of freely falling bodies was formulated by Galileo as a result of his famous experiments from the Leaning Tower of Pisa. He discovered that apart from any wind resistance, all bodies accelerate at a uniform rate when dropped to the earth. Differences in weight have nothing to do with the rate of acceleration. Newton used this and other data in formulating the law of gravity. It says that "any two bodies in the universe attract each other in proportion to the product of their masses and inversely as the square of their distance apart."

Our main concern is not with what gravity is, or what Newton thought it was. For our purposes, gravity is simply a way of describing the attraction between or among heavenly bodies. Our concern is with giving an illustration of the level of metaphysics with a well-known natural law, so we can examine where, what, and how natural laws are apprehended. Clearly, the law in question cannot be seen, heard, felt, smelled, or tasted. That is, it cannot be directly apprehended with the five senses. It applies, however, to bodies in space, bodies that can be seen, at least, if not apprehended by the other senses from earth. The law applies to physical bodies but is not itself physical. It is metaphysical. The same goes as well for the law of freely falling bodies as for all other natural laws.

Could we live without discerning these principles? Absolutely. People did so for centuries before Galileo. But once these principles are discerned and understood, they can be the foundation for all sorts of advances.

Natural laws are in the nature of things, one of the points toward which we have been moving. The law of gravity is in the nature of relationships between bodies in space. The study that deals with laws of bodies or objects is physics, so named because of the physical nature of things affected by the laws it explores. Chemistry deals with another set of laws, those having to do with combinations of differing substances. But regardless of the subject matter, the laws themselves should be thought of as metaphysical.

**natural law**—the natural law exists on the metaphysical level of reality that is mainly understood by reason. It gives form and order to actual classes of physical beings and is the structural part of reality.

## 2.4 The Role of Reason

These laws come to our knowledge either because they are self-evident or by reason. Probably, all precise formulations of laws, such as are made in physics and chemistry, are arrived at by reason. **Reason** is usually classified as either **deductive** or **inductive**. Deduction occurs when the reasoner moves from an already established position to one that follows logically from it but is not otherwise known. The study of geometry with its use of proofs is where most students use this form of reasoning. Inductive reasoning occurs when something is discovered or proved by numerous instances. For example, chemists, are able to demonstrate the character of particular compounds and arrive at principles by numerous experiments. In other words, they observe how combinations of chemicals react with one another to draw their conclusions. That would be inductive reasoning. Actual thought often combines insight, induction, and deduction so swiftly and indiscriminately that the thinker is not aware of what he is using at any particular time. The processes described above occur distinctly in demonstrations, more than in thought. At any rate, reason is the special faculty for dealing with the metaphysical realm, or, as it is more commonly known, the nature of things.

Deduction is probably used most fruitfully in connection with what are called self-evident truths. **Self-evident** truths are those truths that are their own evidence, that is, they are not learned by reference to some other truth. For example, Thomas Jefferson wrote that it is self-evident that all men are created equal. Now if this proposition is true, it must be self-evident, for there is no evidence for it that comes to us from the senses. Nothing is clearer than that the physical evidence about people demonstrates that they are unequal. They are unequal in height, weight, strength, speed, and unequal in all the ways that we may observe with our senses. So what was Jefferson trying to get at? In the Declaration of Independence, he went on to suggest some ways in which they are created equal and the process by which that conclusion is drawn. But the point here is that some things that we know are self-evident in the nature of things and that reason is used in connection with them.

Not all natural laws have the precision of chemistry and physics, indeed most do not. Those formulations called laws in economics do not have the measurable precision of the exact sciences. The same thing goes generally for other areas of social activity, such as politics, society, ethics, etc. Indeed, it is not customary to formulate "laws" for many of these social activities, and such attempts as have been made have not been generally convincing. Thus, in economics, with a few exceptions, the formulations have usually been referred to as "principles," not laws.

One consequence of this relative imprecision has been to deny scientific status to all but the most precise sciences. The more important consequence, however, is as noted earlier, the whole natural law philosophy has been largely abandoned over the past hundred years or so. This has not resulted in denying the validity of laws in what are called the exact sciences. Rather, the terms natural law and metaphysics have been discarded. Instead, people speak generally of scientific laws, or the laws of physics and chemistry, for example. Thus, the metaphysical nature of what they are referring to is ignored or concealed.

Nature abounds in regularities, and these regularities attest to the nature of things. These regularities attest, too, to an underlying order in the universe. Note a few of the most readily observable of the regularities and predictabilities. The seasons of a year follow one another in regular fashion. Then, having completed their cycles, they recur. In the temperate regions, we call the four seasons that occur each year spring, summer, fall,

---

**inductive reasoning**—discovering truth by hypothesis and experimentation using the scientific method. This type of reasoning is used in the hard sciences.

**deductive reasoning**—discovering truth by reasoning from established facts to reach inevitable conclusions. This type of reasoning is used in geometry proofs.

**self-evident**—truths that are self-evident need no proof since any attempt to deny one must affirm it. For example, a person need not prove his awareness of himself. It is an immediately obvious fact. Also, self-evident truths can be driven by logic as in the case of the natural rights of people—the right to life, liberty, and property.

---

### Getting the Point . . .

Suppose someone argues that the only truths we can know for certain are those that are scientifically proven (empirically verifiable).

1. What is wrong with this proposition?

2. Give an example of a truth that is not necessarily proven scientifically.

3. It has been said that the scientific method (testing a hypothesis in a controlled setting) does not really prove something is true but can only prove that something is *not* true.

Can you think of any examples where accepted "science" was proven to be wrong?

and winter. The year of 365-plus days is a fixed regularity, being the time it takes the earth to revolve around the sun. Day and night—another regularity—consist of the 24-hour period it takes the earth to rotate on its axis. But there are all sorts of regularities. For instance, seeds that fall or are taken from a plant reproduce that plant in the right setting. Animals and plants go through a cycle of life: birth, growth, maturity, deterioration, and death. There are the regularities in the movements of the heavenly bodies, the tides go in and out on schedule, and so on and on.

## 2.5 Human Nature Described

Not only do all things, including plants and animals, have a nature, but humans have a nature as well. Like all living things, humans are mortal, though unlike other animals, we believe that humans alone are aware that they will die. This awareness promotes an urgency, a tension, and heightened purpose to life. Humans have a discernible physical nature; they are bifurcated, bipedal, and mammalian. They grow toward a certain physical form, and when it is reached they may be called mature. The feature that has usually been focused upon that distinguishes them from the rest of the animal kingdom is the potential for rationality. (Not that any people always act upon the basis of reason, but that they are able to.) Humans alone of all creation are thinkers by nature, capable of taking thought before acting, rather than acting upon instinct, capable of knowing the universe of cause and effect, of law and order, and making calculation in terms of this knowledge, capable of knowing what is appropriate. Since they can choose, humans are moral beings. Since they can recognize cause and effect, they are morally responsible beings. These mental, moral, and physical traits are only fully developed in those who are mature, of course, and individuals may have defects that make them differ in some respect from what is normal. But there is a normal **human nature**.

The emphasis upon the enduring nature of things, has been made here because this is the realm in which reason works to discover the principles of economics. Economics is a social study, and thus economics involves the interaction of humans within the frame of human nature. We discover the nature of things by stripping away all that is cultural, all that is man made, all that changes over time. It is not that economics does not involve changes as well. Of course, it does but these changes occur within the framework of fixities. Fashions in clothes change, but the form of the body they cover does not perceptibly change. Thus, it is necessary to keep in mind throughout the study of economics the enduring nature of things. That is the only way we can discover or be aware of the principles, the operation of cause and effect, the order that underlies and endures through change. History is the discipline whose peculiar province is change. All other studies either become history or deal with the realms fundamentally of the enduring or the eternal. So it is with economics.

**human nature**—the traits that all humans have in common, especially those that separate them from the other animals.

## 2.6 The Natural Order of the Universe

One other philosophical aspect of this nature of things needs to be examined before leaving the general subject. The metaphysical realm is thought of as the natural order. God created it and provided it with its nature. Thus, it is an order, is harmonious, is good, and is the way it was meant to be. People throughout the ages have often viewed the heavens and earth as the handiwork of God, have looked upon them with awe and wonder, and have gradually come to view them as instructive for man.

This sense of wonder and perception of order is illustrated by the following story told by H. D. F. Kitto in his account of *The Greeks*. It has to do with the order in the number system:

> It occurred to me to wonder [he wrote] what was the difference between the square of a number and the product of its next-door neighbors. 10 x 10 proved to be 100, and 11 x 9 = 99—one less. It was interesting to find that 6 x 6 and 7 x 5 was just the same, and with growing excitement I discovered, and algebraically proved, the law that this product must always be one less than the square. The next step was to consider the behavior of next-door neighbors but one, and it was with great delight that I disclosed to myself a whole system of numerical behavior.... With increasing wonder I worked out the series 10 x 10 = 100; 9 x 11 = 99; 8 x 12 = 96; 7 x 13 = 91 ... and found that the differences were successively, 1, 3, 5, 7 ... the odd-number series.

He draws the conclusion:

> Then I knew how the Pythagoreans [ancient Greek followers of the mathematician Pythagoras] felt when they made these same discoveries.... Did Heraclitus declare that everything is always changing? Here are things that do not change, entities that are eternal, free from the flesh that corrupts, independent of the imperfect senses, perfectly apprehensible through the mind.

> **Getting the Point...**
>
> Some people think that human nature is improving over time. In other words, they believe that modern man is less likely to allow the evil side to win out. Decide if you agree or disagree with this and give some reasons why you think this is true or false.

What was even more exhilarating was the discovery that the behavior and relations of bodies can be comprehended and expressed in numbers. People began to conceive of such an order in the universe as could be expressed in mathematics, and in the seventeenth century the vision gained hold of such men as Galileo, Johann Kepler, Leibniz, and Sir Isaac Newton. Kepler's vision exceeded what he was able to do, but he wrote of his idea: "My aim is to show that the heavenly machine is ... a kind of clockwork..., insofar as nearly all the manifold motions are caused by a most simple, magnetic, and material force, just as all motions of the clock are caused by a simple weight. And I also show how these physical causes are to be given numerical and geometrical expression." In a book called *The Harmony of the World*, he attempted to show that the universe is permeated with relationships that reflect outward into every realm of reality in a great symphony of harmonies. What he attempted to do in describing the motion and relationship of the heavenly bodies, he lacked all the needed tools of mathematics to do. But Newton was able to combine his work, along with that of Galileo, to give mathematical expression to the ratio that explained both the continuing motion of the heavenly bodies and how they were kept in their spheres by the working of natural laws.

## 2.7 The Natural Order and the Roots of Economics

These formulations in physics spurred people to seek out with new zeal the natural laws and the sources of a built-in harmony in other areas as well, both social and physical. Our main concern here, of course, is the discovery of the natural order in economics. In the late seventeenth and in the eighteenth centuries, thinkers began to discern the outlines of an economic order. Some French thinkers, known as **Physiocrats**, declared that there was economic order that would be socially harmonious if government would only cease to meddle with, intervene in, and direct the economy. They described their prescription for bringing about this state of affairs as *laissez-faire*, that government should stay out of it and let the natural order emerge.

It was **Adam Smith**, however, who gave the fullest expression to this conception in *The Wealth of Nations*, published in 1776. Smith vigorously set forth the idea that there is a natural order for economy and economic well-being that involves a natural harmony between the self-interest of the individual seeking his own gain in the production and sale of goods and the general well-being of nations and societies. Smith explained his concept this way:

> But the annual revenue of every society is always precisely equal to the exchangeable value of the whole annual produce of the industry, or rather is precisely the same thing with that exchangeable value. As every individual, therefore, endeavors as much as he can both to employ his capital in the support of domestic industry, and so to direct that industry that its produce may be of the greatest value; every individual necessarily labours to render the annual revenue of society as great as he can. He generally, indeed, neither intends to promote the public interest, nor knows how much he is promoting it. By preferring the support of domestic to that of foreign industry, he intends only his own security; and by directing that industry in such a manner as its produce may be of the greatest value, he intends only his own gain, and he is in this, as in many other cases, led by an invisible hand to promote an end which was not part of his intention. . . .

In sum, as individuals pursue their own advantage in their own production, they produce the most of what they can that is most wanted, and in so doing they increase not only their own supply but that available to others as well. Since originally penning these words, this idea has come to be called Smith's **invisible hand theory** and is really nothing more than what implicitly follows from a natural law perspective of this world.

**Physiocrats**—eighteenth century French thinkers who opposed government intervention in the economy and, more broadly, mercantilism. They believed in laissez-faire, that government should keep hands off the economy and allow natural law to prevail in these matters. In a sense, they were landists, for they usually believed that land is the source of all wealth.

*laissez-faire*—French phrase conveying the idea that government should not interfere in the economy of men. This belief was justified by the concept of human nature and natural law, which would hold sway in economic activity in the absence of government interference.

*The Wealth of Nations*—book written by Adam Smith in 1776 where he set forth the idea that there is a natural order for the economy, which involves a natural harmony between the self-interest of the individual seeking his own gain and the general well-being of societies.

**invisible hand theory**—Adam Smith's theory that there is a natural harmony between the self-interest of the individual seeking his own gain and the general well-being of societies. By pursuing his own advantage in his production, he produces the most of what he can that is most wanted by others. In doing so he increases not only his own supply but that available to others as well.

> **Adam Smith's Invisible Hand Theory**
> In sum, as individuals pursue their own advantage in their own production, they produce the most of what they can that is most wanted, and in so doing they increase not only their own supply but that available to others as well. Since originally penning these words, this idea has come to be called Smith's invisible hand theory and is really nothing more than what implicitly follows from a natural law perspective of this world.

He made clear, however, that this rule not only applied within nations but in trade among people in different nations as well. Thus, Smith said:

> **Adam Smith (1723–1790)**
>
> Scotch economist and leader in setting forth many of the principles of what has since been known as Classical Economics. He was born in Kircaldy, Scotland and educated at the universities of Glasgow and Oxford. Smith taught language and related courses at Edinburgh and Glasgow. He left the university, however, to study economics. In this effort, he was greatly aided and influenced by David Hume and the French Physiocrats, whose attitude toward natural law and its working in economy he fully accepted. Smith's fame and repute rests mainly on his major work, *Inquiry into the Nature and Causes of the Wealth of Nations*. His case against mercantilism was compelling as were his reasoned arguments for free enterprise. He brought together a variety of ideas in one book laying the groundwork of modern economic thought.

...The interest of a nation in its commercial relations to foreign nations is, like that of a merchant with regard to the different people with whom he deals, to buy as cheap and to sell as dear [as high] as possible. But it will be most likely to buy cheap, when by the most perfect freedom of trade it encourages all nations to bring to it the goods which it has occasion to purchase; and, for the same reason, it will be most likely to sell dear, when its markets are thus filled with the greatest number of buyers.

There is, of course, much more to the working of the market and of economics than is contained in the above. The point here, however, is only to call attention to the conception of a natural and harmonious economic order. It was this idea that gave rise to the development of an intellectual discipline of economics in the nineteenth century and that sustains the concept of principles of economics. It is, however, a natural order in an extended analogy to the natural order for heavenly bodies described by Newton. The natural order for an economy does not lend itself to exact mathematical precision, and all attempts to turn economics into an empirical science this way, by statistics or otherwise, are doomed to failure. This is because, unlike the heavenly bodies, economies work through **human action**, through the decisions and choices of individuals. These choices depend on the wisdom, knowledge, and expectations of the people who make them. Since humans are fallible beings and their fallibility—their frailty—appears in actual economies, economic principles can only be generally stated and their working can at best, only be roughly measured in statistics. All mathematical models in the study of economics necessarily suffer from the same defects.

One other thing needs to be noticed before going on to other aspects of the framework of economics. The concept of a natural order in economics buttresses the idea of individual liberty in economic activities, as well as in other areas. That is, if the pursuit of self-interest economically results in promoting the general well-being, or welfare, then it follows that the individual ought to be free to do just that. If there is a natural order of economy, it is not necessary or desirable for government to intervene in the economy continually. Smith said as much himself:

> It is the highest impertinence and presumption, therefore, in kings and ministers to pretend to watch over the economy of private people, and to restrain their expense, either by sumptuary laws, or by prohibiting the importation of foreign luxuries.

So long as people believe in a natural order of economy they can believe as well in a free market and individual liberty. Indeed, both the concept of a natural and enduring order and individual liberty have had rough sledding since the beginning of the twentieth century, and it should come as no surprise that the two things go hand-in-hand.

---

**human action**—people are created with a mind to know. In addition, all people possess a body and can act. Thus, human action is the purposeful pursuit of a defined end by using the ordinary means at hand.

**Human Action**
Economies work through human action, through the decisions and choices of individuals. These choices depend on the wisdom, knowledge, and expectations of the people who make them. Since humans are fallible beings and their fallibility—their frailty—appears in actual economies, economic principles can only be generally stated and their working can at best, only be roughly measured in statistics. All mathematical models in the study of economics necessarily suffer from the same defects.

---

*We hold from God the gift which includes all others. This gift is life—physical, intellectual, and moral life.*

*But life cannot maintain itself alone. The Creator of life has entrusted us with the responsibility of preserving, developing, and perfecting it. In order that we may accomplish this, He has provided us with a collection of marvelous faculties. And He has put us in the midst of a variety of natural resources. By the application of our faculties to these natural resources we convert them into products, and use them. This process is necessary in order that life may run its appointed course.*

*Life, faculties, production—in other words, individuality, liberty, property—this is man. And in spite of the cunning of artful political leaders, these three gifts from God precede all human legislation, and are superior to it.*

*Life, liberty, and property do not exist because men have made laws. On the contrary, it was the fact that life, liberty, and property existed beforehand that caused men to make laws in the first place.*

**Frédéric Bastiat, *The Law***

# Budget Project

Every person lives within a budget, be it intentional or accidental. Trying to function without a plan can lead to a lot of month left at the end of the money. Everyone has limited resources and must make choices about how to use them. Individuals have different values and preferences, and the amount spent in different categories will fluctuate greatly from person to person. Whether you plan it out ahead of time, or completely wing it, you will constantly make choices about how you spend the money you have. This project is designed to help you consider many different options so that you can be intentional about the choices you make to help you plan for your future.

How much income will you need to live the lifestyle you desire? There are a lot of factors that determine the answer to this question. This project will give you the opportunity to design a budget for two different income levels so that you can compare. The project as written will use the amount you would make if you worked full time at your local minimum wage as one income. For the other income we chose $25,000, but if desired your teacher may change this amount.

The project is designed to take place over the course of a semester. Each week you will investigate one category of income or expenses and make decisions about how you think you might budget that area. You should develop a notebook with thorough notes on all your research and document the sources of any information you use. The topics that will be covered are as follows:

- Week 1:    Minimum Wage
- Week 2:    Taxes, Withholding
- Week 3:    Charitable Giving and Gifts
- Week 4:    Savings, Investments
- Week 5:    Housing
- Week 6:    Housing (continued)
- Week 7:    Transportation
- Week 8:    Insurance
- Week 9:    Loans, College
- Week 10:   Personal Care, and Pets
- Week 11:   Food, Groceries
- Week 12:   Entertainment
- Week 13:   Other
- Week 14:   Wrap-up

## Directions

1. Budget Sheets in PDF and Excel formats can be downloaded from the Economics Course Resources on boundarystone.org. Print a copy of the budget sheet to use in recording your budget choices as you go. Use pencil in case you decide to change amounts as you go. You can use the spreadsheet version if you have Excel or another spreadsheet program, and many of the calculations will be made for you.

2. Be sure to document with a written log all your research, recording where you found your numbers. For any item where you need to make a decision on what you will do, you should record all the prices for options in your log as you find them, and put a note as to where you found them in case you need to go back to find them again later. Be prepared to discuss your research and choices at any time.

3. Complete the Budget Sheet, with two different incomes: one higher and one lower. Suggestions are to make the larger salary a typical starting salary in a career you might be considering, or you might research and find the average starting salary for a college graduate. Decide with your teacher at the beginning of the project. For the lower wage, you should use the current federal minimum wage.

4. As a section is assigned, you should make choices for all the items listed that you want, and add/edit other items that you want if they are not listed. Discuss options and your choices for each section with a person you trust who has been self-supporting for a while and let them help you determine if you are being realistic. For each section, you will need to turn in a copy of your budget sheet. If you are filling it in by hand, be sure you always keep your master copy.

5. Your grade on this project will be determined from your written log and final budget. You need to find realistic options that allow you to complete your budget with a zero or positive balance.

# Study Guide for:

# 2  In The Nature of Things

## Chapter Summary

Since the beginning of the twentieth century, there has been a conscious rejection of the metaphysical realm and of natural law in academic circles. This unfortunate rejection of the metaphysical has led to increased ignorance because our grasp and understanding of things depends on there being an order in the universe. Thus, even though it may be fashionable to speak as if there were no fixed principles, such an idea is wholly false. Furthermore, in practice, we cannot operate on such an assumption because everyone acts each day on the basis of the fixed regularities of the universe.

In truth, there are three levels of reality: the physical, the metaphysical, and the spiritual. The metaphysical area of reality is made up of the enduring principles of the universe and is known to us by way of our reason. This is the area of reality that has received little attention in recent years as academicians have focused more and more of their energies on describing change as if there were only change. As already stated, such a presumption is folly for it undercuts all science and hence all substantive knowledge to guide human action.

There are two methods of reason: inductive and deductive. The inductive method observes the numerous particulars, proposes a hypothesis and then tests the hypothesis, gathers empirical data and reasons to general conclusions from that data. Hypotheses only become accepted principles or laws when they are repetitively tested and confirmed over time, and by various people. By contrast, the deductive method of reasoning reaches a necessary conclusion from a set of stated premises. Both methods are used regularly. The result has been an increase in the general understanding of the numerous regularities in creation. This improved knowledge of the universe over time has spawned tremendous advancements as people use their knowledge of regularity to better achieve the ends they have in mind.

The study of economics follows this same method. As a separate study, thinkers first began to consider economic topics during the late seventeenth and continuing into the eighteenth centuries. They were concerned with identifying the metaphysical rules that applied to the economic success of nations. The fullest expression of this work was Adam Smith's *The Wealth of Nations*, which was published in 1776.

Unlike the physical sciences though, the study of economics is focused on how economies work through human action. Individual decisions and choices are of fundamental importance. Since humans are fallible, and always working from a framework of incomplete knowledge of the options their choices are subject to change as they continually learn from their mistakes. Therefore, economics cannot be comprehended solely within the framework of a set of mathematical equations. Rather, it must be understood by examining human nature, the environment within which humans act, and the interplay between the two.

## Points of Emphasis

1. Reality is made up of three levels. We come to gain knowledge of each level by way of a different means and each has a different length of endurance with respect to time as displayed in the table on page 12.

2. Modern existentialists have challenged the existence of the metaphysical realm. The result has been a "flight from reality" that is serving to undermine the educational process and confuse students. The existential position, however, is forced and cannot be held consistently. No one can live practically as an existentialist.

3. Natural laws are an enduring feature of the universe and they are fundamental if we are to gain understanding about any subject.

4. Economics is different from physical sciences in that its focus involves the study of the actions of fallible human beings. Nevertheless, there are principles to be discovered and applied.

## Identification

1. evolutionary ideas
2. metaphysical
3. natural law
4. inductive reasoning
5. deductive reasoning
6. self-evident
7. human nature
8. Physiocrats
9. *laissez-faire*
10. Adam Smith
11. *The Wealth of Nations*
12. invisible hand theory
13. human action

## Review Questions

1. What are some of the regularities in nature that we take for granted?
2. Give some examples of how regularities in nature serve as principles upon which we can act to achieve some purposeful end.
3. List an example of a truth that can be discerned in each of the three levels of reality. How did you come to the conclusion that it is true? Explain the duration of each truth.
4. How have evolutionary ideas departed from the three levels of reality?
5. This chapter listed several characteristics that make up human nature. List as many as you can find.
6. Are there any characteristics on your list in the previous answer that you can make a case for why they should not be included? Or others that should be added? If so, pick one and write out your reasons. Be prepared to discuss in class your case for doing so.
7. Why is it important to understand human nature in the study of economics?
8. What are some of the immediate implications on public policy as we begin to recognize the natural order in economics?
9. People often throw around the idea that in every trade there is a winner and a loser. Use deductive reasoning, to explain why this is not true.

## Activities

1. Prepare a case either to support or oppose the following position: "Everything is relative."
2. Write a one- to two-page paper describing your view of human nature.

## For Further Study

1. Clarence Carson, *The Flight from Reality*, The Foundation for Economic Education: Irvington, NY, 1969.
2. Murray Rothbard. "In Defense of 'Extreme Apriorism'," https://mises.org/library/defense-"extreme-apriorism"
3. Adam Smith, *An Inquiry into the Nature and Causes of the Wealth of Nations*, edited by R. H. Campbell and A. S. Skinner, Liberty Classics: Indianapolis, 1976.

> **CHAPTER CONTENT**
>
> 3.1 The Necessity for Government    24
> 3.2 The Nature of Government    25
> 3.3 How Government Impacts the Economy    26
>     3.3.1 Minimizing the Impact of Taxes    27
>     3.3.2 Describing Just Taxation    29
>     3.3.3 Taxes That Are Commonly Used    31
> 3.4 Constitutional Limits on Government    32
>     3.4.1 Prohibiting Certain Actions    33
>     3.4.2 Separating Powers    35
>     3.4.3 Limiting Involvement in Economy    36

# 3 Government

Let every person be subject to the governing authorities. For there is no authority except from God, and those that exist have been instituted by God. Therefore whoever resists the authorities resists what God has appointed, and those who resist will incur judgment. For rulers are not a terror to good conduct, but to bad. Would you have no fear of the one who is in authority? Then do what is good, and you will receive his approval, for he is God's servant for your good. But if you do wrong, be afraid, for he does not bear the sword in vain. For he is the servant of God, an avenger who carries out God's wrath on the wrongdoer.

**Romans 13:1–4**

According to the system of natural liberty, the sovereign has only three duties to attend to: ... first, the duty of protecting the society from the violence and invasion of other independent societies; secondly, the duty of protecting ... every member of the society from the injustice or oppression of every other member of it ...; and thirdly, the duty of erecting and maintaining certain public works and certain public institutions. ...

**Adam Smith, *The Wealth of Nations***

Every actual economy exists in the framework of a government, or governments. It might be possible to write a book on economics that never mentioned government. Certainly, it is possible to focus on the voluntary system of markets in such a way as to imagine that government is unnecessary. This can be accomplished by focusing attention on all the wants that can be met by cooperation among numerous individuals. But that all this would or could occur without government is largely a mirage. Certainly, it does not go on outside some sort of governmental framework.

There are some who think we could dispense with government, but they are a small minority. Most people appear to be all too convinced of the desirability of government. In a seminar in which the idea was advanced that government could be dispensed with, Professor Gottfried Dietze of Johns Hopkins University observed, dryly: "There is never a time without government. When one government falls, another takes its place." History bears him out. In all societies of any extent for which any record exists, there have been governments. They may not be such elaborate organizations as are common today, but all societies have had some body that acts as the office of government.

Scripture says that governments are ordained of God. Experience shows that they have been around for a long time. Reason can explain why they are necessary. In what follows, both the necessity for and the ways that governments may affect economies will be discussed.

## 3.1 The Necessity for Government

In the nature of things, the need for government arises from human nature. Granted, people are capable of reason. That is, people have the potential to act rightly, to understand that it would be in their best interest to live in peace with others, and to refrain from violence. But there is another side to human nature, as deeply a part of it as his reasonableness, and often more dominant in his actions.

The underside of human nature has been described in many ways. Scripture says that he is a sinner, that he disobeyed God, and is a fallen creature. Humans have been described as fallible (liable to be mistaken), as a weak reed, as having clay feet, as being bent to their own destruction. As an infant, man is observably self-centered, concerned only with his own desires and gratifications. Only slowly, and often painfully, does the child learn more sociable and thoughtful behavior. If **enlightened self-interest** replaces self-centeredness as an adult, considerable progress has been made. Sadly, one does not have to look far to see the many expressions of this darker side of human nature. In truth, man is subject to strong emotions, to fits of temper, and may become violent, aggressive, and destructive. He can be crafty, may cheat, trespass, steal, and commit all sorts of crimes. He may conspire with some to take advantage of, or do great harm to, others. Societies and groups may become so worked up that there is almost no limit to the harm they would inflict on their enemies. The historical record is replete with stories of almost every kind of preying of man on man that can be imagined. It is said, too, that man tends to love power over others, and if he gains it may exercise it in tyrannical fashion.

It is the evil in the nature of man that makes government necessary. That is not to suggest that man is not tamed and inhibited by other than governmental means. Indeed, this may be accomplished to greater or lesser degree by instruction in morality, by conscience, by training in the home and school, by social rewards and punishments, and even by calculation on the part of the individual. But when these fail to achieve their ends, government must intervene to use force and restrain. Government may be the last recourse, but it remains a necessary presence to restrain and punish some men at some times. But even in the absence of deceitful and violent behavior, government would be necessary to settle disputes that arise—to enforce the rules of justice generally.

Government is necessary not only for society in general but for economic activity in particular. It is possible that government is not essential to the economy of individuals and associations who might look after that for themselves. That question can be left for later exploration. But government is essential for the protection of economic activity and for the settlement of disputes. All economic activity involves either the production or transfer of property. Property can be trespassed upon, stolen, abused, or destroyed. Thus, government is necessary to protect it, thereby making economic activity possible.

Markets are the arena of the transfers and exchanges of goods and services. Markets require the protection of government in several ways. First, they require protection against theft and malicious damage of goods while they are being transported or displayed. Second, traders need

> **enlightened self-interest**—reason teaches us that it is in our highest self-interest to behave in accordance with the objective moral boundaries established by God. As enlightened self-interest gains sway in someone's life he becomes more self-controlled.

protection against fraud in their transactions. Third, the smooth functioning of the market requires the enforcement of **contracts.**

All transfers of property that are voluntary are by agreement, or in legal terms by contract. That does not mean that the contract must be a written one or that the terms must be spelled out verbally. Most transfers of property are not by written agreement, though there is an implied contract in the transfer of goods or the sale of services. For example, written agreements on purchases made in stores are unusual except when the purchase is charged. Nonetheless, an implied agreement is involved, and a written receipt is given as evidence of the transaction. Some contracts, however, must be written in the United States in order to be enforceable. That is the case with land transfers, purchases of automobiles in most states, and the sale of copyrights or exclusive rights by authors.

The major problem with enforcement, however, occurs where there is a time element involved. Ordinarily, where an object or service is paid for and bought at the same time, the only problems that might arise would be those having to do with quality. These would usually involve fraud or guarantees of performance. But where longer time elements are involved one or the other party may be unable or not wish to perform all that the contract requires. After all, the reason for entering into contracts of some duration is to assure performance even after the conditions that existed at the moment of the contract have changed or the desire to perform no longer is so strong. It is in these cases that justice may require the use of force to assure performance or some payment by one party to the other. Thus, government is even more essential to assure performance in long-term contracts.

Governments may, of course, perform other functions that may be useful to economic activity, but these may be best described in other connections. Certainly, roads, rights-of-way, and communication facilities are more or less essential to economic activity, and governments have long played a role in providing these. Whether and to what extent that government role may be essential, however, is another matter.

## 3.2 The Nature of Government

By nature, government must be especially suited to perform its basic functions. The basic functions of government are to protect the people under it from foreign governments, to protect their lives and property from domestic enemies, to maintain the peace by settling disputes, and to perform other such public functions as require its special offices. In short, the basic functions of government are those that require the use of force in maintaining the peace. Government is the body that has a monopoly on the use of force within its jurisdiction. Its jurisdiction may extend over a whole nation or kingdom, or it may have a narrower and more limited sphere, as is the case with states in a federal system, or even more narrow as in the case of counties, cities, or towns. Governments do not usually insist upon an absolute monopoly, but rather allow such exceptions as in acts of self-defense by individuals when they are endangered by an attacker.

It may be well to emphasize that governments not only claim a monopoly on the use of major force but also equip themselves for and actually use force. To put it another way, governments operate as government by the use of intimidation and force. Their agents are equipped with such weapons as pistols, nightsticks, blackjacks, tasers, shotguns, assault rifles, tanks, cannons, bombs, drones, and the like. They maintain jails, prisons, and other secured buildings for the purpose of restraining those confined

> **contracts**—legal agreements, whether written, spoken, or implied, between two or more people to do something.

in them. They execute people by firing squad, hanging, electrocution, poison gas, lethal injection and the like. All the laws of government carry with them the threat of the use of force to restrict some measure of the offender's right to life, liberty, or property; else they are not properly laws at all. Government is, in essence, legal force.

> **Basic Functions of Government**
> 1. To protect the people under it from foreign enemies.
> 2. To protect their lives and property from domestic enemies.
> 3. To maintain the peace by settling disputes.
> 4. To perform other such public functions as require its special offices.

What justifies and properly constrains the use of force? The functions of government already noted provide a framework for an answer to the question. The need to maintain justice is what justifies the use of force. **Justice** is giving every person his due. In economic terms, justice is concerned that each person gets what he has earned or has by right. In terms of maintaining the public peace, justice attempts to mete out punishment in accord with the gravity of the offense, how greatly the offender harmed the life, liberty, or property of some other person. Of course, justice is much more complex. Maintaining it is much more varied than these limitations may suggest. However, the main point here is that justice is the business that justifies government.

Regarding the business and nature of government, one other point needs to be made here, since our main concern is with economics. Government does not produce goods or provide services in an economic sense. Its products might better be called "bads," and most of its services are hardly wanted by those on whom they are exercised. That is, the use of force on persons, however much it may be justified, is not in economic terms a good. Nor is imprisonment or execution a service that is much sought after. There are a few situations where governments do produce goods or provide services, but to the extent they do they are generally not performing the functions of governments.

*justice*—giving every person his due. In economic terms, justice is concerned that each person gets what he has earned or has by right.

> **Justice** is giving every person his due. In economic terms, justice is concerned that each person gets what he has earned or has by right.

## 3.3 How Government Impacts the Economy

Governments necessarily have some impact on economy. They may, of course, have a dominating and even controlling impact on economy. But the main concern here is with the impact they have in the performance of their basic functions. As already noted, government, by providing protection for economic activities, performs an essential function that is generally beneficial. But government also impinges upon economic activities in ways that may hamper, burden or disrupt them. The major way by which this is done is by taxation, but two other ways will be discussed first.

While governments are not producers of goods ordinarily, they use an assortment of goods. They use food, clothing, uniforms, a vast assortment of weapons, transportation, building materials, office supplies, and so on through the gamut of goods that police, armies, and the like, may require. So long as they purchase their goods in the market, at prices determined in the market, they are not significantly different from others who make purchases. They may, however, hamper and disrupt the market if they purchase products either well above or below the market price. In a time of war, governments often become major users of goods. Many times they acquire products by seizing goods from those in the vicinity of their armies (sometimes called "requisitioning" them) or disrupt the market by establishing priorities, prescribing what can be produced, rationing goods to the population, cheapening the money by inflation, and other uses of force. In these latter cases, markets cannot perform their normal function of distributing goods very well. In short, government as a consumer of goods may have anywhere from a negligible impact to a dominant one on an economy, depending upon the extent of its requirements for goods and the policies it follows.

Government is also a competitor in the market for workers. That is, government employs people to perform the various jobs it undertakes. The extent of the impact is determined both by how many workers the government employs and the policies it enacts in relation to employment. If government simply goes into the market to employ workers at going rates, it will not differ significantly in impact from any other employer. However, if government sets its pay with little reference to the market, tampers with the market generally by prescribing hours of work, enforcing minimum or maximum wages, drafting soldiers, or prescribing work conditions, it may have a large impact on the economy. The impact of particular interventions will be discussed elsewhere in this work.

### 3.3.1 Minimizing the Impact of Taxes

Taxation, however, is the one area where governments inevitably have some, usually considerable, impact on the economy. As noted earlier, in the nature of things governments do not produce goods. It follows that if they are to make expenditures they must raise the revenue from some other source than the sale of goods. In short, they must levy taxes. They may, of course, temporarily supplement their revenue by borrowing, but if their credit is to be maintained, debts must be paid, and that usually involves even higher taxes.

Taxes unavoidably are burdensome on those on whom they fall. This burden falls upon the economy of individuals and families, and on the economy generally. George Washington put the point this way in his Farewell Address: "that to have a revenue there must be taxes; that no taxes can be devised which are not more or less inconvenient and unpleasant...." Indeed, the burden of taxes can be more than "inconvenient and unpleasant." Chief Justice John Marshall set forth an axiom on the matter in the landmark Supreme Court decision of **McCulloch vs. Maryland**. Marshall wrote, "That the power to tax involves the power to destroy; that the power to destroy may defeat and render useless the power to create...."

Marshall was not using this axiom as a basis for nullifying the power of the United States Government to levy taxes. Instead, he was building his case for nullifying a state tax on the currency of a bank chartered by the United States. If states can levy taxes on an instrument of the United States, he was arguing, they can destroy it. Indeed, if they could tax one

*McCulloch vs. Maryland*—landmark Supreme Court decision that effectively blocked states from taxing the federal government. Chief Justice John Marshall said in his opinion, "That the power to tax involves the power to destroy; that the power to destroy may defeat and render useless the power to create...."

government operation, they could tax others; they could tax all, and thus destroy the United States Government. But he did not rely entirely on the axiom that the power to tax is the power to destroy for his opinion. He went on to deny the power of a state to tax the federal government on the grounds that a state represents only the people in the state and thus cannot properly levy taxes on a much more extensive body composed of many people who are not of that state.

Even so, the power to tax *is* the power to destroy and may render useless the power to create. The general power to tax entails the power to take up to 100% of the proceeds from all undertakings. No undertaking can survive indefinitely if all its proceeds are drained away in taxes. Hence, the motive or incentive for all creative production can be undermined by taxation. This is the potential of the power to tax.

But the power to tax is not the power to destroy only when it is levied on 100% of the proceeds. That only demonstrates the principle by looking at the extreme. Actually, the power to tax involves the power to destroy whether the degree is some fraction of 1% or 100%. It is possible to demonstrate this by **marginal theory**. The marginal theory as it applies to the degree of taxation can be stated this way: any level of taxation will make some undertakings unprofitable or sub-marginal. The idea is that there are always businesses and undertakings that are near the point where they are in danger of going under. In practice, any increase in taxes will drive some people out of business or make it difficult or impossible for them to sustain themselves at whatever they are doing.

The principle of marginality applies to anyone who attempts to produce, provide, purvey, sell, or transport any good or service; it applies to farmers, manufacturers, storekeepers, teachers, artists, industrial workers, or whomever, but the effects may be most clearly seen in business enterprise. Taxation affects whether a business can be begun and whether it will last or not. The failure of any business can be the result of something to do with the costs of taxation whether it is the rate of taxation, the record keeping necessary for tax purposes, or the collection of taxes from employees or customers. And many businesses do fail. Studies over the years have shown that at least one-fourth of all new businesses do not last a year, and about half are unable to make it through the fourth year.

There is no way of knowing how many of these failures are attributable to taxation. Some of them would most likely have failed had there been no taxes to pay, none to collect, and no records to keep. But it is safe to say that taxes were a contributing factor in almost every failure and a determinative one in many, because taxation adds to the cost of doing business.

To observe that the power to tax is the power to destroy, all that is necessary is to drive down almost any road. The empty stores, the abandoned service stations, the factory no longer in operation, the rusting rails on the spur of the main track, the farm that is no longer cultivated, the fading signs that still stand from some undertaking, are mute evidence of the destructiveness of taxation. There should be no doubt that taxation does have an impact on the economy, and it can be a determinative one.

Even though the power to tax is the power to destroy, it does not follow that taxation should be abandoned. The courts have never seen fit to extend to the rest of us the protection from this possible destruction that they have given to the federal government, nor is it likely they ever could or would. The case for some sort of taxes is approximately as good as the case for government. Taxation is as widespread today as the existence of governments. Jesus said, on the matter of taxation, " . . . render to Caesar the things that are Caesar's, and to God the things that are God's"

**marginal theory**—as it applies to the degree of taxation—any level of taxation will make some undertakings unprofitable or sub-marginal. Basically, any level of taxes will make certain undertakings not worth it and will push certain people and businesses into harder financial situations, debt, or bankruptcy.

(Matthew 22:21). Reason will also show that if government is necessary, then taxation is necessary.

The potential destructive nature of taxation shows that great care needs to be taken in levying taxes, and the power to tax must be limited, else it may be used to destroy particular taxpayers. It may well allow legislators the power to pick winners and losers in the market by granting tax breaks to certain favored businesses.

> **Danger in Increasing Taxes**
> In practice, any increase in taxes will drive some people out of business or make it difficult or impossible for them to sustain themselves at whatever they are doing.

### 3.3.2 Describing Just Taxation

Whenever changes to tax policy are considered, there are always going to be some taxpayers who are more affected than others. It is often said that everyone should pay their fair share, but opinions as to what that means in practice vary widely. Too often, tax rates are designed based on ability to pay, and those who have the most ability to pay also have the most ability to pay lobbyists who petition legislators to adopt policies that favor them. When these are the driving factors, the **first rule of taxation** is being ignored. That rule is that taxes should be justly levied. Justice, as noted, means that each person should receive his due. If one of the basic functions of government is to protect property, then it must be acknowledged that the income and property of a person is his own, and not the government's. Especially since government uses force when enforcing law, in the case of taxes justice would mean that as much as possible, the amount a person or business is taxed should be based on the cost of benefits received by them.

Unfortunately, most of the basic functions government performs cannot be charged for directly on the basis of benefits. If a thief is apprehended, for example, all property owners might well benefit, not simply someone who was being robbed at the time he was apprehended. This is simply another way of saying that many of those whom government serves do not want the service (the thieves, for example), and those who benefit are not always directly served. Government does provide some services, and these might well be paid for by users. For a few examples, users could pay for government parks by paying an entry fee. Licenses to drive can be and usually are, paid for by those who obtain them. Gasoline could be taxed to pay for road construction and maintenance. But **user fees** for beneficiaries would only work in a limited number of cases.

To discover which taxes beyond user fees are more just, it is helpful to go back to the basic functions of government. Protecting persons in their lives and property would include services such as military, police, fire, and courts, etc. Two kinds of taxes are closest to being just in taxing the beneficiaries of these governmental functions.

First, since every person is presumably equally protected, a **head tax** on each person would meet the qualifications of justice. Although such a tax has often been imposed in the course of history, it is not familiar to most Americans. (It has also been called a poll tax, but since the poll tax was associated with voting in some states, we will use the term head tax.) In addition to the justice of the head tax, it has other advantages that

**first rule of taxation**—as much as possible taxes should be justly levied, that people should pay an amount of tax that equals the benefits received.

**user fee**—a tax or fee paid for a government function or service that goes directly to financing that service.

**head tax**—uniform tax where amount due is determined by the number of people in a household. It might have a different rate for adults than for dependents.

> **Getting the Point...**
>
> Make a list of government entities that protect lives and property.
>
> Which ones are part of a local (city/county) government? ...a state government? ...a federal government?
>
> Describe taxes that could justly fund them.
>
> What would be required to collect the tax?

**real property**—land and the permanent structures on it. It is distinct from chattels (movable property), personal property, and intangible property.

**tangible property**—the personal property that someone owns that you can literally touch.

**intangible property**—property that is not tangible—touchable or reachable by the sense of touch—but is usually represented by paper only, such as a share in a corporation (no particular piece of property involved) or the good will of a business.

recommend it. It would be easy to levy since it involves only the establishment of the amount of tax per head and the establishment of how many persons are in each household. It involves no extensive intrusion into the lives of people or invasion of privacy. The head tax would probably be as economically neutral a tax as could be conceived. It targets no class or order of persons for special treatment. Since it falls on all alike, it offers a minimum inducement for programs of redistributing wealth. Moreover, in a representative government with an extensive electorate, there should be great pressure to keep the levies low.

The one major objection to the head tax would probably be that it might bear heavily on large families. The assumption here is that the tax would fall on everyone, including children, old, or disabled people and so on, and that the heads of household would pay the tax for dependent children. Undoubtedly, then, large families would pay more taxes than single persons or small families, so far as the head tax went. The aim, however, would be justice, and the assumption is that since each additional person adds to the cost of government protection of persons, it is only just that taxes should fall upon persons.

On the other hand, the other thing protected, property, is not divided evenly among all people. Because of this, in order to be just, it should no doubt be taxed proportionally based on the value of the property owned. The assumption is that more extensive holdings would require more police and court activity and that owners should pay proportionally more taxes. How much and what -kinds of property to tax would be another question. Probably, automobiles would be the easiest to tax, since they are usually registered and licensed by the authorities, and valuation is made relatively easy by the large number of sales of used cars. **Real property** would be the next easiest because land and deeds are registered and houses can hardly be hidden. However, assigning a value to real property is more difficult than for automobiles because there are so many factors that affect the value, and property is not usually bought and sold as often. Taxing **tangible** and **intangible property** runs into both problems of valuation and intrusiveness. Nevertheless, it would be just to levy a proportional tax on the value of all property owned.

> **Ideals of Just Taxation**
> 1. As much as possible, for any particular government function, the people who benefit from it are paying their due portion of the cost.
> 2. The tax does not offer special privileges or advantages to any class of businesses or people.
> 3. The tax does not fall more heavily on any class of businesses or people.
> 4. The tax is relatively neutral in impact on the economy.
> 5. The tax is designed to minimize the intrusion on privacy and time (record keeping requirements) of the taxpayer.
> 6. The tax is designed to minimize the size of bureaucracy and numbers of agents needed for enforcing compliance.

Undoubtedly, levying taxes on property would have some economic impact, other than the burdensomeness of any tax. It would seem to discourage having possessions, or at least those that are to be taxed. Taxing real property might even discourage home-ownership, though the extent to which it would do that would depend upon how high the tax was. It should be noted, too, that it is customary in levying a real property tax to have a **homestead exemption**, which reduces the tax for a home that is a family's primary residence. Such an exemption somewhat violates the principle of equal justice in taxation. In any case, a uniform tax levied proportionally on property would meet the requirements of justice.

**homestead exemption**—a reduction in property tax rate due for the primary residence of the household.

### 3.3.3 Taxes That Are Commonly Used

The above discussion of just taxes was not made in the expectation that legislators will rush out to repeal all other taxes and enact in their stead head taxes that fall equally on all and proportional but uniform property taxes. That is unlikely to happen until there is a revival of concern with justice. They were, rather, discussed so as to provide models and standards for some of the principles of taxation, namely: justice, equality, proportionality, ability to be levied without swarms of revenue agents, ability to be collected without imposing the task upon businesses, and relatively neutral in their impact on economy. Discussion of these principles provides a setting for discussion of taxes that do not stand up well against them. Many taxes have been levied over the years, and a few that are commonly used will be discussed. Most of these have a considerable impact on economy, though that objection alone may not be decisive in avoiding them.

　a. **Tariff.** A tariff is a tax on goods either exported to or imported from other countries. (Since our Constitution prohibits export taxes, they need not be discussed here.) Tariffs clearly would have an impact on economic activity, since that is precisely what they tax. In the nineteenth century, it was customary to distinguish a **tariff for revenue** from a **protective tariff**. A tariff for revenue has relatively low rates and might be levied uniformly on all imports. Its purported purpose is to raise revenue, not to keep foreign goods out, though rates would have to be low indeed not to have some impact on the number of goods imported. A protective tariff, on the other hand, will have high rates (50% was not that unusual), is usually selectively imposed on goods that are also produced in the country levying the tax, and is alleged to protect domestically produced goods from foreign competition. In its favor, the tariff is relatively easy to collect, requiring only customs agents at ports. On the other hand, it tends to drive the price of goods up for domestic consumers. Thus, its impact falls more on domestic consumers than on foreigner producers. So far as the protective tariff dries up foreign imports it may also reduce the foreign market for exports since countries generally try to balance exports against imports in foreign trade. Protective tariffs tend to bring retaliation from other countries, produce enmities, and may even set the stage for war. Above all, they most punish the consumers in the country imposing the tariff because they are forced to pay higher prices for goods.

**tariff**—any list of fixed charges. In economics, it usually refers to a tax levied on exports or imports.

**tariff for revenue**—a tax levied on exports or imports for the primary purpose of raising revenue. It is distinguished from a protective tariff in that it is generally low enough so as not to actually keep foreign goods out.

**protective tariff**—a tax levied by a government, usually on imports, aimed at reducing the amount being imported to protect domestic production from foreign goods. As a result, consumers usually pay a higher price for protected goods, whether they buy domestic goods or foreign imports.

　b. **Sales tax.** The sales tax is another tax that has an economic impact directly because it is levied on trade in the market. It is a tax directly on consumption, is generally paid by the consumer, and even when it is paid by a business, a restaurant, for example, it is then usually passed on to the consumer. Moreover, it makes the retailer a tax collector for the government and increases his record keeping burden. Some states and localities impose the tax selectively, thus discouraging the sale of some goods and making it easier to buy others. The general impact of the sales tax is to raise the price to consumers of goods covered and possibly to reduce sales.

**sales tax**—a tax levied on sales of goods and services at the point of sale in the market.

**excise tax**—a tax levied on specific items. Some of these are referred to as "sin taxes." This tax is often designed to limit the consumption of these products, as well as collect revenue from "sinners" who use them.

**graduated income tax**—a progressive income tax imposed upon an individual's earned income such that the more taxable income that is made the greater the proportion of it is taken as tax.

> **Getting the Point...**
>
> What information currently collected by the government about taxpayers would no longer be necessary if we did not have an income tax?

**corporate income tax**—tax imposed on taxable income earned by corporations. The definition of taxable income is arbitrarily defined and it is usually subject to progressive taxation.

**withholding**—a method of collecting taxes where tax is deducted before the workman receives his paycheck. It has the effect of taking away from the workman any choice as to whether or when he will pay the tax.

c. **Excise tax.** These are taxes on highly selected consumer goods, often referred to as "sin" taxes. They are most often imposed on tobacco and alcohol for consumption, though they are sometimes imposed on luxury goods as well. The purpose of the tax, aside from raising revenue from "sinners," or from the wealthy who can afford "luxuries," is to discourage the consumption of certain products. They do succeed in making some habit-forming products more expensive. If they do not succeed in discouraging consumption, they may have, as a side effect, a negative impact on the families of users because of the increased amount of income spent on them. The consumer is taxed indirectly rather than directly because the tax is usually levied on wholesalers and passed on in the shelf price.

d. **Graduated income tax.** It would take a sizable volume to detail the economic effects and side effects of the individual and corporate income taxes. The graduated income tax is inherently unjust, and disproportionate. It taxes income above certain amounts at higher *rates,* and taxes what one earns rather than the wealth one possesses. Thus, it tends to make it difficult for someone to save and invest in order to accumulate wealth in the first place. It penalizes industrious efforts and abilities. The income tax was expressly forbidden in the original Constitution and was not even legal until the Sixteenth Amendment was ratified. To enforce the tax involves a high level of government prying into the lives of the citizenry, and Americans have become more accepting of this burden over the years. One of the great difficulties of this type of tax lies in determining what income is to be taxed since any definition is somewhat arbitrary in practice. The **corporate income tax** is also graduated and is usually passed on to consumers in higher prices for goods. In addition, it subjects stockholders to double taxation since the dividends they receive, which are determined after the corporate taxes are already paid, must then be declared on their individual income tax forms. **Withholding** is a method of collecting taxes that makes tax collectors of employers and taxes the employee's money before he ever sees it. The graduated income tax can only be kept from working disastrous consequences by allowing all sorts of tax breaks and deductions, thus probably increasing the injustice of it.

Other taxes, of equal import, such as Social Security and inflation, will be discussed elsewhere, but enough has been told here to suggest something of the economic impact of taxation.

## 3.4 Constitutional Limits on Government

Americans used the constitutional device to limit and restrain the governments over them. During the colonial period, they gained familiarity with constitutional protections of their rights. While Britain did not have a single written constitution, there were several documents, including the Magna Carta, to which they might appeal. There were also colonial charters and other acknowledgments of their rights. They lived in an age when the natural law philosophy, as noted earlier, had gained new vigor, and it had been bolstered by the natural rights theory of John Locke.

Indeed, there probably has never been a people more jealous of their rights or more aware of the dangers of government to them than were Americans at the time of the making of the United States Constitution and of state constitutions. The documents of this period are replete with warnings about the dangers of extensive or unrestrained government power. John Dickinson of Delaware declared that it was his conviction "that every free state should incessantly watch and instantly take alarm on any addition made to the power exercised over them." Thomas Jefferson maintained that "The natural progress of things is for liberty to yield and government to gain ground." Power was the danger, not simply the form of government, according to Richard Henry Lee. He thought:

> ...that unbridled passions produce the same effect, whether in a king, nobility, or a mob. The experience of all mankind has proved the...disposition to use power wantonly. It is therefore as necessary to defend an individual against the majority in a republic as against the king in a monarchy.

> **Thomas Jefferson:**
> "The natural progress of things is for liberty to yield and government to gain ground."

James Madison pointed out the dangers of unrestricted majority rule, saying: "In all cases where a majority are united by a common interest or passion, the rights of the minority are in danger." Jefferson described the remedy in which most Americans believed: "In questions of power, then, let no more be heard of confidence in man but bind him down from mischief by the chains of the Constitution."

The limiting of government by constitutions reached its peak at the Constitutional Convention in Philadelphia in 1787, and in the drawing and ratifying of the first ten amendments to the Constitution (the Bill of Rights) a few years later. Government was limited and restrained in three ways in the Constitution by prohibiting government from taking certain kinds of action, by enumerating the powers of the United States Government and prohibiting the exercise of any other powers by it, and by structuring the government so as to require cooperation among the branches, and in some cases the states, in taking action. Some specifics will help to further explain and illustrate.

> **Constitutionally Limiting Government Power**
> 1. Prohibiting government from taking certain kinds of action.
> 2. Enumerating the powers of the United States Government and prohibiting the exercise of any other powers by it.
> 3. Requiring cooperation among the branches, and in some cases among the states, in taking action.

### 3.4.1 Prohibiting Certain Actions

The Constitution prohibits certain kinds of actions by the states as well as the United States. For example, there is this prohibition on states in the Constitution: "No State shall...pass any...Law impairing the Obligation of Contracts...." Or, in the case of the United States Government, the First Amendment says, "Congress shall make no law respecting an establishment of religion, or prohibiting the free exercise thereof...." There are many other prohibitions on both, some of which will be discussed below, but the point needs only to be illustrated here.

It was generally understood by the makers of the Constitution that the general government, while supreme in its realm, would have only a limited scope of governmental activities and that it would be limited to those powers enumerated. Thus, the authorization of certain powers was carefully done in the Constitution. For example, "The Congress shall have Power . . . To establish Post Offices and post Roads." There was, however, considerable concern expressed in some of the state conventions that it was not enough to list powers granted and circumscribe them but that there also needed to be prohibitions on the government. For example, Patrick Henry argued in the Virginia convention:

> I repeat, that all nations have adopted this construction—that all rights not expressly and unequivocally reserved to the people are impliedly and incidentally relinquished to rulers, as necessarily inseparable from the delegated powers. It is so in Great Britain: for every possible right, which is not reserved to the people by some express provision or compact, is within the king's prerogative. It is so in that country which is said to be in such full possession of freedom. It is so in Spain, Germany, and other parts of the world.

Richard Henry Lee, also of Virginia, thought it highly desirable for the people to build and maintain strong structural protections for their liberties:

> Fortunate it is for the body of a people, if they can continue attentive to their liberties, long enough to erect for them a temple, and constitutional barriers for their permanent security: when they are well fixed between the powers of the rulers and the rights of the people, they become visible boundaries, constantly seen by all, and any transgression of them is immediately discovered: they serve as centinels for the people at all times, and especially in those unavoidable intervals of inattention.

In consequence of both views, the first ten amendments were adopted. They not only made additional specific prohibitions on government exercising certain powers but also the Ninth and Tenth Amendments tried to make it clear that the United States Government had only such powers as had been granted. The Ninth Amendment states:

> The enumeration in the Constitution, of certain rights, shall not be construed to deny or disparage others retained by the people.

The Tenth Amendment nails down the point:

> The powers not delegated to the United States by the Constitution, nor prohibited by it to the states, are reserved to the states respectively, or to the people.

---

**The U.S. Constitution Summary**

**Preamble**
We the People of the United States, in Order to form a more perfect Union, establish Justice, insure domestic Tranquility, provide for the common defense, promote the general Welfare, and secure the Blessings of Liberty to ourselves and our Posterity, do ordain and establish this Constitution for the United States of America.

**Article I The Legislative Branch** (Ten Sections)
All legislative Powers herein granted shall be vested in a Congress of the United States, which shall consist of a Senate and House of Representatives. . . .

**Article II The Executive Branch** (Four Sections)
The executive Power shall be vested in a President of the United States of America. . . .

**Article III The Judicial Branch** (Three Sections)
The judicial Power of the United States, shall be vested in one supreme Court, and in such inferior Courts as the Congress may from time to time ordain and establish . . .

**Article IV The States** (Four Sections)

**Article V Amending Process** (One Section)

**Article VI Debts, Supremacy, and Oaths** (One Section)

**Article VII Ratification** (One Section)

## 3.4.2 Separating Powers

The Founders were not satisfied simply with "paper" limitations on government. In their own experience, they were familiar with how these could be ignored or re-construed by those who governed. They tried to go further by building restraints in the structure of the government authorized in the Constitution. One of the principles used for limiting government was the separation of powers among the three branches: legislative, executive, and judicial. In addition, the legislative branch is divided into two houses, the Senate and House of Representatives.

For any act of the government to be put into effect, it usually requires the working together of all three branches, including separate approval action by both houses of Congress. For any law to be passed, it must be approved by majorities in each of the houses of Congress and signed into law by the President. Or, if the President vetoed the bill, it can only become law by being re-passed by two-thirds majorities in each of the houses. Even then, though the Constitution does not say this, if the courts find the law defective, as being contrary to the Constitution, they may not enforce it. Moreover, the courts require the cooperation of the executive branch to use force. The Founders hoped that each of the branches would be jealous of its own prerogatives, and would defend them and put a break on the grasp of power by any other branch.

There is yet another division of power in the United States as well. It is the division of governmental jurisdictions between the United States and the individual state governments. States existed before the Constitution was drawn and were already acting as governments. In effect, they yielded up a portion of their powers to the general government, but they still retained their own jurisdiction for governing while granting a jurisdiction to the general government. That the states would be jealous of their jurisdictions, and the United States would be as well of its jurisdiction, no one could doubt. This would further work to restrain government.

While the branches of the government are dependent upon one another in that they must work together to use force, they are independent in their actions because, at least in the original Constitution, they are selected by different electorates. The members of the House are elected by the voters in their respective districts. The Senate was originally chosen by state legislators (changed by the Seventeenth Amendment) and thus represented their state governments. The President is chosen by the Electoral College, which is a distinct body serving only that function. Federal judges are appointed by the President with the advice and consent of the Senate, but once appointed they serve for life unless they are impeached for violating the Constitution. In this sense, they are independent. None of the branches may coerce the others in the performance of their duties. This independence of the branches in taking their actions, or more precisely, in deciding whether or not to act, is crucial to their role in restraining the other branches.

---

**The Bill of Rights Summary**

Amendment I
Freedom of Religion, Speech, the Press, Assembly, and for Redress of Grievances

Amendment II
Right to Bear Arms

Amendment III
Prohibiting Forced Quartering of Soldiers in Homes

Amendment IV
Prohibiting Unreasonable Search and Seizure

Amendment V
Right to Due Process

Amendment VI
Right to Speedy Jury Trial in Criminal Cases -with Witnesses and Counsel

Amendment VII
Right to Jury Trial in Civil Cases

Amendment VIII
Right to Reasonable Bail and Punishments

Amendment IX
Other Rights Retained by the People

Amendment X
Non-enumerated and Non-Restricted Rights Retained by the States or the People

### 3.4.3 Limiting Involvement in Economy

There are a number of limitations on government in economic and trade matters written into the Constitution. The states are prohibited from coining money, from emitting bills of credit (issuing paper money), or from making anything but gold or silver coin a tender in payment of debt. Nor may they make any law impairing the obligation of contracts. Moreover, the United States was made a free trading area internally by the restrictions placed on the states in taxing goods coming in from any other states, and regulation of commerce among the states was reserved to the United States.

On the matter of money, the United States was not authorized to make any sort of money legal tender. It was authorized "To coin Money, regulate the Value thereof, and of foreign Coin, and fix the Standards of Weights and Measures." Since the states could neither coin money nor issue paper currency, nor make anything but gold and silver coins legal tender, and since the United States was only authorized to coin money, the clear indication was that if government was to have anything to do with money, it would be only to establish gold and silver as the currency.

The taxing power of the United States Government was limited in the original Constitution. Congress was empowered to lay and collect taxes, but the general rule was that they must be uniform throughout the United States. Moreover, all taxes and the like were to be levied only for the "common Defense and general Welfare of the United States." The Constitution also requires that if a head tax, or other direct tax, be levied, it must be apportioned according to the census. (This restriction has been modified by the Sixteenth Amendment.)

Property is otherwise secured by a number of provisions in the Constitution. The Fifth Amendment says that "No person shall be ... deprived of life, liberty, or property, without due process of law; nor shall private property be taken for public use without just compensation." The Fourth Amendment secures persons, houses, papers, and effects from unreasonable searches or seizures by the government. To further protect property from the government, the Seventh Amendment provides for jury trials in civil suits where more than twenty dollars is involved.

While many changes have taken place since the adoption of the Constitution and the first ten amendments, it is well to begin the study of economics from that original perspective on government. The Founders were extremely well versed in the principles of human nature and the nature of things, and they laid down a governing document in accord with these principles.

---

*The state ... tends to expand in proportion to its means of existence and to live beyond its means, and these are, in the last analysis, nothing but the substance of the people. Woe to the people that cannot limit the sphere of action of the state! Freedom, private enterprise, wealth, happiness, independence, personal dignity, all vanish.*

**Frédéric Bastiat, *The State***

# Study Guide for:

# 3 Government

## Chapter Summary

Economies exist within the framework of some form of government. While it is possible to focus only on the voluntary interactions of individuals with one another, to do so without any mention of the role of government would obscure the facts. Government exists because of the nature of man. Though humans are capable of reason and can understand the benefits of living in peace, it cannot be denied that they are also capable of abandoning good reason to gain some immediate pleasure. Man is fallible. He errs and does so to his own destruction. He is self-centered and has a strong propensity to focus only on his own desires. This often leads to errors in thinking as he commits the logical fallacy of composition, which is to rationalize that his own good is the largest good. When this occurs, he is led to inflict pain and hardship on his fellow man in order to achieve his own ends. The history of man provides ample evidence that man is sinful. Violent and aggressive behavior is often the means by which people attempt to achieve their ends, rather than relying on social and civil relationships.

Though people can rationalize cheating, stealing, trespassing, and killing, they can also be tamed. There are many means by which this occurs. Religion, education, and social rewards and punishments are just a few of the means by which a person's behavior is tempered. In addition, government is also a means to limit abusive tendencies. Generally, government is the means of last recourse in restraining behavior.

Economic activity involves the production or transfer of property. As such, government is necessary since property can be trespassed upon. Therefore, its role is necessary to protect property from malicious damage, theft, and fraud, and to enforce contracts that were voluntarily agreed upon.

By its very nature, to accomplish its function in society, government uses force. In essence, government is legal force and this force is to be used to limit unjust behavior. Consequently, governments generally benefit society by protecting lives and property. This, in turn, promotes peaceable cooperation. But even this benefit comes at a cost. Government activities must be paid for and the primary means of raising the funds necessary for financing government is taxation. Taxation is the use of legal force to take property from citizens in order to finance the operations of government. If people were perfect no government would be needed. Since no government would be needed there would be no need for taxes and people would be better off without them. However, "any level of taxation will make some undertakings unprofitable or submarginal" and represent a real cost to individuals. Unfortunately, people are not perfect and government is needed to secure civilization. There is tension as to what the proper amount of government is. There is also a potential threat that government's force might be used to accomplish the very thing that government is instituted to prevent. Namely, the government can be used to steal property rather than protecting it from being stolen. Since this is true, great care must be exercised in the just levying of taxes and in the proper functioning of government.

Historically, Americans have been aware of the dangers of government. This awareness led the Founders of the nation to limit and restrain the government constitutionally. The United States Constitution limits the government in three ways. First, it prohibits government from taking certain kinds of action. Second, it enumerates the powers of the federal government and prohibits the exercise of any other powers. Finally, it structures the government in branches and requires cooperation among those branches for action to be taken.

## Points of Emphasis

1. Government is necessary because of human nature.

2. By its nature, government uses force to accomplish its ends.

3. The government has an impact on the economy.

4. The United States Constitution limits the scope and powers of the government so as to tame and restrain it.

## Identification

1. enlightened self-interest
2. justice
3. contracts
4. *McCulloch vs. Maryland*
5. marginal theory
6. first rule of taxation

## Taxation Terms

1. user fee
2. head tax
3. real property
4. tangible property
5. intangible property
6. homestead exemption
7. tariff
8. tariff for revenue
9. protective tariff
10. sales tax
11. excise tax
12. graduated income tax
13. corporate income tax
14. withholding

## Review Questions

1. What is the basic function of government in society?
2. Why is government necessary?
3. How can government minimize its impact on the economy when it is a consumer of economic goods? When it is a competitor?
4. What does marginal theory tell us generally about the effects of increased taxation?
5. What justifies the government's use of force?
6. What constrains the government's use of force?
7. List some characteristics that make certain types of tax have more or less impact on the economy?
8. An income tax that is not graduated is called a flat tax. Explain the difference between the two.
9. How does the United States Constitution limit the power of the federal government? . . . state governments?

## Activities

The Fifth Amendment of the Constitution says in part: No person shall . . . be deprived of life, liberty, or property, without due process of law; nor shall private property be taken for public use, without just compensation.

1. Prepare a case either to support or oppose the following position: "Environmental restrictions on private property violate the Fifth Amendment."
2. Prepare a case either to support or oppose the following position: "Government programs aimed at redistributing wealth violate the Fifth Amendment of the Constitution."

## For Further Study

1. Frédéric Bastiat, *The Law*, The Foundation for Economic Education: Irvington, NY, 1987.
2. Frédéric Bastiat, "The State," *Selected Essays on Political Economy*, The Foundation for Economic Education: Irvington, NY, 1964, pp. 140–151.
3. Clarence Carson, *Basic American Government*, American Textbook Committee: Wadley, AL, 1993.
4. Philip H. Wicksteed, "The Scope and Method of Political Economy in the Light of the Marginal Theory of Value and Distribution," *The Common Sense of Political Economy*, Augustus M. Kelly: New York, 1967, pp. 772–796.

> **CHAPTER CONTENT**
>
> 4.1 The Necessity of Morality    39
> 4.2 Morality without Authority    40
> 4.3 Imparting Morality    41
> 4.4 Morality Outranks Economy    42
> 4.5 Political Economy    42
> 4.6 Morality in Government Policy    43
> 4.7 Religion and Morality    43
> 4.8 The Problem of Moral Positivism    44
> 4.9 Jeremy Bentham and Utilitarianism    45

# 4 Society and Morality

*But seek first the kingdom of God and his righteousness, and all these things will be added to you.*
Matthew 6:33

*Of all the dispositions and habits which lead to political prosperity, religion and morality are indispensable supports. In vain would that man claim the tribute of patriotism who should labor to subvert these great pillars of human happiness—these firmest props of the duties of men and citizens. The mere politician, equally with the pious man, ought to respect and cherish them. A volume could not trace all their connections with private and public felicity. Let it simply be asked, Where is the security for property, for reputation, for life, if the sense of religious obligation desert the oaths which are the instruments Of investigation in the courts of justice? And let us with caution indulge the supposition that morality can be maintained without religion. Whatever may be conceded to the influence of refined education on minds of peculiar structure, reason and experience both forbid us to expect that national morality can prevail in exclusion of religious principle.*
George Washington, 1797

## 4.1 The Necessity of Morality

The framework of any economy is quite extensive. Government is only one piece among quite an array of social institutions, customs, traditions, ingrained beliefs, and morality within which the production and distribution of goods takes place. While these may be useful to economy, they ordinarily have other reasons for being, and if the two should conflict on any matter, there is no assumption here that the demands of economy should prevail. In short, there are other aspects of life than economy that may be judged to be more important than the economic.

Even so, **morality** and order are essential to economic activity. This is especially so for trade, though it is hardly less so for production. Trade requires basically peaceful conditions, security of property, fulfillment of contracts—that people generally perform as they have promised, a general absence of fraudulent and deceitful intent, and absence of intimidation applied aggressively. Government, as noted earlier, has the basic

**morality**—occurs when someone acts or behaves in accord with the principles or standards of right conduct.

**totalitarian**—see definition, p. 6.

function of maintaining the peace. But the intervention of government in the conduct of trade and production is usually occasional and as a general rule ought to be a last resort. That is, the courts are called upon to settle disputes ordinarily when all other efforts have failed. The courts intervene when the parties cannot reach a peaceful and unforced settlement. Nor can the police be expected, or indeed wanted everywhere that economic activity is going on at all times and places. Thus, government is a last or ultimate resort in maintaining the peace.

This is a way of saying that short of the continual and ubiquitous presence of police to a **totalitarian** degree, morality and order must have other sources. People must commonly respect property, be productive rather than destructive, be honest, just, upright, and faithful. The degree to which people can be trusted varies both with individuals and particular associations and societies, of course, but that varying degrees of trust are essential to extensive commerce cannot be denied. Markets of some sort will exist even under the most unfavorable conditions. When people are less trustworthy, more must be spent to ensure safe transactions. As the cost of security mounts, the prices of goods can increase to the point where many people cannot afford them.

> **Markets** of some sort will exist even under the most unfavorable conditions. When people are less trustworthy, more must be spent to ensure safe transactions. As the cost of security mounts, the prices of goods can increase to the point where many people cannot afford them.

## 4.2 Morality without Authority

There is a notion that is sometimes expressed that if markets are free from government intervention they will develop their own order and morality. The argument for this view would go something like this. The benefits of the exchange of goods among people are so great that when calculating their own well-being, most would generally agree to observe the morality essential to the production and distribution of goods. Hence, a morality based upon calculation and utility would develop and be reinforced by the obvious success of production, trade, and commerce. That is, people would be honest, truthful, faithful in fulfilling their commitments, would not steal, cheat, lie, form gangs to prey upon the defenseless, or otherwise do harm to one another because of the advantages accruing from trade. In short, no authority aside from calculated social advantages would be necessary to induce or reinforce morality.

An obvious disadvantage of this theory is that so far as we know it has not been put to the test. No society of any extent exists, or so far as we know ever existed, without some sort of government. More, no society of any extent has existed without a morality based upon some authority other than personal or social advantage. Undoubtedly, self-interest is a powerful motive, but that the self-interest will be "enlightened" does not follow in the least. Nor is it all that easy to get from individual self-interest to the general welfare of society. There are too many ways to benefit oneself to the harm of others. Stealing, lying, and cheating are not only attractive at times, to the extent they might be expected to succeed, but they can also be done by the individual for his own benefit at the same time they are harming others. Indeed, the very idea of the desirability of the general well-being probably depends upon a highly developed moral or ethical sense.

## 4.3 Imparting Morality

In any case, both reason and experience suggest that it is by no means an easy matter to inculcate morality. After all, even with widely held religious convictions, parental moral teaching, social approval of upright moral behavior, and legal punishments for many kinds of wrongdoing, there has always been more than a little lying, cheating, stealing, killing, and trespassing. Sometimes, it is more open than others, sometimes more widespread, and sometimes and in some places, rampant. Sometimes immorality and lawlessness become so widespread that the continued existence of society is in doubt. In such chaotic times, the evil of which people are capable becomes apparent to everyone. In such circumstances, it is easier to see that morality needs or requires extraordinary, even ultimate, sanctions. In general, it would seem to be desirable to have as many supports of morality as possible.

Children are usually taught the rudiments of morality and of acceptable social behavior in the home. They are also taught, quite often incidentally, the customs and traditions of community and country. Generally, the teaching of morality is, and must be, taught in a framework of parental authority and as an assertion of authority. The child must be taught not to do things that would endanger himself first, and those by which he might harm others later. They are often taught first as "dos and don'ts," and gradually the idea of right and wrong begins to take shape. It depends upon the child, to some extent, but before he has reached school age the child will usually begin to want to know why he should do this and not that. Prohibitions that have to do with self-harm may be easy enough to explain, but various authorities are apt to be invoked for other prohibitions. The parent may assume authority by declaring, "Because I say so." Or, in the case of customs, he may simply say, "Because it isn't done, not in public anyway." Reason is often an uncertain authority, either because of the uncertain grip on logic of the child or parent, or uncertainty as to premises.

In any case, for most children, other sources or authorities on morality will soon begin to come into play. Siblings, peers, school, television, movies, internet, and celebrities, may become either reinforcers or counter authorities to parents. Church or Bible may become supplemental or ultimate authorities. Appeals to conscience may be made, and that something is against the law may come into play.

All this is a way of suggesting how people learn about morality and the authorities for it. The main point here is that society and morality have an impact on economy. Morality provides necessary supports to economy when children learn honesty, trustworthiness, truthfulness, respect for the property and rights of others, and faithfulness in fulfilling obligations. They may also learn virtues that are important to economy, such as hard work, thrift, doing a job well, punctuality, and the like. They may learn also about the desirability of becoming independent, self-supporting, and providing for themselves and those dependent on them. Kindliness, thoughtfulness of others, cooperation in productive activities, acceptance of and obedience to authority may also have bearing on economic affairs. Of course, our reason for learning many of these morals and virtues is not primarily because they have some bearing on economy, but they do. When people act in ways that respect the life, liberty, and property of all others, it positively impacts our economic lives. When people have no

> **Getting the Point . . .**
>
> Create a list of voices that influence teenagers' views of morality.
>
> How do you decide which ones you listen to the most in a given situation?

moral framework for these virtues, it has tremendous costs throughout the economy.

## 4.4 Morality Outranks Economy

It is also possible to learn to place economy in a subordinate role in life. Thus, Jesus taught, in the quotation at the beginning of this chapter, to seek first the Kingdom of God and His righteousness and the things of the world would be provided. Moreover, even though the market may well be the most effective means for producing and distributing goods, there are undoubtedly goods that are harmful to produce and distribute—cocaine and heroin, for example. Of course, if a good is in great and widespread demand—alcoholic beverages, for another example—attempts to prohibit its manufacture and sale may not be effective and if laws are enacted to ban the good it would give rise to lawlessness in general.

> **Respecting the Natural Rights of Others**
> When people act in ways that respect the life, liberty, and property of all others, it positively impacts our economic lives. When people have no moral framework for these virtues, it has tremendous costs throughout the economy.

There should be no doubt, either, that claims about what is moral and virtuous or socially desirable may be uneconomic or dis-economic. For example, there have been many claims over the years about the supposed injustice or wrongness of the distribution of wealth, the extraordinary profits that some people make, of the exploitation of workers, and the like. So far as these claims lead to forceful attempts to redistribute the wealth they may have a harsh impact on economy generally. Envy and covetousness may be licensed, so to speak, by such claims and lead to the taking of property from some and conferring it upon others.

## 4.5 Political Economy

This brings us to a major role that economics has played since it was formulated as a study. It was shaped by the classical economists mainly as an argument against government regulation and control in an economy. The descriptions of the market generally showed that it works most effectively in providing those goods and services that are most wanted if government does not interfere with its working. The principles of economics, as they eventually came to be called, were useful knowledge in themselves, quite often. But economics was called **political economy** from its early inception through most of the nineteenth century, and it developed more as a guide to political conduct than to economic behavior.

Ideas began to be spread from the middle of the nineteenth century onward that the market and unhampered economic activity worked for some classes of people and not well at all for others. Thus, some who called themselves economists began to champion various interferences with and interventions in economic activity by government. Strangely, the phrase political economy was dropped and replaced by economics generally at about the time that economists were increasingly championing various political interventions. In the twentieth century, many economists began

**political economy**—the conditions under which an economy exists in a country. It includes laws and government regulations, customs, traditions, and morality. The early study of economics was pursued in terms of the political context in which the economy operated. All economies have some political context and it is important to understand that framework to appropriately analyze the economy.

to make a living by advising government in what ways to intervene in the economy. Indeed, since immediately after World War II, the President of the United States has had a Council of Economic Advisers. There are still economists, of course, who believe in and support the free market and free enterprise, but they have been a relatively small minority for most of the twentieth century.

## 4.6 Morality in Government Policy

There are questions of morality in government action as well as individual action. A case could be made that unjust taxes are immoral. When government goes beyond taxing to support itself in maintaining the peace to programs for redistributing the wealth, it is certainly doing things that most people would agree are immoral for individuals to do. That is, it is generally accepted that it is wrong to take property from some—steal it—to keep for oneself or give to others. Is it less wrong for government to do so? To put the question in a more pointed American context, may the people, acting through elected representatives, rightfully do what is wrong for individuals to do? These are questions that must be answered, if they are faced, in terms of morality and what ultimately sanctions it. They are ultimately religious or philosophical questions.

In any case, perhaps the main point has been made that society and morality form a major part of the framework of economy. Morality, sanctioned by society and religion, is highly important in the ordinary conduct of economic activities. Society, with its customs, traditions, taboos, prescriptions, and institutions is integrally a part of the background of economic activity. Indeed, in many respects, an economy is an aspect of the society and the prevailing morality and beliefs.

> **Getting the Point...**
>
> Is it moral for people, acting through their elected representatives, to do what is wrong for them to do individually?

> **Morality and Society**
> Morality, sanctioned by society and religion, is highly important in the ordinary conduct of economic activities. Society, with its customs, traditions, taboos, prescriptions, and institutions is integrally a part of the background of economic activity.

## 4.7 Religion and Morality

The discussion of this portion of the framework of economy will be closed by some demonstration of the connection between religion and morality. If a morality is to be effective, it must be supported by powerful rewards for doing right and penalties for doing wrong. Such sanctions usually accompany the prohibitions against wrongdoing and provide an implicit promise of rewards, which usually sustain the virtues of the people. The rationalist may conclude that murder is an obvious evil and that all people will readily concur with him in this opinion. The matter may be otherwise, however. Remove the sense of awe and mystery that people have before God—in whose image they were each created—and who is to say that you do not at the same time remove the awe and mystery that envelops human beings and protects them from one another ordinarily? Thus, murder may become widespread, as it has in our day, when the majority of the people no longer believe strongly in a transcendent God.

So it is, too, with morality and virtue in general. At the time that the United States was founded and for most of the nineteenth century, Americans generally believed strongly in an order in the universe. They believed, too, that it was a moral order, for it had been created by God. It was virtuous, people thought, to act in accord with this order. This belief served as a profound basis for freedom for Americans. Such a belief was conducive to faith. The one who lacks faith will be easily inclined to the view that he must do everything himself or in conjunction with others, that if people are not compelled they will not act in desired ways, and that there must be a master plan conceived by men or else society will come to pieces and chaos will reign. The person with faith in an order higher than himself can be content to leave other people to their devices, secure in his knowledge that God is not mocked, that right will triumph, and that his major task is to see that he is not destroyed in the process. He can believe that an economic order may work justly without society's intervention by way of a master plan. That is, he believes that there is an order in the universe that brings harmony out of the diverse activities of people if government does not interfere with it.

It was beliefs such as these about morality and order that underlay the great achievements in America. It is possible to conceive a vast system of economics without reference to the framework, but unless it is supported by the framework it will not work.

---

**Faith as the Basis for Liberty**

The one who lacks faith will be easily inclined to the view that he must do everything himself or in conjunction with others, that if people are not compelled they will not act in desired ways, and that there must be a master plan conceived by men or else society will come to pieces and chaos will reign. The person with faith in an order higher than himself can be content to leave other people to their devices, secure in his knowledge that God is not mocked, that right will triumph, and that his major task is to see that he is not destroyed in the process.

---

## 4.8 The Problem of Moral Positivism

In addition to the rise of Marxism, which will be considered in greater detail later, another strand of collectivist thought emerged in the nineteenth century. Its impact in Western societies has been profound. In general, it was this mode of thinking that provided the avenue for socialism and communism to spread. It can best be called **moral positivism**.

Moral positivists reject the position that people have certain natural rights. In fact they reject the concept of natural law altogether and argue that there are no moral absolutes. Rather, they view man as if he were simply another animal, a "smart ape" as they would come to view him. This mode of thought developed as a result of the success of science. Using the inductive method (most often called the scientific method) of gathering data and empirically verifying or rejecting certain theories, physical scientists had made numerous discoveries about the world. Early scientists conducted their work based upon a Judeo-Christian view of nature. In fact, they confidently studied nature to gain knowledge about it because they thought it was created by a rational and orderly God who established fixed principles that could be discovered, understood, and

**moral positivism**—a rejection of a natural moral order and of God-given individual rights in favor of a naturalist view of mankind. In the naturalist view, what is right becomes simply what legislatures declare is right.

acted upon. The result of this was that many discoveries were made and many new inventions were created whose usefulness depended on the regularity of the principles in action.

> **Moral Positivism**
> Moral positivists reject the position that people have certain natural rights. In fact they reject the concept of natural law altogether and argue that there are no moral absolutes. Rather, they view man as if he were simply another animal, a "smart ape" as they would come to view him.

However, as the Enlightenment gained acceptance, more and more scientists and other philosophers began to speculate that nature was all that was there. That is, they embraced a view that can best be called **naturalism** and came to believe that the universe operated like a machine going on of its own accord. As such, they embraced atheism as a foundational assumption. The implication of this assumption for the study of history and the social sciences is that man is seen as just another animal whose actions are mechanical and should be studied in the same way as the actions of any other animal.

**naturalism**—the worldview that asserts that nature is all there is and, hence, embraces atheism.

## 4.9 Jeremy Bentham and Utilitarianism

The introduction of this view into the study of political economy was largely due to the efforts of the British philosopher, Jeremy Bentham. Having rejected the natural law foundations of the British legal system, Bentham argued for a new foundation, which came to be called **utilitarianism**. He argued in favor of making public policy decisions on the basis of conducting a **hedonistic calculus**. Based upon the notion that man is just another animal, Bentham claimed that the only public policies that made sense were those that would increase the sum of total happiness in society. He, therefore, argued that the acceptance or rejection of any law should be based on a calculation as to whether the law would add to or subtract from the people's happiness. Good laws were those that increased happiness and bad laws were those that decreased it.

But the problem with this is that it is impossible to measure happiness. What are the measurable units of happiness? Bentham aimed to call such a measure a util. But how much is a util? When we measure things we devise units of measure that have a straightforward meaning. People have a conception of how much an inch is, or a yard, or a meter for that matter. But, how much is a util? While Bentham recognized his problem, he did not give up on eventually finding such a measure. Nonetheless, such an effort is a fool's errand. Happiness is an illusive thing. The pleasure that one person might take in some action is often considered pain by someone else. As such, how do we make comparisons?

> **Jeremy Bentham (1748–1832)**
> English legal reformer, philosopher, and economist. He was a child prodigy, indeed, a prodigy all his life and had a great influence on thought in the nineteenth century. Bentham gave currency to a philosophy known as utilitarianism. The touchstone of his philosophy was the pleasure–pain principle, teaching as he did that people seek to maximize their pleasure and minimize their pain. That is the wellspring, he thought, of human activity. Society ought to operate, he claimed, on the principle of "the greatest good for the greatest number." This underlay his belief in majority rule in politics and to work to extend participation as widely as possible. While he accepted some of the central ideas of utility as the guiding principle. Many economists since his time have followed his lead in stressing utility.

**utilitarianism**—a form of legal positivism that argues that laws should be based on a hedonistic calculus.

**hedonistic calculus**—the idea that any law or government program should be evaluated by adding up all the pleasure it would create and subtracting out any pain it might cause. If the sum is positive, proponents argue that the law or program is good.

In truth, no calculations can ever be made to discern the sum of happiness associated with any public policy or law.

Nevertheless, Bentham's philosophy made its way into the study of economics. One of Bentham's disciples was a man named James Mill who was the father of John Stuart Mill. It was John Stuart who coined the phrase utilitarianism by writing a book by that title. In addition to writing this book, John Stuart also published an economics text that became the most widely used teaching text of the late nineteenth century. As a result, his utilitarianism began to spread through the British school of economics and from there throughout the world.

While Bentham and Mill were largely in favor of policies promoting free enterprise, there is nothing inherent in utilitarianism that would predispose it in that direction. There is no foundational commitment to the individual's right to private property. As a result, utilitarian economists today exist on a spectrum running from those who advocate for economic freedom on the grounds that the market is efficient to those who advocate for heavy regulation or socialism on the ground that the market economy suffers from many foundational failures.

Indeed, among the mainstream of economists today, the focus of the study has essentially become an effort to square the circle, so to speak. That is, having implicitly adopted Bentham's utilitarianism most economists today are engaged in the effort to evaluate public policies on a cost-benefit basis. Thus, **equilibrium price theory** has become the tool that these economists are attempting to employ to achieve Bentham's grand design. Most such thinkers cannot conceive of economics apart from the mathematical models they create and their efforts to measure these through the statistical analysis of econometrics. But this effort is reductionism and it is implicitly atheistic. It reduces our conception of mankind to the animal level. Rather than being seen as individual actors who pursue self-defined ends by purposeful action, human beings are seen as programmed machines whose choices are purely mechanical and can be endlessly redirected.

> ### John Stuart Mill (1806–1876)
>
> English reformer, philosopher, and economist. He was a child prodigy, educated by his father rather than going to school, read the main Greek and Latin works in the original languages, and read virtually all the major histories by the time he was grown. In time, he had picked up at least a smattering of knowledge about all the arts and sciences. He worked for years at India House, which dealt with governing India, wrote widely, and interested himself in a variety of causes. He was a philosophic radical and utilitarian, which meant little more than that he was a nineteenth century English liberal. Among the more important of Mill's works are: *On Liberty, Principles of Political Economy*, and *Utilitarianism*. Mill was the bridge between nineteenth century liberalism and the emerging socialism. Ultimately, he could accept property only as a temporary arrangement, and his reform bent tilted him toward socialism.

**equilibrium price theory**—modern day price theory attempts to enact utilitarianism by way of cost/benefit studies. The problem is that costs and benefits are always subjective and based on assumptions.

> *When law and morality contradict each other, the citizen has the cruel alternative of either losing his moral sense or losing his respect for the law.*
> **Frédéric Bastiat**
>
> *History has taught us that freedom cannot long survive unless it is based on moral foundations. You can get the economics right, but in addition liberty must be cultivated as a moral quality.*
> **Margaret Thatcher**

# Study Guide for:

# 4 Society and Morality

## Chapter Summary

There are many aspects to life. Economics is one of them. Though much of life involves economic activity, other aspects of life are important as well. In fact, the economy operates within a vast array of other social institutions, customs, traditions, beliefs, and moral values. Of these, morality is an essential prerequisite for economic activity to flourish. That is, unless people respect the property rights of others, it is difficult for the economy to operate effectively since the basis of economic activity involves production and trade of property on a voluntary basis. If there is constant trespass on the property rights of others, people will spend far more time, energy, and material resources protecting themselves from abuse than working and trading. Therefore, moral values are fundamental.

Among the important virtues that form this base are honesty, integrity, faithfulness, kindness, thoughtfulness, punctuality, diligence, and respect for legitimate authority. In addition, trust is a key element of the overall success of an economy. To the extent that an atmosphere of trust is prevalent in society, people can believe that their trading partners will live up to their obligations in contractual agreements. Thus, the contracting process requires less time and effort and trade thrives. Otherwise, as trust wanes, more resources will be expended for security measures aimed at protecting property and insuring contractual performance. When immorality and lawlessness become pervasive, the continued existence of society is threatened.

Moral values are best taught to children by their parents. To this instruction, churches, schools, or peer groups may either augment or diminish the morality that has been instilled by parents. The values inculcated in children will have a significant bearing on the eventual success or failure of the economy. Economy works best when the moral values of truthfulness, hard work, thrift, and others are promoted. On the other hand, when these values are not encouraged, then negative side effects in the economy will become prevalent.

This understanding of the nature of things led early economic thinkers to argue against government regulation and control, since they saw that government could easily be manipulated to destroy rather than promote these moral values. They argued instead for active government participation in promoting property rights only, leaving citizens to engage in whatever productive endeavor they thought most appropriate and to trade privately among themselves. However, by the mid-nineteenth century, other writers began to argue that government intervention is necessary to protect some individuals from exploitation. Most twentieth century economists have argued for some degree of government intervention in the economy.

## Points of Emphasis

1. Economics is only one of many aspects of life. Since human beings are spiritual, mental, and material beings, it is not surprising that this is true.

2. Trust is a key element to economic growth and economic well-being. The degree to which people can be trusted to perform according to their word is one indicator of the potential for economic success in a society.

3. Moral values are inculcated primarily within the context of family life. Further, it is highly unlikely that humans would gravitate towards moral behavior simply on the basis of reason alone for it is all too evident that human nature is given more to rationalizing one's actions.

## Identification

1. morality
2. totalitarian
3. political economy
4. moral positivism
5. naturalism
6. utilitarianism
7. hedonistic calculus
8. equilibrium price theory

## Review Questions

1. Who has the final say as to what is right and what is wrong?
2. What are some ways that we act by faith and take for granted that others will do what they say?
3. How is morality learned?
4. In what ways do some supposed authorities undercut the moral formation of people generally?
5. Give one or more examples of how laws might be different when written by legislators who acknowledge human nature from those written by moral positivists?

## Activities

1. Discuss the current transformation of Eastern Europe and Russia from what they were under the Soviet Union. You might want to pick one country to discuss some specifics. If these countries want true free market reform, what changes are necessary? Are these changes taking place?
2. Prepare a case for or against the following position: "The advantages to be gained by peaceful, voluntary trade are so great that no government authority is needed at all for individuals to behave morally."

## For Further Study

1. P.T. Bauer, *Reality and Rhetoric: Studies in the Economics of Development*, Harvard University Press: Boston, 1984.
2. P.T. Bauer, *Equality, The Third World, and Economic Delusion*, Harvard University Press: Boston, 1981.
3. Lloyd Billingsley, *The Generation that Knew Not Josef*, Multnomah Press: Portland, Oregon, 1985.
4. Dennis O'Keeffe, editor, *Economy and Virtue*, The Institute of Economic Affairs: London, 2004. www.iea.org.uk
5. Clarence Carson, Paul Cleveland, and Dwayne Barney, *The Great Utopian Delusion: The Global Rise of Government and the Destruction of Liberty*, Boundary Stone: Birmingham, AL, 2015.

> **Chapter Content**
>
> 5.1  Varieties of Property       50
> 5.2  Origins of Property         52
> 5.3  Legal Protection of Property    55
> 5.4  Assault on Property         56

# 5 Property

*You shall not steal. . . .*
*You shall not covet . . . anything that is your neighbor's.*

**Exodus 20:15, 17**

*In my opinion, society, persons, and property exist prior to the law, and—to restrict myself specifically to the last of these—I would say: Property does not exist because there are laws, but laws exist because there is property.*

**Frédéric Bastiat, 1848**

*The fact that God has given the earth for the use and enjoyment of the whole human race can in no way be a bar to the ownership of private property . . . Men always work harder and more readily when they work on that which belongs to them . . . It is surely undeniable that, when a man engages in remunerative work, the impelling reason and motive of his work is to obtain property and thereafter to hold it as his very own.*

**Pope Leo XIII, 1878**

All economic activity entails the use or transfer of **property**. It is not possible to produce goods without using various sorts of property. All transactions involve exchanges of property. Indeed, it could be maintained that all human activity, or even existence, entails the use of property. Even the occupying of space, which is the minimum any corporeal being can do, uses property. But since the concern here is economic, let us stick with the economic aspect of the use of property. It follows from what has been said that property ownership or control is the essential framework of economic activity.

It is probably essential that most property be privately owned for economic activity to take place. The Austrian economist, **Ludwig von Mises**, says that "Private ownership of the means of production is the fundamental institution of the market economy. It is the institution the presence of which characterizes the market economy as such. Where it is absent, there is no question of a market economy." Mises has, however, introduced a distinction that is not in the nature of property by referring to the "means of production." All property is potentially a means of production, whether it is land, buildings, food, clothing, or what not. Nor is it clear why the distinction would be introduced even if all property were not potentially a means of production, since production is only one aspect of the market and economy. It is probable that it is not simply the existence of the market, nor only the presence of the means of production, but the very possibility of the economy itself that depends upon private ownership. Economy means, most basically, the frugal use of scarce resources. The most crucial aspect of ownership is control. Without ownership, then, there can be no frugal management of resources—no economy.

That does not dispose of the matter, however. There have been claims that property should be held in common. This claim has been most often advanced for landed property, but we are considering the general idea of **common ownership** here. That property could be owned in common is an illusion. Obviously, it could not be used in common, i.e., everyone could not use the same portion of it. Someone has to make the decisions about the use of land or any other resource. That is, someone must be in control of any good. Once resources were parceled out, the common ownership would dissipate.

Sometimes ownership is referred to as public ownership. Actually, public ownership is the same illusion in a different guise. The general public cannot control and use the property at will, nor does it do so. Those who actually control it restrict the use of all so-called **public property**. It is never available at will to the general public. Governments can and do own property, of course, which is what is usually meant in America by public property. Nor is government ownership an illusion, not at least so long as private ownership is also widespread. But if government should proceed to try to own all property, that is, if it controlled everything, it could only succeed in abolishing the market and any effective economy as well. After all, markets are places where transfers of property take place, and if government is not going to transfer property there can be no market. Without a market, there could be no calculation, and without calculation no economy.

The above might appear to be so much idle chatter, but it is hardly that in a world where there have been and are massive movements to establish communism and in the United States where there is much talk of public property. Of course, the economic arguments are not the only ones for private property; there is the matter of right and of the natural character of private property, but that will be taken up later. First, however, it may be helpful to get in mind the different kinds of property.

> **property**—anything that belongs to someone. There are different kinds: labor, money, real property (land, buildings), personal property (clothes, books, furniture, etc.), tangible property, and intangible property (stocks, bonds, etc.).
>
> **common ownership**—true ownership of property would mean that you have the right to determine how it is used or consumed. Ownership of anything cannot be completely common. Common property is generally a public place such as a park—it is open to the public and for the public to use, but the public does not have the right to use it in any way they want. Somebody (typically a government body) oversees the place and makes rules about how it may be used.
>
> **public property**—public ownership is an illusion—it may be open to the public and for the public to use, but the public does not have the right to use it in any way they want. Some government body oversees the place and makes rules about how it may be used.

---

**Economy** means, most basically, the frugal use of scarce resources. The most crucial aspect of ownership is control. Without ownership, then, there can be no frugal management of resources—no economy.

---

## 5.1 Varieties of Property

Generally, when someone refers to property what is most apt to come to mind is land. Undoubtedly, land is the most prominent sort of property, but there are many other forms of property as well, which if they are not equally important are important nonetheless. Land encompasses more than actual land as a variety of property. When someone purchases land, it is done by deed. The deed describes the land purchased and any buildings on it. It also specifies that any future permanent structures erected on it are part of the land. The land and the buildings on it are called **real property**.

> **real property**—see definition, p. 30.

Another species of property, though it is not often referred to as property, is **labor**. Every free person has a property in his labor, a potentially highly valuable property. It is economically a property because it is bought and sold in the market. Granted, it is not the actual labor that is transferred to someone else but rather the fruits of it. Even so, this right of a person to dispose of his labor is in other respects a property right.

It is important, too, that we not think of labor in a common acceptance of its meaning only, that is, that we not restrict it to physical work, such as is done in factories. Labor, properly conceived, includes mental and physical work, includes management as well as production workers, and is not, in short, limited to some category or class of people. In addition, some products of labor are singled out for establishing a property claim in them such as inventions, discoveries, and literary and artistic productions. Inventions can be patented, giving the inventor an exclusive right to exploit them for a period of years. Writings and artistic compositions or productions can be copyrighted, giving the person who produced them an exclusive right in them for a period of years. With newer technology, such as recordings, television programs, videos, these, too, are often copyrighted. Speeches, too, may be copyrighted, if they are recorded or written down.

When labor is sold for remuneration, as in wages and salaries, the fruits of the labor become the property of the employer. That is also the case, generally, for inventions and for literary and artistic productions. Karl Marx, often known as the Father of Communism, referred to this transfer as the alienation of the worker from his product, and made much ado over it, as if it were somehow evil. While there are undoubtedly problems connected with the sale of labor, both for workers and employers, the transaction is usually recognized as legal and not inherently immoral.

Another category of property that is usually distinguished from other kinds is **motor vehicles**, especially those that use public thoroughfares. These are identified as the property of particular owners in a variety of ways. The purchaser usually receives a bill of sale that has the vehicle identification number on it. Vehicles have to be licensed to use highways and waterways as well as airways. In addition, most states issue titles to the vehicle for which they must be registered. Since motor vehicles are most apt to be left unattended away from homes, they are especially vulnerable to thieves, and proof of ownership is more important than for most property.

The category of **personal property** covers the widest range and variety of items, ranging from foodstuffs to beds and bedding to clothing to household appliances to lawn equipment to cosmetics to jewelry to guns to silverware to all kinds of furniture to anything you may own in your residence for your personal use. These are property, however short-lived their possession, as in the case of perishable foodstuffs, and whatever doubts there may be as to which member of the family owns what. It might be doubted that personal property could be a "means of production," but the point remains that they are mostly potential means, even if they are unlikely to be so used. Suppose, for example, that one has a bag of flour in

**labor (as property)**—all people possess themselves and are aware of themselves. Since a person achieves his desired ends through human action, his efforts or labor is his very first and most valuable property. Labor will be discussed and defined more specifically in the next chapter. *See definition, p. 65.*

---

**Ludwig von Mises (1881–1973)**

Austrian economist who was not only influential in his native country but also in the United States. He was born in Lemberg, Austria, educated in Vienna, and received his law degree from the University of Vienna. Mises was economic adviser to the Austrian Chamber of Commerce, 1909–1938, as well as being a lecturer in economics at the University of Vienna 1913–1938. He taught a private seminar over many years at which he taught many young men who would wield considerable influence in the world in political economy. In 1940, Mises moved to New York City, where he lived, taught, and wrote for the remainder of a long and fruitful life. Among his many influential works were these important books: *Socialism, Human Action, and The Ultimate Foundations of Economic Science.* He both opposed socialism during his life and was a compelling advocate of the free market.

---

**motor vehicles**—property that is used to transport people and/or goods, which at times will be left unattended away from the real property of the owner.

**personal property**—anything you own for personal use: your toothbrush, your cat, your books, all the stuff in your home.

the pantry. Although it may be used for making biscuits or cakes for personal consumption, it might be used instead for making these items for sale in the market. Even personal clothes can be sold to get money for investments—a means of production. Or, clothes may be used in the making of fine paper for sale. In sum, then, personal property is potentially a means of production for sale in the market.

**Currency or money** is another category of property. If it is in the form of coins made from precious metals that have intrinsic value, it would be considered **tangible property**. Currency used in the United States today is *fiat* money, which will be discussed in later chapters. It has value only in exchange for other goods, if it has any at all. It may nevertheless be considered as money, and thus as property in its own right.

Finally, we come to **intangible property**. Since paper currency may be a claim on some commodity, such as gold or silver as it once was in the United States, it may be intangible property. But perhaps, the most familiar example of this type of property is shares of common stock. Shares of stock indicate parts of ownership of a corporation. The shareholder, as such, neither owns nor has a specific claim to any particular piece of the property of the corporation. He owns a part of the whole. Should the property of the corporation be sold, the shareholder would have a portion of the proceeds, depending upon the number of shares outstanding and how many shares he held, after all other claimants or creditors had been satisfied. Bonds and notes of debtors are also intangible property of the creditors. Contracts may also constitute intangible property as claims upon future service or goods.

In sum, any and all sorts of things constitute property, as the above listing may suggest. Moreover, the rights in property are subject to many kinds of division and assignment. Property extends from the most tangible and extensive—land—to the least tangible and limited, for example, shares in a corporation. Property is everywhere man is and in all sorts of things.

> **Karl Marx (1818—1883)**
>
> German intellectual, revolutionary, and the philosopher for modern communism. He was born in Germany, studied in several universities, and received a doctorate in philosophy. The academic life was not for him; he was too alienated from his culture and society for anything as ordinary as that. His revolutionary ideas brought him to the unfavorable attention of the authorities, and he was soon shifting from one European country to another for refuge. Finally, he settled with his family in London, where he lived for the rest of his life. Marx's complex ideology can be approached through these three keys. The class struggle was his key to explaining history. The exploitation of the laboring class (resting on the labor theory value) his key to economics. Revolution was the key to power. While Marx led an International Workingmen's Association briefly, most of his life was taken up in disputation and writing. He honed his writing skills in critiques of the works of other socialists before going on to develop his own central concepts. His influence on thought in the twentieth century has been great, not only in communist countries but also throughout the world.

**currency or money**—this will be defined and discussed in detail in the chapter "A Medium of Exchange—Money" on p. 87 ff.

**tangible property**—see definition, p. 30.

**intangible property**—see definition, p. 30.

**property rights**—the right to make decisions about the things you own. A person's rights to his or her own property and the right to protect it.

## 5.2 Origins of Property

**Property rights** are primal. They at least undergird if they do not give rise to all other rights and liberties. They are primal in that they are essential to the maintenance of life on this planet. In that sense, it can be said that claims to or rights in property arise from the nature of things. "Property," the French economist Frédéric Bastiat, writing in the middle of the nineteenth century, said, "is a necessary consequence of the nature of man." Bastiat explained his position this way:

> In the full sense of the word, man *is born a proprietor*, because he is born with wants whose satisfaction is necessary to life, and with organs and faculties whose exercise is indispensable to the satisfaction of these

wants. Faculties are only an extension of the person; and property is nothing but an extension of the faculties. To separate a man from his faculties is to cause him to die; to separate a man from the product of his faculties is likewise to cause him to die.

Indeed, something like property rights could be said to exist for plants and animals. In a sense, plants assert a property-like claim on the soil and the surrounding area in which they are rooted. They send roots down into the soil, claiming it for their portion until they are uprooted or die, and appropriating the minerals in the surrounding soil. Some plants even enrich—improve—the soil with the nodules of nitrogen they form on the roots.

The lower animals, too, appear to have and to hold property, and sometimes even to produce it. Thus, ants have their hills that they attempt to defend from intruders; bees have their hives where they live and make honey, protecting it with their stings. Some of the higher animals even lay claim to more extensive territory that they may mark off in some way, and that they defend against others of their species or any animal they may recognize as a threat. This has been called the territorial imperative of animals, and it is said to apply to many, if not all, animals.

However, all plant and animal claims are subject to human sufferance or pleasure. God gave man dominion over the earth, Scriptures say, and this dominion extends to creatures and plants as well. Man may tolerate, even welcome, some plants and those animals that he reckons to be friendly or harmless, and he more or less endures those plants that are too fecund to be readily got rid of or those animals, such as flies, ants, and various bugs, but in general all animal claims are subject to man's dominion.

Bastiat said that property "has been divinely instituted . . . ." He meant primarily the nature of man as created by God, and the conditions in which he placed man made property essential to him. Beyond that, however, the Ten Commandments give a special place to property. The eighth commandment prohibits stealing, and the tenth condemns the coveting of the possessions of others. Thus, property is given a similar protection to that of life itself.

Somewhat more needs to be said, too, on the natural origins of property, for the Biblical commandments simply assume property rights. One of the earliest attachments of small children is to what they claim as their property. One of the first emphatic phrases that a child usually uses is "that's mine." If it is a prized toy, he will wrestle for it with anyone who has it, announce his claim, and cling tenaciously to it once it has been reclaimed. It is more as if it were instinctual than learned, though, of course the child may have been told it was his and may even have been admonished to take care of "his" plaything. It may be noted, however, that children display no such sharpened sense about the property of others. That, and the respect for it, is something that children have to be taught, and many do not learn it readily.

Reason tells us, or at least confirms to us, that what a person has made from his own materials with his own hands and tools is his. No one

> **Frédéric Bastiat (1801–1850)**
>
> French economist of the mid-nineteenth century. His youth was spent as a country gentleman in the provinces, and, as befitted his position, he became involved in local government. He came to economics by way of a concern about protectionism and free trade. It became his consuming interest from the early 1840s until his untimely death in 1850. Bastiat brought a facile pen, a quick and ready wit, and the skills of a journalist to his voluminous work. Much of it was concerned with refuting socialism and to showing the benefits of free trade and free enterprise. The framework from which he wrote was that of natural law and the rights of property. Many of his works have now been translated into English, among them, *The Law, Economic Harmonies,* and *Economic Sophisms.*

who has ever produced an object in this fashion is ever apt to doubt it. It is likely, too, that if each person had made everything with his own hands from his own materials that he claims to own, no question about property would ever have arisen. Except, of course, his claim to the materials from which the objects were produced might be questioned. Before exploring that further, however, let us stick simply to the matter of property arising from the adding of labor in the improvement or production of it. Those seeking a natural explanation of the origin of property have usually focused upon the mixing of one's labor with something, as in improving it or making it accessible. They say that the labor added gives the claim to property. Thus, Pope Leo XIII (who served 1878–1903) declared that each man:

> ... makes his own that portion of nature's field which he cultivates—that portion on which he leaves, as it were, the impress of his individuality; and it cannot but be just that he should possess that portion as his own and have a right to hold it without anyone being justified in violating that right. ...

While this is an impressive argument, it does not entirely dispose of questions that have been raised about the ownership of land. And, as implied above, ownership of land is crucial to the defense of private rights in property. It happens that the production of any sort of good is dependent upon land. Land provides a place on which and from which all things are produced. Virtually all goods are either drawn from the soil or produced with things derived from the earth. Thus, if they are to be private property, the ownership of the land from which they are drawn must somehow be settled. To put it another way, full-fledged private property depends upon private property in land.

It has been argued that the land belongs to all of us in common, since no man does or can make land, since it is a gift of God. On the other hand, it should be equally clear that the land must be parceled out if it is to be effectively utilized. In fact, that is what has usually happened, and probably always has happened. As soon as any considerable number of people settle in some territory the production of the various individuals involved leads to the division of the land. Sometimes claims to land have been established by those who have lived upon the land and improved it. Sometimes, lands have been purchased from governments who had claims by way of conquest or treaty to the territory. Sometimes, lands have been granted to political favorites by those in power. All of these devices were used at one place or another as people of European background initially claimed lands in the United States. Undoubtedly, many original claims to land were not established by any improvements made on the land by claimants, or the mixing of his labor with the land.

In truth, the claim to private property in land has a different ground generally than that of a maker of some good or provider of some service. It arises from the nature of life on earth, the dominion of man, and the conditions for utilization of land, as well as the establishment of property in the products dependent upon the soil. Property in land is essential to all claims to property, and the sooner justice is established in the matter of land owners, the better for all economic and other activity. That is not to suggest that it has not been established for those generations now living in the United States, who generally had nothing to do with the original claims, but rather to confirm a general rule in the matter.

> **Land as Property**
> Property in land is essential to all claims to property, and the sooner justice is established in the matter of land owners, the better for all economic and other activity.

## 5.3 Legal Protection of Property

According to modern natural law theory, government neither grants nor confers rights in property. At most, it only recognizes rights to particular property and protects or enforces the owner's rights to his property. Even when an individual acquires property from government, he acquires such rights as government had, not the right itself from government. In its ordinary conduct of its affairs, then, government is a protector of property rights, among the other rights of the individual. In the course of the protection of rights, government does indeed often define various sorts of property, and indicate measures to be taken to assure protection. So far as it goes no further than this, property rights may still be inviolate.

A good example of this appropriate government role is the copyright law that went into effect in 1978. In this act, Congress declared that copyright is vested in the author when the work is done, regardless of whether the author obtains a copyright from the Copyright Office in Washington. However, the author's rights will be more effectively established if he does file a copyright application and submit copies of the material copyrighted to the Library of Congress. In connection with this law, the rights of authors in various sorts of materials are defined and set forth. The law also specifies that any transfer of the author's exclusive right to copy to someone else must be by written instrument. Thus, the Congress conferred upon authors a similar kind of protection of their property rights in their creations that landowners generally have in landed property in the United States.

Laws in the United States have generally protected property in ways similar to which they protect persons. That is, the theft of property, whether by taking, fraud, or deceit, is a crime. It is not simply a civil matter. The government itself will proceed against thieves, and, when they are found guilty, they may not only have to make restitution, if they do or can, but also may be fined and imprisoned. Thus, theft is considered not only an offense against a particular property owner but against the public generally. By that, we may conclude that the security of property generally is considered of great public importance. The law not only distinguishes between the amount taken—calling a small amount petty theft and a large amount grand theft—but also may assign greater penalties for more use of force in taking. Thus, breaking and entering is considered a more serious crime than simply taking unprotected property. Assaults or the use of weapons in thievery also incur larger penalties generally, though this may be because of danger to persons rather than to property.

Some species of property are protected more fully than others. A man's house is his castle it has been said, signifying the special protections accorded homes. A man's house may be entered only by invitation of the householder, except under exceptional circumstances, even by the police. Thus, the Fourth Amendment to the Constitution says:

> **Getting the Point...**
> What is the difference between a crime and a civil matter?

> The right of the people to be secure in their persons, houses, papers, and effects, against unreasonable searches and seizures, shall not be violated, and no Warrants shall issue, but upon probable cause, supported by Oath or affirmation, and particularly, describing the place to be searched, and the persons or things to be seized.

The filing of deeds on real property and the requirement that transfers of real estate must be in writing might be considered also as special protections of real property. Real property is further protected in that it may not be taken by government for public purposes without "just compensation."

## 5.4 Assault on Property

The legal protections of private property reached a peak in Western Europe and America in the nineteenth century. Not only was it generally well protected from thieves but also from governments as. Moreover, property was more completely owned by individuals than in earlier times. That is, individuals generally owned property in **fee simple**, which means once they had acquired it they could keep it, divide it up, sell it, bequeath it, join with others in projects by contract, withdraw from these arrangements when they had completed their contractual obligations, and dispose of it at will.

But even as these protections of property were reaching a peak a new assault on property was mounting, especially in Europe. The main thrust of the assault came from those under the sway of some sort of communal idea and socialism. It was mainly a verbal assault for most of the century, though some revolutions were attempted in the middle of the century. Karl Marx emerged at about this time, and he made himself a prophet of a coming revolution with his ideas about "scientific" socialism. All property was not directly attacked at this time, but rather that property used as a "means of production." As already noted, however, all property is potentially a means of production, even, or especially, that property we have in our own labor.

Revolutionists and radical socialists had no notable successes in the nineteenth century. Socialists, even when they were not revolutionaries, had little success with their political parties because they were rejected at the polls. Even so, these socialist ideas began to have a tentative impact on legislatures, courts, and public opinions. By the early twentieth century, if not before, laws were being enacted in many countries of the West, including the United States that intruded upon the rights to property. The legislation was usually called "social legislation." In the early years of this century, the subtle assault on the rights to property was usually mild, limiting the hours of work of children and women, passing only slightly progressive income taxes, regulating only some businesses, and the like. The attack has mounted since, and taken more and more forms, so that for a good while now it has become widely accepted that government should tax to redistribute the wealth, should adopt ever more stringent and universal regulation of the uses of private property, and even empower labor unions to use their tactics to impose their will on employers and employees.

Those who have championed this development have progressively downgraded private property; some of them have alleged that people have no rights to their property. Others have said that while human rights should be inviolate, property rights were of little account. Thus, they have proceeded on their way of downgrading property, while lionizing such "human rights" as freedom of speech and freedom of the press. Property

---

**fee simple**—a term that arose from English Common Law where the lands belong to the owner and his heirs absolutely, without any end or limit put to his estate. Land held in fee simple can be conveyed to whomsoever its owner pleases; it can also be mortgaged or put up as security.

rights are, of course, human rights, if they are rights. No one ever alleged that property, *per se,* had any rights. Humans have rights to their property, and no other point has ever been seriously argued. Property is mostly inanimate, and where it is not, it does not ordinarily contest man's dominion. Thus, it neither has, nor asserts, rights.

Property rights are not inferior to other individual rights. Most other rights, if not all, are dependent upon rights in property for their exercise. For example, freedom of the press is largely an illusion without the right to own printing presses, paper, ink, and the resulting printed material. Significant freedom of the presses is virtually unknown where government owns the presses. Nor is it easy to see how the matter could be otherwise, for someone must make the decision as to what is printed; government decisions about such matters can hardly be called freedom. Even freedom of speech is unlikely if there is not extensive private property, for without private real property there is no place to sit or stand and speak, without permission of government. Such dependency upon government does not beget free speech. Nor is it likely that there could be any significant market without private property, as indicated earlier.

Both evidence and theory point toward the view that private rights in property are essential to and underlay all other rights if they are to be enforced against government intrusion.

> **Getting the Point . . .**
>
> In the United States, lands held by Native Americans are a great illustration of what happens when land is held in common, or trust, versus fee simple ownership.
>
> Watch this video on the website stosselintheclassroom.org for a six-minute explanation. From their home page, go to Streaming Videos and search for "Native Americans." The title: of the video is, "How Government Perpetuates Native Americans' Cycle of Poverty."

> *If a man has the right to self-ownership, to the control of his life, then in the real world he must also have the right to sustain his life by grappling with and transforming resources; he must be able to own the ground and the resources on which he stands and which he must use. In short, to sustain his human right.*
>
> **Murray Rothbard**

## Tips for Preparing for Tests

You are one-fourth of the way through this text. Here are some suggestions that should help you study for upcoming tests.

1. **Ask your teacher** to review and edit this list.

2. Read the **Chapter Summary** and review the **Points of Emphasis** in the Study Guide for each chapter.

3. Review all definitions for **Study Guide Identification** and answers for **Review Questions** from each chapter.

4. Review any **quizzes** that were given and be certain you understand the correct answers.

5. Read over the information in **pull-out boxes** in each chapter and be certain you understand what it means.

6. Make sure you understand how to answer the **Getting the Point** questions.

7. Make a list of any questions you still have and **ask your teacher**.

# Study Guide for:

# 5 Property

## Chapter Summary

All economic activity entails the use or transfer of property. Production requires the use of property and transactions require the exchange of property. At the heart of these activities is the frugal use of scarce resources to achieve as many ends as possible. To accomplish this goal, ownership or control over property is crucial. In fact, it would be illusory to think that frugal management of resources could be achieved through common property. When someone uses property in one way, it precludes its use by others. If the government should attempt to control all property, then there could be no transfer of it and hence no market or market calculations. That is, there could be no economy.

There are many forms of property. People most commonly think of land when the term is used, but, in economics, the term is also extended to refer to an individual's labor services and the fruits of that labor, to personal property such as clothing, and to intangible property such as a copyright on a book. The existence of property is primal. It is a fundamental aspect of our being material beings. For example, plants in the process of growth take control over space. Also, animals mark off territory over which they try to exercise control. But these claims are subjugated to those of humans since God has given man dominion over the earth. Scripture begins with this decree and it is affirmed later in the Decalogue, which merely assumes property in the eighth and tenth commandments.

The right of property, in its fullest expression, thus finds its origin in the Judeo-Christian tradition. This tradition, coupled with insights from the Greco-Roman tradition, served as the informing philosophies that gave rise to the American form of government, which constitutionally protects the right of property. However, there is a growing assault on property in this country as well as in other countries around the world. The communal ideal of socialism is at the root of this attack. Intrusions on private property by way of the law began late in the nineteenth century in the United States. These have increased to the current day and have generally been promoted under the guise of social reform. This intrusion is undercutting a fundamental human right and endangers civilization.

## Points of Emphasis

1. The ownership of property is a fundamental prerequisite to economic activity.

2. There are many types of property.

3. The United States Constitution recognizes the individual's right to property and is meant to secure that right from government intrusion.

4. Nevertheless, the federal government has been engaged in intruding upon property rights through social reform legislation.

5. God's decree is the origin of property. In particular, not only did He give man dominion over the earth as a matter of direct decree, but creation itself, being material, necessitates private property.

## Identification

1. property
2. Ludwig von Mises
3. common ownership of property
4. public property
5. economy
6. real property
7. labor
8. motor vehicles
9. personal property
10. tangible property
11. intangible property
12. property rights
13. fee simple

## Review Questions

1. Why is it important for people to frugally manage their property?
2. What happens when people disregard the property rights of others?
3. According to natural law theory, what is the government's role in regard to property rights?
4. How does the United States Constitution address the individual's right to property?
5. List some general ways government activity has undermined the individual's right to property?
6. How are property rights under assault? Why does this matter?
7. In the nineteenth century, buffaloes were hunted to the verge of extinction. Yet more cattle are slaughtered every year in America today than all the buffalo that were killed during that time period and cows are still abundant. Why are cattle not in danger of extinction?

## Activities

1. List the pieces of social legislation that have been most important in undermining the individual's right to property in the United States.
2. Prepare a case for or against the following position: "Government intervention and control over property is absolutely necessary to protect the environment."

# Section II
# The Production and Distribution of Goods

## Chapters

| | | |
|---|---|---|
| 6. | Scarcity and Economy | 63 |
| 7. | How We Get What We Want | 73 |
| 8. | A Medium of Exchange—Money | 87 |
| 9. | The Age of Inflation | 107 |
| 10. | The Market and Prices | 129 |
| 11. | Failed Attempts to Control Prices | 145 |
| 12. | Competition and Monopoly | 163 |
| 13. | The Elements of Production | 189 |
| 14. | The Entrepreneur and Production | 205 |
| 15. | The Distribution of Wealth | 225 |
| 16. | International Trade | 241 |

*If you wish to prosper, let your customer prosper. When people have learned this lesson, everyone will seek his individual welfare in the general welfare. Then jealousies between man and man, city and city, province and province, nation and nation, will no longer trouble the world.*

**Frédéric Bastiat**

*Men naturally rebel against the injustice of which they are victims. Thus, when plunder is organized by law for the profit of those who make the law, all the plundered classes try somehow to enter, by peaceful or revolutionary means, into the making of laws. According to their degree of enlightenment, these plundered classes may propose one of two entirely different purposes when they attempt to attain political power: Either they may wish to stop lawful plunder, or they may wish to share in it.*

**Frédéric Bastiat, The Law**

*The first lesson of economics is scarcity: there is never enough of anything to fully satisfy all those who want it. The first lesson of politics is to disregard the first lesson of economics.*

**Thomas Sowell**

**CHAPTER CONTENT**

6.1 Economy     63
6.2 Scarcity     64
6.3 Allegations about Surpluses     67
6.4 Fallacy of Abundance     69

# 6 Scarcity and Economy

This section, which is the longest in the book, deals with economics proper. Section I dealt with the framework within which economy occurs. Section III deals with particular types of economies, or in some cases, more nearly *dis*-economies that have existed or do today. Section II does deal primarily with the market economy, but the market should not be given exclusive attention in economics, so the section is called rather "The Production and Distribution of Goods." That captures more completely the subject matter of economics than does market economy. While the market has become the dominant center for the production and distribution of goods in much of the world, it does not encompass all of it, even today.

## 6.1 Economy

Economy has two distinct meanings as employed in economics. The most basic one is that one closely related to such words as economize, economical, and economic. In all these connections, economy has to do with saving, thrift, and careful management of resources. Thus, one dictionary defines economical as "avoiding waste or extravagance; **thrifty**." It "implies prudent planning in the disposition of resources so as to avoid unnecessary waste." To economize is to use sparingly or frugally. Economy refers to thrifty management; **frugality** in the expenditure or consumption of money, materials, etc.

Economy is also used in a broader and more general sense as well. While it keeps some of the idea of thrifty and careful management, it refers to the conditions under which they may be practiced, or are practiced, in a particular country. The conditions under which an economy exists in a country may also be referred to as a **political economy**, but it embraces not only laws and government regulations but also customs, tradition, and morality as well. Such an economy is also referred to as an **economic system**, e.g., capitalism, communism, feudalism, and the like. This aspect of economy will be examined in some detail in Section III.

One dictionary defines economics as "the science treating of the production, distribution, and consumption of goods and services...." More pointedly, **economics** is the systematic study of the effective production of those goods that are most wanted with the least use of the scarce resources available. Undoubtedly, it is also concerned with those political conditions under which this can be accomplished.

> **Economics** is the systematic study of the effective production of those goods that are most wanted with the least use of the scarce resources available.

## 6.2 Scarcity

**thrifty**—avoiding waste or extravagance; being economical.

**frugality**—being thrifty.

**political economy**—*see definition,* 42.

**economic system**—the political structure under which an economy exists. Examples include: communism, feudalism, capitalism, etc.

**economics**—*see definition,* 4.

**scarcity**—the first principle of economics: that although human wants are unlimited, our means for satisfying them are limited. We must make choices as to how to use our scarce means to accomplish the ends we desire most.

Why economize? Why concern ourselves with economics? It is on the answer to these questions that the case for economy and economics rises or falls. The answer to be given here can be stated succinctly. In the nature of things, human wants are unlimited; the means for satisfying them are limited. That is, the means for satisfying human wants are scarce. **Scarcity** is a basic condition confronting all of us on this planet. Thus, we must economize to meet our most pressing wants from the scarce resources available to us.

To say that human wants are unlimited is not to suggest that everyone at every moment is desperately yearning for everything his imagination can conceive. That is not at all the way our wants strike us ordinarily. They may appear to us at any given time or condition as quite simple. For example, the man who is truly hungry may believe that all he wants in this world is food; a full meal and all his desires would be met. He is wrong, of course. Food has only temporarily acquired top priority. As soon as he has eaten his fill, other wants will begin to occur to him. When basic wants have been met regularly for even a short time, his want for them will take on a more subtle tone. Wants vary, of course, with the person, and with his condition at various times, but there is no upper limit on them.

That we are faced with fundamental and enduring scarcity may not be so readily believed by many people, especially Americans. After all, we are continually being confronted with an apparent bounty of goods. Go into any grocery store, and you are apt to encounter tables laden with all sorts of vegetables and fruits, freezers stocked with a great variety of meats piled high, shelves piled with row on row of canned fruits, cartons of milk, packages of cheese, cartons of beverages in large quantities, and so on. Department stores present extensive vistas of clothing, appliances, and sundries. New and used car lots may have acres of automobiles, gleaming in bright or subtle colors, lavishly fitted out, and just waiting to be sold. It would appear that goods abound rather than that they are scarce.

> **Scarcity**
> In the nature of things, human wants are unlimited; the means for satisfying them are limited. That is, the means for satisfying human wants are scarce.

Moreover, advertisers on the internet, in newspapers, on radio, on television, and on billboards urge people to buy and consume great quantities of goods. Young people are pictured guzzling down soft drinks freely, filling their tanks with gasoline, driving all over the place, always carefree and having a great time. If you lack the money to make the larger purchases, lenders market their easy term loans—no money down and repayment spread over sixty months, or whatever. Television and the internet are especially effective in showing pictures of happy consumers enjoying mass quantities of their products, and so on. The very willingness to pay out large sums of money to advertise wares would seem to imply that goods are superabundant rather than scarce.

Yet this is merely an appearance of bountifulness, an illusion. Undoubtedly, the goods exist. And there is no doubt that those who have these wares displayed are eager to sell them. To all appearances, the only thing that is in short supply is the money with which to purchase the goods, or perhaps enough customers. Yet that is only superficially the case, as we shall see, though many have come to believe a fictional monetary theory over the past hundred years or so that suggests that our only economic problem is a scarcity of money. We shall return to that problem, but for now let us examine the evidence for scarcity.

The **means of production** are scarce. For the time being, at least, we can think of that as meaning that the means to replace all those goods on display discussed above are scarce. And, if they were not replaced by new production, soon there would be few, if any, goods on display. In the most general terms, the means of production are broken down into three categories: land, labor, and capital.

**Land** includes all the materials and resources on and under the earth that are a part of it. Land is scarce. In the first place, there is a limited amount of it, and, as real estate agents say, they aren't making any more. The resources in the land are scarce as well, oil, for example, and when they are used up they will not soon be replaced. The fertile topsoil, in which plants can grow, is scarce; it washes away and becomes depleted of minerals. In many places, the topsoil is quite shallow, and rarely is it more than two or three feet deep. Except in such places as tropical rain forests, much of the most fertile soil has been brought under cultivation. Trees that grow in the soil are scarce, though they are continually replacing themselves. In any case, land, which is essential in some degree for all production (as a place to stand, if nothing else), is scarce.

**Labor** is scarce. This may be even harder to believe at first than that consumer goods are scarce. After all, we are continually bombarded with statistics of unemployment. For many years now, unemployment has been considered a major political problem. On the face of it, we might logically conclude labor is plentiful rather than being scarce. As in all other cases these most general statements of scarcity refer to the nature of things. The appearance of plenty of labor is the result basically of politically determined conditions. Labor itself remains scarce, but government by intervening in the market, makes available labor appear to be plentiful.

To see that labor is scarce, it is necessary to look more closely at the situation than those who compile the statistics of unemployment ever do. Let us begin with the individual. Each of us, except possibly small children, knows that his time and energy are limited. We can usually think of a great many more things that need doing or that we want done, than we ever have time, energy, or initiative to get done. It is a rare household that does not have a great many tasks waiting to be done. Most any homeowner can attest to the fact that a great many things are always in need of being done. The windows and door trims, as well as the doors often need painting; driveways need paving or resealing; walkways need a new surface; parts of the lawn need new topsoil and replanting; stumps might need to be removed; bushes on the edge of the yard often need pruning; planks on a rear deck may need replacing; the banisters leading off the deck might need replacing; locks on doors sometimes break and need replacing; living room carpets get worn and need replacing; likewise outside water pipes might need new insulation or to be replaced entirely; dishwashers and other appliances wear out; automobiles need regular maintenance; and there are no end of things that could be done to improve the appearance

**means of production**—the factors or elements that go into the production of any economic good. Producing anything takes some combination of the three means: land, labor, and capital.

**land**—land and all the material on or under it.

**labor**—the work that goes into production. This includes manual labor, but also includes the application of your time, energy, and talents in any way.

### Getting the Point...

Imagine that some disaster occurred that caused the trucking industry to greatly decrease operations for a month.

What items would be the first to become difficult to find?

What impact would this have on everyday life?

of houses and yards. Some of these things that need doing require materials, but all of them require labor.

If the total were added together for the whole United States, it would come to a formidable amount of labor, no doubt. Then, there are businesses that need repairs, churches, schools, public buildings, and so on and on. Beyond that, there are many kinds of jobs for which people might be employed but are not. For example, virtually all gasoline used to be pumped into automobiles by service station personnel. Today, so much of this work is done by customers that new drivers cannot even imagine having an attendant do it for them. Much the same is true in many kinds of self-service stores, which are becoming more and more common. When people's unfulfilled wants are added to what they might reckon to be needs, the potential demand for labor is unlimited. Ultimately, that is the reason for asserting that labor is scarce.

No lengthy argument is probably needed to prove that capital is scarce. **Capital** is best defined as goods used to produce other goods. Moreover, the wealth of a society is largely reckoned by the extent of its capital accumulation since this is the foundation upon which its productive capacity is based. That these are limited in supply is relatively easy to see. Moreover, since any business enterprise incurs the expense of paying for these goods to employ them in the production of other goods, they must be financed. This brings into consideration the cost of the financing in terms of money and credit. Technically, the amount spent for labor and land (including raw materials) is not a capital expenditure, but that is often more a matter of bookkeeping than anything else. At any rate, capital is scarce.

But the clinching argument for scarcity is the general one. Goods—**economic goods**—are by definition those things that are wanted that are scarce. They are those goods for which we must pay a price because they are scarce. If they were not scarce, in the nature of things, we could have them without cost. Air and water are the best, indeed, virtually the only, examples of these. Undoubtedly, air is essential for life, and in that sense, it is a prime good. We can live only a few minutes without air. Yet it is free because it abounds, fills all open places on the earth, and is hardly anywhere on the face of the earth insufficient in quantity. Costs are involved with air only in maintaining pressure on airplanes, cooling it in summer, heating it in winter, purifying it in some instances, humidifying or dehumidifying it, or providing certain components in concentrations, as in oxygen. In sum, air is the best example of a necessity for life that so abounds that it is normally free. Indeed, even in most of the cases where costs are involved in altering the quality of the air, no special charge is usually levied for it.

Water is ultimately as essential to life as air, though it is possible to live for days rather than minutes without ingesting a new supply. Water abounds, as does air, but it is not as accessible and somewhat more likely to be polluted. It is most bountiful in the oceans and seas, but because of its salt content is unfit for human consumption as seawater. Even so, fresh water abounds in most places, in springs, streams, and underground. In any quantity, however, it must be made available where it is wanted by labor, machines, or other equipment. Therefore, there is usually some small charge for water in quantity from public sources or for the machinery or labor to make it available where it is wanted from one's own sources. Filtration and treatment may be desirable also, to make the water safe for human consumption. Thus, water to a certain place, or with some other value added becomes an economic good. Only for fish and other life in water could it be said to abound and be free.

---

**capital**—most broadly defined as wealth used in the production of further wealth. Equally broadly, capital is sometimes identified with money invested in productive enterprises. More narrowly, when capital is considered as one of the three means of production, it refers to tools, equipment, or technology used in production.

**economic goods**—those things that are wanted that are scarce. *See a more detailed definition of goods, p. 4.*

This discussion of air and water may help to clarify, by comparison with commodities that do not abound, what is meant by scarcity.

Why so much attention to prove something that should be obvious, i.e., scarcity? There is good reason for the emphasis. For one thing, as already noted, the great quantities in which goods are often displayed today may give the impression that these products abound. Second, it is essential to debunking the claims about surpluses that have been used to make extensive assaults on economy over the past century. We now turn to these allegations.

## 6.3 Allegations about Surpluses

> **Friedrich Engels (1820–1895)**
>
> Son of and a business agent for a German cotton manufacturer, collaborator with Karl Marx, and co-founder of modern communism. He was born in Germany, but spent most of his adult life in England. Engels not only worked with Marx on some of his writings but also provided him with considerable financial support over the years. He co-authored *The Communist Manifesto* as well as edited and published the last two of Marx's three volume work, *Capital*. Engels wrote several books of his own, but he was almost always second fiddle to Marx.

For more than a century now, claims that abundance has replaced scarcity have been advanced, mostly by people who were supposed to be economists. They have usually not made the claim in quite those absolute terms. They have, for one thing, restricted the claim to particular areas of the world, most commonly Western Europe and the United States, or highly industrialized nations. Moreover, they often do not use such terms as abundance and scarcity, but refer instead to overproduction, unemployment, surplus, and the like.

One of the earliest such pronouncement was made by **Karl Marx** and **Friedrich Engels** in *The Communist Manifesto* in 1848. They claimed that in modern crises "there breaks out an epidemic of overproduction. . . . Because there is too much civilization, too much means of subsistence, too much industry, too much commerce." During the twentieth century, a good number of American economists joined the chorus about there being too many goods, among them, Thorstein Veblen, John R. Commons, Stuart Chase, Rexford G. Tugwell, John Maynard Keynes, and John Kenneth Galbraith. Some examples of what they have said may give the flavor of their claims.

**Karl Marx**—father of Marxism and co-author of *The Communist Manifesto*. See biographical sketch, p. 52.

**The Communist Manifesto**—one of the earliest works to attempt to make the false claim that abundance has replaced scarcity as the problem to be solved..

Stuart Chase held that the United States reached a condition of abundance in 1902. "Abundance," he said, "is self-defined, and means an economic condition where an abundance of material goods can be produced for the entire population of a given community." Chase gives such examples as these in 1931, to support his claim:

> American oil wells are capable of producing 5,950,000 barrels a day, against a market demand of 4,000,000 barrels, according to the figures of the Standard Oil Company of New Jersey.
>
> The real problem in coal is excess capacity. The mines of the country can produce at least 750,000,000 tons a year, while the market can absorb but 500,000,000 tons.
>
> American shoe factories are equipped to turn out almost 900,000,000 pairs of shoes a year. At present we buy about 300,000,000 pairs . . . . Yet if we doubled shoe consumption—gorging the great American foot, as it were—one third of the present shoe factory equipment would still lie idle.

CHAPTER 6: SCARCITY AND ECONOMY

Rexford G. Tugwell, a New Deal economist in the 1930s, said:

> Our economic course has carried us from the era of economic *development* to an era which confronts us with the necessity for economic *maintenance*. In this period of maintenance, there is no scarcity of production. There is, in fact, a present capacity for more production than is consumable, at least under a system which shortens purchasing power while it is lengthening capacity to produce.

**John Kenneth Galbraith**, an economist who began to make an impact in the 1950s, described the condition this way:

> Nearly all [peoples] throughout all history have been very poor. The exception, almost insignificant in the whole span of human existence, has been the last few generations in the small corner of the world populated by Europeans. Here, and especially in the United States, there has been great and unprecedented affluence.

Vance Packard, a popular writer of exposés in the 1950s and 1960s, may have put the case for abundance most emphatically:

> Man throughout recorded history has struggled—often against appalling odds—to cope with material scarcity. Today, there has been a massive breakthrough. The great challenge in the United States—and soon in Western Europe [he wrote in 1960]—is to cope with a threatened overabundance of the staples and amenities and frills of life.

If such abundance were indeed the case, it is clear that economy would no longer be the problem. Instead of economizing, the task would be to find ways of consuming all the goods that we can consume. In fact, a whole new branch of economics has been spurred by this outlook—"**consumer economics**" and consumerism is its motif. The problem is viewed as one of getting consumers to spend, to expand credit to spur consumer spending, and to consume more and more so that businesses can prosper and more jobs can be created to put people to work.

These "new economists" are hardly economists at all. They assume that the real economic problem is consumption and not production. As they see the matter, if consumers will not spend their money, then governments must redistribute income to ensure that it is spent. To achieve that end, they are by and large conceivers, justifiers, and promoters of government programs to redistribute the wealth and promote ever widening consumption. They have, of course, promoted programs to keep the young off the job market as long as possible, primarily through government subsidized education. As for those who are older, the aim is to get them to retire as early as possible and to provide programs that will enable them to

---

**John Kenneth Galbraith (1908–2006)**

American economist, professor, government worker, diplomat, and editor of *Fortune* magazine. He was born in Canada, educated at the universities of Toronto and California, and taught at Princeton and Harvard. He is best known, perhaps, as a writer; most of his works were very much more in the popular vein than scholarly. Among his better-known books were, *The Affluent Society, The Concept of Countervailing Power,* and *The New Industrial State.* Some of his concepts, such as "affluent society" and "countervailing power" became a part of the general language. Galbraith has attempted to maintain that we now have an economy of abundance and that there needs to be a much higher level of government control over the distribution of goods.

---

**consumer economics**—attempting to approach economics from the mistaken view that abundance has replaced scarcity. The problem is viewed as one of getting consumers to spend, to expand credit to spur on consumer spending, and to consume more and more so that businesses can prosper and more jobs can be created to put people to work.

retire early in comfort. All these things are done on the grounds of abundance of goods and of workers.

## 6.4 Fallacy of Abundance

The claims that have been made for general abundance are not valid. That is not to suggest that it is not possible to make more of some particular goods than would be wanted in the market at a particular time. It definitely is possible to do that. It is easily possible, too, to produce more than can be disposed of at the cost of production. It would be possible, for example, to make ten times more horseshoes than there are horse's feet in the world. It would be possible, by concentrating effort on producing milk, to produce more milk than all milk purchasers would want to buy for immediate use or storage. To take a simpler example, it would undoubtedly be possible to produce more copies of this book than could be sold at any price. Indeed, with today's technology, it is quite possible to saturate the market for a good number of items.

None of these examples, or others that could be cited, proves that the problem of production has been solved much less that scarcity has been banished from the earth. Granted, modern printing presses can turn out vast quantities of newspapers, books, magazines, and the like, virtually on command. Modern mass production techniques make it possible to reproduce particular items in huge quantities, many more, at least in some instances, than would be wanted or could be sold. If such reproduction constituted the whole problem of production, it could be argued that the problem of production for at least some reproducible commodities has been solved. But the problem of production does not consist only, or even mainly, of making reproductions. The main **problem of production** is to allocate resources and manpower so as to produce what is most wanted from the scarce materials available. All the ingredients that go into utilizing a printing press, for example, are scarce: that is paper, ink, electricity to turn the machines, graphic designers, artists, writers, oil to grease machines, and so on and on, are scarce. There are many other potential uses for virtually all the materials used in producing printed materials, for the trees used in making pulp for the paper, for the other ingredients used in making paper, for electricity, for oil, for ink, and so on. Thus, they must be allocated. They are scarce.

In the market, the basic problem of production is to produce goods that are in sufficient demand to trade for goods that the producer wants. This is a problem not simply for owners of steel mills, makers of paper products, producers of the legendary widgets, or whatever can be reproduced by machines. It is a problem for everyone who would trade in the market. For if he is truly going to carry his weight, everyone must produce either what he can use or what someone else will want enough to pay his price.

When we return the matter to households, it is not difficult to see that scarcity remains. Virtually every person is aware of the goods that he wants and the difficult choices he constantly has to make for what to purchase now, and what he will have to forgo or wait to purchase. Every person is aware of his economic wherewithal to purchase goods in the market. As a result, every person who shops with any care chooses goods by priority to be purchased, and those with lower priority remain on the shelves, even if they are wanted and available. These unfulfilled wants signify not only his scarcity of means to supply them, but the inadequacies of his production to generate the means to obtain them.

**problem of production**—to allocate resources and manpower so as to produce what is most wanted from the scarce materials available.

> **Getting the Point...**
>
> The basic problem of production for the market is to produce goods that are in sufficient demand to trade for goods that the producer wants.... For if he is truly going to carry his weight, everyone must produce either what he can use or what someone else will want enough to pay his price.
>
> Why would it be important for someone to grasp this principle before choosing an educational or career path in life?

None of these things prove, nor are they attempts to prove, that there is not unemployment, nor overproduction, nor sometimes surpluses of this or that or the other. All these things do indeed occur. They do not, however, disprove scarcity; they have other explanations. Producers do sometimes miscalculate or overestimate how much of certain products can be sold so as to pay for the cost of production and return a profit. Merchants sometimes stock more of particular goods than they can sell in a timely fashion at the price they are offering. Thus, they hold sales to dispose of the excess merchandise. Producers do the same with unwanted stock. Sometimes those who manage factories and the like overestimate either the demand for a product or the share of the market they will get. They develop unused capacity, which they may nevertheless keep for some time in the hope that the market will improve. Employers for these and other reasons sometimes lay off employees, which results in at least temporary unemployment. Those who are seeking employment either for the first time or otherwise may take some time to get located and this happens because we live in a world of imperfect information. We simply do not know about all economic opportunities without a search for that information. Even when we do search, there is always information that is beyond our reach.

For longer-term surpluses—of labor or other goods—there is another explanation. It is the result of government intervention in the market. Anything that is overpriced will be difficult to sell, and will most likely be in surplus. Thus, if government fixes a minimum price for any good that is above the market price, fewer purchases will be made. Additionally, when government subsidizes some products, as it has done in the past, it will most likely result in overproduction. This is as true for labor and minimum wage as it is for any other good. When the minimum wage is set above the market price for lower skilled workers, the least effective workers will not be hired and increased unemployment will be the result. If government action makes credit easy to obtain, it can result in overbuilding, and the like. These matters will be explained in detail later, but they needed to be alluded to here to round out the explanation for the appearance of abundance.

In short, scarcity remains as a basic condition, and economy is essential to survival in this framework.

---

The main **problem of production** is to allocate resources and manpower so as to produce what is most wanted from the scarce materials available.

---

> *One of the most important features of our economic resources is their scarcity: land, labor, and capital goods factors are all scarce, and may all be put to various possible uses. The free market uses them 'productively' because the producers are guided, on the market, to produce what the consumers most need: automobiles, for example, rather than buggies.*
> **Murray Rothbard**

# Study Guide for:

# 6 Scarcity and Economy

## Chapter Summary

The term economy can be used in two different ways. It can refer to the effort to economize resources so as to successfully accomplish more of one's goals or it can refer to all the conditions and arrangements within which people attempt to economize their resource use. In the former case, the term denotes the frugal management of resources that involves the avoidance of waste and extravagance in order to accomplish more end results. The latter usage of the term focuses our attention on the institutional structures, customs, and traditions that may or may not foster the economizing of resources.

People economize because resources are scarce. The wants of human beings are unlimited in the sense that people can always imagine a better situation than the present one. Yet, the resources with which those imagined ends could be pursued are scarce. Therefore, people must choose to allocate resources between competing ends.

If the economizing process is successful, it may give the appearance that the only thing that is scarce is the money needed to buy the output. In these situations, stores are full of products to sell, but the semblance of abundance is an illusion. The reality is that store shelves must be constantly replenished with new goods. These goods must be produced and the resources used to produce them are scarce. If production of new goods should cease for any extended period of time, the scarcity of goods would become very apparent.

Modern production techniques have led many writers to argue that scarcity is no longer a problem in industrial nations. Rather, they maintain that surplus production has replaced scarcity as the fundamental "economic" question. In turn, they assert there is no longer any need to economize. Instead, the focus should be on developing new ways to consume. As a result, it is common to find these writers encouraging government programs that redistribute income from those who would save to those who would borrow and spend in society. Unfortunately, these writers have succumbed to a fiction and can scarcely be called economists at all.

To be sure, it is possible for a businessman to overestimate the size of his market and produce more than can be sold for a profitable price. If this happens, when the businessman realizes his mistake he will cut his production and lower his price to reduce his inventory and cut his losses. This action will mean the unemployment of some of his workers for a time period as they seek a more valued line of endeavor.

In addition, it is possible for government intervention to confuse market signals so as to give the appearance of abundance. For example, government attempts to make credit more readily available will result in over-building in areas where this credit is extended. But these factors aside, it should be abundantly clear to everyone that they desire more than they presently have and that it is the scarcity of resources that forces them to forgo some of their desired ends for a time period. This is in the nature of things.

## Points of Emphasis

1. Scarcity of resources relative to our unlimited wants forces us to economize upon our use of resources in order to accomplish more of our desired ends.

2. Modern technology in production and mistakes by market participants give the illusion of abundance. This illusion has fooled many writers into believing that scarcity is no longer a real problem for industrial nations.

3. The notion of over abundance of goods and services is a fallacy.

## Identification

1. thrifty
2. frugality
3. political economy
4. economic system
5. economics
6. scarcity
7. means of production
8. land
9. labor
10. capital
11. economic goods
12. Karl Marx
13. Friedrich Engels
14. *The Communist Manifesto*
15. John Kenneth Galbraith
16. consumer economics
17. problem of production

## Review Questions

1. A friend of yours who has not had the privilege of studying economics yet hears you talking about scarcity. They say, "What do you mean scarcity? Go to Wal-Mart and look at the shelves. There are sixty brands of toothpaste. There's no scarcity in America!" How do you explain to them what scarcity is and why it is important?

2. Is labor scarce? What plans would you like to accomplish that require labor?

3. "Consumer economics" was mentioned as a term used for an attempted change in economic thought. How have these "new economists" attempted to change the problem being studied in economics?

4. In what ways have journalists promoted the ideas of those who argue that surplus production has become the economic problem of industrial nations?

5. How would economic activity differ when the goal is the most efficient production of the goods that are most wanted from when the goal is getting consumers to spend more money? Explain any moral hazards (temptations to compromise morals) involved for consumers.

## Activities

1. Make a list of all the things you would like to have or do or see accomplished during the next week. Rank them from most important to least important. Develop a plan for achieving the items on your list. Report back the number of things that could not be achieved.

2. Prepare a case for or against the following position: "The fact that businesses must entice consumers to purchase their products by advertising them proves the over production of goods and services in industrial nations."

## For Further Study

1. Frédéric Bastiat, *Economic Sophisms*, The Foundation for Economic Education: Irvington, NY, 1964.

> **CHAPTER CONTENT**
>
> 7.1 Acquisition by Gift    74
> 7.2 Producing for Ourselves    75
> 7.3 Acquisition by Exchange    77
>   7.3.1 Auction in the Market    77
>   7.3.2 Advantages of Market Exchange    79
> 7.4 Theft by Government for Redistribution    81

# 7 How We Get What We Want

To achieve our purposes and ends in this world, we need means. We call the means economic goods. We have already seen that these goods are always scarce relative to our unlimited desires or ends. But the question before us now is, "How can we acquire the economic goods needed to achieve our ends?"

In the nature of things, there are only four basic ways to secure the means that we need:

- we can produce them ourselves

- we can produce something of value for others and use the proceeds to trade for them

- we can receive them as charitable gifts from others

- we can steal them from others through acts of force or fraud.

Each of these methods needs some elaboration. In addition, it should be noted that **theft** can be carried out by individuals, robber bands, or by governments through the forced redistribution of private property. Theft by individuals and robber bands can be disposed of rather summarily as not being economic. On the face of it, stealing things from others might appear to be a very economic method of acquiring what you want. After all, economics is about the employment of the least amount of scarce labor and materials to acquire the goods most wanted. For the individual thief, theft might be thought of as quite economic. It might be possible for an individual to use a $100 handgun to rob a bank and acquire $20,000 in cash in a few minutes. However, there are several flaws in this line of reasoning. This reasoning suffers from a logical fallacy since what is true for the individual thief cannot be generalized to everyone in the economy. If everyone tried to live as a thief there would be nothing produced and, therefore, nothing to steal. Everyone would simply starve to death. For this reason, theft of this sort is rightly considered to be immoral, which is why God prohibits it in the eighth commandment. Thievery, then, requires no further consideration so far as individual theft is concerned. Theft by government is discussed below under a separate heading, as are gifts, producing the goods ourselves, and voluntary exchange.

> **Four Ways to Get What You Want**
> In the nature of things, there are only four basic ways to secure the means that we need:
> 1. We can produce them ourselves
> 2. We can produce something of value for others and use the proceeds to trade for them
> 3. We can receive them as charitable gifts from others
> 4. We can steal them from others through acts of force or fraud

## 7.1 Acquisition by Gift

**theft**—taking property from someone else using force or fraud.

**charity**—the voluntary act of giving to someone without expecting anything in return.

**Getting the Point...**

Can you think of any way to get things you want that does not fall within the four ways listed above?

As a general rule, economists do not consider gifts a matter for economic treatment. This is done for the same reason that theft is not considered economic either. Namely, charity requires previous production if it is to be engaged in. Someone cannot give someone something that he does not possess. Moreover, an economy cannot be built solely on charity. If everyone is waiting for someone else to produce something to give to them then nothing is produced and nothing can be given away.

Nevertheless, **charity** is very important in a free society. This is true because there are always some people in this world who would be unable to live off their individual ability to produce. Gift giving becomes an important means of survival for such people. Altruism means doing something for the well-being or welfare of others. There is no good reason to doubt that this occurs; people do give gifts, with no hope or certainty of a return. Regardless of the motives that the giver might have, this activity has gone on from the beginning of recorded history, and gifts do have an impact on economy.

It is not difficult to understand why. Many people cannot produce the goods to meet their own needs, nor do they have goods to exchange with others to meet them. The most obvious example is that of infants and small children. By the age of eight or nine, many children probably could perform simple tasks by which they might meet a portion or all their needs. Today, however, compulsory school attendance and child labor laws severely limit the work of children until they are at least 16–18 years old. Thus, most young people do not produce much, if any, of the goods to satisfy their wants. They are dependent upon others to provide for them by what amounts to gifts. Normally, parents or relatives provide these gifts; otherwise, they are most likely provided by charitable organizations.

In earlier times, elderly parents who eventually could not work were taken care of by their grown children. It was generally understood that it was an obligation to do so. Moreover, it was common for several generations of a family to live in the same house with those capable of working providing for the rest. These expectations have been rapidly declining or disappearing. Increasingly, children expect to be paid for any chores they do, and if they do any work outside the family, they expect to have all that they are paid for their own use. In addition, parents have typically built up their own financial resources so that they can provide for themselves in retirement. There have also been numerous government programs that have relieved some of the responsibilities of parents for children and children for parents.

These changes over the past several decades have been accompanied, if not caused, by a loosening of family ties generally, widespread divorce, declining birth rates, and increasing parental resentment of children. The loosening of family ties may be the result of declining dependency within the extended family and increasing dependency upon government programs.

Children are not the only ones, of course, who may be dependent upon gifts or charitable giving for goods. This is to a greater or lesser extent true for most of those who are disabled for any number of reasons. Widows and orphans, too, may sometimes be dependent upon others for the means to meet their needs. Historically, the disabled have been cared for within the extended family or by charitable giving. Thus, churches have often supported orphanages and numerous institutions have developed to care for the needs of such people. In recent decades, however, disability aid has been provided by government agencies. Whether this is a good thing or not will be discussed in more detail in later chapters.

Giving to meet temporary needs or on special occasions has long been widespread in America. In the case of natural disasters such as floods, hurricanes, and earthquakes, there is often an outpouring of gifts to the victims. On the institutional side, the American Red Cross has long played an important role in providing temporary relief. People in the community often give goods or money to those whose homes burn down or who suffer some temporary need. At the less drastic level, newlyweds may be aided in setting up housekeeping by showers or other wedding gifts. Those presumed to be about to go out on their own, such as graduates, are traditionally given gifts by relatives and friends. Baby showers are common in churches or neighborhoods, especially for the firstborns. Churches are almost wholly supported by voluntary gifts in America. Schools are often supported by gifts and are beneficiaries of assorted fund-raising activities that entail giving.

While the above examples do not exhaust the kinds of giving that are common, they may help to drive home the point that gifts play a considerable role in the economy of individuals and families. Voluntary giving has customarily helped stave off some of the demands for government to play a role. Voluntary private giving certainly has had many economic consequences, and may be correctly said to be a part of the economy.

## 7.2 Producing for Ourselves

People today generally do not think about relying on their own ability to produce all of the goods they want. There is good reason for this. Can you imagine the limitations one would face if he had to produce everything he consumed? Take for example the production and consumption of something as simple as a ham sandwich. If the consumer had to produce every ingredient in such a sandwich it would require a great deal of time and effort. The consumer would have to raise, kill, and butcher pigs. Then the suitable portion of it would have to be cured before the ham could be sliced. He would also have to grow and harvest wheat. Once that was completed it would have to be milled into flour and then baked into bread for the sandwich. And, of course, making bread requires more ingredients than the flour. These would have to be secured as well. So far we have ignored any condiments or cheese for that sandwich. The whole productive process would be incredibly complex and take an exorbitant amount of labor.

Nevertheless, through much of human history most people lived what is best styled an agrarian life. That is, they were farmers. Most people throughout most of history have probably been farmers, or at least lived on farms. They have been gardeners, shepherds, growers of grain, keepers of vineyards, and have often produced a variety of goods on their farm. It is easy enough to lose sight of this fact, because most histories focus on civilization and its rise and fall here and there, and civilization is usually centered in cities. Thus, cities tend to get the lion's share of attention. But from what we can surmise, farming has persisted and been a major occupation throughout history.

In the United States in 1800, a few years after the adoption of the Constitution, it is estimated that something on the order of 80–90% of the population lived on farms. Whatever the actual percentage, there were only a few cities of any size, and these were port cities. Virginia, which was the most populous of the states, had no city worthy of the name, nor did North Carolina, Delaware, or New Jersey. Farming continued to be the dominant occupation for most of the nineteenth century, though from the middle of the century onward, cities, especially in the Northeast and Midwest grew rapidly, as did manufacturing and other industrial pursuits.

In the nineteenth century, with the exception of the plantations in the South, most farms were small family owned or family occupied endeavors. Many of these farms were more or less subsistence farms. That is, they produced most of the goods consumed on them, both food and clothing. While they did produce a surplus for sale on the market, much of what was consumed on the farm was also produced there. Farmers did buy some goods on the market. For example, pepper and other spices, salt, tea (if they consumed any), perhaps an occasional bolt of fancy printed cloth, trinkets, gunpowder, and the like were bought. But many such farms were not so much dependent on the market as found it convenient or helpful as a supplement from time to time.

More or less **self-sufficient farms** could be found through the fourth decade of the twentieth century, but they were becoming more and more scarce. These farms not only might produce some crop for the market, such as, wheat, corn, cotton, tobacco, meat, or dairy products, but they also produced a great variety of goods besides these for home consumption. They had large gardens for producing vegetables, kept cattle, fowls, such as chickens, geese, and turkeys, hogs, and had fruit trees and vineyards for apples, peaches, cherries, grapes, and many other goods in season. Many had sheep to provide the wool for cloth. Parents, especially the father, were apt to be jacks of many trades, carpenters, wheelwrights, butchers, shearers, plowmen, teamsters, furniture makers, blacksmiths, and doers of every sort of work on the farm. They were the opposite of specialists. Women not only cooked and kept house but also might help with the farm work. They gardened, washed clothes by hand, made soap, canned food, cured meat, and engaged in many other enterprises.

The universal disadvantage of self-sufficient farms was that the farmer was limited to his own skills and what could be produced well on his land. Life on the farm was difficult and the ability of any particular individual to achieve his goals in life largely depended on his ability to master and effectively execute a vast number of skills. This greatly limited the quality of life. The shift to trading with others allowed people to specialize their efforts and this enhanced the number and quality of goods that people could acquire and put to use. Thus, the general dependency on the market has no doubt developed because of the great variety of goods that are available. We turn now to an examination of exchange and the market. As the economy grew, people more and more specialized their productive efforts on those things where they had the greatest comparative advantage and left the production of everything else to others. This resulted in the rapid increase of greater prosperity and the ability to enjoy

---

**self-sufficient farms**—farm that produces most everything it needed to survive without trading with others.

a much wider variety of goods and services than could have been had on the self-sufficient estate.

Before moving on to a discussion of acquisition by trade, it would be good to consider a down side to market exchange. The market is a hard taskmaster. Those who depend entirely upon it are subject to the vagaries of the market with its changing consumer tastes, styles, fashions, and the fickleness of human wants. Someone's success in trade can quickly evaporate because of these changes. People trading in the market do not care how hard the workman labored to produce the articles offered for sale there, with what sacrifice the producer suffered in saving to buy the tools to produce the goods, and so on. The consumer does not concern himself in the least with who will be put out of work by his decision not to buy some good. Speeches such as mothers often give their children about how they have slaved over hot stoves to cook the meal they are resisting eating would be pointless and out of place in the market. The customer in the market is almost wholly bent on supplying his wants without regard to anything else. Indeed, the rigors and uncertainties of the market are such that those who depend upon it often devote much thought to ways of evading the hardest features of their taskmaster. For this reason, free enterprise is often disparaged by people even though it has greatly advanced the well-being of people generally.

## 7.3 Acquisition by Exchange

Exchange or trade is the usual, even normal, means for acquiring goods today. Ultimately, goods are exchanged between those who own them. The main characteristic of trade is that it is a voluntary exchange of goods between owners. As long as those making the exchange are the owners of the goods, they are of an age to make contracts, both parties are mentally competent, and fraud and coercion are absent, the law does not ordinarily inquire into the relative worth of the goods being exchanged. It assumes that the contracting parties may please themselves in making trades. Trading to acquire goods has the general blessing of custom and of law.

The place where exchanges are made is known most generally as a **market**. For our purposes the word market can be used in a couple of different ways. For example, the New York Stock Exchange is a market in which stocks are bought and sold, or exchanged. It is a physical location where parties wishing to buy and sell stocks meet to do so. But when we speak of the stock market, it comprises, or comprehends, all the places and various institutional arrangements where stocks are bought or sold. Examples abound, of course, of particular markets, as well as general markets for particular goods. Economists use the word market most often in the broader sense. For example, they make such statements as, "Prices are determined in the market."

**market**—all the places and institutional arrangements providing for the exchange of an economic good.

### 7.3.1 Auction in the Market

What happens in the market can be conceived best as an **auction**. That most markets are not operated in this fashion may obscure the fact, so we had better begin with an auction. The ideal auction takes place in an estate auction in which household goods, outdoor equipment, and even, perhaps, houses and land are sold. The auctioneer announces the item to be sold, describes it, and may hold it up for examination if it is small enough. Those who expect to bid on larger items will have had an

**auction**—type of trade where would-be buyers bid on items and the sale goes to the highest bidder.

opportunity to examine them before the sale. The auctioneer then asks for bids. When everyone wishing to bid has had an opportunity, the auctioneer usually awards the item to the highest bidder. The owner may, of course, reserve the right to refuse to sell, if in his judgment the highest bid is too low.

In fact, most goods are not sold at such an auction. Rarely are new and reproducible goods sold this way. However, some goods are regularly sold in an auction-like manner. A good example is common stocks. Those who have stocks for sale will quite often offer to sell at an asking price. Those who want to buy may name a bid price. Actual sales often fluctuate between the higher asking prices and the lower bid prices. Many sorts of goods are sold by bargaining between buyer and seller. The sale of houses and land are often sold in this fashion. The seller usually sets a price at which he will sell, and the buyer may then make an offer that is lower than the asking price. The two may then bargain face to face to arrive at a mutually agreed upon price, or do the bargaining secondhand by way of real estate agents. Automobiles are often exchanged after bargaining between seller and buyer. If the buyer is trying to trade-in his old car on a more expensive car, the buyer–seller may change roles to reach agreement on the trade-in allowance, and then reverse them in the process of completing the transaction. Bargaining may occur in transactions involving less expensive items as well. Finally, yard sales are another example of where buyers and sellers negotiate the prices of items traded.

But as pointed out above, most goods are not disposed of either by bargaining or in an auction format. Instead, sellers display their wares—in supermarkets, department stores, hardware stores, gasoline stations, convenience stores, and the like—with the price marked on the goods. Buyers fill their baskets with wares, take them to check-out counters, and pay the asking prices. It appears from the way these goods are sold that no auctioning nor bargaining is taking place. Nor do many who provide services—physicians, lawyers, plumbers, electricians, for example—usually bargain about the prices they charge. The same could be said for many employers; they simply tell prospective employees their pay scale as a take it or leave it offer. There is no obvious auction going on, although all employers compete among themselves to attract workers and are, therefore, constrained in the offer that might attract the workers needed.

It might be easy to conclude otherwise. That is that sellers, providers of services, and employers simply determine the price at which they will sell (or hire) and that no bidding takes place. In a simple sense, this is the way it seems. In a broader sense, however, and behind the scenes, a kind of bargaining is going on. The merchant may simply mark his price on the goods, but that is no guarantee that he can sell them at that price. If buyers reject goods at the price he is offering them, he will have to lower the price in the hope of attracting buyers. Sales are a frequently used device to sell slow moving merchandise. However he accomplishes it, the merchant will eventually have to reduce the price of merchandise to a level that customers will pay if he is to sell all of his goods. In sum, if the merchant does not want to take a loss, he has to attend to prices that customers will pay. The same goes for providers of services and employers. Individual providers of services can, of course, set any price that pleases them for their services. But consumers are apt to use them only if the price set is competitive with that of others offering a similar service and if they want the service enough to pay the price. In sum, the consumer may shun high prices for services as well as for other goods. As for employers, they will generally have to offer enough to get as much skilled labor as they want. An offering wage is nothing more than an employer's estimate of what it will take to do that.

We are not yet, however, examining the whole question of how prices are determined in the market. The point we have been making is a simpler one, namely, that exchanges in the market are done by auction, or something akin to auction, in which both buyers and sellers play a role.

The main point in this section is that exchange has become the major means for acquiring the goods that we want. It has become the main alternative to producing the goods for ourselves. These exchanges take place by something akin to an auction. The places where exchanges take place are called markets, as noted earlier. It may be added that exchanges take place because each of the parties wants what the other has more than what he has. That does not necessarily mean that parties are drooling at the mouth to consume what each other has, as when one is offering cakes and the other succulent peaches, for example. One party may want it more because he believes he can sell it for more than whatever he is offering. **Want** covers a multitude of desires, calculations, expectations, needs, and so on. Whatever inspires it, a human want or desire is translated into demand and this is what underlies all trade.

**want**—all people aim to achieve some purpose or end. To do so they need the means necessary to realize the end. The desire to obtain the means constitute wants.

In the nature of things, people voluntarily exchange goods with one another because they perceive some advantage to themselves in doing so. The market results from the relative advantages individuals seek by trading. The disadvantages of dependence on the market have already been noted. We can now describe the advantages of using the market.

> **Why People Make Exchanges**
> Exchange has become the major means for acquiring the goods that we want. It has become the main alternative to producing the goods for ourselves. These exchanges take place by something akin to an auction. The places where exchanges take place are called markets. In the nature of things, people voluntarily exchange goods with one another because they perceive some advantage to themselves in doing so. The market results from the relative advantages individuals seek by trading.

### 7.3.2 Advantages of Market Exchange

It is probable that markets arose initially as means of disposing of surplus goods by sellers and of obtaining wanted goods by buyers. Actually, however, "buyer" and "seller" are distinctions that occur in a much more complex money economy than that which would have existed when trade originated. The earliest trading was undoubtedly carried on by **barter**; goods were traded for goods; all traders were both sellers and buyers. Since all exchange is ultimately of goods for goods, a point to which we will return in discussing money, some economists refer to **direct exchange** and **indirect exchange.** Direct exchange occurs when goods are directly exchanged for goods as in barter. Indirect exchange occurs when the exchange is made through some **medium of exchange**, as in money. It is in indirect exchange that the distinction between buyer and seller is made; the buyer is the one who offers money and the seller delivers goods in the exchange. To return to the point, it is probable, then, that markets developed as trading places between those who had different kinds of surplus goods for sale.

**barter**—direct trade with someone else where goods are traded for other goods.

**direct exchange**—occurs when goods are traded for other goods.

**indirect exchange**—occurs when the exchange is made through some kind of medium (money).

**medium of exchange**—money or currency that allows trades to take place indirectly.

Markets remain as places for disposing of surplus or unwanted goods, and some of them serve in that capacity to this day. The great

**division of labor**—the dividing up of the tasks of producing goods among those who operate most efficiently. It involves specialization, cooperation, and, in the broadest sense, widespread trade.

**specialization**—the focus of a person's work on some particular operation, skill, or practice. When such specialization is widespread it could be said that a division of labor exists.

advantage of the market, however, is that it enables people to specialize their production and fosters the **division of labor** in society. Through **specialization** goods can both be produced in greater quantity than otherwise and some goods can be produced that could hardly be produced at all without the combination of numerous skills in making them.

Adam Smith gave a classic example of the greater production of goods possible through specialization by his description of pin making in the 1770s in his book, *The Wealth of Nations*. Smith said:

> A workman not educated to this business ... could scarce, perhaps, with his utmost industry, make one pin in a day, and certainly could not make twenty. But in the way in which this business is now carried on, not only the whole work is a peculiar trade, but it is divided into a number of branches.... One man draws out the wire, another straightens it, a third cuts it, a fourth points it, a fifth grinds it at the top for receiving the head: to make the head requires two or three distinct operations; to put it on, is a peculiar business, to whiten the pins is another; it is even a trade by itself to put them into the paper; and the important business of making a pin is, in this manner, divided into about eighteen distinct operations, which, in some manufactories, are all performed by distinct hands, though in others the same man will sometimes perform two or three of them. I have seen a small manufactory of this kind where ten men only were employed, and where some of them consequently performed two or three distinct operations. But ... those ten persons ... could make among them upwards of forty-eight thousand pins in a day.

Thus, by specialization it could be said that one man produced, in effect, nearly 5,000 pins per day. The market makes possible this beneficial specialization.

One man could most likely produce a pin by his own efforts, but the late Leonard Reed, president of The Foundation for Economic Education, suggested in a little essay, "I, Pencil," that no one knows how to make a pencil. No article of use, he suggested is more generally available and casually used than the pencil, but most of us could not supply one by our own unaided efforts. His point was that no man has all the skills and abilities to assemble a pencil. To do so, he would have to be able to mine and refine the materials that go into making "lead," that he would have to cut, haul, and mill the trees used in making the wood, that he would have to mine and refine the metal used in attaching the eraser to the pencil, get the materials and shape an eraser, get and put together the materials from which the paint is made, assemble all the parts into a whole, do the lettering on the pencil, and box them for shipment. That is only a partial list, of course, of all that would go into so simple an item as a pencil. The difficulties would be multiplied in producing a computer, a television, an automobile, or the hundreds and thousands of other products that no one person knows how to do.

Without extensive exchange and markets, it might be added that the complex machinery used in making numerous goods would be too expensive to obtain. That is, if a man had to produce for his own needs alone, he could not begin to have the equipment that is now necessary to do so.

Another great advantage of trading with others for what we want is that we are able to enjoy the gains that arise from what economists call

**comparative advantage.** Such an advantage exists when someone or something has a lower cost of production when compared to someone or something else. For example, because of comparative advantage we can obtain all sorts of exotic goods from distant lands, goods that could be produced locally only at great expense and with much difficulty. It might be possible to grow pineapples and bananas, for example, in the continental United States, but the product would probably be inferior and too expensive for most people. In fact, climate, soils, rainfall, and the like, differ from region to region, and minerals are unevenly deposited around the earth. Thus, it is possible in the United States to produce steel for trade in the United States and other countries and to buy pineapples from Hawaii, bananas from Central America, and coconuts from tropical isles.

Moreover, the hurdle of gains from trade in this fashion is not particularly high. A person need not be the best at producing something to engage in a mutually beneficial trade with someone else. For instance, suppose a surgeon had studied horticulture during his undergraduate education. Though he may be highly skilled at tending a garden, he may well hire someone else to do so for him even though they might be less proficient simply because of the cost to him personally of engaging in the endeavor. For example, if our doctor can earn $700 per hour as a surgeon, that is what he would have to give up to work one hour in his garden. This is what economists call **opportunity cost**. As a result, mutually beneficial trading relationships abound.

The advantages of exchange are so great, especially in a money economy, that exchange has become a major, and generally dominant, means of obtaining goods over the past 100 years. Even so, there are dangers entailed, as already noted, in dependence upon exchange in the market. Specialization can be particularly precarious for the individual. A man who has spent years learning a specialty may find himself without employment because what he has learned has become obsolete or because he has been squeezed out by competitors. Too heavy reliance upon a single specialty leaves the individual exposed to all sorts of changes and circumstances. This is simply another variation of the hazards of dependence on the market, of course. Most people are capable of learning to do a considerable variety of jobs, even of learning to produce some of the goods they need for themselves. Learning to do such things is a wise defensive measure in a market economy.

## 7.4 Theft by Government for Redistribution

As a general rule, when individuals steal things from people we view it with moral outrage. Indeed, governments throughout time have punished thieves and have attempted to limit their actions. That is not to suggest that thievery does not take place, but rather that such actions are minimized in a law-abiding society. It is one of the main functions of government to protect property by apprehending thieves and punishing them.

However, it seems that people are not as outraged when governments use force to take the property of some people for the benefit of others. Nonetheless, it must be recognized that the transfer of property was done by force. These are not acts of voluntary charity. If government steals, so to speak, both the onus and the penalties for theft are removed, and, indeed, some other word is usually used to describe it, such as taxation, confiscation, appropriation, controlling the money supply, and the like. In any case, when government does it, the benefits of thievery may be

> **comparative advantage**—advantage that exists when someone has a lower opportunity cost of production than someone else.

> **opportunity cost**—the highest valued alternative given up to do or get something.

**redistribution**—taking wealth from some to give to others.

### Getting the Point...

Is it a legitimate function of government to take from each according to his ability to give to each according to his need to provide social justice for the unequal distribution of incomes and wealth?

Make a case for or against.

made available to some without their being subject to the legal penalties imposed upon private thievery.

Since the end of the nineteenth century the practice of this forced government **redistribution** of private property on a large scale has steadily increased. Granted, those in power have used government revenues to reward their favorites from time immemorial. Thus, kings often rewarded their courtiers with choice positions, and sometimes with an income for life. Granted, too, governments have often bestowed special privileges that may have verged on being redistributionist in character on some elements of the population. But it has only been in recent history that intellectual justifications for taking property from some and bestowing it upon others by government have been made. The practice has been described in such phrases as "Taking from the rich to give to the poor" or "Taking from the haves to give to the have-nots." Perhaps, the most elegant description was made by Karl Marx, when he said: "From each according to his ability; to each according to his need." The practice has also been described as "distributive justice" and "social justice." The implication of these phrases is that there is injustice in the distribution of wealth and that government is acting to right this wrong by redistributing the wealth. This claim is usually supported by showing that people have unequal incomes and wealth.

In the United States, government programs for redistributing the wealth have been widespread and commonplace for many years now, both by the federal, state, and local governments. These programs have taken many forms and been operated under a great variety of names: they have been called relief, welfare, Social Security, Medicare, Medicaid, food stamps, subsidies, loans, grants, entitlements, insurance, minimum wages, foreign aid, Federal aid to education, public housing projects, small business loans, and many other names. The taking by governments has occurred in a considerable variety of ways as well: taxation, inflating the currency, empowering groups, such as labor unions, to use force to achieve higher wages, price controls, wage controls, and the like. The graduated income tax has been a favorite one for taking from the haves to distribute to the have-nots.

In fact, however, the redistribution has not been simply from the haves to the have-nots. Quite often, the wealthy or prosperous have benefited from the redistribution as well. Examples of this practice abound. Government grants for building airfields and airports in small towns are likely to benefit mostly those who own airplanes, rarely poor people. Even government financed public housing projects may provide the first fruits of benefits to contractors who build the projects, and contractors are rarely poverty stricken. Government grants and guaranteed loans benefit professors by providing students to keep them employed before students even begin to reap any benefits for themselves. Crop subsidies supported by government funds have often gone in larger amounts to large, prosperous farms than to small farms. The loudest voices lobbying for legislation are paid for by the same people who can and do contribute large amounts to political campaigns. Politicians often focus their rhetoric on the poor who are supposed to receive the benefits in their claims and make no public mention of the benefits that go to others.

There may be those who will object to calling the appropriation of wealth by taxation or otherwise for these purposes theft. It is not customary to call it theft, nor do we usually conceive of taxation as theft. Yet a strong case can be made that taking property from the rightful owners to confer it on someone else is theft. One way to approach this subject is to refer to the nature and purpose of government. As noted earlier, government is not by nature a producer. That being the case, it can only confer unearned benefits by taking goods that others have produced from them. In the nature of things, the purpose of government is to maintain the peace, and as Americans used to say, to protect people in the enjoyment of their lives, liberty, and property. Government is not performing its function of maintaining the peace when it takes the property of some to give to others. Far from protecting property, it is confiscating it for purposes not in accord with government's assigned role.

Nor is this use of the Federal Government authorized in the Constitution. The Constitution authorizes Congress "to lay and collect Taxes, Duties, Imposts and Excises to pay the Debts and provide for the common Defence and general Welfare of the United States. . . ." Many people probably believe that taxation for the general welfare includes levying taxes on taxpayers generally in order to redistribute the wealth to those said to be in need. This notion was popularized in the 1930s and afterward, and for two decades thereafter programs to redistribute the wealth were called welfare programs, and departments of government carrying out this redistribution were named "welfare departments." The word "welfare" had no connotation of relief or anything to do with redistribution of the wealth until well into the twentieth century. It simply meant a condition of well-being or faring well in life. When the Social Security program was being considered in 1934–1935, those who were promoting it decided to attach the idea of welfare to it in order to give it the color of constitutionality in the hope that the courts would not nullify it. It worked; "welfare" acquired a new meaning, and the general welfare clause in the Constitution was used as a justification for taxing and spending for this purpose.

From an economic point of view, this sort of theft by government for redistribution is only a slight improvement, if any, over private theft. It obviously works better in that all penalties for government theft are removed for the recipients, and, of course, the onus of theft for those in government is removed in the public mind, since it takes on the character of all other taxation. The other major difference between private and **public theft** on the economy is that levies by government are more or less predictable. That is, the amount being taxed can generally be known in advance, while private thievery cannot be calculated either as to the amount that may be taken or when the confiscation will take place.

Even so, theft by government for redistribution has a negative impact generally upon the economy of a country. If the aim of the redistribution is to relieve the poor, it tends to penalize the productive and reward the unproductive or less productive. This is perhaps easiest to comprehend when the progressive income tax is used extensively to raise the money to redistribute. Other things being equal, we may assume that those with the higher incomes are the most productive and efficient, yet the progressive tax attempts to take a disproportionate amount of their income away. This tends to discourage the productive from becoming more productive. It also takes a larger portion of their means away from productive investment as well. Thus, taking from the haves to give to the have-nots is an uneconomic undertaking.

How uneconomic such programs can be is well illustrated in government payment of unemployment compensation. People are actually paid not to work by unemployment compensation. Thus, workers, who may prefer leisure to work when income is provided, may avoid productive work while they draw this pay. It is easy enough for us to see how uneconomic this is when we recall that the real problem is scarcity—scarcity of labor as well as land and capital.

It would be possible, of course, and is, to give help by redistribution to those in temporary need or who for one reason or another are destitute. It would not be economic to do so, however, by taxation, though it might

**public theft**—theft that is carried out by the government; money is taken by force through taxes from some and given to others through welfare programs.

### Getting the Point . . .

Government programs designed with the best of intentions often have unintended consequences that cause great harm.

List some negative consequences of programs designed to help the poor and temporarily destitute.

be done on other than economic grounds. The question remains, too, as to whether or not government is the proper organization for providing charity, relief, or giving alms. But it would be a mistake to suppose that many government programs billed as aids to the poor actually do aid them. In fact, many of them have not done so. Those who are unemployed need to be finding productive employment, not extensive support in idleness. Many who are unproductive, or do not produce enough to support themselves, need to become more productive. While government programs may provide temporary aid, they do not, and cannot, do much more than expand a lack of productivity.

The main theme of the book, *The War on the Poor*, was that government intervention in the economy had generally harmed the poor rather than helped them. In the most general way, this happens because government intervention makes it much more difficult to discover what it would be economical for them to do, because it sends false signals into the economy. For example, when government makes loans available at low interest (to farmers, for instance), the economic signal these low interest rates send out is that the expansion of farming is a good economic risk. In fact, this is not even the signal that government has wanted to send out. Or, if government tries to raise the price of commodities with subsidies, as it has often done with selected farm products, the signal these higher prices send out is that more of these goods are wanted. The result has been that government then has encouraged a great surplus of goods that cannot be sold at higher prices. In any case, higher prices generally make life harder for the poor than for anyone else.

In sum, government theft for the redistribution of goods is an uneconomic process. It is unconstitutional for the United States Government, because the government is limited in its taxing power to taxing for the general welfare (not for the supposed welfare of some class, such as the poor), and required to make just compensation when private property is otherwise taken for public purposes. It is not the function of government to redistribute wealth, and when it proceeds to do so it abandons some portion of its legitimate authority by taking rather than protecting property. While the language is harsh, the impact of government taking from some to give to others is only in some particulars different from theft. Using government in this function is contrary to its function and is contrary to the well-being of the populace.

---

**Calling Government Redistribution of Wealth Theft**
There may be those who will object to calling the appropriation of wealth by taxation or otherwise for these purposes theft. It is not customary to call it theft, nor do we usually conceive of taxation as theft. Yet a strong case can be made that taking property from the rightful owners to confer it on someone else is theft. While the language is harsh, the impact of government taking from some to give to others is only in some particulars different from theft. Using government in this function is contrary to its function and is contrary to the well-being of the populace.

## Study Guide for:

# 7 How We Get What We Want

## Chapter Summary

There are only four ways to acquire the economic goods we need to pursue our wants and desires. We can produce the item ourselves, produce something of value to others and trade it for what we want, steal the item from someone else, or receive it as a charitable gift. The first two means of acquisition are economic while the last two are not. That is, an economy cannot be founded on the last two ways of acquisition.

Though gift giving and receiving is fundamental to human experience in America, little attention has been devoted to examining its role in the economy. Yet children are totally dependent upon their parents to provide for all their needs until they can begin to work for themselves. Likewise, we find numerous charitable organizations whose purpose is to meet individual needs. These organizations provide gifts for orphans, widows, and many others who, for one reason or another, cannot at the moment provide for their own needs. In addition, we give gifts for numerous other reasons. For example, gifts are given to newlywed couples to help them establish a home, and later gifts are given when those couples begin to have children. Whatever the case, gift giving is a significant part of the acquisition of goods and services. Nevertheless, charity always relies on prior production. You cannot give something you do not already have.

Historically, people tended to be more self-sufficient. In America, a rural farming family would provide for most of their needs. This required the members of the family to perfect their skills in numerous activities ranging from agriculture to carpentry to the canning of produce. However, specialization and division of labor have led to a greater dependency upon the market. The advantage of this has been an increase in the variety and affordability of a vast number of goods and services. The major disadvantage has been the fluctuations of the market. From time to time these fluctuations and changes render certain skills and certain products obsolete and of no value regardless of the investment of resources in them.

Nevertheless, the advantages seem to outweigh the disadvantages and people have come to rely more and more upon the market for acquiring the things they want. The market itself can be thought of as an ongoing auction whereby sellers seek buyers for their products. Actually, trade was initially accomplished by way of barter or direct exchange so that every seller was also a buyer and vice versa. However, the introduction of money has obscured this fact somewhat because money allows for indirect trade. Trade in essence remains the same. It is fundamentally two parties voluntarily agreeing to exchange items of value at some specified rate.

Theft by the individual and by groups of individuals has generally been viewed with disdain. Further, it has been the role of government to catch and punish those individuals who would steal from others. However, a strange change has been transpiring. Government has more and more become involved in efforts to redistribute wealth from some individuals to others. The various programs promoted to accomplish this have been established by an appeal for social justice. Yet it is odd that people would argue that government could justly do that which would be manifestly unjust for the individual to do—namely take someone's property by force in order to give it to someone else. Though these programs are strictly at odds with the Constitution, they have gained the general approval of government officials and voters. Unfortunately, these programs have created numerous economic hardships and rather than promoting the welfare of the poor have actually served to undermine their welfare.

## Points of Emphasis

1. There are only two ways to get what we want. We can either produce it ourselves or acquire it from someone else. If we acquire it from others, there are only three modes through which such procurement can be effected. It can be received as a gift from that person, or as a voluntary exchange, or by some form of theft.

2. Gifts are an important part of the economy but are often neglected in economic analysis.

3. Modern day economies have substantially moved away from self-sufficiency toward market exchange in order to get what we want. An advantage of this approach stems from the gains to be made from specialization and division of

labor. The major disadvantage is that market fluctuations can render someone's product or labor invaluable.

4. During the twentieth century in the United States, the government has increasingly passed legislation that systematically redistributes income even though the action is in conflict with the Constitution. This change exemplifies government theft.

## Identification

1. theft
2. charity
3. self-sufficient farm
4. market
5. auction
6. want
7. barter
8. direct exchange
9. indirect exchange
10. medium of exchange
11. division of labor
12. specialization
13. comparative advantage
14. opportunity cost
15. redistribution
16. public theft

## Review Questions

1. What would it be like if you had to live in a totally self-sufficient manner? What goods that you currently consume would you have to give up because you could not produce them yourself?

2. During the past fifty years, what occupations have vanished as a result of the changing market place? You might want to ask someone who is older than you.

3. When advances in technology are making jobs obsolete, should the government step in to subsidize those jobs to allow people to keep producing?

4. What are the advantages of market exchange? What are some dangers of dependence on market exchange?

5. List some people who would not survive on their own apart from the charity of others?

6. Why are government redistribution programs widely accepted even though they could be considered to be public theft?

## Activities

1. Make a list of the government programs enacted in the twentieth century that represent public theft.

2. Suppose you want to send a text message to a friend. Make a list of all the people and resources needed to make that possible.

3. Prepare a case for or against the following position: "The government should provide health care for everyone because health care is a right."

## For Further Study

1. Frédéric Bastiat, *The Law*, Foundation for Economic Education: Irvington, NY, 1987.

2. Frédéric Bastiat, *Selected Essays on Political Economy*, Foundation for Economic Education: Irvington, NY, 1964.

3. Clarence Carson, *The War on the Poor*, American Textbook Committee: Wadley, AL, 1991.

4. F.A. Hayek, *The Fatal Conceit: The Errors of Socialism*, University of Chicago Press: Chicago, 1988.

5. Stephen Littlechild, *The Fallacy of the Mixed Economy*, Cato Institute: San Francisco, 1979.

> **CHAPTER CONTENT**
>
> 8.1 The Function of Money  88
>     8.1.1 As a Medium of Exchange  88
>     8.1.2 As a Standard of Calculation  90
>     8.1.3 As a Store of Wealth  91
> 8.2 The Origin of Money  93
>     8.2.1 Gold and Silver as Money  94
>     8.2.2 Gresham's Law and Government Interference  95
> 8.3 Government and Money  96
> 8.4 Paper Money  98
>     8.4.1 Origins of Debt Money in Europe  99
>     8.4.2 Fractional Reserve Banking  101

# 8 A Medium of Exchange—Money

It is not practical to go very far in the discussion of exchange and the market without taking up the medium of exchange, or, in common terms, money or currency. We must do this because most exchanges have long since come to be performed by the use of money. Moreover, many of the ideas that economists deal with, such as price, interest, and supply and demand are understood today in the context of a money economy. Indeed, the very distinction between supply and demand is usually made because we think in terms of money. In a money economy, demand is made with money, and supply consists of goods. Without money, both supply and demand would be expressed in terms of goods. Granted, some goods would be more plentiful than others, and some would be more urgently wanted than others, but demand would have no distinctive object by which it could be expressed. In any case, money is the lubricant that makes the market function smoothly and effectively.

Without money, we would have to resort to barter to effect exchanges. While barter is still sometimes used in making exchanges, it is easy to see that it could not be used for most exchanges and that a complex economy would not be possible. Small children often make exchanges by way of barter, quite frequently to the embarrassment of their parents. One child, usually the younger one, will trade a toy whose cost of replacement is much larger than the one he gets in return, such as trading a tricycle for a toy gun. That points to one of the difficulties of barter, even for adults—i.e., finding two goods of equal replacement cost to trade. It is often difficult to find someone who wants to acquire what you have, and who has the object that you want. For example, suppose you want a dentist to pull your tooth, yet the only thing you have to offer in return is a bushel of potatoes. The price might be right, so to speak, but it might happen that the dentist grew his own potatoes and had no need of any. Undoubtedly, trades would be made under such a system, but they would be time consuming, primitive, and generally rare.

The obvious solution would be some medium of exchange. It turns out that this solution was hit upon well before people developed much in the way of advanced culture or civilization.

# 8.1 The Function of Money

**money**—a commodity or the promise to pay in some specified amount of one or more commodities.

The medium of exchange in the United States today is incredibly complex. **Money** itself is not difficult to understand, but the system of currency and credit that we use for money is extremely complicated. That is not to say that the dollar as a monetary unit poses any special difficulties in calculation or in making change or closing a transaction. On that score our currency is both simple and convenient. But to grasp how it is issued and on what supposed basis that it is done is both obscure and complex. In fact, it is doubtful that we should call what we use money at all. It would be much more accurate to refer to it as currency and credit rather than money. Money, as we shall see in a later section, has usually been some commodity that has a market value based on demand for it (e.g. gold or silver). What we call money today in the United States is not a **commodity** nor is it backed by any. It is, as noted, **currency**—consisting of paper bills and base metals—plus credit. If it is based on anything, it is based on debt. As a result, it does not serve very effectively as money in all its functions, but to understand that, we first need to understand the traditional functions of money. Before taking those up, it should be noted that while it probably should not be referred to as money, it will be done so here in accord with custom. Money has usually performed three basic functions.

**commodity**—an economic good.

**currency**—that which circulates as money in a country usually consisting of paper bills and base metals. But it can be said that any medium of exchange is currency, whatever it happens to be.

## 8.1.1 As a Medium of Exchange

**medium of exchange**—*see definition*, p. 79.

The primary function of money is to serve as a **medium of exchange**. In other words, we use it to buy and sell things. As early civilizations developed in river valleys, caravan merchants traveled up and down the rivers with pack animals engaging in trade with the people living in various places. Initially, the trade was simply accomplished through bartering, as some things that could be had in one place were not available in another. In time, it became apparent that some goods were more acceptable in trade than other goods and if you wanted to increase your trading opportunities it would be worthwhile to always possess some inventory of the most accepted commodity.

There were characteristics that made some commodities better money than other commodities. For instance, a good commodity money needed to be relatively scarce to hold its value in trade. It also needed to be easily recognizable, divisible, and durable. Finally, you needed to be able to carry it around with you. For these reasons the precious metals of the world—gold, silver, and copper—emerged as the commodity monies of the world used in trading relationships. Until very recently in human history these commodities have served as the backbone of money transactions.

To understand the basic function of money better it will be useful to consider the work of an early economist. In 1803, a French economist, **Jean-Baptiste Say**, published *A Treatise on Political Economy*. In that book Say argued that goods are always exchanged for other goods and that this reality is often overlooked in a money economy. When money is used, the trade is simply an indirect exchange instead of a direct one. Thus, money can tend

### J. B. Say (1767–1832)

French journalist and economist. He was born in Lyon but lived in England as a young man where he engaged in business. Say became interested in and helped to spread Adam Smith's ideas on economics. His major contribution, which is named for him, is Say's Law. In its simplest form it holds that production creates its own demand. To see this, it is necessary to realize that money is only a medium of exchange, that ultimately goods are exchanged for goods, though money often postpones the completion of the process. If his law be accepted, it becomes clear that general overproduction can never be a problem so long as there are human wants unmet. His most important work was a book on the principles of political economy.

to take our eyes off what we are actually doing. What usually happens in a market economy is that we sell our labor services (which is an economic good) to an employer in exchange for money. We then use that money to purchase other goods from sellers of other things like groceries. In sum, goods are ultimately exchanged for goods, and money only temporarily defers the completion of the transaction.

Since goods are ultimately traded for other goods, Say argued that whenever anyone produces more of a good than he personally wishes to consume, it becomes his demand for other goods in the market. To take a simple example, suppose I grow apples and my neighbor grows pears. If we use our surplus apples and pears to trade with one another, my apples become a demand for my neighbor's pears and vice versa. To put it in economic terms, my supply of apples is my demand for pears. The price of the exchange is the number of apples I give up per pear that I receive.

The use of money in this example would tend to obscure this fact. Suppose that instead of trading directly with each other we both choose to sell our fruit to a grocery chain. The grocery store offers to buy our fruit from us in exchange for a certain amount of money. Now suppose that I would like to have some pears. In this case, instead of going to my neighbor I merely go to the grocery store and pay the money price for the pears. In this case, my apples are still being exchanged for pears but it is done indirectly.

Since goods are always being exchanged for other goods, Say observed that in an unhindered market place, where every individual is free to trade with others, there cannot exist a general overproduction of goods. This conclusion is often referred to as **Say's Law** and rests on the fact that market exchange will result in money prices of goods that will, in turn, result in profits and losses for the various business enterprises. Profits provide a clear signal that what is being offered in the market is more valuable to customers than the cost of its production while losses signal just the opposite. As a result, all businesses have the incentive to do more of that which is profitable and less of that which is not. In other words, market exchange is self-regulating. However, if people are hindered from being able to trade with one another freely for some reason, there may well be a lack of coordination in the market.

This is not to say that no one will ever make a mistake by producing too much of something. The truth is that people make mistakes all the time. Nevertheless, when such mistakes are made there is ample incentive arising from the pain inflicted by the loss to adjust one's productive efforts. These incentives are strong enough to keep overproduction from occurring generally across the broader market.

**Say's Law**—no one would ever produce more of whatever they are producing than they could use unless they intended to trade the surplus for something else.

> **Say's Law**
> Goods are ultimately exchanged for goods, and money only temporarily defers the completion of the transaction. Because of this, in an unhindered market place, where every individual is free to trade with others, there cannot exist a general overproduction of goods.

If people kept their eyes on this reality they would not be swayed by a number of economic fallacies that are all too widely believed. Unfortunately, when money is used to effect transactions it tends to be thought of as demand itself. This gives rise to the recurrent illusion that

**shortage of money**—the illusion that there is less money in the market than there needs to be, and that if we increase the money supply, we will reach a better equilibrium point where more people can afford to live.

there is a **shortage of money.** That is, when some producers cannot sell their goods for a profit in the market they tend to believe that their problem is simply that there is not enough money. To remedy this situation, they call for increases in the money supply. But, when this is done it does not relieve the problem. Instead, it merely cheapens the value of money. The real problem is that some of what is being produced is not sufficiently wanted while many other goods are in too short supply. The real solution to the problem is an ongoing adjustment in amounts produced to match the desires of consumers. As we will see later, when governments attempt to control the money supply by embracing this faulty understanding of market exchange, they confuse the market signals and disrupt market exchange.

Undoubtedly, money is scarce. That is its chief usefulness as an effective medium of exchange. If it were not scarce, it is most doubtful that people would exchange goods for it. All people feel varying degrees of its short supply, as individuals, as families, and within organizations. We all face times when money seems to be in short supply relative to the ends we wish to pursue. Does this indicate a general shortage of money? Certainly not! That is, not in a market sufficiently free to adjust to the general supply of money. Any amount of money will do because prices will adjust to the amount available as people make their individual choices. The important factor is that the money supply stay stable so that the market signals are clearer.

> As long as the market is sufficiently free to adjust to the general supply of money, **any amount of money will do** because prices will adjust to the amount available as people make their individual choices. The important factor is that the money supply stay stable so that the market signals are clearer.

The main point of this discussion thus far needs now to be stated. In its primary function, money is the medium through which exchanges are made. While money may be a commodity that is generally wanted, in its monetary function, it is not an end, only the means of exchanging goods for goods. It has other functions, of course, and these are discussed below, but as a medium of exchange its only use is in facilitating trades. Increasing or diminishing the general supply of it will not make it function better; it will only disrupt its function and send false signals into the market. Money makes a complex economy possible, but because it allows for indirect trades, it obscures the fact that all goods are ultimately exchanged for other goods.

### 8.1.2 As a Standard of Calculation

Money has two other fairly distinct functions, though they are secondary to, and a result of, its primary function as a medium of exchange. One of these secondary functions is as a standard in making calculations. This is basically the **pricing function of money**, the reducing of the cost of a thing to a money price. When something has been reduced to a monetary figure, it can then be compared to other objects as if they were the same in kind.

An example will illustrate this function. A man who goes to the bank to make an unsecured loan may be asked to calculate his **net worth**. This

**pricing function of money**—the comparison of money to other goods via trade gives us a relative standard to compare goods with other goods.

**net worth**—total assets minus total liabilities.

is accomplished by listing his **assets** (what he owns) in one column and his **liabilities** (what he owes) in another, then subtracting his liabilities from his assets. Most people have little difficulty in calculating their liabilities, for these consist in the sum of his outstanding debts, which are already expressed in money. But his assets are usually another matter entirely, because they have no current price tag on them. His list might include a house and lot, an automobile, a lawn mower, an assortment of tools, furniture, appliances, books, paintings, silverware and china, televisions, computers, a sound system, clothes, cell phones, and so on. It is not possible, of course, to add these items and arrive at a sum. They must first be reduced to a monetary value (an estimate of what they would bring in the market) before they can be added to arrive at a sum. Money enables us to make such calculations.

In a money economy, goods for sale are usually marked with a price. This not only makes it possible to engage in comparison shopping for particular goods of the same kind but also to get an easily calculated notion of the relative price of different goods. For example, if a television set costs $500, a motorcycle $15,000, an automobile $30,000, and a house $240,000, then we can plot their costs relative to one another. In this example, a motorcycle is thirty times as expensive as a television, an automobile is twice as much as a motorcycle, and a house is eight times as much as an automobile. In any case, a price for one good stated in the same terms as all other goods is one of the functions performed by money.

As a standard for calculation, money is invaluable in keeping records and accounts. Thus, loans are made and records are usually stated in amounts of money. Taxes are levied and reckoned on the basis of valuations made in terms of money. Bookkeepers work almost exclusively with sums of money. The profits and losses of businesses are determined in terms of money. Plans are made for future activity, especially economic activity, on the basis of past monetary calculations. Calculations regarding the future are nothing more than projections of the past, and few things are more certain than that there will be changes in the future. However, it is important to emphasize that the use of money makes it possible to engage in extensive economic calculation.

### 8.1.3 As a Store of Wealth

The other secondary function of money is as a means of storing wealth, or, as some would have it, maintaining cash holdings. The preference for cash holdings is sometimes referred to as **liquidity preference**. That is, it is the preference for having money over having goods that might be difficult to dispose of to raise money, or that might be perishable or subject to fairly rapid deterioration. There are many reasons for wanting cash rather than other goods. In the most general terms, the future is always uncertain, making it difficult to predict future needs. Money is, therefore, held for a "rainy day," as people say. People may also use money to postpone present consumption for future consumption by saving. In order for saving to take place, financial markets must serve as a means of transferring resources via financial contracts. These contracts are often called securities. Such contracts, including stocks and bonds for example, are more liquid than other sorts of assets. As will be explained later, the shortest-term bonds are extremely liquid and are used as a basis for credit money in our economy. Nevertheless, financial markets allow us to benefit from postponing consumption by earning interest.

To better explain how financial markets work and the benefits of postponing consumption, let's look at an example. Suppose that you want

**assets**—what someone owns.

**liabilities**—what someone owes.

**liquidity preference**—the preference for having access to money quickly over access to other goods, which might take time to sell for money, might be perishable, or subject to rapid deterioration. When liquidity preference is widespread, people generally avoid long-term or risky investments.

to purchase a new car with a walk out the door price of $20,000 after your down payment/trade in. There are three main methods of doing this. You can lease the car, borrow from someone else to finance the car, or pay cash for the car.

First, you could lease the car from a dealership or some third party. In this method, you do not own the car and will never own the car. Instead, you are paying monthly payments for the right to use someone else's car. If you decide to purchase a new car at the end of five years, the current car will not have any trade-in value because it is not your car. Now think about this method for a second. How did the person leasing you the car acquire it? Certainly, not by leasing it because they have ownership of it and the authority to lease it to you. So, if they own the car, why are they leasing it to you? It is clear that they intend to profit. If they purchased the car in some other way and intend to profit by leasing it to you, then it can be concluded that the other way of purchasing must be less expensive.

Second, you could finance the car through a loan from the dealership, bank, or some other third party. In this example, you make monthly payments over the course of some period of time. While financing may seem like the best option because it breaks up the payments over a longer period of time, using someone else's money has a cost. This cost comes in the form of interest. If the car costs $20,000 and you agree to make monthly payments of $368 for 60 months at 4% interest, you will pay a total of $22,099.80 over the 60 months. The extra $2,099.80 is the cost of using someone else's money. In essence, it is the cost of acquiring the use of the car immediately without spending the entire $20,000 up front. After making payments for five years, you own the car. It is important to note that the value of the car would have depreciated significantly since its purchase, but some of the money paid for the car would be retained in the value of the car and could be used in trading for the next car.

Each of the previous methods satisfy the desire for immediate consumption. They provide the use of the car without necessarily having access to the $20,000 it costs to purchase the car up front. In the case of leasing, the cost is never having ownership of the car. In the case of financing, the cost comes in the form of interest. This illustrates an important rule for us; immediate consumption always has some cost. Around 87% of all vehicles are acquired using one of these first two methods.

The third method of acquiring the use of a vehicle is paying cash for it. In order to pay cash, you must have first saved $20,000. This method requires delaying consumption until you have saved the money. It is not always easy to choose this method. It may require using public transportation, a bicycle, or a cheaper, used car for the four or five years it takes to save the money needed. However, there is a benefit to paying cash. You do not have to pay $2,099.80 in interest. You also get the benefit of earning interest on the money you save. The amount of interest earned depends upon the financial vehicle you use for saving, but there is at least the potential to earn interest.

There is, however, a cost involved when paying cash that most people never consider. In order to purchase the car, you must decide to give up the future possibility of earning interest on the $20,000. This concept is known as **opportunity cost**, and was briefly touched on in the previous chapter. Opportunity cost is often ignored in decision-making, but it is vitally important to understanding the concept of money and financial markets. If you decided to further delay consumption, and invested the $20,000 somewhere earning 4% interest for 60 months, you would make $4,419.93 in earned interest. So, in order to pay cash for the car, you must give up the opportunity of earning $4,419.93.

opportunity cost—*see definition*, p. 81.

Also, notice that the opportunity cost of $4,419.93 is greater than the cost of financing the car by paying $2,099.80 in interest. So, after saving the $20,000 to purchase the car, if you decided to finance the car anyway and keep your money invested, you would end up paying $2,099.80 in interest to a third party, but earning $4,419.93 for yourself. You would come out of the transaction earning a net gain of $2,320.13! This is an example of the power of **compound interest**. Compounding interest is the effect that takes place when you earn money on an increasing balance by delaying consumption. If you aren't confused yet, then you are well ahead of most of your peers. Those who are able to understand and utilize compounding interest to their advantage will be well equipped to create wealth for themselves and those around them.

In a free market the encouragement to save is fairly obvious. Such savings provide the economic wherewithal for the increase in capital goods and this provides the foundation for enhanced productivity. As a result, banks and other financial institutions provide numerous contractual arrangements that allow people to effectively save for the future. With all this said, one must not confuse money with these financial securities. Money is merely the medium by which financial exchanges are made. But as we shall see, in recent times governments have actively blurred the dividing line between the two by establishing fiat currencies (paper money not backed by a commodity such as gold or silver) and promoting easy money schemes that artificially alter market prices in financial markets. This has harmed the economy in some specific ways.

One attack on sound economic thinking is the recent attack on savers who have been charged by political powers with "hoarding" their money. This happened during the Great Depression in the United States, when New Dealers charged people with keeping their money in secret hiding places. Actually, there was a widespread liquidity preference, with good reason. In the early 1930s people were afraid of banks because they were either failing or being forcefully closed by government. In any case, saving is saving, whatever its motive, and none is more a case of "hoarding" than any other. As we shall see in a later chapter, saving does not harm the economy, as some would suggest, but rather, is a primary catalyst for a healthy economy.

Money is fully effective so far as it performs well in three functions. It must first be acceptable as a medium of exchange. Then, it must serve the subsidiary functions of providing a standard for calculation and as a means of storing wealth.

**compound interest**—when some principal amount of money is deposited in a financial account at interest and left there over many years, the interest earned in the first year will itself earn interest in future years, thus compounding annually.

> **Three Functions of Money**
> Money is fully effective so far as it performs well in three functions:
> 1. Its primary function: it must first be acceptable as a medium of exchange.
> 2. Two subsidiary functions: providing a standard for calculation (pricing function of money) and
> 3. as a means of storing wealth.

## 8.2 The Origin of Money

Two things seem reasonably certain about the origin of money. One is that it came into general use in many different places around the world because as a medium of exchange it was greatly superior to barter. Second, it originated as a commodity among commodities. Indeed, we know that a variety of commodities that would not now appeal to us as money have been used as a medium of exchange. Examples include tobacco, sugar, salt, cattle, nails, copper, grain, beads, tea, shells, and even fishhooks.

It is hardly strange that commodities of one kind or another should have been used as a medium of exchange. After all, it is unlikely that people would have traded their goods for something they viewed as worthless, or virtually so. What is much more likely is that they traded them for something of greater perceived value in the market. Nor was it essential that only one commodity serve a monetary function. For example, in colonial Virginia where tobacco served widely as the unit of account, gold and silver coins also circulated. This particular diversity undoubtedly had a political explanation, but different varieties have circulated in some places without political intervention.

### 8.2.1 Gold and Silver as Money

In general, however, wherever they were available and as civilization advanced, precious metals tended to replace other media of exchange. More especially, gold and silver became widely used as money and tended to replace other commodities. It should be made clear that gold and silver are commodities that are valued for other uses than as money. For example, people use them as jewelry and other highly valued decorations. It is also important to emphasize that those who traded for them generally expected that the quantity of metals they received was at least as valuable to them as the goods they exchanged for them. Otherwise, there would have been no reason to engage in the trade.

As mentioned above, both gold and silver possess properties that make them especially appealing as money. (It should be noted that copper has also been used as money, but since it is not so precious a metal, it lost out to them, except as a subsidiary coin.) They are both relatively valuable for their weight relative to most other commodities. They are durable and not at all perishable, and thus make not only good media of exchange but also an excellent means for storing wealth. They are malleable and easily divided into various sizes of **coins** by weight. They are metals that are difficult, indeed almost impossible, to **counterfeit**. The supply of gold has generally been much less than that of silver, at least relative to the demand. So, gold has typically been more valuable. This, in itself, has not kept them both from circulating as media of exchange in the same places. In fact, they tend to supplement one another. When made into coins, gold could be used for more expensive purchases (and for storing more extensive wealth), while silver could be used to make change and to make less expensive purchases. Where both silver and gold serve as currency, the system is sometimes referred to as being **bimetallic**.

Generally speaking, gold and silver were the dominant currencies in the modern world through the nineteenth century. This dominance of gold and silver has been ascribed by some economists to the working of voluntary exchange in the market. Gold and silver came to dominate because of their superiority in performing the functions of money. One other superiority, which has not been mentioned yet, is that so long as people can claim gold in return for any substitutes used, government is quite limited in its power over the money by the amount of gold they possess.

---

**coins**—originally instituted as certain weights of precious metals. Today's coinage is made mostly of base metals and are thus cheap imitations with no inherent value other than what the issuing government declares.

**counterfeit**—creating fake money with the intention of passing it off as real.

**bimetallic**—system where both gold and silver are used as money in trade.

## 8.2.2 Gresham's Law and Government Interference

The most prominent and long standing economic principle dealing with money, if not understood correctly, would appear to deny the possibility that the superior money could have been established in the market. **Sir Thomas Gresham** advanced this principle in the sixteenth century, and it has since become known as Gresham's Law. **Gresham's Law**, stated most generally, holds that bad money tends to drive good money out of circulation. If that rule holds true in the market, then the most inferior money, surely not precious metals, would eventually dominate.

> **Sir Thomas Gresham (1519–1579)**
>
> He was born in London and was the son of Richard Gresham, a merchant. He was well-educated, eventually pursuing studies at Cambridge. He became especially adept at financial management and served the British Crown in that capacity. Gresham's Law takes its name from him.

Undoubtedly, Gresham grasped and stated a principle that applies under certain conditions. What Gresham had observed was that worn and debased coins tended to circulate, while those that were of full weight tended to disappear from circulation. The rule probably should be stated in this way: in cases where money has a stated value, and one kind of it is actually less valuable than the other but will buy the same amount of goods in the market place, then the less valuable will drive the more valuable out of circulation. In sum, people will tend to hold on to the more valuable and spend the less valuable. There are numerous examples that illustrate the validity of this principle.

For example, gold coins, despite their availability, cannot become a currency in the United States and win out over paper money. Clearly, gold coins are quite valuable, and the paper money should be to all intents and purposes worthless. The bad money is keeping the good money out of circulation. Why should this be so? The answer is simple enough. The worthless paper money is **legal tender** for all debts, public and private. Who would choose to pay a debt in gold instead of paper money? The answer is that no one in his right mind would. Even if gold and silver were made legal tender, as well as paper money, it probably would not circulate, following Gresham's Law unless, of course, the paper could be readily redeemed at par with a specified amount of the underlying metal.

**legal tender**—money that is legally enforced as having a certain value by law, regardless of if a commodity backs it up.

> **Gresham's Law**
> In cases where money has a stated value, and one kind of it is actually less valuable than the other but will buy the same amount of goods in the market place, the less valuable will drive the more valuable out of circulation.

Another example that bears out Gresham's Law occurred in the early years of the United States under the Constitution. Hamilton persuaded Congress to authorize the minting of both gold and silver coins at a ratio of 1 to 15. That is, a gold dollar was fixed at 24.7 grains of gold and the silver dollar at 371.21 grains of silver. This ratio represented the approximate prices of the two metals at the time, in relation to one another. However, since gold and silver are commodities and their prices fluctuate in the market, the price of silver soon fell, whereas gold remained steady. In consequence, the silver coins were overvalued and the gold coins were undervalued. The result, in accord with Gresham's Law, was that the silver coins (the "bad" money) drove gold (the "good" money) out of circulation. People held on to the gold coins. The main point of this example is that Gresham's Law is typically evoked by government efforts to dictate monetary values.

Clearly, Gresham's Law is valid for certain cases. That does not prove, however, that bad money would drive good money out in the market, or that the superior money would not become dominant in a free market. In all the above instances, governments tampered with the market. To see what would occur in the market, it will be helpful to return to the example of an auction. Keep in mind that money is basically a commodity, and so far as the determination of its value is concerned, it is subject to the rules of the market. In the market, the price of any particular commodity is determined by quality and quantity. Imagine a cattle auction. There are all sorts of cattle for sale: cows with calves, young cows, old cows, yearlings, bulls, and so on, with great differences in quality and weight. No one is apt to bid on a cow without the knowledge of his weight or quality. A healthy male weighing 1,000 pounds is apt to bring twice as much as one weighing 500 pounds, and so on. The case for money as a commodity in the market is no different. In the case of precious metals, the price will depend upon weight and fineness of the metal. There is every reason to believe, then, that the superior money would survive and dominate the market. It is only when government has tampered with the money that Gresham's Law comes into effect.

The origin of paper money—warehouse receipts, bills of exchange, bills of credit, bank notes, or whatever form it may take—has not yet been discussed. That will be taken up after some discussion of government's involvement with the money supply.

## 8.3 Government and Money

Most Americans, indeed, most people anywhere in the world today, would probably find it difficult to imagine money without the imprint of government upon it. No one now living can remember when government did not play a dominant role in authorizing or issuing money. The Federal Government has played a dominant role in monetary matters since the Civil War and was from time to time involved in it before that. Indeed, governments have a long history of playing a major role in money.

There is nothing in the nature of government and little enough in the nature of money to account for this fact. Granted, government would be expected to punish fraud, deception, and theft of money as well as of other goods. There is no need, however, to use the power of government to force people to have some sort of money. After all, the convenience and utility of money are enough to commend a medium of exchange to people generally. Basically, money is a commodity among commodities in the market, as noted before, but there are some differences between commodities as media of exchange and other commodities. Some of these differences may have led to government involvement in money.

For one thing, government as a tax collector may specify in what commodity taxes may be paid. In doing this, government would be most likely to specify the superior money, if there were any choice. For another, it can at least be argued that it would be convenient for a single medium of exchange to prevail throughout a country, so that uniformity exists in usage. This argument is less compelling than it might appear to those who are used to a single medium. As already noted, the superior money would tend to prevail in the market. Also, trade is not simply within a country but also among peoples of different countries. The best medium of exchange is the one that generally prevails over the widest possible area. Gold and silver had established that position in the modern era in virtually all civilized countries. The other reason often advanced for governments to specify money is to ensure the quality and weight of it. This probably led governments, or could be used by governments, to argue for minting and guaranteeing the contents of coins. That function is not essential either, though many may consider it convenient for government to do it.

At any rate, governments for many centuries have minted coins, specified a unit of money, and in various ways attempted to control the use of money in exchange. Often an image of the head of a monarch was stamped upon the coins of his realm. This practice was republicanized in the United States, where likenesses of Presidents, usually past ones, appear on coins and on paper money. Such decorations hardly affected the value of the coins, except possibly for coin collectors, nor did they have much effect on their circulation. They did suggest the nationality of coins, but that in itself was not greatly significant, since gold and silver coins used to circulate regularly from country to country without much distinction. Moreover, it was the weight and fineness of the precious metals that counted most and not whose picture was on the coin.

A much more important government involvement was in the establishment of a standard **unit of account**, a practice that was widespread by the nineteenth century. These monetary units of account arose generally from the name of some coin, that itself was often tied to a certain weight in some metal. The British pound sterling, for example, signified a pound of silver. The dollar was the corruption of a word used generally in Germany and central Europe for a coin consisting of an ounce of silver known as the **thaler**. It originated in the sixteenth century in Bohemia, named more or less for a well-trusted silversmith, and was the common unit of Germany until the latter part of the nineteenth century. When the United States revolted from England they abandoned the British pound and took the Spanish peso as their unit of account. Americans, however, referred to the Spanish coin, not as a peso, but as a dollar. In 1792, the United States defined the dollar in terms of a certain weight and fineness of silver, though much later the dollar was defined in gold. The government has always played a major role in defining the content and backing, if any, for the standard unit of account, the dollar.

Governments do not have a good record in their monetary interventions. Their record is especially bad with maintaining a standard unit of account. When commodities serve as money, quantity and quality are the only significant measures. Yet once a standard unit of account has been established, governments have a tendency to view this as a value distinct from quantity or quality. Thus, monarchs sometimes called in the gold coins and clipped or shaved them, thus reducing the metal content and using it to issue additional coins. Thus, they departed from weight as a standard basis of the unit of account and tried to circulate them as if the denomination of the coin determined its value. In fact, they had debased the coinage. Another ploy was to establish a fixed ratio between silver and gold. The result of this, as already noted, is that one or the other of these will not circulate when the market price varies significantly from the ratio set by the government. It should be noted, too, that metal coins tend to wear with circulation, and older ones typically weigh less than new coins. The simple solution to these problems is to keep accounts in weight and fineness of metal, not in arbitrary coins that will lose weight in the course of time. But there would be no need for government intervention to establish such units of account, something that does not necessarily please rulers.

We have not yet come to the most serious interventions by government in the money supply, but to do that we must take up a new topic.

**unit of account**—the standard monetary unit that is widely accepted and used for calculations of accounts.

**thaler**—sixteenth–nineteenth century German word for a coin consisting of an ounce of silver.

## 8.4 Paper Money

**paper money**—paper used to represent money in exchanges.

**debt money**—money issued on the basis of debt. There are two basic types. One promises to pay in an actual commodity on demand. The other has no inherent value, but can be traded for something of value. Federal Reserve notes in the United States today are the second type.

**fiat money**—money that has no commodity backing it, and only has value because a government entity has declared it so.

**Great Khan**—ruler in China who was first recorded as using paper money, and required its acceptance by threat of death.

Strictly speaking, there is no such thing as **paper money**, any more than there is such a thing as a paper horse, paper potato, paper apple, paper rose, paper man, or paper any other commodity, except paper paper, which is clearly a redundancy. Since paper has been used to represent money and as a substitute for money, however, it will be treated as money here, but with considerable misgiving.

Paper money is also referred to by some writers as **debt money** or credit money. The term is generally accurate enough, but it can nevertheless be misleading. Debt money, as paper money, has to cover two distinct kinds of debt. It can stand for promises to pay in actual commodities, and when it is fully backed up with the promised commodities, it could be said to be as "good as money." However, we have another kind of debt money today, which is issued upon the basis of debt, yet which promises to pay no commodity or anything else. How this is done will be explained in more depth in the next chapter. This should be more accurately described as **fiat money**. It has value only because a government entity has declared it so—by fiat.

One of the early accounts made of such a fiat money was made by Marco Polo in the thirteenth century in the account of his travels in Asia. In his book he described the paper money system of the **Great Khan** of China. It seems that the Khan had a kind of paper made from the bark of the mulberry tree. The paper was cut into different sizes, each size representing a different denomination of money and described as follows:

> All these pieces of paper are issued with as much solemnity and authority as if they were of pure gold and silver; and on every piece a variety of officials, whose duty it is, have to write their names and to put their seals. And when all is prepared duly, the chief officer deputed by the Khan smears the Seal entrusted to him with vermilion, and impresses it on the paper, so that the form of the Seal remains imprinted upon it in red; the Money is then authentic. Any one forging it would be punished with death.

Marco Polo went on to say that a vast quantity of this paper money was printed each year and then tells how it was distributed:

> With these pieces of paper, made as I have described, he causes all payments on his own account to be made; and he makes them to pass current universally over all the kingdoms and provinces and territories, whithersoever his power and sovereignty extends. And nobody, however important he may think himself, dares to refuse them on pain of death. And indeed everybody takes them readily, for wheresoever a person may go throughout the Great Khan's dominions he shall find these pieces of paper current, and shall be able to transact all sales and purchases of goods by means of them just as well as if they were coins of pure gold....

> Furthermore all merchants arriving from India or other countries, and bringing with them gold or silver or gems and pearls, are prohibited from selling to anyone but the Emperor. He has twelve experts chosen for this business,

men of shrewdness and experience in such affairs; these appraise the articles, and the Emperor then pays a liberal price for them in those pieces of paper. The merchants accept his price readily, for in the first place they would not get so good an one from anybody else, and secondly they are paid without any delay. And with this paper money they can buy what they like anywhere over the Empire, whilst it is also vastly lighter to carry about on their journeys. And it is a truth that the merchants will several times in the year bring wares to the amount of 400,000 bezants, and the Grand Sire pays for all in that paper. So he buys such a quantity of those precious things every year that his treasure is endless, whilst all the time the money he pays away costs him nothing at all. Moreover, several times in the year proclamation is made through the city that anyone who may have gold or silver or gems or pearls, by taking them to the Mint shall get a handsome price for them. And the owners are glad to do this, because they would find no other purchaser give so large a price. Thus the quantity they bring in is marvelous, though these who do not choose to do so may let it alone. Still, in this way, nearly all the valuables in the country come into the Khan's possession.

When any of these pieces of paper are spoilt—not that they are so very flimsy neither—the owner carries them to the Mint, and by paying three per cent, on the value he gets new pieces in exchange. And if any Baron, or anyone else so ever, hath need of gold or silver or gems or pearls, in order to make plate, or girdles, or the like, he goes to the Mint and buys as much as he list, paying in this paper-money. (George B. Parks, ed., *The Travels of Marco Polo* [New York: Macmillan, 1927], pp. 143–44.)

There are several things that are worth emphasizing in this account of a paper money system by Marco Polo. First, it is clear that it was tyrannically imposed, because of references to the death penalty for counterfeiting or refusing to accept it as payment for goods. The latter provision made this paper money legal tender. Second, if Marco was right, the emperor had greatly enriched himself with this system, drawing in vast quantities of precious metals and gems with it. We have no inkling of what economic consequences followed from this, and Marco Polo gives no indication of how increases in quantity would affect prices generally. In any case, this provides us with a kind of model of a fiat money system using paper money, to which we may refer later.

### Getting the Point . . .

How did the Great Khan's paper money get into circulation?

Over time, where did much of the country's precious metals and stones end up?

## 8.4.1 Origins of Debt Money in Europe

Even if Europeans generally had read and believed Marco Polo's account of the Great Khan's paper money scheme, it is highly doubtful that any country would have tried to imitate it. The technology for carrying it out—paper and printing—was either new to Europe or not yet fully developed. More important, perhaps, Europe had a long Christian history both of condemnation of great wealth and of exchanges in commodities. To be compelled to exchange goods for pieces of paper was far too remote from their experience to be contemplated. It would be several centuries before Europeans would advance fraudulent paper money schemes.

However, a kind of paper or debt money did begin to develop in Europe in the late Middle Ages and became fairly widespread in the fifteenth, sixteenth, and seventeenth centuries. This debt money is usually described by two different phrases: bills of exchange and warehouse receipts. Bills of exchange became important items in some of the Italian city-states first. A **bill of exchange** is a paper on which the receiver or buyer of something of value promises to pay a certain sum of money, either upon demand or at some specified maturity date. It may have come into use with merchants as a device for transferring sums of money from one place to another, or, more precisely, having sums of money available where they are wanted. For example, a merchant might be traveling to some distant or foreign city to do business. It might be dangerous or inconvenient to carry the money—precious metals—with him. He might leave the money with some trading house with a branch in the place to which he was going, taking in its place a bill of exchange. Or, he might have sold some goods in a distant land and taken payment in a bill of exchange rather than taking the money with him.

Bills of exchange might be made out to a specific person or made payable to the bearer of it. In any case, such bills might become negotiable instruments, i.e., transferable at will from one person to another, by endorsement or otherwise. Bills on reputable companies might be widely accepted and serve as a kind of paper money, though no one but the issuer might be required to accept them in payment. There were dangers of abuse, of course, since it was possible for an issuer of bills of exchange to issue more bills than he could redeem. In any case, they were an early form of debt or paper money arising out of private transactions. They differ only in degree from the modern check written against a bank deposit. The major differences are that bills of exchange were (and are) used in foreign exchange, may involve different currencies, and were more apt to circulate than checks usually do.

The **warehouse receipt** was much more closely tied to banking than was the bill of exchange. It was the forerunner, too, of fractional reserve banking, but in origin it did not usually entail that feature. A bank simply issued a receipt for gold or silver deposited there, and paid out the money on the demand of the owner. That these receipts might be used as a medium of exchange is obvious, so long as there was any great confidence that the receipts would be redeemed. The receipts, of course, signified a debt of the bank or issuer. The idea was practiced for some time by a bank in Venice, Italy, in the sixteenth century, described in the following way by Elgin Groseclose:

> [It] was founded upon the principle of safe deposit, a principle unfortunately largely submerged in modern banking practice. Lending of deposited funds was not practiced. The bank sought to make no profit from the use of its credit, and merely undertook to keep the money of depositors in safety, and to pay it out or transfer it to others at the will of the owner.

The bank's income came "from fees for effecting transactions on its books, for the negotiation and discounting of bills of exchange . . . and from the bank's services as money changer."

In fact, however, many such banks frequently loaned out deposit money, and began practices associated with fractional reserve banking. While any paper issued promising to make payment in the future and

**bill of exchange**—paper on which the buyer of something of value promises to pay a certain sum of money either on demand or on some specified maturity date.

**warehouse receipt**—receipt detailing an amount of some commodity stored in a warehouse or bank.

circulating as a medium of exchange in any degree may be described as debt money, so long as the money kept on deposit equals the obligations there is nothing immoral or illegal about it. The warehousing of precious metals, whether as coin, bullion, or in whatever form need not be any different from the warehousing of tobacco, cotton, household goods, or any sort of merchandise. Nor is there anything amiss in issuing receipts for such goods, or these receipts being used as payment for other goods, so long as they are fully redeemable. But there grew up a practice by some banks, goldsmiths, or other warehousers of precious metals, of making loans with these deposits. To make the loans, in effect, they issued warehouse receipts for goods that had not been deposited, thus contracting obligations they could not fulfill, if everyone demanded his deposits at once.

It is easy to see how such practices began. Banks and other depositories often had large amounts of precious metal on hand at any one time. It might be, too, that deposits often equaled or exceeded withdrawals. Thus, in the normal course of events, the bank could commit to redeem more of its receipts than it had deposits, or so it has often been held. And, so long as the bank continued to redeem its pledges, it need have no particular fear of being caught short. Of course, any "run" on the bank by depositors would spell inevitable bankruptcy. Debt money had been put into circulation for which no assets existed to redeem it. This is the essence of fractional reserve banking, which we must now discuss in detail.

### 8.4.2 Fractional Reserve Banking

The great engine that has produced the vast quantities of paper money inundating particular countries from time to time, and that in our day swamps virtually the whole world, is banking. The tremendous increases in the money supply, which now come regularly, can usually be ascribed to fractional reserve banking. Granted, governments have sometimes issued such paper and caused it to circulate themselves, but the norm has been for banks to do so, usually with charters from governments and more or less under the control of government. At any rate, fractional reserve banking is the key to the paper (and usually debt) money that now holds sway.

**Fractional reserve banking** is quite simple, though the variety of devices can be quite complex. Fractional reserve banking is the practice of keeping only a fraction of its deposits on hand to redeem the claims against them. The size of the fraction—whether 90%, 50%, 20%, 10%, 5%—does not alter the character of the practice, though the bank's position is relatively stronger when the percentage is higher. Nor does it matter, so far as determining that it is fractional reserve banking, whether what is being held on reserve is gold, silver, warehouse receipts for precious metals, bank notes, or whatever. Obviously, it matters to the depositors that what is on reserve is the same in kind as what they deposited. In sum, it is fractional reserve banking when a bank holds on reserve only a fraction of what has been deposited.

Fractional reserve banks are of two kinds, in terms of function, though they have often been united in single banks. There are banks of issue and checking account, or commercial, banks. A **bank of issue** is a bank that issues currency, commonly called bank notes. These bank notes are payable on demand or redeemable at some specified date in the future. They are secured by various sorts of assets, and in a fractional reserve bank, only a portion of the means for redeeming the outstanding notes is kept in reserve. The bank expects that these bank notes will circulate as currency, in short, as a kind of paper money, for that is their main

**fractional reserve banking**—a system in which banks keep only a small portion—a fraction—of deposits on hand to meet the demands of the depositors. The system is vulnerable before the depositors, because if large numbers, or most of them, demand their money, the bank cannot do what it promised.

**bank of issue**—bank that issues bank notes intended to serve as a currency. By law in the United States today Federal Reserve banks are the only banks of issue, but in earlier times banks generally issued such bank notes, especially in the first half of the nineteenth century.

function. This is the most pernicious form of fractional reserve banking as it is essentially financial fraud since some of the paper notes have no claim to actual assets.

Checking account or **commercial banking** is well enough known but we need to discuss its operations here. A commercial bank is simply a bank that accepts deposits, cashes checks, issues debit cards, makes loans, and the like, from those deposits. The essential business of a commercial bank is to act as a financial intermediary between borrowers and lenders. When depositors put their money into checking accounts they are basically saving their funds in a short-term manner. The bank then holds some of this money in reserve and lends out the rest to ready borrowers at interest. Thus, the bank has a **fiduciary** responsibility to the depositors.

The main problem that arises in this activity is that banks are borrowing the money in the short-term and generally lending it over longer terms. For example, suppose the bank lends some money it has on deposit from its customers to someone over a five-year period to purchase an automobile. The result is that there is a mismatch in duration. Since depositors can demand their money at any time, if too many depositors demand too much money it will deplete all the reserves and the bank will not be able to meet the demand. Such a situation can result in a rapid loss of confidence and promote a run on it by all the depositors at once. In such cases, banks have failed and been put out of business.

What could be done to mitigate against this possibility? One option would be for the bank to hold all of its deposits on reserve. To do this it would have to charge its customers fees to cover the cost of the services it is providing. The problem here is that the depositors are likely to prefer to accept some risk of investing to avoid these fees. A second option would be for the bank to avoid lending in longer-term markets choosing only to make short-term highly liquid loans. In this case, the bank could readily cover the demands of the depositors. Banks have generally avoided doing this since the rate of return on such loans is lower. A third option would be for the banks to attract depositors willing to save money over a longer period of time. This would tend to correct the mismatch in duration on the depositors' end. This has not generally worked even though banks do offer certificates of deposit, which offer higher interest rates for savers willing to deposit money for longer terms. A final option would be for bank owners to maintain a significant equity stake in the business thus providing the ready resources to meet depositors demands. As a general rule commercial banks have been highly leveraged businesses maintaining only a small fraction of equity to its debt. Nevertheless, in a free market where people are left free to choose some, or all, of these options, there would be a move to greater stability in time. But that has not happened.

What has happened is that banks of issue and commercial banks have been radically separated in the United States. Federal Reserve banks are the only banks of issue. More will be said about them later, but, for practical purposes, they are quasi-government bodies owned technically by member (private) banks. They have a monopoly of the issue of bank notes in the United States, and their notes are legal tender by law for all debts public and private. Commercial banks, on the other hand, are privately owned but heavily regulated by government.

Fractional reserve banking as it is currently practiced is an awesome, dangerous, and devious practice. No amount of legalizing it can change that fact. The most obvious danger is that any bank engaging in fractional reserve is always in potential bankruptcy, since the claims on it exceed its liquid assets. Checking account banks that hold fractional reserves against their deposits can be brought down at any time when the demands for cash exceed their reserves and they are unable to acquire the needed

---

**commercial bank**—bank that takes deposits, cashes checks, and makes loans.

**fiduciary**—individual who has been placed in a position of trust to manage money or property. A fiduciary is permitted to treat people's money in many respects as their own. However, they must still be able to meet any demands the original owner might make to withdraw the money or else be subject to bankruptcy.

liquidity because of the duration of their loan portfolio. In sum, the banks have obligations that they cannot meet. No other business is authorized by law to carry on its business in this fashion. Indeed, a bank customer who writes checks knowing that he does not have the full amount to cover his outstanding checks is subject to legal prosecution. No such penalties exist for officers of banks for what is for them a normal condition, recognized by law. Thus, banks enjoy a highly privileged position.

The most awesome power of fractional reserve banks, however, lies in their ability to expand and contract the currency through the issuance of new notes coupled with the lending practices of the commercial banks. Banks of issue can increase the bank notes in circulation, or they may reduce them. When commercial banks loan out to other customers all but the reserve fraction of their current deposits, they are expanding credit. This in effect, increases the total amount of money available for use to individuals and organizations. This power may be best described as the power to inflate or deflate the currency. The full impact of the use of this power will be illustrated later but that it can have a great impact on the economy needs to be asserted here. Banks can increase or decrease the exchange value of money. They can cause depressions or create a temporary aura of prosperity. They can wipe out savings, virtually, by inflating the money supply and destroying the value of the paper money. Many of the depressions in history have been set off by rounds of bank failures; indeed, these have been the most prominent causes of depression.

> **Getting the Point...**
>
> Explain how when banks make loans it inflates the currency. Are there potential negative consequences in this?

The greatest damage has usually come from combining fractional reserve banking with the use of fiat money, and the use of legal tender laws. The problems created by printing money out of thin air are compounded in commercial fractional reserve banking. Inflation creates an even greater aura of prosperity and results in an even deeper depression. This idea will be discussed in more detail in Boom-Bust Cycles in the next chapter.

Moreover, fractional reserve banking leads a very precarious existence so long as its money has to be redeemed in commodities, in modern times, usually gold or silver. The pressure of depositors to redeem their paper money in precious metals if they are in doubt about the stability of the bank would lead prudent bankers to keep large reserves. So long as paper money has to be backed by a fixed percentage of precious metal reserves it tends to limit the amount of paper currency in circulation. In any case, banks are dramatically called to account from time to time when their currency is redeemable in precious metals, but that is no longer the case in the United States today.

It may not have escaped the attention of even the young and relatively inexperienced that banks usually occupy expensive and pretentious buildings and that the atmosphere within them is one of an almost reverent hush and solemnity. The reason for these things is now before us. Fractional reserve banks are absolutely dependent upon depositor confidence for their continued existence. The aura of wealth and respectability is essential to them, and they go to considerable expense to maintain them. None of this is meant to suggest that individual bankers are personally dishonest or even devious, but rather that they are engaged in an enterprise that is precarious and potentially dangerous to the public if and when they fail.

**Fractional reserve banking** as it is currently practiced is an awesome, dangerous, and devious practice. No amount of legalizing it can change that fact.
1. The most obvious danger is that any bank engaging in fractional reserve is always in potential bankruptcy, since the claims on it exceed its liquid assets.
2. The most awesome power of fractional reserve banks, however, lies in their ability to expand and contract the currency through the issuance of new notes coupled with the lending practices of the commercial banks.

The greatest damage has usually come from combining fractional reserve banking with the use of fiat money, and the use of legal tender laws.

---

*Money is different from all other commodities: other things being equal, more shoes, or more discoveries of oil or copper benefit society, since they help alleviate natural scarcity. But once a commodity is established as a money on the market, no more money at all is needed. Since the only use of money is for exchange and reckoning, more dollars or pounds or marks in circulation cannot confer a social benefit: they will simply dilute the exchange value of every existing dollar or pound or mark.*

**Murray Rothbard**

# Study Guide for:

# 8 A Medium of Exchange—Money

## Chapter Summary

In man's efforts to obtain what he wants from others by way of exchange, money serves as the basic medium by which most of these exchanges are negotiated. Why this is the case is not hard to understand. If people had to rely upon bartering goods for goods directly, then each individual seeking to trade would be forced to find a suitable trading partner. That person would have to possess the particular good desired and want the good being offered in order to make the exchange. Obviously, this situation greatly limits the benefits that can arise from trade by limiting the number of suitable trades that would be likely to occur.

Money facilitates a tremendous expansion in the market by serving as a common denominator for trade. Thus, its primary purpose is to serve as a medium of exchange. Initially, various commodities were used as money. Certain characteristics made some commodities more useful as money than others. In particular, an exchange can be better facilitated by a commodity that is portable, durable, divisible, and more easily measurable. Money serves three basic functions. It serves as:

- a medium of exchange,
- a standard of calculation, and
- a store of wealth.
- Given these functions it is easy to see why gold and silver became so prominently used as money.

One drawback with the use of gold and silver was the need to weigh it in each exchange situation. To overcome this problem, coinage of money became popular. The coins would then be marked according to their weight, and the seal of the coin's maker would be applied to its face to authenticate the coin. Historically, governments have shown a strong interest in control over the money supply and have engaged in coining activities.

The use of paper money to execute exchanges is associated with the development of commercial banking. Gold and silver are not as portable as paper. Therefore, banks developed as depository warehouses that held precious metals for people. In return they would issue bank notes that were redeemable in gold to depositors. Depending on the reputation of the issuing bank, the notes were accepted for making exchanges.

Commercial banks in turn began the practice of holding only a fraction of gold deposited in reserve and lending out the rest at interest. The process is called fractional reserve banking. The practice significantly increases the amount banks can lend and has led to numerous problems and bank failures. This is especially true when their depositors generally seek to redeem their deposits. Such bank runs can produce instant bankruptcy.

## Points of Emphasis

1. Money functions as a medium of exchange, a standard of calculation, and as a store of wealth.

2. Say's law is a proposition by a French economist, J.B. Say, that production creates its own demand. That is, people produce things and enter the market because they have an interest in acquiring some other goods. Though money may lead an individual to misread the market, there can never be a persisting overproduction in the economy.

3. Fractional reserve banking dramatically increases the level of debt in the commercial banking system and creates uncertainty.

4. Today, government involvement with money is immense. By declaration or fiat they declare certain paper to be legal tender. As a result, we no longer have a commodity based money.

## Identification

1. money

2. commodity

3. currency

4. medium of exchange

5. Say's Law
6. shortage of money
7. pricing function of money
8. net worth
9. assets
10. liabilities
11. liquidity preference
12. opportunity cost
13. compound interest
14. coins
15. counterfeit
16. bimetallic
17. Sir Thomas Gresham
18. Gresham's Law
19. legal tender
20. unit of account
21. thaler
22. paper money
23. debt money
24. fiat money
25. Great Khan
26. bill of exchange
27. warehouse receipt
28. fractional reserve banking
29. bank of issue
30. commercial bank
31. fiduciary

## Review Questions

1. Why do some people believe that there is a shortage of money? What is wrong with this belief?
2. Why were gold and silver favored above other commodities as money? Does Gresham's Law apply to this historical development?
3. Why have governments been so interested in controlling money throughout history?
4. What is fractional reserve banking?
5. What is really meant by the following statement: "There is no such thing as paper money"?

## Activity

1. Prepare a case either to support or oppose the following position: "The only scarcity is the scarcity of money with which people can buy goods and services."

## For Further Study

1. Henry Hazlitt, *The Inflation Crisis and How to Resolve It*, 2nd edition, University Press of America: Lanham, MD, 1983.
2. Richard Maybury, *Whatever Happened to Penny Candy?*, Bluestocking Press, Placerville, CA, 2004.
3. Hans Sennholz, *Age of Inflation*, Western Islands: Belmont, Massachusetts, 1979.
4. Hans Sennholz, *Gold and Money*, Greenwood Press: Westport, Connecticut, 1975.
5. Barry Siegel, editor, *Money in Crisis*, Pacific Institute: San Francisco, 1984.
6. Lawrence White, *Competition and Currency: Essays on Free Market Banking*, New York University Press: New York, 1989.
7. Leland B. Yeager, *International Monetary Relations*, Harper and Row: New York, 1966.

> **CHAPTER CONTENT**
>
> 9.1 Eighteenth Century Inflationist Schemes  108
>     9.1.1 John Law's Mississippi Stock Inflation  108
>     9.1.2 The Continental Currency Inflation  111
>     9.1.3 The French Revolution Inflation  113
>     9.1.4 Lessons Learned  115
> 9.2 The Twentieth Century Age of Credit and Inflation  116
>     9.2.1 Paving The Way for the Federal Reserve  117
>     9.2.2 The Federal Reserve Act  119
> 9.3 Abandoning the Gold Standard  120
>     9.3.1 Boom–Bust Cycles  121
>     9.3.2 Living on Credit  122
>     9.3.3 Federal Reserve Notes as Money  125

# 9   THE AGE OF INFLATION

In twentieth century American political lingo, the term inflation was made to mean a general rise of prices. Contrary to this popular use of the term that continues today, **inflation** is simply an increase of the money supply. It is accomplished by debasing or devaluing the money supply. The general rise in prices is the effect of inflation and not inflation itself. This distorted meaning was undoubtedly promoted by politically motivated people in order to shift the blame for the rise of prices away from a government that was inflating the currency toward the producers of goods who were charging higher prices. In any case, inflation will be used here mainly to refer to increases in the money supply, which was its agreed upon meaning until the middle of the twentieth century.

Infationist schemes have abounded throughout history and have been especially prominent since the eighteenth century. Indeed, even before that, inflation had been carried out both in banking activities and by monarchs who called in and **"clipped"** the **coins**. Clipping a coin involved shaving off some of the metal, thus reducing the weight of the coin. The shavings were then used to create more coins. Inflation really began to come into its own in the eighteenth century—and it has been very much a way of life since the twentieth century.

Increasing the money supply—inflation—has a strong appeal because of its early effects. At the beginning of a vigorous inflation, it usually creates an aura of prosperity. There is much new money in circulation. Trade expands, becomes brisk, and all sorts of goods command high prices. The initial rise in prices, including wages, only increases the sense of well-being generally, or so it seems. The whole country may begin to develop a false sense of prosperity. It is false because it is ill-founded upon an increase in the currency, which is only a medium of exchange, and not an increase in the production of the goods and services that people really want. The prices of those are rising as well. They do not want their money devalued, of course, but that is what is really happening. In any case, it takes larger and larger doses of inflation to keep the aura of prosperity going. Meanwhile, the value of the money is being progressively destroyed; it ceases to be useful as a store of wealth as the value of savings is decreased, and no longer serves effectively any of its functions. Governments tend to become tyrannical in forcing this devalued currency on people. A very common consequence is runaway inflation, followed by ruinous deflation, usually called a depression.

> **The Appeal of Inflation**
> Increasing the money supply—inflation—has a strong appeal because of its early effects. At the beginning of a vigorous inflation, it usually creates an aura of prosperity. Trade expands, becomes brisk, and all sorts of goods command high prices. The initial rise in prices, including wages, only increases the sense of well-being generally. But it is false.

## 9.1 Eighteenth Century Inflationist Schemes

**inflation**—has historically meant an increase of the money supply. However, for the past 50 years there has been a politically inspired effort to have inflation mean the general rise in prices that follows upon a monetary inflation. This change in terminology helps to obscure the cause of the rise of prices.

**clipped coins**—coins that have had some portion shaved off in order to make more coins with the scraps. Many coins have ridged edges to make it more difficult to hide clipping.

Probably, the most extensive, and as yet unfinished, inflation in the United States got underway in the 1930s and is still going on. Some account of that must await the discussion of the Federal Reserve System, which will be made in a following section. At this point, however, three eighteenth century inflations will be described because they illustrate both the various methods and the usual consequences of inflations.

### 9.1.1 John Law's Mississippi Stock Inflation

The first one to be described was a major French inflation in the early eighteenth century. It was almost certainly the most extensive and devastating inflation to have been brought off in any country in Europe up until that time. This inflation grew out of a plan advanced by John Law and was associated with a project for the development of the Mississippi territory then owned by France. John Law was a Scotchman, an advocate of paper money inflation, and an international gambler. He was driven out of several countries and was wanted for manslaughter, at least, in England. Law took up residence in France, where he soon became well known to the French nobility, including the Duke of Orleans, for his gambling exploits and bold ideas. He pushed the idea that France could only achieve prosperity through a great increase of the money supply. Indeed, in the waning years of Louis XIV, the government was head over heels in debt, and the means of even paying the interest on the debt was limited. On the death of Louis XIV (1715), Law's friend, the Duke of Orleans, became Regent (ruler during the years that Louis XV was a minor) of France. Law persuaded the Duke to charter a bank under his control.

John Law followed very cautious banking policies at first. He gave his bank notes a premium value by paying more for French coins than they would bring elsewhere and promising to redeem all his bank notes with precious coins. Law even let it be known that he thought any banker ought to be hanged who did not redeem all notes when they were presented. Thus, Law built confidence in his bank notes, which he issued in relatively small quantities at first. He was greatly admired for his banking prowess, and it was with this background that he put forward his Mississippi scheme. This was an alleged project for the development of the Mississippi territory by his company, which had trading privileges there. Law sold shares in the company, which quickly became worth much more than their face value. He issued fewer shares at first than the market would have absorbed, promised spectacular dividends, and set off a frenzy of trading activity in the stocks.

The whole thing came to a head in 1719–1720. Law used his bank notes to foster the speculative mania in the Mississippi stocks, making ever larger bank note issues. The government cooperated by making his the official currency of France. The inflation did indeed create an aura of prosperity in France, as the country enjoyed a temporary boom. Charles Mackay, who wrote of this substantial inflation in a book, *Extraordinary Popular Delusions and the Madness of the Crowd*, described the boom this way:

> For a time, while confidence lasted, an impetus was given to trade which could not fail to be beneficial. In Paris especially the good results were felt. Strangers flocked into the capital from every part, bent not only upon making money, but on spending it.... The looms of the country worked with unusual activity to supply rich laces, silks, broad-cloth, and velvets, which being paid for in abundant paper, increased in price fourfold. Provisions shared the general advance. Bread, meat, and vegetables were sold at prices greater than had ever before been known; while the wages of labor rose in exactly the same proportion. The artisan who formerly gained fifteen sous per diem now gained sixty. New houses were built in every direction; an illusory prosperity shone over the land, and so dazzled the eyes of the whole nation, that none could see the dark cloud on the horizon announcing the storm that was too rapidly approaching.

Inflationary prosperity, even when the feeling of prosperity is dominant, resembles nothing so much as the gain a dog makes when he is chasing his tail. After all, the higher prices one receives for his goods mean nothing if he must pay equally high prices for what he buys. That is not to say that monetary inflation affects the whole population equally. It does not; there are winners and losers. In a speculative mania, much of the gain goes to those who have the time, wealth, and credit to speculate. So it was in this inflation. As Mackay says,

> **Who is Able to Take Advantage of Inflation**
> The higher prices one receives for his goods mean nothing if he must pay equally high prices for what he buys. That is not to say that monetary inflation affects the whole population equally. It does not; there are winners and losers. In a speculative mania, much of the gain goes to those who have the time, wealth, and credit to speculate.

> It was remarked at the time that Paris had never before been so full of objects of elegance and luxury. Statues, pictures, and tapestries were imported in great quantities from foreign countries, and found a ready market. All those pretty trifles in the way of furniture and ornaments which the French excel in manufacturing were no longer the exclusive playthings of the aristocracy, but were to be found in abundance in the houses of traders and the middle classes in general. Jewelry of the most

costly description was brought to Paris as the most favourable mart. . . .

Nothing could or did sustain the Mississippi stock or the paper currency indefinitely. Larger and larger issues of bank notes were made in desperate attempts to keep up the price of near worthless Mississippi stock. Eventually, the price dropped. Not even the might of the tyrannical French government could sustain the bubble. There was not enough gold coin in all of France to redeem the paper currency. Thus, the government eventually ceased redeeming any but small amounts of the currency. They called in all but small amounts of personal precious metals and forbade the acquiring of expensive jewelry or other ornaments in a sustained, despotic attempt to restore the declining value of the currency. Nothing helped. The Mississippi stock was now virtually worthless, and fortunes were wiped out. The bank notes, which were supposed to enrich the nation, had driven it much nearer to bankruptcy, as most of the precious metals had been drawn out of the country as larger and larger issues of bank notes were made. John Law was so hated by the French that he left the country for his safety, and the French government was as near discredited as a monarchy could be. Revolution was still more than half a century away, but the ground for it was being prepared.

What had happened in France can be succinctly stated from an economic point of view. The creation of paper money adds nothing of use, value, or worth in society. It is only worth what it can be exchanged for, and that is dependent on what the money represents in terms of commodities and how much of it is in circulation. If it can be redeemed in specific amounts of gold, it is always known to be worth what the gold is worth. As more paper currency is created, each unit of it buys fewer goods and services. In sum, what a given unit of money will purchase in the marketplace is a ratio between the quantity of the money in circulation and the quantity of goods and services available. This is modified by the strength of the wants of all who wish to either buy or sell goods.

> The **creation of paper money** adds nothing of use, value, or worth in society. It is only worth what it can be exchanged for, and that is dependent on what the money represents in terms of commodities and how much of it is in circulation. If it can be redeemed in specific amounts of gold, it is always known to be worth what the gold is worth. As more paper currency is created, each unit of it buys fewer goods and services.

To put the matter concretely, if a bushel of wheat brings one dollar this means that the relative supply and demand conditions for money and wheat is such that a one dollar bill is the price that will satisfy both buyer and seller. If the quantity of money in circulation is increased, and all else remains the same, the price of wheat may be expected to rise in proportion to the increase of money. This is all especially so in the case of paper money, where the increase in quantity has added nothing else of value.

## 9.1.2 The Continental Currency Inflation

During the American War for Independence, a major paper money inflation occurred. It can at least be argued that the reasons for issuing large quantities of paper money by the Continental Congress during this war were better than those in France in 1719–1720. After all, the united colonies were engaged in a war to obtain their independence from Britain. The revolt had been, in some measure, a reaction to taxation, and the states were reluctant to levy high taxes. There were divisions between Loyalists and Patriots within the states, and high taxes might have alienated the people even more from the cause. The Continental Congress, which was conducting the war, did not have the power to tax, and relied, instead, upon requisitions on the states. Thus, paper money was used as an expedient to raise money for conducting the war. The motives for the actions, however, did not significantly alter the consequences, as we shall see.

In any case, Congress did make successive issues of paper currency during the war. This currency consisted of bills of credit, called Continental notes. They were issued on authority of the Congress and paid out directly into circulation by Congress, not through banks. They were supposed to be redeemed by the states at some later date. In short, they had nothing to back them except vague promises of future redemption. They were debt money—so far as they circulated as money—with no great probability that the debt would ever be paid.

Congress issued $6 million in Continental currency during 1775—before the Declaration of Independence. The initial issue was $2 million, but it was followed by another $1 million before it had all been put into circulation, then by another issue of $3 million before the end of the year. Benjamin Franklin, who was in Congress, said: "After the first emission I proposed that we should stop, strike no more, but borrow on interest those we had issued. This was not then approved of, and more bills were issued." Indeed, the pace was stepped up in the ensuing years. Estimates have it that $19 million was issued in 1776, $13 million in 1777, $63.5 million in 1778, and over $90 million in 1779. It should be noted that Congress was not the only source of paper currency during the war. Some of the states issued bills of credit, and the British counterfeited the Continental currency, with the purpose of hastening the destruction of the currency.

The more paper money that was issued the less it was worth in the market. It was not long before there were difficulties in getting the paper accepted in exchange for goods. Thus, efforts were made in the states to make people take the paper money. For example, the Council of Safety in Pennsylvania declared in 1776 that anyone who refused to accept the Continental currency would forfeit whatever he refused to sell and be subject to a penalty besides. All this was for a first offense. For a second offense he would be banished from the state. In the same year, Rhode Island made both state and Continental notes legal tender. In addition to providing penalties for not accepting this paper, that state prohibited the buying of **specie** with paper or differentiating in prices of goods when offered gold or silver instead of paper.

One of the first and most notable of the effects of the successive issues of this paper money was a general rise in prices. In an attempt to stop the rise in prices, Congress recommended that the states hold a convention to adopt price controls. Conventions were held from the states north of Maryland and these states developed a list of prices to be fixed. After the conventions set the prices, it was up to the states to enforce the price controls. For example, Rhode Island recommended that anyone violating the price controls should be fined 20 shillings for each violation.

**specie**—precious metals used as money.

The price controls, where they were at all effective, resulted in shortages. John Eliot wrote from Boston in June of 1777, "We are all starving here, since this plaguy addition to the regulating bill. People will not bring in provision, and we cannot procure the common necessaries of life. What we shall do I know not." What they did, of course, is what people always do when governments adopt regulations severely hampering the operation of the market. They evade the regulations, barter with one another, engage in black-market exchange, produce money from hiding that will be accepted, and find a variety of means to obtain goods and services necessary for life.

The paper money did not succeed for long in making the necessary provisions for the army available. Many people would not even take the paper money in return for their goods and services. When they could be persuaded to take the paper, George Washington noted in 1779, "a wagon load of money will scarcely purchase a wagon load of provisions." The army had to be provisioned by direct confiscation of goods, a method that was both wasteful and unjust in its application.

In fact, the whole paper money inflation worked many injustices. It favored debtors, for they could pay off their debts with depreciated currency to those who had loaned them money. Likewise, it hurt creditors who had to take much less to satisfy their loans than they had originally loaned. John Adams put it this way, in 1778, saying that

> ... every man who had money due him at the commencement of this war, has been already taxed three-fourths part of that money [that is, has lost it by way of the depreciation of the currency].... And every man who owed money at the beginning of the war, has put three-fourth parts of it in his pockets as clear gain. The war, therefore, is immoderately gainful to some, and ruinous to others.

Inflation tends to reverse the rules of economic behavior: where once it was prudent to save money, it becomes expedient to spend it; where once it was good business to supply customers with durable goods, it becomes profitable to delay the sale for the rising prices; where once creditors were those who were better off generally, it now becomes good business to borrow money and repay it with a currency that is less valuable than when the loan was made. When the money supply is stable, the solid citizen who is cautious and prudent can do well over the years by hard work, careful investments, and saving. His prosperity may even be described as virtue rewarded. Inflation sets the stage for wealth to be gained in a different fashion: by borrowing, by holding on to goods for the inevitable higher prices, and by attending closely to the swift changes in the value of the money. Of course, there are many losers in this game: those who have saved for old age may find their lifelong savings wiped out, and so on. In essence, monetary inflation sets in motion the redistribution of wealth from the prudent to the prodigal

In the late 1770s, the country was faced with runaway inflation. Prices rose too swiftly to be taken into account. The bills became worth $1/40^{th}$ of their original face value. Congress devised an elaborate plan in 1780 in order to solve this problem. They attempted to introduce a new currency that was not devalued into the market to replace the old currency. The plan did not work. There was no reason why it should. If the new money was more valuable than the old, it would not circulate. In fact, the new money quickly fell to the same value as the old, and both became virtually worthless by 1781. In March of 1781, Congress abandoned the acceptance of its own currency at face value as legal tender. It was now to be accepted only on a sliding scale that was supposed to represent its depreciation. Thereafter, the paper money depreciated so rapidly that it shortly ceased to circulate at all. Gold and silver coins came out of hiding and replaced paper money as the currency of the land. Debts contracted during the inflation were difficult to repay, and the country was afflicted by the depression, which is the deflation of the money supply.

> **Rewarding Prodigality**
> When the money supply is stable, the solid citizen who is cautious and prudent can do well over the years by hard work, careful investments, and saving. His prosperity may even be described as virtue rewarded. Inflation sets the stage for wealth to be gained in a different fashion: by borrowing, by holding on to goods for the inevitable higher prices, and by attending closely to the swift changes in the value of the money. Of course, there are many losers in this game: those who have saved for old age may find their lifelong savings wiped out, and so on. In essence, monetary inflation sets in motion the redistribution of wealth from the prudent to the prodigal.

The paper money inflation in the United States had run its course in a period of six years. For the first year or so during the early issues, there had been the flush of prosperity. Then as more and more of the currency was issued, prices rose, the currency fell in value, and people no longer wanted to accept it. Draconian laws were adopted to make people accept the money and to impose price controls. The more Congress issued, the less it was worth, and the money eventually became worthless. The correction to this inflation came by way of a depression.

### 9.1.3 The French Revolution Inflation

No account of paper money inflations in the eighteenth century would be complete without some mention and discussion of the one that occurred during the French Revolution in the 1790s. It might be supposed that the French would have been immune to paper money after the experiment under John Law's tutelage. Or, that they might have learned from more recent events of the past decade or so in the United States. That did not prove to be the case at all. France went through the whole inflationary spiral at an accelerated pace between 1790–1796. Just as in America in the 1770s, the first issue provided an aura of prosperity, and the pressures mounted for further issues, and eventually for greater and greater quantities of paper currency. The first issue in 1790 was for 400 million livres. By the last issue in 1796, the money supply had ballooned to 40 billion livres or francs in circulation. Tyrannical measures were undertaken to force the currency into circulation at par, and the same depreciation as in other countries took place in France.

One difference in the French Revolution inflation was that some effort was made to make it appear that the paper money was backed by land. The first issue was used, in some part, to pay for Church lands confiscated by the government. There was an attempt also to sell these lands to reclaim the paper money issue. There was even the claim that the paper money would then be retired from circulation. Nothing much came of all

> **Getting the Point...**
> List the reasons a country would want to avoid inflating their currency.

this, but the government pledged the land of the realm as support of further issues of paper money. In fact, however, the land was not generally available for any such redemption, and if it had been, it would hardly have served as a medium of exchange. In short, the land and money were not interchangeable, and the paper money was not redeemable in anything of value. Redeemability is a crucial feature if any paper money is to be restrained in its issue. Such restraint is necessary if currency is to maintain a reasonably stable value. Claims that government is backing paper money with all of the land in the country, all the buildings, or what not, are of no account, if the currency is irredeemable.

Andrew Dickson White made a fascinating study of *Fiat Money Inflation in France*, and in it he made some interesting points. One was the extent to which prices rose under the pressure of more and more paper money issues and as the currency depreciated in value. On this point, White wrote:

> The writings of this period give curious details. Thibaudeau, in his Memoirs, speaks of sugar as 500 francs a pound, [translating one franc as one dollar gives some idea of how extraordinary these prices were], soap, 230 francs, candles, 140 francs. Mercier, in his lifelike pictures of the French metropolis at that period, mentions 600 francs as carriage hire for a single drive, and 6,000 francs for an entire day. Examples from other sources are such as the following: a measure of flour advanced from two francs in 1790, to 225 francs in 1795; a pair of shoes, from five francs to 200; a hat, from 14 francs to 500; butter, to 560 francs a pound, a turkey, to 900 francs.

White makes another interesting point about who was hardest hit by the runaway inflation:

> The answer is simple. I shall give it in the exact words of that thoughtful historian whom I have already quoted: "Before the end of the year 1795, the paper money was almost exclusively in the hands of the working classes, employees and men of small means, whose property was not large enough to invest in stores of goods or national lands. Financiers and men of large means were shrewd enough to put as much of their property as possible into objects of permanent value. The working classes had no such foresight or skill or means. On them finally came the great crushing weight of the loss. After the first collapse came up the cries of the starving. Roads and bridges were neglected; many manufacturers were given up in utter helplessness."

White described well also how the whole paper money business came to an end:

> The financial agony was prolonged somewhat by attempts to secure funds . . . ; but when all was over with paper money, specie began to reappear—first in sufficient sums to do the small amount of business which remained after the collapse. Then as the business demand increased, the amount of specie flowed in from

the world at large to meet it, and the nation gradually recovered from that long paper-money debauch.

That makes the recovery sound easier or fuller than it was. Business and economic relations had been so greatly harmed by this six years of playing with paper money that it took many years to get back to the point France was in before the Revolution. In White's own words:

> But though there soon came a degree of prosperity—as compared with the distress during the paper-money orgy—convalescence was slow. The acute suffering from the wreck and ruin brought by . . . paper currency in process of repudiation lasted nearly ten years, but the period of recovery lasted longer than the generation which followed. It required fully forty years to bring capital, industry, commerce, and credit up to their condition when the Revolution began.

### 9.1.4 Lessons Learned

In these three examples from the eighteenth century of paper money inflations, the ruin that follows upon them should be clear. Much was learned from these experiences by at least some of those living then and afterward.

Indeed, there were men in the French National Assembly when the issuing of paper money was debated who called up the experience during John Law's time and warned repeatedly that any new currency would lead to similar excesses and the consequent ruin. As Andrew Dickson White noted,

> Against this tendency toward the issue of irredeemable paper Necker contended as best he could. He knew well to what it always had led, even when surrounded by the most skillful guarantees. Among those who struggled to support ideas similar to his was Bergasse, a deputy from Lyons, whose pamphlets, then and later, against such issues exerted a wider influence, perhaps, than any others. Parts of them seem fairly inspired. Anyone today reading his prophecies of the evils sure to follow such a currency would certainly ascribe to him a miraculous foresight, were it not so clear that his prophetic power was due simply to a knowledge of natural laws revealed by history.

Moreover, one member arose during the debate to hold "up a piece of that old paper money and to declare that it was stained with the blood and tears of their fathers."

The experience with paper money during the War for Independence left such an imprint on the minds of some of the men that they took care to leave no opening for it when they drew up the Constitution in 1787. The matter came up on the question of whether or not the United States Government should have the power to "emit bills of credit." The decision was that the government should not have the power to issue such paper money or make it legal tender, and no such power was granted. Some who voted against giving such a power had very strong views. Oliver Elsworth of Connecticut, for example, declared that this was:

> ...a favorable moment to shut and bar the door against paper money. The mischiefs of the various experiments which had been made were now fresh in the public mind and had excited the disgust of all the respectable part of America.... The power [to issue unbacked paper money] may do harm, never good.

James Wilson of Pennsylvania thought that not granting the power "will have a most salutary influence on the credit of the United States to remove the possibility of paper money."

It should be noted that the United States, by the Constitution, is authorized to mint coins from precious metals. In addition, the states are prohibited from making anything but gold or silver legal tender. No power was granted to the United States to make any money legal tender. It was generally understood that bank notes could be issued if they were redeemable in gold or silver, but that if they specified any other mode of redemption they could not be legal tender. There were early differences of opinion as to whether the United States Government could charter banks that could issue currency.

In sum, much had been learned from the various experiments with paper money inflation in the eighteenth century. The general trend in Europe and the United States was toward the use of gold and silver as money throughout the nineteenth century. Bank notes were common, but they were usually redeemable in precious metals. The United States departed briefly from this rule during and immediately after the Civil War by issuing Greenbacks, which were not redeemable. However, in the mid-1870s Congress resolved to redeem them in gold, and the Treasury began doing so in the latter part of that decade. Gold emerged as the dominant basis of currency from that time until World War I.

## 9.2 The Twentieth Century Age of Credit and Inflation

The whole world appears to have increasingly ignored the earlier lessons about paper money inflation. The twentieth century onward has become known by some as the Age of Inflation, and that is hardly an exaggeration. Moreover, the base for this inflation, especially from the 1930s onward, has been irredeemable paper money. In terms of the total amount of money, bank credit, of one sort or another, has been the dominant factor. Thus, ours could more aptly be styled the Age of Credit and Inflation. The United States has played a key role in this since World War II.

What we have in the United States today is unbacked paper money, commonly called fiat money. That is, it is money by government decree. We must now focus upon how this situation came about, and in the course of telling the story it should become clear what sort of money or substitute for money, we now have. Since our paper currency now consists of Federal Reserve notes, the discussion properly begins with the establishment of this system.

The Federal Reserve Act, which established the **Federal Reserve System**, was passed in 1913. It was pushed as a means for setting up a "flexible" money system in the country, a system that could increase or decrease the money supply according to the commercial and agricultural needs of the country. It quickly became an engine of inflation, in

**Federal Reserve System**—system of banks put into place in order to create a flexible money supply. This system can increase or decrease the money supply as they see fit.

conjunction with the privately-owned banking system. Before describing the provisions of the act, however, it will be helpful to describe a little of its political background.

> **Money in the United States**
> What we have in the United States today is unbacked paper money, commonly called fiat money. That is, it is money by government decree.

### 9.2.1 Paving The Way for the Federal Reserve

Woodrow Wilson, a Democrat, had just become President, and the Democrats controlled both houses of Congress when the act was passed. Political reformers in favor of radical inflation, including such parties as the Greenback-Labor Party and the Populist Party of the late nineteenth century, had pushed for a government backed paper money. The Populists had also pushed for the free coinage of silver. They had more or less merged with the Democrats during the election of 1896, and thus provided an inflationary push within that party, paving the way for the passing of the Federal Reserve Act.

Just the same, the roots of the act lay in the report of the National Monetary Commission, which was a Republican controlled body set up in 1908. They represented the banking interests, though it should not be supposed that all bankers were in agreement as to what, if anything, needed doing. In any case, banks had an ever-recurring problem, and it was at least potentially worsening in the late nineteenth and early twentieth centuries. The root of the problem was fractional reserve banking, though that is hardly how they would likely have described it. As noted earlier, so long as banks maintain only a fraction of reserves against the whole of the demands that can be made for currency or precious metals, they are always potentially bankrupt. That potentiality becomes an actuality when there are "runs" on banks. Both in the mid-1890s and in 1907, there were pressures on banks, which demonstrated this weakness. Before telling the story of these, however, two trends in fractional reserve banking need to be explained.

The first trend involved national banks of issue. The American government was struggling to pay for soldiers, weapons, and food during the Civil War. In order to overcome this problem without heavily taxing the American people, Congress authorized a national banking system. That is, the Federal Government began chartering what were called national banks. These banks were allowed to issue paper currency so long as they used it to buy **government bonds**, which they were required to hold in reserve of those notes. In other words, they were able to print as much money as the government needed to fight the war, so long as they exchanged it for government bonds. The government then used the printed currency to pay for the war. In addition, Congress levied a tax on the currency issued by state banks that was so high that it drove them out of the business of issuing currency. While these notes were in circulation, people could redeem them for precious metals if the Treasury reserves of such metals were sufficient. However, such redemption of the notes for precious metals was not in the government's best interest. They recognized the need for retiring the excess currency in order to prevent a run on the Treasury. After the conclusion of the Civil War, as taxes were collected, the government used some of the revenue to buy back its bonds. The banks

government bonds—a debt security issued by a government to pay for its expenses. It is sold with a guarantee of interest to be paid when redeemed.

**commercial banking**—a system of financial institutions that accept deposits and process checks.

would then "retire" the currency, or in other words, burn it or store it for the next bond issuance.

The other major trend was a tremendous growth in **commercial banking**. After the Civil War, that became the main business of state chartered banks, which were quite numerous. By late in the century this was also the main business of national banks. The deposits were generally payable on demand, basically in gold after the late 1870s, and the gap between gold reserves and deposits widened more and more during these years. Bank liabilities (deposits plus bank note issues) increased from approximately $750 million in 1865, to $1.46 billion in 1880, to $2.8 billion in 1890, to $4.75 billion in 1900, to $10.77 billion in 1910. The greatest increase was in checking account deposits. By contrast, the ratio of gold to bank liabilities declined over the years: from 25.3% in 1865, to 23.9% in 1880, to 20.4% in 1900, to 14.2% in 1910. In short, in 1910, there was $1.00 in gold to redeem every $7.00 or so in demands upon banks. Actual cash reserves in banks were even lower than that. The lower the ratio of reserves held, the greater the danger of the banks failing as a result of a run on it, all things being equal otherwise.

This situation grew increasingly precarious, and a major crash occurred in 1893, when the pressure for cash became more than the banks could bear. A number of major Chicago banks failed followed by closings and suspensions around the country. As Elgin Groseclose has described the situation,

> Banks all over the country were refusing to make payments except in the form of certified or clearing-house checks. This was no more than exchanging one form of bank obligation for another. Currency went to a premium, and many factories were obliged to shut down for lack of money to pay their employees.... Thus, the whole fabric of money disintegrated under the strain of a vast weight of credit obligations payable on demand in money.

Banks relieved themselves of many of their obligations by defaulting on payments, or suffering bankruptcies and foreclosures.

The country did not have to wait too long, for another banking crisis occurred in 1907. It was not so severe, or at least did not last so long, but once again many banks suspended cash payments to one degree or another. In any case, it provoked a rising concern that something needed to be done.

Exactly what should be done, however, was not so easily decided. The main problem was that banking in the United States had never really been left to the free market and so no free market solution was advanced. As discussed in the previous chapter there were real free market solutions that would have led to greater stability. In any case, the country was already becoming hooked on inflation as it was provided by expanded bank credit, which will be discussed below. Thus, the focus was upon how to reform banking so as to provide a "flexible" (i.e., expansive) money supply, at less risk to depositors and banks. Among bankers, the idea of a central bank, such as many European countries had, was gaining hold. Probably, many bankers would have preferred a private central bank, holding reserves on which troubled banks could call. On the other side, there were politicians calling for a break-up of an alleged money monopoly of private institutions on Wall Street. Above all, though, there was a desire to have money available in the quantity wanted to prevent future money panics and depressions. The Federal Reserve System was a compromise of these various directions.

### 9.2.2 The Federal Reserve Act

The **Federal Reserve Act** did not exactly set up a central bank, at least not on the European pattern, but it tended in that direction. It provided for twelve regional banks, called Federal Reserve Banks, by dividing the country into twelve Federal Reserve districts. Technically, these banks are owned by the private banks who are members. All national banks must be members of a Federal Reserve Bank, and state chartered banks may become members if they meet certain requirements. Member banks are required to hold 3% of their capital as stock in their Reserve Banks. Control over the banks is vested, however, in the Federal Reserve Board, which is composed of the United States Comptroller of the Currency, Secretary of the Treasury, and five other members appointed by the President of the United States. In short, the Federal Reserve System is an organ of the United States Government.

Federal Reserve Banks are basically bankers' banks. That is, they deal nearly exclusively with banks, neither accepting deposits from the general public nor making loans or providing checking accounts. Federal Reserve Banks are banks of issue; that is, they issue bank notes, and each Federal Reserve Note indicates which bank has issued it. The close relation to the United States Government is evidenced even in this, however, for the bank notes are printed by the Treasury Department and signed by the Secretary of the Treasury and the Treasurer. It should be noted that the Federal Reserve Banks were not, however, given a monopoly of the paper currency by the act of 1913; there continued to be other bank notes and paper currency in circulation until these were called in, in the 1930s.

The Federal Reserve System did provide a central reserve system for commercial banks. All depository institutions in the United States, whether they are members of the Federal Reserve or not, are subject to System regulations and are required to keep a percentage of their deposits in reserve. Non-member institutions would include savings banks, savings and loans, and credit unions.

Most of all, however, the Federal Reserve System provided for a more "flexible" money supply. By issuing Federal Reserve notes (printing them and using them to purchase securities in the open market) it can increase the supply of cash, or more precisely, paper currency. If this new cash is deposited in a member bank it will expand the money supply by loaning out all but the required reserve portion. The size of the credit expansion depends on the percentage of deposits held in reserve. The smaller that percentage the greater the expansion.

In essence, the Federal Reserve maintains three tools by which it controls the supply of money. These three are:

- setting the required **reserve ratio,**
- setting the **discount rate,**
- and **open market operations.**

The required reserve ratio is the percentage of deposits that commercial banks must hold in reserve. For example, if the requirement is 20% then every bank must meet a daily requirement of holding that percentage of deposits in reserve. The discount rate is the rate at which the Federal Reserve is willing to lend money to the banks to meet their daily reserve requirement should they otherwise fail to do so. If this rate is lowered, it

---

**Federal Reserve Act**—law passed in 1913 to set up the Federal Reserve System.

**reserve ratio**—the mandated fraction of deposits that commercial banks must hold in reserve. Remember that because of fractional reserve banking practices, they are permitted to loan out all money they have deposited by customers except this percentage, which is determined by the Federal Reserve..

**discount rate**—interest rate that the Federal Reserve charges to lend money to a bank that it needs to meet their reserve requirements when they for any reason fail to do so.

**open market operations**—buying debt securities such as bonds, Treasury bills, or others, from securities dealers or large banks. When the Federal Reserve issues new currency, it uses it to buy these securities, and transfers money to a bank, which increases that bank's total deposits.

makes it more attractive for banks to lend money generally. Finally, the Federal Reserve can expand the money supply simply by purchasing debt securities in the open market.

As it was originally conceived, this last tool was meant to add another level to the fractional reserve system. Thus, the Federal Reserve originally had to keep a 40% reserve in gold against all its bank notes. This meant that for every dollar in gold it had, it could issue 2.5 dollars in bank notes. However, this limitation was abandoned in the 1930s when President Roosevelt took the nation off any gold standard. As a result, there is nothing backing Federal Reserve notes and it can expand the money supply at will simply by purchasing additional debt securities in the open market. For the most part the Federal Reserve has done so by buying United States Treasury notes, which have been issued by the Federal Government to finance its ever-expanding national debt. However, in the financial debacle of 2008 with the housing and real estate bust, it turned to buying other kinds of debt. In particular, it purchased a great deal of mortgage debt in the market. All these things added to the inflationary powers of the banking system since the Federal Reserve is essentially creating new money out of thin air. While the Federal Reserve was supposed to control the money supply, its main impact has been to inflate the money supply and to greatly expand credit.

To see this process at work is fairly easy. Since the banks only keep a fraction on reserve they can expand the money supply by way of making loans. Suppose, for example, that the Federal Reserve requires banks to hold 20% of its deposits as reserves. Thus, 80% of a new deposit could be loaned out. If all banks held this minimum, and the resulting loans eventually ended up back in the banking system as additional deposits, the money supply could expand by a maximum of five times an original deposit. Economists refer to this ratio as the **money multiplier**. It is equal to one divided by the required reserve ratio. In this case that ratio is 20%, which gives rise to a money multiplier of five. While it is not likely that all loans would necessarily return to the banking system via new deposits, it is likely that the larger share would. For instance, suppose an individual borrowed money from a local bank to purchase an automobile. The dealer would most likely deposit that money in his own banking account rather than holding it in cash. As a result, this new deposit could serve as the basis for that bank to expand its own loans.

**money multiplier**—the multiplier effect on money in the marketplace in a fractional reserve banking system. (When someone borrows from a bank, that money normally ends up back in a bank, a portion of which can be loaned out again.)

---

**Multiplying Money**
With a 20% reserve requirement, 80% of a new deposit could be loaned out. If all banks held this minimum, and the resulting loans eventually ended up back in the banking system as additional deposits, the money supply could expand by a maximum of five times an original deposit.

---

## 9.3 Abandoning the Gold Standard

To complete our discussion of money and the Federal Reserve System, it will be helpful to consider how it was that the gold standard limitation came to be abandoned and to consider further the ramifications of this change. Whatever its purposes, the Federal Reserve System neither saved fractional reserve banking nor prevented future money panics nor ended deflation and depressions. On the contrary, it set the stage for continued financial debacles and monetary panics. The first great panic occurred because it increased the amount of debt money in circulation and provided a weak basis for a greatly increased **credit expansion** by the banks. There were tremors in 1921 and 1925, but the whole system began to collapse after the stock market crash in 1929. By early 1933, the credit expansion banks had created became an overwhelming crushing weight on the fractional reserves of the banks still in operation and they were either shut down by state governments or closed their doors. More recently we have also had the dot com bust in 2000–01 and the real estate bust of 2008. These, too, were caused by the actions of the Federal Reserve.

**credit expansion**—the increasing of the money supply by increasing credit. Most of monetary inflation occurs by expanding credit, not by increasing the currency, though both may be going on at the same time. Both fractional reserve banks and the Federal Reserve can expand credit.

### 9.3.1 Boom–Bust Cycles

At this point it is worthwhile to examine how it is that an easy money policy and credit expansion gives rise to a **boom** that must necessarily **bust** in the future. In fact, it is the bust that we call a recession or a depression but it is actually nothing more than a return to economic reality. The problem arises in the following way.

First, as we discussed in the previous chapter, we must recognize that all people have ends they want to pursue, and all people prefer to accomplish their ends sooner rather than later. Economists refer to this fact as **time preference**. As a result, there is a requirement that people must be benefited if they are to postpone their consumption. That is not to say that we care nothing about the future, but simply that we all prefer a dollar's worth of consumption today over a dollar's worth of consumption one year from today. The existence of time preference in turn gives rise to a positive rate of interest in financial markets. Such a positive reward provides the incentive needed for some people to postpone consumption from the present to the future. In an unhindered free market the interactions of people based on their willingness to lend and their converse desire for consumption now gives rise to this rate as borrowing and lending take place.

**boom–bust cycle**—cycle started by government interference in the money supply that continues as long as government continues its interference.

**time preference**—the preference for present goods over future ones. The degree of the preference is said to be the prime ingredient in the interest rate. At least, it is a major factor in the determination of whether or not to lend goods or what they would accept as payment for doing so.

> **Consume it Now or Later**
> We all prefer a dollar's worth of consumption today over a dollar's worth of consumption one year from today.

The market rate of **interest** serves an important function in a market economy because it is a key factor in business decision making. All businesses incur expenses before revenues and, therefore, must be financed. Moreover, all business decision makers are forever faced with decisions about which capital projects make the most economic sense. Some capital projects are more intensive and more indirect in production. While they are typically more productive in the long run, they are also more expensive as compared to more direct methods of production. As a result, all business decision makers must decide whether the longer term, more productive projects are better than shorter term, less productive projects. This is where the interest rate is an important market signal. The lower the market rate, the lower the general time preference in the economy, and the longer people are willing to postpone consumption and wait for the payoff. Thus the longer term, more capital intensive projects are likely to be selected when interest rates are low. In this case, the

**interest**—usually expressed as a percentage, it is a fee paid for use of someone else's money for a time period.

accumulation of capital brings about economic growth and an expansion in the economy as people save more resources for future use.

Suppose, however, that the monetary authority intervenes in the market by making money cheaper simply through a credit expansion. Is this action the same thing as people generally deciding to save more resources for future consumption? The answer is obviously no. Indeed, if the rate of time preference in the economy is unchanged, then such an artificial reduction in the market rate of interest via easy money would actually provide the incentive for people to save less today and to enhance their current consumption. This distorts the market signal relied on by business decision makers. From their vantage point it appears that people are willing to wait longer for their rewards, but in truth the opposite is actually the case. As a result, there is a shortage of resources to support the capital that is being produced. During the capital build up, the economy appears to boom, but the boom cannot be sustained. Businesses will soon realize that there is insufficient demand for their products and that their capital investments cannot be sustained. At this point a bust occurs and some capital must liquidate and be reallocated.

> **Danger of Manipulating Interest Rates**
> If the rate of time preference in the economy is unchanged, then an artificial reduction in the market rate of interest via easy money would actually provide the incentive for people to save less today and to enhance their current consumption. This distorts the market signal relied on by business decision makers.

### 9.3.2 Living on Credit

Living on credit became a more common way of life in the 1920s. On consumer borrowing, Elgin Groseclose has said that:

> ...after the enactment of the Federal Reserve System, the use of credit grew at an astounding rate. In 1910, of total retail sales of twenty billion dollars, approximately 10 per cent are estimated to have been made on credit. By 1929, half the sixty billion dollars of retail sales in that year were credit transactions, and of the thirty billion dollars worth of goods sold on credit in that year, some seven billion dollars were sold on installments. Sales made on open account were financed by the store itself, generally by resources supplied by the commercial banks; sales made on installments were financed through installment finance companies which in turn discounted a large part of their paper at the banks.

More to the point, a large portion of the expanded credit in the 1920s went into speculative booms, most spectacularly into common stocks. Much of this stock was financed by buying stocks on margin—paying 10% or more down and borrowing the remainder against the stocks. When the stock market fell in 1929, great sums of wealth that existed only on paper disappeared overnight and there was a great crunch for cash. It was followed by a prolonged liquidity preference, people preferring cash or other liquid assets, and this kept pressure on the banks, who were struggling to collect their loans and build up their reserves. Bank failures increased: there were 1,352 in 1930 and 2,294 in 1931. Bank failures dropped to 1,456 in 1932. But in the interval between the election of Roosevelt to the presidency and his inauguration the banking system rushed headlong toward collapse. Federal Reserve banks generally did what they could to prevent runs on banks from closing them, rushing armored cars first here and then there where runs were developing to provide large amounts of currency. Governors in state after state called banking holidays or imposed severe restrictions on how much cash could be paid to depositors. When banks opened for business after state ordered closings, it was generally on a limited basis. The great credit contraction was running its course. Over four thousand banks failed in 1933, mostly in February and March. The crunch finally became too great for Chicago and New York City, the great financial centers, and early on the morning of March 4, the governors of New York and Illinois proclaimed banking holidays. Banking was at a virtual standstill in the country. One of Roosevelt's first acts as President was to proclaim a national banking holiday. It looked like the death knell of fractional reserve banking.

That was not to be, of course. Instead, the President stopped the redemption of any and all currency in gold, called in all gold and gold certificates, and nullified all private obligations to pay in gold. To round out this action, the dollar was devalued by raising the price of gold in dollars from approximately $20 an ounce to $35, thus drawing much of the gold in the world into the United States over the next several years. All this was preparatory to an inflation that has run from the 1930s to the present. Fractional reserve banking was vigorously revived to carry out this long running marathon inflation. After the closing of all banks, those judged by examiners to be "sound" were allowed to reopen. Confidence was restored by the guarantee of bank deposits up to a maximum amount. Reserves in gold held by the Treasury were greatly increased, and national bank reserves were increased as well.

The United States did not, however, abandon commodity money entirely at this point. Since money was no longer redeemable in gold, the United States no longer had an effective gold standard. Since no claims could be made on the gold within the country, the reserve could be reduced over the years—which is what has taken place—without any noticeable effect. Ultimately, silver now replaced gold as a potential commodity money. The government issued a large number of silver certificates, which were redeemable in silver. All the old currency was called in, and Federal Reserve notes now served as the only paper currency besides the silver certificates. The silver certificates could not, however, compete effectively with the Federal Reserve notes, because the silver certificates were only $1 bills. Since they were of such small denomination they could not drive the Federal Reserve money out of circulation. In addition to the silver certificate commodity money, the larger subsidiary coins, mainly half dollars, quarters, and dimes, had significant percentages of silver, which made them commodity money as well. Since anyone who wished to could trade larger denominations of Federal Reserve notes for silver certificates (or coins) and redeem them in silver, the United States still had a commodity money of sorts.

The United States Government and American consumers provided the market for a vast credit expansion over the ensuing decades that would eventually drive the country off commodity money. This credit expansion can be viewed most graphically in the rise of the national debt over the years. Here are some figures for that. Federal debt is shown for the end of fiscal years.

| End of Fiscal Year | Federal Debt | Outstanding Consumer Credit |
| --- | --- | --- |
| 1930 | $16.2 Billion | |
| 1940 | $43 Billion | |
| 1950 | $256 Billion | $19.1 Billion |
| 1960 | $284 Billion | $56.1 Billion |
| 1970 | $370 Billion | $127.8 Billion |
| 1980 | $907 Billion | $351.7 Billion |
| 1990 | $3.2 Trillion | $802.8 Billion |
| 2000 | $5.7 Trillion | $1.55 Trillion |
| 2010 | $13.6 Trillion | $2.5 Trillion |

Sources: St. Louis Federal Reserve, and U.S. Treasury

In essence, the national debt is exploding. Private debt has also risen considerably over the years. Coupled with the vast increases in debt, the savings rate of Americans has become among the lowest among industrialized nations in the world.

These mountains of government and private debt are built basically upon credit expansions with a fraction of reserves of one sort or another to cover the borrowing. They are the result mainly of a vast expansion of the money supply. A part of the money supply consists of the actual currency in circulation, but it is only a very small part. The Federal Reserve Banks are authorized to issue currency on the basis of certain credit instruments—i.e., notes signifying debt—and they do create money this way. But the money supply consists mainly of deposits in banks and savings institutions, and, as already noted, commercial banks can create deposits on the basis of loans that they make, provided they have the necessary fraction of reserves against the deposit. When they do so, they not only expand the credit but also the effective money supply. From one point of view, then, much of the increase of the money supply is created out of thin air by credit expansion. In effect, however, the expansion is achieved by **debasing the currency**. The process is properly called inflation. What happens is that the expansion of the money supply, whether by bank notes or creating bank deposits, is accomplished by depreciating all of the then existing money supply. In short, the value that the new supply of money has is subtracted from the value of the then existing money supply. Prices do not necessarily rise to reflect all of this inflation, nor do they always rise evenly. But whatever happens to prices, the debasing of the currency is going on.

The debasement of the money supply reached a point in the late 1960s at which the silver certificates and silver coins were seriously undervalued. To put it another way, the amount of silver in the dollar became worth much more than a dollar in paper currency. Following Gresham's Law, the bad money—Federal Reserve notes—drove the good money—silver commodity money—out of circulation. In practice, people began to

**debasing the currency**—reducing the worth or value of the currency. When currency consisted primarily of coins made from precious metals, the coins were literally debased when they were melted down and recast with an addition of base metals. Also, when cupronickel coins were substituted for those with silver content, they were literally debased. Today, the currency is often figuratively debased by increasing the amount of paper money and by credit expansions.

take the silver certificates out of circulation and redeem them in silver, and to take the coins out of circulation, possibly to melt them down for their silver content. The government set a date after which the silver certificates would not be redeemed, and replaced the silver coins with base metals—cupronickel.

The United States then had—from the late 1960s to the present—fiat money only, money by government decree. It is, of course, not real money at all. It is not a commodity, not redeemable in any commodity at a fixed rate, not redeemable in gold or silver, not based on any commodity. The fact that the government may have some gold in reserve is of no account, for there is no promise to pay in gold or anything else. It is a paper currency or credit, based on debt. As a result, our money is worthless.

Why, then, will people trade labor and other goods for this paper currency? There are two intertwined reasons for this. One is that government has made these Federal Reserve notes a legal tender in payment of all debts public and private. Thus, no other money, no commodity, will replace it. The other reason is that there is a strong desire and need for something like money, and these Federal Reserve notes are all that we can have. It may help some that people became used to it while they still had real money, that at one time it was redeemable in gold, then silver, and that the change to pure fiat money was gradual. The main reason remains, however, that ours is an exchange economy, and we must have something like money to use as a medium of exchange.

### 9.3.3 Federal Reserve Notes as Money

It remains now only to evaluate this paper currency and our credit system of money more generally, as to how well it performs the function of money. We may recall now that there are three functions of money, the main one being as a medium of exchange. Federal Reserve notes do serve money-like functions; they are in that sense as-if money. They can be used to some extent as if they were money. And, Federal Reserve notes do serve in a fashion as a medium of exchange. We exchange them for goods, and take them in exchange for our goods. That is more appearance than reality, however. What we actually do is give credit for payment to those who give us the notes in return for some good or service, or receive credit in payment for some good or service. Federal Reserve notes are a vague representation of a medium of exchange, not a fully effective or valid one. They provide credit only in exchange for goods, not a ***quid pro quo***, more nothing-for-something than something for something. It is only credit. The fact that the note bears a legend that it is so many dollars does not change that fact. A dollar undefined in a certain quantity of commodities is only a name.

But if our bills of credit, as Federal Reserve notes should be called, are unsatisfactory in their prime function as a medium of exchange, they are even less so in performing the other functions of money. The second function of money, as described above, is as a standard for calculation. It serves for pricing and for relative valuations of goods and services generally. Our Federal Reserve notes perform these functions poorly. Rather than serving well as a measuring rod for other things, in an ongoing credit expansion they are continually changing by devaluation themselves. Thus price changes may indicate mainly that the money is declining in value, not that changes in supply and demand have taken place.

In regard to the third function of money—as a store of wealth—bills of credit tend to be much more nearly anti-money devices than they do money. In an ongoing credit expansion such as ours, the currency is

***quid pro quo***—literally, "this for that." When something is given or done in exchange for something else.

> **Getting the Point...**
>
> When credit is made more easily available on a massive scale for college expenses, what effect would that be expected to have on prices for tuition?

almost continually depreciating. As the credit expands, any given unit of the currency tends to buy less and less. In consequence, storing it is somewhat like storing a perishable commodity. It must be used immediately after it is obtained, or it will become progressively worth less and less. A dollar earned in 1970, say, and simply saved without interest, would have shrunk in purchasing power to about 30 cents by 1984 and is worth even less today. Such fiat money creates an economy of living for the day, of spending rather than saving, and ultimately leads to a flight from the currency. It has also set the stage for an endless series of booms and busts. In the late 1990s there was a boom in technology. There was the establishment of a host of new companies called dot-coms because of their supposed efforts to take advantage of the new internet services. However, many had no substantive business plans and when the bust came, as it did in 2000–2001; many vanished as quickly as they came. Rather than allowing capital to reallocate, the Federal Reserve responded with a rapid monetary expansion that fueled another boom. This one centered on the real estate market as credit for purchasing homes became easier and easier to obtain. Housing prices increased beyond all economic sense until the bust arose in 2008. Once again, despite the failure of its policies, the Federal Reserve intervened in an effort to re-inflate the money supply and to prop up failing ventures.

In sum, then, our Federal Reserve notes serve very poorly as a kind of money. There are many other objections to and weaknesses of fiat paper currency, of course. Most of them have been discussed in connection with great paper money inflations. One question, however, might still remain. While it cannot be fully answered here, it can at least be expressed. How could an inflation in paper currency go on for so long without producing runaway inflation? One answer is that it has been better controlled than in the earlier inflations. That may be true, at least to some extent. A broader answer is that it has relied much more heavily on credit expansion than on currency creation. That does not mean, however, that a runaway inflation cannot occur. It can. It requires only an extended **liquidity crisis** in which those who have cash on deposit that is supposed to be available on demand, demand it. When that happens, the government will be under great pressure to print all the Federal Reserve notes needed to meet the demands. If it does so, it will most likely produce runaway inflation, among other potentially greater consequences.

**liquidity crisis**—occurs when large numbers of people need to turn their assets into cash. The causes of such a liquidity preference may vary (for example, some people prefer cash to any other means of holding on to their assets at all times), but the cause of the crisis is usually fractional reserve banking or the holding by some institution of only a fraction of reserves against the potential demand.

> **Our Vulnerable Situation**
>
> Massive credit expansion has put us in a vulnerable position were we to face an extended liquidity crisis in which those who have cash on deposit that is supposed to be available on demand, demand it. When that happens, the government will be under great pressure to print all the Federal Reserve notes needed to meet the demands. If it does so, it will most likely produce runaway inflation, among other potentially greater consequences.

# STUDY GUIDE FOR:

# 9 THE AGE OF INFLATION

## Chapter Summary

In the course of time, many nations abandoned the convertibility of the currency into gold or silver. As governments have taken control over printing and circulating paper money, there have been numerous examples of countries inflating the currency so badly as to destroy all its value as money. The U.S. has followed this practice by creating the Federal Reserve System, which issues its notes by purchasing federal government debt.

A significant problem of this system is the ease with which governments can debase the money. Since this is accomplished by the extension of greater credit, a false prosperity is created. The general population is willing to go along with this process because they believe the common myth that money is demand. That is, they believe in an illusion that there is a shortage of money with which to buy goods and services and that there is a need for monetary expansion in order to facilitate more consumption. Initially, such an expansion gives the impression that things are better. As a result, people make business decisions based upon a false understanding of the value of things. For example, a retail merchant might initially think that there is a real increase in the demand for his merchandise as inflation occurs. Rather than raise his prices immediately, he may act upon this perception by increasing his inventory of products, by hiring new personnel, and perhaps by expanding the size of his store. However, the real preferences of consumers have not necessarily changed and the inflation will eventually cause all prices to rise. If other things remain the same, this increase would be in proportion to the inflation itself. At any rate, as prices begin to rise, the store owner will begin to realize his errors in judgment. When these mistakes are realized, resources will have to be reallocated to account for the real economic situation since all exchanges are ultimately made on a goods for goods basis and money merely serves as a common denominator to facilitate the trade.

## Points of Emphasis

1. The Federal Reserve System is essentially the United States' central bank. Federal Reserve Notes are legal tender and are issued by way of purchasing federal government debt in financial markets.

2. While the creation of paper money may lead to short-term prosperity, it cannot sustain it.

3. The boom–bust cycle inevitably redistributes wealth from savers to borrowers. The chief borrower benefiting from it is the government.

## Identification

1. inflation
2. clipped coins
3. specie
4. Federal Reserve System
5. government bonds
6. commercial banking
7. Federal Reserve Act
8. reserve ratio
9. discount rate
10. money multiplier
11. open market operations
12. credit expansion
13. boom–bust cycle
14. time preference

15. interest
16. debasing the currency
17. *quid pro quo*
18. liquidity crisis

## Review Questions

1. What were the three great paper money inflations of the eighteenth century, and what can be learned from them?

2. What are the Federal Reserve's tools for adjusting the money supply? How do they function?

3. Explain how monetary inflation redistributes wealth from the prudent to the prodigal.

4. What is a credit expansion? How does it create an economic boom that cannot be sustained?

5. Explain why increasing the money supply (the number of dollars in circulation) does not increase the wealth of a nation generally? What actions, and by whom, would increase a nation's wealth?

## Activities

1. Suppose you owned a hamburger stand and the Federal Reserve announced that green dollars and account balances would be replaced two for one by new red dollars. As a business owner what would you do as a result of the action of the Federal Reserve? What would happen at a hamburger stand that did not double its prices as a result of the change?

2. Find a current events article related to inflation and comment in writing on the events/article in a few sentences using what you have learned so far.

## For Further Study

1. Henry Hazlitt, *The Inflation Crisis and How to Resolve It*, 2nd edition, University Press of America: Lanham, MD, 1983.

2. Richard Maybury, *Whatever Happened to Penny Candy?*, Bluestocking Press, Placerville, CA, 2004.

3. Hans Sennholz, *Age of Inflation*, Western Islands: Belmont, Massachusetts, 1979.

4. Hans Sennholz, *Gold and Money*, Greenwood Press: Westport, Connecticut, 1975.

5. Barry Siegel, editor, *Money in Crisis*, Pacific Institute: San Francisco, 1984.

6. Lawrence White, *Competition and Currency: Essays on Free Market Banking*, New York University Press: New York, 1989.

7. Leland B. Yeager, *International Monetary Relations*, Harper and Row: New York, 1966.

## Chapter Content

10.1 Who or What Determines Price?    130
10.2 Diversity of Products and Prices    131
10.3 Going Prices    132
10.4 Factors that Determine Prices    133
    10.4.1 Supply    133
    10.4.2 Demand    134
    10.4.3 Elasticity    137
    10.4.4 Taxes    138
    10.4.5 Monetary Inflation    138
    10.4.6 Competition    139
10.5 Wages    141

# 10 The Market and Prices

    The functions performed by the market in an economy could not be fully discussed without some basic understanding of money, or more precisely, the purpose of money as a medium of exchange. Money makes possible distinctions between buyers and sellers, which are not clearly there when goods are simply bartered for goods. In the latter case, every person operating in the market is both a buyer and seller. When a medium of exchange is in use, buyers are ordinarily those offering money for goods and sellers are those offering goods for money. The use of money also makes possible a distinction between supply and demand. Thus, supply is thought of as goods and demand arises from the willingness to pay money for them. The distinction between supply and demand is very important in understanding how "going prices" are established and on what basis they are most likely to change. Indeed, prices are ordinarily recorded in terms of money.

    **"The Market,"** as ordinarily used by economists, is a generalized or abstract concept. Thus, economists are given to saying, "The market performs this or that function;" "The market is the prime institution in advancing social cooperation;" and the like. In such cases, they are referring to the nature and function of the market in general. Economists are well aware, of course, that particular markets exist in great variety and numbers, but they find it useful in discussion to discuss things common to markets, and to refer to them as "the market." "The market," then, is a useful concept that leaves out of account the peculiarities of any particular market. In truth, it would be best to think of the market as simply a process by which people achieve their individual economic ends. Indeed, this concept captures all the ebb and flow of institutional arrangements of the exchange of goods and services.

    The kinds and varieties of markets are at least as extensive as the kinds and varieties of goods sold in them. There are wholesale and retail markets, markets for raw materials and for finished goods, and markets for every sort of particular good—for wheat, for toys, for books, for movies, for appliances, for stocks and bonds, and so on and on almost infinitum. Thus, the market is any place or arrangement where trading takes place. It performs a central role in an exchange economy and is pivotal for establishing prices.

# 10.1 Who or What Determines Price?

Price plays a key role in apportioning goods through the market. That is, how much and what kind of goods are bought is price dependent. The decision to buy or not to buy a good often depends upon its price. One of the questions economists have wrestled with over the years has been who or what determines price. Why does a painting by a famous artist bring $2,000,000 while a large well-shaped diamond brings $100,000, a Mercedes brings $75,000, and an economy car brings $17,000? When the question is asked in this way, the most direct and least debatable answer is that the above prices were arrived at in the market on the basis of supply and demand. We shall return to supply and demand and prices later on, but for this discussion, it should be noted that many of those who have been aware of supply and demand as the answer have sought to pursue the question at a deeper level.

Probably, a major reason for pursuing the question at deeper levels has come either from a desire to justify—ethically or morally—the prices that are generally reached in the market, or in order to substitute some other basis for determining prices than the market. The attempt to fix prices on the basis of religious authority or political power has a long and checkered history, and there have been many experiments in **price fixing**. To justify or oppose such efforts, economists have toiled in deeper and murkier realms to establish some position. In the Middle Ages, philosophers wrote of a "**just price**." Such a price, it seems, was one in which the things exchanged had some sort of equality of worth or value. Thus, Thomas Aquinas, a medieval Christian philosopher, thought it wrong to "buy cheap and sell dear" (high), a practice much preferred by sharp tradesmen through the ages. He admitted that the "just price of things is not absolutely definite, but depends rather upon a kind of estimate; so that a slight increase or decrease does not seem to destroy the equality required by justice." It might be observed as well that this concept did not help in deciding what price ought to be charged for a good.

Modern thinkers have sought some underlying justification or explanation of prices as well. Adam Smith posited the idea of a "**natural price**" for goods, which frequently varied from the market price. While Smith believed that the natural origin of price was the labor that went into producing a good, "natural price" was indistinct from the cost of production, as we might think of it. Smith put it this way:

> When the price of any commodity is neither more nor less than what is sufficient to pay the rent of the land, the wages of the labour, and the profits of the stock employed in raising, preparing, and bringing it to market, according to their natural rates, the commodity is then sold for what may be called its natural price.

While many people, most of whom are not economists, may agree that cost of production is a kind of natural price, it is not at all clear how this answers the question about what determines price. To be sure, many things sell for prices well above their cost of production while others sell for short time periods well below their cost.

Natural price provided a standard for Adam Smith. Others have sought a standard more recently in what is called an "**equilibrium price**." This is the price at which supply and demand converge in the market so as to clear the market of goods for sale and satisfy the demands for them. It may well be objected that neither of these things actually occurs, though both buyers and sellers may aim at it as a goal.

---

**the market**—a market is any place or arrangement where trading takes place. When economists refer to "the market" they are referring to the general nature of the market as a whole, or the process by which people generally achieve their economic ends.

**price fixing**—when governments mandate the price of something.

**just price**—the concept of the pricing of something such that justice is served.

**natural price**—the idea that any economic good has some inherent price. Some think this price is its cost of production.

**equilibrium price**—the price of an economic good such that the amount of it that consumers desire to buy in a time period is equal to what sellers wish to sell.

All attempts to reduce the complexity of market trades to one simple explanation with mathematical precision have failed. That is not to say that there are not economic principles. There are, and this has been affirmed. But these principles must leave the actual complexity and diversity intact. Before making any further observations about the determination of prices, something of the range of prices and diversity of products that actually exist in the market should be examined.

## 10.2 Diversity of Products and Prices

The variety of products and services in a complex market economy, such as the United States, is amazingly extensive. In its size, the product can range from something as minuscule as a microchip to something as massive as a cruise ship. Almost anything and everything is on sale or available somewhere. Anyone who doubts the variety might go through an internet search for products available, but even that would only be the tip of the iceberg. The number of people who perform common as well as exquisite and highly specialized services is almost unending. They range from audiologists, to fruit pickers, to ornithologists, to chimney sweepers, to well drillers, to airplane flying crop dusters, to ballet dancers, to weavers, to the whole vast number of occupations and specialties.

This variety and diversity is important to keep in mind because there is an even greater range of prices than there are products and services. It should be emphasized at this point that wages, salaries, and all compensation for services are prices, just as much as the price paid for a product. Although wages are often treated separately from other prices, they are in fact subject to the same principles in their determination in a free market. This greatly increases the range of prices that we have to consider, for each person is substantially different from every other, and where differences in skill and competency are involved we may well expect that these are often expressed in different wage prices.

The most basic rule for the determination of price is this: a **price** in a free market is the amount that a willing seller will take and a willing buyer will pay. That is, prices are arrived at by agreement between buyer and seller. Not every sale, of course, entails either a formal or even an articulated agreement between buyer and seller. Nor need it have been preceded or accompanied by any bargaining between them. Even the simplest purchase involves a tacit agreement between the two parties on price. Suppose, for example, that a person goes into a supermarket, selects a tube of toothpaste priced for $1, goes to the checkout counter, lays a dollar bill down, and the sale is rung up. Not a word need be spoken, yet a tacit agreement was made and carried out. The store management decided upon a price and caused it to be marked on the box. Thus, it offered the toothpaste for sale at that price. The purchaser agreed to buy it at that price when he selected it. Otherwise, he could have chosen some other size or brand, or, simply could have decided to make no purchase at all.

**price**—in a free market is the amount that a willing seller will take and a willing buyer will pay.

> A **price in a free market** is the amount that a willing seller will take and a willing buyer will pay.

There are better examples of much more explicit agreements in determining prices, of course, and we may now examine some. Take, for example, a husband and wife making the purchase of a house. They have gone to a real estate agent, looked at several houses, and found one to their liking in their price range. The owner of the house is offering it for sale at $250,000. The prospective buyers decide to try to get a lower price. They ask the real estate agent to make an offer for them to the owner of $225,000. The owner makes a counter-offer of $240,000. The prospective purchasers still think that price too high, and they counter with an offer of $235,000. The owner accepts, and both parties proceed to the execution of the agreement. Both buyer and seller have clearly agreed upon a price in this case.

Similar situations occur in arriving at wages and salaries. In many kinds of employment, no bargaining ever takes place. Suppose a builder of houses wishes to hire a carpenter. He lets it be known, and several more or less experienced carpenters apply. The builder is offering $20.00 an hour, a figure he has already decided upon and announced before the hiring. The successful applicant accepts the offer, is given no opportunity to bargain, and agrees to come to work. On the other hand, there is sometimes extensive bargaining, especially where more skilled work or individual performance is at a premium. So it is with professional football players. Outstanding players often have their own agent or lawyer, and bargaining may take place between the player's agent and the owner's agent. The haggling over all sorts of terms may go on for days, or intermittently for weeks or months. If agreement is finally reached, a detailed contract is drawn and signed by both the owner and the player. Again, there is explicit mutual agreement between buyer (owner of the team) and seller (the player).

Given the great multitude of products and services, the individuality of the participants, and the variety of things to be priced, it would be rash indeed to make any generalization as to why willing buyers and willing sellers agree upon a particular price. People are informed with different understandings and different motives in their actions. Some may and probably do believe in a just or equitable price for particular goods and services, and that may well affect what goods they will offer or what services they will provide in the market. Some may believe that they should only have to pay so much for a product as to cover the cost of production, including some profit, and they will offer goods or buy goods based on this estimation. Others may believe in charging whatever the traffic will bear regardless of the circumstances. For example, some people may take advantage in cases of emergency, occasioned by freak storms or catastrophes to enrich themselves at the expense of those in need. Others may believe that they should maintain prices at the regular level in disposing of what goods they have on hand. In short, many different beliefs and motives may affect particular prices.

## 10.3 Going Prices

**going price**—that range of prices at which sellers can dispose of most of their goods and at which buyers with some intensity of demand for the good can be satisfied.

**loss leader**—offering a product at a price where the seller is actually losing money to draw people into the store in hope they will purchase enough other products while there to more than make up for the loss.

Even so, there tends to be **going prices** for particular goods and services. For example, it is possible to observe at a particular place and time that eggs are bringing $2.00 per dozen, that bananas are selling for 60 cents per pound, that a handy man can be employed for $15 per hour, and so on. In fact, the most that can be correctly stated about any extensive free market is that goods and services are being bought and sold within a more or less narrow range of prices. Anyone shopping in several stores may find that eggs of roughly the same size might be offered from $1.90 to $2.10 per dozen, or that bananas range from 50 to 65 cents per pound. Merchants often offer one or more items as a **"loss leader"** to draw customers into the store, and that alone often plays havoc with the going price, at least briefly. Thus, going price is little more than an average of a range of prices at best.

Several things may alter or affect the going price. Clearly, not all goods or services bearing the same name are alike in quality. An hour's work from one carpenter may be worth an hour and a half's work from another. Bananas that are over ripe may not be reckoned by most people to be worth 60 cents per pound, while nearly ripe bananas might move briskly at 65 cents per pound. Products similar in kind are often graded so as to give at least a rough indication of their quality, and prices are differentiated accordingly. Experienced workers in a particular line may be valued over beginners. Going prices, so far as they could be said to exist, may reflect all sorts of differences in quality or customer preferences.

Differences in the character or quality or customer preference for some goods or services may be so great as to challenge the very concept of a going price. There is, for example, no going price, or even a narrow range of prices, for landscape paintings. A landscape by an unknown painter of ordinary skill might bring $50 while one by a recognized master, long since deceased, might bring millions of dollars in the market. Seats remain empty at a concert by an unknown band, while tickets to a world famous band may be sold at a premium of hundreds of dollars by "scalpers." Reproducible goods are much more likely to have a going price than those that are not. Even so, in an antique market, going prices, of sorts, get established where there are many similar items that exist but they are no longer being reproduced.

While going price is a somewhat imprecise concept and it can usually be much more correctly described as a going range of prices, something to that effect does tend to be established in the market. It can even be described in general terms. It is that range of prices at which sellers can dispose of most of their goods and at which buyers with some intensity of demand for the good can be satisfied. This rule generally only holds over some extended time period and for reproducible goods. When the quantity is small and the good is not reproducible, there may be no going price.

## 10.4 Factors that Determine Prices

Particular prices—it may be repeated—are determined by agreement between a buyer and a seller. Again, there tends to be a going range of prices for goods available in an extensive market. All other considerations now set aside, or as the saying goes, all other things being equal (***ceteris paribus***), these going prices are the result of the interplay of changing supply and demand. The cost of production will undoubtedly play a role in the pricing of reproducible goods, but it must be made clear from the outset that cost of production is subsidiary to supply and demand. In brief, it is quite possible that there may be no demand at all for some good at someone's cost of production. In short, supply and demand are the dominant factors in pricing.

*ceteris paribus*—this Latin term will be used often in this book. It simply means that while examining the effects of one factor of an issue holding that all other factors are held equal or constant.

### 10.4.1 Supply

Economists define the **supply** of a good to be the various amounts of the good that would be offered for sale in the market at various prices, other things being equal. In this sense, the concept of supply is that of a functional relationship between price and quantity that is specified for some time period, say a day, week, month, or year. As such, supply is considered a flow of goods into the marketplace. Since sellers are interested in

**supply**—the various amounts of the good that would be offered for sale in the market at various prices, other things being equal.

getting the highest price possible for their goods, the relationship is positive. That is, sellers would be willing to offer more for sale at higher prices, *ceteris paribus.*

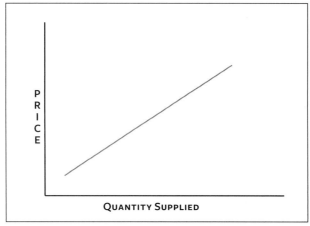

Figure 1: Supply

Among the factors that we might consider constant in such a definition are the prices of resources used to produce the good, the technology of the production process, natural phenomena, and price expectations of the sellers. Any changes in these factors would readily alter supply in this sense. For example, suppose the price of labor is bid up. It would now be more expensive to produce the good and sellers would not be willing to produce and sell as much of the good at any given price than before the wage increased. The same could be said for changes in technology that may increase or decrease the costs of production. Likewise, changes in

**Some Factors Being Held Constant in Supply Graph**
1. The prices of resources used to produce the good
2. The technology of the production process
3. Natural phenomena
4. Future price expectations of the sellers

nature such as a hurricane or earthquake might deplete some resource, or a change in the seller's expectation about the price he might get at some future date. If he believed that the future price would be higher tomorrow than today, he might well hold his product off the market today.

10.4.2 Demand

**demand**—the relationship of prices and the various quantities that people would desire to purchase in the market per unit of time, *ceteris paribus.*

On the buyer side of things, the **demand** for goods is defined as the relationship of prices and the various quantities that people would desire to purchase in the market per unit of time, *ceteris paribus*. Once again, the concept of demand is a functional relationship between price and quantity. Only now it applies to buyers and not sellers. In the case of buyers of goods, people always prefer to purchase goods for lower prices. As such, there is an inverse relationship between the price of the good and the quantity that would be demanded per unit of time, other things constant.

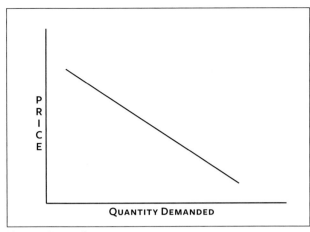

Figure 2: Demand

Among the other factors that would affect demand are the prices of related goods in the market. These goods can be either substitutes or complements. That is, some goods can be substituted for each other while some are used in conjunction with one another. If the price of a substitute increases, people may well desire to purchase more of the good in question as they substitute it for the now more expensive good in the market. In addition to prices of related goods, consumers' desires are also shaped by their income, taste, preferences, and expectations about future prices.

> **Some Factors Being Held Constant in Demand Graph**
> 1. The prices of related goods in the market
> 2. Consumers' income level,
> 3. Consumers' taste and preferences
> 4. Consumers' expectations about future prices.

Given these definitions of supply and demand, and holding all other factors constant, a simple graph captures the essence of these functional relationships. It is given in the graph below:

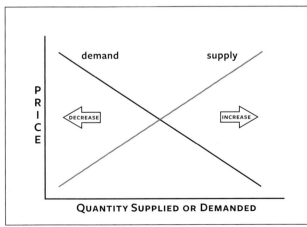

Figure 3: Supply and Demand

CHAPTER 10: THE MARKET AND PRICES

For any given product, consumers will demand less of the good as its price increases. On the other hand, sellers will tend to offer more for sale as the price they can get for the good increases. Within this framework, both buyers and sellers are generally disposed to accept what they reckon to be going prices at any particular time. In a money economy, prices are expressed in monetary terms. (Money also has its demand and supply, in some quite complicated senses, but let that wait for a bit.) You will notice in Figure 3: Supply and Demand that supply and demand intersect at only one price. Moreover, if the price varies from that price, competitive forces will tend to push it back in the direction of the intersection. For instance, if the price is above that price, sellers will be trying to sell more of their good than consumers wish to buy. As a result, there will be a build-up in inventories and competition among sellers will tend to force the price down. Alternatively, if the price is below the intersecting price, consumers wish to purchase more than sellers are willing to offer for sale. As a result, there is a shortage in the market and the competition among buyers will tend to drive the price up.

Of course, the very concept of such an intersection of supply and demand is based on the notion that other things in the market are constant. In truth, they never really are equal and so the concept of a market equilibrium price is an illusion. New products come and displace older products, prices of goods and resources readily change, people's taste and preferences vary from day-to-day and year-to-year, the information available to make one's exchange decisions is always very imperfect, and expectations about the future are often highly variable. For these and many other reasons it is best to think of the market for any good as a process of dynamic change. The main benefit of conceiving of the market in terms of supply and demand is that it allows us to consider how various factors would influence the direction of change of the going price for any given alteration in the circumstances of life. This is why it is more useful to think of the going price of any good as a range of prices for which the good currently exchanges in the economy. Put simply, supply and demand is merely a useful tool for analyzing changes in the market.

For example, consumers tend to prefer the highest quality of a good they can get for a given price. Therefore, in analyzing quality we think of it as price differences of related goods and people trade down in quality to take advantage of a lower price. Thus, if the price of a good thought to be of a higher quality went down, it would result in a reduction in the demand for the lower quality good and lead to a reduction in its price as well.

One general rule of demand and supply is this: if the demand for some good increases and the supply remains the same, the price will rise. Price is the major means by which supply and demand are adjusted to one another. The rise in prices sends a signal to producers of those goods. Those who are already producing the good will be likely to increase their production, and others may be lured into producing the product because of the increased opportunities for profit. The second rule is: if the demand remains the same and the supply increases, the price will decline. This, in turn, tends to increase the amount demanded. Once again, supply is adjusted to effective demand in the market.

> **General Rules for Supply and Demand**
> 1. If the demand for some good increases and the supply remains the same, the price will rise.
> 2. If the demand remains the same and the supply increases, the price will decline.

### 10.4.3 Elasticity

One other concept that needs to be introduced with respect to supply or demand is what economists refer to as **elasticity**. Demand, for example, is described as being elastic or (relatively) inelastic. An elastic demand is one in which there is a sharp response to an increase or decrease in price. That is, if the price rises by some percentage and the amount demanded falls by a greater percentage, demand is said to be elastic. Suppose, for example, that a car dealer increases the price of a particular model by 10%, but subsequently observes that he sells 20% less of this model. Economists would say that the consumers' demand for this kind of automobile is elastic.

On the other hand, the demand for light bulbs is relatively inelastic. A minor increase in the price of light bulbs, supposing all suppliers raised their prices accordingly, would probably have little impact on sales. The same could probably be said for gasoline. A minor rise or drop in the price of gasoline would have little impact on the amount of gasoline sold. Generally speaking, there is probably no such thing as a totally inelastic demand (that is no consumer response to a price change), but what we would find on careful examination would be that there are many different degrees of elasticity and inelasticity of demand.

All this may not make it entirely clear how prices reflect the interplay of supply and demand. An example might help to clarify some matters. It might be supposed that sellers ordinarily determine prices rather than supply and demand. For example, many goods sold in stores have prices marked on them in one way or another. These may be described as quoted prices. Let's take the example of a publisher offering a book in the market. It will illustrate both the working of supply and demand in pricing and how the seller cannot stick to one price if he wants to sell all of the copies of a particular book.

Suppose that a publisher has printed 10,000 copies of a history book on the Civil War in the United States. The publisher does not know in advance how many copies he will sell at what price, if any. He has been able to calculate his costs and he knows what comparable sized books are selling for, or at least the range of quoted prices on them. Given this information, he concludes that if 10,000 copies could be sold at a quoted retail price of $20 per copy, his company would make a profit, albeit a relatively small one. He could make a considerably larger profit at a somewhat lower price, if he could sell 30,000 copies. In any case, the publisher sets a quoted price of $20 for the book. After a few months trial, he concludes that the book is moving much too slowly at that price, and that it is unlikely he can dispose of his stock. He can do one of at least two things at this point. He can suggest a lower sale and dealer price, in the hope that will move the book, or he can remainder his copies (sell them to dealers at printing costs or

*elasticity*—the responsiveness of buyers and sellers to price changes.

whatever they will pay). At the sale price of $17 per copy the books move briskly, and most of his supply is soon sold. The publisher may decide to print an additional 25,000 copies that he subsequently hopes to sell at the new lower price. He may or may not be able to move this new stock at that price. The above illustrates the following point. The demand for the book was elastic in that sales did respond to lower prices. The publisher could not stick with the original price if he wished to move his stock of the book. Supply and demand tended to determine the price in the market.

### 10.4.4 Taxes

There have been and often are other factors included in prices. One of these is taxes. Taxes generally tend to increase the price of the goods whose manufacture, transportation, and exchange are taxed. The clearest case of a major impact on prices occurs when an excise tax is levied. These are taxes often levied for the purpose of discouraging the consumption of certain goods. The most familiar examples are taxes on cigarettes and alcohol. Obviously, if the total taxes, Federal, state and local, amount to three or four dollars per pack this will have a large impact on the price to the consumer of a pack of cigarettes. If liquor is taxed at the rate of $10 per quart, the same is true. That does not mean that supply and demand will not play its role in determining the final price to the consumer. It means, rather, that the tax provides a basic minimum price for the good before supply and demand can play any role. Supply and demand in the market will tend to determine how much is added to that base price before the product reaches the consumer.

### 10.4.5 Monetary Inflation

Even more bothersome to the market is the impact of monetary inflation on pricing. As noted earlier, variations in the supply of money also alter prices. An increase in the money supply tends to increase the price of goods. It could even be said that the amount of money demanded declines as the supply increases; the result is a general rise in prices. Rises in prices due to monetary inflation do not necessarily signal a rising demand for goods, however. Thus, price does not perform one of its major market functions. The fault lies with inflation, of course, not with the market, nor with supply and demand. It would be an error, however, to suppose that a monetary inflation has a uniform impact in raising prices throughout the market. The greatest impact on prices will occur where more of the new money is spent. This rise in price typically attracts a great deal of speculative purchases by people hoping to profit from future price increases. When this happens, the price of the underlying good is bid up beyond its actual economic price, and this cannot be sustained indefinitely.

A few examples will illustrate this point clearly. Credit expansion in the late 1920s and the late 1990s fueled a precipitous increase in stock prices only to crash later. The rapid monetary expansion following the crash, precipitated by the terrorist acts of September 11, 2001, fueled a widespread speculation in real estate. Real estate prices rose well beyond their economic fundamentals only to reset in 2008. Since this point a revived effort at monetary expansion with a sluggish economy has made it much easier to obtain student loans. This has led to a rapid expansion of student loans as more young people remain in college in an effort to obtain credentials and ultimately a job. However, it is unlikely that any job they might find would be sufficient to pay off these extra loans. In truth,

---

**Getting the Point . . .**

Have you ever heard anything about monetary inflation being a cause of rising prices from the media?

If people understood this principle, how might it change what types of policies that are supported?

such concentrated spending is seen as an increase in demand, but it is driven by market confusion and marks a disruption in the ordinary functioning of supply and demand. There is no way to separate the two, which is one of the reasons why inflation is so troublesome in the market, and is why it is no surprise that this has sparked a rapid increase in prices for college.

Government intervenes in the economy in a variety of ways that interfere with the orderly working of the market. But these other ways must be taken up after finishing the discussion of the determination of prices in the market. Supply and demand play an important role in that, but there is another important market factor. It is competition.

### 10.4.6 Competition

**Competition** is the balance wheel of the market, so to speak. It provides the spur to efficiency by weeding out the inefficient producers. Thus, it keeps prices always moving in the direction of the costs of the most efficient producers. It is competition that tends to keep prices low. In truth, the desire to attract customers for one's products keeps the producer ever vigilant as he seeks a better and cheaper means of production so that he can make a better offer than his competitors. Competition is the friend of consumers (which includes everyone). It should be noted that however beneficial competition is to us in our capacity as consumers, most of us would much prefer not to have to contend with competitors in our capacity as producers. A much fuller discussion of competition is made in a later chapter, however; only that aspect of it having to do with the determination of prices need be discussed here.

People often say that the price of this or that or the other is too high. Sometimes they also argue that the profits of particular individuals or companies are too large. Sometimes, they form organizations to push for political action to control prices, or even profits. It is in some ways a curious argument as well as a curious way to go about solving the problem. If prices are too high or profits too great, we might suppose that people would see that the producing of whatever is at issue would be a great opportunity and go into the business. After all, if profits are too great, whatever that should mean, it would tend to attract someone else into the market as a competitor and to make those high profits as well.

Actually, it may be no simple matter to go into a particular business. It may be well beyond the resources of most people making the complaints, and that organizing a company all the way to going into a particular line of production takes too much time and effort. Suppose, for example, that the complaint is lodged that automobiles are too expensive, that the companies make inordinate profits, and that the managers are overpaid. Still, it is by no means easy to organize a new automobile company to compete with the ones already producing them. It would undoubtedly cost billions of dollars to get into production and distribution on a level to compete with the major automobile makers such as Ford, Honda or Toyota. Even so, it must be said that competition is the most effective device for keeping prices in the vicinity of costs since the profits of any one company tend to spur greater innovative efforts of the others. As a result, product quality relative to price improves over time as people are left free to trade on terms they find mutually agreeable. We would always prefer to pay less and get more for our money as consumers, which is really why people are likely to complain about price in the first place.

In any case, competition generally works to provide the largest supply that can be disposed of in a reasonable period of time, to hold prices

**competition**—occurs when there are two or more sellers or buyers of similar goods or services in a market. Substitutes should also be taken into account when deciding whether competition exists in a market or not. It is well, too, to keep in mind that so long as anyone who wishes may offer the good or service, and so long as there are no prohibitions against offering the goods, the market is at least open to competition.

---

**Getting the Point . . .**

What are the most dominant two factors in determining the price of goods?

From the list below, which of these would tend to most effectively lower the price of goods while ensuring that enough is produced to meet the market demand?

- price fixing
- regulations
- taxes
- monetary inflation
- competition

Which would tend to increase the price?

Which would lower the amount produced?

down, and to provide the answer for rising demand. When demand increases and prices rise, not only do those already in the field increase production when they can, but others will enter the field to supply the goods or services.

How competitors enter an industry in response to a demonstrated demand can be illustrated in almost any field and undertaking. A successful product or service quite often has many imitators and competitors. This phenomenon is best seen in crazes, fads, trends, and styles. As soon as the popularity of whatever it is has been demonstrated, competitors quickly abound. For example, when the Beatles had phenomenal success on the American concert and record market in 1964, it spurred many other rock groups to the market. It would be difficult to determine exactly what it was about them—their Britishness, their lower class background, the style of their music, the fact that they took such a strange name for the group, or what have you. In any case, other British rock groups were soon trying to compete with them—the Rolling Stones, Herman's Hermits, the Zombies, the Yardbirds, the Animals, and others. The phenomenon caught on, became trendy, and then a virtual fixture, as competitors proliferated. From an economic point of view, the significance of this competition—in whatever field—is that it tends to stabilize the market, fill the demand, appeal to a broad range of tastes, offer alternatives, and eventually bring prices into range of more and more people.

Competition plays its role effectively only if there is a free market. A free market is one that is open to all buyers and sellers, in which none are prevented by force—legal or otherwise—from making exchanges. Not all markets are free, of course, and, to the extent that they are restricted, competition may not be able to play its regulatory role. This will be made clearer in connection with a fuller discussion of competition in a later chapter.

---

**Competition** is the balance wheel of the market. It provides the spur to efficiency by weeding out the inefficient producers. Thus, it keeps prices always moving in the direction of the costs of the most efficient producers. **It is competition that tends to keep prices low.** In truth, the desire to attract customers keeps the producer ever vigilant as he seeks a better and cheaper means of production so that he can make a better offer than his competitors. Competition plays its role effectively only if there is a free market. A free market is one that is open to all buyers and sellers, in which none are prevented by force—legal or otherwise—from making exchanges.

---

## 10.5 Wages

The determination of compensation for work may be determined in the market as are the prices of goods and services. The price of labor is the result of the interplay of demand and supply under competitive conditions as it is for anything else. Thus, **wages** and salaries are prices of labor, work, service, or whatever, and need not have been discussed separate from the discussion of the determination of the prices of other goods. That is, except for the fact that they have been treated differently from other prices in the United States since the early twentieth century.

Congress declared in the **Clayton Antitrust Act**, passed in 1914, "That the labor of a human being is not a commodity or article of

**wages**—payment to an employee for his or her labor services.

**Clayton Antitrust Act**—antitrust legislation that provided special legal privileges to labor unions.

commerce." By this rather confusing assertion, Congress was clearly attempting to assert a distinction between labor and other sorts of goods where pricing was concerned. Congress did not go on to define labor; rather, it used the assertion as the basis of exempting industrial labor and agricultural unions from the prohibitions of the antitrust laws. As the act said,

> Nothing contained in the antitrust laws shall be construed to forbid the existence and operation of labor, agricultural, or horticultural organizations . . . ; nor shall such organizations, or the members thereof, be held or construed to be illegal combinations or conspiracies in restraint of trade, under the antitrust laws.

Labor is probably not a commodity in the usual meaning of the word. It may not even be an article of commerce, though it is by no means certain, since "article," in this sense, is imprecise and rather indefinite. But this much is certain: labor has been bought and sold in the market from time immemorial. It is bought and sold directly when a person is hired as an employee or servant. It is bought and sold indirectly when products are sold with which labor is mixed. More precisely, labor is bought and sold more or less directly in several ways. One way is when a person is hired for definite periods of time, by the hour, by the day, by the week, by the month, and so on. In such cases, what is bought and sold is work-time. Or, the workman may be paid for his production, as in piece-work or for a particular job. Or, labor may be bought and sold as a part of the payment for a product, for example, for a watermelon that a farmer has grown.

Since labor is indeed bought and sold in the market, and since that was the only point with which Congress could have reasonably been dealing at the time, Congress was engaging in a rhetorical obfuscation, muddying the waters, so to speak, so as to conceal the matter at issue from view. Congress was hardly ready to prohibit the buying and selling of labor in the market, which would have been the only occasion for its opening remark about labor not being a commodity or article of commerce, but it did wish to legitimize labor unions, and the like. The assertion by Congress was a rather poorly conceived tactic to obfuscate or confuse the issue.

In any case, labor is bought and sold in the market. As for labor unions, we will return to them shortly. As already affirmed, to the extent that labor is bought and sold in a free market, the price of labor—i.e., wages, salaries, price per piece produced, or job—is determined by supply and demand. Moreover, the general rules that apply to other goods apply to labor as well. That is, if the demand for labor increases, the price of labor will rise, other things being equal. If prices rise, they may well result in drawing more labor into the market—i.e., lure people out of retirement, bring more mothers of other caregivers into the market, and so on. In any case, price tends to adjust supply and demand so that those seeking employment can expect to find it at some price, and those wanting more workers can employ them at some price. That is not the case, of course, if price is made inflexible, a point that will shortly be examined.

Competition is the balance wheel in the open market for labor as it is for other goods. But who are the competitors? The answer to that question needs to be spelled out now, since it has generally been obscured in the labor market. Buyers compete with buyers for the available supply, and sellers compete with one another to attract buyers. The buyers, in the case of labor, are employers, or potential employers. The sellers are workers, or potential workers. Competition among workers for jobs has been denied by labor unions, who have sought to unite workers in unions and have them present a more or less solid front to employers. Society has muted the competition as well, so that it is considered bad form, poor taste, or even unethical for workers to compete directly with one another for jobs. That is why it must be emphasized here that if the market is performing its function in seeing that those seeking employment get it or that employers find workers to fill their positions, employers must compete with one another for workers, and workers must compete with one another for jobs. In their competition with one another for workers, employers tend to drive wages up. In the competition of workers with one another for jobs, they tend to drive wages down. A "going wage" tends to result in the market, a wage at which those seeking workers and those seeking jobs can satisfy their wants. Of course not all workers will necessarily compete with one another. Some people possess unique skills that others do not have and only compete with those who possess similar qualifications. These differences lead to a dispersion of wage rates in an open market.

> **Labor** is bought and sold in the market. To the extent that labor is bought and sold in a free market, the price of labor—i.e., wages, salaries, etc.—is determined by supply and demand. Moreover, the general rules that apply to other goods apply to labor as well. Buyers compete with buyers for the available supply, and sellers compete with one another to attract buyers. The buyers, in the case of labor, are employers, or potential employers. The sellers are workers, or potential workers.

The idea of a labor market may be somewhat more difficult to grasp than that for commodities or other articles of commerce. After all, actual formal auctions for workers are not held. Workers are not displayed in the market, as are automobiles, groceries, dry goods, or thousands of other items. No catalogs are issued with pictures of workers and offering prices. The market for labor is somewhat more subtle and indirect than that. Employers do advertise their needs in various forms and fashions. There are employment agencies, head hunters, and job search websites with which those seeking jobs register. Businesses sometimes place notices on their premises or websites that they are hiring. But much of the business of hiring and being hired is carried on out of public view. Those looking for jobs may hear of openings from friends or neighbors. In short, potential employers and employees find out about one another in a variety of ways, formal, informal, and casual. In whatever ways it may differ from other markets in its operation, it is still a market, and so far as it is free, determinations of price are still made in terms of supply, demand, and competition.

# Study Guide for:

# 10 The Market and Prices

## Chapter Summary

Following the discussion of money, it is now possible to discuss the development and functioning of the market. Money makes it possible to distinguish between buyers and sellers and, hence, between demand and supply. Because of the use of money to execute a trade, we typically refer to the individual offering money as the buyer and the individual receiving the money in exchange for a good as the seller. Further, the amount of money given in trade in effect becomes the price.

The question of how prices are determined has long been of interest. There have been discussions of just prices, natural prices, and, most recently, equilibrium prices. Yet in a market economy, it becomes clear very quickly that prices vary as a result of the diversity of products available for sale and as a result of the diversity of individuals who vary with respect to their motives, beliefs, preferences, and values. Therefore, the concept of price can only mean the amount of money that the buyer is willing to pay to the seller and that the seller is willing to accept in exchange for the good being offered.

A going price arises for a product that sells regularly in the market. Thus, similar products of roughly the same quality will tend to sell for roughly the same price in the market. Some of the differences in price can be explained by differences in quality and by the differences in the costs associated with effecting a transaction. Still, even with these in mind, it is not unusual to find a difference in the price of a similar item from one store to another. Yet, these differences are typically small.

Through the repeated interactions of buyers and sellers, going prices for products arise. The interaction of buyers and sellers is often thought of abstractly as the interaction of demand and supply and the resulting going price as that price for which the amount demanded by buyers is just equal to the amount offered for sale by producers. If the price varied from this price, then competition either among buyers or sellers would tend to push the price towards this market price. That is, if the price were higher, sellers would have difficulty finding enough buyers to sell all of their produce. Competition among them to sell their product would serve to drive the price down. Alternatively, if the price were lower than the market price, buyers would have difficulty purchasing all of the product that they would like. As buyers compete among themselves for the product the result would be to cause the price of the product to rise.

The market price will also adjust as changes in the supply and demand conditions occur over time. On the demand side, change can occur from a number of different factors. These factors include consumer preferences, prices of related goods in consumption, consumer incomes, and expectations about future prices. On the supply side, change can occur as a result of changes in resource prices, in the number of producers competing in the market, in the technology employed in production, and in the sellers expectations about future prices.

In addition to adjustments to supply and demand, the magnitude of the adjustments from change will depend on the responsiveness of buyers and sellers to change. This concept is often referred to as elasticity. For example, we might consider how responsive consumers are to a price increase or decrease. The greater the consumer response to a price change, the more elastic the demand.

## Points of Emphasis

1. Money makes it possible to distinguish between buyers and sellers in trading relationships.

2. Economic trade has resulted in a multitude of products. The concept of the price of a product can only be understood in the final analysis as the amount of money willingly exchanged from the buyer to the seller to effect a trade of some product.

3. A going price, or a market price, arises when a product is traded often. Repeated transactions between buyers and sellers tend to establish a price range within which the product is traded. This price range is subject to change as other factors in the market change. However, inflation may create false expectations among both buyers and sellers.

4. Competition among sellers leads to an increased variety of products and to increased efficiency in production. As such, competition benefits all consumers. However, competition causes stress for producers. As consumers we are all thankful for competition, but as producers it is not unusual to find individuals seeking special privilege to relieve them from the headaches of competing with others.

## Identification

1. the market
2. price fixing
3. just price
4. natural price
5. equilibrium price
6. price (in a free market)
7. going price
8. loss leader
9. *ceteris paribus*
10. supply
11. demand
12. general rules of supply and demand
13. elasticity
14. competition
15. wages
16. Clayton Antitrust Act

## Review Questions

1. What makes something valuable?
2. Why do people have a love and hate relationship with competition?
3. How are prices determined?
4. When producers increase the supply of a good available on the market, how does it affect the price?
5. When more consumers want a particular good, how does it affect the price?
6. When new producers see high profits being made and begin making a comparable product, how would that affect prices?
7. As competition increases, in order to gain a larger market share what other actions might a producer take?

## Activity

1. Make a list of several common grocery items and visit several local stores to compare the prices of the items on the list and report the findings. If the prices vary, ask the class to consider why.

## For Further Study

1. Frédéric Bastiat, *Economic Sophisms*, Foundation for Economic Education: Irvington, NY, 1964.
2. Roger Garrison, "Intertemporal Coordination and the Invisible Hand: An Austrian Perspective on the Keynesian Vision," *History of Political Economy*, 17.2, 1985, pp 309–319.
3. Friedrich A. Hayek, *Unemployment and Monetary Policy*, Cato Institute: San Francisco, 1979.
4. Friedrich A. Hayek, *Prices and Production*, Kelley: Clifton, NJ, 1967.
5. Stephen Littlechild, *The Fallacy of the Mixed Economy*, Cato Institute: San Francisco, 1979.
6. Israel Kirzner, *Competition and Entrepreneurship*, University of Chicago: Chicago, 1973.

> **CHAPTER CONTENT**
>
> 11.1 Protective Tariffs     146
> 11.2 Labor Unions     149
>     11.2.1 Government Support for Unions     153
>     11.2.2 The Impact of Wage Controls     156
> 11.3 Consumer Prices     157

# 11 FAILED ATTEMPTS TO CONTROL PRICES

However effective the market may be in setting prices, there is always some degree of dissatisfaction with anything approaching a free market. It is easy enough to see how this could come about. After all, the market is neither sentimental nor compassionate. We are each all too familiar with how hard we work. However, we are also prone to undervalue the efforts of other people in fields that we do not understand. Because of this, we tend to value our labor over that of others and are likely to conclude that the price of whatever we have to offer is too low and the price of whatever we wish to buy is too high. The market is a hard taskmaster (which is a way of saying that tradesmen often drive hard bargains).

In any case, there have been many efforts throughout history to control the market, to reduce competition, to restrict the entry of suppliers, or to intervene otherwise in the market. Our focus will be on efforts to alter the market by implementing restrictions through the use of intimidation or force in order to control prices. It is true that individuals often use other various means in an attempt to raise the price of what they have to sell. For example, a workman may go from employer to employer seeking higher wages or better working conditions. Or, a farmer may keep a part of his produce off the market for a time in the hope that the price will increase. But, such strategies are not generally reckoned to be harmful to others, and are, in any case, an exercise of the basic rights of a person. After all, one cannot be a *willing* seller in the market until he is willing.

The use of intimidation or force, however, introduces a new dimension. Any such attempt interferes with what others may do and produces unforeseen consequences. The focus will be on **government intervention to control prices** or alter them. The reason is that while individuals or non-governmental organizations may use intimidation or force, they cannot do so for long without the help of government. In fact, most of the force that is regularly used to control prices is exerted by governments. There are hundreds of ways governments have and do intervene in the market so as to alter prices. But, only a few of these will be discussed in detail here. Those chosen will be ones that have been prominently used over the last hundred years in the United States, and whose economic consequences can be explored.

## 11.1 Protective Tariffs

The **protective tariff** has been around for a long time. Indeed, it is older than the United States, and was in vigorous use at the time of the early settlements in North America. The protective tariff has been most closely associated with a system known as mercantilism, a system of government promotion of manufacturing and other commercial activity within a country. The primary aim of the protective tariff is to keep foreign goods that are in competition with domestic products out of the country. In economic terms, it is an attempt to keep foreign competitors off the domestic market. The result would be, if it worked, to raise the prices of those goods, thus resulting in prosperity for domestic manufacturers, merchants, and possibly other producers. The harm of such action is imposed on the buyers of the products who must now pay more for the products they wish to purchase.

A great many arguments have been advanced for the protective tariff. A major argument of the mercantilists was the **bullionist** theory. Bullionists claimed that the way for a nation to become wealthy was through an increase of precious metals in foreign trade. They could do this, bullionists held, by exporting finished goods, importing raw materials, where necessary, and keeping as much of the domestic market as possible for domestic producers. That way, they would draw in precious metals in exchange for their goods, and the nation would become more prosperous. This assumed that in trade there was a winner and a loser, and that the winner in foreign trade was the nation that increased its holding of precious metals, especially gold.

Another argument, not so broad in its claims, was the infant industries position. This was the idea that when a country was just developing manufacturing that they needed protection from foreign manufacturers who were already well established. Alexander Hamilton advanced this idea in support of a protective tariff as the first Secretary of the Treasury of the United States. Congress did not act on it, but the idea crops up from time to time. A related claim is that the protective tariff is necessary to keep foreigners from "dumping" goods on the market, presumably to drive down prices and thus ruin their competitors.

A more recent justification of the protective tariff is to protect domestic workers from having to compete with foreign laborers who receive lower pay. This is an argument that the protective tariff will work to hold up domestic wages. A related argument is that by excluding foreign goods, it will provide employment for more domestic workers.

Frédéric Bastiat, the nineteenth century French economist, did a delightful parody of the arguments for the tariff in "The Candlemakers' Petition," which was included in his *Economic Sophisms*. This imaginary petition was addressed to the French National Assembly, and begins this way:

> We candlemakers are suffering from the unfair competition of a foreign rival. This foreign manufacturer of light has such an advantage over us that he floods our domestic market with his product. And he offers it at an absurdly low price. The moment this foreigner appears in our country, all our customers desert us and turn to him. As a result, an entire domestic industry is rendered completely stagnant. And even more, since the lighting industry has countless ramifications with other national industries, they too are injured. This foreign

---

**government intervention to control prices**—legal mandates by government to set prices. *See definition of price fixing, p. 130.*

**protective tariff**—*see definition, p. 31.*

**bullionist**—someone who believed that increasing one's personal holdings of gold and silver money necessarily made one wealthy.

> manufacturer who competes with us without mercy is none other than the sun itself.
>
> Here is our petition: Please pass a law ordering the covering of all windows and skylights and other openings, holes, and cracks through which the light of the sun is able to enter houses. This free sunlight is hurting the business of us deserving manufacturers of candles. Since we have always served our country well, gratitude demands that our country ought not to abandon us now to this unequal competition.

Bastiat proceeded to describe all sorts of advantages that will supposedly result from shutting out all sunlight. There will be a great increase in the demand for tallow for making candles, for oil for lamps, and for resin from trees. "The manufacturers of lighting fixtures will be especially stimulated—candlesticks, lamps, candelabra, chandeliers, crystals, bronzes, and so on. The resulting warehouses and display rooms will make our present shops look poor indeed." Bastiat was, of course, poking fun at a whole body of notions about the advantages of restricting foreign competitors.

Adam Smith had preceded Bastiat by three-quarters of a century in a devastating analysis of the fallacies of all sorts of restrictions on trade, including the protective tariff. The underlying notion behind such arguments is that there is a loser and a gainer in trades either between individuals or nations. This idea struck Smith as simply wrongheaded. When people trade, he held, they are each seeking to better their conditions. When the trade is entered into freely, both parties believe that it is mutually advantageous. Moreover, they would not continue to trade unless this belief was born out in practice. To clinch the larger point, he explained the matter this way:

> The interest of a nation in its commercial relations to foreign nations is, like that of a merchant with regard to different people with whom he deals, to buy as cheap and to sell as dear as possible. But it will be most likely to buy cheap, when by the most perfect freedom of trade it encourages all nations to bring to it the goods which it has occasion to purchase; and, for the same reason, it will be most likely to sell dear, when its markets are thus filled with the greatest number of buyers.

Those who are most directly injured in the attempt to reduce or exclude foreign trade are consumers. Since everyone is a consumer, everyone suffers from such restrictions. However, not everyone benefits from a particular tariff. If the tariff works as it is supposed to, it can only result in higher prices for the protected goods. If some of the goods come in from abroad anyway, it is not the exporter but the final purchaser who will be forced to pay the tariff. If the goods are excluded by the tariff, then we can only assume that the consumer will pay a higher price for the domestic goods than he could have bought them from some foreign country. The argument is a **fallacy of composition** since it promotes the special interest of some while undermining the general welfare of the populace.

To look at it in yet a broader way, protective tariffs reduce or remove the advantages of the **division of labor** on an international scale. For all sorts of reasons, higher quality and less expensive goods of one kind or another are produced in some countries. One country may produce fine

**fallacy of composition**—believing that what is good for the individual, or one particular case, is always good for everyone, or all cases generally. This is logically inconsistent. It may or may not be true.

**division of labor**—see *definition*, p. 80.

linens, for example; another produces cheap woolen goods. It is to their mutual advantage to exchange with one another. Because of climate or soil, one country can produce grain much less expensively than another, while another country may produce dairy products with greater ease. They can each benefit by trading with the other.

> **Who Pays the Costs of Protective Tariffs**
>
> Those who are most directly injured in the attempt to reduce or exclude foreign trade are consumers. Since everyone is a consumer, everyone suffers from such restrictions. However, not everyone benefits from a particular tariff. If the tariff works as it is supposed to, it can only result in higher prices for the protected goods. If some of the goods come in from abroad anyway, it is not the exporter but the final purchaser who will be forced to pay the tariff. If the goods are excluded by the tariff, then we can only assume that the consumer will pay a higher price for the domestic goods than he could have bought them from some foreign country.

As to increasing employment in a country by excluding the goods of another, the notion is an illusion. Granted, if one country could exclude all automobiles produced in other countries, automobile workers might be employed in greater numbers to serve the domestic market. But that does not mean that employment will generally be greater. In truth, the higher prices of automobiles will limit the consumption choices of people and tend to undermine economic activity thus eliminating a wide variety of employment that will now never occur. In addition, local exporters will suffer. In general, foreign countries are more or less dependent on the goods they export to pay for those they wish to import. If imports are restricted widely, the result must be that other countries will be unable to buy the domestic goods from that country.

There is an even more prohibitive disadvantage of restrictions on foreign trade. It is that trade restrictions adopted by governments promote enmity and jealousies among nations, and may lead (and sometimes have led) to war. Adam Smith observed that by the doctrines of mercantilism,

> ... nations have been taught that their interest consisted in beggaring all their neighbours. Each nation has been made to look with jealous eye upon the prosperity of all the nations with which it trades, and to consider their gain as its own loss. Commerce, which ought naturally to be, among nations, as among individuals, a bond of union and friendship, has become the most fertile source of discord and animosity.

Smith blamed this state of affairs in his day upon merchants and manufacturers. They have since been joined by other groups, such as labor unions.

The case for free trade is a strong one, indeed. In the nature of things, trade extends to all peaceful people as far as it may reach. George Washington, in his Farewell Address, set forth what may well be considered the high principles of foreign trade, when he said:

> **Getting the Point ...**
>
> Someone suggests to you that in order to keep jobs in the United States we should implement tariffs on certain imports that are being sold for less than similar products made here. List arguments you could use to help them see why this may not be a good idea.

Harmony, liberal intercourse with all nations are recommended by policy, humanity, and interest. But even our commercial policy should hold an equal and impartial hand, neither seeking nor granting exclusive favors or preferences; consulting the natural course of things; diffusing and diversifying by gentle means the streams of commerce, but forcing nothing....

## 11.2 Labor Unions

Wages, salaries, and payments for work, whether by the piece or by the job are prices, as already noted. In a free market, they are determined in terms of supply and demand and agreements between willing buyers and sellers. However, labor unions have endeavored to hamper the market for labor by controlling the price of labor, usually to raise the price. Indeed, the primary purpose of a **labor union** is to raise the price of labor of its members, and sometimes more broadly, those within a craft, trade, profession, or even a whole industry. They have most often described their aims as higher wages, shorter hours of work, and better working conditions, but the latter can usually be translated into prices as well. Unions may have other functions, such as presenting grievances to employers, arbitrating disputes among workers, serving as a social club, and the like, but these are at best secondary functions. Their basic appeal is to the purses of their members.

**labor union**—an organization of employees aimed at bargaining with employers for the collective.

Labor unions attempt to accomplish their primary purpose by reducing the supply of labor available to employers. Now in and of itself the reducing of supply to hold up or raise the price of some good or service is neither exceptional nor out of the ordinary. Individuals frequently withhold some good or service in the hope of raising the price, as noted earlier. A farmer may keep a portion of his harvest off the market in the hope that prices will go higher later on. An individual worker may do likewise, refusing such offers as he gets in the hope of finding a better job. Unions go beyond this, of course; they join together to withhold the labor of their members from the market. Though courts may have sometimes questioned such behavior, this is not why labor unions are discussed in connection with attempts to control prices.

Labor unions go beyond withholding the service of their members from employers. They try to prevent others from working for those who were employing them. In short, they attempt to reduce the supply of labor to their employers by preventing others from working for them. More, they have, and often will, use threats, intimidation, force, and even terror to prevent others from working. By using force at crucial points, unions act as if they were governments. But even that is not the strangest aspect of union tactics. The strangest thing is that while outwardly declaring they are the voice of workers, they usually use force against other workers. They use force against unorganized workers, members of their union who try to work when a strike has been called, and members of other unions when conflict arises. Thus, the major and central contest is among workers.

There is a sort of logic to this behavior. After all, the most direct way to limit the supply of labor to an employer is to prevent others, who might be willing to work for lower wages from doing so. When others are prevented from competing for work, the supply of labor decreases and the price of labor, or a person's wage, increases. It should be recalled here that in the market employers competing with one another for workers bid the price of labor up. Workers competing with one another for jobs bid it down. Labor unions try to reverse this process by organizing workers and acting for them to bid the price of labor upward. To do that, they attempt to exclude all competitors.

> **Role of Labor Unions in Determining the Price of Labor**
> It should be recalled here that in the market employers competing with one another for workers bid the price of labor up. Workers competing with one another for jobs bid it down. Labor unions try to reverse this process by organizing workers and acting for them to bid the price of labor upward. To do that, they attempt to exclude all competitors.

That is not how unionists usually describe the process. It does happen, however. John L. Lewis, when he was a young union man, once described the process this way:

> As I understand it, it is for the purpose of wiping out competition between us miners first, viewing it from our side of the question; next for the purpose of wiping out competition as between the operators in these four states. When we have succeeded in that and we have perfected an organization on both sides of the question, then as I understand the real purpose of this movement, it is that we will jointly declare war upon every man outside of this competitive field....

In short, Lewis understood that union representatives and coal companies were meeting with the purpose of removing all competition among either workers for jobs or employers for workers that would prevent their setting prices. Usually, however, the contest is described as if it were between union and management, or, in Marxist terms, between capital and labor. These are alleged to be the contestants when unions are organizing, when they go on strike, or when negotiations are underway.

The reality, however, is that unions are basically organized against any workers who might compete with them for jobs or pay. That is not to suggest that unions do not have contests with companies. They do, especially in seeking union recognition by a company and also vigorous negotiations when contracts are being made. But once the company has arrived at an agreement with a union, they enter into an alliance against non-union workers.

This is not to deny that companies may suffer various economic disruptions because of union activities. But such intimidation and violence as usually occurs in strikes or boycotts by unions is directed toward other workers. Only rarely are managers or foremen attacked or harassed by union pickets; they are usually permitted to go about their business unharmed and unthreatened. That is not the case for workers who try to work at struck plants or businesses. Some examples will help to show what happens in a strike, and who is most likely to be intimidated or coerced. Here is one from a Teamster strike against Bowman Transportation in 1962, as reported in *Time* magazine:

> It was just past midnight when the two big tractor-trailers, loaded with cheese and butter, pulled out of a

terminal in Birmingham, Alabama, to start on a 10 hour 365 mile run to New Orleans. At 2:45 they were barreling along Alabama 5 when a cream-colored car passed them, raced on to a junction, turned and sped back. From the car a shotgun was fired point-blank at the cab of the lead truck, critically wounding driver Charles Warren, 31.

It was the latest in a series of bloody episodes that have marked a 12 week strike.... Turning down the union's demands on wages and working conditions, the firm hired non-Teamster drivers. Since then, Bowman trucks have been shot at more than 70 times in Alabama, Georgia, Tennessee, North and South Carolina. Four drivers besides Warren have been wounded....

More dramatic are the confrontations at struck plants sometimes, when pickets mass in front of the plant gates. What follows is an account of such mass picketing before the struck Kohler plant in Wisconsin, as described by Sylvester Petro:

Kohler Village was not quiet on April 5, 1954. Marching in solid ranks before the main entrance to the plant early that morning were some two thousand persons. They were there to prevent anyone from going to work, and they succeeded. As one eye-witness put it, "employees attempting to enter the plant were slugged, kneed in the groin, kicked, pushed, and threatened," almost always by the group of militants who had come from out of town to "help".... It was many... months before persons might return to their jobs in peace without fear of reprisals to themselves, their homes, and their families.

While threats may do less harm, they are also widely used in labor disputes to intimidate those who oppose unionists in one way or another. The following are threats selected from many cases in courts and hearings by Armand J. Thieblot, Jr. and Thomas R. Haggard and compiled in a book entitled *Union Violence* (published by the University of Pennsylvania, 1983), minus the profanity and obscenity in many of them:

- "The next time I catch you in that plant I am going to give you a whipping."

- Union agent said that the mine will stay union, "if it takes bloodshed to do it."

- Union agent told employees that they intended to organize the store and that "wives and children of employees had better stay out of the way if they didn't want to get hurt."

- Non-striking employee told he was "'liable to wind up' in a funeral home."

- Non-striking employee told he would not "get out alive" if he went back to the plant.

- Employee told that he "might be pulled off the road one night and get his brains knocked out."

- Union agent asked employee who refused to honor the picket line, "Do you know you could have bodily harm done to you?"
- Union attacking employee, saying "I'm going to beat your _____ _____ head off."

Professor Sylvester Petro, who has studied unions extensively, has concluded that "Coercive conduct has been characteristic of trade unions in this country throughout the history at all levels of union action." Much of it is neither open violence nor even coercive threats, however. Instead, it is the known possibility that if companies try to operate during a strike by hiring replacements that bad things may happen.

The main point here, however, is that when coercion is used it is usually against other workers by unions. The point has been emphasized not only because unions claim to be for the working man and against management but also because workers are ultimately likely to be the ones to receive the most direct unfavorable economic consequences of union activity.

The aim of the unions, as already noted, is to raise wages, reduce hours of work, and improve working conditions only for its members. They attempt to control prices of labor by artificially reducing the available supply of labor. The most direct result is unemployment. If workers are kept from accepting employment at wages lower than the union demands that causes unemployment directly. If the unions succeed in driving wages up above what they would have been in the market fewer workers can be employed. Any increase in the price of anything is likely to reduce the amount demanded, and when the rise is accomplished by forceful intervention to keep supply down, less can be sold. This is as true for labor as it is for anything else.

> **Effect of Price Increase on Supply**
> Any increase in the price of anything is likely to reduce the amount demanded, and when the rise is accomplished by forceful intervention to keep supply down, less can be sold. This is as true for labor as it is for anything else.

It must not be supposed, however, that organized labor necessarily benefits in the long run from this situation. Labor unions are usually hard hit by depressions (or deflations). Factories that are unionized are often the first to shut down in hard times. Indeed, in the early 1980s many factories with unions closed their doors for good, and, when possible, the plants and equipment were sold. Moreover, when capital decisions are made companies are likely to choose to locate their factories in non-unionized locations. Thus, union workers often find themselves unemployed as well.

Indeed, a whole train of unwanted economic consequences follows from union activities. Unionists misconceive the nature of the economy by supposing that there is a **surplus of labor** and hence of goods in general. That is a faulty premise because both labor and goods are scarce. Yet, on the basis of the false premise that a general surplus exists, unionists strive to reduce the available supply of labor and thus of goods. They not only reduce the number who can be employed to the extent that they raise wages above the market level, but also work in various ways to hold down production. The only way to increase the real wages of workers in the market is to increase **productivity**. Yet unions often strive to decrease the

**surplus of labor**—when there are more people willing to work for a particular wage rate than there are employers willing to hire them.

**productivity**—the rate at which a worker can accomplish a particular task. The more productive, the greater the output in a given time frame.

productivity of workers. For example, they may try to limit the number of hours someone is allowed to work.

In addition, unions press to reduce competition among workers on the job. "Eager beavers" are discouraged. Unions have often encouraged "featherbedding," employing more workers than the job may require. Work rules written into union agreements often describe the tasks to be done by workers of particular classifications and prohibit them from doing other jobs. For example, an electrician may not move furniture on a stage set, and possibly those who are employed to move furniture may be unable to move lamps. All such prescriptions tend to reduce the productivity per worker and make labor much more expensive.

### 11.2.1 Government Support for Unions

Beyond these activities, unions have also sought government intervention to limit the supply of substitute labor in other ways. For example, government has intervened in the market by setting **minimum wages.** When a minimum wage is established above the going wage for unskilled labor, it prices that labor out of the market thus eliminating a potential form of substitute labor from the market. Such **price floors** always create a surplus of the good being offered in the market. A price floor simply being the situation where the government has decreed that the price of some good in question should be set above its current going price. In the case of such a restriction in the labor market there would be a surplus of unskilled labor resulting in a higher rate of unemployment.

Furthermore, unions lobbied the government to establish the maximum hours a person can work and to prescribe the working conditions. By doing so, the government has removed these matters from the realm of agreement between employer and employee in the market. Indeed, government has intervened in the situation both by directly passing laws on the subject and indirectly by empowering unions. As noted earlier, unions can use their coercive tactics only if government either ignores them or aids them. Beginning early in the twentieth century, the federal government began making tentative moves toward aiding or empowering labor unions. During World War I, the government generally upheld the right of workers to organize and engage in **collective bargaining**. It was in the 1930s, however, before government lent its full weight toward unionization. This move came to fruition with the passage of the National Labor Relations Act in 1935. By this act, the national government became deeply involved in questions of union recognition by companies. The act held that employees had the right to organize, bargain collectively, and engage in concerted activities. Employers were forbidden to interfere with, restrain, or coerce their employees in regard to any of these undertakings. They were not to "dominate or interfere" with the formation or running of the labor organization or to encourage or discourage membership in any labor organization. "*Provided*," however, the act stated, "that nothing in this Act . . . shall preclude an employer from making an agreement with a labor organization . . . to require as a condition of employment membership therein." In short, employers could agree with unions to force employees to become members of that union in order to get a job. Most important, employers could not "refuse to bargain collectively with the representatives of employees. . . ."

To oversee and enforce this law, Congress authorized a **National Labor Relations Board** (NLRB). The NLRB certifies elections, holds hearings on labor disputes, and makes what is called administrative law by its decisions. It requires that employers recognize and bargain with the

**minimum wage**—a governmentally mandated lowest wage rate that can be paid to an employee. When set above the market wage it results in unemployment and a surplus of labor.

**price floor**—setting a government mandated lowest price that can be charged for an economic good. The minimum wage is an example.

**collective bargaining**—when an employer bargains on working conditions and wages with a labor union that represents a group of its employees.

**National Labor Relations Board (NLRB)**—established in 1935 by the National Labor Relations Act (also known as the Wagner Act), it is a government institution empowered to enforce the provisions of the legislation.

majority union and that non-union employees accept it as bargaining agent. This is coercive both on employers and any employees who may not belong to the union. One writer describes the situation this way: "Not only must an employer recognize a labor organization the representative of all employees in the appropriate unit, but he must bargain collectively with the union for all employees in the unit regardless of whether all are members of the union or not."

Perhaps the most coercive aspect of all upon employers is that they are required to bargain in "good faith." The NLRB has taken this to mean generally that employers must make concessions when bargaining with unions. Fred Witney in *Government and Collective Bargaining* describes the requirement to bargain in good faith this way:

> Employers must do more than just meet with the representatives and merely go through the motions of bargaining. To satisfy the requirement of collective bargaining, an employer must bargain in "good faith." In defining the term, the Board held that an employer to bargain in "good faith" "must work toward a solution, satisfactory to both sides, of the various proposals and other affirmative conduct." In another case, the Board declared that "... the obligation of the Act is to produce more than a series of empty discussions, bargaining must mean more than mere negotiations...." The Board has considered counter-proposals so important an element of collective bargaining that it has found the failure to offer counter-proposals to be persuasive of the fact that the employer has not bargained in good faith."

To fail to bargain in good faith can make an employer guilty of an "unfair labor practice," thus subjecting him to penalties.

There is no doubt that the intent of the law was that labor unions should have every opportunity to win in their contests with employers. The original act listed a number of unfair labor practices employers could be guilty of, but none for unions. (That part of the act has been since amended to include some unfair labor acts for unions as well.) Unions were empowered to utilize the coercion implicit in the numbers of their members, but employers were prohibited to use any. When the National Labor Relations bill was being considered before the Senate, an amendment was presented to prohibit coercion or interference with or by any person. It was defeated by a vote of 21 to 50. In the House, there was an attempt to add an amendment to prohibit coercion from any source. It was rejected. In short, the Congress was not about to prohibit union coercion.

Government has aided unions, too, by reducing the labor supply, thus reducing the effective competition from other workers. Compulsory school attendance in most states has kept most young people off the labor market until the age of 16 at least. Child labor laws passed in the late 1930s kept young people off the market until 16, and in some dangerous employments, until 18. That age has been extended for many young people who have gone to college and trade schools, often subsidized to do so by government programs. At the other end of the age spectrum Social Security, passed in 1935, made retirement possible at an earlier age for many people. Unemployment compensation and disability payments by government that are higher than the market wage would be have eased some of the burden of the unemployment that is one of the consequences of union wages. Unemployment tends to reinforce the union view that there is a surplus of labor as well.

Meanwhile, however, the government went more directly into the business of controlling the price of labor itself. In 1938, Congress passed the **Fair Labor Standards Act** that prescribed minimum wages and maximum hours in covered industries. Initially, the minimum wage was set at 25 cents per hour and scheduled to advance to 40 cents per hour over a period time. The act did not actually limit the number of hours per week a person could work. Instead, it prescribed the number of hours—initially 44 hours per week, to be reduced eventually to 40 hours—a workman could be paid at his regular wage. Any work over this maximum had to be compensated at time-and-a-half for overtime. Over time Congress has had to increase this minimum to try to keep up with the devaluation of the dollar. It now stands at over $7.00 per hour and will no doubt be increased again in the future. Moreover, the number of employers subject to the law has been increased over the years.

Fair Labor Standards Act—federal law aimed at controlling and restricting voluntary exchange in labor markets.

Government has mandated other payments by employers, which add to the cost of labor, even if they are not called wages. Employers are required by law to pay one-half of the Social Security levy on wages. Those in covered industries are required to contribute to the fund for Unemployment Compensation. They also have to deduct employee income tax and Social Security taxes from wages, keep records and accounts for all of these, and make the appropriate payments to state (sometimes city or county) and federal treasuries. All these things are a direct cost of labor to employers, however they may be thought of by others.

Working conditions in various kinds of employment are also mandated by state and/or national governments. These also add to the cost of labor, and, from the employer's point of view, the price of labor, or, in common terms, wages. One of these employer costs is usually for liability insurance to cover claims by their workers. The general trend is for employers to be held liable for any accident or injury that occurs on the job. Negligence by employees is not usually much considered to relieve an employer of liability, though there is some variation about this from state to state.

Another example, where government has tended to drive the cost of labor up has been Equal Employment Opportunity for women. This act, passed by Congress in 1972, prohibited discrimination in hiring by most employers on the basis of sex, color, religion, or national origin. Pressure has especially been applied in cases of female employment, and the doctrine of equal pay for equal work has been pushed as the standard. How this helped to drive up wages or costs of labor may be seen best by a little historical analysis. Historically, women have competed with women for jobs, and men with men, and not nearly as many women as men have been employed for wages or salaries as men. The division of labor in times past generally resulted in men being hired for certain kinds of employment, and women for others. For example, women were usually employed as elementary school teachers, nurses, and (in the twentieth century) for secretarial and clerical work. By contrast, men were usually employed as construction workers, as over-the-road drivers, garbage collectors, in shipping, and more often than not in managerial positions and for professional work. That is not to say that there were not employments open to men and women, but it often happened that where women were hired in these areas they received lower wages. Although the reasons for this are complex, the most basic reason, economically, at least, was that women competed with other women for these jobs, rather than with men. To put it another way, women usually accepted lower pay to work than men could or would in similar employment. There has usually been a much larger pool of potential women workers not employed for wages or salaries than men. Thus, women bid down the price of jobs by competing with one

**price ceiling**—the maximum legal price that can be charged as mandated by the government.

**shortage**—when the price of something is legally held below the market clearing price, then people desire more of the good than sellers are willing and able to sell. The result is called a shortage.

another. Any attempt to change this artificially by paying equal pay for equal work, for example, would drive up the wages of women and, in the long run, tend to drive the wages of men down. This would create surpluses of women in the market for the kinds of jobs they are seeking while resulting in shortages of men to do the kind of work they tend to be employed in doing. The truth is that a **price ceiling**; government restrictions keeping the price of a good below its going price, results in a **shortage** of the good. In this case, if employers cannot legally offer potential workers a higher wage, fewer people will have the necessary incentive to seek employment.

### 11.2.2 The Impact of Wage Controls

The most general impact of driving wages above the market level is unemployment, whether it is done directly or indirectly by government, labor unions, or what not. More, all payments made by employers in behalf of employees, whether Social Security, to retirement funds, for insurance, or whatever, are in effect wages to the employee. Thus, the actual cost of labor to the employer is often much more, as much as double or sometimes more, than the wage shown on the paycheck stub.

The significance of these facts is that the employer must recoup more than enough to pay the wages of each of his employees, plus all his other expenses connected with producing and disposing of his good or service, or else lose money in the operation. The crucial factor in hiring any person is usually whether or not what he contributes to production will more than compensate for the added cost. According to marginal theory, the breaking point on whether to hire an additional employee comes when his additional production will no longer provide such compensation. The same rule applies when an employer is laying off workers, i.e., he will have to lay off all those workers whose additional production does not more than compensate for the cost. That is why the minimum wage, whether it is the union wage in a particular plant or government mandated tends to cause unemployment.

The unemployment that results from attempting to control wages falls most heavily upon the least productive in a society, as the above analysis indicates. It falls upon those with the least skills, the slow learners, and those who are in some manner disabled. It falls upon the young, the partially incapacitated for whatever reason, the weak, and often upon older persons. The inexperienced, the unskilled, and the partially disabled are not sufficiently productive to warrant paying them the minimum or union wage when all fringe benefits and other payments have been added. Statistics on unemployment over the years confirm the above analysis of who is most likely to be unemployed.

How the minimum wage works to place the unskilled and less productive at a disadvantage can be documented in other ways. What follows are quotations from actual employers published by the National Federation of Independent Business:

A laundry in Utah reported its problem this way:

> We have some choice and loyal employees but we have some who are not able to produce to the necessary capacity, so we are forced to replace them. This is a most difficult thing to do to an old employee, but the dollars just won't reach.

An automotive electrical shop in Nebraska reported:

> I have helped four men through the ranks giving them education needed for a better job. Under the minimum wage I cannot afford to hire anyone to train because I cannot absorb the cost or charge to the customer.

A plant in Wisconsin reported on the difficulties of hiring students:

> The minimum wage and hour law keeps me from employing high school and college students. Many students seek work in this area but have no experience. An employer like myself cannot train the students and pay [the minimum wage]. We could use them for clean-up personnel and they would be happy to work for less but it puts our cost too great.

This last account points toward another aspect of pushing wages above the market level. It tends to create both a surplus and a shortage of labor. It creates a surplus that appears as unemployment. On the other hand, the hand in which someone might hire workers, it creates a shortage, because people simply cannot be found to work for or are not permitted by law to work for those who might employ them at lower wages. For example, *service* stations for dispensing gasoline and other motoring aids have almost all become self-serve stations. Services such as windshield washing, free air and water, dispensed by station attendants have virtually disappeared. This is a result both of the high cost of labor and the willingness of customers to do-it-themselves rather than paying the higher cost for gasoline and oil. The self-service supermarket has replaced the grocery store in which clerks gather the groceries from the shelves for customers. Probably, most people now living have never even been served in such a store. More and more stores are using self-checkout to eliminate the need for cashiers. Do-it-yourself production, more generally, has become commonplace as the price of labor has risen. Thus, many people do most of their own plumbing, carpentry (of the repair sort), and do the mechanic work on their own cars. Tool and material makers have increasingly supplied this growing market with easy to work with materials. Cooks, gardeners, and the like have virtually disappeared as servants became too expensive for all except the very wealthy. Of course, many of the people who might perform such work are now unemployed and some of them are dependent upon a variety of government aid programs.

> **Controlling Wages Causes Unemployment**
> The unemployment that results from attempting to control wages falls most heavily upon the least productive in a society. It falls upon those with the least skills, the slow learners, and those who are in some manner disabled. It falls upon the young, the partially incapacitated for whatever reason, the weak, and often upon older persons.

## 11.3 Consumer Prices

Wages are prices, as has been sufficiently emphasized. All prices tend to fall under the same rules of determination in the market; that is, they are a result of the interplay of supply and demand under competitive conditions. The rules are the same, whether for work of human beings or for any other sort of goods. But in the discussion of attempts to control prices, wages are treated separately here as elsewhere because they have been treated differently from other sorts of prices. Since the twentieth century, government policy has been in the direction of trying to raise wages, or at least to establish minimum ones. In the case of consumer goods, when government has intervened it has often tried to keep prices down by establishing maximum prices. But even in this, government has hardly been consistent over the years. More often than not, government has attempted to raise prices for farm goods above the market level, while it has sometimes attempted to keep other sorts of prices for consumer goods down.

The general rules concerning these activities are as follows:

- If prices are raised above the market level, there will be a surplus of such overpriced goods.

- If they are made lower than they would be in the market, there will be a shortage of goods.

- Prices serve as signals in the market.

  - Low prices in general signal abundance of goods, and tend to increase the amount of the good consumers of it demand.

  - High prices signal a greater scarcity of the good and discourage consumption of it.

  - If prices result in profits for producers, the producers will increase their production or new producers will be attracted into the field.

- When government intervenes in the field by artificially making prices high or low, the signals are crossed.

In other words, while the going market price remains, it is artificially denied the legal right of being revealed. Thus, the market is distorted and the desires of people are frustrated. In reality, if prices are too low, producers reduce their production while consumers demand more; if they are too high, consumers cannot clear the market of goods that producers offer in it. Either way, there is an imbalance that the market cannot correct.

There have been many examples of both of these effects in the twentieth century. For instance, the New Deal government of the 1930s made a concerted effort to raise the prices of many farm products, such as that of hogs, wheat, cotton, dairy products, and the like. The first major effort was to reduce the supply on the market. The best example was in making acreage allotments for the planting of certain crops. This, it was thought, would result in curtailing production and raising prices. But as the price rose, those growing the crops found other ways to increase production, as using better seed and more fertilizers. The result, eventually, was large surpluses of farm goods, warehoused at government expense. At the unnatural higher prices, produced by subsidies and other devices, many of the goods simply could not be sold.

The eventual result of prices fixed in one way or another above the market is to drive the product wholly or partially out of the market. One product that has tended to be priced out of the market is butter. Government price supports on dairy products accomplished this. Margarine was developed as a substitute, but it took a good many years before it began to displace butter in the market. For one thing, margarine is naturally white, and governments prohibited artificially coloring it yellow

**Getting the Point . . .**

Why is it a problem that signals get crossed when government intervenes and sets prices artificially higher or lower than the market going price?

for years. The taste is different, too, but eventually artificially colored margarine replaced butter. Cotton prices have been driven up for many years by price supports, and cotton has been increasingly replaced as a major fabric, replaced by such chemical substitutes as rayon, nylon, and other synthetic fabrics. This is, of course, a similar effect to what happened with artificially high wages, where technological substitutes for labor were developed. There has been some revival in cotton clothing as textile manufacturing has moved away from the domestic market. As a result, cotton clothing in the market has reappeared since foreign producers of cotton are not subject to the crop limitations imposed by the U.S. government.

There have been many examples as well of government setting prices lower than they would be in the market. While this has most often happened during wartime, there have been peacetime examples as well. The result, as noted, is a shortage of the particular good. During World War II, the United States Government adopted price ceilings, as they were called, for numerous goods, for example, sugar, coffee, shoes, and so on. Some of these goods might have been in short supply anyway, because of war conditions, but all of them were soon in short supply. Thus government turned to rationing to allocate the limited supply of goods. The market response to a shortage is a higher price, and this often happened on what is called a "**black market**," in which goods in great demand could be purchased in larger quantities. Such illegal markets arise because there are always customers willing to pay a much higher price than the legal price to obtain the desired good.

**black market**—when economic goods are bought and sold in illegal markets.

**Rent controls** are a particularly pernicious variety of price controls, because they have sometimes been continued long after the wars that were made the occasion for them. New York City is the most horrendous example of perpetuating rent controls, for they are still in effect even though World War II has long since faded into the past. The most direct result of New York's rent controls has been a perpetual housing shortage. It has also resulted in many rundown and abandoned buildings because landlords could not afford to keep them in good repair for the low rents. It has discouraged building rental apartments, since they cannot compete well with older apartments whose rents have been kept far below the market level. Some people benefit, of course, those who have long term leases on good apartments. William Tucker described it this way in an article in *The American Spectator* (February, 1987):

**rent controls**—when property rental rates are mandated by government below market rates. This is an example of a price ceiling.

> Make no mistake, there are thousands and thousands of winners under rent control. Typically, they are affluent tenants with small families who have been able to stay in the same apartment for many years. Their rents will be more reflective of 1968 than 1986. Often they have been able to use their savings to buy a second home in the country. Using the apartment less and less these days, they are now letting their daughter and her friends live in it while attending college. Soon they will try to get the daughter's name on the lease so that the apartment will stay in the family for another generation.

In conclusion, prices are basically a market phenomenon. Fundamentally, they are the result of an agreement between a willing buyer and seller. In the broader frame, they take shape within the interplay of supply and demand and are kept within a relatively narrow range at any given time by competition. Any attempt to establish prices by force results in an imbalance that results in either a shortage or surplus of the good whose price is controlled. In such circumstances, price cannot effectively perform its role in giving signals to producers and consumers or of allocating goods among them. When governments go further in trying to make their prices work, they raise the level of compulsion, and the direction of this movement is toward the destruction of the market, the destruction of the people's liberty to choose, and, ultimately, the rise of tyranny and despotism.

---

**General Rules Concerning Government Manipulation of Prices**

- If prices are raised above the market level, there will be a surplus of such overpriced goods.

- If they are made lower than they would be in the market, there will be a shortage of goods.

- Prices serve as signals in the market.
  1. Low prices in general signal abundance of goods, and tend to increase the amount of the good consumers of it demand.
  2. High prices signal a greater scarcity of the good and discourage consumption of it.
  3. If prices result in profits for producers, the producers will increase their production or new producers will be attracted into the field.

- When government intervenes in the field by artificially making prices high or low, the signals are crossed.

---

*Falling prices through increased production is a wonderful long-run tendency of untrammeled capitalism.*
**Murray Rothbard**

# Study Guide for:

# 11 Failed Attempts to Control Prices

## Chapter Summary

Inflation creates a problem for market participants. When government increases the money supply, prices must adjust. Unfortunately, market prices are always in flux as other factors change in the market place. This coupled with inflation creates an additional problem since the inflation tends to create a false sense of prosperity where producers are led to believe that the demand for their products has increased. In turn, business decisions to expand production at this point will have to be accounted for later. Thus, it is common that economic recessions follow periods of inflation as mis-allocated resources are reallocated to some other use.

Competition is at the foundation of the working of the market. As individuals use the process of trade to gain what they want, participants naturally compete with one another as producers in an attempt to establish and maintain trading relationships with buyers. As a result, sellers are always thinking about how to produce the product a little better, at a lower cost, in order to attract customers who are also attempting to more effectively achieve their own ends. From the consumers' perspective, competition is a close friend that tends to produce variety and quality at affordable prices. However, as producers, competition serves as a taskmaster. As sellers, we must be continuously working to improve the product of our efforts if we hope to find and maintain buyers for our product or our services. Therefore, it is not uncommon to see people seek special privileges to protect them from the rigors of the marketplace.

Special privilege is often sought by promoting government control over some price. In fact, price controls have been established over a wide range of goods and services. For example, protective tariffs, labor union activities, and control over a wide range of consumer goods prices have all served to establish special privilege.

## Points of Emphasis

1. Governments often intervene in the economy to artificially control prices, This activity is always a hindrance to an efficient market.

2. Price floors create surpluses while price ceilings cause shortages.

3. While the federal government has intervened in many ways, labor markets have been particularly affected. Labor unions have sought and obtained numerous political favors aimed at decreasing the supply of substitute labor.

## Identification

1. government intervention to control prices
2. protective tariff
3. bullionist
4. fallacy of composition
5. division of labor
6. labor union
7. surplus of labor
8. productivity
9. minimum wage
10. price floor
11. collective bargaining
12. National Labor Relations Board
13. Fair Labor Standards Act (1938)
14. price ceiling
15. shortage
16. black market
17. rent controls

## Review Questions

1. What is wrong with the protectionist argument that restricting trade by imposing tariffs on imported goods promotes the welfare of the nation?
2. How do labor unions attempt to achieve the goal of increasing the wages of their members?
3. Why is the central conflict in a strike generally between the striking union members and potential non-union workers?
4. What is the fundamental economic misconception of unionists?
5. What are some types of actions that government might use in an attempt to control prices? What are the effects or consequences of these actions.

## Activities

1. Prepare a case either to support or oppose the following position: "Working conditions would be horrendous if it were not for the efforts of labor unions."
2. Describe some of the major pieces of government legislation that have affected labor markets in the United States during the twentieth century.
3. Make a list of items whose price government has tried to control. Examine the impact of such efforts.

## For Further Study

1. Frédéric Bastiat, *Economic Sophisms*, Foundation for Economic Education: Irvington, NY, 1964.
2. Roger Garrison, "Intertemporal Coordination and the Invisible Hand: An Austrian Perspective on the Keynesian Vision," *History of Political Economy*, 17.2, 1985, pp 309–319.
3. Friedrich A. Hayek, *Unemployment and Monetary Policy*, Cato Institute: San Francisco, 1979.
4. Friedrich A. Hayek, *Prices and Production*, Kelley: Clifton, NJ, 1967.
5. Stephen Littlechild, *The Fallacy of the Mixed Economy*, Cato Institute: San Francisco, 1979.
6. Israel Kirzner, *Competition and Entrepreneurship*, University of Chicago: Chicago, 1973.

# 12 Monopoly and Competition

**Chapter Content**

12.1 Monopoly    164
    12.1.1 The United States Postal Service (USPS)    165
    12.1.2 The Tennessee Valley Authority (TVA)    166
    12.1.3 Government Grants of Monopoly    167
    12.1.4 Private Monopolies    169
12.2 Competition    171
    12.2.1 First Class Mail Delivery    172
    12.2.2 Organization of Petroleum Exporting Countries    172
    12.2.3 Railroads    173
    12.2.4 Business Strategies to Lessen Competition    176
12.3 Government Regulation of Monopoly and Competition    178
    12.3.1 The Sherman Antitrust Act    179
    12.3.2 Rate Fixing the Railroads    180
    12.3.3 Flood of Regulatory Legislation    181
    12.3.4 Government Monopoly of Schooling    184

Probably, no other two terms in economics have been used in more ways to confuse than competition and monopoly. The concepts themselves are easy enough to understand, but when it comes to applying them to the complex realities of trade and government regulation confusion tends to spread. This is especially so for monopoly, a term that has more often been used to castigate or denounce; but competition has been too narrowly understood as well. It may well have been that a portion of the confusion has been deliberate by those who had some ax to grind. But deliberate or not, the terms are often used in confusing ways.

Take monopoly, as the prize example of this confusion. The term has often been specialized in such a way as to make moral or legal judgments. Monopoly had an especially bad name in the seventeenth and eighteenth centuries, when many people thought of monopoly as bad, or even an evil. What they had in mind by the use of the term is what the dictionary describes this way: "the exclusive privilege to carry on a traffic or service, granted by a sovereign or state, etc." In sum, a monopoly was an exclusive trading privilege granted by a king or government. There was an attempt in the late nineteenth and early twentieth century to assign the revulsion connected with monopoly to large private businesses or corporations that were often referred to as "**trusts**." During much of this time monopoly was supposed to be bad, and competition was good. Even competition got a bad name in the 1930s, during the New Deal days. At least, that kind of competition designated as "**cutthroat competition**" was labeled as being bad. However, based on this assertion, it is more than a little difficult, if not impossible, to define what is ordinary and beneficial competition, or to discern what variety can be called "cutthroat competition."

In any case, monopoly and competition are often juxtaposed in such a way as to make them mutually exclusive concepts. This is a result of overspecializing words and making them apply to only designated portions of the reality with which they deal. They are not mutually exclusive forms of behavior in the market. Both monopoly and competition are essential to the effective function of the market. Every tradesman is a monopolist in that he has, as a seller, exclusive rights to dispose of his wares. And, every buyer is at least a potential monopolist in that he is trying to gain exclusive control over some good or service. Further, sellers are generally in competition with other sellers, and buyers in competition with buyers. Thus, the existence of the

**trust**—a business holding company. It can be a combination of businesses of similar products, or in the same stream of a production process, or a combination of diverse business enterprises.

**cutthroat competition**—competition that is excessive or mean spirited in nature. It is difficult to distinguish between "cutthroat competition" and regular competition.

**monopoly**—the absence of competition of a supplier of particular goods or services in a market. Historically, it has consisted of an exclusive right to sell some good or class of goods in particular markets, a right, or privilege that could only be granted by the ruling powers.

market depends upon monopoly, and its effectiveness in performing its function depends upon competition.

That is not to suggest that all forms of monopoly are beneficial or desirable, or that tradesmen relish competition. On the contrary, some kinds of monopoly do indeed exclude competition or greatly reduce it, and tradesmen do often try to avoid the rigors of competition. It is rather to suggest that there are multiple kinds of monopolies, and competition is a much more complex matter than it is often portrayed as being. Above all, though, both monopoly and competition are essential to the market, and to an understanding of the market. We have already examined the role of competition as the balance wheel of the market and touched upon the private property aspect of monopoly. Now the discussion of both need to be rounded out and completed.

## 12.1 Monopoly

It might be supposed that competition should be discussed first, but logically, monopoly is more basic and comes first. In its broadest meaning, **monopoly** means the "exclusive possession or control of something." Thus, we may say, for example, that a child is monopolizing a particular toy. In Greek, the root of the word meant the "exclusive right of sale." We may rightly conclude from definitions that private property is a monopoly of its owner. As sole possessor, he not only controls it but has an exclusive right to dispose of it, i.e., to sell it in the market. It is this aspect of monopoly that makes it important to discuss monopoly prior to competition, for the competition between sellers, or buyers, is only possible because they have a monopoly on goods to dispose.

The most basic of all monopolies is the exclusive right of free people to sell their labor services. Indeed, it is the specific difference between freedom and slavery. It is a natural right, hence, a natural monopoly. The individual is the only one who can direct the constructive use of his labor. Granted, some people are induced by coercion to use their faculties constructively for someone else's purposes, but that is an abuse of power rather than a natural use. Those who oppose monopoly indiscriminately, whether they are aware of it or not, are voting by their attitude for slavery. It is this monopoly that enables individuals to dispose of their labor to others at a mutually agreeable price.

> **Monopoly of Individual Labor**
> The most basic of all monopolies is the exclusive right of free people to sell their labor services. Indeed, it is the specific difference between freedom and slavery. It is a natural right, hence, a natural monopoly. The individual is the only one who can direct the constructive use of his labor.

All landed property is a monopoly of its owner. That is, he who owns it possesses, controls, has dominion over, and may alone dispose of the land and structures thereon. The monopoly of land has usually been qualified in one or more ways by governments. The most general qualification is that he may not use his land so as to do demonstrable harm to others (except, possibly, in self defense, though self defense is in no way restricted to private property). In the United States, governments may exercise the power of **eminent domain**, or, as the Constitution says, take private property for public use, provided the owner is awarded just compensation. Unfortunately, this power has been much abused in recent years as local communities have exercised it for commercial development purposes to increase their tax base. This activity is quite different from what the American Founders had in mind. When governments go beyond these limited qualifications, they tend to erode away the monopoly character of property and, thus, undermine the voluntary trade and exchange of it.

All other private property, whether tangible or intangible, whatever form it may take, whether a share in a corporation, an automobile, a copyright or patent, or currency, is a monopoly of the owner. The point needs to be emphasized because this aspect of monopoly is often overlooked in public discussion and debate. Moreover, so far as the owner's monopoly is observed in law and practice, the owner is sovereign over what he owns. If he offers it for sale in the market he is, as seller, sovereign, in that he alone may determine at what price he will part with it. Some economists refer to consumer sovereignty in the marketplace. Some even refer to the market as the arena of consumer democracy. In fact, neither buyer nor seller is sole sovereign in the market. Each is sovereign over whatever property he has to exchange there. Consumers are no more sovereign than producers; each has a veto over what he may offer in exchange. It is true that if consumers generally veto something a producer is offering it will not sell well, if at all. It is equally true, however, that if a producer ceases to offer a line of goods they may no longer be available. In any case, the crucial factual point is the **sovereignty of owners** over their goods is paramount to free enterprise. The issue is not how one or the other parties in the market may somehow manage to dominate over the other.

But however important it may be to understand that all ownership constitutes monopoly in the strict sense of the word, most of the public discussion and debate about monopoly has not been cast in those terms. Rather, it has dealt with what the dictionary describes as "exclusive control of a commodity or service in a particular market, or a control that makes possible the manipulation of prices." Two different kinds of monopolies have dominated the discussion over the years. They are sufficiently different as to warrant separate discussion.

**eminent domain**—provision in the United States Constitution for government to take private property for public use, provided the owner is awarded just compensation.

**sovereignty of owners**—the right of property owners to treat their property however they wish. In other words, they have a monopoly over their property.

### 12.1.1 The United States Postal Service (USPS)

As noted earlier, one of the definitions of monopoly is the grant by government of an exclusive privilege to carry on the traffic in some good or service. The government may grant such a privilege to some organization it has created, i.e., to some part of the government, or to some private person or organization. The most familiar grant of such a monopoly in the United States today is the grant of the exclusive privilege to the United States Postal Service to deliver first class mail. The Postal Service is, of course, a creature of the United States Government. The Postal Service does not, however, perform all the functions of delivering mail everywhere in the United States. It may, and does contract with private carriers to deliver mail to post offices, and the like, and sometimes private carriers have contracts to deliver mail to homes. In any case, the Postal Service illustrates many of the aspects of a government granted monopoly.

Actually, the Postal Service claims a monopoly only of delivering personally inscribed messages, known generally as First Class mail. However, the manner of its enforcement of the monopoly tends to give it a monopoly of the delivery of all sorts of advertisements and messages. It claims the exclusive privilege to deliver to postal or mail boxes and denies their use by all other carriers. This it does despite the fact that mail boxes are generally privately owned and postal boxes at post offices are privately rented. Nevertheless, any other carrier has to deliver to the door and, if delivery is not made personally to the tenant, he must find some place to leave the material.

The Postal Service demonstrates in practice most of the objections to monopoly. In the absence of direct competition, prices are arbitrarily set. It is sometimes asserted that the monopolist may charge as much as the traffic will bear. That has not necessarily been the case with the Postal Service (or the Post Office Department that preceded it), but it is true that high or low prices are arbitrarily set. They are in no real sense the result of voluntary agreement between buyer and seller. The seller—the Postal Service—sets the prices, and the potential buyer can take it or leave it. There is really no way to determine whether prices are high or low, to the extent that other sellers are excluded from the market. It is possible, of course, to know whether or not the Postal Service makes or loses money. But we cannot know that when the Postal Service makes money it is efficient.

Even so, it is possible to know in a number of its policies that the Post Office is arbitrary, political, or ideological, and not economic. It is surely not economical, for example, to charge the same price to deliver a letter to your next door neighbor as for delivering one to Hawaii or Alaska, for example. At least, the Post Office is overcharging for its service in the case of the local delivery and undercharging from Alaska to Florida, for example. Indeed, the Post Office did at one time charge a lower rate on letters delivered in the same town than for those posted from other locales, but even that sensible distinction was abandoned. While the Postal Service does charge more for parcel post deliveries in its zoned system for those in more distant zones, this sensible arrangement is not even applied to all packages. For example, the rate for shipping books throughout the United States is uniform rather than being graduated by zones. In fact, judging by the rate system, the Postal Service appears to have either set many of them arbitrarily or on the basis of political or ideological motives.

Governments tend to monopolize any good or service they offer for public sale. This might even be called a natural tendency. After all, governments generally have a monopoly of the use of force within their jurisdictions, and it could hardly be otherwise, as explained earlier. Thus, those who govern think in terms of monopoly even when they operate in the market, even though competition, not force, regulates the market. Governments also tend to be bureaucratic, regulation ridden, and to be governed by other than economic considerations. All these things follow more or less from the nature of government and its basic role. If government is not operated by strict rules, then its power will most likely be arbitrarily and despotically used. In performing its task of maintaining the peace, its function is not to make a profit but to enforce the law. When government intrudes in the market, it tends to bring habits formed in another arena with it.

### 12.1.2 The Tennessee Valley Authority (TVA)

The tendency to monopolize can be illustrated by another example of government providing a service. The Tennessee Valley Authority demonstrates the point well. The TVA, as it is called, was authorized in 1933, at the beginning of the New Deal. It is a government organization founded to develop that region known as the Tennessee Valley, encompassing much of Tennessee, north Alabama, and western Kentucky. Critics have charged it over the years with being socialistic. It is that, of course, for it involves government ownership of a means of production—electricity in this case. But the point that concerns us most directly here is that it has been monopolistic. Actually, the production of electricity was supposed to be a by-product of the taming of the river and making it navigable. A series of dams was to be built on the Tennessee River and its tributaries. These dams with their locks would not only make navigation easier or possible but also produce hydroelectric power.

It was not many years, however, before the production and distribution of electricity became a dominant activity of TVA. Private companies producing electricity were excluded from the region claimed by TVA. TVA sold its electricity to municipalities, cooperatives, and other non-profit organizations. It was not many years before the demands for electricity exceeded the capacity of the dams to produce it. TVA turned to building and operating coal fired steam turned turbines for producing more and more of its electricity and in more recent times built nuclear plants as well. Thus the TVA established and maintains its monopoly over electricity in that region.

### 12.1.3 Government Grants of Monopoly

Government grants of monopolies to private individuals and organizations have been much more common historically than to actual government organizations that provided goods and services. Ordinarily, governments have provided few goods and services themselves, though the practice became much more widespread in the twentieth century with the spread of socialism. In some periods of history, this practice has been especially rampant. During the seventeenth and eighteenth centuries, under mercantilistic ideas, the practice was especially widespread. Trading companies were granted monopolies of trade with respect to transporting particular goods or trading in specific products. The British East India Company was such an organization, whose monopoly of exporting tea to America sparked the Boston Tea Party and other colonial resistance. There were other kinds of government granted monopolies as well. Road and bridge building was often fostered in early America by granting monopolies over these undertakings and the right to collect tolls to particular companies.

In more recent times, state and local governments have been the most prolific granters of monopolies to individuals and private companies. This is done most often by granting exclusive franchises to provide some good or service. Probably the best known of such monopolies are those granted to what are often called public utilities, for example, electric companies, telephone companies, light rail transportation, city bus, garbage collection, and the like. The usual argument made for granting such franchises is that the good or service that they perform is a **natural monopoly**. That is, in the nature of things, it would be impractical to have more than one supplier of electricity, land-line telephone service, or street cars. To say the least, it would get very crowded if more than one company strung electrical or telephone wires, laid down street car tracks, or laid natural gas lines in the same locale. However, the case for granting a monopoly franchise grows weaker and has little or nothing compelling about it when it is done for buses, garbage collectors, trucking companies, and the like. Garbage collection is no more a natural monopoly, if there is such a thing, than is home delivery of any other good or service. In any case, governments have granted a variety of such franchises or assumed the service over the years.

> **Getting the Point...**
>
> Briefly explain the significance of the USPS and TVA in understanding government monopoly.

**natural monopoly**—a natural monopoly provides a service that, in the nature of things, would be impractical to have multiple companies provide. Examples include electricity, streetcars, or anything that involves laying down wires, tracks, or pipelines.

**registration**—buying a license to permit operation of a certain business.

**certification**—occurs when government recognizes the expertise of an individual by issuing a certificate, but does not restrict the practice to only those holding a certificate.

**licensing**—restricts entry to the field and tends to give at least some of the conditions of monopoly to those who are licensed.

Licensure is another area where government has promoted a kind of near monopoly over the years. Again, state governments have been leaders in this field. Now, there are multiple types of licenses, and by no means do all of them promote a kind of monopoly. For example, businesses are usually licensed by municipalities and other local governments. But in most cases, the fees are nominal; anyone may obtain a license upon paying the fee; and the requiring of such licenses is more a taxing device than anything else. In most cases, it does not substantially restrict entry to the field, which is our concern here. Economist Milton Friedman says there are three different categories of government recognition or authorization of doing business in a trade or profession: **registration**, **certification**, and **licensing**. Thus, buying a license to operate a grocery store, he would call registration. Certification occurs when government recognizes the expertise of a person by issuing a certificate, as occurs with Certified Public Accountant, but does not restrict the practice of accounting to those holding the certificate. Licensing, as Friedman uses the term, does restrict entry to the field and tends to give at least some of the conditions of monopoly to those who provide the licenses.

Such licensing is widespread in most states for a considerable variety of trades and professions. Walter Gellhorn explored licensing extensively in a book, *Individual Freedom and Governmental Restraints*, and noted that:

> One may not be surprised to learn that pharmacists, accountants, and dentists have been reached by state law as have sanitarians and psychologists, assayers and architects, veterinarians and librarians. But with what joy does one learn about the licensing of threshing machine operators and dealers in scrap tobacco? What of egg graders and guide dog trainers, pest controllers and yacht salesmen, tree surgeons and well diggers, tile layers and potato growers? And what of hypertrichologists who are licensed in Connecticut, where they remove excessive and unsightly hair with the solemnity appropriate to their high sounding title?

Whether or not there is some justification for licensing some or all of the above or other professions and trades, such as that of physicians and plumbers, is an interesting question. Undoubtedly, many people may be persuaded that it is highly useful to have physicians, for example, licensed to practice, thus indicating, we might hope, that they have at least minimum competence to do so. However, it is by no means clear why this kind of certification could not be accomplished privately. There are good points that might be made on both sides of this question, but the main concern here is to make clear the economic consequences of such licensing. Clearly, such licensing restricts the number of those who offer goods or services in particular fields. The two most immediate consequences are: (1) some people who might make a living or increase their income are denied the opportunity; (2) it tends to raise the cost of the service or good involved. To the extent that it reduces the quantity being offered, it makes the good or service unavailable or difficult to obtain for some people. In short, such licensing causes unemployment, higher prices, and a greater scarcity of goods and services.

On the face of it, licensing does not appear to grant a monopoly to any person or group, however. After all, there are many physicians, lawyers, plumbers, dentists, and the like, offering their services in competition within their trades or professions with one another. This is somewhat deceptive, however, for admission to standing in the field is often overseen by craft and professional organizations, or their members. The American Medical Association, for example, plays a leading role in recognizing medical schools, and local medical associations do the same in admitting physicians to practice in hospitals. The boards that admit physicians to practice are dominated by physicians. The same holds sway generally in the practice of craft or professions. Thus, the various craft and professional organizations often have similar effects to those of labor unions, though they are achieved in a more dignified manner.

> In short, **licensing** causes unemployment, higher prices, and a greater scarcity of goods and services.

### 12.1.4 Private Monopolies

Strictly speaking, a monopoly of the sort we are now discussing can only exist by government grant or establishment, or by the use of non-governmental force. In the absence of the use of force, others would be free to enter the field and offer similar goods or services. Imagine, for example, a village in which there is only one grocery store. Some might suppose that the grocer would be the sole supplier of groceries, and hence have a monopoly. That would only be the case, even superficially, if other grocery stores were inaccessible, either because of lack of roads or waterways. Even in that extreme case, however, so long as others were free to open up grocery stores in the area, his would be at most a temporary monopoly, pending the entering of the field by a competitor. Neither legally nor illegally would the grocer have a monopoly so long as others could enter the field.

Be that as it may, there has been much contention and controversy in the United States about the alleged monopoly status of privately owned businesses. It has not been about single grocery stores in small villages, of course. Rather, it has been about large businesses operating on a nationwide scale. In the late nineteenth and early twentieth centuries, very large businesses grew in America, some of them selling goods throughout the United States. Actually several meat packers grew quite large during and after the Civil War: Armour, Swift, and a few others. But it was the formation of the **Standard Oil Trust** in the 1880s that aroused the popular fear of private monopoly. Within a decade or so after the Civil War, John D. Rockefeller and associates formed a nationwide oil distributing business. The company was set up as a trust company in the 1880s. Standard Oil got much of the stock of other oil companies by the decision of the controlling boards to allow them to hold their stocks and pay dividends on them. General estimates have been that at its height of dominance in the industry, Standard controlled somewhere between 80 and 90% of the oil market. The trust device was abandoned very shortly. One reason was the assault upon Rockefeller and his associates by way of congressional investigations, and the like. The other was that more effective methods of control became available. John D. Rockefeller thought the solution for nationwide businesses was to have the United States Government charter corporations to do business throughout the nation. That did not happen, however. Instead, New Jersey offered incorporation that allowed the corporations to do business throughout the country. These corporations could also buy stock in other corporations, thus becoming holding

**Standard Oil Trust**—nationwide oil distributing business started by John D. Rockefeller in the 1880s. It was the first of its kind and controlled between 80–90% of the market.

companies. These provisions of incorporation enabled large corporations to grow and spread throughout the United States.

Other companies, too, had moved to dominant positions in other industries. Robert Heilbroner (in *The Economic Problem*) described the situation this way at the beginning of the twentieth century.

> In the locomotive industry, two companies ruled the roost in 1900, contrasted with nineteen in 1860. The biscuit and cracker industry changed from a scatter of small companies to a market in which one producer had 90 percent of the industry's capacity by the turn of the century. Meanwhile in steel there was the colossal U.S. Steel Corporation, which alone turned out over half the steel production of the nation.... In tobacco, the American Tobacco Company controlled 75 percent of the output of cigarettes and 25 percent of cigars. Similar control rested with the American Sugar Company, the American Smelting and Refining Company, the United Shoe Machinery ...

Some perceived great danger to state and national government from these huge businesses. To quote Heilbroner again: "By the end of the nineteenth century some business units were already considerably larger than the states in which they were located." More than that, however, the Pujo Committee in 1913,

> ... pointed out that the Morgan banking interests held 341 directorships in 112 corporations whose aggregate wealth exceeded by three times the value of *all* the real and personal property of New England. And not only was the process of trustification [?] eating away at the competitive structure of the market, but the emergence of enormous financially controlled empires posed as well a political problem of ominous portent. As Woodrow Wilson said: 'If monopoly persists, monopoly will always set at the helm of government. I do not expect to see monopoly restrain itself. If there are men in this country big enough to own the government of the United States, they are going to own it.'

It should be pointed out that the above quotations have somewhat exaggerated the factual situation to draw some dubious conclusions. It does not follow, for example, that if a man sits on the board of two or more corporations, that he uses his power for some particular corporation. More precisely, the fact that people connected with the House of J.P. Morgan held directorships in a large number of corporations does not tell us that they controlled all these corporations. That is highly unlikely. Nor does wealth necessarily translate itself into political power. The quotations were made to demonstrate two points. First, during this period of time large companies obtained dominant positions in some industries, and some described these dominant positions as monopoly. Second, this dominance was often described as if it somehow constituted political power, and thus endangered republican government. The question of the relation of corporations (large or small) to government will be left mainly for discussion later in the section on economic systems. The issue here is competition and monopoly, more precisely, private monopolies.

---

**Getting the Point . . .**

Briefly explain the significance of OPEC, Standard Oil Trust and J.P. Morgan in understanding monopoly.

There is no doubt that large corporations attained leading roles in a number of industries in the late nineteenth and early twentieth centuries. There should be no doubt, either, that where large amounts of capital are necessary, as in the manufacture of automobiles or building of transcontinental railroads, for example, it is difficult for competitors on that scale to emerge. American history tends to indicate, however, that given time other large companies emerge to compete. It is true that the United States Government did try to break up Standard Oil, with only limited success. What is much more significant is that other companies emerged in the early twentieth century to compete with Standard, such companies as Gulf, Texaco, Sunoco, and others. Given time, too, competitors take on large companies.

Some economists, however, do not describe the situation that way. Rather than seeing several large companies as competing, they persist in seeing monopolistic behavior, although they describe it as **oligopoly**. Oligopoly is said to exist when several large firms dominate the market rather than one. One alleged example of this kind of monopoly was the dominance of the big three—General Motors, Ford, and Chrysler—in the automobile industry during a large part of the twentieth century. Although a variety of charges have been made about oligopoly, the most common one is that the several firms administer the prices of their product, generally to keep prices above what they would be under "pure" competition. They are said to do this usually in one of two ways. Either, they tacitly agree not to lower prices, or they enter into actual (secret) agreement with one another not to lower prices.

**oligopoly**—a condition in which two or more producers or distributors dominate the market in providing some particular good or class of goods and are thus able to control prices. While the claims have doubtful validity, and even the use of the term is suspect, the idea has nonetheless caught on.

Occasionally, companies have and do enter into agreement with one another either to divide up markets or otherwise keep prices at a certain level. Such agreements are now generally illegal, but they have never been enforceable (except when government administered the prices). In any case, it is unlikely that whether agreements are tacit or actual, they have never been known to work for long. If a company involved in such an agreement could greatly increase sales and profits by lowering its price, it will not delay long in doing so. It is by such price competition that a business may gain a larger share of the market.

In any case, much of the alleged evidence for administered prices is flawed. The United States has had almost continual monetary inflation since the mid-1930s. In those conditions, prices tend to rise rather than fall. It is not surprising, in those circumstances, that one or another company in an industry may raise prices first, and others follow suit. Such things do not prove **collusion**, administered prices, nor "oligopolistic" behavior.

**collusion**—when multiple firms come together and decide to manipulate their prices in the market.

Indeed, the whole case against private monopolies is less than convincing, either that they should be called monopolies or that they are. Much of the talk about private monopolies does not proceed from a clear understanding of either competition or monopolies. Competition, in all its breadth, is much more extensive than those who speak of "pure" competition have fully understood. We must turn then to a much fuller examination of competition.

## 12.2 Competition

Perhaps the best approach to understanding **competition** is to look at it first from the monopoly angle. How successful are so-called monopolies—even government monopolies? Can the provision of some good or service actually be monopolized? The possibility of such monopolization is doubtful absent government privilege. It is certainly no easy matter to

**competition**—see *definition*, p. 139.

monopolize a good or service. And, even if that could be temporarily accomplished, as soon as prices rose sufficiently, or service declined, substitutes would surely gain ground. Moreover, as soon as a commodity is sold, and if the buyer has a property in it, he can presumably compete with the monopolist by offering it for sale himself. Thus, if government manufactured automobiles and prohibited all others to enter the business, if used cars could be sold, the government's monopoly over the automobiles would be compromised, to say the least. (A totalitarian government might try to prohibit all trading, of course, but that is a form of tyranny that has rarely been practiced before the present century.)

> **Monopolizing**
> It is certainly no easy matter to monopolize a good or service. And, even if that could be temporarily accomplished, as soon as prices rose sufficiently, or service declined, substitutes would surely gain ground.

### 12.2.1 First Class Mail Delivery

Let us take an actual example, however, that of the government's monopoly over the delivery of first class mail. Defined the way it has been, that monopoly is fairly complete, though it extends only to the commercial delivery of mail, and, even then, only to letter boxes designated as recipients for such mail. But the service actually involved is communication, and letters are only one of many ways people may communicate. They may, of course, go in person (though that would not be commercial), send a messenger, a telegram, telephone, text, or even talk to them by radio or internet. At the present time, the closest general competitors with first class mail are the telephone and email service. In fact, as the cost of mailing a letter rose precipitately in the 1970s and 1980s, there were many indications that the telephone was increasingly being used in place of letter writing. In the 1990s, email service exploded. Indeed, these two means of communication have virtually replaced the personal letter. In recent times, cell phones and texting have gained significant ground in the communication industry.

It is well to note, too, as the above example illustrates, new technology often supplies substitutes, especially where so-called monopolies are involved. The telegram, telephone, radio, and computer technology illustrate such inventions. The Postal Service continues to act in many ways as if it had a monopoly, could pay as high wages as it wishes, and raise prices at will. This is not true, of course, as developments are beginning to show.

### 12.2.2 Organization of Petroleum Exporting Countries

The main point here, however, is that even where governments appear to have a monopoly it is quite limited by substitute modes of providing the good or service. Another example of this, involving governments acting as monopolists, was the reaction to the actions of OPEC (Organization of Petroleum Exporting Countries), an international **cartel** of oil producing and exporting countries, mainly in the Middle East. The Middle East countries embargoed oil to the United States for a period in the mid-1970s, as punishment for certain American policies, including its aid to Israel in a war with the Arab countries and Richard Nixon's decision

**cartel**—an association of manufacturers or suppliers with the purpose of maintaining prices at a high level and restricting competition.

not to redeem foreign holdings of dollars for gold. Afterward, OPEC raised the price of oil precipitately by restricting production. Gasoline, motor oil, and kerosene prices rose, as did that of electricity and all sorts of things made from oil derivatives. Many ways of conserving fuel were devised, and many substitutes were sought as well. The insulation of houses was increased, new ways to use sunlight for heating explored, and many people conserved fuel by changing the settings on their thermostats. Smaller cars became commonplace, and alcohol was added to gasoline in some instances to make it go farther. Some people adapted or bought new furnaces to burn less expensive fuel to heat their homes. Vast new sources of oil, especially in the North Sea and Alaska, were developed to compete with the OPEC countries. Most of the OPEC countries soon saw that they were losing revenues by overpricing their oil, and the cartel could not maintain its prices. Given time, human ingenuity, and the great variety of potential substitutes, even attempts by government to monopolize particular goods or services tend to break down.

### 12.2.3 Railroads

Competition is often much too narrowly conceived. This is especially so where the allegations of private monopoly and oligopoly have been concerned. For example, the assertion that the railroads in the late nineteenth and early twentieth centuries were engaging in monopolistic practices was especially misplaced. The pressure to have federal regulation of rail rates mounted in the 1880s. Some states had attempted to regulate rates as early as the 1870s, but the Supreme Court held that states could not regulate interstate rates. As a result, the pressure for Congress to do something mounted. Congress responded with the Interstate Commerce Act, which made a stab at regulating them. Both the pressure and the legislation were inspired by more than a little tunnel vision about competition and the railroads. Let us take a little deeper look into the matter.

The railroads are a form of transportation. In economic terms, they add value by moving people and goods from one place to another. In this respect they are like all other means of transportation. The purpose of transportation is to bring people and goods together. Ideally, a transportation system would make available at one's doorstep goods and people from all over the world upon command, and without differential charge based on distance transported. At least, that is what consumers would prefer, though, of course, no such system has ever existed except in fantasies. Railroads never had a monopoly of transporting either people or goods. People could, in the latter part of the nineteenth century travel on foot, on horseback, in carriages, and on boats, as well as by rail. Goods could be transported by persons walking, on pack animals, in wagons, and on boats, as well as by rail. Undoubtedly, rail transport had certain advantages over the other modes for transport by land, as travel by boat continued its great advantage over swimming across expanses of water.

But even if there had been no competition with the railroads in land transport, railroads would have had incentives to offer attractive rates and good services. That would have been true to a considerable extent even if railroads were not often in competition with one another, which they were. To see this, it may be helpful to look further into the economics of railroading.

Railroads have unusually high **fixed costs**—i.e., those costs that precede the performing of the service. Fixed costs are higher for railroads as a rule, than for any other means of transport; and they are probably as much or more than for any other industry. They include such items as

**fixed costs**—costs that precede the performing of the service. Example: purchasing a building.

laying and maintaining tracks, building and keeping up passenger stations and freight depots, paying for switchyards, rights-of-way, bridges and crossings, rolling stock, safety devices, sidings, and the like. Railroads usually even own and operate their traffic signals, something unheard of in other large transport operations. Hence, their costs in preparation for operation are very high.

On the other hand, railroads have unusually low **variable costs** compared with other means of transport. That is, railroads can increase the amount of service with declining costs for each additional unit to a point much beyond what is common in other businesses. A train of fifty cars, say, can be hauled for very little more than one of ten cars, both in terms of fuel and personnel costs. Moreover, the cost per mile traveled declines precipitately as the distance is extended, since most of the fixed cost is in loading, unloading, and related activities. To put it another way, given the fixed costs and the fact that a train has been made up, each car added and each additional mile traveled costs less than the one before. Thus, railroads have tremendous incentives to increase the length of their trains, the frequency of them, and distance traveled. By so doing, they are enabled to recover their fixed costs, take advantage of low variable costs, and increase their income. When they operate in this fashion, they are serving the consumer in the optimum fashion.

The economics involved in railroading are such that railroads may adopt practices that on their face appear to be discriminatory. For example, it is undoubtedly less expensive for railroads to haul people or goods, per unit, on much traveled lines than on those that are little used. In like manner, it may be quite expensive for a train to stop at a station for one passenger or at a depot for one or two packages. Even so, Congress included a provision in the Interstate Commerce Act of 1887 virtually prohibiting the charging of more for a short haul than a long haul over the same line. Such a provision completely ignores the economies of railroading. Actually, railroads did discriminate among customers, as do many businesses; it is, for example, less expensive to supply large quantities of goods to a single buyer than small quantities to many buyers. Producers usually pass some of that saving along to quantity buyers (including governments, who regularly expect discounts when they buy in quantity). Henry Fink, writing in 1905 about railway rates, insisted the railways did and must discriminate. He said:

> Discrimination is the underlying principle of all railroad tariffs, whether they have been established by State railroad commissioners, or by the railroads themselves. This is so necessarily. Were it otherwise, railroads could not be successfully operated. Instead of promoting and facilitating commerce, they would hamper and obstruct it, and cause great injury to the public.

For example, people at different distances from a particular market need to be able to offer the same sorts of goods at competitive prices if they are to serve that market. Take providing milk for New York City, as an illustration. If the railroads had charged strictly on the basis of miles the milk was transported, then farmers near Poughkeepsie might have to pay twice as much per unit for transportation as those near Peekskill, those near Albany four times as much as those from Poughkeepsie, and those near Syracuse three times as much as those from Albany. If such rates had prevailed, the more distant producers simply could not have afforded to compete in the New York City market. Railroads had to be aware of the competition among producers for particular markets in setting their rates.

---

**variable costs**—the change in the cost of producing an additional unit of some good. When costs are highly variable, it means each additional unit can be produced at a significantly lower cost than the one that preceded it.

This was not a great inconvenience to the roads, for, as we have seen, it does not cost railroads that much more to haul goods long distances than short ones.

The important point, however, is that it is not only competition among railroads that tends to keep down prices but also competition of producers who use the railroads who try to sell in the same market. The competition is not only between those who produce the same product but also among producers of different products that may be chosen as substitutes. Not only are human wants extensive but also the means for gratifying them are numerous and diverse. The number of foods that either singly or in combinations with a few others will sustain life is so great as to be unnumbered. There are numerous fibers from which to make clothes, a great variety of building materials, a considerable number of different fuels, and so on. If the price of any one of these is raised significantly, alternative means may be used to gratify the want. For example, if oranges become more expensive, apples may be substituted. The consumption of commodities for which the demand is elastic will decline as the price rises, particularly if it rises in proportion to the prices of substitutes. Or, if prices of some good or service is lowered, consumption of it may be expected to increase.

The above point takes us beyond railroading to the market in general, and suggests how broad competition actually is among goods and services. If railroads are to benefit fully from their high fixed costs and low variable costs, they need to make transportation costs competitive for as many goods as possible. Additionally, for railroads, it might be supposed that if a town had only one railroad, it would be at the mercy of that railroad. The thought is that a single railroad could significantly raise prices because of the lack of other railroad options. However, that logic does not follow. "Backhauling," as it is called, is most important to railroads. The incentive is to haul loaded cars both in and out of any locale, and, in order to do that, charges must be sufficiently low for goods coming in as well as those going out.

The above examples of the variety and breadth of competition suggest some conclusions. So long as the market is generally free, the dangers of monopoly are not great. Indeed, even government monopolies or government grants of monopoly are restrained by substitute means of satisfying wants. New technology tends to offer competitive means of breaking monopoly, even where it does exist. In the case of railroads (even though they were never able to charge what the traffic would bear, as we have seen), other means of transport were soon developed to compete with them. The truck was available from the early twentieth century on to compete in the transport of commodities. The automobile was busily supplanting it in the transporting of passengers by the third decade of this century, supplemented by buses, which hauled passengers for hire. The airplane provided swifter transport than either and eventually replaced the trains as carriers of first class mail.

### Dangers of Monopoly
So long as the market is generally free, the dangers of monopoly are not great.

None of this is meant to suggest that producers and sellers do not seek ways to avoid the rigors of competition. They do so, and in their efforts they often thrust toward monopoly, in however small a way. They try to differentiate their product from all others and attract more customers by selling a better product at a lower price. They establish temporary monopolies and take advantage of these by raising prices. However, if people are left alone the forces of competition will eventually erode any short-term advantage.

### 12.2.4 Business Strategies to Lessen Competition

One way that businesses sometimes try to extend their influence over customers is through extending **store credit**. A department store sometimes issues its own credit cards, which are only good for its own merchandise. This tends to give the store an advantage over those stores that do not use them, and, if it works, the store gets a larger volume of business than otherwise from those who hold its credit cards. Indeed, the whole business of extending credit has long been used as a means of getting a greater volume of a customer's business, with the additional revenue arising from interest charges. General merchandise stores in times past used credit in this fashion. The offering of easy terms has for many years been used to lure customers.

> **store credit**—allowing customers to buy now and pay later. Some stores issue a credit card that can only be used in their store.

A very important way that producers and sellers try to gain customer loyalty is to distinguish and differentiate their product from all other similar products. Indeed, this is one purpose of having name brands. In fact, many products do not differ significantly from those of their competitors. A good example is gasoline. The main difference between kinds of gasoline is the octane rating, and this is made insignificant by the fact that most gasoline companies offer approximately the same octane ratings for the "regular" and "premium" products. The only other differences are such additives as companies may put in their brands. But additives are of little account, except for lead, which is now regulated by government. Even so, each brand makes its own claims to superiority, and brands have many loyal customers.

This brings us to the business of **advertising**. Undoubtedly, advertising is used most extensively to differentiate between competing products. The basic function of advertising, of course, is to inform people of the existence of some product and what it can do or provide those who might want it. In fact, however, advertising today goes much beyond informing to persuading or salesmanship. Advertisements are often used to move people to some action, commonly to purchase some good or service. Quite often, the aim of advertising is to develop or solidify consumer loyalty to some particular product or service by providing a promise of consistent quality to the customer.

> **advertising**—promoting a product or service to the public.

Some writers have painted advertising and salesmanship in rather somber hues. For example, Vance Packard published a book in the 1950s in which he charged them with being *Hidden Persuaders*. In his opening remarks, Packard described his thesis this way:

> This book is an attempt to explore a strange and rather exotic new area of American life. It is about the way many of us are being influenced and manipulated—far more than we realize—in the patterns of our everyday lives. Large-scale efforts are being made, often with impressive success, to channel our unthinking habits, our purchasing decisions, and our thought processes by the use of insights gleaned from psychiatry and the social sciences. Typically, these efforts take place beneath our

level of awareness; so that the appeals which move us are often, in a sense, "hidden"....

This depth approach... is being used most extensively to affect our daily acts of consumption. The sale to us of billions of dollars' worth of United States products is being significantly affected, if not revolutionized, by this approach....

What the probers are looking for, of course, are the *whys* of our behavior, so that they can more effectively manipulate our habits and choices in their favor. This has led them to probe why we are afraid of banks; why we love those big fat cars; why we really buy homes; why men smoke cigars; why the kind of car we drive reveals the brand of gasoline we will buy; why housewives typically fall into a hypnoidal trance when they get into a supermarket; why men are drawn into auto showrooms by convertibles but end up buying sedans; why junior loves cereal that pops, snaps, and crackles.

Indeed, John Kenneth Galbraith, an economist, published a book, *The Affluent Society*, about a year later in which he argued that advertising and salesmanship were changing the nature of economic development. They were, he claimed, being used by producers to create wants and desires that did not exist before. Rather than producing to fulfill the needs and wants of people, they were creating wants to sell whatever they decided to produce. "So it is," he said, "that if production creates the wants it seeks to satisfy..., then the urgency of the wants can no longer be used to defend the urgency of the production. Production only fills a void that it has itself created." It seemed to him that the very size of advertising efforts tends to prove his thesis. He calls up the following scenario:

A new consumer product must be introduced with a suitable advertising campaign to arouse an interest in it. The path for an expansion of output must be paved by a suitable expansion in the advertising budget.... The cost of this want formation is formidable. In 1956 total advertising expenditure... amounted to about ten billion dollars. For some years it had been increasing at a rate in excess of a billion dollars a year. Obviously, such outlays must be integrated with the theory of consumer demand. They are too big to be ignored.

But such integration means recognizing that wants are dependent on production. It accords to the producer the function both of making the goods and of making the desires for them. It recognizes that production... actively through advertising and related activities, creates the wants it seeks to satisfy.

Actually, Galbraith's thesis is much less compelling than it may appear on first examination. There is considerable evidence that wants are more independent of advertising than he suggests. A frequently cited example is that of the Edsel, introduced by the Ford Motor Company in the 1950s. It did not sell well, despite abundant advertising, and production was abandoned a few years later. Actually, many products do not survive their early introduction; hundreds and thousands go out of production, regardless of the amount of advertising. Others survive on the market for long periods of time with little or no advertising. Undoubtedly, the amount of exposure consumers have to a product will have some effect on its sales, if there is any need or desire for it.

The main point here, however, is monopoly and competition. The point has been made that as producers, people generally try to avoid the full rigors of competition. They try to differentiate their products from one another, attempt to solidify consumer loyalty to their particular products, offer special inducements, such as easy credit, to extend the number of their patrons, and even to gain monopolies, at least in particular times and places. In fact, however, most of their efforts only increase the level of competition. If one seller increases his sales by advertising, others join the fray by advertising as well. If one merchant extends credit, even issues his own credit card, many others do likewise. The most important point to be learned here is that competition is simply the other side of the coin of attempts to monopolize trade in any relatively free market.

---

**Monopoly and Competition**

As producers, people generally try to avoid the full rigors of competition. However, most of their efforts only increase the level of competition. If one seller increases his sales by advertising, others join the fray by advertising as well. If one merchant extends credit, even issues his own credit card, many others do likewise. The most important point to be learned here is that competition is simply the other side of the coin of attempts to monopolize trade in any relatively free market.

---

## 12.3 Government Regulation of Monopoly and Competition

Since the 1880s, the Federal Government, as well as the state governments generally, adopted many **regulations** controlling and restraining business and trade. Many of these regulations had to do with monopoly and competition, though even some of those that did were not advanced under those names. The most prominent of these regulations were the antitrust acts, the fair trade acts, and the expanding regulations of interstate commerce. During the late 1970s through the 1980s, there was a movement toward **deregulation**, though since this time a revival of regulatory control has occurred. Therefore, we should consider the nature and impact of regulatory control in the market.

Reformers who pushed for these regulations were more than a little ambiguous in their attitude toward competition. They usually claimed to favor competition in the 1890s and the early twentieth century. On the other hand, reformers who promoted the regulation in the 1930s were outspokenly opposed to that competition that they called "cutthroat," whatever that might mean. But even during the earlier period when they generally praised competition, they were, if not ambivalent, at least confused as to what competition was and how it could be promoted.

That the reformers were ambiguous in their posture toward competition, however, should not be surprising. They wanted to use government and legislation in their efforts to regulate. Government is, after all, monopolistic by nature. It performs its most basic functions by monopolizing

**regulation**—government controls set by legislation or agencies of the executive branch of government. They are put into place to restrain certain activities of businesses.

**deregulation**—the act of removing the controls government has previously put into effect restraining businesses.

the use of force within its jurisdiction. The more it extends its power the more monopolistic it tends to become. Moreover, it is not at all clear that competition can be forced. Buyers are in competition with one another, whether they intend it or not, and sellers are in competition with one another, even when they try to avoid it. Competition is elemental to the market. That is not to suggest that government may not prohibit certain practices, but it must be clear that when it does so it is more apt to be inhibiting than promoting competition.

### 12.3.1 The Sherman Antitrust Act

The ambiguity can be seen even in the language of the **Sherman Antitrust Act of 1890**, the first major anti-monopoly act passed by the United States Government. Even the opening sentence is vague and ambiguous. It reads: "Every contract, combination, in the form of trust or otherwise, or conspiracy in restraint of trade or commerce among the several States, or with foreign nations, is hereby declared to be illegal." As Henry Steele Commager said, in his introduction to the act in *Documents of American History*,

> The first federal act ever passed which attempted to regulate trusts, it was couched in general and often ambiguous language. The bill contains no definition of a trust, of a monopoly, and no indication of the meaning of the term 'restraint'. Nor was it clear at the time of the passage of the act whether its terms were meant to embrace combinations of labor as well as capital.

**Sherman Antitrust Act**—The first major anti-monopoly act passed by the U.S. government. It was vague, ambiguous, and poorly defined.

Certainly, the failure to define restraint is critical. Ordinarily, the word connotes the use of force or coercion to prevent some actions, and in this case would appear to refer to the use of coercion or force to prevent interstate trade or trade with foreign nations. Such acts are ordinarily illegal, of course, whether committed by individuals or private combinations. "Combination," not mentioned by Commager, is an even vaguer word, and could be construed to mean a corporation, a union, or any sort of association. But in the following section there is, even greater ambiguity, as it might apply to competition.

It reads, in part:

> Every person who shall monopolize, or attempt to monopolize, or combine or conspire with any other person or persons, to monopolize any part of the trade or commerce among the several States, or with foreign nations, shall be deemed guilty of a misdemeanor....

This sentence is a disaster, so far as its intent is concerned. What does attempt to monopolize trade or commerce mean? The crime here is not simply establishing an actual monopoly but even "attempting" to monopolize "any part of the trade or commerce among the several States...." Any attempt to compete in commerce could be construed as an "attempt to monopolize." True, the tradesman may not have in mind a monopoly, but if he does anything to best his competitors, and if it succeeds, he is surely making a move toward monopolizing the trade. Imagine a store located near a state line, with customers from two states. If the owner lowers his prices, offers credit to his customers, delivers goods to the home, or even supplies carts to transport goods to cars, is he not attempting to monopolize some part of the trade and commerce between two states? Could he not, therefore, by the terms of the Sherman Antitrust Act, be found guilty of a misdemeanor and "be punished by fine not exceeding five thousand dollars, or by imprisonment not exceeding one year, or by both said punishments, in the discretion of the court"?

The law evinced a profound misunderstanding, if not ignorance, of both monopoly and competition. Ostensibly, the act declared war on competition in the name of prohibiting monopolistic combinations. Actually, the courts never held that it prohibited competition. Neither, however, did they incline to hold businesses guilty of restraint of trade simply because they combined to increase their portion of trade. Indeed, the Sherman Antitrust Act was not applied with any vigor until a decade and a half later, then only very selectively. The act has never been more than selectively and arbitrarily applied on occasion to this or that business. It has not prevented the formation of holding companies, various sorts of combinations, and competition in general, though it may have inhibited and occasionally prevented some of these.

### 12.3.2 Rate Fixing the Railroads

**rate fixing**—the effort of the government to regulate prices of some product or service.

Before taking up other antitrust regulations, another aspect of regulatory interference with competition needs to be discussed—that of **rate fixing**. The effort to regulate rail rates had begun with the establishment of the Interstate Commerce Commission in 1887. The Interstate Commerce Act had not given much, if any actual rate fixing authority to the commission, and it had none of consequence until the early twentieth century. It should be pointed out in advance that the setting of prices by sellers is one of the major ways that they can compete. The Elkins Act, passed in 1903, prohibited the giving of rebates by railroads. Rebating is the practice of returning a portion of what has been paid for a good or service to the buyer. As a general rule, the giving of rebates is a silly (which is not to suggest it should be illegal) way of giving a reduction in price. Except when it is selective, which rail rebates were, and many of those offered by companies today are. Today, companies often require the sending in of a coupon and a long wait before receiving the rebate. This makes the reduction less than it appears, because many people will not bother to send in the coupon, and allows the company to return the money when it will. The rail rebates were even more selective. They were usually competitive reductions given to large shippers. Prices might simply have been lowered for bulk shippers, but the Interstate Commerce Act required the publication of rates. It was these published rates on which rebates were given. The practice was no doubt discriminatory, but then so are all prices arrived at by agreement based on larger amounts of something bought. In any case, the Elkins Act effectively removed one of the ways railroads could compete.

In 1906, the Hepburn Act empowered the Interstate Commerce Commission to set "just and reasonable" maximum rail rates. In theory, railroads could still compete with one another, or with other means of transportation, by lowering rates. In practice, however, the maximum rates tended to become the minimum rates also. The Mann–Elkins Act, passed in 1910, made it much more difficult for the railroads to alter their rates. By this time, or before, the railroads were increasingly intent on surviving rather than competing, because of the financial bind many of them were in. Their great need in the years just before World War I was a general increase in rates. Prices were rising in general during these years. Labor costs increased greatly for the railroads. Meanwhile, the ICC was not allowing them to adjust their rates to their rising costs. John F. Stover, in *The Life and Decline of the American Railroad*, describes what happened this way.

> In 1910 the railroads filed new freight rate schedules with increases of from 8 to 20 percent. The new federal regulation had transferred the burden of proof to the railroads in such rate cases, and the ICC suspended the increase while conducting an investigation.... After long hearings the ICC unanimously refused the rate increase request early in 1911. During 1911 and 1912 ... general prices continued to inch upward, and railroad labor made new demands for higher pay. A second request made in 1913 to the ICC for increased freight schedules eventually resulted in a modest 5 percent hike in rates. The ICC again was slow in its deliberations, and when the moderate increase was authorized it was clearly inadequate.

Thus, the rate regulation was used both to impoverish the railroads and reduce competition.

### 12.3.3 Flood of Regulatory Legislation

The federal government was moved by new antitrust fervor just before World War I. Two new acts were passed in 1914: the Federal Trade Commission Act in September and the Clayton Antitrust Act in October. The first of these acts created a Federal Trade Commission whose task was to oversee corporations in particular and business conduct in general. The act declared "That unfair methods of competition in commerce are hereby declared unlawful." The act did not, however, either describe in general or list in particular what methods of competition were unfair. This was left to the Commission to decide, and when they had so decided they were authorized to issue a cease and desist order to the offending company. If the company did not do so the case could be taken into the federal courts. This was supposed to be an anti-monopoly measure, since unfair trade practices were alleged to be the sources of monopoly. Actually, the commission's activities did not notably retard the growth of large businesses. The main tendency of the act was to reduce competition, since competitive acts could be declared unfair.

This comes out clearer in examining the companion act, the Clayton Antitrust Act. This act is best known for its supposed exemption of labor organizations from the provisions of antitrust laws, for declaring that labor is not a commodity, and, thus, presumably, not to be bought and sold in the market in the manner that commodities are. In any case, the thrust of this provision was to reduce competition among workers for jobs, whether it succeeded or not. But labor was not the only reduction in competition involved in the act. The act made it "unlawful for any person engaged in commerce" to cut prices if the effect of such discounts or rebates "may be to substantially lessen competition or tend to create a monopoly in any line of commerce...." While the wording of this statute is more complex than the summary might suggest, it still appears to be in the direction of restraining competition. Granted, Congress may have had in mind the kind of situation in which a company drives out competitors by cutting prices. Even so, the reduction of prices is a time honored way of competing; it is a way of selling slow moving goods; it is a way of increasing one's customers. Congress was caught once again in the illogic of trying to prevent what does not so clearly exist, i.e., private monopolies, and doing so by hampering competition.

Congress reached something of a peak in its assault on competition among the railroads in 1920. In that year, it passed the (Esch–Cummins) Transportation Act, probably the most thorough regulatory act ever passed. The most amazing provisions of the act were those having to do with rates and incomes of the railroads. For the first time, Congress authorized the ICC to set both minimum and maximum rates, thus virtually removing that means of competition from them. It hardly mattered, however, for much of the incentive for competing was removed. Rates were supposed to be fixed so as to assure a "fair" return upon investment if the railroad were efficiently run. Initially, Congress declared that a fair return in most instances would be 5.5% annually of the aggregate value of railway properties. Any railroad that earned more than 6% on the aggregate value of its properties in a given year was to have one-half of the excess placed in a reserve fund for its own future use and the other one-half to be turned over to the Commission to place in a general contingency fund to aid ailing railroads. In short, the more successful railroads were to subsidize the less successful ones.

The Transportation Act of 1920 did not encourage railroads to compete with one another in services either. The rules under which the railroads operated were so restrictive that roads could hardly compete in this way. In order to build or expand a railroad, the managers had to have a "certificate of convenience and necessity" from the ICC Nor would it be possible for railroads to do any long term borrowing for expansion or improvements without approval of the Commission. No more could railroads compete with one another for traffic interchanged with other rail lines. The ICC was now authorized to decide what routes interchanged traffic should go on. Even if a railroad owned well located terminal facilities, or built them, it was not at all certain it would be able to use them to gain an advantage over competitors. The law provided that if the Commission should find that it would be in the "public interest" "it shall have the power to require the joint or common use of terminals, including mainline trace or tracks for a reasonable distance outside of these terminals...." The act abandoned any concern with monopolies and focused virtually the whole attention on restricting competition.

In the early 1930s, under the New Deal, the government abandoned even the facade of concern with monopoly to focus virtually its whole attention on reducing competition. The crowning piece of legislation was the National Industrial Recovery Act passed in 1933. This act authorized industries to develop their own codes. For example, the coal mining industry, the auto-making industry, the cotton textile industry, and so on, were each to confer, organize, and develop their own particular codes for their industries. If an industry failed to produce such a code, the President was authorized to promulgate one for it. These codes were supposed to have the force of law within each covered industry. While the act declared "that such code or codes are not... to promote monopolies or to eliminate or oppress small enterprises," it is clear that such industries were to behave like monopolists are alleged to behave. The declared purpose of the act was to provide:

> for the general welfare by promoting the organization of industry for the purpose of cooperative action among trade groups, to induce and maintain united action of labor and management under adequate governmental sanctions and supervision, to eliminate unfair

competitive practices, to promote the fullest possible utilization of the present productive capacity,...

In short, they were to cooperate with one another to eliminate competition.

Many of the industries moved eagerly to do just that by establishing quotas of production, setting prices both for labor and products, and the like. Arthur S. Link summed up the activity of this sort in *The American Epoch* this way:

> Although the NRA tried to discourage outright price fixing, the bituminous coal, petroleum, and lumber codes contained schedules of minimum prices; most of the codes forbade sales below cost; and over half the codes required the establishment of the open-price system, that is, a system of prices openly published and adhered to. Production control was achieved in various ways in the codes. The petroleum, copper, and lumber codes, for example, set definite production limits and assigned quotas to individual producers. The cotton textile code limited mills to two eight-hour shifts daily. Other codes forbade the expansion of plant without approval of the code authority.

So far as workers were concerned, the codes, as well as the National Industrial Recovery Act specified the right of workers to organize into unions, and codes often specified minimum wages and maximum hours of labor.

The act was declared unconstitutional in 1935, and the program of requiring industrial codes was abandoned by the government. Much of the reduction of competition was continued by other devices, however. The National Labor Relations Act, passed in 1935, placed the government even more firmly behind the formation of labor unions. These, in turn, were often organized by industry and pushed for standard pay scales within an industry. Moreover, the Fair Labor Standards Act passed in 1938, prescribed minimum wages and maximum hours for industrial workers generally. Competition among workers was being drastically reduced.

Throughout the 1930s, the New Deal took steps to remove competition among farmers. Moreover, the government devised all sorts of programs for raising prices of farm products, so that farmers could do what monopolists have generally been accused of doing, setting prices above the market level. Among the devices used by government were: crop quotas, crop allotments, government loans for storing crops, and an assortment of subsidies. The general thrust of this regulation was to reduce or remove competition in agriculture.

Other laws enacted during this period show a definite tendency to limit competition. Congress passed the Motor Carriers Act in 1935. This act placed common carriers in trucking under the Interstate Commerce Commission. The act contained a kind of "grandfather" clause providing that those who were common carriers before the act was passed would be automatically issued certificates upon application. After that, common carriers would have to meet the following requirements for certification: "(1) the applicant is fit, willing and able properly to perform the service proposed and to conform to the provisions of the laws and rules of the Commission; (2) the Commission finds the 'proposed service . . . is or will be required by future convenience and necessity.'" Contract carriers would also have to have permits and those were to be issued upon somewhat similar grounds. The purpose of these restrictions was clearly primarily to limit competition. The Robinson–Patman Act of 1936 "prohibited sales at unreasonably low prices for the purpose of destroying competition or eliminating a competitor." Again, the act seems to be aimed at preventing monopoly, but what it actually limits is competition. Fair trade laws enacted by many states during the same era limited competition by prohibiting price cutting and the underselling of competitors.

In sum, government regulations aimed at restoring and particularly at enforcing competition have hardly had that effect over the years. Part of this failure may be attributed to an ambiguous attitude of reformers toward competition. More seriously, however, they have misunderstood both monopoly and competition. So far as there can be long term monopoly, it is a creation of government policy. Private monopolies and oligopolies are largely figments of the imagination. In any case, the cure for monopoly is freedom of entry to the field of competitors. However, government attacks monopoly by restraining competition, thus tending to create what it is supposedly preventing. Ultimately, government by its very nature tends to establish monopolies, and the more extensively it extends its sway over an economy, the more the undesirable results attributed to monopoly gain ground.

> **Unintended Consequences**
> The cure for monopoly is freedom of entry to the field of competitors. However, government attacks monopoly by restraining competition, thus tending to create what it is supposedly preventing. Ultimately, government by its very nature tends to establish monopolies, and the more extensively it extends its sway over an economy, the more the undesirable results attributed to monopoly gain ground.

In any case, government is hardly qualified to lay down rules of fair competition for others, even if such rules could be drawn. (None of this is meant to suggest that deceit, fraud, character defamation, and coercive restraint should not be prohibited by law. These things are wrong in themselves without regard to their impact on market competition, and cannot, by nature, be fair.) When government enters into business, it is notoriously unfair toward competitors, using its power to exclude them, underselling them, and sometimes compelling people to use its services. Competing in a field in which government has entered has even less prospect of success than gambling against the house in a casino.

### 12.3.4 Government Monopoly of Schooling

All this should be obvious, of course, and probably would be except that governments often conceal what they are doing by a barrage of verbiage and propaganda. Let us examine in some detail only one example of government involvement in business. The example is a major one, that of **schooling**, and it is especially appropriate because it has been dominated by state governments, and these have been little noticed thus far. Let us begin by dispelling some notions that have been deeply embedded in the public mind. There is nothing in the nature of schooling to dictate that it could not be sold in the market like any other good. The materials used in schooling—buildings, classrooms, desks, books, audio visual materials,

**schooling**—instruction or education received inside a school.

and the like—can be and are bought and sold in the market. The people who perform the services, such as teaching, can be and usually are paid. Moreover, the costs can be apportioned among the prime users or beneficiaries. Nor is the need for schooling more urgent than for many other goods that are regularly bought and sold in the market. Surely, bread, or some sort of food, is much more necessary to survival than schooling. Yet the production and distribution of the staff of life is usually left to the market, where competitors vie for customers and offer a great variety of foodstuffs. Nor is it clear that compulsory schooling is essential to education. After all, there are many other ways to be educated than in schools, but if schooling commends itself so strongly, and is so demonstrably superior to other approaches to education, it should succeed without compulsion.

In any case, schooling, or the providing of schools, is not by nature a function of government. Governments throughout the long span of history have neither usually provided schools or much concerned themselves with it one way or another. Historically, such education was usually provided for children by churches or parents. States occasionally took an interest in colleges or universities, chartered them, and sometimes provided some support. In the Middle Ages and in the early modern era, governments and churches were often intertwined, and thus government might have been tentatively involved with schooling. In early American history, there were here and there some town schools that probably received some local government support. Schooling, as such, began to catch on more generally in the course of the nineteenth century. Although there were variations from region to region, and sometimes from state to state, governments at the state level had little to do with schooling. Local communities built school buildings and hired a schoolmaster. Parents frequently provided the financial support, and this was sometimes augmented by local governments. Churches also provided schools; this was especially so for Roman Catholics, Lutherans, and Episcopalians. But by or before the early twentieth century, most states were becoming more and more involved with schooling, both at the higher and lower levels.

The main point here is how state governments behaved as competitors. One conclusion can be stated at this point: they behaved much worse than any private company ever has toward its competitors. Far from providing examples of fair competition, they did not truly compete at all. By the early twentieth century, the thrust was on for states to have monopolies of education within their boundaries. The power of the state was used to compel attendance at school. In itself, this would not necessarily have led to virtual state monopolies. This was accomplished by their pricing policies. Accompanying compulsory attendance was the thrust to provide free public schooling. Private and church schools (home schooling was rarely considered at the time) were usually heavily dependent for their existence on tuition payments.

Local community schools were usually driven out of existence by a combination of the carrot and the stick. States began to subsidize them, and they became dependent upon state funds. Then came the "consolidation" movement, as school buses became commonplace. Numerous schools in local communities were closed. (This happened at different times in different states.) States not only provided free schools but also free transportation to them, free books, and eventually inexpensive lunches. It was difficult, and often virtually impossible, for privately funded schools to stay in the field. The states funded all this schooling by force; they levied taxes on everyone, whether they had children in the schools or not.

States moved less slowly or resolutely to monopolize college and university education. College attendance has never been made compulsory. Moreover, the practice of charging tuition has been continued, even in state supported colleges and universities. Even so, states have generally undersold private and church-related colleges, and have heavily subsidized theirs with tax derived money. Moreover, since around the middle of the twentieth century, they have gone heavily into vocational and junior college education. They have made it extremely difficult for private profit-making trade schools to survive. Many fields, such as barbering, secretarial, refrigeration, and others were once dominated by these schools. They are being replaced by state supported schools, which charge little or no tuition for similar schooling.

Most states exercise some supervisory role over most schooling, however private it may claim to be. They oversee content of courses, sometimes the books to be used, the qualifications of instructors and the like. The brute force of the state is sometimes used against these interlopers on the state's monopoly. Home schoolers have been sent to jail in some states. Those who would not hire state certified teachers for lower schools have sometimes had their school closed, and teachers or administrators have sometimes been jailed when they persisted with their school. Generally, however states have been content to impose their rules on their competitors and allow them to survive as best they can.

Governments are monopolistic in tendency, as has already been pointed out. They are never for very long fair competitors. What reformers and politicians have often charged about large businesses is indeed true of governments. Moreover, they generally charge as much or more than the traffic will bear when they enter a field. They do not, of course, usually charge the way businesses do, and leave it up to the customer to decide whether he will pay it. They levy most of their charges as taxes, and collect them by the use or threat of force.

---

*Competition is the keen cutting edge of business, always shaving away at costs.*
**Henry Ford**

*The truth is that economic competition is the very opposite of competition in the animal kingdom. It is not a competition in the grabbing off of scarce nature-given supplies, as it is in the animal kingdom. Rather, it is a competition in the positive creation of new and additional wealth.*
**George Reisman**

# Study Guide for:

# 12 Monopoly and Competition

## Chapter Summary

In the seventeenth and eighteenth centuries, the term monopoly was used to refer to the situation where an exclusive trading privilege had been granted by the ruling authority to an individual or business firm. The classic example was the British East India Company, which maintained such privilege in shipping. It was this company's monopoly privilege that sparked the Boston Tea Party.

Today, the term monopoly is used to describe the situation where there is a single producer of a good or service. However, rather than providing a clearer conception of monopoly, this usage has resulted in greater confusion. This confusion has spilled over into numerous policy debates, which usually abound with misconceptions of not only monopoly but of the concept of competition as well.

Broadly speaking, competition is to be conceived of as a natural process that transpires when people are free to trade with one another. This should be rather self-evident since as producers people must compete amongst one another for customers. Therefore, they find it in their interest to produce a product of superior quality when compared to similar items that might serve the same purpose for the consumer. Also, producers must continually consider new methods that are more cost effective lest someone else should discover such methods and attract their clientele. The whole process of competition among producers, as well as competition among consumers, is the push for greater coordination of the plans of individuals.

Based upon this understanding, early writers criticized government for extending special privilege to some firms and individuals since such mandates undermine the process of competition. Thus these writers advocated *laissez faire* government policy in which the government was to take a neutral position. The influence of these writers set the stage for the development of relatively free markets during the nineteenth century in England and the United States. It should be noted that trade has never been fully free. For example, the delivery of mail has continued to be run by government in both places by creating a government monopoly. Furthermore, governments in both countries have moved significantly away from free market policies during the twentieth century.

Government intervention in the United States increased substantially from 1880 to 1970. During this period the government created numerous regulatory controls that had the effect of creating special privileges for some producers at the expense of others. Rather than remaining neutral, the government increasingly pursued an active role in people's economic affairs. These efforts have fundamentally circumscribed the process of competition.

## Points of Emphasis

1. The use of the term monopoly in the twentieth century is different from its usage during the seventeenth and eighteenth centuries. Instead of providing greater insight, the new usage has created greater confusion.

2. Competition is a process among all producers in their quest for customers. It is not necessarily limited to some particular product for which there might be one or more producers. As such, competition tends to promote improvements in the quality and variety of products available in the market.

3. Government production or control over an industry limits competition and undermines potential economic gains.

4. Antitrust legislation, along with other regulatory control, is arbitrary and is always ambiguously applied. This follows because the position taken by advocates in arguing for the need of such policies is ill-conceived.

## Identification

1. trust
2. cutthroat competition
3. monopoly
4. eminent domain
5. sovereignty of owners

6. natural monopoly
7. registration
8. certification
9. licensing
10. Standard Oil Trust
11. oligopoly
12. collusion
13. competition
14. cartel
15. fixed costs
16. variable costs
17. store credit
18. advertising
19. regulation
20. deregulation
21. Sherman Antitrust Act
22. rate fixing
23. schooling

## Review Questions

1. The fact that one firm raises its price in an oligopolistic industry and that other firms follow suit shortly thereafter does not prove either the theory of price leadership or of collusion. Why not?

2. What is wrong with the concept of unfair competition as used by those who advocate government control over the economy?

3. Who is helped and who is harmed by antitrust legislation? . . . by regulatory control? . . . by government subsidy? . . . by tariffs?

4. When are the dangers of monopoly the most pronounced?

## Activities

1. Define and discuss Friedman's three categories of government authorization of business.

2. Prepare a case either to support or oppose Galbraith's contention that human wants are so readily met that advertising is only necessary to arouse some interest in new products.

3. Choose a very large corporation and describe any government actions that are contributing to their maintaining such a large share of the market. Identify any factors you see that are keeping competitors from effectively competing with them?

## For Further Study

1. Dominick Armentano, *Antitrust and Monopoly: Anatomy of a Policy Failure*, Independent Institute, www.independent.org, 1990.

2. Harold Demsetz, "Industry Structure, Market Rivalry and Public Policy," *Journal of Law and Economics*, April 1973.

3. Friedrich Hayek, *Individualism and Economic Order*, Henry Regency: Chicago, 1948.

4. George Stigler, "The Theory of Economic Regulation," *Bell Journal of Economics and Management Science*, Spring 1971.

> **CHAPTER CONTENT**
>
> 13.1 Land     190
>     13.1.1 Natural Resources     190
>     13.1.2 Common Ownership of Land     191
> 13.2 Labor     192
>     13.2.1 Labor as a Class of People     194
>     13.2.2 Clarifying the Meaning of Labor     194
> 13.3 Capital     195
>     13.3.1 Fixed Capital     195
>     13.3.2 Circulating Capital     196
>     13.3.3 The Process of the Use of Capital     197
>     13.3.4 Saving and Investment     198
>     13.3.5 The Multiplier Effect of Capital     199
>     13.3.6 The Importance of Capital     200

# 13 THE MEANS OF PRODUCTION

The means of production are land, labor, and capital. Some writers list others, but on examination they will be found to be merely a part of one or the other of the above, usually labor. Each of them is essential to extensive and orderly production of goods. Some people and even whole societies have over-valued one or the other of these, and undervalued the others. In the Middle Ages, for example, land was so highly valued that virtually all political power was based on its control. In the contemporary world, capital occupies the dominant role, though people often view it suspiciously and are rather ambiguous in their attitude toward it. In fact, they are each essential, and one could hardly be said to be more important economically than the other.

> **The means of production** are land, labor, and capital.

This is not to suggest, however, that one element cannot be more scarce than the others at a given time resulting in a higher cost in the market. Indeed, economy in production involves the greater or lesser use of each of these elements depending upon their relative scarcity or plenty. For much of the nineteenth century, land was the most abundant of the elements in America. In much of Europe, during the same period, labor was relatively more abundant than land or capital. Thus, in America, land was much more prodigally used than in Europe. By contrast, in Europe, land was conserved, intensively cultivated, heavily fertilized, and used generally only for its highest uses. Capital was generally the scarcest of the elements in America; thus, it was sparingly used. Economy of production dictates that the "mix" of land, labor, and capital vary depending upon which is relatively scarcer and which is relatively more plentiful. Thus, which is more valuable is not a question to be decided once and for all. They are all ultimately essential and hence equally valuable. At any given point in time, the value of one or the other depends upon relative scarcity. In other words their value depends upon their supply and demand.

We turn now to an examination of each of the means of production in detail.

## 13.1 Land

land—*see definition, p. 65.*

**Land** is essential to all material production. That is, all material goods are made from ingredients found on or beneath the surface of the earth. Some goods are referred to as man made, but that is somewhat misleading, for they are still made from materials drawn from the land. For example, shoes may be made from oil derivatives, and the oil from which the derivatives are made is found beneath the surface of the earth usually. Paper may be made from wood pulp, but it is grown as trees on the surface of the earth. Water, which is used almost universally in all production, might be thought to be an exception. After all, it comes to the earth as precipitation. But the water we actually use is drawn from collections on the surface of the earth or beneath it.

The role of the land in material production is so universal that it is no surprise that some people have rated it as most important. Farmers are likely to value the land highest of the three elements. They are the ones that usually work closest with the soil and can see how much their produce depends on it. After all, nothing grows, or at least produces food itself, unless it is either rooted in the soil or otherwise has access to the minerals that are found in soil. Coalminers are also dependent upon the land for their livelihood, for the coal is found in deposits in the land. Every undertaking requires the use of land in some way. Land is necessary as a place from which to operate. It contains the material ingredients with which we work. However, many people do not deal with the land as directly as farmers and spend their time working with materials that have been greatly altered by man. Thus, they travel in automobiles, made by man, on streets paved with concrete, asphalt, and the like, work with machines that are products of human technology, and so on. Thus, they are apt to be more impressed with man's alterations than the original ingredients of what they use.

> **Land** is essential to all material production. That is, all material goods are made from ingredients found on or beneath the surface of the earth. Some goods are referred to as man made, but that is somewhat misleading, for they are still made from materials drawn from the land.

### 13.1.1 Natural Resources

**natural resources**—materials that exist in nature, such as coal or oil, for which valuable uses have been found. It should be pointed out, however, that whether a material is a resource or not generally depends upon some use having been discovered or made of it.

Some of the materials found in the land are referred to as **natural resources**. This is especially so for some of the minerals found beneath the surface of the earth. The phrase is somewhat misleading and can lead to dubious conclusions. Materials found in nature only become resources when some use is found for them. Whether a river is an obstacle or a resource depends much on whether you are traveling by land and wish to cross it, or have a boat and are using it as a navigable stream. Oil was considered a natural pollutant and hardly used at all until after the 1860s, yet today it is thought of as a prime natural resource. That is because ways were found for refining and using it, ways that did not exist in 1860. Drilling rigs were devised and developed that would bring the oil to the surface from ever greater depths. It was first refined to produce such products as kerosene for lamps, and grease for axles. It could also be burned for heat as well, once furnaces had been developed. The invention of the internal combustion engine provided a greatly expanded market for gasoline, another derivative of oil refinement. Oil became the main lubricant for motor oil. None of these things existed in nature except crude oil; they were the results of mechanical and other inventions and developments. It was only after these things had occurred that oil became a prime natural resource.

The notion of natural resources has been mischievously applied to account for the wealth or poverty of nations. Many American historians, for example, have attributed the wealth of America to the abundant natural resources. It is true, of course, that various sorts of natural materials are unevenly distributed among the nations of the earth. Some countries, such as Saudi Arabia, have abundant reserves of oil. Especially fertile land is located in large concentrations only here and there on the earth. The United States does have great reserves of coal. Some Pacific islands have an abundance of tree and bush bearing fruits. However, the larger truth is that any extensive country has a considerable variety of natural materials. The great difference lies in how well a people use their ingenuity, inventiveness, and industry to turn natural materials into usable goods.

Britain was the most prosperous nation in the world for much of the nineteenth century, yet the tight little isle is not now thought to be especially blessed with what are called natural resources. The prosperity of the Japanese from the 1960s through the 1980s is legendary, yet Japan has few "natural resources." Moreover, Hong Kong is built on nothing more than a large rock and yet became one of the wealthiest places on planet earth. By contrast, the vast natural materials of the former Soviet Union and of Africa in general have not resulted in widespread prosperity for the inhabitants of those places. Nations do have different degrees of natural advantages, but we must look elsewhere to explain wealth and poverty.

> The notion of **natural resources** has been mischievously applied to account for the wealth or poverty of nations. However, the larger truth is that any extensive country has a considerable variety of natural materials. The great difference lies in how well a people use their ingenuity, inventiveness, and industry to turn natural materials into usable goods.

### 13.1.2 Common Ownership of Land

One way that land is distinct from the other means of production is that it cannot be expanded or increased. There is only so much of it on the planet. It can be improved, of course, by cultivation, by terracing, or by planting legumes on it. The amount of land under cultivation can be increased by cutting down the forest, draining swamps, or even building dikes to hold back the sea. It can be intensively cultivated, or not. It can be put to different uses. More people can live on a particular acreage by constructing multi-storied buildings. But, ultimately, the amount of it is fixed.

There is another and perhaps more distinctive feature of land. Alone among the goods of this earth, it was not made by man. It was here before man and is of God's provenance. Ever since people began to think in economic terms, or in politico-economic terms, these facts have posed a considerable economic problem. Why, if humans did not make land, should particular people have the rewards from producing something on a particular piece of it? Should all land not be considered the common property of all people, and its produce equally shared? Those who argue from these premises do not usually cut so wide a swath with their arguments. In the contemporary world, at least, they are much more apt to confine themselves to gross inequities in land ownership in some particular countries. The cry has often been raised against large landlords, whose lands, it is charged, should be broken up and distributed among those who occupy them. Communists, of course, generally claim that all except one's own personal possessions should be commonly owned. Marxists have focused upon the instruments of production, and land is certainly one of those.

The conclusions do not necessarily follow from the premises. We can all agree that the land is a given, so to speak, that man did not make it, and that any claim he may lay to it does not arise from his having produced it. It does not follow, however, that he may not have a good title to it. The basic situation is this. Someone, or some authority, must have the disposal of the land if it is to be utilized. Someone must decide who is to occupy it. If it is to be cultivated, someone must decide when it is to be planted, when cultivated, and when harvested. Moreover, someone must decide how the harvest is to be distributed. Someone must perform such work as occurs upon the land, and his compensation must be determined. There is yet one other stubborn fact. Much of the land is now owned by those who either purchased it or acquired it by inheritance. Is that which has been legitimately acquired by the present owners to be taken from them by force?

What all such theories entail is something like this. If we could begin anew, wipe out all civilization and developed cultures, strike all deeds to property, alter all the prejudices, inclinations and beliefs of men, a just distribution of the land would be to hold land in common. Such assaults on civilization have been and are being made. They are usually undertaken by dictators who claim to be acting for some political party, usually the communist cause. It is of more than a little interest that their activities have not resulted in anything resembling **common ownership** of land. On the contrary, the government usually owns the land, and some sort of bureaucracy disposes and directs the use of it. Common ownership is a will-of-the-wisp. It is contrary to the nature of man and the nature of things.

In any case, land is an element of production. It is essential to production, but there is no way to calculate its contribution except for its price in the market, which includes the value of all of its fruits.

> **Getting the Point...**
>
> Is common ownership of land a reasonable policy suggestion? Why or why not?

**common ownership**—*see definition*, p. 50.

## 13.2 Labor

It is not difficult to understand why earlier economic thinkers might have concluded that **labor** is the prime element of production. Throughout the long span of history, labor (both of human beings and of beasts of burden) has probably been the most obvious component of all production. Labor is what we do, and because we receive the payment for all goods, it is easy enough to suppose that we are being paid for our labor in exchanges. Adam Smith quoted with approval a statement made by David Hume, a philosopher whose work preceded his, to the effect that "Everything in the world is purchased by labour," Smith himself said:

**labor**—*see definition*, p. 65.

> The value of any commodity, therefore, to the person who possesses it, and who means not to use or consume it himself, but to exchange it for other commodities, is equal to the quantity of labour, which it enables him to purchase or command. Labour, therefore, is the real measure of the exchangeable value of all commodities.

Smith went on to elaborate on his position:

> The real price of every thing, what every thing really costs to the man who wants to acquire it, is the toil and trouble of acquiring it. What every thing is really worth to the man who has acquired it, and who wants to dispose of it or exchange it for something else, is the toil and trouble which it can save to himself, and which it can impose upon other people. What is bought with money or with goods is purchased by labour, as much as what we acquire by the toil of our own body. That money or those goods indeed save us this toil. They contain the value of a certain quantity of labour which we exchange for what is supposed at the time to contain the value of an equal quantity. Labour was the first price, the original purchase—money that was paid for all things . . . .

It is by no means clear exactly what Adam Smith meant by the term "real price." He seems to be saying that when we boil it all down, remove all other considerations, the price of a thing is how much we would have to labor to acquire it—the "quantity" of labor that goes into acquiring the article. But he certainly did not mean that prices in the market are determined by the quantity of labor that goes into them. In a later chapter, he makes clear prices in the market are determined by bargaining and that they tend toward a price that would cover not only the wages but also the rent on land, the cost of capital, and profits of the producer. Supply and demand are taken into account as well in his equation. He probably meant no more than that labor is the prime element in the production of goods.

Even so, the notion that labor is the source of exchangeable value has proved to be a mischievous one. Later in time, Karl Marx developed a full-fledged **labor theory of value**, virtually ignoring the other means of production. As a result, he concluded that laborers were being exploited, i.e., taken unjust advantage of, not being paid what was their due. He developed an ideology of laborism, and it is this ideology that undergirds modern communism.

Labor is an essential element of production. Everything that is made available for human use or consumption is done so in some part by labor. This is true whether someone is gathering berries in the woods or producing automobiles in a factory. Even wild berries have to be picked before they are consumed, and anyone who has done that for very long has become aware of the fact that it is labor. Every good is produced or done by some mix of labor. Today, when so much of production is done by machines, those jobs that require a great deal of human labor are called **labor intensive**. But even where most of production is done by machines human labor remains a crucial and essential element.

**labor theory of value**—says that value is entirely determined by the amount of labor that goes into the production of the good. Or as Marx himself thought, the value of anything was the value of laboring power used in the production of it. Exactly what the value of laboring power is, is not known.

**labor intensive**—an undertaking that uses labor much more than land or capital in producing a good or service. For example, the writing of a book is by its nature labor intensive. By contrast, the transport of coal by railroad is capital intensive. The growing of cattle is land intensive.

> **Labor** is an essential element of production. Everything that is made available for human use or consumption is done so in some part by labor. This is true whether someone is gathering berries in the woods or producing automobiles in a factory.

### 13.2.1 Labor as a Class of People

By labor as an element of production, we mean much more than what is meant by Marxists and unionists. Labor unionists and Marxists refer to an alleged class of people when they say "labor." By labor they mean those who actually perform the work of production or directly providing services. Thus, laborers constitute factory workers, miners, operators of machines, teachers in the classroom, steamfitters, plumbers, truck drivers, barbers, and the like. They do not generally include members of professions, such as, physicians, dentists, and lawyers, though their exclusion appears to be arbitrary. In sum, when Marxists and labor unionists usually speak of the "working man" or "laborer" they generally refer to the hands-on producers and providers of goods and services.

All of the above are, of course, laborers, but the term "labor" in economics comprehends much more than hands-on work. It comprehends all labor of mind or hands that goes into the providing of goods and services. It comprehends inventors, managers, entrepreneurs, scientists, technicians, salesmen, architects, engineers, clerks, clergymen, farmers, cooks, and on through all those who have a part in the providing of goods and services. Labor, in these terms, is not a class concept at all. It embraces the human element that goes into production.

### 13.2.2 Clarifying the Meaning of Labor

Technically, and in economic terms, labor does not include the work of lower animals or of human slaves. Slaves and lower animals, such as draft horses, would be classified as capital among the means of production. This point may become clearer after the discussion of capital and the distribution of wealth, but it needed to be made here nonetheless. The crucial distinctions for classification is that human slaves and horses (or other beasts of burden) are bought and sold in the market and are not compensated for their work. Thus, they are capital, not labor. To enslave another human being is to steal his labor, thus turning him into a commodity. This is clearly immoral, and now, thankfully, an illegal act.

Labor, it may be repeated, is an essential of production. In this regard, it is ranked with land and capital, but not necessarily more important than the other elements. All payments, whether for land, labor, or capital, are made to human beings, of course. Thus, the fact that labor is provided by human beings does not place it in some more basic or more important category than the other elements. Quite probably, some people do think in terms of how much time they had to spend at work to earn their money and even make calculations among other goods as to how much they cost in terms of hours or days of work. Estimates of such things sometimes appear in the news or in books, especially in comparing the time a worker in some communist land must work to acquire some good with the time of American workers. But such calculations, it must be emphasized here, involve only one of the means of production.

## 13.3 Capital

**Capital** is any good that has been produced that is then utilized in the production of some other good. Once labor is applied to land, it becomes capital. It is a somewhat blurrier concept than are the other means of production, or at least its meaning is rather easily blurred. One reason is that the term is often not used with much precision, but part of the difficulty lies in the concept itself. We all understand what land is. Moreover, we grasp what labor is, though it is not itself a physical object. Capital, on the other hand can only be defined, or delimited, by function. The traditional definition is that capital is "produced wealth used in further production." Since land is not produced, it is distinct from capital in that regard. And, human beings are not wealth, absent slavery, and thus their labor is distinct from capital. The role of money in relation to capital is more difficult to sort out. Undoubtedly, money is used to invest in capital goods and, thus, is often confused with capital. The truth is, however, that money is merely serving its purpose as a medium of exchange as we have already seen. It is, therefore, best to restrict capital to the capital goods themselves, and treat any money that has not yet been spent on them as neutral.

One thing should be clear: capital has become increasingly important during the modern era. It has always been important, but it has played an ever more dominant role in recent times. In the minds of many people it has come to dwarf both land and labor in production. We must insist, however, that land and labor remain essential to production and that whatever may be its present standing in some people's evaluation capital is like them only to be rated as a coequal element in production. All the above may become clearer by examining some of the aspects and kinds of capital.

*capital—see definition, p. 66.*

> The traditional definition is that **capital** is "produced wealth used in further production." Since land is not produced, it is distinct from capital in that regard. And, human beings are not wealth, absent slavery, and thus their labor is distinct from capital. The most basic way to think of capital is as goods used in the production of goods.

### 13.3.1 Fixed Capital

The most basic way to think of capital is as goods used in the production of goods. Often times these goods take the form of tools. In this sense, capital may equally well be thought of as the implements or instruments of production. Although we may think of tools mainly as hand implements, such as a hammer, used to perform relatively simple operations, machines and much else may also be thought of as tools. All tools are not capital instruments, of course. Knives, forks, and spoons, for example, are usually implements for consumption when used in the home. However, there are times when they are capital. The difference is determined by whether the tool is used to produce a good for sale in the market rather than for the ends of the final consumer. If they are used in the preparation and provision of a meal by a restaurant then they are capital. It is all a matter of use in deciding whether a given tool is a capital good or a consumer good. Even so, it is helpful to think of capital as tools. In this sense, these capital goods are best referred to as fixed capital.

To understand the role of tools, it will be helpful to think at first of performing some of the operations of production without tools. Some could be done without some sort of tools; others could hardly be done at all. We might consider how farming was once done without certain tools. It involved the pulling, tying, and drying of fodder from corn. Fodder was dried and fed to horses and mules. It was made from the blades or leaves on the cornstalk. These blades provided the food for the growth of the ear of corn. When the ear was grown, the blades that were still green and could be stripped away with little harm to the ear. When enough blades of the corn had been stripped away to make a handful, these were tied into a "hand" by using a few of the blade tops. The tassel of a cornstalk was broken off by hand and the "hand" of fodder was hung on the stalk to dry. When the "hands" had dried, they were tied into a bundle, three or more hands to the bundle, tied again with the blades of corn. The bundles were then stacked for transporting to shelter. Actually, the bundles could have been carried to shelter by someone, but usually tools were brought into play at this point. A wagon pulled by one or more mules or horses was brought into the field to haul the fodder to the barn.

It is difficult to imagine performing many tasks, even simple ones, unaided by tools. Imagine, for example, driving a nail into wood without a hammer! It simply could not be done with the bare hand, at least not through very hard wood for much depth. The most we can think of, when presented with the problem, is some poor substitute of a primitive instrument, such as a rock, for driving the nail. Or, try to imagine cutting down a tree, or cutting away dead limbs, or cutting the tree into lengths without an ax or a saw. These are not simply labor-saving tools, they are essential to doing the job. The hammer is essential to the carpenter. The ax and saw are essential to the woodsman, though power driven chain saws can now do most of the work once done with an ax. The ax, or something like it, is still essential to splitting wood.

There are some tasks, that can be done by hand alone, but they are laborious, time consuming, and not very productive. Others are very nearly impossible to do without tools. Simple hand tools, while invaluable in many instances, may not take us very far either. Hand power is quite limited as are simple tools for production. To understand the full role of capital we must look not only to more complicated machines but to technology and methods as well.

### 13.3.2 Circulating Capital

Before doing so, it would be well for us to consider another distinction in our discussion of capital. Namely, some capital is best categorized as circulating capital. That is, production processes use fixed capital; factories, equipment, tools and the like; to work with various materials that eventually become a finished product. All of the inventories of materials and finished products are also capital assets. The difference is that these goods are flowing through the production process rather than remaining stationary in it. This is the reason for referring to them as circulating capital goods. For example, consider an automobile manufacturing plant. The factory itself along with all the machines and tools in it represent the fixed capital. Those tools are used on and with other goods that move through the process that ultimately results in a finished automobile. For instance, coils of steel arrive at the plant and are placed at the foot of large machine presses. The sheet metal is used to stamp out fenders, hoods and other parts that will later be used in the assembly process. The steel is a form of circulating capital that will eventually leave the plant as a part of the automobile being made. The final automobiles will be held in inventory until they are sold to dealers. The dealers will then hold them in inventory until they are sold to the final consumers of the product.

### 13.3.3 The Process of the Use of Capital

The making of goods or the provision of a service entails all the tools, machinery, equipment, and shops or buildings used for the purpose. These constitute the capital of any particular undertaking. The actual process of production brings all of this equipment into play. We are discussing the array of equipment, or capital goods, at this point, not the organization of personnel that provide the labor. The discussion of the latter will come in the following chapter. The idea here is to view how different equipment is used in the production process and how goods flow through it.

Take a plumber, for example. His basic work is to provide an assortment of services having to do with plumbing. To that end, he will probably have a shop in which he may store his equipment as well as some merchandise he may have for sale. He will have a van or some sort of truck to enable him to take the necessary equipment to a particular job. He will have among his equipment such devices as a blowtorch, plunger, a variety of wrenches, pipe, glue, hacksaws, seals, seating devices, washers, and parts of plumbing that customarily wear out. These things constitute his capital for completing a service known in general as plumbing.

At much more complex levels, there are great factories, housed in huge buildings, having many complex machines, a multitude of motors, even perhaps assembly lines. There are steel mills, flour mills, cereal mills, cotton mills, factories in which television sets, washers and dryers, motors, hand tools, and every sort of thing is made or assembled. Each of these will have its complement of equipment for the process of making and assembling whatever may be involved, designed and assembled with that process in view.

As common as this business of assembling tools and machinery to assist in producing goods may be, there is an important aspect of it that may not be noticed at first. It is an indirect way to go about obtaining goods, or, as the Austrian economist, **Eugen von Böhm-Bawerk**, said, it is a **roundabout** way to produce goods. Let him describe the roundaboutness, as he did in his work, *Capital and Interest*:

> A farmer needs and desires drinking water. There is a spring at some distance from his house. In order to meet his requirements he may follow any one of several procedures. He may go to the spring and drink from his cupped hands. That is the most direct way. Satisfaction

---

**Eugen von Böhm–Bawerk, (1851–1914)**

Austrian economist and finance minister in the government. He was born in Austria, studied law at the University of Vienna, and political science at several German universities. Böhm-Bawerk taught economics for a while but then entered government services where he was appointed Finance Minister. He left government in 1904 to teach at the University of Vienna. As an economist, he helped to develop the economic theory known as Austrian Economics and emphasized free markets, free trade, and the primacy of the consumer. His best known work is the three-volume Capital and Interest. He contested the theories of Karl Marx and other socialists, rejected the labor theory of value and emphasized instead the subjective nature of value.

---

**roundabout**—in economics, roundabout refers to how much labor went into producing capital needed to produce some good. When a great deal more labor is required to produce the capital needed, the method is more roundabout.

is the immediate consequence of his expenditure of labor. But it is inconvenient, for our farmer must travel the distance to the spring as often during the day as he feels thirsty. Moreover it is inadequate, for this method never enables him to gather and store any considerable quantity such as is required for a variety of purposes. Then there is a second possibility. The farmer can hollow out a section of log, fashioning it into a bucket, and in it he can carry a full day's supply of water to his house all at once. The advantage is obvious, but to gain it he must go a considerable distance on a roundabout course. It takes a whole day's carving to hollow out the pail; to do the carving it is necessary first to fell a tree; to do the felling he must first procure or make himself an axe, and so forth. Finally, there is a third possibility for our farmer. Instead of felling one tree, he fells a number of them, hollows out the trunks of all of them, constructs a pipe line for them, and through it conducts an abundant stream of spring water right to his house. Clearly, the roundabout road from expenditure of labor to attainment of water has become considerably longer, but to make up for it, the road has led to a far more successful result. Now our farmer is entirely relieved of the task of plying his weary way from house to spring burdened with the heavy bucket, and yet he has at all times a copious supply of absolutely fresh water right in the house.

To put the matter simply, the use of capital to produce goods is a roundabout way to get them. Certainly, production processes can be more complex and, therefore, more roundabout. Such roundabout production extends the time or cost greatly between the want and its fulfillment in consumer goods. There are goods that can only be produced in this roundabout way of assembling the tools or machinery to assist in doing the job. But whether we could have the good by another route or not, the use of capital is a roundabout, time consuming, and costly way to produce goods. Undoubtedly, there are advantages that may more than compensate for the roundabout production by capital but they do not change the distance, or the waiting time, between the want and the production of the consumer good.

### 13.3.4 Saving and Investment

The roundaboutness of production by using capital is important in several ways. It serves as justification for profit to those who provide the capital. If money is invested in capital it serves as part of the justification for interest on it. But, above all, it explains the role of saving and investment.

All capital must be acquired by **saving**. Capital is an indirect way to produce consumer goods—its object. The cost of all the indirection must be paid from savings. Savings are accumulated by deferring the gratification that consumer goods provide. This is easy enough to see where money is concerned. It may be more difficult to appreciate that the time spent in providing capital goods is an act of saving. For example, suppose a man stranded on an island spends time making a spear, which he plans to use to catch fish. His act of investing in the spear is also an act of saving, though monetary exchange is not involved. In basic terms, savings arise by

**saving**—the act of postponing consumption.

devoting time to producing capital goods rather than producing for consumption. Thus, the farmer who spent the days felling trees and hollowing them for pipes was not getting consumer goods directly. He was devoting his time to a project that would only bear fruit in the future. The plumber obtained his equipment by saving, or by borrowing from others who had saved. In the plumber's case, monetary exchange was involved as financial markets came into play to finance the purchases of capital. The owner of the saw mill and all the various equipment used in turning trees into planks bought it with savings, his and/or those of someone else. The principle remains the same whether the capital involved is that of a single carpenter or a huge system of factories owned by a giant corporation, whether the money raised was borrowed from a relative or was obtained by selling large numbers of stock.

The roundaboutness also accounts for our referring to money spent for capital goods as investment. If we buy a hamburger, a chocolate bar, a movie ticket, or a record, whether the money has been saved or not, the expenditure is *not* an investment. Only money put into some roundabout process in which the hope or expectation is that you will receive more in return is generally an investment. In one way, at least, the farmer providing water for his home could be a misleading example. He was to be a direct beneficiary of the consumer good that resulted. Many investors, however, may not want or have any particular desire for the consumer good that is to be produced. In a sense, the investment is made for others. From the investor's point of view, he is probably making it in the hope of profit. In any case, it is an investment because there is a time lapse between the spending of the money for capital and any return that may be realized.

### 13.3.5 The Multiplier Effect of Capital

Capital differs from land and labor in yet another important way. The amount of land is fixed and cannot be increased, though it can be utilized for higher (or, at least, more productive) purposes. Nor can the production of a given worker be greatly expanded. True, a given worker may become more skilled. Through specialization workers may produce considerably more individually than they could if they had to engage in all the processes of making everything they wanted. Still, the increase in the amount of work by a given worker is limited. There are only so many hours in the day, and all workers must spend some of them resting or sleeping, eating, and taking care of bodily needs.

By contrast, capital can be greatly expanded. As a result, production can be multiplied many times over. There are no known limits to the increase of production by the use of tools and machines. The limits at any particular time are the state of technology, the existence or availability of materials, and the limited wealth that can or will be disposed as capital. There is no need, however, to exaggerate the extent to which production can be expanded with capital. Capital is scarce, after all, as are labor and land. The important point is capital has a **multiplier effect**. Moreover, as savings expand, capital tends to be accumulated, enhancing the productive efforts of people generally.

**multiplier effect of capital**—when it is used, capital multiplies the output that is possible by labor. The effect is typically greater for capital that is more roundabout. For example, using a chainsaw greatly increases the number of trees a lumberjack can fell as compared to an ax.

This is easy enough to see where hand operated machinery is involved. When Eli Whitney invented the cotton gin and it came into use there was a large increase in the productivity of labor. Suddenly, a single man might separate as much lint from the seed as 50 people could do without it. Thus, we could say that the effect of the cotton gin immediately was to multiply by 50 the amount of the product from a given quantity of labor. Suppose, for example, that one woodsman with a chainsaw could cut 5 times as many logs as two men could with a crosscut saw. In that case, the chainsaw multiplied the product of one man's labor in cutting logs by 10. Or, a farmer operating a large tractor that pulls multiple fertilizer distributors and planters, gang plows, and large harvesting machines may produce a hundred or even a thousand times as much of some crop as could a large family without such equipment. It is not so easy to see that the effect of a given amount of labor is being multiplied in more extensive or more indirect processes. For example, a great printing press may be activated to print hundreds of thousands of books by pressing a button. Did the labor of pressing the button get multiplied by such an exponential figure? In a sense, it did, even if the amount of labor of doing that was small. In a larger sense, the labor of all those who had been involved in producing the book—the writer, the editors, the cover design artists, and all who had a hand in it—had been multiplied.

And, of course, the use of capital multiplies the goods that can be made available to consumers. There simply is no way that the population of the United States could have all the array of goods in the quantities that now pour forth with the technology that existed 50 years ago, to say nothing of the technology of a hundred or two hundred years ago. Americans today have goods that were not available to emperors 300 years ago. That is not because people work harder today, nor because there is more land available today. It is because of inventions, the advance of technology, or, to state it more directly, it is because of the extensive and intensive use of capital.

Let us take an example to illustrate the point. In a 2015 annual report, Delta Airlines stated that it had assets worth just over $53 billion. During that same year, it employed a full-time equivalent of 83,000 employees. This works out to a capital investment of around $640,000 per employee. Of course, some employees work with less capital than others while some use much more. Take for instance the flight crew of a Boeing 777–200 aircraft. The purchase price for this aircraft was around $262 million, which means a sizable capital investment was put into the hands of a relatively few employees. What has been multiplied has been the number of people that can be transported at high speed and usually in great comfort. Henry Grady Weaver described the process by noting that "man's material progress *depends* on natural resources *plus* human energy *multiplied* by tools."

What this multiplier effect means for workers is that their income tends to increase as the amount of work they can do by using machines is multiplied. People who operate huge earthmoving machines are usually paid much more than a person using a shovel. The main reason for that is that the man operating the machine can move thousands of times as much dirt as can a man with a shovel. Wages tend to rise as more capital is effectively employed. A pilot of a large airliner earns far more than, say, a cab driver. The reason why he earns more is because the capital he uses greatly enhances his productivity.

### 13.3.6 The Importance of Capital

It is hardly surprising that the multiplier effect of capital combined with the relative ease of operating machines has produced a great enthusiasm for capital. The rapid rise of computer technology and the devices that use it, capture this enthusiasm at the level where it is the greatest. Today, everyone uses these devices in some capacity. In fact, most people cannot imagine a world without cellphones, automobiles, washing machines, microwaves, computers, or the many other machines we use daily. True, the everyday person may not think of these devices as capital.

---

**Getting the Point . . .**

Summarize some characteristics of capital that make it important to production.

Nevertheless, whenever they are used to produce other goods they are a means of production.

More broadly, the whole world in the twentieth century is engrossed in, or, at least, busily seeking for and spending capital. That is not to suggest capital has gone unchallenged in this century. Opponents have ranged from those who have denounced mechanical contrivances as gadgets to communists who vociferously denounced capital. The Austrian economist, Ludwig von Mises, once wrote a piece entitled "The Anti-Capitalist Mentality," which pointed out how capitalists have often been depicted as villains in movies, plays, stories, and the like. Unionists, too, have often denounced those whom they described as "capitalists." Undoubtedly, private capitalists have been portrayed badly, since the late nineteenth century. But much of this was opposition to big business or businessmen of great wealth, to capitalists of the more conspicuous variety, rather than to capital, *per se*. Since the mid-twentieth century the thirst for capital has been evinced by most of the nations of the world, and they have exerted themselves in many ways to obtain it. Much of the opposition to private capitalists may remain, but it hardly entails any aversion to capital.

The broader aspects of this will be discussed in the following section of the book. The matter is brought up here only as it concerns the relative value of land, labor, and capital. There have been economists who were so pro-capital that they believed that expenditures for capital were always socially beneficial. Looking at the matter from the point of view of the multiplier effect, it is not difficult to see how they might arrive at this conclusion. Some who are inclined to this view have even denied the possibility of **technological unemployment**, i.e., people put out of work by machines. Undoubtedly, machines may replace humans in the production of certain goods; else they would not be labor-saving devices. Nor does it necessarily follow that other jobs, such as making and servicing the machines, would offset the loss of jobs to machines. If that were so, it could hardly be argued that the machines had saved labor.

Just the same, in a world of scarcity coupled with economic freedom, such labor savings give rise to a host of new entrepreneurial efforts that produce goods henceforth unavailable. These activities do give rise to new employment opportunities in the course of time. There is no need for artificial interference by outside or governmental forces in favor of any of these means of production.

It is one of the virtues of a free market that it tends to signal the relative scarcity of the means of production. For example, when wages rise relative to rents and interest, we might conclude that labor has become scarcer than land and capital, as a rough measure. Shifts to other elements might then be indicated. Or, if interest rates rise in relation to wages and rents, we can conclude that capital has become scarcer.

To return to the point at hand, any ingrained preference for capital is a prejudice. If this prejudice becomes the basis of political action or otherwise results in greater use of capital than a free market would indicate, technological unemployment could indeed result. Such prejudices and such government interventions have been widespread in the twentieth century, and they will be surveyed in the following section of the book. It is appropriate here only to call attention to these possibilities.

Here, it is only necessary to reiterate a point about capital that has already been made about land and labor. All three of the elements are essential to extensive production. Land and labor remain essential regardless of the advance in technology. The surge of invention and technological innovation in our era has dramatically illustrated the dramatic impact of the multiplier effect from the effective use of capital. It is not surprising that many should have become enamored of capital. But the purpose of

**technological unemployment**—idea that people can be put out of work with the increase of technology and the use of machines.

economy is not to achieve greater production, as such. Economy is concerned primarily with producing those goods that are most wanted with the *least* expenditure of the scarce means of production. That includes capital as well as land and labor. To turn the point around, it is economical to employ available workers so long as their contribution will cost less than the generally highly expensive roundabout approach of using capital. To overvalue either production or capital will tend to result in imbalances.

---

*We do not assert that the capitalist mode of economic calculation guarantees the absolutely best solution of the allocation of factors of production. Such absolutely perfect solutions of any problem are out of reach of mortal men. What the operation of a market not sabotaged by the interference of compulsion and coercion can bring about is merely the best solution accessible to the human mind under the given state of technological knowledge and the intellectual abilities of the age's shrewdest men.*

**Ludwig von Mises**

*What our generation has forgotten is that the system of private property is the most important guarantee of freedom, not only for those who own property, but scarcely less for those who do not. It is only because the control of the means of production is divided among many people acting independently that nobody has complete power over us, that we as individuals can decide what to do with ourselves.*

**Friedrich August von Hayek**

*Whoever prefers life to death, happiness to suffering, well-being to misery must defend without compromise private ownership in the means of production.*

**Ludwig von Mises**

# Study Guide for:

# 13 The Means of Production

## Chapter Summary

There are three factors of production. They are land, labor, and capital. All material goods are ultimately made from raw materials. Thus the category of land not only includes the use of the term in the common way, but also includes raw materials that are used in production.

Regarding the resources of a nation, it is not so much the availability of particular resources that makes a country wealthy, as it is the ingenuity of the people of the area to make good uses of them. The truth of this proposition can be made apparent by numerous historical illustrations. For example, the Soviet Union at its height controlled tremendous natural resources, yet its economic productivity lagged far behind that of Japan, which is extremely limited in its land mass and the natural resources at its disposal.

Labor is another fundamental factor of production. As used by economists, the term is not limited to those individuals who are working in some manual endeavor under the supervision of managers. Rather, the term is meant to embody all work of the mind or body that goes towards the provision of some good or service. Therefore, all professions constitute labor.

In the past, many economists theorized that labor was the sole factor giving rise to the value of a product. But this labor theory of value is significantly flawed and fails to adequately explain market prices. Furthermore, it ignores the contribution to production made by the other factors and also ignores the subjective values placed on different goods by consumers.

Capital is the other factor of production. Capital is produced wealth that is used in further production. It may also be thought of as the tools used in production. Thus, a personal computer with a word processing package is capital equipment for the writer. Or, a table saw is capital equipment when used by a carpenter in the process of making cabinets. But it also includes eventual consumer goods that are moving through the production process. Thus, we can distinguish between the fixed capital of tools and equipment and the circulating capital of inventories.

There are a variety of ways to accomplish most productive endeavors. Yet when one method has been decided upon it usually requires specific capital arranged in a specific way. The more capital employed the more roundabout production is said to be. Furthermore, the use of capital has generally increased the fruits of production.

Capital is amassed by saving. Saving is the postponement of present consumption to a future date. If all goods produced today were consumed today then it is obvious that there could be no new capital produced. Thus, if we are to employ capital we must first save. Capital tends to be consumed by use as do other goods. Therefore, its eventual replacement must be prepared for in advance if production is to be maintained.

## Points of Emphasis

1. There are three means of production: land, labor, and capital.

2. The term land is used broadly and refers to all raw materials that are used in production.

3. Among economists, the term natural resources has become a popular synonym for land, but this use may be misleading since not all actual resources in nature are used in production. Furthermore, some resources are a hindrance to production.

4. The term labor refers to all work of the mind and body that goes towards the production of some good or service.

5. The labor theory of value is untenable.

6. The production of capital requires saving, which is postponed consumption.

7. One benefit from capital is that it tends to multiply the productive efforts of labor.

## Identification

1. land
2. common ownership
3. natural resources
4. labor
5. labor theory of value
6. labor intensive
7. capital
8. roundabout
9. saving
10. multiplier effect of capital
11. technological unemployment

## Review Questions

1. Why are the terms "land" and "natural resources" not interchangeable?
2. Why is there an incentive to conserve the use of raw materials for production?
3. The wealth of a nation is not the direct result of the abundance of natural resources available in the country. Why not? Give an example that illustrates this point.
4. Why is saving necessary for the production and use of capital? What would happen if people stopped saving? What are some ways to obtain needed capital without saving your own wealth?
5. Select a particular business and describe the different means of production they use. Show examples of land, labor, and capital.

## Activities

1. Prepare a case either to support or oppose the plausibility of the following reasoning: "Last night Arthur Deco finished painting a picture that he spent 48 hours working on. He recently read that one of Rembrandt's paintings sold for $2,400,000. From his study of history, Art knows that it only took Rembrandt 32 hours to complete his masterpiece. Based on his estimates of how much work he has put into his painting, Art expects to sell it for $3,600,000. If the art gallery fails to find a buyer at this price he is thinking of suing the gallery for discriminating against artists."

2. Historically, socialism has sought government control and/or ownership of the means of production. Write a one- to two-page paper describing the differences you see between government and individual ownership/control of one or more particular means of production.

> **Chapter Content**
>
> 14.1 The Role of the Entrepreneur 206
> 14.2 Raising the Money 208
>     14.2.1 Partnerships 208
>     14.2.2 Corporations 209
>     14.2.3 The Stock Market 211
>     14.2.4 Lending Institutions 213
> 14.3 Organizing to Produce 214
>     14.3.1 The Factory System 214
>     14.3.2 The Downside of the Factory System 216
>     14.3.3 Home Based Businesses 217
>     14.3.4 Segregating Commercial and Residential Areas 219
>     14.3.5 Economies of Scale and Specialization 220
>     14.3.6 Managers 221

# 14 The Entrepreneur and Production

At this point, we should put greater emphasis upon the human elements in production. Thus far, the elements that go into production have been discussed more or less abstractly, minus the flesh and blood, the uncertainties, the risks, and much that is particularly human. Such things are dependent upon individual traits, and are subject both to genius and to error. The point is to see the business of production pulled together, to see it as a unified process under the control of people. Much of economics has to do with analysis, with taking things apart, but it is necessary also to show how they are brought together to result in particular goods and services. This is the main subject matter of the organization of production.

Of course, all production is done by people, directed by people, and for people. It is possible to speak of producing for the market, but that is only an intermediate stage, for ultimately all production aims at producing for consumers, i.e., for people. It is possible to speak of people either as producers or consumers, but these are aspects of human activities, not classes of people. Everyone is a consumer. Not all people produce during the whole course of their lives. Infants cannot ordinarily produce in an economic sense; some people are or become disabled at various times in their lives. Even so, most people at most times are both producers and consumers to some degree. At any rate, consumption is dominant in all economic activity; it is the end of production. The differences, peculiarities, and varying tastes and wants of people are continually at work in the market. Just so, the differing inclinations, aptitudes, temperaments, skills, and means of people are at work in production, either advancing or retarding it.

The main concerns here are with how the means of production are brought together, how they are organized for production, how the means of production are obtained, and how workers are managed or directed in producing goods. There are a great many ways of doing these things, and these ways will be surveyed here.

## 14.1 The Role of the Entrepreneur

**entrepreneur**—an individual who undertakes to organize the production of a particular good at his own personal risk of economic loss.

The central role in the organization of production belongs to the **entrepreneur**. The term is derived from a French word that means to undertake, and is most precisely defined as "one who undertakes to carry out any enterprise." More broadly, his role is that of the "person who assembles the various means of production, and by mobilizing them, renders them operative and useful. He is a promoter or initiator of production." In short, the entrepreneur pulls together the means of production and arrays them in such a way that a product or service is the result.

The entrepreneur is the decision-maker of an enterprise. He decides the mix among land, labor, and capital, the amount to be spent for a location, for raw materials, for equipment, and for workers. He decides as well how all these are to be brought into play to produce goods. In contemporary business language the entrepreneur is the chief executive officer (CEO) of an enterprise. Directors of business, however, may range from a farmer who does all his work to the head of a large diversified corporation. What may strike an outsider about him are his independence and the power he wields over an organization. To the entrepreneur himself, he is apt to be much more aware of the perilous risks that he must take in making his decisions.

Undertaking to produce any good is a risky business. There is no certainty that it will sell well, even if it has sold in the past. The taste and wants of the buying public may shift and change. He may produce more than he can sell at the price he has in mind. Investment in new equipment may not work out. If he is making raincoats, the season for which he has produced them may be unusually dry. He may be producing a good that many buy on credit, and interest rates may rise. He must change to meet the competition, yet any change he may make increases his risks. Thus, the entrepreneur is a risk taker.

In the nature of things, the entrepreneurial role is performed in any enterprise by one person. That is not to suggest that he may not have assistance in performing his function. He may have a board of directors, accountants, technological experts, managers, company officers, budget directors, and other advisers to aid him. It is rather that ultimately someone must make the final decision, bear the responsibility, and take the risks. That person, whatever his title, is the entrepreneur in a firm. He may not personally have put up the money, manage the detailed operation, or have much knowledge of the technology. But he is the one person who has the final say. Two people cannot have the final say in the operation of a plant or firm. If there were three or more, they might operate by majority vote, of course, but committees are hardly well suited to the entrepreneurial function.

---

**The Role of the Entrepreneur**
In the nature of things, the entrepreneurial role is performed in any enterprise by one person. That is not to suggest that he may not have assistance in performing his function. It is rather that ultimately someone must make the final decision, bear the responsibility, and take the risks. That person, whatever his title, is the entrepreneur in a firm. He may not personally have put up the money, manage the detailed operation, or have much knowledge of the technology. But he is the one person who has the final say.

An entrepreneur may have the assistance of many advisers in performing his function. He may be the owner and operator, and the task of making decisions is the least of his work. Suppose he is a farmer, who has no hired help in farming. He must still decide what crops he is going to plant on which plots of land, when he is going to prepare the land, and when he would like to plant them. He must allot his time to see that the work of tending crops gets done as near the right time as possible. He must decide what new equipment to buy, how much he can afford to pay for it, when to harvest, and when to sell his crops. In short, he must make all the sorts of decisions that an entrepreneur must make, bear all the risks, and do the work as well.

Or, an entrepreneur may be a great industrialist, as **James J. Hill** was in building the Great Northern railroad. This was a vast undertaking, finally stretching from St. Paul–Minneapolis to the Pacific. He completed this great undertaking between 1878 and 1893, first buying small lines and linking them, then surging across the plateaus and mountains to the northern Pacific with a new roadbed. It is not possible to capture in one paragraph all he had to accomplish to finish this project. At a minimum, he had to persuade financiers to put up the money, hold off creditors with promises to pay, purchase the needed equipment, and hire and supervise the employees who completed the work. Albro Martin describes some of the energy that was required for this endeavor in his biography of James J. Hill, as he tells of an interlude during which Hill acquired a steamship line to transport goods on the Great Lakes to Buffalo, New York:

### James J. Hill (1838–1916)

American railroad builder and magnate who was born in Ontario province in Canada, but eventually settled in St. Paul, Minnesota. He began work in a village store at the age of 14 and eventually got involved in transportation as a clerk in a steamboat company. His earliest interest was in river transportation between Minnesota and Canada, but his future lay with the railroad, as did that of the country. He joined with other investors to buy the St. Paul and Pacific railroad, a company operating in Minnesota, and this road became the nucleus for his vast Great Northern system. The Great Northern reached from Lake Superior to the Puget Sound on the Pacific, was a landmark for free enterprise in transcontinental railroad building because he received no government aid, and was remarkably successful for such undertakings. Hill was known as the "Empire Builder" of the Northwest for his contribution to railroad building in that region.

> So the Manitoba road was going into the steamship business. Grain would proceed eastward, on the company's own line of Lake steamers, from Superior all the way to Buffalo, from which point it would enjoy highly competitive rates to the seaboard; and the steamers would return laden with coal, which the Northwest was demanding in vaster quantities each year. But what did Hill know about Lake steamers? He had kept abreast of shipbuilding . . . , in which the reduction in the cost of steel had revolutionized the industry, and he knew that steel ships, although they would cost twice as much as wooden ones, would pay for themselves that much faster. Mark A. Hanna, his old friend, was building steel Lake steamers at Cleveland, and when Hanna got wind that Hill wanted a fleet he wrote him that that moment, when steel prices were depressed, was the time to buy. . . . Hill wired him to lay the keels for four vessels at once. He sent his own man to oversee construction, but, as usual, took a direct hand in design and construction. . . .
>
> . . . Hill, in his haste to launch his fleet had done nothing about dock facilities at Buffalo, but he was greatly relieved to learn that Kennedy [an aide] had: "I saw Mr.

Sam Sloan, President of the Delaware, Lackawanna & Western Railroad Co., a short time ago . . . and he [said] that they would be very glad to give you all you need at Buffalo." The new ships were all to contain the word "Northern" in their names. . . . Hill met Hanna's request to pay up delinquent bills. . . .

Thus, in this side venture Hill busied himself in conceiving a steamship line, ordering the ships, overseeing their building, naming them, and seeing to it that the bills were paid. James J. Hill was an entrepreneur, *par excellence.*

## 14.2 Raising the Money

One of the tasks of an entrepreneur is to raise money. Sometimes individuals decide to fund their business through the saving of their own money. A man may save money until he has enough to buy a farm, open a service station, or start a restaurant. Undoubtedly, many people dream of doing such things, and some actually go through with it. More often than not, however, entrepreneurs will find it necessary to raise more money than they can possibly raise themselves. There are several ways he can do this and they mostly deal with how he organizes his business. Each way has its own advantages and disadvantages, which will be discussed further here.

### 14.2.1 Partnerships

A common way to start and maintain a business is to form a company with others who have put up money to finance it. One device for doing this is a **partnership**. Partners generally each put up the same amount initially and share equally in any profits of the firm. However, many businesses cannot be operated well as partnerships. As noted earlier, there is usually one head of an organization and to have two or more often poses problems, especially where entrepreneurship is involved. Thus, usually a company will have a single head. In a strict partnership, on the other hand, each of the partners shares in running the business. Typically, each may enter into contracts, commit funds, and make binding business decisions. If a partner knows there will be disagreement on some issue, he could decide to move forward without the consent of the other(s). Partners are also jointly responsible for the debts of the business. This extends beyond what each partner contributed to the business. In this case, the damage arising from one partner's poor decision exposes the others to unlimited liability.

**partnership**—a form of business organization where two or more people partner in an enterprise together.

> **Partners** generally each put up the same amount initially and share equally in any profits of the firm. They are also jointly responsible for the debts of the business. This extends beyond what each partner contributed to the business. In this case, the damage arising from one partner's poor decision exposes the others to unlimited liability.

It should be obvious from what has been said thus far that partners must have a great deal of trust in each other. Not only must partners trust one another with the money and reputation of the business, but, because of the joint responsibility, they must also trust each other with their own money and reputation. They must trust that no partner will act rashly, or be drawn into unwise schemes of one kind or another. Generally speaking, the partnership arrangement only works well when each partner is a working member of the firm, has a common background with the others, and is well known by the others.

While partners have more freedom when it comes to working out agreements internally, law governs certain rights and liabilities of the partners. Both the **common law** and some statutes passed by states govern partnerships. For example, partners have the option to limit their liabilities by switching from a full partnership to a limited liability partnership or LLP. However, with limited liabilities comes limited rights. Limited partners can share in the profits of the firm, while their liability is limited to the amount of their investment. They may not, however, make decisions binding upon the firm nor participate in the running of it.

> **common law**—the law that the King's courts began to develop in the twelfth century—a law common to all England. It replaced many local customs that frequently had the force of law and tended to bring all those in England under the same legal rules.

The partnership is, then, a very limited device for raising money to start and run a business. Very large undertakings have rarely, if ever, been financed that way. It works best for relatively small undertakings such as stores, garages, small shops, law firms, medical clinics, and the like. It can also work within family businesses where a father may admit one or more of his children as partners. Such arrangements may work well so long as the authority of the father is accepted, for they may not depart from the rule that a business should have a single head. But, in general, partnerships are only practical when all partners are actively involved in the business, and are as near as possible equals.

### 14.2.2 Corporations

The most widely used device for raising the money for business enterprises today is the **limited liability corporation**. Technically, a corporation is a fictitious "being" brought into existence by agreement of several individuals by legal authority. The corporation has an existence distinct from the individuals who formed it, invested in it, or comprise it in any way. At law, a corporation is a "person" in many respects. It can receive money, sue or be sued in the courts, own property, engage in undertakings in accord with its "charter" or certificate of incorporation. In earlier times, corporations were creatures of a monarch or king. At the present time, however, most corporations are formed by filing of articles of incorporation with the legal record-keeping body for the jurisdiction in which the corporation is located.

> **limited liability corporation**—a form of business organization whereby a legal entity is formed. The resulting firm's financial liability is limited to the funds invested in it.

---

A corporation is a fictitious "being" brought into existence by agreement of several individuals by legal authority. The corporation has an existence distinct from the individuals who formed it, invested in it, or comprise it in any way. At law, a corporation is a "person" in many respects. It can receive money, sue or be sued in the courts, own property, engage in undertakings in accord with its "charter" or certificate of incorporation.

The corporation has large advantages over other forms of organization as a money raising device. Its greatest attraction is that the liability of investors is limited, usually to the amount that they have actually invested. That is, those who invest in corporations are not usually personally responsible for the debts and obligations it may acquire. Their personal wealth cannot be tapped to pay the bills. If the corporation should go bankrupt, for example, the investors can usually walk away with their reputations more or less intact, their credit rating unaffected, and their personal belongings otherwise untouched. This is certainly much more attractive to an investor than a personally owned business or than being a partner in a business in which all that he has may be at risk. Indeed, a stockholder in a corporation may, if he chooses, not concern himself in the least with the business, if he is not an officer or director of it. Thus, it sometimes happens that hundreds of thousands, or even millions, of people own shares in some corporation.

The corporation did not, however, originate as a device for raising funds for private businesses. On the contrary, corporations were conceived as bodies "clothed with a public interest." Most often they were governmental or semi-governmental bodies. That usage continues to this day as most towns and city governments incorporated. On the basis of their incorporation, city officials are elected, ordinances are passed, taxes are levied and collected, and some of the powers of government are exercised. In like manner, charities, educational institutions, and the like, were also incorporated long before there were any business corporations.

In early America, businesses were sometimes incorporated for undertakings such as building bridges, roads, and other matters of public concern. They were usually incorporated for the express purpose of being able to raise funds by virtue of the limited liability. They were sometimes given a monopoly and were usually permitted to charge fees to recoup their investment and make a profit. During the various embargoes on trade from 1807–1811 and the following the War of 1812, many states wished to encourage domestic manufactures. Thus, a large number of business corporations were formed. At that time, an act of a state legislature was required for incorporation. Such a limitation invited corruption of public officials since incorporation was a special privilege. Such special privileges came under increasing political attack in the 1830s during the Jacksonian period. The result was that states began to pass general acts of incorporation making it available to any group of three or more people who filed articles of incorporation in accord with the general law. By the mid-nineteenth century, most states had such laws. Incorporation was still a privilege, but it was no longer a special one.

Corporations can raise money by selling stock or shares in the corporation. Two kinds of stock can be issued: **common stock** and **preferred stock**. Shares of ownership of the corporation are obtained by buying common stock. Common stockholders may vote in corporate elections. Preferred stock does not convey ownership but rather acquires a preferred position in any profits of the corporation. Common stockholders receive the remainder after obligations to preferred stock have been met. Corporations may also raise money by issuing bonds or by borrowing from lending institutions. Creditors have a claim on the assets of corporations should debt payments not be made. All the various securities, including common and preferred stock, are transferable at will, and there has been a great deal of activity in corporate securities as this form of business enterprise increased.

There are other aspects of the corporation that need mention as well. They may endure long beyond the life of their founders. Corporate charters today do not usually contain a termination date, and many of

**common stock**—shares in the ownership, control, and residue of the profits of a corporation. The liability of such owners is generally limited to the amount of their investment.

**preferred stock**—shares in the first claim to receive a dividend out of the profits of a corporation according to the terms of the contract. Preferred stockholders, as such, do not own or take part in control of the corporation.

them are specifically established in perpetuity. Even if they are not, the charters are easily renewed. Management of corporations is not tied to ownership. That is, managers need not own stock in the corporations that they manage. Stockholders choose a board of directors, who technically control it. They, in turn, appoint the operating managers who deal with the day to day business of the company. These frequently do own stock in the firm. The chief executive officer may, and sometimes does, own controlling interest in the corporation. But this is not necessary, and often managers only own a small portion of the stock, if any.

Nevertheless, the managers are responsible to the board of directors for their stewardship over the assets of the company. As such, their main concern should be to promote the interest of the shareholders of the firm since they own the company. Certainly, there can be conflicts of interest at this point since the managers are generally only partial owners. Whatever other criticisms that can be made against the corporate form of organization, it does provide a means of the formation of a large-scale business enterprise. The economic value of this is found in what economists call economies of scale (this will be defined and discussed more fully later in this chapter). That is, a large-scale business often makes it possible to produce a large volume of a product at a much lower cost per unit.

A simple example can help illustrate this point. Before the modern assembly line, automobiles were basically made in garages. Each car began by laying a frame on the floor and then parts were added to it until the car was complete. Henry Ford observed that he could assemble cars on a much larger scale at a much lower cost per unit by dividing the needed tasks between more workers. He accomplished this by moving the car through a process and stationing workmen at various places assigned with the tasks of adding specific parts. Ford's vision proved to be true and he was able to subsequently sell his cars to the public at a much lower price, thus gaining a much larger customer base than his competitors.

While the benefits of economies of scale are possible, there is a down side to the corporate structure. Let us call it "**corporate drag**." Large firms must be managed. To do so, they must set up various rules. In the process of doing this, they become bureaucratic. This results in inevitable inefficiencies of operation and tends to stifle the entrepreneurial spirit that once fueled their success. As a result, it is not uncommon to see large scale enterprises rise and fall over time.

**corporate drag**—large businesses develop rules and regulations to govern those acting in it. These typically become bureaucratic and tend to impede entrepreneurial human action.

### 14.2.3 The Stock Market

When most people say "the **stock market**," they are usually referring to some **stock exchange**. Most often, they are referring to the **New York Stock Exchange**. It is not the only stock exchange in the United States, much less the world. There is the American Stock Exchange, as well as stock exchanges in various cities. Moreover, there are great exchanges elsewhere in the world, such as London, Paris, Tokyo, and so on. But the New York Stock Exchange is the great exchange in the world, the bellwether of stock exchanges, though only a selected number of stocks are even offered for sale, or listed on it. Moreover, the **Dow Jones Industrial Average**, which is the most widely recognized barometer of stock prices, is calculated from a very small list of stocks.

The main point, however, is that the various stock exchanges, including the "over-the-counter" market do not constitute *the* stock market. Instead, they constitute the major portion of what we might more properly refer to as "the used stock market." That is, what is ordinarily offered for sale on stock exchanges is "used stock" that has come into the ownership

**stock market**—the broad array of institutional arrangements that allow for the trade of existing shares of stock issued by corporations.

**stock exchange**—a physical location where individuals meet together to buy and sell stock.

**New York Stock Exchange**—a private stock exchange located in New York City.

**Dow Jones Industrial Average**—a market measure of the prices of thirty of the largest corporations.

of someone who wishes to sell it. Newly issued shares of stock are not, as a rule, offered on stock exchanges. Indeed, new companies cannot get their "used" stock listed on most exchanges. The New York Stock Exchange lists only a highly selected number of older established companies whose stability and dependability has been demonstrated over a period of time.

So far as newly issued stock is concerned, the market is anywhere there is anyone interested in or willing to buy such newly issued shares of stock. There are investment banking houses that make offerings of and serve as brokers for newly issued stocks and bonds. They make it a business to deal in such securities. Anyone licensed to market securities may offer them for sale. Someone who is starting a company may sell shares to willing parties, members of his family, friends (or enemies), business acquaintances, or whoever.

The point of the above is that the financing for American business is not raised directly in stock exchanges. The funds do come, at least initially, from the sale of shares in corporations and the sale of bonds. This occurs, however, in what is called the investment banking process. Undoubtedly, the stock exchanges are an adjunct or an aid to the sale of stock for financial needs, though they are at some distance from the actual process. People who buy stock often wish to sell some portion or all of it from time to time. The decision to buy stock newly issued is no doubt affected by the transferability of the stocks and the possibility that they can probably be sold in some stock exchange. For stocks listed there, stock exchanges provide a ready market both for buyers and sellers, and enable owners of stock to liquefy their assets by selling them.

> **The Stock Market**
> The various stock exchanges do not constitute the stock market. Instead, they constitute the major portion of what we might more properly refer to as "the used stock market." That is, what is ordinarily offered for sale on stock exchanges is "used stock," which has come into the ownership of someone who wishes to sell it. The market for stock in new companies and for newly issued shares in older companies is anywhere there is anyone interested in or willing to buy such stock.

There are, however, social, economic, and possibly moral problems that arise from the activity on the stock exchanges. One of these problems arises from the fact that people tend to interpret prices and their fluctuations as signifying something for the economy generally. For example, rising stock prices are taken quite often to signify a coming period of prosperity. On the other hand, declining stock prices are interpreted sometimes as indicating depressed economic conditions. Strangely, people do not interpret the price of other goods that way, as a rule. If the price of potatoes falls, most people are glad enough, will buy more, if they like potatoes, and may even store some for future use. People flock to sales, looking for bargains. It is true that those who have some commodity for sale will not be likely to relish declining prices, but those who buy their potatoes, or whatever, are not apt to worry very much about the sellers.

Why should stocks be any different? They are, after all, a good, i.e., an investment. Unless the decline in the price follows a drop in dividends or signifies that the company is in trouble, declining prices should be good news for those buying stocks. They can now buy more shares than formerly, at no greater cost. No doubt, there are those who view the matter that way. But the prevailing interpretation, both among those who play the stock exchange and those who do not, is that declining prices generally signify economic trouble ahead. When stocks are rising it is called a "**bull market**;" when they are declining, it is called a "**bear market**." The bull market is generally preferred.

**bull market**—the situation where the prices of common stock are generally rising.

**bear market**—the situation where the prices of common stock are generally falling.

When people buy stock on the exchange they do so in hopes of gaining a return either through dividends or through an increase in the future price of the stock. As a general rule there should be some connection between the stock's current price and the likelihood of such gains.

However, this connection does not always hold true. As we have already seen, an artificial increase in the money supply disrupts market prices. This is especially true in the used stock market. As it most generally occurs, a monetary expansion by the Federal Reserve is most likely to give rise to a bull market that sends stock prices up well beyond the likelihood of any return to the owner that would warrant the price paid. Thus, such an expansion generally promotes an air of prosperity in stock ownership that will not be sustained. Nevertheless, the rapid speculation of increasing stock prices in the short term drives prices ever higher only to eventually crash. This is what took place in the 1920's and many times since. **Speculators** drove prices up from 1926–1929, but the game ended in October of 1929 when prices crashed. Once again we see the pernicious effects of the monetary expansion of the Federal Reserve.

**speculators**—people who buy or sell shares of stock based on expectations about their future prices.

> **Effects of Monetary Expansion on the Stock Market**
> As we have already seen, an artificial increase in the money supply disrupts market prices. This is especially true in the used stock market. As it most generally occurs, a monetary expansion by the Federal Reserve is most likely to give rise to a bull market that sends stock prices up well beyond the likelihood of any return to the owner that would warrant the price paid. Thus, such an expansion generally promotes an air of prosperity in stock ownership that will not be sustained. Nevertheless, the rapid speculation of increasing stock prices in the short term drives prices ever higher only to eventually crash.

### 14.2.4 Lending Institutions

Corporations raise money by issuing and selling common and preferred stock, by issuing bonds or debentures, and by borrowing it in more direct fashion. Two major sources of concentrated funds are banks and insurance companies. Fractional reserve banking has already been discussed at length and does not need further discussion here. It should be noted that banks are themselves limited liability corporations. In times past, however, bank stock was subject to double liability. That is, a stockholder could not only lose the amount he had invested but could be held liable for that much again if the bank got in trouble. That practice has generally been abandoned. At any rate, banks make operating loans and the like to businesses. Fractional reserve banking has long been considered as a means of fostering business expansion both directly and indirectly, directly through loans to businesses, and indirectly by sparking demand through loans to consumers.

Insurance companies take in huge amounts of money regularly through the payment of premiums. A portion of this money, especially that for life, term, and burial insurance, is not expected to be paid out for many years. Thus, a life insurance company may collect hundreds of millions, even many billions of dollars over the years. Some of it will be paid out, but much of it needs to be invested for shorter or longer periods of time. Insurance companies are a major source of business finance, by buying stocks and bonds and by making loans to businesses, as well as through money kept on deposit in banks. Insurance companies are often large businesses themselves. They are often private corporations, though there are mutual companies also, which are owned by their policyholders.

## 14.3 Organizing to Produce

How the money is raised for financing an organization tells us little about how it is organized to produce. In that sense, a family owned business need not differ in its organization for production from a partnership or a corporation. Nor does whether money is personally saved or borrowed from a lending institution tell us anything about the organization. A corporation may be a manufacturing company, run a railroad, be a medical clinic, be a nursery school, make movies, be a rental service, be a service station, or be a brokerage firm. Regardless of how a business is financed, it may be small, middle-sized or large. In short, financing is a separate and distinct activity from what is produced or how the production is organized.

All efficient production is organized, whether it is performed by one person or ten thousand, whether it is producing firewood or building jumbo jet airplanes. How it is organized depends on the product, the scale of the production, the technology used, the decisions of entrepreneurs, and probably custom. A farm is organized differently from a flour mill, for example. A cattle ranch is organized differently from a crop farm, and so on. Indeed, the production and sale of goods and services is almost as varied as the goods and services themselves.

There is not necessarily any one best way to organize to provide goods and services of particular kinds. Take the building of a house, for example. A house can be stick built. That is, assembled on the spot from lumber and other materials. On the other hand, houses can be prefabricated, transported to the site on trucks and assembled there by workmen. Or, if a mobile home be considered a house, they can be manufactured in a factory, prefabricated, assembled, finished, and furnished, before they are pulled to their sites. Or, it is possible to stick build the house generally but use certain pre-built or prefabricated parts, such as trusses for the roof, cabinets, and bathtub-shower cast units. Each of these approaches has its advantages and drawbacks; none of them has replaced older ways of building a house.

Despite the great variety of organizations for production, however, some approaches have loomed large both in economic literature and influencing other organizations. Such concepts as machine mass production, the assembly line, and computerized or robot production come to mind. Perhaps the most influential of all has been the factory system, so it needs to be considered a little more fully.

### 14.3.1 The Factory System

**factory system**—a process of production where goods are produced in a large volume in a factory thus consolidating the use of labor.

The **factory system**, as we know it, developed in the textile industry. The basic inventions that set the stage for it were made in Britain. These included spinning machines and power looms. They required more power to operate than a person could supply with his hands or feet. The development of the factory for textile manufacturing was largely an accident of the state of technology at the time. The most common means of supplying power for turning machines was the water wheel and connecting belts. They were already in use for sawmills, gristmills, and the like. The water wheel was usually placed beneath swiftly flowing water impounded by a dam. The textile mill was in an adjoining building that housed the spinning and weaving machines. Such mills were built in considerable number, mostly in New England, in the early nineteenth century.

Before these inventions, spinning and weaving usually occurred in homes. In Britain, where the making of woolen goods was a major industry, it had been organized into a system by entrepreneurs. The machines belonged to the workers and they operated them in the home. With a regular procedure, known as the "putting out system," the organizers took the materials around to the homes and picked up the finished products, paying for the work and the use of the machines. The carders, spinners, and weavers provided a portion of the capital, while the entrepreneur provided part of the capital, the transportation, and the outlets to the market.

The textile factory system changed much of that. The factory owners provided the capital—the dam, the water wheel, the building, the belts, and the machines. The workers now worked in the mill or factory, where they had been congregated. Generally, they no longer provided any of the capital and were paid wages—whether for the piece or by the hour or day—for their work. They were brought under new and often harsher discipline than that under which they had formerly worked. They were under the authority of the foreman, came to work and left by the sun or the clock, and were driven by the machines to a certain pace in their work. As far as control of the system was concerned, capital, i.e., those who provided the capital, occupied the dominant control over labor, i.e., the workers, in the factory system.

It is not clear that many of the workers in these factories lost as much of their independence as might be supposed. Many of the textile workers were women and children. These were the ones who had customarily done such work, and there are those who say that the work with the fibers was especially suited to the limberness and agility of young hands. In any case, women and children were accustomed to working under the authority of men, so the change in that regard may not have been so great. In the United States, men generally resisted working in factories, saw it as a loss of independence, if not manhood, and continued to farm when they could, or do outside or heavy work.

The important social and economic point about all this is that the factory system caught on, spread, and eventually became the dominant means for providing a great many goods. Its development coincided with the development of economics as a discipline, and many economic theories were either built around the factory system or illustrated with it. The role of capital was greatly increased as the factory system spread as the means for making more and more goods. It generally succeeded to the position that land had held when farming occupied the center of the economic stage.

**Specialization** of workmanship and machines was as well suited to the factory system as it was ill suited to farming. Uniform and interchangeable parts combined with assembly line methods gave a new dimension to specialization. Workers could be set to shaping particular parts of some good, and others to assembling the parts, with each worker adding one piece to the whole. Since the factory brought together in one place many workers, they could be put to doing whatever task was wanted done, and specialization could be taken to its most efficient level. Of course,

specialization—*see definition*, p. 80.

> **Getting the Point...**
>
> Schools, hospitals, and fast food restaurants were mentioned as imitators of the factory system.
>
> - List some characteristics of those endeavors that are similar to the factory system. List a few that are not mentioned in the text if possible.
>
> - As you read the next section, keep a written list of the disadvantages mentioned for the factory system.
>
> - How would these factors impact the American school system? What strategies would help avoid any of these issues?

specialization has many dimensions: the specialization of physicians in a clinic or of scholars in a university is different in degree and skill than the specializations involved in assembling an automobile. But specialization has proceeded from the factory into many other areas of work.

The factory system provided the setting, too, for another practice: the payment for work-time. Payment for work-time is payment for the amount of time the worker is available for work at the work site, and is usually stated in terms of an hourly wage rate. This is such a familiar practice today that it would hardly seem worth calling attention to it. Yet payment for work-time has only become commonplace over the past few hundred years. It is true that in earlier times servants and hired help were sometimes paid for intervals of work, such as by the day, the week, the month, or year. Most people, however, received their pay either when they sold their products or by the piece for whatever they produced. Services have often been compensated for whatever was performed, such as a physician's fee for an office visit, a dentist's fee for extracting a tooth, a well digger's fee for digging a well, or whatever.

To the extent that it can be economical, workmen can only be practically compensated for work-time when they are under more or less direct supervision throughout the period. The use of machinery turned by external power has added to the practicality of paying by work-time because the movement of the machinery often sets the pace of the work.

On its face, paying by work-time is neither especially logical nor economical, though it may be easy to track. After all, it is hardly a workman's time that either employers or consumers want. Rather, they want the product he produces or the service he performs. Justice, too, would seem to require that a workman be paid for what he does rather than the time it takes him to do it. Payment for work-time can only in the grossest fashion compensate for skill and efficiency. In any case, the hourly pay of workers and the number of hours to be worked in a day have been points of controversy almost since the factory system became widespread. Undoubtedly, labor unions prefer the compensation for the work-time approach because it becomes a common ground for complaint among workmen. Probably many managers prefer it, too, because it tends to increase their authority over the other workmen.

In any case, the factory system so far succeeded as a method of operation that it was abstracted and extended into many lines of endeavor. It has become so common that it is imitated in schools, with their rows of desks, their timed periods for classes, the specialization of teachers, the discipline, and the emphasis more on the time spent at schooling rather than the quality of the learning. The factory is emulated in the large modern hospital, with its numerous specialized personnel, its routine, and its very size and complexity. The factory has even been imitated in fast food restaurants.

### 14.3.2 The Downside of the Factory System

Even so, the factory has not been an unqualified success. Indeed, it has had its critics from the outset; many have so far resisted in working in the factory atmosphere that they have managed to live without doing so. Critics early weighed in with the view that factories were no places for children to work, and eventually laws were passed, at first limiting, then prohibiting child labor. Legislatures sometimes attempted to limit female work in factories. Both labor unions and legislatures worked, too, to limit the hours of work in factories as well as the length of the work week. That the factory was often focused upon as the villain has been glossed over since then because hours of work and work weeks have been generally limited in more recent times, either by law or custom.

Undoubtedly, workers organized in factories have provided a cornucopia of goods in this era. To put the matter more broadly, people using machines have produced a wide variety of goods, whether they were working in a factory setting or not. No doubt, either, that factory organized work has many unfortunate side effects, though not all of them are economic in character. It has already been noted that it placed workers generally under the direction of those who provided the capital. That manner of organizing activities goes far beyond manufacturing and is so commonplace that it now seems inevitable. The factory tends, in a sense, to straitjacket those who work there, to have an appointed time for work, to have a set manner for performing tasks, to reduce work to a routine, and for many people to use only one or a few of their skills and capabilities.

From an economic point of view, however, the most wasteful aspect of factory-like employment is that much of it does not engage the intellectual capabilities and potential skills of those working there. By necessity workers are directed toward ends and ways of doing things that they had no hand in formulating. Suggestion boxes are hardly a substitute for actual decision making as to how best to do things. Moreover, payment by worktime, which is epitomized in punching the clock, tends to turn workers into time servers and clock watchers. The main economic result is what we have called "corporate drag."

The point has sometimes been argued that machine production is repetitious and boring. The counterpoint is that much work has always been repetitious and boring, whereas, machines now do much of the work that is repetitious. This is certainly the case. Undoubtedly mechanical cotton pickers do work that once was done by hand in the most repetitious and boring manner imaginable. The same is true for numerous other kinds of machines. In any case, the problem being addressed here is primarily that of organized production in a factory setting.

### 14.3.3 Home Based Businesses

Actually, the advances of technology have increasingly made it possible for production to take place in settings other than the factory. The widespread availability of electricity, and the development of gasoline, diesel, and electric powered engines, made the water driven wheel and steam power obsolete. Particularly, the great wheel turned by water, made necessary or practical the concentration of workers in a factory near the waterway. Machines to do many kinds of production can now be placed in almost any location: the home, the home workshop, basements, or wherever. It is true that many of the machines now in use are too large and cumbersome for such locations, and some operations require more space and special skills than any one or several people can provide. But, the use of computers, the miniaturization of parts, and the building of much smaller machines are helping overcoming many of these difficulties.

These things are making possible an industrial counter-revolution, so to speak. They are making practical the dispersion of capital for producing many goods and providing services. They are making technologically feasible the location of many kinds of production in homes, in home workshops adjacent to homes, and even small assembly plants operated by one or more families. The technology for much of this transformation is already available. There is no reason to doubt that many families would much prefer to work at or near home, or that it would be economical to

> **Getting the Point . . .**
>
> Make a list of all the obstacles mentioned to home based businesses.

fully engage workers in production, leaving them more or less free to choose their own times and places for working and resting.

> **The Move Toward Capital Dispersion**
> Actually, the advances of technology have increasingly made it possible for production to take place in settings other than the factory. These advances are making possible an industrial counter-revolution, so to speak. They are making practical the dispersion of capital for producing many goods and providing services. They are making technologically feasible the location of many kinds of production in homes, in home workshops adjacent to homes, and even small assembly plants operated by one or more families.

At the present time, however, there are a number of obstacles to such a counter-revolution or change. There is custom, habit, an assortment of laws, and union opposition, among other things. It may be instructive to recall that there never was any compelling reason why the ready-made clothing industry should have been centered in factories. When the sewing machine was first invented, the power for it was provided by a foot operated treadle. When an electric motor was developed to turn it, thus replacing foot power, increasing numbers of homes were being provided with electricity. While clothes were undoubtedly made for sale in homes at first, most of this was short-lived. For one thing, unions were opposed to piecework pay and work in the homes, characterizing such arrangements as "sweatshops," or "sweated" labor. It is clear that the factory setting with its concentration of workers is better suited than any other to unionization. It is easier to sell the idea in that setting that management and labor are at odds with one another and that those who work with their hands are the true laborers and have a common interest. For another thing, no extensive system was developed generally for putting out materials and collecting the finished product by factors. Indeed, transportation for such an arrangement only existed in towns and cities in the latter part of the nineteenth century. In America, in contrast to England, most people did not live in villages, towns, and cities but rather on separate farms. The widespread use of the automobile by the second or third decade of the twentieth century changed that, but long before that, most ready-made clothing manufacturing was done in factories.

Meanwhile, other obstacles to locating shops in or near homes were being written into law. **Zoning laws** today probably stand as the major obstacle to the use of new technology in the making of goods. The main purpose of zoning is to separate commercial from residential areas, though other purposes have also been behind creating zones for this or that or the other from time to time. The push for zoning laws got underway in the 1920s. Initially, most zoning laws were municipal ordinances, but in more recent times, counties, states, and more indirectly the United States Government have become involved in it. In most cities and towns today, most commercial activities are prohibited in areas zoned for residential use. In some communities, there have even been strenuous objections to locating churches there. Some states, counties and townships have zoning regulations that prescribe what sorts of activities may be located in particular zones. Some states mandate zoning throughout their jurisdiction. Environmental regulations and occupational safety and health

**zoning laws**—local laws that restrict the uses of land within particular zones of the city.

restrictions, both by the United States and by local governments, make it difficult to start a business even in areas zoned for them.

Zoning is not the only government obstacle to producing goods in the home or adjacent to it. Any family-sized business will encounter a variety of restrictions and discouragements from government. Record keeping in order to satisfy governments for tax purposes may put considerable strain on a very small business. There are self-employment taxes to be paid, including the whole of the Social Security tax (called a "self-employment" tax). There may be sales taxes to collect and account for, inventory records, and the like may also be required. Safety and health regulations may be virtually impossible to meet. Product liability, whether insured for or not, is now a major problem for all businesses. This latter is the result of government efforts to shift virtually the whole responsibility for safety and health on the manufacturer. The necessary licenses may be, and often are, quite expensive.

In contrast to many of the obstacles to small businesses by governments is the active quest for large businesses by state and local governments. State governors are expected to make business seeking trips to other states and foreign countries. Many municipalities go to all sorts of lengths to lure large businesses to their locale. Senators and Congressmen join state officials in proudly announcing the decision of some business to locate there. Cities acquire land on which such businesses may locate; special tax concessions are made by state and local governments; and special loans may even be made to lure the business. Media sources announce not only the decision of some business to locate there but also proclaim projections of the number of people to be employed and the increased business activity the business will generate. Large businesses are at a premium, and the coming of a great corporation is virtually a signal for dancing in the streets.

In sum, the legal and other obstacles to small business and home business utilization of the latest technology if not prohibitive, are at least formidable. The segregation of commercial activity from life in general is, to say the least, well advanced. That is not to suggest that small businesses do not continue to exist or even play a considerable role in American production. They do. Moreover, many people work in or out of their homes in making a living. There are states and locales, too, where the laws are laxer or hardly exist on the local level to discourage or prohibit home production. Overall, though, the obstacles are a difficulty that must be overcome or worked around.

## 14.3.4 Segregating Commercial and Residential Areas

There are, of course, arguments on both sides of the question of whether or not to segregate commercial activity and residential areas. These arguments are too extensive to examine in detail here, but a few need at least to be noted. The arguments for zoning and the like are generally well known, though it should be noted they are hardly economic ones. They are, in large, that the noises and chaos of much of commercial activity would be disruptive of quiet neighborhoods and many things that go on in the home. Undoubtedly, many people prefer not to live adjacent to railroad switching tracks, next to great furnaces belching smoke, truck terminals, and the like. Some kinds of production, too, are so inherently noisy that sleep might be difficult in the immediate vicinity. Property values may and sometimes do decline when some "undesirable" business is located nearby. A good example is houses located along the flight paths into and out of busy airports.

A counter argument to these is that zoning does not actually protect against these things happening. Anyone who follows zoning controversies soon realizes that whatever can be zoned, can be, and sometimes is, rezoned. Great interstate highways have sometimes been driven through the midst of residential areas. Moreover, many people do not object to living near factories, especially if they work in them. Ultimately, zoning politicizes and collectivizes the decision over the location of property rather than providing guarantees about who or what will win in the ensuing political contests.

There should be no doubt the factory-like setting and the segregation of commercial from home activity has fragmented family life. Work life tends to be separate from family life, with all the consequences that follow from that. This segregation is quite expensive at the level of family economy as well. Much of the traffic that clogs highways and city streets is of people going to and fro, often for considerable distances, between homes and commercial areas—whether to work, to shop, to places of entertainment, or what not. Probably, more noxious fumes are emitted and noise is made by this traffic than comes from factories.

Every arrangement of things, indeed every decision, has its own particular line of consequences and results. None are without drawbacks, nor can it be expected that everyone will agree as to how best to accomplish the production of goods, or how to organize to do so. The point here is that how production is organized has many social and economic consequences that we tend to be unaware of so long as we conceive some pattern that was actually historical in origin as rooted in the nature of things.

> **Organizing for Production**
> How production is organized has many social and economic consequences that we tend to be unaware of so long as we conceive some pattern that was actually historical in origin as rooted in the nature of things.

### 14.3.5 Economies of Scale and Specialization

One of the considerable costs of the expansion of businesses beyond the size that can be personally managed by a single owner or two or more partners is that of paying hired managers. (The shareholders in corporations are not, as a rule, expected to participate directly in management.) The basic idea is that the company will be more than compensated for this outlay by economies of scale coupled with the possibilities of specialization in large companies.

The basic principle of **economy of scale** is that in the production of a large amount of a particular good, each additional unit can be produced for less than the one that preceded it, other things being equal. Other things do not remain equal indefinitely, of course. Each time an additional employee is put on the payroll, an additional manager is hired, an additional machine is bought, or a new factory is built, the benefits of economy of scale are disrupted, until these additional costs have been absorbed in a new stream of economy of scale. Some economists approach the decision making process on this from the angle of **marginal utility**, that is, they attempt to determine the point at which an additional unit of whatever would cost more than any return that could be expected. (Markets are not unlimited, of course, nor can the cost of production ever be brought to zero.)

**economy of scale**—refers to the reduced cost of production for each additional unit produced. In the broadest terms, it refers to the economy of producing larger rather than smaller amounts of something.

**marginal utility**—the additional utility derived from consuming an additional unit of some good.

In any case, that there are economies of scale is easy enough to illustrate. Take the printing of books, as an example. It is conceivable that a single copy of a fair sized book could be printed today for $10,000. Another copy might be run off at a cost, let us say, of $10. The cost of the printing of the two books averaged is $5,005 per copy. So, with the production of one additional copy, the cost has been nearly halved. If the run were increased to 1,000 copies the total cost (which included typesetting, proofreading, paste-ups, photography, paper, ink, binding, and so forth) might be, let us say, $11,000. The cost of printing one book would then be reduced to $11 per copy. Ten thousand copies might be run off at a cost of $16,000, say. In which case, the printing cost for each book would be only $1.60. The illustration could be extended, but the point emerges. Each successive copy is less expensive to print than the one before it, other things remaining equal. On the other hand, the decline in cost per copy is less and less as more copies are printed.

Thus, economies of scale and specialization that is made possible with a larger work force tend to lead to expanding facilities and increasing the number of employees. These and other considerations have led to expanding the number of managers.

### 14.3.6 Managers

The task of the manager, at whatever level, is to overcome what is elsewhere referred to as corporate drag. His duty is to act in place of the owner(s) with the same care and diligence that the owner would himself exercise if he were present. In a large organization, the manager is somewhere in the chain of command and is held responsible, at least in theory, for the performance of those working under him. In practice, however, this responsibility may not be matched with the correlative authority to do what he believes needs to be done to get the best performance out of those under him. He may, for example, not have the authority to fire an ineffective worker without the approval of his superiors. He may have to contend with disruptive work rules or "featherbedding" by unionized workers in terms of contracts that top management has entered into with unions. In any case, in a large organization the system will have been to greater or lesser extent "bureaucratized." That is, it has been brought under more or less fixed rules. Thus, in the attempt to overcome corporate drag he may be caught in the toils of bureaucratic drag. Of course, not all managers are alike. Some are diligent, some are lackadaisical, some are eager to do an effective job, others seek to fit in and produce only the minimum quota in order to get along within the organization.

> **The task of the manager**, at whatever level, is to overcome what is elsewhere referred to as corporate drag. His duty is to act in place of the owner(s) with the same care and diligence that the owner would himself exercise if he were present. Much of the work of the manager is motivational, to motivate workers to come to work regularly, to give their best effort, and to stay on after they have learned their jobs.

Large organizations in this century have called forth a great variety of managers, ranging from the top boss to the shop foreman (or fore-lady).

Colleges and universities have accommodated the demand by turning out ever larger numbers of Business Administration majors, some of whom go on to get a master's degree before they go to a middle rank position in some organization. The function of these managers is to make the organization work, to organize production, to see that whatever is supposed to be produced does indeed get produced. The managers are assisted by an assortment of experts, many of them college or university trained. There are personnel managers, efficiency experts, auditors, accountants, computer programmers, and so on, as well as economists, psychologists, guidance counselors, and the like.

Perhaps the assistance of efficiency experts may help to bring the work of the manager into focus. These are people who come into a plant to figure out how the most can be accomplished with the least land, labor, and capital. They come in with their spreadsheets, tape measures, stop watches, and the like, to determine how wasted effort may be turned into productive effort. They are often despised and resented by workers because they have the audacity to tell workers who have done the job for many years how it can be done better. This is often resisted when their recommendations require changes in habits and routines.

Much of the work of the manager is motivational, to motivate workers to come to work regularly, to give their best effort, and to stay on after they have learned their jobs. To this end, the manager is often assisted by a program of benefits that he can use as rewards or enticements, such as seniority, paid vacations and holidays, Christmas bonuses, retirement programs, and so on, many of which are based on length of service with the company. The manager is, in a sense, a disciplinarian, whether this is apparent by his manner or not. It is his job to see that the work gets done.

> *Opportunity is missed by most people because it is dressed in overalls and looks like work.*
> **Thomas A. Edison**

# Study Guide for:

# 14 The Entrepreneur and Production

## Chapter Summary

In the previous chapter the means of production were defined and considered in an abstract form. The focus of this chapter is the human element, which brings the factors of production together in specific ways for the purpose of production. That is, production is organized and fashioned by humans. As human beings, people think, plan, and act upon their plans to accomplish their desired ends. We use our ingenuity to orchestrate the production of a good or service in a world filled with uncertainty and risk.

The entrepreneur is an individual who pulls the means of production together and arrays them in a particular form to produce the product he has in mind. As such, he is an initiator and a promoter. As production proceeds, he needs to be aware of changing market conditions that either give rise to new opportunities or eliminate earlier ones. This is no easy task in an environment marked by change.

To compound the entrepreneur's difficulties, production always requires financing because costs always precede revenues in the process. Therefore, funds must be raised to pay for the means of production needed to produce the product and bring it to market.

There are basically two categories into which we can classify business organizations. One is the proprietorship\partnership and the other is the corporation. The first of these involves either a single owner or two or more owners. Individuals doing business in this form include business income on their personal income tax returns and are each unlimitedly liable for the obligations of the firm. That is, should the firm incur some obligation and be unable to pay, the personal assets of the owners can be attached by the firm's creditors.

The corporation is a fictitious being brought into existence by a legal agreement between a group of individuals. Under the law, owners of the firm are identified as the stockholders. This form of business organization is to be differentiated from the previous category in that the owners face only limited liability. That is, they only risk the price they paid for the purchase of the stock. This form of organization allows for the development of much larger firms since stock ownership may be quite diverse.

The diversity of ownership poses a real problem since the managers of the business are not necessarily owners of the firm. As a result, these managers are acting in an agency relationship on behalf of the owners. Thus, the potential for a conflict of interest is always present since the interests of the managers may not be the same as the interests of the shareholders. However, in spite of this difficulty, this type of organization does allow firms to reap economies of scale, which reduce the average cost per unit of production by producing in large volume.

The move toward large scale production during the last part of the nineteenth century and through the twentieth century is centered around the factory. A factory is a central location that brings together large scale capital assets along with labor and raw materials to mass produce goods. Large scale manufacturing has led to the development of a vast array of products that are widely available to many people at an affordable price.

Along with the development of this form of business activity, came increasing levels of government taxation and regulation. Public policies during this period essentially created artificially high fixed costs for business activities and hence created artificial economies of scale thereby erecting an artificial advantage for large business enterprises. However, the recent proliferation of computer technology has undermined some of the inherent advantages of large scale production. Nevertheless, a move back toward smaller organizations will be hindered due to government policies that have developed over time. The end result will be greater economic inefficiencies than would have existed were government activities eliminated.

## Points of Emphasis

1. Entrepreneurial activity is fundamental to production and the process itself is carried on in a world filled with risks and uncertainties about the future.

2. Business organizations must raise funds to pay for production because expenses always precede revenues in the production process.

3. Though the owners of partnerships are generally liable for the obligations of the firm, the owners of corporations only face limited liability. As a result, the owners of corporations need not be as concerned over business decisions.

4. The factory system of production took advantage of economies of scale, which exceeded their inherent disadvantages that existed at the time of their proliferation. Though some technological advancements have served to reduce those advantages, government policy has served to reinforce them artificially.

## Identification

1. entrepreneur
2. James J. Hill
3. partnership
4. common law
5. limited liability corporation
6. common stock
7. preferred stock
8. corporate drag
9. stock market
10. stock exchange
11. New York Stock Exchange
12. Dow Jones Industrial Average
13. bull market
14. bear market
15. speculators
16. factory system
17. specialization
18. zoning laws
19. economy of scale
20. marginal utility

## Review Questions

1. What role(s) does the entrepreneur serve in the production process?
2. What is the difference between the unlimited liability of partners and the limited liability of the shareholders of a corporation?
3. Why is it necessary to raise money to engage in a productive process?
4. In what way is the New York Stock Exchange similar to a used car dealer?
5. What are the disadvantages of the factory system? In what ways and to what extent can they be overcome?

## Activities

1. Write a report on some modern-day entrepreneurs. For example, Bill Gates or Sam Walton.
2. Prepare a case either to support or oppose the following position: "Modern technology is making the factory system obsolete."

## For Further Study

1. A. Alchain, *Economic Forces at Work*, Liberty Press: Indianapolis, 1977.
2. M. Jensen and W. Meckling, "Theory of the Firm: Managerial Behavior, Agency Costs and Ownership Structure," *Journal of Financial Economics*, October 1976, pp. 305–360.
3. Israel Kirzner, *Competition and Entrepreneurship*, University of Chicago Press: Chicago, 1973.
4. Fritz Machlup, "Theories of the Firm: Marginalist, Behavior, Managerial," *American Economic Review*, March 1967, pp. 1–33.

**CHAPTER CONTENT**

15.1 Rent    228
15.2 Wages    230
15.3 Interest    231
    15.3.1 Time Preference    233
    15.3.2 Impact of Government on Interest Rates    234
15.4 Profit and Loss    234
15.5 Inheritance    237

# 15 THE DISTRIBUTION OF WEALTH

*You shall not covet your neighbor's house; you shall not covet your neighbor's wife, or his male servant, or his female servant, or his ox, or his donkey, or anything that is your neighbor's.*

**Exodus 20:17**

It may well be that the distribution of wealth is the most interesting matter with which economics deals. Certainly, it involves issues that concern all of us at some time or another. The **distribution of wealth** deals with who gets what, when they get it, and why. This is not a replay of the chapter entitled "How We Get What We Want." Rather, it deals with income in terms of the means of production, as well as that received by inheritance. The justice of the distribution also comes in for discussion.

The first observation to be made under this heading is that wealth is unequally distributed, within countries and among the inhabitants of the earth. Most basically, this unequal distribution arises from the nature of things. The materials for producing wealth are unevenly distributed on the earth's surface and in the deposits beneath it. The fertility of the soil varies from place to place, ranging from highly fertile, producing luxuriant growth, to barren, unable to sustain any but the hardiest of life. Some regions have bountiful rainfall while others get very little; temperatures vary from harsh cold for much of the year to almost unbearable heat. The same variations occur in mineral deposits, in topography, in plant cover, and on and on. Of the justice of this distribution, there is not much to be said. That is the way it is.

In like manner, individuals are unequal in ability, talent, strength, intelligence, interests, vigor, and all those things with which they may be said to be naturally endowed. They differ as well in what skills they develop, how much they learn, their training, their inclinations, the degree to which they give thought to the future, health, tenacity, how industrious they are, and in almost every way imaginable. One man may carefully plan his activities, saving against future needs by making investments, applying himself diligently to all his undertakings, and wasting little that comes to him. Another, by contrast, may be a slovenly wastrel who lives for the day, is lazy, takes little interest in what goes on around him, and puts aside nothing either for a rainy

**distribution of wealth**—the result of economic action in determining who gets what. It also answers the questions of when and why he receives it.

day or for the future. In short, people are not only differently endowed but also differently motivated in the extent to which they use what they have.

It follows, then, that if people get approximately, or roughly, what they are due or have earned, wealth will be unequally distributed. It is difficult to see how it would be otherwise. Nor do we have to resort to speculation to arrive at this conclusion. In fact, wealth is unequally distributed among the inhabitants of the earth, in every land, in every country, and at all times. True, utopian schemes have been devised in fiction in which the wealth was evenly distributed in some land. But these are fiction. They are fantasies. Even so, redistributionists abound in our era. There are plenty of people today who claim that the power of government should be used to redistribute the wealth until it is more evenly distributed. For that reason, it is necessary to explore how wealth tends to get distributed in the market in the absence of force.

> **The Nature of Wealth Distribution**
> Wealth is unequally distributed, within countries and among the inhabitants of the earth. Most basically, this unequal distribution arises from the nature of things. The materials for producing wealth are unevenly distributed on the earth's surface and in the deposits beneath it. In like manner, individuals are unequal in ability, talent, strength, intelligence, interests, vigor, and all those things with which they may be said to be naturally endowed. They differ as well in what skills they develop, how much they learn, their training, their inclinations, the degree to which they give thought to the future, health, tenacity, how industrious they are, and in almost every way imaginable. It follows, then, that if people get approximately, or roughly, what they are due or have earned, wealth will be unequally distributed. It is difficult to see how it would be otherwise. Nor do we have to resort to speculation to arrive at this conclusion.

That each man was getting his just due would be easy enough to determine in the simplest form of economy. Suppose that each person lived on his own land and received for his own use all that he produced. That is, he used only the materials on his own land, fashioned all his own tools, did all the work, and consumed only what was produced on his own land. Whatever inequalities of wealth there might be would be easy enough to explain. One person's land might be less fertile than that of some others. Or, any number of natural mishaps might have befallen someone. Or, this person might have eaten all the seed rather than saved some for the next year's planting, or any other of many reasons having to do with one's own industry or location. In any case, the inequality of distribution would involve no complex question of justice, for each person was able to keep and use all that they had produced.

The matter is not so easily disposed of in the complex economies of the contemporary world. Indeed, once a market had developed, a medium of exchange was available, and some division of labor had taken place, the determination of the justice of who gets what, when, and why becomes more complicated. To take a contemporary example, how much of the dealer price of a new automobile should the man get who installed the left front wheel of it working on the assembly line? What payment for the work would be his just due? When should he be paid for the work? As soon as he has finished his work? Or as soon as the automobile has been sold by the dealer and the money is available?

There is no objective quantifiable answer to these questions. We could say, for example, that the workman should be paid what his work has contributed to the final price of the car. Well and good, we might all agree that this would be his just due. But how much did he contribute to the final cost of the car? How do we calculate that number? The only way to arrive at a numerical answer is to calculate what each person who contributed land, labor, and capital to the car received for his contribution, including the person who installed the wheel. But this answer begs the question. We wished to know the just due of the worker, not what he was actually paid. Nor would it serve to take the figures from the assembly of numerous cars in times past and reduce them to average amounts paid for each contribution. No doubt, such figures are sometimes bandied about, but they, too, beg the question. They do not tell us what installers of tires were due, only the average of what they got. What other people get for their work may be of interest to those who pay and to those who are trying to arrive at an acceptable figure, but what justice requires cannot be quantified in an objective fashion.

Prices, as was explained earlier, are determined by agreement between the parties. They are undoubtedly influenced by going rates, which are in turn influenced, if not absolutely determined, by supply and demand as modified by the extent of the competition. This is true of all that has gone into building and marketing a car, wages included. An employer will undoubtedly offer such wages as he has to in order to get the quality of employees he needs and can afford. An employee will no doubt accept such pay as he finds satisfactory in the condition of the market.

What is due the worker who installed the left front wheel of an automobile is whatever he was promised, and accepted, for his work. If he is paid by the hour, what he would get is whatever portion of an hour he worked to install the wheel. When he is due to be paid for the work is also a matter of agreement, however formal or informal. This is how the determination of prices is made by free people in a free market. In the market, the answer to the question, what price is just, is determined by the mutual agreement of both parties.

Of course, the above answers do not satisfy those who believe that prices should be determined by some other criteria. Karl Marx suggested, for example, that people ought to be paid for what they produce, or help to produce, according to their needs. Some people believe that workers ought to get a living wage or that farmers ought to get high enough prices for their crops to bring them up to parity with other producers. In short, they propose to locate the decision as to what prices shall prevail outside the market. Two observations are in order. First, determining prices in any way other than through the free market will be arbitrary and disruptive to the market. The other point is that what follows in this chapter will be a discussion of the distribution of wealth by free people in a free market. Most of the consideration of those who reject the market to greater or lesser extent will be taken up in the discussion of economic systems. The ways that wealth is distributed other than the outright buying and selling of goods, which has already been discussed, will be discussed below in several categories.

## 15.1 Rent

**rent**—the payment to someone to use his property for a specified period of time.

**Rent** is the fee paid to the owner for the temporary use of his goods. By custom and by law anything that can be owned can be put out to rent. However, by custom the fee paid for the temporary use of money is called interest rather than rent. Rentals are usually made for specified periods of time, such as a day, a week, a month, a year, or some portions thereof, and the rent is for a fixed period of time. Some rentals of a more complex nature or involving longer periods of time are called leases, but they are still rental agreements. The renter acquires the right to use the property for the specified time in the manner agreed upon in the rental agreement. At the end of the rental period, the renter is expected to return the property to the owner in good condition, less normal wear and tear. (Sometimes, security deposits are required in advance to cover damages that might occur to the property.)

Rent is a way of distributing surplus wealth to its highest use for the best return. Economically, it serves both the owner and the renter, providing the owner with a return on his property and the renter with goods that he may be unable to afford.

All sorts of things are put up for rent today, including apartments, movies, heavy equipment such as earth-moving machines or tractor-trailers, furniture, appliances, office machines, and lawn mowers. Some people, and companies, go into the rental business, while others make rentals only occasionally.

Putting property out to rent has been most prominently considered as an alternative use for property by economists. Indeed, it is *the* alternative use, either to keeping it or to selling it. In determining the cost of production, the potential rent is an opportunity cost when the owner foregoes rent to use the property himself. In other words, when the owner decides to use the property himself he must give up the possibility of earning money from potential renters. Or, if he decides to sell, the rent that he foregoes when he parts with it may be a part of his calculation of an acceptable selling price. In any case, when property is rented for production purposes, it is a direct part of the cost of production. When an owner decides to use his property for production instead of putting it out to rent, the rental income he has foregone may be thought of as a part of his cost of production.

Economists often focus on the rental of land in their discussions of rent. There are several explanations for this focus. First, the rental of land was commonplace long before the technology to produce most of the goods now available to rent existed. Second, rent is a way of discussing the cost of one of the means of production, though it should be pointed out that capital may be rented as well as land. Third, and probably most important to them, there have been far more controversies about land rental than the rental of other goods. These have hinged on the rightness or justice of the private ownership and rental of land.

While the right to the ownership of property has already come up for discussion elsewhere, it has to occupy our attention again in this connection. The particular context here is the right or justice of the landlord drawing rent on land. As noted earlier, land differs from the other means of production because man does not make land; whereas, he does provide labor and produce the equipment that constitutes capital. Adam Smith, and after him other classical economists, had held that labor was the origin of the value of goods. Socialists seized upon this claim to denounce private property in land as theft, or the taking for personal use what they had not created. In that view the landlord could be pictured as an idle man who soaked his tenants for rents to which he had no right. In consequence, economists have spilled a great deal of ink over the years to prove economically the case on one side or the other.

In practice, the question of private property in and rental of land has no different standing than private property in and rental of any other inanimate object. That is, the man who owns land may well have bought it from someone else, just as the one who owns a lawn-mower did. Indeed, the two may have earned their money in exactly the same way; the one having as great a right to his possessions as the other. Or, the landlord may have inherited the land. In any case, ownership confers upon the owner the right of disposal, whether by gift, sale, or as rental property.

Nor does it follow that because man did not make the land he cannot own some piece of it. It is no more logical to conclude that the land belongs to everyone or to no one than that it can be owned by people individually. Indeed, it is less logical. Land is scarce; it is an economic good. In the nature of things, the use of the land must be directed by someone. Everyone cannot use a given amount of land in common, as pointed out earlier. Some means has to be employed to distribute it among users. It has to be distributed or its use allocated by somebody. In short, the role of landowner or landlord has to be occupied by somebody.

> **The Nature of Land Use**
> Land is scarce; it is an economic good. In the nature of things, the use of the land must be directed by someone. Everyone cannot use a given amount of land in common. Some means has to be employed to distribute it among users. It has to be distributed or its use allocated by somebody. In short, the role of landowner or landlord has to be occupied by somebody.

There is more than logical necessity involved in this, too. The land needs attention and care; it must be improved if it is to be put to its highest use. For this to occur with any predictability there must be inducements to the improvement and care of land. What inducement is there for a man to build a house upon the land if the house is not his? And, how can the house be his if he does not own the land on which it is situated? The same goes for every kind of improvement, whether it be clearing the land of trees and growth, draining it, terracing it, rotating crops, planting legumes upon it, and so on. Undoubtedly, the greatest inducement is the ownership; that the owner shall continue to enjoy the fruits or benefits of improvements; that he can sell the land, rent it, or pass it on to his heirs. Private property in land is sanctioned by usage, by long experience, by necessity, by common practice, and is rooted in the nature of things. It is the most basic property, that which they are most likely to mean when people refer to property. All property is sustained by it, for without private property in land there is no private place to store and keep all other varieties of property.

Any other than private ownership of land would be likely to result in exploitation of the land without regard to its future value and would most likely lead to serfdom or slavery. Those who have no stake in the land are likely to mine it of its minerals, plant the easiest tended crops year after year and make only the most temporary of improvements. Indeed, tenants do not usually do more for the land than they are required to do for its immediate future. But at least, under private ownership, there is the landlord to see to such improvements as he deems desirable or necessary.

Rental fees on land are determined just as other prices are in the market. That is, they are the result of the interplay of supply and demand under competitive conditions. The more fertile and better situated lands bring higher prices in the market. In competition with one another, tenants bid the price of land up, and landlords in competition with one another bid the price down. That process proceeds until the least desirable land has been put out to rent to the tenant who cannot or will not pay more than the margin that covers the cost of using the land in a particular way.

Finally, then, rent is the means of distributing land to users. To put it another way, it is the price that occupants and users of the land pay for it. Since there is usually a reciprocal relationship between the rental fees and the purchase price of land, it can be said that the owner who also uses his land pays rent for doing so in the amount of rent he foregoes by his use of the land. Then, rent is the price of land used in production.

> Rent is the means of distributing land to users. To put it another way, it is the price that occupants and users of the land pay for it. Since there is usually a reciprocal relationship between the rental fees and the purchase price of land, it can be said that the owner who also uses his land pays rent for doing so in the amount of rent he foregoes by his use of the land. Then, **rent is the price of land used in production.**

## 15.2 Wages

*wage—see definition, p. 140.*

A **wage** is a price paid for labor. It is the means of distributing a portion of the wealth to those who have contributed to its production. Customarily, wages are payments made to employees by an employer for their work. Quite often, the term is restricted to those who work by the hour or day, and most often to those who do physical labor. Economically, however, wage is a much broader term, referring to the payment for all sorts of work, mental, physical, or spiritual (if that is the right term). Not only do factory workers receive wages but so also do those who receive salaries, commissions, are self-employed, or who work in any capacity for remuneration. Every person who works for pay has a wage, then, whether as a bricklayer, real estate salesman, writer, physician, waitress, minister, or solid waste collector. Some get their wages in specific sums from employers. Others get theirs as a designated percentage of the price they receive for some product (commissions). Some wages are so lumped together with what they receive for land (rent), interest, and profit that the concept of receiving a wage for their work may not even occur to them. Even so, if they work and receive compensation for it, some portion belongs to wages.

A wage in a free market is the amount paid. This allocates labor to the positions of employment where it is in greatest demand. Since labor is scarce, as emphasized already, not every way it might be employed will have a sufficient wage to induce someone to work for it. On the other hand, some wages must be sufficiently low to enable those who can produce little of what is wanted to get some form of employment. Any effort to fix them higher or lower than those amounts will result either in unemployment or labor shortages.

Since wages have already been discussed in some detail, it is unnecessary to deal with all aspects of them here. Suffice it to say that there is no such thing as an "Iron law of wages," as some classical economists thought. Nor does society have a "wage fund" from which wages are to be paid. There is no fixed proportion as to how much is to be allotted to land, labor, and capital, or to use the terms that we are now using, among rent, wages, interest, and profit or loss. It is possible, of course, to project a budget in which expenditures are allocated in proportions to each of these except profits. But such things are only projections, not faithful reflections of what actually occurs in the market. What is paid in the market depends upon supply, demand, and competitive conditions.

It should be noted here that the market does not allocate wages on the basis of some objective standard of the merit of the work. No doubt some rap artists, for example, may be grossly overpaid for their work according to an objective standard for musicianship. Highly popular rap stars may get paid more for a few hours spent in the recording studio than a classical cellist will get for a lifetime of work devoted to his exacting music. Some would place the blame for this disparity on a free market economy. If blame is due, it would appear to be the fault of those who bought the recordings, along with those who produced them. The market can only *reflect* the taste of those who trade in the market, not monitor nor alter it. It does not redistribute wealth; it only distributes it in the way that those who had it choose to allocate it. One of the ways this is done is in the payment of wages.

> A **wage** is a price paid for labor. It is the means of distributing wealth, a portion of it, to those who have contributed to production. Customarily, wages are payments made to employees by an employer for their work. A wage in a free market is the amount paid. This allocates labor to the positions of employment where it is in greatest demand. Since labor is scarce, not every way it might be employed will have a sufficient wage to induce someone to work for it. On the other hand, some wages must be sufficiently low to enable those who can produce little of what is wanted to get some form of employment. Any effort to fix them higher or lower than those amounts will result either in unemployment or labor shortages.

## 15.3 Interest

**Interest** is the payment made for the use of someone else's money. If the money goes into productive equipment, it could be said to be a cost of capital beyond the price at which it was purchased. At any rate, interest is a means of distributing money from those who have accumulated it to those who want it and are willing to pay a price for it. Generally speaking, people do not accumulate large hoards of money that they store in counting houses, as King Midas was supposed to have done. Ordinarily, they invest or loan out any surplus they have to earn interest.

interest—*see definition*, p. 121.

The taking of interest was once a suspect activity. Indeed, the taking of interest and the amount or rate charged has almost certainly been the most regulated and controlled by government of all economic undertakings, except possibly prostitution and gambling. In the Middle Ages the taking of interest was widely condemned and often made illegal for Christians. Jews, since they were not Christians, were sometimes allowed to reside in Christian lands and lend money out at interest. While prohibitions on charging interest were generally abandoned beginning with the Renaissance, regulation of rates has been common, and some relics of this still remain in the United States.

In the United States, interest was never prohibited. However, the maximum rate that could be charged has often been fixed by state law. While many restrictions have been removed, the charging of high rates of interest is still a contentious issue. It is often referred to as **usury**. Federal regulations have partially supplanted state laws, especially with regard to interest on savings accounts. A part of the prejudice, if that is what it is, survives in references to some lenders as "loan sharks," in the social view that pawn shops are "seedy" institutions, and to some distaste for finance companies.

It would be an error, however, to view any social opposition to indebtedness as simply prejudice. There is good reason to be wary of going into debt, and long-term debts are especially suspect. Shakespeare's "Neither a debtor nor lender be" contained considerably more than a grain of common sense. The man who is in debt has not only given commitment to a portion of his future earnings but also has compromised his independence of action. He has lost some of his flexibility, while the man with savings has gained, depending on his liquidity.

Be that as it may, interest is a way of paying for and obtaining at least a temporary distribution of wealth. Lending and borrowing is another way of distributing wealth. Moreover, the prejudice has shifted away from opposing the practice to general approval and widespread practice. Moreover, it is widely understood, or at least accepted, today that interest is the "price of money" and that it may be expected to fluctuate as do other prices. Political emphasis has shifted away from fixing maximum rates to the monetary policies of the Federal Reserve, and the impact of these on interest rates.

At any rate, interest is the price of savings, which is accomplished in monetary terms, as rent is the price of land and wages the price paid for labor. It is the price, that is, for the temporary use of money. There are many different ways of borrowing money and many different sorts of lenders. There are long term loans and short term loans, secured loans and signature loans, commercial loans and consumer loans. Money can be borrowed on personal items at pawn shops, for consumer goods from merchants, from finance companies and from banks. There are savings and loan institutions that have for many years made loans primarily on real estate. Money can be borrowed on notes, by issuing bonds, from insurance companies, and from banks in general. Loans from individuals have become difficult to acquire, except when owners finance something that they are eager to sell, such as real property. Individuals have become reluctant to make loans to other individuals because they lose their liquidity when they do so, whereas they retain most of it when they deposit it with lending institutions. It generally requires a high interest rate to induce an individual to make loans that he cannot readily sell at a discount to someone else. As a result, larger financial institutions have developed to connect borrowers and lenders.

The price of money for hire is determined in the market much as other prices are. That is, it is the result of supply and demand under competitive conditions. The interest rate is basically determined by the rate that will induce lenders to supply enough money to meet the effective demand. Would be borrowers bid the price up, so to speak, and would be lenders bid it down, though each is seeking the opposite result. In the absence of some sort of external control, the price of interest will finally reach a rate at which the least promising of borrowers finds someone who will make him a loan.

**usury**—the charging of interest on a loan. In today's use it has come to mean the charging of excessive interest on a loan.

There are going rates of interest, of course, just as there are going rates or prices for other things. In fact, at any given time, there are several going rates. There are, first of all, "wholesale rates" and "retail rates." The wholesale rate is what the depositor in a lending institution receives on his principal. Today, there are several wholesale rates: the passbook rate, the money market rate, and the rates on certificates of various durations. All of these deposits can be withdrawn at will, but the certificate-holders are penalized if they withdraw their funds before the maturity date. There are rates on government securities, on business bonds, on prime commercial loans, on other business loans, on real estate loans for long term, and on consumer loans.

There are economic—and sometimes political—reasons for these different rates. They are more or less closely tied to the reason for interest in the first place. One reason is the cost of handling the loan. If it is necessary, there is the cost of investigating the credit rating of the borrower before the loan is even approved. There are papers to be prepared, sometimes lawyers' fees to be paid, and there will be origination costs if it is a brokered loan. (In the case of real estate loans, these initial costs are often collected when the loan is closed and are not counted in the interest. On other types of loans, they are usually absorbed in the interest payments.) On installment loans, the payments have to be recorded. Sometimes, bills or reminders may have to be mailed to the borrower.

Then, there is the risk that the loan will not be repaid, or that major efforts may have to be made to collect payment. Even government guaranteed loans will cause inconvenience to the lender, though there is no ultimate danger that the principal will be lost. It is easy enough to suppose, if you do not look much into the matter, that the danger of loss is the main reason for interest, but that is not the case. It is rather a variable cost, added on and becoming larger as the risk is reckoned to be greater.

A third reason both for interest and for variations in the rates is the inconvenience of having money tied up for a period. Granted, notes are ordinarily transferable and there may be a market for them, but as a rule debt instruments can only be sold at a discount. That is, the holder of a note may have to take less than he was promised if he is to get his money before the note matures.

### 15.3.1 Time Preference

The basic reason for interest, therefore, is the **time preference** of lenders. To put it another way, the lender must be without those goods for which he might have exchanged his money during the period before the loan matures. All people prefer present goods to future goods, and the extent to which this is the case is considered by economists to be the rate of time preference. As market participants enter financial markets with their varying rates of time preference, supply and demand for loanable funds gives rise to a going market rate of interest.

Time preference is often cited as the justification for charging interest. Perhaps, it is a better explanation than justification. The best justification is that postponing consumption by accumulating money as property, like land and labor, and that interest is the payment for parting with it temporarily. Granted, there have been those who find fault with taking interest, and even more commonly with charging interest above a certain rate, which they have been pleased to call usury. They may be economically ignorant, covetous, envious, busybodies, power hungry, socialists, or whatever. In any case, they have not come to grips with or choose to ignore

> **Getting the Point...**
>
> List at least three reasons for differences in interest rates for loans.

time preference—see definition, p. 121.

the case for private property, time preference, and, one other point, that money is a good that has alternative uses.

Rather than lending his money to someone else, the man who has it may choose to invest it on his own account. In which case, he may receive as great a return as he would have received in interest, and a profit above that. In any case, alternative uses affect decisions about the use of money, how much will be loaned, and ultimately the rate of interest, or vice versa.

### 15.3.2 Impact of Government on Interest Rates

There is yet another factor that affects interest rates. It is not in the nature of things, and so it may best be considered separately. Monetary inflation has a decided effect on the interest rate, and is the main means by which governments in this day attempt to intervene in them. There is a time element involved in the various effects of inflation that makes inflationist policies so attractive to some people. Initially, the effect of an inflation would be to lower interest rates. It increases the supply of the currency, and thus of money to lend. But, this will also cause prices to rise, and as they rise, a unit of money begins to lose value. What this means is that present money, i.e., money held at the initial stage of the inflation is worth more than future money. Lenders begin to discount future interest, and the price of money, or interest rate, will rise. This effect can occur over and over again in an ongoing inflation.

One final point needs to be made on the setting of maximum interest rates by government. Those who are apt to be most hurt by such regulations are those with the lowest credit ratings and possibly in greatest immediate need of a loan. They are the ones who have to pay the highest rates to induce someone to lend them money. It should be made clear, too, that those determined to borrow money can usually find someone who will lend it, either illegally or through some provision or loophole in the law. Consumer, installment loans have usually cost much more than the stated or legal rate of interest, and still do. This has been considered quite legal because they simply charge the legal rate on the initial amount borrowed for the whole term of the loan, without reducing the principal amount in the calculation, though the principal has been progressively paid off. If such loans are paid off before maturity, a penalty is charged by the lender to collect the add-on interest lost through early payment. As for illegal rates, there are always "loan sharks" around glad to charge higher interest, many of whom have no qualms about the methods they use to collect it. These are the step-children, so to speak, of government intervention in the money market.

## 15.4 Profit and Loss

**profit**—the residual funds left from producing and selling an economic good in the market after all other costs are met.

**Profit** is what is left over after *all* the costs of an undertaking have been met. It is that amount above the payment for rent (land), wages (labor), and interest (money for capital, etc.). If all these costs have been capitalized by investment, then profit is the return on investment. That is, if the land is owned by the producer, the wages are paid out of savings, and the equipment and materials are paid for by investment money, these have all been capitalized, and profit is a return on capital. Even so, rent, wages, and interest must be taken into account, for they are all alternative ways of getting a return on labor and wealth. That is, investors have foregone rent, wages, and interest for such money and time as they have put into the undertaking. This may be easier to see in the case of rent and wages than in that of labor.

If so, look at it this way. Imagine a proprietor who owns and manages his own business. He manages his business himself: making all the decisions, purchasing all the materials, hiring help, and so on. Other firms might hire him to do similar work to what he does, and pay him, say, $70,000 per year. Thus, it is proper for him when he does his accounts to add that amount to costs to see if he has made a profit. (Undoubtedly, for tax purposes he would actually have to pay himself that amount, but we are considering the economics of the situation here, not making records for the government.) The same principle applies to rent and interest, of course, whether they have been actually paid out or not.

Profit can and needs to be considered from other angles than a return on investment. In terms of the distribution of wealth, profit is the reward for rightfully predicting the market, for prudent and frugal use of materials and labor, and for what turns out to be a wise investment. It is the reward for successfully risking capital in an enterprise. Some writers call it entrepreneurial profit to call attention to its venturesome character. Not all enterprises make a profit. Indeed, when land, labor, and rent are fully taken into account, many businesses go from year to year and even survive for generations without making significant profit.

Profit is the economic incentive for business enterprise. Every entrepreneur strives to operate the business so as to make a profit. Profit is the lifeblood of an enterprise; if it is losing money that lifeblood ebbs away. Capital is consumed without being replenished, and if there are multiple investors, some of them, at least, will begin to shift their funds elsewhere. Investors are always seeking the most profit for their money. They move funds from the less or unprofitable to those opportunities they judge to have greater prospects for profit. The quest for profits provide the incentive for the most efficient use of land, labor, and capital, to reduce expenses where possible, to purchase new labor saving devices, and to adopt better techniques of production.

> **The Profit Incentive**
> Profit is the economic incentive for business enterprise. Every entrepreneur strives to operate the business so as to make a profit. Profit is the lifeblood of an enterprise; if it is losing money that lifeblood ebbs away.

Much misunderstanding exists regarding the effects of profits on prices. Some people suppose that profit is something added to the price of goods. It is easy to see how that idea arises. After all, a merchant buys goods from a producer or wholesaler and marks up the price in the hope of profit. Thus, if he makes a profit, it is clearly from that which he has added to the price he paid. The same would be true of the wholesaler who bought from the producer and sold to the retailer. In a competitive situation, however, profit tends to lead the other way in the long run. Indeed, John Chamberlain, a business historian, has said:

> Profits, like rent, do not figure in selling price under properly competitive conditions. For, just as the price of wheat is set at the margin by the wheat grown on no-rent lands, so is the price of an industrial product set at the margin by the output of the no-profit company.

Profits, then, are the special creation of the ability, the knowhow, the inventiveness, the foresight, the imagination of the superior executive. They are, in effect, not added into price but taken out of cost.

This may be hard to believe at first, but an example or so may make clear how this can happen. Let us take as the first example, the early producer(s) of refined products from petroleum. The most important of these products was kerosene for lamps and eventually for heating purposes. The competitive product when kerosene was first introduced was whale oil. Undoubtedly, whale oil was quite expensive, for ships had to be outfitted, the whaler had to find and harpoon whales, and these, in turn, had to be processed for oil and other products. Kerosene could be extracted from petroleum much more simply and dependably. There were no long weeks at sea to get crude oil. The first refiner to market kerosene did undoubtedly reap a handsome profit. Other refiners were quickly lured into the business by the desire to earn these profits as well. To get a portion of the market, they sought ways to offer the kerosene cheaper. They sought or developed better refining processes, cheaper ways of transporting the materials and products, less expensive ways of drilling, and so on. The profits that they made, if any, could then be said to be taken out of cost rather than out of the price of the kerosene to the consumer, since the price fell due to competition and improvements.

A similar process can occur in retailing, so we may return to the place where the discussion began. Some time back, retail discount department stores began to make an appearance. Some of the early ones were quite profitable and were probably begun as local ventures. Others entered the field, and before long national chains of retail discount department stores were built, such as J. C. Penny, Sears, Woolco, and Montgomery Wards were common. Eventually new competitors entered the retail market as deep discounters, such as K-Mart and Wal-Mart. The competition brought by these firms pushed companies like Woolco and Montgomery Wards out of business. The deep discounters were able to sell their goods for much less than these stores. The appearance and growth of online retailers such as Amazon is bringing a whole new form of competition to the retail industry. While no one knows for sure how the industry will change and who will survive, one thing is sure. Like all market endeavors, the competitive process is sure to change what, when, and where people engage in trade.

The above examples call attention to other common phenomena. As competitors enter the field, not only do prices tend to drop but also profits decline. Indeed, many economists hold that competition tends to reduce profits as prices continue to fall to a level at which there are no longer any true profits left. The actual situation is usually more diverse than that. The less effective companies are progressively squeezed out. Some of the most efficient may still make something that could be denominated profit, so long as demand holds up. Companies diversify, develop new products, have extensive advertising campaigns, try to develop customer loyalty, appoint new executive leadership, and attempt any number of things in order to get or maintain an edge over the competition. This tendency of profits to decline or disappear partially explains, too, the capital hunger of corporations. With more money and more advanced technology, they hope to restore profits.

The above are the ways wealth gets distributed in the market. They are, to sum up, rent, wages, interest, and profit. It should be pointed out, however, that while all people desire to increase their wealth, many wish to avoid the rigors of competition to get it. One way to do this is to get government to redistribute wealth. Such a **redistribution of wealth** does

---

**Getting the Point...**

Once an entrepreneur develops a new profitable enterprise, how does competition develop, and what generally happens?

---

**redistribution of wealth**—a governmental forced effort to take wealth from some people and give it to other people.

not create anything new and in the end is like theft. In essence, it is a forced redistribution of wealth.

Another way of avoiding competition is to get government to place regulatory restrictions on one's competitors. This method simply stops wealth from being created in the first place. There are, first of all, businesses exclusively franchised to provide some good or service. These are called public utilities, and usually do such things as provide electricity, telephone service, transportation, water, garbage pickups, and the like. Their rates or charges are usually fixed or regulated by government. Sometimes, an effort is made by the regulators to provide for a profit in the rates, although no satisfactory way has ever been devised for doing that. The rates (prices) themselves are largely guesswork, since competition, either potential or actual, usually determines prices. Comparing the rates of utilities from one state or region to another provides all too little information as to what rates would be if there was competition. In such cases, any profits are indeed simply added on to the costs in the price. The decisions made are likely to be political, not market ones.

There are undoubtedly profits to be made in illegal enterprises such as gambling, drug-dealing, prostitution, and the like. Profits in these enterprises, however, are indistinguishable front payments for the risk of being caught and punished. No doubt some distribution of wealth takes place this way, but it is rather clearly distinguishable from the distribution in the legal market.

## 15.5 Inheritance

Strictly speaking, **inheritance** is a redistribution of wealth rather than a distribution, but the time factor ordinarily involved between the acquisition and the redistribution gives it at least some of the character of a distribution. At any rate, the question of inheritance has long been a subject of controversy and government policy.

**inheritance**—the gift of one's property to one's heirs.

The question of large inheritances has especially raised the ire of redistributionists in general and socialists in particular. They claim not to see the justice of it at all. The children of wealthy parents may come into great wealth and yet may not have lifted a hand in producing it. Why should they have all that wealth when there are so many in need? They would tax away all, or nearly all, of any but the smallest amount of wealth left by its owner in order to meet the needs of the poor.

These are not, strictly speaking, economic questions, though economic justifications have sometimes been made for concentrations of wealth. Wealth does not, after all, usually lie idle in the modern age. Where there are concentrations, the wealth is usually loaned out or invested. Quite often, it may be used as capital in some enterprise, thus providing goods for consumers and better jobs for workers. After all, much of investment comes from concentrations of wealth, and hardly any from those who live from day to day and hand to mouth. But inheritance may be more of a question of right or equity than of economy.

Inheritances come from the distribution of the property of an owner after his death. (If he makes the actual distribution during his lifetime, it would be gifts.) If it was his property at the time of his death and he has left a will disposing of it, given that it was the owner's choice of how to distribute his property, the case for respecting that will is very strong. This was his will and how he wanted his property disposed. If he died intestate (without a will), the general rule in the United States, by state legislation or otherwise, was that the estate would go to the heirs according to formula. Only if there are no heirs, and the owner dies intestate would the property go to the state. Two considerations have then held sway in legal consideration in the United States: first, the will of the owner, and second, the priority of the family. There is no assumption in all of that, that the property somehow belongs to the state.

However, in this century, heavy taxes have been levied by the states and especially by the United States on all except small estates. In consequence, much of the wealth in great estates is confiscated by governments. This clearly discriminates against accumulations of wealth, against the will of the owner, and against families, for inheritances are the economic cement of families across the generations. To avoid such a fate for their wealth, some people of property create private foundations or trusts committed to charitable and other government approved purposes. These may, or may not, serve worthwhile purposes. However that may be, the subject deserved some discussion in connection with the distribution of wealth.

> *To take from one because it is thought that his own industry and that of his father's has acquired too much, in order to spare to others, who, or whose fathers have not exercised equal industry and skill, is to violate arbitrarily the first principle of association-the guarantee to every one of a free exercise of his industry and the fruits acquired by it.*
> **Thomas Jefferson**

# Study Guide for:

# 15 The Distribution of Wealth

## Chapter Summary

This chapter deals with who gets what, when, and why. That is, people receive income from numerous sources. In the market place that income is derived from their ownership of resources and the sale of those resources in the production process. Thus, rent is a payment for land, wages a payment for labor, and interest a payment for borrowed money.

Some writers have argued that rent charged for the use of land should not be allowed because no one's labor produced the land. But this argument is not persuasive since all land has numerous competing uses and has typically been acquired by individuals through some market transaction. Therefore, rental payments for its use in a particular productive endeavor serve a very real function.

The determination of wage rates was discussed before and need not be considered again here. It might be added though that all attempts to fix wages will either cause a surplus of labor and hence unemployment or a labor shortage.

The interest rate is the price charged for borrowing money. Money can only be borrowed from those who have postponed consumption today in order to provide for some future purpose. Since people prefer to meet their desires sooner rather than later, a potential profit is needed to induce people to save. The interaction between borrowers and lenders gives rise to a market rate of interest against which individuals act according to their own preferences.

People and organizations borrow money for three reasons. First, individuals borrow against expected future income in order to consume today. Likewise, governments borrow money in order to finance current spending programs. Finally, businesses borrow money to pay for capital investment projects that they hope will generate a return greater than the cost of financing them.

As government has moved to control money through the creation of fiat currency, inflation has become a significant problem for lenders. This is due to the erosion of purchasing power that follows the unexpected inflation of currency. In recent years lenders have become much more interested in speculating on the likelihood of the Federal Reserve engaging in a new round of inflation.

The residual business income that is left after paying for the factors of production is called profit. This residual is claimed by the owners who were risking the most in the production process and had no guarantee of success. Individuals who see clearly an opportunity in the market and take advantage of it can reap substantial rewards for their insight. In fact, it is this entrepreneurial insight that drives the market and leads to an increase in the variety and quality of goods available in the market.

## Points of Emphasis

1. Rent, wages, and interest are payments for land, labor, and money. Each payment serves a valuable economic function in the production process. Arbitrary attempts to alter one or the other leads to adverse economic side effects that distort market activity and inhibit trade generally.

2. Profits provide the incentive for entrepreneurship, which is the life blood of the market. It prompts individuals to look for ways of providing a little better product at a little cheaper price than their competitors.

3. Unexpected inflation tends to lead to a mis-allocation of capital since it makes borrowing money cheaper than it really should be. As a result, it leads to a redistribution of wealth from savers to borrowers.

4. Taxing an individual's inheritance is another example of the twentieth century assault on private property.

## Identification

1. distribution of wealth
2. rent
3. wage
4. interest
5. usury
6. time preference
7. profit
8. redistribution of wealth
9. inheritance

## Review Questions

1. Describe the socialist argument against the private ownership of land (or all property). How can this argument be answered?
2. How do rents insure the conservation of land?
3. What determines the cost to you of using land you own for your own purposes, rather than renting it out?
4. Why is it that a professional athlete can command a multi-million-dollar salary while a college professor with far more education earns only tens of thousands in salary?
5. What are the effects of the heavy taxation of inheritances in the United States?
6. Compare and contrast activities that:
   —create wealth,
   —distribute wealth,
   —redistribute wealth
   in such a way that explains what each one means. Why is this important to understand?

## Activity

1. Prepare a case either to support or oppose the following position: Because the heirs in an inheritance did not earn the wealth, it should be subject to heavy taxation.

## For Further Study

1. George Reisman, *The Government Against the Economy*, Caroline House Publishers: Ottawa, IL, 1979.
2. Hans Senholz, *Death and Taxes*, Libertarian Press: Spring Mills, PA, 1976.
3. Mark Skousen, *Economics on Trial: Lies, Myths, and Realities*, Business One Irwin: Homewood, IL, 1991.

> **CHAPTER CONTENT**
>
> 16.1 Advantages of International Trade     243
> 16.2 Money and Trade     244
>      16.2.1 Precious Metals     244
>      16.2.2 Fiat Money in Trade     246
>      16.2.3 The International Monetary Fund (IMF)     248
>      16.2.4 Government Obstacles to Trade     248
>      16.2.5 The Impact of Socialism on International Trade     251
>      16.2.6 Effects of Internal Redistributionist Policies     252

# 16 INTERNATIONAL TRADE

Economic principles are the same everywhere. The law of supply and demand works in determining prices in a free market the same in Afghanistan as in the United States. In the absence of different governments and, perhaps, some cultural differences there would be no occasion for having a separate chapter on international trade. We could assume that *the* market that is the crucial instrument in trade is simply the world market, and go on from there.

Actually, there are many differences from land to land: cultural, geographic, linguistic, ethnic, sometimes racial, and in customs and traditions. There are clothing, dietary, life style, religious, and ornamental differences. They often have different histories, heritages, heroes, and recreational pursuits. Peoples are separated from one another by political boundaries, generally referred to as nations. These national boundaries are sometimes accidental rather than essential so far as these differences are concerned. That is, within a single nation there may be peoples of different languages, customs, traditions, ethnic backgrounds, and so on. Moreover, there are sometimes several nations with essentially the same background, as, for example, Great Britain, Australia, and Canada (excepting the French speaking provinces).

However convenient it might be, there is no reason that it would be best for all people to be the same and ruled by one world government. The case for free trade is a persuasive one. There are great advantages to all nations to have as free a movement of people and goods as possible. George Washington laid down some wise rules for freedom of trade that would leave political systems largely undisturbed, in his Farewell Address in 1796, rules worth quoting again. He said:

> The great rule of conduct for us in regard to foreign nations is, in extending our commercial relations to have with them as little *political* connection as possible. . . .
>
> Harmony, liberal intercourse with all nations are recommended by policy, humanity, and interest. But even our commercial policy should hold an equal and impartial hand, neither seeking nor granting exclusive favors or preferences; consulting the natural course of things; diffusing and diversifying by gentle means the streams of commerce, but forcing nothing; . . .

He implied, what is indeed the case, that trade or commerce is a peaceful thing by its nature, while political entanglements can and do tend to lead to conflicts. But the thought here may well go beyond what he had in mind. It is that even if differences among peoples and nations may sometimes hamper trade that is not necessarily a compelling reason for trying to obliterate all distinctions. It may well be that differences have merits of their own, and greater or lesser value, which may rightly overrule the economic advantage. To hold otherwise would be to give to economy a greater priority in public affairs than it has, to fall sway to **economicism**, to maintain that the economic tail, so to speak, should wag the dog that is life. Jesus said that "Man does not live by bread alone." Economics describes the rules by which bread may be most effectively attained, but it has no place in prescribing whether bread is what is most wanted or not.

> **economicism**—an ideology or economic theory that makes economics the centerpiece in thought and gives it priority over moral, ethical, or other philosophical or religious considerations in the making of decisions.

> **Limits of Economics**
> Jesus said that "Man does not live by bread alone." Economics describes the rules by which bread may be most effectively attained, but it has no place in prescribing whether bread is what is most wanted or not.

The developments in transportation and communication over the past century have greatly expanded the opportunities for contacts among people around the world and the expansion of world trade. Indeed, there is truly a world market for many goods today, though it is still greatly hampered by political barriers and other differences. The development of the steamship put travel and transportation across the seas on a scheduled basis. The development of the telegraph, telephone, radio, and internet placed communication on a virtual instantaneous basis to the places where it reached. Satellite transmissions have brought the whole world into instantaneous reach. Air travel and transport with jet propulsion have placed virtually the whole world within reach within 24 hours, though scheduling and stops might extend that slightly for more remote areas.

Advances in technology signify a kind of progress that makes it appear that not only a world market but also a world government is within reach. That, however, is an illusion. It is by no means clear that man makes substantial or continual cumulative progress in any other arena than technology. There is all too little evidence that manners and morals progress with continual improvement. By almost any standard, they have been in a constant decline. Diplomatic manners, i.e., behavior among nations, have gone downhill from what was probably a high in the nineteenth century. The most obvious example might be the increasing failure of nations to declare war when they actually go to war, and the appearance of massive surprise attacks. As for music, to take another example, there has been great progress in reproducing it over the past century, that is in the technology, but the quality of music produced has been in decline since the mid-nineteenth century. Nor do relations among peoples and nations necessarily improve with contact. In the nature of things, each child that is born has to be trained and civilized, and that is an ever renewed task for parents, communities, and cultures, which are all also subject to decay, deterioration, and disintegration. The analogy from technological progress does not apply well to communities and peoples. Moreover, technological change often strains and disintegrates cultures.

All this is a way of suggesting that advances in technology may tell us very little about what can or will happen in international relations. There, the differences are great and have been aggravated even more by political ideologies that have thus far separated people rather than uniting them. And, as we shall see, these ideologies have tended to hamper rather than extend free trade. Some people become enamored of the possibilities of harmony among peoples when they study economics, but it must ever be kept in mind that much of economic thought is an abstraction from the whole reality that must be seen in context to see the limitations.

In any case, collectivist, socialist, and communist ideology and practice have greatly altered the character of international trade. From time immemorial, trade has been mostly between people acting as individuals, or occasionally as organizations, usually privately owned. Socialist policies within countries have altered trade to make it more in the direction of being between and among nations rather than individuals and private organizations. That is most pronounced in countries with Communist controlled governments. These do not permit individuals to engage in **foreign** trade for resale, as a rule. Moreover, private property is so circumscribed that individuals own little to trade, in any case. This will be discussed more fully below, but it needed to be called to attention at this point. In such cases, trade among nations is primarily politically, not economically, motivated, and as we turn now to the examination of the advantages of foreign trade, we need to keep in mind that those enumerated are mainly economic, not political, in character.

**foreign**—situated outside one's own country.

## 16.1 Advantages of International Trade

The great economic advantage of international trade is that it expands the market, expands it from the **domestic** scene to as many countries and peoples as participate in it. It makes a greater variety and supply of goods and services available. It should be kept in mind, too, that this greater supply is a greater demand for domestic goods as well. Recalling Say's Law, remember that goods are ultimately traded for goods. Thus, the supply of goods being offered by foreigners to Americans is a demand for American goods as well, directly or ultimately.

**domestic**—situated inside one's own country.

Nor should the market be thought of only as a trade of commodities for commodities, as would occur if Americans traded appliances for bananas to Costa Rica, for example. Some economists talk about foreign trade in these terms, as if that were all that were involved. Not only does international trade involve all sorts of goods and provide an outlet for the output of the skills and craftsmanship of all people, but in its broadest sense it entails the free movement of people as well. The country that carried out the most thoroughgoing free trade ever known was the United Kingdom (England, Scotland, and Wales) for much of the nineteenth century. How far it went is suggested by the following quotation from A. J. P. Taylor, *English History, 1914–1945*:

> Until August 1914 a sensible law-abiding Englishman could pass through life and hardly notice the existence of the state, beyond the post office and the policeman. He could live where he liked and as he liked. He had no official number identity card. He could travel abroad or leave his country for ever without a passport or any sort of official permission. He could exchange his money for any other currency without restriction or limit. He could buy goods from any country in the world on the same terms he bought them at home....

In sum, he could move and trade freely in the world without penalty from his country.

In any case, all sorts of things get exchanged between countries besides manufactured products and exotic produce. Undoubtedly, the United States does buy bananas, coconuts, Brazil nuts, coffee, tea, cocoa, and Turkish tobacco from abroad, but in addition to exotic products, Americans import music, books, wine, Scotch and Irish whiskey, Persian rugs, paintings, automobiles, steel, beef, oil, and numerous other goods of all sorts. In addition to commodities, many highly skilled and learned persons have migrated to the United States.

Among the advantages of international trade is that it disperses the fruits of specialization or division of labor. It enables peoples and countries to produce what they produce best and less expensively and to import from other countries that which they produce best and less expensively. It would be possible, for example, to grow bananas in the United States, but it would be prohibitively expensive to do so. It might be possible, too, to grow cherries or apples in the tropics, but again it would be quite expensive. Many countries have **natural advantages** in producing particular goods. There are other sorts of advantages than natural ones, but the principle remains the same. Some people have developed over long periods particular kinds of skills, have acquired and mastered the technology earlier, and so on.

Over time, international trade tends to reduce the apparent inequities in the distribution of materials and goods over the earth. There is an important qualification to this, however; this works if trade is not greatly hampered by political forces. Technological advances, machinery as well as consumer products, get distributed ever more broadly. As this happens, differences in wages tend to decline as well. As a normal process of trade, however, this may take a long time, for many people not only lack machinery but lack as well the training and tradition of learning for adapting it to their use. Even so, free trade does tend to reduce economic disparities among countries and peoples.

**natural advantage**—an advantage owed to something unique to a particular location.

### Getting the Point . . .

List as many advantages of international trade as you can. Why would we want to encourage it?

## 16.2 Money and Trade

One of the biggest problems for international trade is a medium of exchange. Common ground in some sort of medium of exchange is as essential to extensive international trade as it is for domestic trade. As has been demonstrated, national monetary systems can pose major obstacles to trade. At best, they can introduce great complexities in trade; at worst, they return trade to virtual barter. Some sort of common currency for accounting purposes is almost essential. That is one of the functions of money, of course, and a prime one. In the absence of a common currency, roundabout ways can be worked out to arrive at something like one. That is what exists in the world at the present time. Before going into that, however, it will be helpful to review a little the system for an international medium of exchange that preceded the present situation.

### 16.2.1 Precious Metals

By common and widespread acceptance, the precious metals became the media of exchange among civilized peoples. Most often, gold emerged as the standard of account or reckoning, but silver was widely used as well, and pieces of copper served well for making small change. Jewels might have served almost as well, so far as being widely valued and being acceptable in exchange, but they did not have malleability, could not readily be divided into standard sizes, and thus were inferior to gold and silver as media of exchange.

Kingdoms, nations, or empires often had their own particular systems of coinage. Their coins were often stamped with the likeness of some monarch or leader, too. These differences mattered little for international trade, however. Precious metals traded by weight in international trade, regardless of the will of the sovereign whose image might adorn them, or the name or the alleged weight of the coin. In such an extensive empire as the Roman Empire, which at one time encompassed all the known civilized peoples, Roman coins undoubtedly held sway. But in the more diverse situations that have been more usual, precious metals often moved with ease from one country to another. Only two things usually concerned tradesmen, the weight and fineness of the metal. Otherwise, they could not have cared less what was stamped upon the coins.

> **Precious Metals in International Trade**
> In the more diverse situations that have been more usual, precious metals often moved with ease from one country to another. Only two things usually concerned tradesmen, the weight and fineness of the metal. Otherwise, they could not have cared less what was stamped upon the coins.

As national paper currencies became commonplace, backed more or less by gold and/or silver, the circulation of gold and full valued silver coins declined. International accounts were often settled in gold or silver ingots, which moved freely from country to country. The important point, however, is not the mechanics of exchange but that accounting and exchanges between countries were effected by precious metals. Gold was the standard for exchange in the nineteenth century, and continued to do so into the twentieth century. But after the first third or so of the twentieth century, paper currencies were so loosely backed by gold, when they were backed by it at all, that gold was decreasingly used in international exchanges and ceased to be the basis for international accounting.

The gold standard proved itself as the best one for international exchange; indeed, it has proved itself over and over again as the choice of peoples in civilized countries. The term, however, is somewhat confusing, since it might convey the notion that it was a standard established by government, as a standard of weights and measures may be. That, however, is not the basic meaning of a gold standard. It means, rather, the standard medium for accounting among nations, however it came to play that role. It means that under it gold is the ultimate medium of exchange. The gold standard is what evolved as the standard in as much of a free market internationally as has existed. Gold is almost universally prized by tradesmen and people generally. It has use as a commodity; hence, its monetary use is by no means the sole determinant of what it will bring in the market. It is not an arbitrary standard but one that arises from its natural place among precious metals.

Two major developments of the twentieth century set the stage for or led to the abandonment of the gold standard. They were: world war and socialism. War always disrupts trade. The more extensive and intense the war, the more trade is disrupted. There were two world wars in the first half of the twentieth century: World War I and World War II. Although the fighting in World War I was concentrated, it was vastly destructive of lives and property and had worldwide impact. World War II was even more destructive and disruptive. It was total war, and in both wars governments had tended to become totalitarian, using the power of government to mobilize all resources. Governments did not raise much of the wealth for fighting the wars by regular taxation, but resorted instead to monetary inflation. Most of them went off the gold standard during World War I, and many of them virtually destroyed their money by vast inflations during World War II.

Socialist ideas were gaining ground in a number of countries before World War I, and totalitarian socialism—Bolshevism or communism—came to power in the Soviet Union during the war. While most socialists promote the idea that they are internationalist, socialistic governments have tended to be highly nationalistic in impact. Socialists have sought to control the economies of their countries to a greater or lesser extent. In order to do so, they have found it desirable to control the money supply and necessary to control trade in one way or another. The most drastic control over trade was introduced in the Soviet Union under Joseph Stalin, who sought, as he said, to "build socialism in one country." In effect, he closed the borders of the Soviet Union, dropped an Iron Curtain, in the phrase of Winston Churchill, and virtually wiped out what remained of trade with the rest of the world. Domestically, the old money was destroyed, to be replaced by a rigidly controlled paper currency that was fiat money. Other countries, in Europe and America, moved more gradually toward controlled economies in the interwar years. The partially revived gold standard was abandoned generally during the Great Depression.

Governments turned to deficit spending to finance their increasing welfare programs. To do this, countries turned to their control over the money supply as a means of getting borrowed money to cover the deficits. **John Maynard Keynes**, an Englishman, proposed that governments should engage in deficit spending during recessions and depressions and increase the money supply to promote economic prosperity. Many countries, including the United States, took his advice. The ongoing inflations could not be sustained by gold, and countries eventually abandoned such relics as remained of any gold backing of the currency.

### 16.2.2 Fiat Money in Trade

Fiat money does not travel. That is, it generally has no value outside the country in which it is issued. Fiat money, it may be recalled, can be exchanged for goods within a country because it has been made legal tender by the government of that country. Because a medium of exchange is essential to make all but the simplest exchanges possible. The acceptance of such paper possibly stems from the time when it was backed by or exchangeable for precious metals. Obviously, a country has no power to make its money legal tender in another nation. That might be sufficient reason to explain or account for the failure of fiat money in traveling. In fact, however, governments do not usually approve, i.e., they prohibit, the use of another nation's money within their borders,

---

**John Maynard Keynes (1883–1946)**

English economist and adviser to the government. He was born in England and studied at Cambridge University. Keynes first came to public notice as the result of a little book he wrote about the peace settlement following World War I. It was called *The Economic Consequences of the Peace* and dealt with the difficulties countries would encounter in attempting to enforce the scheduled reparations payments on Germany. The most important and influential work by Keynes, however, is his *The General Theory of Employment, Interest and Money*. He claimed that by deficit spending and money management governments could maintain prosperity. He offered a theoretical justification for at least some of the inflationary policies that most governments have followed since the book appeared, though some countries were apparently already embarked upon such a course.

and they often limit or prohibit the taking of their own money outside their borders.

While it is accurate to say that virtually all the currencies in the world, including the dollar, are fiat money, in a sense they still have a residue of backing. That is, they are backed by the commodities, land, and labor for which they can be exchanged in countries. Indeed, precious metals still constitute a residue of the backing, especially in international trade. Gold, held in central banks or by nations, is still used sometimes to make up for an imbalance of trade. But the backing is floating, not fixed, and uncertain or indeterminate. That is to say, this money is no longer worth any certain amount of any commodities (including gold or silver), land or labor. What anything will bring, including the currencies themselves floats and may change by the minute or hour on international exchanges. It is possible to buy gold with dollars, but how much gold with how many dollars is subject to ongoing changes. Even so, at least some, perhaps all, of the values of fiat money derive from the floating backing they have in commodities, land, and labor.

These things may help to explain why some national currencies have a higher standing in international trade than others. It might be supposed that all national currencies would have an equal standing, or lack of it, in international trade. Since the early 1970s that has been largely true in the international market for currencies, where currencies have floated in value in relation to one another. None of them have any fixed value, and they are all equal in that. Even so, the United States dollar and the British pound occupy a special position in trade. After World War II, the dollar came to be used by a large portion of the countries in the world as the currency for settling international payments. The British pound continued to play that role for Commonwealth countries. Communist countries have not usually participated in international arrangements for making payments. The dollar was stable internationally until the early 1970s. Between 1934 and 1971, or thereabouts, it was supported by gold at the rate of $1/35^{th}$ of an ounce. Internationally, it was not a fiat currency, but supported by gold. Since the early 1970s, it has no longer been supported by gold at a fixed rate and is as unstable as most other major currencies.

**Fiat money does not travel.** That is, it generally has no value outside the country in which it is issued.

Now it is necessary to back up a bit to clear up some matters. How international exchanges are actually made has not yet been explained. Ordinarily, currencies do not leave the countries of issue in international trade. Trade is basically of goods for goods (excluding money); those who buy the goods pay in their own currency, and those who sell them are paid in their own currency. Large banks and money dealers have foreign currency credits held in the country of origin, and these countries, in turn, have dollar accounts, by way of example, on deposit in the United States. These accounts build up or decline, depending upon whether the money dealer pays for something bought from a foreign source by an American (decline) or pays an American for goods bought abroad (build up). Trade is multilateral, consisting of all foreign countries that trade with one another. Thus, a country only has a problem when there is an imbalance between its total exports and imports.

### 16.2.3 The International Monetary Fund (IMF)

**International Monetary Fund (IMF)**—an international organization created in the Bretton Woods treaty to provide for currency exchange in a world of fiat money.

When a country has an imbalance at the end of an accounting period, the difference must somehow be made up. In 1944, an **International Monetary Fund** was set up to deal with this situation, a fund with which all member nations make deposits. They can draw on the Fund a portion of their assessment to meet these imbalances. The Fund also requires member nations to deposit in currencies that are relatively stable, i.e., they only fluctuate a given percentage over a prescribed period. Since the currencies of most countries usually lost value swiftly in the midst of their frequent inflations, most countries kept dollars rather than their own currencies on deposit. Thus, the dollar gained its preeminence among the currencies of the world. It was obviously a case, as the saying goes, that in the kingdom of the blind the one-eyed man is king. Since the early 1970s, when the United States stopped backing the dollar with a fixed amount of gold, the dollar, too, has fluctuated as well, though not as wildly as the currencies of many countries, although that may well change in the future as the U.S. debt rises and the Federal Reserve's monetary expansion escalates.

The above gives much too pretty a picture, however, of international trade as it has been carried on since World War II. The fiat currencies of virtually every country in the world are a cross between play money and national bills of credit. They are not even true bills of credit because they are not promises to pay in fixed amounts of anything. For most of the period, the United States has fostered a great redistribution of wealth, by way of foreign aid, the World Bank, and, in recent years, by huge bank loans from large American banks. Virtually all the governments in the world are fiscally irresponsible. They pile up huge debts and repudiate them by destroying whatever value their money might have through monetary inflations and failure to make payments when they fall due. There are degrees of fiscal irresponsibility, of course; some countries are wildly irresponsible, while others mask their irresponsibility.

At any rate, international trade is a charade carried on upon a foundation of debt, credit, currencies continually being devalued, unpaid loans, and deficit spending. A degree of honesty exists regarding the worth of these currencies in relation to one another. Other than in communist countries, official exchange rates have generally been abandoned, and they are bought and sold in the market. It is true, too, that actual goods are traded between countries, and that is not a charade. The charade lies in what is traded for the goods within countries and in making up imbalances between countries. This is a charade of paper, debts, loans, and credits.

To all appearances, international trade was quite vigorous in the 1980s. A great deal of ingenuity has gone into providing a framework within which the insubstantial currencies—growing progressively less substantial—can sustain the trade. The system appears to work. Yet national currencies based upon fiat money are, by their nature, obstacles to trade. They are made to appear otherwise by the will and power of governments, mainly the United States. How great obstacles the national currencies really are awaits only the withdrawal or fall from power of such nations as sustain it for demonstration.

### 16.2.4 Government Obstacles to Trade

If governments are primarily maintaining law and order, then most of the obstacles to trade are natural. That is they are associated with the costs of engaging in trade. These include the costs of information, communication, and transportation. Such costs are more efficiently and effectively overcome when law and order are maintained. Thus, governments are necessary for extensive trade to be carried on.

> **Natural Obstacles to Trade**
> If governments are primarily maintaining law and order, then most of the obstacles to trade are natural. That is they are associated with the costs of engaging in trade. These include the costs of information, communication, and transportation. Such costs are more efficiently and effectively overcome when law and order are maintained. Thus, governments are necessary for extensive trade to be carried on.

Yet, governments themselves often erect many obstacles to trade. When they prevent or prohibit private ownership of something within their country they are interfering with trade. For example, the United States prohibited private ownership of gold except for certain commercial or decorative purposes during the years from the early 1930s to the early 1970s. When a government makes paper currency legal tender and makes that currency inconvertible into gold, it makes the international currency—gold—unavailable for trade. Tradesmen must go through all the hassle that may have been set up to effect trades.

Anyone who ever goes through the customs inspection of his own or another country has got at least a whiff of the obstacles. His bags are subject to inspection. He may have to pay duties on goods bought in one country and taken into another. Even the mailing of packages from one country to another entails the filling out of papers and attachment of customs stickers. Such things may be only minor inconveniences, but importing some goods may turn out to be quite costly. Suppose, for example, that an American who is traveling abroad decides to buy a sports car in that country and have it shipped to the United States. He will, of course, have to pay any duties levied by the United States on such imports. Worse, possibly, he will have to pay for making such changes as are required (such as bringing it to American standards for emissions, and the like) before it can be licensed for use on public roads in the United States. What may have looked like an attractive bargain when he was abroad may turn into a costly nuisance in this country.

It sometimes appears that governments are determined to offset the advantages of foreign trade. Historically, the device most often used to this end has been the **protective tariff**. The tariff has already been discussed in some detail elsewhere, though one economic point needs to be made about it here. Most arguments advanced for protective tariffs are made by those who have some particular interest or hope of gain from the tariff. Take the argument for the protection of infant industries as an example.

The argument goes something like this. A new industry is at a considerable disadvantage when it begins competing with products from well established industries in other countries. Undoubtedly, new firms often have difficulty in competing with older established ones, but it is hardly a conclusive argument for making customers pay a higher price for the goods of the established firms. Nor is it a matter only of firms separated by national boundaries from one another. After all, an American automobile company starting out now would have great difficulty in competing with

**Getting the Point...**

As you read through the rest of the chapter, keep a written list of actions by government that create obstacles to international trade.

protective tariff—*see definition, p. 31.*

General Motors or Ford. Yet most of us would be unmoved by the argument that General Motors car buyers should be taxed 50% above the list price in order to give the new company a chance. For that matter, a new dentist or physician in town may have difficulty in getting customers for his services. The older established professionals, if they have good reputations, undoubtedly have an advantage over beginners. Should we tax their services with a 50% surcharge in order to give the newer ones a chance? Those are the economic questions involved in the infant industries argument. National boundaries do not alter the economics of what is involved, though they may arouse nationalistic prejudices or partisanship.

The point should be made, as well, that a domestic producer will have some advantages over a foreign producer whether he is starting out or established. In competing in his home market, he is at least somewhat nearer the market—reducing the cost of shipping—and may be many thousands of miles nearer than any foreign competitors. He is apt to be much better acquainted with the market. He knows the language, the customs, and the tastes of his customers better. He may even have some success in appealing to the national pride of his countrymen in getting them to purchase his goods rather than those of foreign firms. In any case, the economics of starting a new business are approximately the same whether the beginner is competing with domestic or foreign producers or both. If he is entering the business, he must feel that he can offer the product at a lower price or of higher quality at a competitive price, or that he is offering something sufficiently different from others that it will fill a gap in the market.

Let us return, however, to the question of national interest, which has often been raised as a justification for protective tariffs. The most persuasive case, at least in our day, is that a country must maintain its industrial, and, perhaps, its agricultural base in case of war. If we become dependent upon other countries for industrial or other goods, the argument goes, we may confront a situation where these goods will not be available in time of war, either because we were buying them from countries that are now at war with us or from countries whose trade is cut off by the enemy. Looked at closely, this is substantially an argument against virtually all foreign trade. Every independent country in the world is at least a potential enemy who might go to war against us. Almost any good or service has some possible use in war. Moreover, almost any sort of production machinery or technology of anything could be altered in war to contribute to the war effort.

The above is basically a fear tactic employed by manufacturers, and others, who wish to avoid the rigors of competition. It may well be an antiquated argument as well. This is an age of jet planes, rockets, and atomic missiles. There is great doubt that weapons not available at the outset of a war might ever have any relevance. This would almost certainly be the case in an nuclear war, and it might well be true in a more conventional war among great powers. In any case, unless war is imminent, it is a rather strange argument. What it amounts to is that a nation should forego less expensive or better quality goods from foreign countries for ten, twenty, thirty, or a hundred years, either until the protected industry has become competitive or the awaited war has come. In sum, the national interest argument makes more sense as a self-interested argument for non-competitive producers than for the defense of a country.

The market and economic approach to this question, in any case, is not to seek dis-economic solutions to failing businesses or industries by devising means to reduce foreign imports, whether the means are tariffs, quotas, or other obstacles to trade. If an industry is producing goods that are in demand in the United States, it is economic to look to the causes of failure rather than for devices to hamper trade. As noted earlier, a domestic manufacturer has some advantages in any case in producing for the home market. If it is a business that has long been in operation, it may also have the advantage of being well established.

> **Domestic Industry that Cannot Compete**
> The market and economic approach to this question, in any case, is not to seek dis-economic solutions to failing businesses or industries by devising means to reduce foreign imports, whether the means are tariffs, quotas, or other obstacles to trade. If an industry is producing goods that are in demand in the United States, it is economic to look to the causes of failure rather than for devices to hamper trade.

Our inquiry takes us once again over ground that has been at least partially covered. As noted earlier, if a business is a good-sized corporation, it probably suffers more or less from corporate drag. The larger it becomes the greater the likelihood that it will also suffer from bureaucratic drag, the weight of its own procedures for doing things. The entrepreneurial spirit may be long gone from the organization. It may have been replaced by the managerial spirit, people intent upon maintaining their power, thus determined to keep out those who are brighter, more innovative, and bolder. In short, failing businesses, or even industries, may have their own internal weaknesses. Businesses that survive in perpetuity may in theory be unworthy candidates for protection from competition. Instead, competition is the cure for incompetence. But the problems of international trade are much broader than that.

### 16.2.5 The Impact of Socialism on International Trade

Socialism and welfarism, as noted earlier, not only present obstacles to international trade but also for competition in domestic and world trade. The United States has hardly been hardest hit by the onset of socialism and welfarism. Indeed, America has been spared the worst extremes of these ideologies thus far. Even so, the thrust of socialism is worldwide, and the United States has been bitten as well.

Socialism is, at its center, an assault on private property, and the rights that pertain to it. The property it is most apt to focus on is that used in the production and distribution of goods. Doctrinaire socialist governments are often committed to the nationalization of productive property when they come to power. They especially like to nationalize the property owned by foreigners within their country. That is especially popular with voters who have listened to the harangues of demagogues and believe that their economic ills have been caused by foreign investors. These are alleged to have plundered the wealth of the country for their own benefit. However that may be, the property of foreign investors is a favorite early target of socialistic governments. The result is that potential investors are reluctant to invest in countries that have gone or are in danger of going socialist. Private foreign investment is the market way of distributing the benefits of technology around the world. It is a crucial aspect of freedom of trade. If investments cannot move freely then trade is hampered and cannot fully work its altruistic effects.

Socialists do not necessarily confiscate property, either of their own people or of foreign investors outright. Instead, they may seize the property but promise to pay for it over a period of time. Either way, of course, they discourage foreign investors. Or, they may leave the owners nominally in control over their property but tax away most of the profits, prescribe the wages to be paid, and regulate the property in other ways. In short, they may leave the substance of private property but divest the owners of the fruits and rights of ownership. All these types of assaults upon property have occurred. They have been especially common in what are called Third World, or less developed countries.

> **Socialism** is, at its center, an assault on private property, and the rights that pertain to it. The property it is most apt to focus on is that used in the production and distribution of goods. Doctrinaire socialist governments are often committed to the nationalization of productive property when they come to power.

### 16.2.6 Effects of Internal Redistributionist Policies

Socialist or welfarist policies within countries also hamper international trade. These are basically redistributionist policies by which governments in one way or another redistribute wealth. They may or may not entail taxation and welfare payments by governments directly. Governments may, for example, give special privileges to labor unions, enabling them to organize and establish union wages well above what they would get in the market. Or, they may restrict the production of certain farm products, so as to drive up prices. In such cases, they will need to be insulated from the world market. Goods produced at these abnormally high prices probably will not sell on the world market, nor can goods produced and offered on the world market be permitted to compete with them on the domestic market.

Various devices have been used by countries to enable them to have trade under these or similar circumstances. One of these is the **European Common Market**. This is a regional agreement among neighboring nations to reduce or remove barriers of trade as they apply to member nations. Since these countries are more or less socialistic and welfarist, this enables them to keep their redistributionist policies in effect while having a good-sized market within which to buy and sell their products. This enables them to enjoy some of the advantages of free trade without giving up their redistributionist policies. Meanwhile, they can still have barriers to trade with other countries in the world.

The discussion of internal obstacles to trade brings us back to contemporary difficulties of American businesses in competing in foreign trade. Aside from difficulties inherent in large organizations, especially corporations, welfarism under the thrust of socialism has placed large burdens upon business in general. This has been especially true for corporations and large, once profitable, businesses. Perhaps, the single largest burden has been the **corporate income tax**. For large profitable corporations the tax has sometimes been more than 50%, though it is now less than that. In effect, this is meant to be a tax on profits. If it were, it would actually be subtracted from the profitability of the corporation, since at the point that it is taken, the actual investors have had no return on their

---

**European Common Market**—the European Union was formed to allow for the smooth, less hindered trade of goods among the European nations that have joined it and this is their trade agreement.

**corporate income tax**—*see definition, p. 32.*

investment for the taxpaying period. Actually, the corporate tax is a cost of doing business for the corporation, though it does not have to be paid if there are no profits. In order to make a reasonable return to investors, it has to be added to the cost of products or services. It should be noted that when the profits are paid out to investors, they are subject to the income tax already. Thus, the whole of the alleged profits are taxed at the corporate level, and what remains is taxed again when it reaches the investors. The tendency of these taxes is either to drive up the cost of products or reduce profits, or both. If it drives up the cost of products that may mean that the company may find it quite difficult to compete with foreign companies either in price and quality of products or for investment money.

But the corporate and private income tax is only the most visible of the burdens placed upon businesses by redistributionist activities in the United States. Since the 1930s, the government has generally supported labor unions. There is no doubt that the cost of labor is a cost of production, and, as such, may drive up the price of goods produced. To the extent that union prices are higher than they would be in the market, then, they tend to price American goods out of the market. The Social Security tax paid by the employer is another cost added to the cost of production. The same is true for any company contribution to a union or other retirement plan. Company contributions to health or hospitalization insurance, paid holidays and vacations, and any other fringe benefits are costs of labor, and thus of production.

It is often claimed in defense of a protective tariff that higher paid American workers cannot compete with foreign labor that is often much cheaper. Beyond a certain point, that is undoubtedly true. To the extent that higher American wages can be attributed to higher productivity, owing to skill, better technology, and more effective techniques, it would not be true. When government intervenes to redistribute wealth, however, any additions it makes to the cost of labor are likely to be above any payment for the greater efficiency of American work. The problem should, however, be attributed to its source. It should be attributed to welfarist and redistributionist measures by the government. Heavy corporate and individual income taxes take away from investment in technology as well. Obstacles to trade will only aggravate, not cure, these problems.

*We need to fight protectionism with everything that we have because when there's a level playing field and when you have open markets and when free trade is flourishing, American workers, American farmers, Americans are going to benefit.*
**Condoleezza Rice**

*In a world dependent on international trade and commerce, and staggering under a heavy load of international debt, no policy is more destructive than protectionism. It cuts off markets, eliminates trade, causes unemployment in the export industries all over the world, depresses the prices of export commodities, especially farm products of the United States. It is the crowning folly of government intervention.*
**Hans F. Sennholz**

*You don't need a treaty to have free trade.*
**Murray Rothbard**

*If goods don't cross borders, armies will.*
**Frederic Bastiat**

# Study Guide for:

# 16 International Trade

## Chapter Summary

International trade is really no different from any other kind of trade. Yet, there are factors that complicate the process. This is especially true in modern times when fiat currencies have been established in most countries around the globe. The problem of trade thus encompasses the need to trade these fiat currencies. As each country's central bank manipulates its own currency, fluctuations in exchange rates result. This adds to the uncertainty of trade.

Governments have created other obstacles to international trade. These include the imposition of tariffs and quotas. Tariffs are taxes that drive up prices of foreign goods while quotas limit the entry of goods into a country. These policies are pursued in order to provide some special interest businesses protection from competition. The major problem of these policies is that competition serves a positive function because it promotes excellence and leads to higher quality products at lower prices.

## Points of Emphasis

1. The advantages of international trade arise for the same reasons that we trade at all: namely because trade is mutually beneficial.

2. When precious metals were used as money, currency exchanges were unnecessary. When paper money was redeemable for precious metals, exchange rates were established.

3. The development of fiat currencies in the twentieth century has resulted in flexible exchange rates since no currency has a fixed value based on the quantity of gold for which it can be redeemed. Thus, the values must fluctuate and this can lead to trade imbalances. For this reason, the International Monetary Fund was set up in which member nations can make deposits of some stable currency to meet these imbalances.

4. Governments have served as formidable obstacles to trade because of the artificial barriers that they have erected.

## Identification

1. economicism
2. foreign
3. domestic
4. natural advantage
5. John Maynard Keynes
6. International Monetary Fund (IMF)
7. protective tariff
8. European Common Market
9. corporate income tax

## Review Questions

1. Why do people trade? What is the advantage of international trade?

2. What complication to international trade arises as a result of the introduction of fiat currencies?

3. Why do governments create laws that reduce international trade?

4. Why is government necessary for an efficiently functioning market?

5. What types of government actions create additional obstacles to international trade?

## Activity

1. Prepare a case either to support or oppose the following position: "We can't open our borders to foreign products because other countries would flood our markets with their goods."

## For Further Study

1. Frédéric Bastiat, Economic Sophisms, The Foundation for Economic Education: Irvington, NY, 1964.

2. P.T. Bauer, Reality and Rhetoric: Studies in the Economics of Development, Harvard University Press, 1984.

# Section III
# Politico-Economic Systems

## Chapters

| | | |
|---|---|---|
| 17. | The Manorial-Feudal System | 261 |
| 18. | Mercantilism | 273 |
| 19. | Free Enterprise | 289 |
| 20. | Corporatism | 309 |
| 21. | Welfarism | 331 |
| 22. | Communism | 347 |

# Politico-Economic Systems

In Section II, the focus was on the principles of economics largely within the framework of a free market with free enterprise. This approach was modified somewhat by the discussion of some of the ways that government has intervened and the impact the interventions may have on economy. The approach was through breaking economy up into parts analytically, such as, money, scarcity, markets, etc., and outlining the principles as they apply to the various parts. Section III will treat economies systemically, as wholes, rather than in parts. This is possible because actual economies are to some extent integrated and comprise systems of sorts. These systems may be national, imperial, or extend more or less across a whole civilization.

As noted earlier, every actual economy exists in a political, legal, social, and perhaps a religious framework. The social framework includes customs, institutions, folkways, and traditions. The framework may be as broad as a civilization in many respects or as restricted as a small community on a small isolated island. The framework will usually adjust somewhat depending upon what it is most economical. That should not be taken to mean that the principles of economics are different from one political or cultural system to another. The principles remain the same, but how they can be applied or practiced does change. In considering economic systems, then, something much more than economy has to be taken into account, though the impact on economy is still the focus of attention.

Individuals tend in all circumstances to do what is economical for them. That is, so far as they are able, they tend to produce as much of what they most want as they can with the least cost. Following the principle of scarcity, they use those elements that are scarcest most frugally and those that are less scarce more freely. There is no great mystery why they do so; they do it because it is in their self-interest to do so. People must act ordinarily in their self-interest in order to survive, endure, or prosper. They must be on guard against the dangers that may beset them at any time, against stepping into holes, against falling prey to some dangerous animal, against attacks when they are in a helpless position, as when asleep. Their self-interest dictates, too, that they must behave economically in producing or acquiring goods.

> **Acting Out of Self-interest**
> People must act ordinarily in their self-interest in order to survive, endure, or prosper. They must be on guard against the dangers that may beset them at any time, against stepping into holes, against falling prey to some dangerous animal, against attacks when they are in a helpless position, as when asleep. Their self-interest dictates, too, that they must behave economically in producing or acquiring goods.

These rules hold whatever the social or political system, though people may sometimes be limited or thwarted in behaving economically. Examples may illustrate that they are likely to do so. Imagine a man living close to a state line in the United States. Suppose that the state in which he lives enacts a tax on gasoline that is 4 cents per gallon higher than in the adjoining state. If gasoline is that much cheaper in the other state, and other things being equal, he will probably buy his gasoline there. In this case, no legal penalties are likely to be imposed on him since it would hardly be worthwhile for state laws to prohibit bringing in gasoline not taxed there. In some other cases, however, state laws do get passed to prohibit such otherwise economic behavior. For example, at one point, Pennsylvania added 5 cents per pack to its tax on cigarettes, making them that much higher than in Ohio. The newspapers reported that some Pennsylvanians were going into Ohio and stocking up on cigarettes. Pennsylvania promptly passed a law prohibiting the bringing in of more than two packs of cigarettes not bearing the Pennsylvania tax sticker. Probably, this law did not deter many people from engaging in the illicit traffic, though little is known on the subject. In any case, people tend to behave economically as individuals despite the system under which they live.

There are cases where individuals can be shown to act in their own interest, despite the intent of the law, in ways that may harm others within the system. Extensive examples of this occurred under the crop allotment and subsidy system for cotton in the 1930s and afterward. The government attempted to reduce cotton production by limiting the amount of land that farmers could plant of the crop. On the other hand, the government subsidized the price of cotton to drive it up and make the production of cotton more profitable. With these signals sent into the market, many farmers redoubled their efforts to produce more cotton per acre, allotting their best land to the effort, increasing their use of fertilizer, and buying the most productive seed. The result was that much more cotton was produced than could be sold at the subsidized price. The government was stuck with a great surplus of cotton. It hurt Americans by diverting taxes to pay for what could not be sold. People in general were denied cotton goods, and chose what were probably less desirable synthetics, because of the high price of cotton. Granted, the fault lay on the government programs, but the principle was still illustrated that people will tend to act in ways that are individually economic even though within the system it is socially harmful.

However that may be, a considerable variety of politico-economic systems have been developed over the centuries. Some of these have been organized with little or no attention to or knowledge of economics. Others have been devised with considerable understanding of economics, and some have been devised to change the character of behavior regarding economy. Six systems will be considered here—the Feudal–Manorial system, Mercantilism, Free Enterprise, Corporatism, Welfarism, and Communism. They range in time from the Middle Ages in Europe to the present. They probably encompass most of the practices that have been utilized in politico-economic systems, except for outright slavery, though they may not cover some of the more primitive of practices.

It should be emphasized at the outset that the discussion of these systems has been simplified. All systems are operated by humans, with all their individuality, weaknesses, lack of discipline, slovenliness, and imperfections, as well as aspirations. Politico-economic systems entail greater diversity than can be suggested in any brief account. This is especially so in the account that follows, where there is an attempt to describe the essentials only. There is more freedom in totalitarian systems than the rulers intend, and more compulsions in the freest of systems than may immediately meet the eye. Human imagination is never completely contained within any system, nor are people ever completely freed to do as they will. Systems do, however, tend toward integrating around some ideas, principles, beliefs or purposes.

In addition to treating economies as wholes, there are other reasons for examining several politico-economic systems. They provide us some prototypes for characterizing economic practices. Moreover, many practices are not confined to any one system. They crop up in others as well. The protective tariff, for example, has its systemic justification within mercantilism, yet it has persisted to a greater or a lesser extent to this day. Sometimes, the words and justifications change more than the practices. To see these practices in their historical settings is the best way to understand them to the fullest.

Finally, to look at economics in this way is necessary to offset economicism. Economics is an aspect of life and thought, but only a single aspect. Separated from other aspects and values, it may assume a haughty role that is not, nor ever has been, its place. To say this is not to demean either economics or economic thought, but rather to put it in its place. Without the chastening of the context of actual systems, it is subject to overstating its case in whatever direction it happens to take. Within context we can appreciate both economic ideas and their limitations.

---

*Self-interest is not myopic selfishness. It is whatever it is that interests the participants, whatever they value, whatever goals they pursue. The scientist seeking to advance the frontiers of his discipline, the missionary seeking to convert infidels to the true faith, the philanthropist seeking to bring comfort to the needy—all are pursuing their interests, as they see them, as they judge them by their own values.*
— **Milton Friedman**

*Where self-interest is suppressed, it is replaced by a burdensome system of bureaucratic control that dries up the wellsprings of initiative and creativity.*
— **P. J. O'Rourke**

> **Chapter Content**
>
> 17.1 Feudalism     262
> 17.2 The Manor     264
> 17.3 The Revival of Trade     266
> 17.4 The Growth of Towns     267
> 17.5 Medieval Guilds     268
> 17.6 The Lasting Impact of Medieval Ways     269

# 17 Manorial-Feudal System

The Middle Ages was in many respects the opposite of the age in which we live. It was static in orientation, not wedded at all to change and progress. That is not to suggest that change and even some progress did not take place. On the contrary, great changes took place over a period of nearly a thousand years, from the sixth century to the fifteenth century. Some historians have referred to the first two or three of these centuries as the Dark Ages and separate this time period from the Middle Ages. From the crude beginnings of the early centuries, a civilization was developing, which began to emerge and bear fruit in the twelfth and thirteenth century. This civilization was the product of the intermingling of Roman and Germanic cultures under the vitalizing influence of Christianity. Indeed, the rude and barbaric peoples of Western Europe were being Christianized during a considerable portion of the Middle Ages, or at least brought under a powerful overlay of Christian teaching and practice. Indeed, Will Durant has called the Middle Ages an *Age of Faith*. There were many other changes, as well, economic and otherwise.

Still, it was a culture, a civilization (to the extent that it was), and had an economy that was static and stable. Its organization was hierarchical. Position and place were hereditary, except in the church. In contrast to our age, equality was neither the aim nor goal; not equality before the law, not equality of opportunity, not equality of sexes, not equality of wealth, or anything else. That all humans might be equal before God was not a common thought during the Middle Ages because on earth all people were more or less unequal. A man was born to his place and that was where he was expected to live out his life. If a man was born the son of a serf, he was expected to be a serf, absent some higher calling in the church. A calling to the clergy was the only route of escape for most serfs. There were occasional exceptions and these increased as towns and trade grew, but we speak here of the general rule and of the animating ideal.

All these things had a profound effect on the economy of the Middle Ages. There was little place or reward in the society for technological innovation. Indeed, capital is one of the means of production, except in the most rudimentary economic undertaking. Capital played hardly a role at all, except at the very margins of the economy. Some coins did circulate, but money was largely irrelevant to the basic exchange of the medieval economy until the late Middle Ages. Land was central in the economy, as well as to government. That might

**landism**—an established preference for land over capital and labor. The preference must be supported by government policy to prevail. Such a preference for land and those who controlled it was established by the feudal system.

be expected since it was basically an agricultural society. But in the Middle Ages the centrality of land was much greater than that might suggest. In terms of the means of production, the system might well be called **landism**. Most people not only tilled and lived upon and off the land but were more or less bound to it. The serfs were attached to the land in the sense that they could not ordinarily move away from it of their own will. Nor could the landlord ordinarily move them off the land. Political power was based on control of the land.

In short, the Middle Ages were different from, and in many ways the opposite of our age. Yet to study them is to see some of our practices and ways in relief. This is especially so regarding their governmental institutions and economy.

## 17.1 Feudalism

**feudal system (feudalism)**—a system of political and economic control that prevailed for much of the Middle Ages in Europe. Economic control of the land was linked to political control over the people and vested in the feudal nobility, who were primarily warriors.

**estates (feudal)**—the three classes of people in feudal times, which included the nobility, the clergy, and the serfs.

**serf**—a person bound to the land on which he lives, owing work to the lord of the manor, and generally entitled to the land that he works and the hut in which he lives.

**vassal**—a Medieval term referring to the fact that a person owed loyalty and military service to some overlord. It does not signify any rank that the vassal might hold, since kings might be vassals as well as knights. Indeed, it was sometimes held in the Middle Ages that every man should have an overlord.

**homage**—a ceremony in which a vassal pledged his loyalty and service to his overlord. It might also involve some symbolic transfer to him of his fief or feudal estate.

**fealty**—the obligation of a vassal to be faithful—maintain fidelity—to his lord. Most often this required military service.

**subinfeudination**—process by which a vassal might extend his holdings by obligating himself to two or more overlords. This was only possible legally when the vassal limited his loyalty to particular overlords.

The **feudal system** was the system of government that emerged during the earlier Middle Ages to provide such government as they had in Western Europe. There were three **estates** (in a sense, classes): the nobility, the clergy, and the **serfs** or peasants. The nobility was the governing class. According to an old saying, the nobility fought, the clergy prayed, and the serfs did the work. While this greatly oversimplifies the role of the nobility and the clergy, it is substantially accurate for the serfs. There were many ranks in the nobility from highest to lowest. Depending upon when and where, they might include: emperor, king, dukes, earls, knights, and such other ranks as might exist. Indeed, in the early thirteenth century, Pope Innocent III asserted the claim that various monarchs in Europe were his **vassals**, and he was their overlord. That claim undoubtedly confused the estates, but it illustrates how far the feudal principle was extended that every noble must be a vassal of some overlord.

The government of feudal lords was based on control of land. It was a system of personal loyalty pledged from the vassal to the overlord in return for his recognition or grant of land to the vassal. It could hardly be said that the land belonged to anyone outright—as we say, in fee simple—for most land holders owed **homage** to someone for the land. Moreover, title to the land was often hereditary, and the question must at least some time arise as to whether the noble holding it could sell it and thus alienate it from his heirs. Think of it this way. A king might grant to a duke a large parcel of land. The duke then became his vassal and owed him **fealty** (loyalty) in return. The duke might in turn parcel out (subinfeudinate) the land to his own vassals. Such **subinfeudination** might go on until the land had been broken up into parcels no bigger than what would support a knight on horseback. Smaller parcels could serve no useful purpose in providing a mounted army for the overlords. Whose land was it, after all the divisions and subdivisions had been made? Was it the king's? The duke's? Or the lowest of the vassal's? In some sense, it could be said to belong to each of them in his particular capacity, but that would be to overstate the case.

It was the duty of the lords and vassals to protect the property and persons of those living on their lands. To that end, they were primarily warriors. They were judges, too, in effect, for the lord of the manor might hold court for the trying of his serfs. Overlords also held court, which their vassals were required to attend, and in which they might be tried by their peers. The church had its own courts for such trials or other hearings as might be necessary for the clergy, and the clergy were not ordinarily subject to the authority of the civil courts. While feudal lords were charged with keeping the peace, they were the main disturbers of the peace as well.

Feudal wars were frequent occurrences, if not incessant, for many times force was the only means for settling disputes. Rights were often intertwined, complex, and numerous, and to protect them war was a frequent resort. Take a case such as this. An overlord held court with his vassals in which he determined that one of his vassals had repeatedly failed or refused to perform his feudal obligations. The court would decree that the lands of this vassal were forfeit, that they must be returned to his overlord. But if the vassal chose to defend his holdings, the overlord must take them from him by force. Thus, a feudal battle or war might take place.

> **The feudal system** was the system of government that emerged during the earlier Middle Ages to provide such government as they had in Western Europe. There were three estates (in a sense, classes): the nobility, the clergy, and the serfs or peasants. The nobility was the governing class. According to an old saying, the nobility fought, the clergy prayed, and the serfs did the work.

Wars were neither necessarily large nor lengthy, they might involve no more than a few men and might last for an hour, a day, or whatever short periods they might take. **Feuds** were common, of course (the very term is Medieval in origin), and the battle might be renewed and discontinued many times. The most important point for economics is that these feuds consumed much of the wealth of Europe, particularly in the tenth and eleventh centuries. At least, the wars, *and* the preparation for them, consumed much of the wealth. A knight, as well as other lords, must be constantly ready to go to war, either on his own behalf or that of his overlord. He must have and maintain not only a fine horse worthy of the battle, but also replacement horses should his be killed or wounded. He must maintain servants to support and look after him. He must be fitted out with the required armor for battle, which in the course of time became more elaborate and expensive. And, he must have the tools of battle, swords, shields, axes, or whatever was in use. Thus, most of the wealth produced on his lands went to sustain him in or for battle.

Much of the wealth that did not go to the feudal lords went to the Roman Catholic Church. Indeed, many of the farm lands came under the control of the church in the course of time. Since the church let them out in the usual way, it was often involved in the feudal system to greater or lesser extent. Now undoubtedly, the church performed many useful and important services with the wealth that came its way. The church provided religious services, of course, maintained monasteries, nunneries, hospitals, and schools, and built many beautiful edifices, especially cathedrals, in larger towns. Nor did the church generally approve the continuous warfare of the feudal system. Eventually, it began to proclaim periods of peace during the year, when no fighting was to take place. In time, fighting was restricted to the hottest and coldest months of the year, periods when fighting was least attractive. It may be that such proclamations were often honored as much or more than the actual observance of them, but at least the church tried to limit and restrain the fighting. The codes of chivalry, which often bore earmarks of religious influence, attempted as well to soften the harshness of conflict by trying to limit it to the combatants and requiring that women be respected and that the poor not be robbed nor oppressed.

**feud**—a dispute as to who holds the rightful claim to a parcel of land, which was usually settled by force.

> **Getting the Point...**
>
> How was the wealth of Europe consumed during the Middle Ages?
>
> Why was more wealth not created during this period?

What also tended to restrain some of the excesses of feudalism was the rise of strong kings in the twelfth and thirteenth centuries, especially in England and France. Henry II of England appointed and sent judges all over England to hold court. These King's Courts began to formulate a common law for all of England by their rulings. Before that time, local custom had usually held sway, and differences in custom had undoubtedly made warfare more likely and common. The courts of the king offered a means for settling feudal disputes without resorting to combat. This did not, of course, mark the end of either feudalism or feudal warfare, but it did offer a means of reducing conflict.

## 17.2 The Manor

The **manor** was the economic unit of medieval agriculture. Indeed, it was a capsulized version of the whole economy for much of the Middle Ages, and remained throughout the period. It was also the local unit of feudal government, at least the village was. The lord of the manor, or his appointees—for a lord might have several manors—ruled the village. He held court at which serfs might be tried and punished. Fines usually went into the pocket of the lord. In theory, the lord's word was law, but in practice local custom usually held sway and modified the arbitrariness of the rule of the lord.

A manor consisted of several hundred acres of land, probably a minimum of enough to support a knight in armor. The land was divided into arable land that was cultivated, pastures, meadows, and woods. A manor ordinarily had a manor house, which was the largest and best appointed house in or around the village. It would also have a church and perhaps a parsonage as well. Villages were usually built near a stream, on which a dam would be constructed to back up waters in a mill pond. These would be used to turn the wheel for the grist mill. Most villages also had an oven for baking, a wine press, and perhaps a shop. The main part of the village consisted of the huts of the serfs or peasants. These were crude buildings that ordinarily sheltered a family and the various animals they might have, such as chickens.

Serfdom was a condition somewhere between slavery and tenant farmers. They were not free; rather, they were bound to the land. They could not leave it without the permission of the lord. On the other hand, the serfs could not be dispossessed, or driven off the land. It was their lot to work, year in and year out, winter and summer. They did, however, have many days when they did not work: there was Sunday, Saint's days (which were numerous), and other holidays.

The manor was a subsistent or self-sufficient farm. Virtually all that the inhabitants had or could get was grown or produced on the manor. Sometimes, there were surpluses and some trade in the market, but basically the manor supported a mounted warrior, the lord of the manor, his assistant, a priest, and the serfs. The farm usually had a variety of animals in addition to the horses of the lord. The land was tilled by oxen that pulled the plows and carts or wagons. They were usually scrawny creatures, and it would take four or more of them to pull the plows. In addition to the oxen, there were cows, sheep, hogs, chickens, and other barnyard animals. These were killed when the time was right for beef, pork, mutton, and chicken, and meat that was not to be eaten immediately was salted or cured to preserve it until it was eaten.

The arable land was divided into three large fields: one for spring planting, one for fall planting (wheat, rye, or other winter grains), and one to lie fallow for a season. These were then rotated from year to year. The

---

**manor**—an estate of a size and wealth reckoned to be sufficient to maintain a mounted warrior and his household. A manor consisted of the land, the manor house, the mills and shops, and the huts of the peasants. The serfs themselves could also be said to belong to the manor, since they were bound to the land.

serfs did not have their plots of land separate from that of the others. Instead, all of the arable land was divided into strips containing about an acre each. These strips were allotted to the serfs, to the lord, and possibly to the church. A serf's strips would be scattered about over the land. The strips were marked off from one another by a balk, which is an unplowed area, or other marking but were not otherwise separated from one another. The plowing was often done in common because no serf would have enough oxen to pull the heavy plow. Otherwise, each serf might tend his own plot, but all the serfs had to tend the church and the lord's strips as well. The serf not only had to pay rent on his harvest, provide his labor on church lands, but also had to pay a tithe (a tenth) of what he produced to the church. In addition to the labor on the lord's lands, serfs might be called upon to do other work for the lord. Moreover, he had to use the lord's grist mill to grind his grain, his oven and baker to bake his bread, his wine press to make his wine, and to pay tolls for the use of all these. There was some division of labor on the manor, at least for part of the time. There were plowmen, dairy maids, cowherds, shepherds, wheelwrights, and other specialists such as bakers and millers.

There was little chance that a serf might improve his condition, even marginally, under this system. He had to spend probably better than half his time providing free labor for lord and church, pay rent on what he produced and pay an assortment of special fees on various occasions. It was a system designed to drain him of what he produced and to make him work as hard as he could to make even a bare livelihood. He worked under the supervision of an overseer who might beat him if he was not industrious enough in working the land of the lord. If he fled from the manor, the lord had the right to pursue him and, if caught, return him to the manor. But often there was little reason to flee, for that would only take him away from his livelihood to a life of great uncertainty elsewhere.

Undoubtedly, it would be possible to present a prettier picture than this of the Middle Ages. People today may find such manor houses as are still standing charming or attractive, and especially gaze in awe at the great castles and cathedrals. These certainly adorned a life that is remote from our own. It is possible, too, to see in some Medieval institutions or practices the genesis of some that are still used and admired, such as trial by jury or the separation of powers, which certainly had its origin in the powers of the vassals, the monarchs, and the church. Even the peasant life had its more pleasant side. People may have whistled while they worked, drank with considerable gusto, and danced and pranced on the numerous holidays.

But the economy of the Middle Ages was cramped and slanted. The manorial system gave those who controlled the land the power over those who labored on the land. It was a labor intense system. Land was used extensively and labor intensively. Such capital as there was—such as water wheels, grist mills, and the like—was usually a monopoly of the lord, and he had little economic incentive to improve the equipment, since he could compel the use of it. A considerable portion of the labor on the land was forced labor, which is notoriously inefficient in production. The serfs had no direct interest in the yield of the lord's crops and might be expected to give them the minimum attention required to get the job done. The cost of government provided by feudalism was formidably expensive, since it probably took as much as 60–70% of the labor of the serfs. The surplus, if it could be called that, was largely spent on warfare and adornment. While the feudal lords were interested in improving the technology of warfare and the church in improving the technology or techniques of building, they paid scant attention, if any, to improving the technology of production, i.e., to capital.

> **Getting the Point...**
>
> Describe life on a manor for people in different positions: lord, knight, farmer, blacksmith, baker.

> **The Elements of Production in the Manorial System**
>
> The manorial system gave those who controlled the land the power over those who labored on the land. It was a labor intense system. Land was used extensively and labor intensively. Such capital as there was—such as water wheels, grist mills, and the like—was usually a monopoly of the lord, and he had little economic incentive to improve the equipment, since he could compel the use of it. A considerable portion of the labor on the land was forced labor, which is notoriously inefficient in production.

## 17.3 The Revival of Trade

Trade never entirely died out in Europe, but it was insignificant from the sixth to the beginning of the eleventh century. The conditions were hardly favorable to trade during this long era. The towns and cities that had once harbored trade had been largely abandoned and fell into decay. Most of Europe was almost entirely dependent upon agriculture, and farming was so entangled in the manorial and feudal system that little surplus was available for trade. As for a medium of exchange, there were some coins in circulation, but they were used for rare purchases or the payment of fines and the like. Perhaps the greatest deterrent to trade was the lack of effective government to maintain the peace. The feudal lords were not necessarily opposed to trade, but their incessant warfare made it dangerous to travel with goods. Merchants often became the prey of thieves. Moreover, the numerous feudal lords exacted tolls and charged fees for passing through and using their facilities. Tradesmen and artisans require freedom of movement and clear ownership of goods for going about their business. The feudal system had no place for them at first. Every vassal was supposed to have a lord and every serf a master. As a result, rights and privileges were limited.

The situation began to improve in the eleventh century, and was at least reasonably favorable in the twelfth and thirteenth centuries. Strong monarchs gained power and began to consolidate their kingdoms. The Roman Catholic Church also asserted its authority more firmly. Feudal squabbles did not end, of course, but with authority covering larger areas, the local feudal lords were somewhat restrained. The trade with the Near East increased considerably, and goods from Asia and Africa began to reach Europe in larger amounts. Europeans especially prized the spices from the East, the silks, linens, jewelry, precious stones, paper, and the like that came through from this trade. The Italian coastal cities were major ports of entry from the Near East, but traffic by way of Russia into northern European cities or ports played an increasing role as well. The French port of Marseilles on the Mediterranean was also a major medieval port of entry.

The merchants themselves were the greatest promoters of trade. They were very active, too, in improving conditions for trade. From earlier times, merchants had traveled in groups to carry their goods from one place to another. Groups of merchants took on permanent organization generally referred to as **merchant guilds**. These guilds gave the merchants a position alongside, if not within, the feudal system. The guild resembled in some ways a trade union, in other ways a trade association, and in

**merchant guilds**—associations of people engaged in selling goods to promote the interests of the guild members.

others ways a government. These guilds sought to get roads approved, feudal fees reduced or at least regularized, and sought to make travel safer.

The great medieval institution for trade was the fair. **Fairs** were organized by merchants and were places where they assembled to display, trade, and sell goods. Some fairs were large, lasting for many weeks, and drawing merchants and customers in great numbers. Others were much smaller, of course, and were less of an international event. The fairs were highly organized events featuring particular goods on display and sale during particular periods. The fairs operated under their own particular rules and had their own special courts to settle disputes. The law that held sway there was trade law rather than feudal law.

One of the great obstacles to trade in the early Middle Ages was that Western Europe produced no great surplus of goods to exchange for those from other lands. Nor could the feudal-manorial system change this, since the basic aim on the manor was self-sufficiency. What made Europe much more prominent in trade was the development of production largely outside, or free, of feudal restrictions. This took place as towns and cities emerged.

**fair (medieval)**—an event organized by merchants to draw people together to promote merchant trade.

> **Role of Merchants in Promoting Trade**
> The merchants themselves were the greatest promoters of trade. They were very active, too, in improving conditions for trade. From earlier times, merchants had traveled in groups to carry their goods from one place to another. Groups of merchants took on permanent organization generally referred to as merchant guilds. These guilds sought to get roads approved, feudal fees reduced or at least regularized, and sought to make travel safer

## 17.4 The Growth of Towns

The merchants were clearly a class apart in Medieval Europe. They were not nobles, clergymen, nor serfs. They were people outside of the feudal system, yet much valued from the early days for the goods they made available. They were free; they came and went at will; owned property in their goods, and were neither vassals nor overlords. These merchants became the instruments of freedom in Europe. The device by which they achieved what they did was mainly the town. The town was ultimately the place where free labor produced goods for trade and sale, where merchants sold their wares, and found the goods that could be sold in foreign markets.

Towns emerged gradually and became distinct legal entities as they received charters from feudal lords and high churchmen. The charters were usually obtained by merchant guilds. Towns grew up around fortified buildings, such as castles, manor houses, monasteries, and cathedrals. They usually began outside the walls of the forts, as places where the people lived who served the needs of people in the fort. The inhabitants became more numerous at crossroads or places to ford streams along trade routes. As the number of merchants, artisans, and workers increased, such places were granted charters, became towns, and the inhabitants built their own walls, thus becoming walled cities.

The main object of the town was to have a place for the production and sale of goods freed from feudal restrictions. As Professors James

W. Thompson and Edgar N. Johnson said in *An Introduction to Medieval Europe*,

> Everywhere, the object of the towns was the same: freedom from serfdom and all its entanglements. The townsman was to have freedom of movement, freedom of trade.... Town charters not only granted these privileges but, to help attract settlers, commonly provided that any serf who had taken refuge in a town should, after residing there unmolested for a year and a day, be regarded as a freeman, quit of all the claims of his former lord upon him."

Townsmen could own property, buy and sell, and were generally relieved of feudal dues or obligations, though fees or rents often had to be paid. In a sense, towns were citadels of freedom as they developed in the Middle Ages.

---

**Towns** emerged gradually and became distinct legal entities as they received charters from feudal lords and high churchmen. The charters were usually obtained by merchant guilds. The main object of the town was to have a place for the production and sale of goods freed from feudal restrictions.

---

## 17.5 Medieval Guilds

The extent of freedom or opportunity of the towns should not be exaggerated. The town was certainly not a citadel of equality for the very notion was foreign to the Middle Ages. The town, also, was medievalized—brought within the framework of hierarchy and under the sway of rules aimed at stability. This was done mainly in the guilds. The town charters had usually been obtained by the merchant guilds. In turn, they often took over the government, levied taxes, provided defense, and occupied the leading political role in the towns. Beneath the merchants and their guilds an assortment of craft guilds were formed as well. As they developed, they tended to try to monopolize and control whatever their line of endeavor was, whether it was work as tailors, weavers, masons, candlemakers, bakers, or what not.

There were hierarchies of guilds, and within particular guilds, they had their own hierarchies of standing. There were three different levels in craft guilds: **apprentice**, **journeyman**, and **master**. An apprentice had to spend a specified period, often 7 years, under a master before he could become a journeyman. During the period of apprenticeship, his work belonged to the master, though the master usually provided him some sort of livelihood. A journeyman could work for hire, usually under a master's direction. A master was his own man, usually had his own shop, produced goods, and offered them for sale.

As noted above, the purpose of the guild was to give its members the monopoly of some endeavor within their locale. A merchant guild attempted to monopolize trade within the city. For example, a merchant guild in Southampton, England proclaimed that "no one of the city... shall buy anything to sell again in the same city unless he is of the guild merchant or of the franchise." Craft guilds also tried to keep out everyone

**master craftsman**—one who had mastered his trade, could go into business for himself, train apprentices, and hire journeymen to work under him.

**journeyman**—a person who has completed his apprenticeship in some trade. At that point, he can work for hire, usually under a master craftsman.

**apprentice**—a workman who is learning a trade, such as carpentry or plumbing. In feudal times, apprentices often were required to work under a master for seven years before they could hire out to others in practicing their trade.

who had not worked their way up through local masters. The guilds sought stability by preventing competition so far as they could.

Indeed, opposition to competitive activity was the hallmark of the guilds. Their basic idea seems to have been to keep everyone at an equal level, restrain the ambitious, and assure a general level of competence. They regulated or fixed the hours of labor, wages, number of workers an employer could have, prices of products, and trade practices of their members. The merchant guilds required that each member should have an opportunity to buy materials at the price that any member did by bargaining. They opposed all efforts by any member of cornering the market or making purchases without the knowledge of the others. The merchant guilds (often manufacturers) opposed improved methods of production unless all other members could use the same devices. Their attitude toward new technology was profoundly anti-capitalistic. It was considered unfair trade for a guildsman to cut his prices, raise his wages, or in any other way lure away another member's customers or workers.

The guild system, especially that of the **craft guilds**, tended toward **laborism**, in terms of the means of production. They were largely free of the landism of the feudal system, and they were not capitalistic, in the sense that they gave any prime emphasis to capital. Even their laborism was hedged since they limited the wages to be paid to workers. Still, if one element of production received emphasis under this system, it was labor.

**craft guilds**—a guild organized around a specific craft or product.

**laborism**—an established preference for labor over land and capital. The preference must be supported by government policy to prevail. Marx provided an ideology in support of laborism, but communist practice favors state capitalism.

## 17.6 The Lasting Impact of Medieval Ways

The growth of trade, the rise of the towns, and the emergence of a class of producers and tradesmen that were largely freed from the feudal system did contribute to economic growth and some increase in prosperity in Europe. Trade brought in exotic and useful products from many lands. The development of many crafts not only provided goods for trading with the East but also made available a much greater variety of goods locally. The great Gothic cathedrals and magnificent castles attest to the skill and craftsmanship of the age. Undoubtedly, too, there was much advance in the quality and adornment of furniture, metalworking, clothing, and of many articles of use. The cities offered a greater degree of freedom to their inhabitants than could be had elsewhere. Moreover, these freer spirits did make economic and other innovations, such as the fair, before the guilds had become set in their ways and determined to strangle competition.

Still, these developments did not fully break the hold of feudalism on Europe, at least not until the Renaissance, that is, not until the fifteenth or sixteenth centuries. Granted, they did not fit into the feudal system, but it remained a dominant factor in the government and economy of Europe for several centuries. These trade activities were held in abeyance and medievalized by the guilds, by the church, and by their dependence on a governmental system that was basically feudal.

The economic patterns of the Middle Ages are not studied only because they once played a leading role in Europe. They are studied because they serve as archetypes, models, or patterns that recur in history, are recalled and used in various ways in new or revised economic systems. Even feudalism, the most medieval of these institutions, left remnants and relics in later periods. The code of chivalry was transmuted and survived in the ideal of a gentleman. It may be in the nature of things that wealth and political power tend to be joined, but the feudal system incarnated that mode by having them almost completely or fully linked.

The manor survived and has been revived in other systems. Remnants of the manor can still be seen in many European villages. The plantation in the American South that emerged during the colonial period had many facets that showed its lineage in the feudal manor. It was tended by slaves rather than serfs, but many of the differences were not great. The owner was a gentleman rather than a feudal lord, but the one had roots in the other. The plantation was much more commercial in orientation than the manor. But the manor house of the lord and the Greek revival or Georgian mansion of the Southern planter played much the same roles, as the slave cabins did to the village of the serf.

> **Medieval Archetypes**
> The economic patterns of the Middle Ages are not studied only because they once played a leading role in Europe. They are studied because they serve as archetypes, models, or patterns that recur in history, are recalled and used in various ways in new or revised economic systems.

The town of the Middle Ages had its antecedents in the cities of the Mediterranean, but it had its descendants, too, for example, in the self-governing New England towns. The guild system survived too, and can be seen in part in modern trade unions. Indeed, modern socialism was at least partially contrived from archetypes from the Middle Ages.

The main point, however, is that to understand economic systems, and the things within them, it is helpful to have studied them in earlier and clearer forms.

> *Feudalism made land the measure and the master of all things.*
> **Lord Acton**
>
> *Feudalism, serfdom, slavery, all tyrannical institutions, are merely the most vigorous kind to rule, springing out of, and necessarily to, a bad state of man. The progress from these is the same in all cases—less government.*
> **Herbert Spencer**

# Study Guide for:

# 17 Manorial-Feudal System

## Chapter Summary

Economic growth was hampered by the feudal system during the Middle Ages. This was largely due to the socio-political structures within which people lived their lives. The structure was hierarchical and one's position was largely determined by heredity. The system is called Feudalism and is made up of three primary classes of people: the nobility, the clergy, and serfs. Feudal government was exercised through the nobility whose duty was to uphold the peace. However, the means by which peace was to be promoted actually led to ongoing unrest rather than peace.

The various ranks of nobility held varying degrees of control over land. The lowest rank of noble would pledge his loyalty to the noble above him and so forth up to the king who ruled over a kingdom. It was up to the noble class to maintain control over the land by way of force. As can be imagined, outbreaks between competing nobles were common place. The resources needed to engage in warfare were essentially taxed from the peasants or serfs who were attached to a particular piece of land. Thus serfs were somewhere between slaves and tenant farmers. As such, the serfs had little incentive to work toward improving their lot since the product of their labor was often taxed at rates as high as 70%.

Production centered on the manor, which amounted to land enough to support a knight. The manor was fundamentally a self-sufficient community that rarely engaged in trade with outsiders. Even if they had desired to trade, little could have actually occurred because these communities had little surplus for such purposes. As a result, trade was limited and economic growth through technological development and capital accumulation was largely thwarted.

The situation began to change during the eleventh century. The influence of Christianity, as well as the effective rule of some stronger kings created an environment less prone to ongoing war and provided an atmosphere within which merchants could move more easily. Merchants were a class of people apart from others. They were outside the feudal system. Since they owned the property they traded and were free to travel, trade began to flourish. Towns developed as the centers of trade. These towns attracted more freemen who engaged in trade through the guild system. It also attracted a number of serfs who had fled the manor hoping for something better.

## Points of Emphasis

1. As much as they are able, people tend to produce as much of what they most want, or acquire it in other ways, as they can with the least expenditure of the means of production.

2. The social or political system in which individuals live and act will determine to a large degree the outcome of their behavior.

3. People will tend to act in ways that are individually economic even when within the system they may be socially harmful.

4. Feudalism was essentially a static economic environment that tended to thwart any advancement.

5. The civilizing influence of Christianity eventually reduced a number of obstacles to trade. As a result, merchants traveled more broadly in Europe and trade expanded. This expansion led to the growth of towns and greater general freedom.

6. Guilds developed during this time and they were the forerunner of the modern day union.

## Identification

1. landism
2. feudal system (feudalism)
3. estates (feudal class system)
4. serf
5. vassal
6. homage
7. fealty
8. subinfeudination
9. feud
10. manor
11. merchant guilds
12. fair
13. master craftsman
14. apprentice
15. craft guilds
16. laborism

## Review Questions

1. Who owned the land in the feudal system?
2. Why did feudalism limit technological innovation and economic growth?
3. List four–five conditions of the sixth–eleventh centuries that severely limited trade.
4. What developments in the twelfth–thirteenth centuries made the situation more favorable to trade?
5. When trade finally expanded in Europe, how did the guild system function?
6. What were the three levels of standing in the craft guilds?
7. Give a more modern recurrence of each of these medieval ideas: chivalry, manor, town, guild system, and anti-capitalism.

## Activity

1. Develop comparisons between feudalism and socialism and between the craft guilds and modern-day labor unions.

> **Chapter Content**
>
> 18.1 The Theory of Mercantilism        275
> 18.2 Mercantilism in England        276
>     18.2.1 By Granting Monopolies        277
>     18.2.2 By Passing Laws        278
> 18.3 Mercantilism in France        279
>     18.3.1 Prior to Colbert        280
>     18.3.2 Colbertism        282
> 18.4 Mercantilism in Colonial America        283
> 18.5 The Consequences of Mercantilism        284

# 18 Mercantilism

Mercantilism is the name most often applied to the monarchical and nationalistic economic systems that generally held sway in Western Europe in the sixteenth through the eighteenth centuries. Before describing these systems, however, they need to be placed in the context of the other great developments of this period. It was this era that contrasted in almost every way with the age that preceded it, and it is usually described by historians as the early modern period. Rather than stability as the goal, growth, expansion, and development were the aim and tenor of this new age. Capital began to come into its own in the economic realm, but the age of technology still lay largely in the future. The communal manorial life of the people of the Middle Ages was replaced by increasing individuality. Trade largely replaced the focus on land as the source of wealth and power.

The nation-state generally replaced the numerous feudal provinces of the Middle Ages. The process was very nearly completed in several countries before the end of the fifteenth century. Monarchs consolidated their kingdoms, disentangled them from feudal obligations, and generally made the feudal lords subservient to them. For example, English kings were rid of their feudal ties and connections with France by the end of the Hundred Year's War (1453). The feudal nobility was decimated and brought to heel as a result of the War of the Roses. Ferdinand and Isabella united much of Spain as a result of their marriage to one another. In general terms, monarchies independent of all other earthly powers became the general rule.

Trade grew mightily in the late Middle Ages and the early modern era. The center of what was virtually a trade explosion was the Italian cities and city-states, such as, Venice, Genoa, and Florence. Great wealth was made by the leading merchants and traders of this area. The finishing of woolen goods imported from northern Europe became a thriving business. More and more ocean-going vessels were being built, larger than before, and capable of longer voyages. Institutions of trade, such as banking houses, bills of exchange, double entry bookkeeping, and the like made their appearance or became more important. International trade was increasingly the route to wealth in Europe.

The great merchant wealth set the stage for the Italian Renaissance, and as the Renaissance spread northward, it set the stage for that other great development, the Protestant Reformation. The focus of the Renaissance was upon re-awakening an interest in the ancient Greeks and Romans. What Renaissance scholars learned and concentrated on was the ancient concern with the good life in this world. The study of Greek and Roman literature gave rise to a humanism that emphasized worldly attainments and pursuits. The study of old documents and attempts to find original ones also increased the awareness of how far the original might differ from later interpretations. Northern Renaissance scholars especially turned to the task of studying how far Christianity had changed since the early days. This helped to spark the Protestant Reformation, which swept over Northwestern Europe in the first half of the sixteenth century. The Catholic Church also underwent its own reformation in the ensuing years.

As rulers and countries became Protestant, they swept away much of the separation and balance of powers of the Middle Ages. Though the balance shifted from time to time, power had been somewhat restrained and balanced between feudal lords and kings or emperors, who were themselves subject to the hierarchy of the Catholic Church, especially the pope. Now with these restraints largely removed, the result was the development of more or less absolute monarchy. Such monarchs as Henry VIII in England and Louis XIV in France personified the development. It is of much importance to economic systems, too, that monarchs increasingly needed money for the affairs of state, since they could no longer rely on the service of feudal lords. This explains both their promotion of trade and increasing alliance with the merchants.

The last half of the fifteenth, the sixteenth, and seventeenth centuries was an age of exploration. Except for the Norsemen and an occasional wanderer, such as Marco Polo, Europeans had shown little interest in the rest of the world during most of the Middle Ages. Nor, had most of the rest of the world shown much interest in Europe. Then, toward the end of the fifteenth century, there was a great burst of exploration that did not finally cease until virtually the whole world was known to and by Europeans. The Portuguese took the lead, exploring the coast of Africa farther and farther down. In the last decade of the century, several startling voyages of discovery were made. In 1492, Christopher Columbus, sailing for Queen Isabella of Spain, sailed to and discovered islands off the coast of the Americas. Not only did Columbus make repeated voyages to the New World for Spain, but in 1497 John Cabot, sailing under contract to King Henry VII, reached islands off America far to the north of Columbus' voyages. In the same year, Vasco da Gama, sailing for Portugal, sailed around the southern tip of Africa and landed in India, thus finding an all sea route to the Far East. To cap off these daring voyages, Ferdinand Magellan led an expedition that sailed around the world (1519–1522). In the wake of these voyages of discovery came the overland journeys of exploration, conquest, colonization, and the establishment of trading posts, not only in North and South America, but also in Africa, Asia, and many islands of the oceans.

The trading and seagoing focus of Western Europe shifted from the Mediterranean to the Atlantic. Kingdoms with ports on or leading directly to the Atlantic became the leading trading and colonizing countries in the world, notably, Spain, Portugal, Great Britain, the Netherlands, Sweden, and France. Only large consolidated kingdoms usually played significant roles in this development. Thus, Germany, which at the time was divided into many principalities, did not participate, nor did Italy with its small city-states. Spain was ideally located for this new commerce and sea-going activity in the Atlantic, as was England with its numerous excellent ports.

People from many nations took part in the voyages, explorations, and settlements in the New World in the sixteenth and seventeenth centuries. However, the Spanish or those acting for the rulers of Spain were far and away the most successful in finding and taking what was most wanted. Undoubtedly, many things prompted Europeans to brave the furious Atlantic, make long overland journeys, and conquer or settle in the New World. One thing more than any other led monarchs to sponsor and commission these undertakings. It was the hope of discovering large quantities of precious metals, especially gold. Europe was gold hungry, so to speak, in the fifteenth and sixteenth centuries. Gold was the most widely accepted medium of exchange. That is to say, gold was the most widely recognizable form of ready wealth in the world. The king who had great quantities of gold was wealthy and could translate that wealth into power. The country that had much gold could command the goods of the world. The Spanish found gold in the New World in great quantities, in Mexico, in Peru, and to a lesser extent elsewhere. Spain dominated the seas for much of the sixteenth century, and Spanish galleons plied the Atlantic from the New World to Spain laden with gold.

It might be an oversimplification to say that other countries adopted mercantile practices to lure Spain's gold away, but the statement is surely near the mark. Countries did other things as well. They built powerful navies and great fleets of merchant vessels. And, of course, gold from the New World and elsewhere had spread across Europe before mercantilism had reached its peak. Still, it was the abundant new gold that became the target of national activity, and Spain was the richest nation in gold in the sixteenth century.

## 18.1 The Theory of Mercantilism

**Mercantilism** was a theory of using the power of government to direct economic effort so as to increase the wealth of a nation. Many of the practices associated with mercantilism preceded such economic theorizing. Even the term itself was a latecomer devised more to condemn than describe the practices. No matter, the term is convenient, even if it does suggest greater cogency than mercantile practices ever had. The term itself suggests that what we are dealing with is merchant*ism*, a theory or ideology designed to foster the interest of merchants. It did that all right, though monarchs supposed that they benefited also.

There are two key concepts that are usually ascribed to mercantilism. One is **bullionism**. This is the idea, possibly parodied by Adam Smith, that maintained a nation's wealth consisted of its holdings of precious metals. Probably, there were few enough who held literally to this idea. What Europeans generally, and mercantilists in particular, did recognize was that gold was the most valuable form of wealth. Granted, you could not eat gold, drink it, live in it, nor even wear much of it. But it could be most readily used to exchange for food, clothing, shelter, the adornments of life, and even the munitions that might lead to victory in war. Mercantilists believed that it should be the policy of the nation to obtain as much gold as they could and to let as little of it get away as possible.

The other concept is a favorable **balance of trade**. The terms favorable and unfavorable balance of trade are basically mercantilistic concepts, though they are still very much in use in our day (and, as is our tendency, calculated in voluminous statistics). Mercantilists preferred a favorable balance of trade. That is they wanted their nation to sell more in goods to other nations than they bought in return. The difference would be paid in gold, and, by their reckoning, would increase the wealth of the nation. Thus, monarchs, or their governments, promoted policies that would be most likely to enhance their favorable balance of trade.

Mercantilism was clearly nationalistic, not individualistic. That is, it was concerned with the wealth of the nation rather than of individuals. An individual trader or merchant has no preference for foreign over domestic trade, other things being equal. He can become as wealthy dealing with those near at hand as in other lands. Mercantilism is nationalistic, too, in that its theory pits each nation against all others. One nation's gain is viewed as another nation's loss.

**mercantilism**—a politico-economic system that is nationalistic, usually involves an alliance, in effect, between the rulers and the merchants, seeks a favorable balance of trade, and tends to operate on the principle that a nation's wealth consists of its holdings in precious metals.

**bullionism**—a system in which the government focuses upon getting and keeping precious metals within the realm. Thus, the government may attempt to get a favorable balance of trade in order to collect the difference in precious metals while it prohibits the export of gold. Thereby, the nation heaps up unto itself gold and silver, so to speak.

**balance of trade**—a concept developed in connection with mercantilism, in which nations sought to have a favorable balance of trade. This meant to them that the nation in the favored position was one that exported more goods than it imported. An unfavorable balance of trade, then, was for a nation to import more than it exported.

**planned economy**—an idea associated with overall government planning for and control over an economy. Probably, the best (or worst) examples of this were Stalin's Five-Year Plans. The idea is somewhat misleading, however, for it implies that anything less than an overall planned economy is unplanned. Actually, all economic activity is planned, whether by individual owners or by the state.

Although the phrase was not used in earlier times, mercantilism tends in the direction of what is now called a "**planned economy**." That is, government policy is bent toward directing economic activity in particular directions. For example, mercantilists argued that a country would be better off to import raw materials and export finished products. Thus, government promoted the development of manufacturing, on the one hand, and encouraged the import of raw materials, on the other. Manufacturing would enhance the price to foreigners, and thus be more likely to result in a favorable balance of trade. The planned economy is now associated with socialistic governments, and mercantilism was not socialist in the usual ways. But in form, mercantilism was a variety of a planned economy.

---

**Mercantilism** was a theory of using the power of government to direct economic effort so as to increase the wealth of a nation. The term itself suggests that what we are dealing with is merchantism, a theory or ideology designed to foster the interest of merchants. It did that all right, though monarchs supposed that they benefited also.

There are two key concepts that are usually ascribed to mercantilism.
1. One is bullionism, the idea that a nation's wealth consisted of its holdings of precious metals. Mercantilists believed that it should be the policy of the nation to obtain as much gold as they could and to let as little of it get away as possible.
2. The other concept is a favorable balance of trade. Mercantilists preferred a favorable balance of trade. That is they wanted their nation to sell more in goods to other nations than they bought in return. The difference would be paid in gold, and, by their reckoning, would increase the wealth of the nation.

---

## 18.2 Mercantilism in England

**Getting the Point...**

Summarize the characteristics of mercantilism.

Before taking up those regulations that are associated with mercantilism, it may be well to emphasize that from the sixteenth century onward England was emerging as a leading productive and trading nation as well as a naval power in the world. This new vitality and industrial activity was ongoing, however mercantilism may have altered and concentrated it. As noted already, England was favorably located to take part in the commercial activities, especially with the New World. The Medieval restraints on economic activity were loosened or removed earlier in England than in many continental countries. Landed property was well on its way to private ownership. England had a well-established and vigorous woolen and textile industry.

The ingenuity, daring, and vitality of the English were erupting in a variety of ways by the reign of Elizabeth I in the latter part of the sixteenth century. It was the age of Shakespeare, the first great era of English literature. Sir Francis Drake sailed around the world, showing the English flag in the ports of many strange lands. Sir Walter Raleigh made the early but futile attempts to plant colonies in the New World. The British defeated the Spanish Armada in 1588, signaling the emergence of England as a sea power. Undoubtedly, mercantilism channeled and fostered certain kinds of industrial and commercial activity, but the vitality was already there.

During Elizabeth's reign, William Cecil, her chief minister, was busily using the power of government to foster desired economic activities. He encouraged the development of a munitions industry in England to free the country from having to import them. He gave monopolies to individuals and companies that would undertake to mine sulfur and saltpeter. He brought foreigners into the country to teach English workers the art of working with metals. Farmers were subsidized to grow flax and hemp for making much needed canvas. In general, he tried to make business conditions sufficiently attractive that entrepreneurs and adventurers would make capital investments.

## 18.2.1 By Granting Monopolies

Indeed, the key to British mercantilism, if not all mercantilism, was monopoly, the monopoly of British ships carrying merchandise to and from the colonies, the monopolies of manufacturers in some line of endeavor, the monopolies of domestic merchants in the trade in some goods, and the monopoly of trade with foreign countries granted to trading companies. The Stuart kings of the first half of the seventeenth century (James I and Charles I) were notorious for their sale of monopolies. Monopolies were or had been granted to foreign trading companies, such as the East India Company. Monopolies were granted or maintained to numerous manufacturers and domestic importers. Christopher Hill, in *The Century of Revolution,* suggests how far these monopolies went, in the following examples:

> It is difficult for us to picture to ourselves the life of a man living in a house built with monopoly bricks, with windows (if any) of monopoly glass; heated by monopoly coal..., burning in a grate made of monopoly iron. His walls were lined with monopoly tapestries. He slept on monopoly feathers, did his hair with monopoly brushes and monopoly combs. He washed himself with monopoly soap, his clothes in monopoly starch. He dressed in monopoly lace, monopoly linen, monopoly leather, monopoly gold thread. His hat was of monopoly beaver, with a monopoly band. His clothes were held up by monopoly belts, monopoly buttons, monopoly pins. They were dyed with monopoly dyes. He ate monopoly butter, monopoly currants, monopoly red herrings, monopoly salmon and monopoly lobsters....

The list goes on—"In Ireland one could not be born, married, or die without *6d* to a monopolist"—but perhaps his point emerges. Almost all trade and commerce, foreign or domestic, was in the hands of some one or a group of monopolists. Monopolies were usually established by a grant from the monarch to someone to engage in some activity. (Our word patent stems from this root, but these were not patents granted to inventors, but to every sort of producer, middleman, or tradesman.) The advantage to the king of this system was that he could charge for these patents or monopoly licenses. They fitted into mercantilism in that they were supposed to encourage the development of industry at home and trade abroad. To domestic consumers, they were simply monopolies that tended to drive the prices of goods upward.

They could sometimes play havoc in foreign trade as well. One of the most notorious examples occurred during the reign of James I. It is known as the Cokayne Project, for Sir William Cokayne who undertook it. The project had to do with the export of woolen cloth to northern Europe. Before 1614, the year a change was attempted, the Merchant Adventurers, a company that exported cloth, had sold large quantities of cloth to the Dutch, which they finished and shipped to the north. King James withdrew the license for the Merchant Adventurers, and created a new company, under Cokayne, called the King's Merchant Adventurers. James prohibited the export of unfinished cloth, and expected that the English would finish and dye cloth before shipping it out of the country. The Dutch retaliated by prohibiting the import of British cloth of any sort. The British had neither the know-how nor capital to do the finishing on such a large scale, nor the shipping to move goods in that quantity to northern Europe.

The project was a fiasco during its brief span from beginning to end. It fit well enough the mercantilist prescription. The British should have increased the value of their exports, thus increasing the chances of having a favorable balance of trade. Of course, the Dutch were mercantilists, too, and could hardly be expected to cooperate with the British project that would have reduced their income from the profitable business of finishing and dyeing cloth. But the British were not prepared to carry out the whole operation, and Cokayne was almost certainly incompetent. (The ability to obtain a monopoly from the king was hardly related to entrepreneurial skill.) The king, under pressure, shut down his new licensee, and re-licensed the old Merchant Adventurers. King James made out well, even if the country suffered, for he collected a large sum from the Merchant Adventurers to allow them to do business again.

The British monarch also made grants, issued patents, or granted charters for colonies in the New World. The first successful planting of a colony was at Jamestown, and this was authorized by James I in 1606. The colony at Plymouth, and then at Massachusetts Bay was authorized by the monarch, as was the one in Maryland. The actual settlements were undertaken by private companies, which was usual in the mercantile era. Whatever the purpose of the monarch or settlers, it was not long before they were being fitted into mercantilism by the mother country. The mercantile hope was that the colonies would, first of all, be a source of gold to the mother country. In England's case, that did not work out, since no significant deposits of gold were found in British America. After that, the hope was that colonies would be a source of raw materials and products not grown in England.

### 18.2.2 By Passing Laws

The British did not rely simply on the market to bring this about. Instead, they passed laws to insure it. The first major legislative action by the British along these lines was the navigation acts. The first of these was passed in 1651 during the Interregnum (the period following the British Civil War when England had no monarch). This Navigation Act was re-passed in 1660 with the Restoration (of monarchy). It was later modified in some particulars, but the basic legislation was in place. The aim of these acts was to give British ships a monopoly of trade with their colonies and to give British merchants the advantage in acting as middle men in exports from the colonies to other nations. The acts declared that no goods could be imported from Africa, Asia, or America except in ships belonging to Englishmen, Irishmen, or English colonists, and the ships had to be manned by crews that were 75% English. Moreover, no goods could be exported to or imported from English colonies except in such ships. Alien merchants were excluded both from colonial trade and the coastal trade with Britain. While the trade and shipping of European countries carrying their own goods were not excluded from Britain, some of them were subjected to very high tariffs. Certain enumerated articles—sugar, tobacco, cotton, ginger, indigo, and dye-woods—from English colonies could only be shipped directly to England. This was to give the British the profits of selling them to other countries.

About the same time, Charles II established a committee of the Privy Council to collect information and give directions to the colonies. This became in the course of time the Board of Trade to oversee trade activities with the colonies. The British also tightened control over the colonies by making them Royal or Crown colonies. That way, the governor of a colony would be appointed by the monarch and might be expected to govern with English interests in mind. In addition, the British sometimes paid bounties to colonists to produce some good especially wanted in England. The British paid a bounty on indigo, used in making dye, and the production of indigo thus became an important crop in South Carolina. Bounties were also paid on naval stores, since the ship building industry was so important to England.

Over the years, the British passed numerous measures aimed at assuring that the colonies benefited the mother country within the mercantile system. Prior to 1663, the British were prohibited to send either bullion or coins to America, and after that date the prohibition on coins was continued. In short, the shipping of coins was to be a one way street from America to England. The colonists, however, were very short of English coins. The king never set up a mint in America, and when minting was attempted by the colonists, the British ordered its work discontinued.

Several other British regulations were aimed primarily at preventing the development of manufacturing in America. The Woolens Act, passed in 1699, prohibited the export of wool or woolen goods from a colony either to other colonies or other countries. The Hat Act of 1732 prohibited the exportation of hats from the colony in which they were made, and limited the number of apprentices a hat maker might have. This was clearly an effort not only to limit competition in a product the mother country wanted to export but also to discourage the development of an industry. The Molasses Act of 1733 placed high duties on molasses, sugar and rum from any source other than British colonies. This was an attempt to give the British West Indies a virtual monopoly of the trade. The Iron Act of 1750 permitted pig iron to be exported from the colonies to England duty free but prohibited the erection of new iron mills for the finishing of products in the colonies. This was a mercantile type of regulation.

Finally, it should be pointed out that tariffs, or customs duties, were probably the most common of the mercantile devices. A tariff on imports could be used to price foreign goods out of the market or to reduce their impact. A tariff on exports could be used to prevent or reduce the exportation of goods in which the country did not wish to compete. However, governments are apt to be ambiguous about tariffs, for they are often a source of revenue as well. They work best as a source of revenue when they do not significantly reduce exports or imports. But so far as they are a protective tariff, they are mercantile measures.

## 18.3 Mercantilism in France

France was in many ways an unlikely candidate to adopt any thoroughgoing mercantilism. It was probably more medieval in the Middle Ages than any other country, and many of the remains of medieval ways remained strong until they were finally crushed in 1789 and thereafter during the French Revolution. The nobility had not been so decimated or brought to heel as in England. Thus, France remained in many ways a country of provinces. Each had its own customs duties and other restraints on trade. The guilds remained much stronger there in the early modern period than they were in England. Nor was foreign trade so common in France. They were not great colonizers or sea faring people and did not manage to acquire many of the prizes in overseas conquest.

Even so, some French thinkers did become enamored with mercantilistic ideas, and once public policy was directed by them their mercantilism was probably more thoroughgoing than in any other country. Indeed, French thinkers are nothing if not logical, or at least rationalistic. Once under the sway of mercantilism, it was predictable they would out mercantile everyone else, or try to. The man who did this most fully was Jean Baptiste Colbert, a leading minister of Louis XIV for a large portion of the latter half of the seventeenth century. In fact, what has gone by the name of mercantilism elsewhere was Colbertism in France, and mercantile practices were still described that way in France long after his death. In any case, Louis XIV, the "Sun King," was as near to being an absolute monarch as France ever had. The Estates General, the French Parliament, did not meet between 1614 and 1789. Thus, a minister acting with the will of the king could go a long way in imposing mercantilism on France. Colbert did, but before taking that up, some background to it is in order.

### Jean B. Colbert (1619–1683)

French mercantilist, minister to the king, and administrative reformer. He was born in Reims, France, entered government service at the age of 20, advanced by making himself valuable to the ministers for whom he worked, and eventually became himself Louis XIV's most dependable and powerful minister. As a mercantilist, Colbert promoted production, expanded the navy, removed some of the interior obstacles to trade, and launched a major road and canal building program. His plans for the development of industry were so detailed that he could justly be called the forerunner of government economic planning. In any case, his determined mercantilism stood out so much that the French referred to these practices as Colbertism.

### 18.3.1 Prior to Colbert

Mercantile practices were introduced long before Colbert was even born. In 1540, a royal ordinance forbade the export of bullion from France because the export of gold would supposedly impoverish the people. There was also legislation to discourage the importing of luxuries, since that would give French wealth to foreigners. The justifications, as well as the measures, were mercantilistic. Moreover, in the sixteenth century the French government gave subsidies, granted monopolies, gave tax exemptions, made loans, and otherwise supported the development of glass making, sugar refining, and textile industries. These things were a beginning, of a conscious mercantilism in France, but they fell far short of what Colbert attempted in the latter part of the seventeenth century.

Underlying and undergirding what was done early and late were a number of thinkers of an economic and nationalist bent. They promoted an idea of trade that emphasized the importance of manufacturing, and hoped to see France enriched at the expense of other countries. How trade was supposed to benefit all Frenchmen was suggested by Jean Eon, a churchman who was secretary to the governor of Brittany. He said,

> Maritime towns, are like general depots where adjoining cities and bourgs [villages] bring their fruits, produce and manufactures to obtain a good price. They are the centers where diverse peoples and artisans bring their work to completion, and earn their subsistence by the salaries given them.

> ... Commerce puts everyone to work, [all people] need fruits, provisions and manufactures, Trade brings general utility to all communities and to all kinds of persons in the realm. Great and small, rich and poor are universally obliged to devote themselves to commerce according to their condition and to their facilities.

He was including farmers, as well, for he referred to their produce as fruits.

Writers did not fail to make clear that the monarchy and government would benefit from all this commerce. It would fill the tax coffers of the government. An anonymous writer in 1658 pointed out that though the money might come into many hands along the way, much of it would make its way to the royal purse. He was describing specifically the commerce with Spain in this description of how the government would benefit from an expansive trade:

> All money coming back finally to the King by the ebb and flow of trade which makes it pass from one hand to the other, to return ultimately to the Prince, because at the very time money arrives from Spain merchants distribute it in the countryside to buy wheat and cloth and the villagers no sooner receive it than they carry it to the Receivers [of taxes], and from there to the treasury which pays all necessary expenses.

Undoubtedly, the writer overstated the extent to which all the money came to the government, but it may be better understood as a process by which a monarch increased his power by adopting mercantile practices.

Some mercantilist writers also set forth the possibility that by building a diverse economy that supplied all the needs of France, the French would be able to supply all their needs at home, which enriched themselves at the expense of their neighbors through exports. The Marquis de la Gomberdière presented this supposedly pleasant prospect by addressing Louis XIV in this way:

> Sire, God has so abundantly strewn his sacred blessings on your Kingdom that it appears He has designated it to have authority and command over all others in the universe. He has so well constituted it and provisioned it with all things necessary and useful to the life of your peoples and with such abundance that we can truly say that this Monarchy is the only one which can do without all her neighbors and no single one can get along without her.

> But Sire, it will be in vain that your Kingdom is the most beautiful, the most opulent in the universe (as she truly is), if the French (your subjects) do not reestablish their work in manufacture and apply themselves to the gifts God bestowed on them.

### 18.3.2 Colbertism

Jean Baptiste Colbert made it his work to see to it that God's bestowing of resources upon France should not have been in vain, that they should be fully developed to the enrichment of the kingdom. He is reported to have said that "One of the most important works of peace is the re-establishment of every kind of trade in this kingdom and to put it in a position to do without having recourse to foreigners for the things necessary for the use and comforts of the subjects." Colbert was the son of a French clothier and the nephew of a rich merchant. He was not of noble birth, but for nearly two decades (1664–1683), he lorded it over much of France that had been smothered by nobility. He did not go into trade but rather into government service, where he rose to the top by applying himself vigorously to the appointments that came his way. He may not have been Louis XIV's chief minister technically, but he was certainly the foremost in asserting himself. The king brought him into government to reorganize government finances, but he eventually made him superintendent of manufactures, commerce, and fine arts, controller general of finances, secretary of the navy, and secretary of state. Above all, though, Colbert took it as his task to apply a thoroughgoing mercantilism in France by developing manufacturing and trade.

Colbert exerted himself least in regard to French agriculture. Probably, he was more concerned with drawing workers away from farming and into industrial pursuits than with making it more attractive. He did, however, sponsor some legislation beneficial to farmers. The seizure for debt of farm animals, carts, and farm implements was prohibited, even if the debts were taxes owed to the government. Stud farms were established to provide superior breeding animals, service free, to farmers. Hunters were prohibited to ride or otherwise cross planted fields, and tax exemptions were offered to those who would bring idle lands into cultivation. To the extent that the means of transporting goods to market were improved under Colbert's administration, farmers were benefited as well as others who had goods for sale.

Colbert concentrated most of his attention and effort, however, on promoting manufactures. It should be kept in mind, however, that "to manufacture" means, literally, "to make by hand," and that this meant mainly the promotion of the production of goods by craftsman with the use of such equipment as was then available. Ordinarily, the work did not take place in what we would call factories, nor was anything other than human power ordinarily used in the production. It might mean anything from carpenters and mechanics building sea going vessels to the production of fine tapestries. At any rate, the government under Colbert's direction took all sorts of actions to promote manufactures, usually mercantile measures. Protective tariffs were kept high enough to keep foreign competitive products off the French market or to greatly reduce the volume of such trade. He encouraged new enterprises by offering tax exemptions, offering government loans, and holding the interest rate down. New industries were given a monopoly until they were well established. Moreover, Colbert made special concessions and other inducements to get skilled workers to settle and work in France. Thus, glassmakers were brought in from Venice; ironworkers from Sweden, and at least one cloth maker from Holland.

Above all, Colbert tried to impose order and discipline upon workers and the workplace. The main organization he used in imposing this discipline was the guild; he tried to transform it from a protective organization for workers into a means of spurring workers on to produce more and better goods. Wages, hours of work, and periods of rest were

> **Getting the Point...**
>
> Make a list of mercantilist practices used in France before, during, and after the time of Colbert.

prescribed. Wages were kept low, hours long, and breaks brief. To improve the quality of French goods, Colbert prescribed the manner of their manufacture in infinite detail. For example, an edict on the dyeing of cloth had 371 articles. Nothing must be left to chance; everything must be done according to rule. Special boards were established in towns to inspect and look for defects in articles of manufacture. If any were found, the article containing the faulty workmanship was exposed alongside the name of the guilty workman or manager. If the workman made a similar error again, he was subject to censure by his guild. For a third offense, he could be tied to a post in public view and thus disgraced.

That Colbert meant business, there should be no doubt. If he had his way there would have been no idle persons in France. Beggars on the streets were rounded up and put to work, and it was a boast of the day that even small children could do productive work. The power of the master or employer over the workers was great and even intruded into what we would describe as the private life or life style of the worker. All sorts of things were forbidden—laziness, incompetence, cursing, irreverence, drunkenness, and the like—and could be punished by whipping.

Colbert made a major effort to remove the provincial tolls that had continued since the Middle Ages. It was difficult to develop a national economic system with all the local tolls. For example, goods moving from Switzerland to Paris were subject to the payment of tolls at 16 points along the way. However, Colbert's efforts to abolish the tolls met with stiff resistance in the provinces, and the best he could do was reduce their number. He met with somewhat greater success in improving roads and waterways. A system of royal highways was planned, and construction of them begun. Major canals were built as well.

Colbert tried to build up foreign trade as well. The French navy was greatly increased in size and strength, providing much greater support and protection for merchant shipping. As he saw it, the merchant fleet must be greatly expanded if France was to compete with the Dutch and English in overseas trade. He encouraged shipbuilders in France by giving a bounty to those who bought ships at home rather than abroad. Great trading companies were either organized or reorganized to trade in the Americas and Asia. Colonization was promoted where colonies had been established. The trading companies never managed to compete very successfully, however, due as much as anything to the fact that they, like so much of the French business, were over-regulated.

France retained its basic mercantilistic emphasis long after Colbert had passed from the scene, indeed, for most of the eighteenth century. It maintained high protective tariffs, encouraged exports, and sought new industrial techniques. But mercantilism was coming under increasing intellectual attack from the middle of the eighteenth century onward. French thinkers were more and more praising liberty, not the government control of mercantilism.

## 18.4 Mercantilism in Colonial America

It might be supposed that colonists disliked mercantilism. After all, colonists were supposed to enrich the economy of the country that founded them. Rules were passed, as already noted, to restrict and restrain manufacturing in the colonies. The colonists in English America, however, were more than a little ambiguous about mercantile practices. They did not like those English imposed restrictions on enterprise or limitations on the market. Nor were they favorably disposed to the monopolies of land or trade granted to the early companies that settled in Virginia and Massachusetts.

On the other hand, they took advantage where they could of British mercantile rules, and sometimes imposed their own in the colonies. New England, for example, took advantage of the British promotion of trade and the opening provided by the Navigation Acts. There was a large demand for ships by the latter part of the seventeenth century, both in England and America. Massachusetts especially developed a large and thriving shipbuilding industry. Many of their ships were sold in America, but the British also bought large numbers of ships. The prices of American ships were lower than those built in England, and no restrictions were placed on colonial shipbuilding.

Some of the colonies also placed tariffs on exports or imports from time to time and even prohibited the export of goods needed within a colony. Some colonies even attempted to prohibit the export of coins. Monopolies and tax exemptions were sometimes granted to new industries. For example, Massachusetts granted a 21 year monopoly to iron makers in Braintree. They also freed them from taxes for the same period. Virginia passed a law in 1661–62 exempting tradesmen and artisans from the payment of taxes. Skilled craftsmen were in great demand in the colonies, and such acts were designed to lure settlers to particular colonies. In short, colonists were often as mercantilistic as the mother countries, but more limited in the extent to which they could impose such restrictions or offer privileges.

## 18.5 The Consequences of Mercantilism

Mercantilism was much more a nationalistic than an economic system. The economic measures it promoted, so far as they were economic, were more often than not tied to the political aims of the rulers. It was capitalistic in emphasis, in that it tended to use the power of government to promote capital expenditures. Mercantilists tended to ignore or undervalue land. Ordinary labor was usually harshly subjected to governmental control and the control of masters and employers. Thus, in terms of the means of production, mercantilism was capitalistic, but the concept of economics was so narrowly focused that it could hardly be said to be an economic system at all.

The fundamental flaw in mercantilism is that it misconstrues what it most highly values, i.e., trade. To a thoroughgoing mercantilist, every trade must have a winner and a loser. The loser, on the bullionist theory, is the one who gives up precious metals for some other good; the winner is the one who gets the precious metals. Of course, mercantilists generally applied this theory at the national level, but if it is true at that level it must be equally true wherever two parties are involved in a trade. However, the truth is that each party to a trade gets something he wants more than what he gives up to get it. This is as true when one party gives up coins as it would be in barter. For example, a man who is clearing his land of trees may sell his fallen trees to a man who wishes to saw them into lumber for sale. Each gets something he wants more than what he gives up. It does not matter at all that one gave up silver coins while the other gave up trees. The same is true for trades among people of different nations. In the sense that each party to a trade gets what he wants more than what he gives up, both parties are winners. Prudent traders often consult more than their desires or wants, of course, before making a trade. They may wish to know if there is a rough parity or equality in the things traded. To discover this, they may review the market both for what they are parting with and what they might get. In any case, this is as true for precious metals as other commodities, and it is fallacious to conclude that the one who receives gold or silver is the winner and the other the loser, as a general rule.

The ultimate logic of mercantilism, as some French writers apparently saw, is that in the contest of nations for a favorable balance of trade, there should be one winner and the rest losers. At any rate, they argued that the French were best situated to occupy that position. Trade is multilateral, i.e., it tends to involve all nations, and there is no economic reason to assume some ultimate winner.

> **The fundamental flaw in mercantilism** is that it misconstrues what it most highly values, i.e., trade. To a thoroughgoing mercantilist, every trade must have a winner and a loser. The loser, on the bullionist theory, is the one who gives up precious metals for some other good; the winner is the one who gets the precious metals. However, the truth is that each party to a trade gets something he wants more than what he gives up to get it. This is as true when one party gives up coins as it would be in barter. The same is true for trades among people of different nations. In the sense that each party to a trade gets what he wants more than what he gives up, both parties are winners.

Nevertheless, the mercantilists thought that the wealth gained by a favorable balance of trade would augment the power of the state. Thus, consistently maintaining a favorable balance of trade should produce wealth to turn into power of a dominating state. Just the same, mercantilism was a prescription for international catastrophe. Its consequence was world war, as conflict among nations spread. Mercantilism puts government power behind the commercial activities of a nation, uses government power to support the trade of one nation against the trade of others, and prohibits trade activities of foreigners in order to give advantages to native tradesmen. In order to support or protect their tradesmen, other nations retaliated with similar restrictions and sought colonies that would be protected trade areas for their people. If trade is free, competition is peaceful, but mercantilism shifts the contest into the realm of governmental power. When governments contest for advantage in this way they are moving in the direction of the ultimate recourse—war.

War was the most tangible result of mercantilism in the seventeenth and eighteenth centuries. War followed upon war with monotonous regularity as naval and colonial powers contested with one another for dominance. The British and Dutch fought three wars that were clearly mercantilist in origin from the 1650s to mid-1670s. The result was that the British drove the Dutch from North America and any significant participation in the trade in America. From the 1690s through the Napoleonic Wars (early nineteenth century), Britain and France were the major contestants, but most of them involved so many other nations and colonial powers that they are most helpfully thought of as world wars. The wars often involved dynastic questions—who should succeed to what throne—but they generally involved the colonies and who should dominate them or their trade. The wars between the 1690s and 1760s were King William's War, the War of the Spanish Succession, the War of the Austrian Succession, and the Seven Year's War (known as the French and Indian War in America). Britain steadily gained in dominance in North America as a result of these wars. In 1700, the English held only a relatively narrow strip of the eastern coast of North America from New England to Georgia, with claims running back to the Appalachians. As a result of the Treaty of Paris of 1763, the British now had all the French Canadian holdings and the French and Spanish claims east of the Mississippi.

By the mercantile theory, Britain was triumphant. It certainly had the most powerful navy in the world, and the government should have been resplendent in wealth. The latter was hardly the case, however. Britain was caught in the ultimate contradiction of mercantilism. It tends to embroil nations in war, as it had done Britain and France. Wars are often frightfully expensive. Indeed, not even counting the cost of the dead and wounded, there is good reason to believe that the wars cost much more than mercantilism brought into the treasury. The growing British debt in the middle of the eighteenth century gives some indication of how inadequate the revenues were in meeting the expense of wars as well as the other costs of government. The British debt in 1755, just after the outbreak of the French and Indian War, stood at £75,000,000. By 1766 it had mounted to £133,000,000. The French debt had grown greatly during these years as well, though the French had been the loser in the colonial wars.

The consequences of a great movement in history followed in the wake of this situation. As a result of the British debt and resistance in England to higher taxes, Parliament made attempts to levy taxes on the American colonists. This precipitated resistance that led eventually to the American revolt against and separation from Britain. The French debt, the oppressive taxation, and the declining fortunes of the monarch in colonial contests helped to set the stage for the French Revolution.

It should be emphasized, too, that mercantilism tends to skew and constrain the domestic economy of the nations that practice it. It generally resulted in special privileges and advantages to some merchants and tradesmen, those possessing monopolies in trade. It placed a premium on manufactures and expenditures to develop them, thus giving advantages and subsidies to capital outlays. While merchants were sometimes enriched, farmers and those who worked for wages were often impoverished. Taxes tended to take a heavy toll on the wealth produced.

Mercantilism left a legacy of programs, policies, and practices that have been revived in new or old forms ever since. Colonial empires did not end with the eighteenth century. Indeed, colonialism was mightily revived in the latter part of the nineteenth century and still has a tenuous existence to the present. Tariffs, one of the most conspicuous of mercantilist practices, have played a prominent role, more or less, since the eighteenth century. It should be noted that justifications and stated purposes for instituting derivatives of mercantilism have shifted over the years. Thus, the idea of a government planned and directed economy has been greatly revived in the twentieth century, though the alleged beneficiaries are supposed to have changed. Governments have intervened in economies with renewed passion. Subsidies have been much used by governments, in aid of all sorts of things from airports to public housing to selected crops. The relics of absolute monarchy have assumed more virulent forms in twentieth century totalitarian dictatorships, which continue today.

In sum, the ghost of mercantilism has haunted the nineteenth and twentieth centuries and continues to play a pivotal role in economic affairs. This has taken place despite the massive intellectual effort to discredit mercantilism root and branch in the eighteenth and nineteenth centuries. Indeed, systematic economics arose in the wake of opposition to mercantilism and has generally tended, until the middle of the twentieth century at least, to expose the economic fallacies of mercantilism.

# Study Guide for:

# 18 Mercantilism

## Chapter Summary

The term mercantilism is used in connection with the monarchical political system that was largely adopted by most Western European nations during the period of the sixteenth through the eighteenth centuries. On one hand, growth and expansion were displacing the stagnation of the feudal period as focus on trade expanded. On the other, the nationalistic character of mercantilism gave impetus to regulations that created monopolies and tended to limit the actual amount of trade that could take place.

There are a number of historical developments that set the stage for mercantilism. First, during the fifteenth century, monarchs in several places were successful in consolidating power. They achieved this by subduing feudal lords, which provided for more widespread peace and freer trade among people in the nation. These monarchs also became interested in exploration. Exploration brought Europeans in contact with peoples in other lands and opened up opportunities for trade.

Unfortunately, the monarchs were primarily interested in building their own political power and position. They tended to view gold as the quickest means by which to develop this power since gold was the common medium of exchange in trade. Therefore, they focused on developing large stocks of gold and believed that this formed the basis of the wealth of the nation. As a result, they were constantly concerned with maintaining a "favorable balance of trade," which was supposed to augment the supply of gold in a country. It is most interesting that even though this idea has been largely discredited by economists, it still is used by some today.

At its heart, mercantilism was the focused use of government to direct and plan the economy. It is the forerunner of modern day economic planning favored by many social reformers. However, rather than promote the general welfare, such practices ended up establishing monopolies over trade that tended to keep prices of goods and services higher than they would otherwise have been. The fundamental misconception of the mercantilists was the notion that in every economic trade someone benefits at someone else's expense. Thus they only saw winners and losers in trade and assumed that trade was analogous to warfare. Consequently, mercantile practices led to hostilities between nations and wars tended to expand into world wars.

## Points of Emphasis

1. Mercantilism is a politico-economic system in which the power of government is used to direct economic effort. The term is most often used to describe the nationalistic economic practices in Europe from the sixteenth century through the eighteenth century.

2. Even though economic activity was directed by the monarch under mercantilism, there was more freedom of movement and trade than had existed during the feudal period. This trade provided for increased economic growth and expansion.

3. Mercantilistic monarchs were preoccupied with a desire to expand their holdings of precious metals. Though there is no economic rationale for this position, they believed that the wealth of a nation consists in the amount of money it possesses rather than in its ability to produce.

## Identification

1. mercantilism
2. bullionism
3. balance of trade
4. planned economy

## Review Questions

1. Why were European monarchs fundamentally interested in stockpiling gold and other precious metals?

2. Why were nations so interested in maintaining a favorable balance of trade?

3. How was monopoly used as the key to British (and probably all) mercantilism?

4. What were some of the methods used by Jean Baptiste Colbert in France? Did they have a positive or negative impact? Explain.

5. What was the fundamental flaw of mercantilism? What were some of its other negative consequences?

6. What current practices are parts of the legacy of sixteenth to eighteenth century mercantilistic practices?

## Activities

1. Compare and contrast the nature of mercantilism in England, France, and Colonial America.

2. Prepare a case for or against the following position: "Government planning is essential in promoting economic activity and preventing economic chaos."

> **CHAPTER CONTENT**
>
> 19.1 Economic Freedom       291
> 19.2 Free Enterprise in Britain       293
>     19.2.1 The Industrial Surge       295
>     19.2.2 The Workshop of the World       296
>     19.2.3 How British Workers Fared       298
> 19.3 Free Enterprise in the United States       300
>     19.3.1 1789–1860       302
>     19.3.2 After the Civil War Through World War I       303
> 19.4 Conclusions       305

# 19 FREE ENTERPRISE

> All systems either of preference or of restraint, therefore, being thus completely taken away, the obvious and simple system of natural liberty establishes itself of its own accord. Every man, as long as he does not violate the laws of justice is left perfectly free to pursue his own interest his own way, and to bring both his industry and capital into competition with those of any other man or order of men. The sovereign is completely discharged from a duty, in the attempting to perform which he must always be exposed to innumerable delusions, and for the proper performance of which no human wisdom or knowledge could ever be sufficient; the duty of superintending the industry of private people and of directing it towards the employments most suitable to the interest of society. . . .
>
> **Adam Smith, 1776**

An idea began to gain hold in the eighteenth century of restraining or limiting government and freeing individuals. Adam Smith argued forcefully for natural liberty in the economic realm. Undergirding this idea was the belief that there is a natural order. In that order when people pursue their own interests justly all of society benefits. For this order to prevail, it does not require any positive acts of monarchs, legislatures, or decrees of courts. On the contrary, those who govern must keep their hands off and leave people to their own peaceful pursuits. The French Physiocrats had a similar belief that they called *laissez-faire*, which meant to let people go their own way in managing and directing their affairs.

Did this mean that human beings are naturally good, that they are naturally inclined to pursue the public interest? Some thinkers jumped to that conclusion, but Adam Smith did not, nor did most of those who were in the Anglo-American tradition and who subscribed to this natural law view of natural liberty. On the contrary, they generally subscribed to the view that humans are flawed beings, fallen creatures, if you will, in keeping with the Judeo-Christian tradition. Smith argued rather that when a man pursued his interest justly in the market, it was in the nature of things that he not only benefited himself but others as well. Beyond that, however, the view that humans are flawed could be, and was, turned against rulers as well as the ruled. Thinkers of this era dared to penetrate the mystic veil behind which those who rule have always tried to hide. They are only human beings, the thinkers argued, no more free from flaws than the rest of us. Thus, they are unfitted to use power to direct our lives.

At any rate, the idea of a **natural order** and **natural liberty** was used as a basis for a sustained assault on mercantilist practices and dogmas. By the early nineteenth century, many mercantilist ideas and practices *laissez-faire*—see definition, p. 17.

**natural order**—the idea that God had established natural principles of conduct that comprise a moral code to be acknowledged and followed.

**natural liberty**—the idea that God created people to be free to choose their way in this world as long as they did not violate the rights of others.

had been discredited. That is not to say, of course, that mercantilism had been swept into the garbage bin of history. We already know that it continued to be carried on to some extent, and has since been revived, often under other guises. But the idea of a natural order served as a basis also for limiting government. The British had already limited the power of the monarch during the Glorious Revolution near the end of the seventeenth century. By the Constitution, the United States went much farther to limit the powers of government much more thoroughly.

> **The Rise of Liberty**
> An idea began to gain hold in the eighteenth century of restraining or limiting government and freeing individuals. Adam Smith argued forcefully for natural liberty in the economic realm. Undergirding this idea was the belief that there is a natural order. In that order when people pursue their own interests justly all of society benefits. For this order to prevail, it does not require any positive acts of monarchs, legislatures, or decrees of courts. On the contrary, those who govern must keep their hands off and leave people to their own peaceful pursuits. The French Physiocrats had a similar belief that they called *laissez-faire*, which meant to let people go their own way in managing and directing their affairs.

The nineteenth century was the great era of attempts to carry into effect the idea of natural liberty that Adam Smith had expressed. It was an era of free enterprise, as near as there has ever been such an era. It was an era of the spread of liberty, of the limiting of monarchy, of the adoption of written constitutions in many lands, of great growths of population, and of the increase of production to exceed even the increase of consumers. The latter is a way of saying that more people had more goods than ever before. Much of this, perhaps in the broader sense all of it, could be attributed to the freeing of enterprise.

All of this can be made to seem easier than it actually was and more complete than it is ever likely to be. Strange as it may seem, freedom is not easy either to convince people to want and accept or to install in practice. Of course, in a vague, general, and imprecise way, many people over the past two hundred years have rallied around the banner of liberty. The profession of the belief is not difficult. But the details of liberty in practice are another matter entirely. Something in the nature of both liberty and power tends us to the restraint and inhibition of liberty. It is not too difficult to see what it may well be. We all want perfect liberty and freedom for ourselves. Where others are concerned, we easily become ambiguous, if not outright opposed to their liberty. In fact, their freedom sets bounds to ours, and *vice versa*, for it works both ways. Each person's property sets limits or bounds to its use by others. My right to use my faculties sets limits to others in the use of theirs. As the saying goes, my right to use my fists ends where another person's nose begins.

The root of the problem is that social man is not by nature content merely with managing his own affairs. He is inclined to take a more or less lively interest in the affairs of his neighbors, those with whom he comes in contact, and whom he hears about. Anyone with some experience soon learns, of course, that other people just will not always act in a way that pleases them. At its mildest level, this interest may be nothing more than friendliness, but it easily becomes nosiness, busybodiness, or worse. Such attitudes and behavior may be tolerable, however, until people gain power over others. The spirit of the **busybody,** when combined with power, easily becomes oppressive. This reaches its apogee in government, where the rulers may use their power to direct the affairs of the ruled. It is not necessarily the case that those who govern even have the same interest as those who are governed. In any case, in the long history of humans and government, the generality of people have been to greater or lesser extent oppressed by those who govern. Restrained government and free people has been the exception, not the rule. In like manner, it has been true that even a moderate degree of free enterprise has been rare in the course of history.

Indeed, the economy is an especially attractive target for government intervention and control, as has already been demonstrated during earlier periods. The linkage of wealth and power has been common. Monarchs often rewarded their favorites with sources of wealth, and conquerors have often plundered the wealth of peoples in their conquests. Wealth may not only activate the spirit of the busybody in power but also arouse the envy of people both high and low. Governments have often placed obstacles in the way of attaining wealth for much of their population and made the acquisition of wealth relatively easy for some favored class. Nor did republican governments, especially those with a democratic bent, cure the ills of envy and jealousy, not for long anyway. When the poor have been enfranchised, they have often sought to use the power of their vote to obtain programs that redistribute wealth. All this contributes to the rarity of free enterprise.

It must be emphasized again, however, that no politico-economic system is ever purely this or that. Some elements of freedom remain in the most totalitarian of systems. In like manner, some elements of restraint remain in the freest of systems. Thus, free enterprise can be said to have existed relatively. In all systems there have been some preferences and/or government interventions. The best examples of free enterprise, then, are examples of freer enterprise as a matter of degree.

That said, it can be affirmed that the nearest thing to a time when free enterprise was widely the rule, or becoming so, was in the course of the nineteenth century. And the best examples of this trend were Great Britain and the United States. Enterprise was sufficiently free during this period in both these countries. These examples serve to illustrate both what it entailed and to demonstrate its benefits and consequences. Before turning to this, however, it is necessary to define and clarify some terms and ideas.

**busybody**—someone who mettles in the private affairs of another person.

> **Getting the Point...**
>
> Moses commanded the Levites to call out certain blessings and curses on the people as they crossed the Jordan and entered the Promised Land. One of these curses had to do with property: "Cursed is anyone who moves his neighbor's boundary stone." (Deuteronomy 27:17) A boundary stone was used to mark property lines.
>
> What are some examples of government policies that violate this principle?

## 19.1 Economic Freedom

**Economic freedom** is essentially free enterprise. **Free enterprise** entails the freedom of persons to use their minds, faculties, and materials to produce and dispose of their goods as they will or choose, subject only to such obligations, responsibilities, duties, and restraints as they may have contracted or as are inherent in their undertaking. A man who is married, for example, has contracted an obligation to provide for his wife according to his means. As a corollary of that, he is responsible to help look after and provide for the children born from this relationship. His duties may extend to aged or infirm parents, to the repayment of his debts in a timely fashion, and to support the government that protects him in the enjoyment of life and property. The most obvious restraint is that he may not use his faculties and property to injure other people. For example, free enterprise does not entail the freedom to dump hazardous waste on his

**economic freedom**—being at liberty to produce and trade goods and services on mutually agreeable terms.

**free enterprise**—see economic freedom.

property so that it may harm his neighbors. Nor does it entail the use of fraud, deceit, or damage to the reputations of others. All this is a way of saying that freedom is always counterbalanced by responsibility.

Free enterprise encompasses the free market and free trade. If there is no market for his goods or services in which he may offer them for sale, his freedom of enterprise is severely limited. It is also limited if he can only trade in a limited area. The freer the market and the broader the arena, the freer enterprise is. But basically, free enterprise means the freedom to undertake to produce what he will with his materials and to offer them for sale at whatever price he chooses, to go into and out of business without arbitrary restraints.

Free enterprise is the logic of **private property**. To turn the statement around, private property is the precondition of free enterprise. Without private property there can be no free market. Without private property there can be no free trade. Without private property, there can be no freedom of enterprise. Indeed, without private property, as pointed out earlier, it is highly doubtful that freedom can be anything but something that has been arbitrarily granted and can be arbitrarily withdrawn. In any case, private property is absolutely essential to free enterprise, and given private property—the right to use and dispose of it—free enterprise follows. Restraints on the use of property are restraints upon enterprise.

All this may be more easily grasped by examples of restraints and how they hamper enterprise. A simple and familiar example of government restraint upon enterprise is the zoning of property. The simplest form of zoning would be to divide all the land within a city into one of three zones: (1) residential, (2) commercial, and (3) industrial. Let us suppose, too, that all commercial or industrial activity had been prohibited on residential property. Those who owned property in this section would be severely limited in how they could use it. Presumably, a person could not use his home as a beauty parlor, a workshop in which he produced goods for sale, nor have on his land a booth in which he offered vegetables or flowers for sale. Obviously, he could not use it as a store or place of manufacture. Of course, there are arguments in favor of and perhaps justifications for such restrictions, but the point here is that they are nonetheless restraints upon enterprise.

**private property**—the acknowledgment that property is the result of human action and that the individual has a right to acquire it through production and voluntary trade.

---

**Private Property and Free Enterprise**

Free enterprise is the logic of private property. To turn the statement around, private property is the precondition of free enterprise. Without private property it is highly doubtful that freedom can be anything but something that has been arbitrarily granted and can be arbitrarily withdrawn. Private property is absolutely essential to free enterprise, and given private property—the right to use and dispose of it—free enterprise follows. Restraints on the use of property are restraints upon enterprise.

---

Or, to take another type of example, suppose that government authorization is required to go into business, such as in licensing and certification. If licensing requires only the payment of a minimal fee, which is essentially a tax, it would still be an obstacle to enterprise, though a small one. In this regard, it should be kept in mind that the Twenty-fourth Amendment to the Constitution was adopted in 1964 prohibiting the states to pass a poll tax, though the usual tax was only a dollar or so per year. If this was an obstacle to voting, then even the lowest fee for a business license could certainly be considered an obstacle to enterprise. Even so, it is not such taxes that ordinarily pose major obstacles to enterprise. But when licensing or certification require schooling and/or the passage of a government administered examination, such as the bar examination for lawyers, the medical license for physicians and surgeons, licensing for dentists, optometrists, veterinarians, hearing aid salesmen, beauty operators or cosmetologists, barbers, and so on, they can pose more or less formidable obstacles to enterprise. It may be objected that requirements such as these are desirable to protect consumers from poorly trained or unqualified practitioners. That may well be, but the point here is to grasp the full meaning of free enterprise.

Free enterprise means the freedom to produce and offer for sale any good or service that one chooses without hindrance from any source. It does not mean, of course, that anyone is obligated to buy it or otherwise avail himself of it. It means also freedom to price the good or service however the person offering it will. This is, of course, to take the words literally and absolutely. It is only by doing so that we can get a clear conception of free enterprise. It helps us to understand, too, why it is unlikely that there ever will be full free enterprise. Almost everyone who says he favors free enterprise will, upon examination, be found to have an assortment of exceptions in mind. He may, for example, be concerned that some sorts of drugs or similar substances not be readily available, such as cocaine, heroin, and others. Moreover, anyone who has a license or certificate that protects him from competition generally can come up with arguments for maintaining the restrictions.

There is only one class of people who could be said to benefit always from free enterprise. They are called **consumers**, and the category includes all of us who are among the living. In our classifications as **producers** we pursue a great diversity of occupations or callings, professions, trades, and skills. In the pursuit of these, our interests follow numerous divergent paths. As consumers, however, we have a common economic interest in free enterprise, a free market, and free trade. We want a great variety of goods offered at the lowest possible prices of the quality we prefer. That is what free enterprise tends to provide when property is generally privately owned. Undoubtedly, there are goods that many of us would rather not be generally available or traded. On such questions, there are often differences, though these, it should be emphasized are not economic questions. For example, probably most of us would not wish machine guns to be generally available (though there are some who might). Hence, we do not want a free market, free trade, or free enterprise in the production or use of them. The economist has no argument against prohibition of the private ownership of machine guns, or of other goods generally adjudged to be harmful. But where the goods are wanted and approved or accepted, the common economic interest is for the widest freedom in the making and offering for sale of these goods and services.

We turn now to an examination of two of the nearest systems to free enterprise that have yet occurred, to those of Great Britain and the United States in the nineteenth century.

**consumers**—those who purchase goods and services in the market economy.

**producers**—those who produce goods and services for sale in the market.

## 19.2 Free Enterprise in Britain

The main thrust of the British from 1689 to the mid-nineteenth century was toward individual liberty and private property. Free enterprise was not always at the forefront of this movement, but it was of increasing concern from the 1780s through the 1830s. The first major step came with the limiting of powers of the monarch that came with the Glorious Revolution in 1688–89. The Parliament definitely asserted its dominant role by determining descent to monarchy and limiting the powers of the king. The king thereafter had to act in conjunction with Parliament in most governmental functions. So far as English monarchy had been absolute monarchy, it was at an end. This was very important for the politico-economic system, for it should be remembered that monarchy and mercantilism were deeply entangled. It was the king who had granted the privileges that had been the hallmark of mercantilism. In addition, the settlement of 1689 contained a bill of rights, as it was called, for the English people. Mercantilism was not abolished in 1689 but it was definitely restrained after that because Parliament had been the center of resistance to mercantilist privileges. The thrust toward individual liberty mounted in the course of the eighteenth century and bore fruit in a number of directions.

Indeed, Voltaire, the French philosopher, dramatist, and historian, wrote in 1769 that:

> The English constitution has in fact arrived at that point of excellence whereby all men are restored to those natural rights of which, in nearly all monarchies they are deprived. These rights are: entire liberty of person and property; freedom of the press; the right of being tried in all criminal cases by a jury of independent men; the right of being tried only according to the strict letter of the law; and the right of every man to profess, unmolested, what religion he chooses while he renounces offices which only the members of the Established Church may hold. These are . . . invaluable privileges. . . . To be secure on lying down that you will rise in possession of the same property with which you retired to rest; that you will not be torn from the arms of your wife and your children in the dead of the night, to be thrown into a dungeon or be buried in exile in a desert; that . . . you will have the power to publish all your thoughts. . . . These privileges belong to everyone who sets foot on English soil. . . .

While Voltaire left out of his account the mercantilistic restrictions and privileges that still remained, he did capture the tenor of the British system. Moreover, after the successful revolt of the American colonies (1776–1783), British policies shifted away even more decidedly from mercantilist restraints. Even before that, however, individual enterprise had been substantially freed from most restrictions. Great Britain—England, Scotland, and Wales—was the largest free trading area in Europe. There were no tolls or fees to hamper tradesman as they moved merchandise from one county or country to another. The guilds had largely lost their power to exclude manufacturers from producing goods they had once monopolized. The old open fields, with plots claimed here and there by tenants, were either in the process of or had been enclosed. This was the process where the complete control of farm land came to the landlord, whereby land became full-fledged private property. Nobles in some countries were prohibited to engage in manufacturing, but in England they were free to invest in whatever sort of enterprise they chose.

There was a new spirit of enterprise, of innovation, of seeking improvements in eighteenth century England. This spirit evinced itself in many new inventions, in a willingness to venture capital in unproved undertakings, and in conceiving of ways to improve how goods were produced. The British took the lead in contriving devices to improve manufactures, in providing power to turn machines, and the like. In the making of iron, Abraham Darby built a blast furnace in 1754 that provided extra air to the process with a bellows turned by a water wheel. The first iron bridge was built by John Wilkinson in 1779. In the 1760s, James Brindley, a self-taught engineer, began the building of canals that made inland cities available to cheap shipping. Toll roads were built extensively, thus making the transport of goods much swifter and less expensive. Spinning and weaving were greatly sped up and eventually mechanized by a series of inventions by John Kay, James Hargreaves, Richard Arkwright, Edmund Cartwright, and Samuel Crompton. The overshot waterwheel replaced the undershot wheel, thus using the power from moving the water to turn machinery much more efficiently. James Watt perfected the steam engine in 1765, and thereafter worked with various entrepreneurs to develop and market it.

What was the source of this spirit of enterprise and innovation? Perhaps the best way to put the answer is this: As the privileges and restrictions of mercantilism were removed, people turned away from seeking preferences as a route to wealth to more economical means of providing goods and services. As monopolies were broken they sought new ways to wealth through innovation. The practices of economy became both privately and socially beneficial under a free system, as Adam Smith said. Many of these enterprisers not only enriched themselves but also made goods more readily available at lower costs than before.

### 19.2.1 The Industrial Surge

There was a great industrial surge in the course of the eighteenth century in Britain, and it became much more pronounced as time wore on. Since "industrial" tends to connote manufacturing, it may be well to emphasize that both farm methods and productivity greatly improved during the same period as well. The statistics for the period are inadequate to discover how much grain production increased, but there is good reason to believe that it increased considerably. Not only was more land brought under cultivation but also production per acre increased, as much as one third in the yield of wheat between 1750 and 1800.

There appears to have been a similar increase in the production of cattle for market during the same period. In 1750, a little fewer than 71,000 head were sold at the major market at Smithfield. In 1794, there were over 109,000 offered for sale. It is generally held, too, that the average weight of cattle offered for sale had greatly increased. One writer says that the average weight of oxen offered at Smithfield had increased from 370 pounds in 1710 to 800 pounds in 1795. Thus, the amount of meat actually offered may have more than tripled. Sheep for sale at this market did not increase quite so dramatically: from approximately 656,000 earlier to about 718,000 in 1794, but sheep were getting much heavier on the average than formerly.

Undoubtedly, the improvement of pasture land contributed to much heavier animals. In row-crop farming, there was a major shift from using oxen to pull the plows to horses. This greatly increased the productivity of the plowman by using the swift moving horses rather than the plodding oxen. As iron became more plentiful and less expensive, it began to be used on plows to replace or cover the wooden parts.

The surge in manufacturing production, however, was much more marked than in farming. The most dramatic increase occurred in the making of cotton goods. For example, at Yorkshire, the annual average number of pieces of broadcloth produced was 34,400 from 1731–40. From

1791–1800, it was 229,400. Printed cloth production increased from 2.4 million yards in the first decade of the eighteenth century to 25.9 million in the last decade.

Mining and iron and steel manufactures increased especially rapidly in the last decade or so of the eighteenth century. In 1788, pig iron production in Great Britain was only 68,000 tons. In 1796, it had grown to 125,000 tons for England and Wales alone. By 1806, it had risen to 258,000 tons for all of Britain. Coal production probably quadrupled between the beginning and the end of the eighteenth century.

Perhaps the best indicators of the great surge of production, however, are the shipping and trade figures. The most reliable statistics have been gathered for these undertakings also. The tonnage of boats leaving English ports in 1700 was 317,000 registered tons; by 1751 it was 661,000 tons; it had reached 1,924,000 tons in 1800. In pounds sterling, the value of English exports in 1700 was about 7.5 million; in 1750, 15 million; in 1800, 42 million. Imports had risen comparably, as might be expected. The export of cotton goods rose precipitately in the last years of the nineteenth century. The total value of such goods was only about 360,000 pounds sterling in 1780. By, 1800, it was more than 5.5 million. The import of cotton as raw material for manufacturing showed a similar increase: in 1781 it was 5,300,000 pounds of cotton, and by 1800 it has risen to 56 million pounds. The invention of the cotton gin in the early 1790s undoubtedly made cotton available in much larger quantities.

But this first industrial surge of Britain in the last years of the eighteenth century was only the beginning of a larger economic expansion. The great century of British manufacturing and trade dominance was yet to come. Much freer enterprise was yet to come as well. In some ways, these last years of the eighteenth and the early ones of the nineteenth involved setbacks for Britain and even more for some of Britain's neighbors. Between 1793–1815, Britain was more often at war with France than not. This was the period of the wars connected with the French Revolution and Napoleon. Wars are destructive of lives and materials, and are not themselves productive. This should not be taken to mean that much of British productivity did not continue to rise, for it did. Foreign trade was greatly hampered during parts of this period, however, and much of the production was consumed in war.

In the 1820s, however, Britain was headed toward free trade, and markets were opening up around the world. Britain lowered or removed tariffs, and other countries followed suit in the ensuing decades. The early policy of Britain had been to prohibit the export of machinery for manufacturing. The prohibition was removed and the export of machinery became a major business as well. The final symbol of British mercantilism—the Corn Laws—were also repealed as well.

### 19.2.2 The Workshop of the World

Britain was the exemplar of the free market, free trade, and free enterprise in the nineteenth century. That century was surely the golden age of European Civilization, if it has ever had a golden age. It was an age when the outcroppings of that civilization were being extended to the rest of the world. It was an era of peace generally—such wars as occurred were usually brief and on the periphery of Europe, or beyond. Britain was the center—the heart, so to speak—of this civilization. The nineteenth century—the period from the end of the Napoleonic Wars to World War I anyway—might well be called the *Pax Britannica*—the Peace of Britain. The British navy ruled the seas. But much more important, Britain advanced the arts of peace around the world, for trade is fundamentally a peaceful undertaking. Britain retained various colonies, but the main object was not now to monopolize but to expand and civilize. Britain was the leader in maintaining order and peace in the world, in literature, in thought, and in commerce.

> **Nineteenth Century Britain**
> Britain was the exemplar of the free market, free trade, and free enterprise in the nineteenth century. The nineteenth century was surely the golden age of European Civilization, if it has ever had a golden age. It was an age when the outcroppings of that civilization were being extended to the rest of the world. It was an era of peace generally—such wars as occurred were usually brief and on the periphery of Europe, or beyond. Britain was the center—the heart, so to speak—of this civilization.

Britain's commercial leadership was first asserted in the realm of manufacturing. It was this particular leadership that led J. D. Chambers to refer to Britain as *The Workshop of the World* in his book by that name, which was an economic history of Britain during the period from 1820 to 1880. The surge in the growth of manufacturing was quite noticeable by the 1780s, as has already been shown, and would continue to mount for much of the nineteenth century. One estimate has it that there was in general a tenfold industrial output increase between 1820 and 1913.

England had long been a major producer of woolen goods, but as cotton became the leading fabric, Britain took the lead in cotton textiles. They were the major export item of the country throughout the nineteenth century—amounting to nearly one-half of Britain's exports in the early nineteenth and one-fourth in the early twentieth century. In 1912, an English economist declared that "the export trade in manufactured cotton goods from this country is in money value the greatest export trade in manufactured goods of any kind from any country in the world."

Another area of dramatic increase was in coal production. About 10 million tons were mined in 1800. This had increased over the years until it was 154 million tons in 1880. Iron production rose mightily during the century. It is estimated that in 1740 about 17,000 tons was produced. The annual production in 1827 was 690,000 tons; in 1840 1,390,000 tons, in 1854 3,100,000 tons, and by the end of the century it had reached 8 million tons annually. In the course of the century, precision tool making had become a major industry.

To show Britain's place of leadership in the world, however, it is necessary to compare British economic activity with that of other leading countries. Great Britain's percentage of manufacturing production in the world was 31.8 in 1870. By comparison, that of the United States was 23.3, that of Germany 13.2, and that of France 10.3, among the leading countries. In 1860, Britain had 23% of world trade, compared with 11% for France and 9% for the United States. In 1880, Britain had more than 6.5 million tons of shipping plying the seas, compared to its nearest competitor, the United States that had only 1.5 million tons. Britain, too, was banker for much of the world. The pound sterling was generally the measure for international trade. Investments poured out of Britain to developing and underdeveloped countries. Britain was the gold capital of the world, and the major insurance firm internationally was Lloyd's of London.

Though agricultural products played little role in British exports, it is indicative of general British productivity that for much of the century, production continued to rise. Despite the growth in population in the country, up until the middle of the nineteenth century Britain grew most of the wheat consumed in the country and almost all animal products.

The commercial leadership of Britain was not only the result of free enterprise but of freedom and free people. Not only were entrepreneurs and enterprisers free but those who toiled in factory, mine, mill, and shop were too. Thus, the commercial and productive leadership of Britain was the accomplishment not only of statesmen, inventors, engineers, entrepreneurs, financiers, industrialists, and shipping magnates but also of miners, millers, factory workers, sailors, steam fitters, mechanics, spinners, weavers, day laborers, farmers, and so on through an almost interminable list of all who contributed with their minds, hands, skills, and will to the effort.

### 19.2.3 How British Workers Fared

This brings us to a question that has often been raised about this period. Namely, how did the workers fare in the workshop of the world? More specifically, did the toilers in factory, mine, and mill receive their due reward for their contributions to British productivity? To put the question in more general terms, did the English people profit from this great productivity, or was the productivity achieved at the expense of and by the exploitation of a large portion of the working populace, as has sometimes been alleged?

From that day to this, there have been charges that the workers generally were the losers in this great industrial achievement. Robert Owen, a mid-nineteenth century British reformer, claimed that all the "splendid improvements" had "hitherto been to demoralize society through the misapplication of the new wealth created." A recent historian has said,

> The initial growth of these industries could only be achieved by the regimentation of vast armies of cheap labour. Herded together in the slum towns of the nineteenth century, these victims of industrial progress had to wait until hard-won experience in handling the new problems of urban life slowly rescued them from their unhealthy squalor.

A leader of Chartism in the nineteenth century reported the following about the lives of some of the poor in London.

> In whole streets that we visited we found nothing worthy of the name of bed, bedding or furniture.... Their unpaved yards and filthy courts, and the want of drainage and cleansing, rendered their houses hotbeds of disease; so that fever combined with hunger was committing great ravages among them.

Undoubtedly, much that was said about the conditions of workers, especially in the first half of the nineteenth century, lacks any perspective. Much of it was written by reformers, some of them under the influence of utopian visions, beside which the lot of workers was indeed hard and poor. To put the matter in perspective, it should first be said that hardship and suffering have been the common lot of most people throughout the ages. Hours of work have been long and often unremitting for those who would produce much throughout history. The disparities between the wealthy and the poor have always been very great. For example, the vast wealth of Louis XIV was mostly wrung from the poor peasants and squandered on his projects and mistresses. Housing has been squalid from time immemorial. Death by disease and malnutrition greatly antedates the awareness of these as causes of death, and, indeed, no doubt, goes back to the very appearance of life on this planet. The squalid housing of industrial towns was probably superior to that in the countryside from which many of the inhabitants came.

What was different about life in the nineteenth century was not that there was hard work, hardship, and suffering, but those conditions were improving. The great British productivity was finding its way in increasing amounts to the homes and lives of those who most directly produced it.

One of the best evidences for the general improvement that came in the wake of these developments is the growth of population. Estimates indicate that there were about five and a half million people in England in 1700, and that the population had increased to about six and a half million in 1750. When the first census was taken in 1801, the population was a little under 8,900,000. By 1831, it had reached 13,897,000; by 1851, 17,928,000; by 1901, 32,528,000. In short, the process of industrialization was accompanied by a rapidly increasing population.

Such evidence as we have indicates that the increasing population could be attributed to improved living conditions that accompanied the freeing of enterprise and industrialization. T. S. Ashton, a careful student of these matters, has pointed out that the growth in population should not be attributed to any extensive change in the birth rate in England. The birth rate remained at about the same level for the years 1740 to 1830. Nor does inward migration from other countries play any significant role in the increase, since there were as many or more migrating from England as were coming in. Ashton maintains that the growth of population can be explained mainly by such improving conditions as the,

> ...substitution of wheat for inferior cereals..., an increased consumption of vegetables..., [better] standards of personal cleanliness, associated with more soap and cheap cotton underwear..., the use of brick instead of timber in the walls.... The larger towns were paved, drained and supplied with running water; knowledge of medicine and surgery developed; hospitals and dispensaries increased; and more attention was paid to such things as the disposal of refuse and the proper burial of the dead.

Another historian, David Thompson in *England in the Nineteenth Century* says of the early years,

> Even in the slums of the new industrial towns expectation of life was better than ever before. People were already, on the whole, better fed, better clothed, less likely to contract disease and better cared for when they did, than during the eighteenth century.

In sum, improved living conditions account for the growth in population. Many more people were surviving birth and early childhood diseases.

Perhaps, there is even more direct proof of the benefits of free enterprise and industry to workers generally. There was a general trend for wages to rise. Of course, this trend was not universal. The skills of some

> **Getting the Point...**
>
> When looking back in time at how workers in nineteenth century Britain fared, what mistake in analysis is made to claim they were mistreated and what facts expose it?

workers were outdated by the use of machines. Machinery was adopted at different paces in different industries. There were always workers and processes that were marginal, and wages would reflect this status. Nevertheless, the trend was up. One survey indicates that if wages were taken as 100 on the average in 1790, they had risen to 137.4 by 1845. In the third quarter of the nineteenth century there was probably the most dramatic sustained improvement in wages and living conditions that had ever occurred in English history. Llewellyn Woodward (*The Age of Reform*) says that,

> Money wages, with a few slight lapses, rose steadily between 1850 and 1874. From a base of 100 in 1850 it has been calculated that the general level rose to 156 by 1874.... For these reasons the standard of living and prosperity of the mass of the workers rose greatly throughout the period.

How did workers fare, then, in the Workshop of the World? They fared well, indeed. They fared well in comparison with workers of other ages and times. They fared well in comparison with their parents and grandparents. They fared well in comparison with workers in other countries, if not all other countries. Their wages were rising in relation to the prices of what they bought with them. Housing and sanitation were improving. If a workman did not like his employer, he could seek out a different one, or go into business for himself. Some did, and many more could have. If he did not like conditions in England, he could migrate. English workmen could hope, and they were free.

---

**How did workers fare in the Workshop of the World?**
They fared well, indeed. They fared well in comparison with workers of other ages and times. They fared well in comparison with their parents and grandparents. They fared well in comparison with workers in other countries, if not all other countries. Their wages were rising in relation to the prices of what they bought with them. Housing and sanitation were improving. If a workman did not like his employer, he could seek out a different one, or go into business for himself. Some did, and many more could have. If he did not like conditions in England, he could migrate. English workmen could hope, and they were free.

---

## 19.3 Free Enterprise in the United States

The rise and growth of the United States in the course of the nineteenth century was even more spectacular than that of Great Britain. It was more spectacular because the emergence of the United States to agricultural, industrial, commercial, and financial leadership came much more suddenly and swiftly. After all, England had been a major European nation since the sixteenth century. By contrast, the United States did not even exist as a nation until the late eighteenth century. Before that time, there had only been some English colonies, caught in the toils of British mercantilism, remote from commercial centers, and of little account in world affairs. The population was little more than 3 million in 1776, and a portion of these were African slaves. Henry Adams, a descendant of John Adams, writing as an historian, had this to say about *The United States in 1800*:

> Even after two centuries of struggle the land was still untamed; forest covered every portion, except here and there a strip of cultivated soil; the minerals lay undisturbed in their rocky beds, and more than two thirds of the people clung to the seaboard within fifty miles of the tidewater, where alone the wants of civilized life could be supplied. The centre of population rested within eighteen miles of Baltimore, north and east of Washington....

As Adams noted, transportation by land was rugged and primitive. There were few improved roads south of Baltimore, most rivers had not been bridged, and travel was by coach, wagon, or on horseback. In comparison with Europe, Adams said,

> America was backward. Fifty or a hundred miles inland more than half the houses were log-cabins, which might or might not enjoy the luxury of a glass window. Throughout the South and West houses showed little attempt at luxury; but even in New England the ordinary farmhouse was hardly so well built, so spacious, or as warm as that of a well-to-do contemporary of Charlemagne. The cloth which the farmer's family wore was still homespun. The hats were manufactured by the village hatter, and nearly every article of dress was also homemade.... The plough was rude and clumsy; the sickle as old as Tubal Cain, and even the cradle [for cutting grain] not in general use; the flail was unchanged since the Aryan exodus; in Virginia, grain was still commonly trodden out by horses.... Stock was as a rule not only unimproved, but ill cared for. The swine ran loose; the cattle were left to feed on what pasture they could find....

Yet, in the course of the nineteenth century, the United States was transformed from a fledgling nation lately freed from colonial status into one of the leading commercial nations in the world. Americans in large numbers had crossed the Appalachians (this movement was already underway in 1800), pressed on to the Mississippi, occupied the Great Plains, forged across the Rockies, and settled in growing numbers on the Pacific coast. The forest, much of it, had fallen to ax and saw; the land, where it was sufficiently fertile, had been tamed by the plow. Americans made or utilized inventions unprecedented in number. The rivers and streams had been bridged, canals dug, and roads built. Railroads had been built from the Atlantic to the Pacific. Great cities with large populations could be found in every section of the country. Mines, mills, and factories provided much of the livelihood of the inhabitants of towns and cities. Manufacturing had replaced farming as the major producer of wealth long before the end of the century. Farmers now had mowers, reapers, binders, threshing machines, gangplows, mechanical planters, and fertilizer distributors. Steam power had largely replaced water power for turning machinery, and electricity was in the offing. The internal combustion gasoline fueled engine was already propelling a few automobiles and would soon be doing so for trucks and tractors as well.

Much of this heady development could and should be ascribed to free enterprise. Most of the building had been done by private entrepreneurs—the factories, mines and mills. Even the vast railroad system, spanning the country in every direction and surely one of the great marvels of the world, was almost entirely privately owned and operated, though there had been government grants and subsidies in the building of some of the systems. The inventions were the result of free enterprise, and their exploitation was usually undertaken by private entrepreneurs.

> **Nineteenth Century United States**
> In the course of the nineteenth century, the United States was transformed from a fledgling nation lately freed from colonial status into one of the leading commercial nations in the world. Much of this heady development could and should be ascribed to free enterprise.

### 19.3.1 1789–1860

Enterprise was about as free as it has ever been anywhere during the years 1789–1860. However, before discussing that, one notable exception must be acknowledged. That exception was the chattel slavery of blacks. It is the perfect illustration of the cost of ignoring God's moral principles, which we must never forget. It was largely restricted to the Southern and Border states during this period. The Continental Congress had prohibited slavery in the Northwest Territory by the Northwest Ordinance before the Constitution was adopted. In the 1780s, the states north of Maryland generally abolished such slavery as existed there. Even so, slavery was a major exception to freedom of enterprise, and its practice kept the farming industry of the plantations from investing in innovations.

Slaves were not independent decision-making persons economically; they were considered chattels—property of their masters. Although they worked, they were not laborers in an economic sense. In the conditions of the time they were more nearly classified as capital—property used to produce other goods. Indeed, they were a major capital investment of plantation owners, both large and small. While slave owners could be said to have a considerable measure of free enterprise, this tended to be qualified by their being more or less locked into a system that could be slave operated. Rather than investing money in improved equipment, they tended to tie more and more of it up in land and slaves. Moreover, the power to own and use slaves was protected by special laws that empowered owners and disabled slaves. Thus, legal status, not enterprise, was the key to the slave-plantation system.

Otherwise, free people and free enterprise were the rule during this era. There were some relics of indentured servitude in the early years of the Republic, but these were soon dispensed with. The break from England had cast off the bulk of mercantile regulations—all that were imposed by Britain. Such monarchical privileges as the king's right to certain kinds of trees for shipbuilding were, of course, removed, as were medieval relics, such as quitrents, the rule of primogeniture (first son) in the inheritance of real property, and entailment of estates. Land thereafter was generally owned in fee simple. Most established churches were disestablished in the 1780s, though some aspects of establishment were retained for several decades in some of the New England states. The economic significance of this is that people were no longer taxed to support churches. The Constitution prohibited the granting of titles of nobility, thus cutting away the ground of any hereditary aristocracy. The Constitution also prohibited taxes on exports, thus completely freeing the export side of foreign trade. No powers were granted in the Constitution for the United States Government to pay subsidies or bounties to encourage any particular kind of production. Tariffs on imports were imposed, but with a few exceptions, they were low up until the Civil War, and were usually what were called tariffs for revenue rather than for protection from foreign goods.

Property was generally privately, most often, individually, owned and transferable at will. The owner could bequeath it to whomever he chose. In case he died without a will, which is referred to as "intestate," his property would be divided among his heirs according to formulas established by the states. If he died intestate and without heirs, his property might then, and only then, **escheat** to the state. People might enter whatever business or undertaking they chose, generally without notice to or approval from government. No license or certification would ordinarily be required. They could produce what they chose, work for whom they chose, sell their goods or services at whatever prices pleased them. There were, it is true, some relics of guilds or incipient labor unions, but the courts usually made short shrift of any efforts they might make to control prices or entry into the field. Regarding such union attempts, a New York court ruled in 1835 that:

**escheat**—the reversion of property to the state. This usually occurs when there are no surviving heirs or none who lay claim to an estate.

> The man who owns an article of trade or commerce is not obliged to sell it for any particular price. He may say that he will not make coarse boots for less than one dollar per pair, but *he has no right to say that no other mechanic shall make them for less.* . . . If one individual does not possess such a right over the conduct of another, no number of individuals can possess such a right.

In short, the owner of a good or service could set whatever price he chose for them, but no other person or group could do so.

The above are strong indications that enterprise was free in America from 1789–1860. The point can be made perhaps more emphatically by turning it around and stating it negatively. Enterprise was *not* regulated or controlled or directed by government. There were neither minimum nor maximum prices set by government for goods or services. There was no minimum wage, no rent controls, no quality controls generally, no environmental control, no zoning ordinances, and little to no competition by government enterprises. Monopolies were rare and more apt to be abolished than allowed to endure or prosper. Taxes were low throughout the nineteenth century. The United States Government usually managed with revenue from tariffs and the sale of land, except during and immediately after wars. The debt of the United States was finally retired in the 1830s, and government was more apt to have a surplus than deficit of funds. The currency of the country was gold or silver or paper money redeemable in these. The United States had no tender laws, and the states prohibited making anything other than gold or silver legal tender in payment of debts.

## 19.3.2 After the Civil War Through World War I

Free enterprise remained the rule from the Civil War down to World War I, though interferences with it were becoming more important during this period. The freeing of the slaves during and after the Civil War removed that blot on freedom from the earlier period. Blacks were now free to engage in enterprise, to sell their labor and the use of their skills, or to produce as they could and would. It should be noted, however, that by the end of the nineteenth century a system of segregation by race, generally imposed by some of the states, limited the opportunities and tended to restrict the enterprises in which they could hope for much success.

Movements were afoot to restrict enterprises or regulate and control them from many other directions as well. Compulsory schooling for the young limited the extent to which they could work. Free public schools, which tended to become the rule as compulsory attendance rules were adopted, made it increasingly difficult for private entrepreneurs to enter the school business and limited the opportunities for free lance teachers and tutors. High protective tariffs restricted imports and interfered with foreign trade. Governments were also moving toward regulating many businesses and even regulating prices in what were coming to be called "public utilities." Throughout most of the nineteenth century the United States had steadily divested of its land holdings, often selling land at near give away prices. Toward the end of the century, the government began to reverse this policy and to acquire land once again. Labor unions were gaining power in some industries and attempting to restrict the hours of labor and set minimum wages.

Even so, free enterprise was the rule or dominant practice from 1789 to 1914. And, the great growth and achievements economically owe much to this system.

Some figures will indicate how dramatic the growth often was. While growth of production occurred throughout the nineteenth century, it was more dramatic from mid-century on. This table shows a few example statistics for American farm production.

| Crop | 1850 | 1900 |
| --- | --- | --- |
| Wheat (bushels) | 100 Million | 600 Million |
| Cotton (bales) | 4.59 Million | 10.226 Million |
| Corn (bushels) | 590 Million | 2.6 Billion |

All this represented a considerable increase in productivity per acre, for land in cultivation had less than tripled.

The value of the annual product of manufacturing increased from approximately $2 billion in 1850 to $13 billion in 1900. This represented great increases in consumer goods. In 1859, men's clothing manufacturers turned out a product worth slightly over $73 million; in 1899, they made a product worth over $276 million. The worth of the factory produce for women's clothing was 20 times as great in 1899 as it was in 1859. In 1849, flour and grist mill products were valued at approximately $136 million; in 1899, this had increased to about $560 million. These figures represent increased goods rather than rising prices due to monetary inflation. In fact, prices declined generally during the period under consideration. One writer notes that if wholesale prices were indicated by the figure of 100 for 1860, they had fallen to 95.7 in 1890, and would decrease somewhat more during the next decade.

There is considerable evidence that much of this rising income was spread widely throughout the populace. Private production income (all income except that from government sources) increased from about $4 billion in 1859 to $28 billion in 1899. Per capita income, in terms of actual money, rose from $134 in 1859 to $185 in 1899. Of course the figures for per capita income are only averages and do not indicate distribution. But there is evidence that real wages rose over this period, much greater than did per capita income. At any rate, the industry of Americans had transformed the country in a century or so from a largely undeveloped outpost of the British Empire into a thriving prominent nation in the world.

## 19.4 Conclusions

It is doubtful that free enterprise should be thought of as a politico-economic system. It is true that every economy operates within the framework of government, and free enterprise does as well. But under free enterprise the economy and government are distinct and separate entities, performing different functions. The government maintains peace, order, and performs protective functions. The economy provides goods and services, and under free enterprise those functions are performed without government intervention, control, coordination, or direction. In the first half of the nineteenth century, the United States Government made a determined effort to keep the government and economy from being entangled. Under the Jacksonians—1830s and 1840s—repeated efforts were made even to keep the money in the treasury out of the stream of commerce by having an independent treasury rather than depositing government money in banks. The efforts of the Jacksonians were not entirely successful along these and other lines, but they carried the principle about as far as it has ever been taken. For a while, free enterprise in America was as near as it has come to being an economic, and not a politico-economic system.

Under full-fledged free enterprise, there would be no institutionally established preference for land, labor, or capital. That means mainly that government would not follow policies giving preference or support for one or the other of these. Individual and private economy will, of course, dictate that whichever of the elements is scarcer be used most sparingly, and the one that is most plentiful will be used more bountifully. Thus, if land is more plentiful than capital or labor, it will be used more freely than the other two elements. There may be times in a country's history when one of the means of production is scarcer than the others and thus it will be used more sparingly. But whether that is the case or not, individuals and organizations will often find that in their own particular case one or the other is harder for them to come by. Thus, it was the case that land in America was more plentiful in the nineteenth century than the other means of production. In consequence, land was relatively less expensive and more extensively used (some critics have claimed wastefully) than the other elements. On the other hand, land was never plentiful for long near the docks in port cities, and the price of such land rose. This soon led to the building of multi-storied structures, hence the using of land intensively. The main point, however, is that under free enterprise, there is no instituted preference for one or another element of production and that people are free to make their own economic decisions in terms of which elements are scarcer and which are available in greater plenty.

Two other conclusions about free enterprise can be drawn. One is that it is a highly productive. It is possibly the most highly productive means of mustering the ingenuity, skills, and labor of a people. Potentially, it puts more minds and hands behind producing what is wanted, or most wanted, than any other arrangement. Surely, free men, using their own materials, or receiving the rewards of their labor, have the highest incentives for doing their best. This is most likely to be the case, of course, when land and equipment are widely owned, but whatever the case may be, many minds applied to their own particular projects are apt to be much more productive than when they are confined in systems where those who hold the political power are directing them.

Second, under free enterprise, people must be basically responsible for their own well-being. To put it more broadly, people who are old enough to work and able to do so must provide for their needs and wants by their own efforts. Those who are unable to do so must be provided for by families and voluntary organizations. Freedom carries with it responsibility. Indeed, responsibility generally precedes freedom both chronologically and logically. Unless free people assume these responsibilities, they lose their freedom to the powers that provide for the needs and wants of those who cannot or will not.

**The Nature of Free Enterprise**

- Under free enterprise the economy and government are distinct and separate entities, performing different functions. The government maintains peace, order, and performs protective functions. The economy provides goods and services, and under free enterprise those functions are performed without government intervention, control, coordination, or direction.

- Under full-fledged free enterprise, there would be no institutionally established preference for land, labor, or capital. That means mainly that government would not follow policies giving preference or support for one or the other of these.

- Free enterprise is highly productive. Many minds applied to their own particular endeavors are apt to be much more productive than when they are restricted to plans designed by those who hold the political power.

- Under free enterprise people who are old enough to work and able to do so must provide for their needs and wants by their own efforts. Those who are unable to do so must be provided for by families and voluntary organizations. Freedom carries with it responsibility. Indeed, responsibility generally precedes freedom both chronologically and logically. Unless free people assume these responsibilities, they lose their freedom to the powers that provide for the needs and wants of those who cannot or will not.

> *My belief in free competitive economic enterprise does not rest solely or even mainly on arguments of economic efficiency, though, heaven knows, these are cogent enough. It rests essentially on the view that the free market is the only safe way of ensuring that productive effort is directed towards supplying what individuals actually want, and in a way which secures the dignity and independence of the worker.*
> **Margaret Thatcher**

# Study Guide for:

# 19 Free Enterprise

## Chapter Summary

The concept of free enterprise began to gain hold in the eighteenth century. In the Anglo-American tradition, the notion of free enterprise is that even though man is a fallen creature and given to self-interest, he will nevertheless work to the benefit of society at large if he is free to pursue his own interests in the market. This occurs since trade in the market is voluntary. Therefore, if an individual is to pursue his own interests he must also serve the interests of his customers. Furthermore, competition among individuals leads to increases in product quality, greater efficiency in production, and lower market prices for goods and services.

On the other hand, it was recognized that since man is flawed, he is just as flawed when he becomes a ruler. Since this is the case, and since it is much easier to use a position of power to promote one's own selfish desires, it was recognized that government must be restrained. Thus, a counterpart to free enterprise was to limit the role of government so that it mainly functioned to preserve order in society so that people could trade freely.

By nature people prefer freedom and liberty more for themselves than for their neighbors. As a result, this type of freedom has never been very widespread. Rather, the historical norm has been toward the oppression of those who are ruled by those who govern. In addition, there is some reluctance to accept the responsibility that necessarily counterbalances freedom. When people are free to engage in any constructive activity and to trade freely with others they become more responsible for the consequences of their actions.

As a politico-economic system, free enterprise has never been completely established, but its most thorough implementation occurred in England and the United States during the nineteenth century. The results were an amazing increase in productivity and in the general standards of living of the people of those countries. Yet for all the benefits, both nations have moved away from freedom toward government regulation, control, and socialistic practices.

## Points of Emphasis

1. Free enterprise means that people are free to use their minds, faculties, and property to accomplish any end desired so long as their actions do no harm to their neighbors in the process.

2. Private property is a prerequisite for free enterprise.

3. In free enterprise human behavior is restrained naturally so that in pursuing one's self-interest, the individual promotes the interests of his neighbor as well.

## Identification

1. *laissez faire*
2. natural order
3. natural liberty
4. busybody
5. economic freedom
6. free enterprise
7. private property
8. consumers
9. producers
10. escheat

# Review Questions

1. What is the counterbalance to freedom?

2. What was the source of the spirit of enterprise and innovation in eighteenth century Britain?

3. How did workers fare in the Workshop of the World? Explain how a lack of perspective lead to the widespread acceptance of the views of the reformers who were critical of working conditions of the time.

4. What was the one notable exception to free enterprise that existed in the United States during the period from 1789–1860?

5. The last section of the chapter laid out three conclusions that can be drawn about free enterprise. What are they?

6. Even though the benefits of free enterprise are great, historically government control and oppression generally prevail. Why is this the case? Are there aspects of human nature that contribute to this?

7. Why have Great Britain and the United States systematically abandoned their free enterprise economies in favor of greater government control?

8. How does free enterprise restrain self-interested behavior and encourage behavior that promotes the interests of others as well?

# Activities

1. Prepare a case for or against the following position: "In every trade someone benefits at the expense of someone else."

2. Compare and contrast the free enterprise in Great Britain with that in the United States.

> **Chapter Content**
>
> 20.1 The Meaning of Capitalism 309
> 20.2 Private Corporatism 312
>     20.2.1 Corporatist Legacy of Alexander Hamilton 312
>     20.2.2 Federally Chartered Banks 313
>     20.2.3 Corporatism of Early Republicans 314
>     20.2.4 Increasing Use of Regulation 316
>     20.2.5 Corporatism of the New Deal 317
>     20.2.6 Entanglement of Business with Politics 318
>     20.2.7 Corporatism in the Farm Industry 320
>     20.2.8 In Sweden 324
> 20.3 State Corporatism 325

# 20 Corporatism

Socialism has been the central ideology that has given rise to or been the basis for imposing the politico-economic systems in many lands since the early twentieth century. But socialism underwent transmutations and changes both before and after those professing it came to power. In retrospect, we can discern that socialism is divided into two basic camps. The milder camp is sometimes called **evolutionary socialism**, but has also been known by a variety of other names: gradualism, democratic socialism, and progressivism. In general, those of this persuasion have sought to move toward socialism by gradual means within a democratic framework without radically altering the existing political framework. The other camp is **revolutionary socialism**. Communism has been the most prominent brand, but it should also include Nazism and Italian Fascism, for they were both revolutionary in character and socialistic in tendency.

All of this has caused the light of freedom to dim in the twentieth century. Revolutionary socialists not only assaulted freedom but also civilization itself. The totalitarian systems they imposed by terror were remote from the civilized order that made free enterprise work so well. Indeed, by the end of the first third of the twentieth century the remains of free enterprise were being replaced by government imposed systems in almost every land. The task here is to try to get to the essence of these systems, or at least to their economic character. To do so, this and the following two chapters, will deal with their central features. The developments will first be discussed under the heading of Corporatism, then Welfarism, and Communism.

Actually, the dominant economic feature of all the present-day politico-economic systems is that they are collectivist. Both in the communist and non-communist portions of the world, corporatists aim to control the economy by regulating or capturing control over the capital resources in it.

## 20.1 The Meaning of Capitalism

When asked what the economic system of the United States is, the majority of Americans by far would say **capitalism**. Confusions or differences about the meaning of words are manifold in modern times, but perhaps no word has more confusion surrounding it than capitalism. Karl Marx, the ideological father of modern communism, gave popularity to the word capitalism. He used it as an ideology, a complex of ideas, concepts, and practices, by which the **bourgeoisie** exploited (took unfair advantage of) workers. In Marx's own ideology, capitalism was an exploitative system in which the rich got richer and the poor grew poorer, and

**evolutionary socialism**—a political movement whereby socialism is imposed gradually upon a nation by implementing new rules and regulations legislatively.

**revolutionary socialism**—a political movement whereby socialism is imposed all at once in a revolution that overthrows the existing political structures.

**capitalism**—an imprecise word coined by Karl Marx aimed at deriding the free market as a system of exploitation. Many mistakenly use the term interchangeably with free enterprise.

**bourgeoisie**—a French word that means, literally, townsmen or burgers. The word has come to be used to refer to members of the middle class. In Europe, that means the class between the aristocrats at the top and the peasants or proletariat at the bottom. Marx used the term specifically to refer to the capitalistic class, i.e., those who owned the instruments of production.

**crony capitalism**—the ongoing result of evolutionary socialism whereby political privileges are bestowed on a few while restricting people generally.

in which all wealth would eventually be concentrated in the hands of the wealthy.

On the other hand, many defenders of the private ownership of capital and free enterprise have championed the notion that such a system should be called capitalism. For example, Ludwig von Mises, a leader of the Austrian school of economics, said in a lecture in Argentina (reprinted in *The Freeman*, December, 1979):

> The capitalist system was termed "capitalism" not by a friend of the system, but by an individual who considered it to be the worst of all historical systems, the greatest evil that had ever befallen mankind. That man was Karl Marx. Nevertheless, there is no reason to reject Marx's term, because it describes clearly the source of the great social improvements brought about by capitalism. These improvements are the result of capital accumulation; they are based on the fact that people, as a rule, do not consume everything they have produced, that they save—and invest—a part of it.

What Mises observed was that the general direction of free enterprise is for a consistent increase in the amount of capital that people have at hand to enhance their labor efforts. That is, left free to do so, people recognize that more and better capital goods will advance their material well-being. As a result, he had no problem with the use of the term as being synonymous with economic freedom, free enterprise, free markets, freedom of trade, and private property.

However, capitalism does not necessarily mean economic freedom. It neither denotes it nor connotes it. While it is certainly true that capital will have its most beneficial uses under economic freedom with free enterprise, free markets, freedom of trade, and private property, that does not make the system necessarily capitalism. After all, the same argument can be made regarding the other means of production, i.e., that under economic freedom these will have their highest, best, and most beneficial uses. Yet no one has ventured the opinion that such a system should be called landism or laborism. The basic problem here is that capitalism means something different in the minds of different people. This difference leads to more than a little confusion. Indeed, what some people have in mind is a sort of **crony capitalism** in which certain business interests are given preferential treatment. When used in this fashion, capitalism means something very much different from free enterprise.

---

### Misconceptions around Capitalism

Capitalism does not necessarily mean economic freedom. It neither denotes it nor connotes it. The basic problem here is that capitalism means something different in the minds of different people. This difference leads to more than a little confusion. Indeed, what some people have in mind is a sort of crony capitalism in which certain business interests are given preferential treatment. When used in this fashion, capitalism means something very much different from free enterprise.

This kind of use is easy to understand. The root portion of the word is capital and its supposed underlying meaning drives the meaning of the whole. Capital refers most specifically to economic goods used in the production of other goods. Sometimes capital is referred to as wealth invested in the production of goods, but that is a derivative use and not the basic economic use. When an *-ism* is added to a word, it usually denotes an ideology or some sort of thought system. Thus, capital*ism* can mean a system of ideas in which capital is given preference over the other means of production. It is, then, a political preference for these resources over land and labor in production. In such a system, capitalism is the establishment of that preference by the exercise of government power. In the absence of government power there is no established preference for any one of the means of production over the others except by the choices made by private individuals. When used to denote political preference capitalism cannot be associated with economic freedom since it is a system that must be forced by government. To put the whole matter into more precise terms, such capitalism is the forced transformation of some greater or lesser portion of the wealth of a people into capital as directed by the state. If this is one's understanding of the term then it is a linking of government to capital, a practice that was noted earlier in the discussions of feudalism and mercantilism. In political terms, this sort of capitalism is the legalization and instituting of a preference for capital generally or specifically. To mitigate the confusion in the use of the term capitalism, **corporatism** will be the word used to denote preferential government treatment of certain business or capital interests since this word more directly exposes the underlying actions of government that undermine individual human action.

As will be shown below, such preference is widespread worldwide in the twentieth century. It must be made clear, however, that this ordinarily involves something as simple as governments passing laws requiring the preference of equipment over land and labor, or prohibiting the use of land and labor, though there are more subtle instances when such things have actually been done. For example, if money for capital investment is made cheaper by law and labor made more expensive, this does establish a preference for capital in pricing. Ordinarily, though, the preference for capital may be expected to take more indirect forms.

Actually, with the above definition and explanation in mind, it should be clear that much of mercantilism was corporatist in tendency. The subsidies and exemptions granted to manufacturers were examples of a kind of corporatism. The attempt to import raw materials—especially since this often involved the use of government power in acquiring colonies—and export finished or manufactured products was an example of preferential corporatism. The main difference between mercantilism and corporatism was that the main beneficiary was the monarch rather than the corporate special interest.

Corporatism in the contemporary world is of at least two kinds, though there are variations within these. First, there is what can be called **private corporatism**. That is, there is corporatism in which both capital and property generally are at least technically privately owned. Second, there is what can be called **state corporatism**. That is, there is corporatism in which capital and productive property is generally owned by government, though such euphemisms as public ownership or common property are often used to describe it. This occurs predominantly in socialist and communist countries though admixtures are common as well. It should be emphasized, however, that the government plays a crucial and often determinative role in both private and state corporatism.

**corporatism**—the advancement of the special interests of some by governmental means.

**private corporatism**—occurs when the special privileges are granted to certain private interests.

**state corporatism**—occurs when the productive property is owned by the government and special privileges are granted to government entities.

## 20.2 Private Corporatism

Private corporatism may be somewhat of a contradiction in terms. If a government establishes a preference for certain capital resources over the other means of production, how can the ownership of capital be considered private? What private corporatism means is that capital is technically owned and disposed of by private individuals. It is conceivable, though barely, that government might simply encourage the private accumulation of capital and its investment in private enterprises and that it would stop there and not become involved in the control, direction, and regulation of the enterprises themselves. The government might even provide loans and subsidies to privately owned enterprises and keep hands out of or off the businesses. Such things would be economically possible, but they are not politically likely even if they are theoretically possible.

Government aid tends always to be followed, if it is not accompanied by, government control. Government operates according to different laws or tendencies than economics. Government is force. The *quid pro quo* of government in any deal is power or control over anything or anyone to whom it extends favors or aid. Economists may criticize politicians for behaving that way, but their behavior is no more exceptionable than that lions should kill and eat jackals. That is the nature of the beast. Moreover, it is logical and probably proper that government should supervise, i.e., control in some measure, the disposal of funds that it has in some way made available to otherwise private enterprises. Government has used force in one way or another to extract these funds from their owners. It has, therefore, a public obligation to see that the funds are used in accord with the purposes for which they were granted. In any case, governments have generally extended more and more control over private businesses over the past century whether they have aided them directly or not.

In practice private corporatism tends to become more regimented and less private. More precisely, government usurps more and more of the rights of control that pertained to ownership. This process has followed from countless government programs that made large amounts of capital available in one way or another, hence the corporatist connection. It is typical of corporatism, too, that the rights and the responsibilities of ownership are separated and reassigned. Sometimes, owners have full responsibility for the successful operation of a business while divested of many of the rights of control. On the other hand, sometimes owners retain some of their rights while being free of responsibilities for the operation. The splintering of the rights and responsibilities of ownership is a typical result of private corporatism. All this should become clearer in the following discussions of private corporatism in particular countries.

### 20.2.1 Corporatist Legacy of Alexander Hamilton

As emphasized in the previous chapter, free enterprise was the dominant motif in the American economy in the nineteenth century. Even so, there were repeated attempts to have government adopt programs to aid in capital accumulation, to promote the development of transportation and manufacturing, and to skew the economy in one direction or another. These efforts met with increasing success during and after the Civil War, so that a case could be made that the economy was becoming less free and more corporatist in the last three or four decades of the nineteenth century. A better case can probably be made that free enterprise was still the dominant approach in the production and distribution of goods down to 1933 though the seeds for the change had been clearly sown much earlier.

However that may be, the new United States Government under the Constitution had hardly got underway in the 1790s before the Secretary of the Treasury, Alexander Hamilton, was making proposals for corporatist type programs (as well as mercantilist). In his Report on Manufactures (1791) Hamilton made the following observations, among others:

> The employment of machinery forms an item of great importance in the general mass of national industry. It is an artificial force brought in aid of the natural force of man; and, to all the purposes of labor, is an increase of hands, an accession of strength, unencumbered too by the expense of maintaining the laborer. May it not, therefore, be fairly inferred, that those occupations which give greatest scope to the use of this auxiliary, contribute most to the general stock of industrious effort, and, in consequence, to the general product of industry?

What Hamilton was leading up to was that government should promote the development of manufacturing with positive programs. He went on to point out that as American agriculture grew, it would need a domestic market. "To secure such a market," he declared, "there is no other expedient than to promote manufacturing establishments. Manufacturers, who constitute the most numerous class, after the cultivators of the land, are for that reason the principal consumers of the surplus of their labor."

To encourage the development of manufacturing and provide the capital for it Hamilton proposed several policies. They included a United States bank as well as the development of banking generally, a protective tariff to promote new industries, the use of subsidies by government to encourage the development of new factories, the establishment of factories by the government to build military supplies, and the encouragement of foreign investment in American industry. Most of his proposals fell on deaf ears in Congress. Congress had already levied a tariff for revenue, but there was not any will to make it protective. In addition, there was little support for subsidizing domestic manufacturing.

> **Hamiltonian Corporatist Policies**
> To encourage the development of manufacturing and provide the capital for it Hamilton proposed several policies. They included a United States bank as well as the development of banking generally, a protective tariff to promote new industries, the use of subsidies by government to encourage the development of new factories, the establishment of factories by the government to build military supplies, and the encouragement of foreign investment in American industry.

### 20.2.2 Federally Chartered Banks

One measure was passed from among Hamilton's proposals—the chartering and establishing of the First United States Bank. Its stock was partially owned by the government and the remainder by private investors. By law, government funds were to be kept on deposit with it, and it was authorized to issue its own currency. Thomas Jefferson vigorously opposed the bank on the grounds that the Constitution did not authorize it. Hamilton argued for a broader interpretation of the Constitution, and his view convinced both President Washington and the Congress.

The bank was chartered for twenty years, but it led a checkered career down to 1836. Thomas Jefferson, who had opposed the bank, became President in 1801, but he left the bank undisturbed. However, when its charter ran out in 1811, it was not renewed. The bank received new life when it was re-chartered for twenty years in 1816. It had a rocky time after that because in the 1830s it ran afoul of Andrew Jackson. When Congress approved a new charter in 1832, four years before the old one expired, Jackson issued a stinging veto, and proceeded to remove government funds deposited in it and place them in state banks. Indeed, sentiment against banking was running so strong in the 1830s that several states adopted constitutional provisions prohibiting the chartering of banks.

The main problem associated with banking in this era was the practice of maintaining only **fractional reserves**. At this time gold and silver served as the commodity monies used and the state chartered banks were issuing more bank notes into circulation than they held in gold or silver reserves. The bankers assumed that not everyone would demand redemption of their notes simultaneously. This action is of course fraudulent and any fly-by-night scamp who did this would have all his personal wealth and possessions seized to make good his promises when his misdeeds were exposed. Indeed, any bank would suffer being driven from the market by its competitors. In short, fractional reserve banking could not withstand the rigors of market competition in a system of genuine free enterprise. However, in practice, state chartered banks in America were given special privilege and kept from bankruptcy by state government bailouts when competitors sought to redeem their notes in excess amounts.

This kind of state intervention allowed the depositor to pay less attention to the practices of the bank than would have ordinarily been warranted. A depositor may deposit his money in a bank for safekeeping, though he may also like the convenience of checking or have other reasons. So far as he is ordinarily aware, his money is being held until he calls for it and in a completely free market he would only wish to do business with a reputable institution. However, if he believes that the state will bail the bank out regardless of its business practices he will be less likely to engage in the **due diligence** that would otherwise be called for. As a result, fraudulent banking practices expanded beyond what the market would have allowed. This ongoing problem in banking is perhaps the most serious departure from free enterprise that plagued the early Republic.

### 20.2.3 Corporatism of Early Republicans

The Civil War marked the next big divide in the business history of America. Major changes in the policies of the national government took place between 1860–1877, the latter date being undertaken to supposedly Reconstruct the South. Many of these changes were the result both of the loss of power by the Democratic Party and the absence of Southerners from national councils. The Democrats had been the main exponents of free trade and opponents of any expansion of federal government power in economic matters. The Republicans, as political heirs of Hamilton, favored high protective tariffs, federal government aid for internal improvements, and government promotion of transportation and manufacturing. They held the power during the Civil War and Reconstruction and enacted their programs of corporatism.

One of the first acts of the Republicans in power was to impose a protective tariff. Major tariff acts were passed in 1862 and in 1864. The act

---

**fractional reserves**—the fraction of deposits that a bank keeps on deposit and does not loan out. *See definition of fractional reserve banking, p. 101.*

**due diligence**—the practice of engaging in the thorough, prudent investigation of a matter before making a decision to act in a certain way.

### Getting the Point...

As you read this section, develop a written list of the corporatist actions of the Republicans in the Civil War and Reconstruction years.

of 1862 imposed an average tariff rate on goods of 37%, which was raised to 47% in 1864. Protective tariffs remained in effect and were usually quite high down to World War I. They were intended to protect American manufacturers and promote mechanical production. The tariff was undoubtedly corporatist in intent and certainly provided special benefits to some industrial business interests at the expense of the general welfare.

The Morrill Land Grant Act was passed in 1862. It was also at least partially corporatist in purpose. The act provided that each state should receive from the public domain 30,000 acres of land for each of its Representatives and Senators. The proceeds from the sale of the land were to be used to help fund agricultural and mechanical colleges in each of the states. While the agricultural programs of these colleges have often been emphasized, the colleges have also focused on mechanical techniques and learning to use machinery, training engineers and the like. Thus, they were at least adjuncts to a greater use and emphasis upon capital. It should be noted that Alexander Hamilton had proposed that the federal government support in some way programs similar to these.

The federal government also made tentative moves toward the support of private railroad building during the war. A number of state governments had done so in previous decades, but the federal government had withdrawn even from the support of building improved highways during Jackson's administration. At any rate, the **Pacific Railway Act of 1862** was the first federal legislation of its kind. It authorized two corporations to undertake the building and operation of a railroad from the Midwest to the Pacific: the Union Pacific from Omaha westward to a junction with the Central Pacific from the west coast eastward. Each was granted a hundred-foot right-of-way, sections of land in alternate sections along either side of the track, and construction loans figured at the rate of $16,000 per mile in level country, $32,000 in the foothills, and $48,000 in the mountains. Even this support did little to lure builders, for there were grave doubts among investors that such a road would be profitable in the foreseeable future. So, in 1864, Congress doubled the amount of the land grants, in the hope of spurring building. The road was built after the war, and large grants and loans were made by the government to build some of the other transcontinental routes as well.

Indeed, there is good reason to believe that these perverse incentives led to perverse results. The transcontinental railroads constructed in this fashion were typically of poor quality and were not suitable for hauling goods or people. Far more track was laid than was needed. Rail lines were often built in remote locations that were unwarranted viewed from a private enterprise point of view. But whatever the merits of the undertakings, it was probably a profitable venture for the government. Much of the land granted was very nearly worthless until the railroads were built making it accessible. As for the loans, they were eventually repaid in one way or another. The important point here, however, is that the government became more or less deeply involved in private business undertakings.

The federal government became entangled in the banking business once again during the war. A National Bank Act was passed in 1863 and revised the following year. The act provided for the federal chartering of national banks. These banks were authorized to issue currency, i.e., national bank notes, on the basis of their holdings in government bonds. Moreover, these bank notes circulated as legal tender. The Congress moved also to drive the state banks out of the business of issuing bank notes by taxing them. When a small tax did not do the job completely, Congress levied a 10% tax on state bank notes, thus making it unprofitable for their issuance. Even so, it could hardly be said that the United States now had a national banking system, for there was no central bank to coordinate the effort.

**Pacific Railway Act of 1862**—federal legislation that authorized two corporations to build and operate a transcontinental railroad.

The original purpose of the banking act was undoubtedly to provide funds for the Union to finance the war effort. Since the banks could issue notes on the basis of government bonds, they could monetize the debt and issue as much currency as the government might want to borrow. The inflation of the money supply eventually brought about the consequences that such an expansion invariably causes. In addition, the government also issued Treasury notes (Greenbacks) and made them legal tender—another inflationary thrust. The inflation worked its usual initial magic: a glow of prosperity, increasing capital investment, and increased production occurred, which was followed by rapidly rising prices and economic recession. The government also fostered capital accumulation by selling bonds for the debased currency, paying interest in gold, and eventually, redeeming the Treasury notes in gold, in effect, giving them a par value with gold. These were relatively short-run effects over two or three decades. It did not remain profitable for the banks to issue currency against 100% backing in bonds, and as the government retired its debt, they gradually reduced the amounts of the outstanding currency. However, banks had long since discovered another and more profitable way to profit by inflation—fractional reserve banking on the basis of deposits in checking accounts. Many of the state chartered banks did not give up their charters when they were driven out of the bank-note issue business. They went more industriously into the deposit-checking account and loan business. National banks followed suit. Thus, both remained as engines of inflation and supplied at least a portion of capital funds.

### 20.2.4 Increasing Use of Regulation

**regulation**—*see definition, p. 178.*

While the government did not cease to provide institutions that augmented capital accumulation and expansion, it did begin turning toward **regulation** in the 1880s. Banks were already regulated to some extent, but the government turned next to regulating the railroads by the Interstate Commerce Act. This regulation reached its peak in the 1920s after the passage of the Transportation Act of 1920. The story is told elsewhere, but the point needs to be emphasized that government had gone full circle from promoting railroad building to control of the industry. Technically, the roads were still privately owned and operated, but government regulation had divested them of much of their control over their enterprises. Government control had followed government aid. That has been the story of corporatism. It could be argued that without the surge of reformism in the late nineteenth century, spurred at least in part by socialist ideas, the regulation might not have followed the aid. On the other hand, it could be argued just as cogently that the government privileges to certain business interests gave reformers and socialists their toehold on the system. The most cogent argument of all is that government control either accompanies or follows in the wake of government aid, and there is logic in that.

> **Government control** either accompanies or follows in the wake of government aid, and there is logic in that.

## 20.2.5 Corporatism of the New Deal

At any rate, government regulation reached a new peak in the 1930s during the **New Deal**. The policies adopted during this decade were largely harmful to businesses with a few exceptions. While the Federal Reserve System had already provided what almost amounted to centralized banking, fractional reserve banks were rescued from the debacle of bank runs by the Federal Deposit Insurance Corporation (FDIC). But a host of new regulations were imposed on the stock exchanges and loans on margin were closely regulated as well. Government control over the economy was greatly expanded during the brief period of the National Reconstruction Administration until it was declared unconstitutional in 1935. Nevertheless, the Roosevelt administration was intent on forcing businesses to heel to its commands. The currency was debased and the gold standard was abandoned, thus setting the stage for an ongoing inflation. The inflation often has other explanations or justifications than supplying money for use as capital, but it often does that as well. The government attacked private investment by promoting union power and adopting a minimum wage. At the same time, it attempted to encourage investment with low interest rates, but the general direction of the era was to put fear into potential private investors. As a result, the end of the recession that began with the collapse of the stock market in 1929 was postponed as greater government involvement in the economy stifled entrepreneurial human action.

What the government gives with one hand it often takes away with the other. Thus, while government making cheap credit available to certain business interests it was at the same time, or not long afterward, levying ever higher taxes on profits and income. The corporate tax rose to the 50% level on profits and the individual income tax was moved progressively higher on large incomes. Those seeking an acceptable motive for these policies could say the government was attempting to destroy the independence of private capitalists, perhaps to make them entirely dependent upon institutions the government controlled. This was certainly the tendency of what happened. On the other hand, the government also embarked on major redistribution programs and was soaking up at least some of the wealth where it was. In any case, capital was both politically attacked and backhandedly supported. There is no reason to doubt that there has been much ambiguity and an assortment of contradictions in the policies of those who have governed in the United States in the twentieth century and continuing today.

In some measure, these ambiguities and contradictions probably should be attributed to faulty analytical tools. The blurring of the definition of what capitalism is provided for more than a little confusion in the minds of the people. There is no doubt that the New Dealers and their political descendants were not in favor of free enterprise. They have tended to favor government regulation and control, sometimes outright government ownership of businesses. Those who have favored free enterprise, on the other hand, or at least campaigned under that banner, have hardly been much clearer for they have often identified it with corporatism. Those who progressively hampered and restrained, even to the point of penalizing, businesses have been more than a little ambiguous in their policies toward business enterprise.

**New Deal**—political program of the Roosevelt administration of the 1930's supposedly aimed at addressing the economic issues of the Great Depression.

> **New Deal Corporatism**
> There is no doubt that the New Dealers and their political descendants were not in favor of free enterprise. They have tended to favor government regulation and control, sometimes outright government ownership of businesses. Those who have favored free enterprise, on the other hand, or at least campaigned under that banner, have hardly been much clearer for they have often identified it with corporatism. Those who progressively hampered and restrained, even to the point of penalizing, businesses have been more than a little ambiguous in their policies toward business enterprise.

### 20.2.6 Entanglement of Business with Politics

From the 1950s down to the present, the pursuit of special privileges by political means has grown largely unchecked. Special interest groups have consistently increased their political support in order to promote some political action that would direct public funds their way. Economists refer to this activity as **"rent seeking"** noting that such expenditures of resources are nothing short of a dead weight economic loss in society. That is, people are said to be "rent seeking" when they use their scarce resources to promote policies and programs that redistribute tax dollars toward their private interests. When people use money in this fashion it does not produce anything of value. Rather, it merely consumes resources for the purpose of influencing the government to use its power to redistribute private property their way. The process continues since voters are largely ignorant of what goes on in Washington. Their single vote in political elections is not likely to make the difference in the outcome and the costs of gaining information about what government is actually doing is high. As a result, the average person pays little attention to politics. This leaves the door open for the vested interests of the lobbyists, politicians, and bureaucrats to pursue policies and programs that further the degree of corporatism in the nation.

**rent seeking**—when private individuals and businesses use their resources to lobby Congress for special legislative privileges.

> **Lobbying for Federal Dollars**
> People are said to be "rent seeking" when they use their scarce resources to promote policies and programs that redistribute tax dollars toward their private interests. When people use money in this fashion it does not produce anything of value. Rather, it merely consumes resources for the purpose of influencing the government to use its power to redistribute private property their way. The process continues since voters are largely ignorant of what goes on in Washington. This leaves the door open for the vested interests of the lobbyists, politicians, and bureaucrats to pursue policies and programs that further the degree of corporatism in the nation.

In sum, corporatism has gained significant ground in the United States. As such both private citizens and their political leaders actively seek taxpayer dollars. For example, the industrial parks, provided by municipalities with such federal and state aid as they can get, have become commonplace. Potential new businesses are wooed more avidly than ever did Prince Charming pursue the Fair Maiden. Not only will these communities provide land on which the manufacturer may build but also they will often provide the building built to his specifications for rent. The manufacturer may find himself relieved of a variety of taxes for a period of years as a further inducement to locate his business there (shades of mercantilism). Governors of some states make forays not only into other states seeking businesses to locate in their states but also into foreign countries courting potential investors. The news that some manufacturer is going to locate in some town or city is announced not only locally but by the state's governor, two Senators, and at least the Representative in Congress for that district. The local paper publishes glowing accounts of the new business, describes the products that will be made, the size of the building (square feet), the number of employees the company will hire, and so on.

Why should politicians become so involved in seeking these commercial enterprises? The usual reason given is that they will provide remunerative work for local workmen. They may do that, of course, as well as provide more customers for merchants, more depositors for banks, more demand for housing for realtors, contractors, and mobile home dealers. It may or may not be emphasized that these infusions of money will also provide more tax receipts for tax collectors, and the workers may be even sufficiently grateful that they will re-elect the politicians. Investors of capital are widely viewed as benefactors, though those who work in the factories may not always be as enthusiastic about that as are members of the Chambers of Commerce.

This has much of the look of a revived mercantilism with its alliance between commercial undertakings and government. Indeed, pressures are now mounting for a new round of protective tariffs, or something of the sort, though negotiations among national leaders for restraints within nations are more the mode these days. The monopolies of mercantilism are all around, though they are called by different names today. Some of them are called public utilities—electric companies, telephone companies, railroads, bus companies, and the like—but they are no less monopolies for all that. Their alliance with government is often obvious, though state governments and the United States Government have elaborate regulatory mechanisms. The institutionalized providers of capital—insurance companies, banks, savings and loan organizations—are also deeply entangled with government. Not only are they regulated, at least in name, but they are empowered by government as well.

Indeed, regulated companies often act as if they were extensions of government—empowered to do whatever government requires—often without regard to the desires of customers. More often than not, issues of morality in behavior are pushed to the side. Instead, decision makers concern themselves with what is legal. In effect, if some government rule did not require a business to conduct its affairs with its customers openly and honestly, then the business simply does not do so. Government rules essentially become the standard for behavior.

The main economic point, however, is not that government entanglement with the economy by way of an instituted preference may cause inconvenience or even oppression of consumers generally speaking. It is important to note that such preference sets the stage for ever greater government regulation that will further exasperate the situation. Moreover, it is very important to recognize that these things tend to undermine property rights and take authority and control away from owners thus destroying the free enterprise system. In truth, governmental privilege for some

> **Getting the Point...**
>
> As business interests invest more money in lobbying efforts and financing political campaigns, business and politics become more entangled.
>
> List some of the consequences of this increased corporatism.

interests lead to dislocations, imbalances, and uneconomic allocations of funds in the economy. These, in turn, produce shortages and surpluses of goods, unemployment, and bankruptcies. It is no small matter, either, that government catering to special interests helped to produce huge government debts, ongoing monetary inflation, and the destruction of the medium of exchange, a story related earlier.

### 20.2.7 Corporatism in the Farm Industry

No single example can illustrate all these consequences. However, it is worthwhile that we consider at least one. Agriculture has always been an important part of the economy and government intervention since the 1930s has resulted in a host of unintended and perverse consequences.

Farming is much like any other business and the successful farmer must produce and sell his crop at a profit in order to stay in business. One of the chief problems in doing so is that the farmer receives low prices in years when his crops are very good. There is no particular mystery about this. When the supply increases, the price tends to fall, other things being equal. The competitive nature of farming led politicians to pay attention to farmers in regard to this inherent business problem in the late nineteenth century. They began to advocate policies they claimed were solutions that would alleviate the problem. Among the alleged causes of the **"farm problem"** were high transportation costs, exorbitant rates for storage facilities, a shortage of money, the fact that farmers growing particular crops are apt to put them on the market at about the same time, thus depressing prices, and their own overproduction. There were sporadic political efforts to "aid" farmers from the late nineteenth century on, such as by inflating the currency, which made more money available, regulating rail and storage rates, and even government credit programs.

However, it was not until the 1930s that the federal government made a concerted effort to raise prices. Programs were enacted to make monetary inflation easier, to make loans, to store crops in warehouses until prices increase, to subsidize prices of certain products, and to restrict the number of acres on which some crops could be planted. The New Deal even paid farmers to plow up cotton and kill little pigs, in an effort to achieve a nearly instant rise in prices. These efforts did succeed in steadying or raising farm prices over the short term, at least. But that only produced another unwanted effect, namely, that as prices rose farmers attempted to increase their production. After all, higher prices are the market signal to increase production. By their method of allotting crops, the New Dealers made it difficult to do that, however. Allotments were usually based on a percentage of the total land in cultivation. Thus, if a farmer was cultivating 40 acres, he might be allotted 10 or 12 acres for cotton, if that was his main commercial crop. The result was that the government could overrule the individual decisions of private farmers.

What this system did was to shift the economic mix from labor to land, and ultimately to capital for successful farming. He had to have more fertilizer, better seed, and more equipment (i.e., capital) and cultivate more total land to produce more of his main crop. Farmers who lacked the capital for this had to give up farming. Indeed, from the 1930s onward there was an increasing flight from farming, born out by the statistics. According to census figures, the total number of farms in the United States declined from 6,102,000 in 1940 to 2,808,000 in 1980. The most dramatic decline for any decade was in the 1950s, when the number of farms dropped from 5,388,000 in 1950 to 3,962,000 in 1960. The total farm population declined from 30,547,000 in 1940 to 8,864,000 in 1980. The number of hired farm

**farm problem**—farmers work in a highly competitive industry that keeps profit margins low. As a result, it is difficult to succeed in the farming business.

workers declined from 3,391,000 in 1920 to 2,679,000 in 1940 to 1,303,000 by 1980. Farms have, of course, been increasing in size over the same period, and farm production is much greater today than it was in the 1930s.

This huge production has been accomplished with perhaps one-third of the labor and no comparable increase of land under cultivation. In short, it has been accomplished largely by vast infusions of capital into agriculture. In terms that can be visualized, it has been largely the result of vast quantities of fertilizer, improved seeds, such as highly productive hybrid corn, and above all, by farming equipment. Tractors had virtually replaced all mules and horses as power for farm equipment by the 1950s. Ever larger tractors have been bought since then to pull and operate gang plows, huge cotton pickers and other harvesting machines, and rows of planters and distributors. Herbicides and pesticides have largely replaced the work done by hoe and individual applications of poisons. The shift from labor and land toward capital has been decisive.

Farmers were pushed toward this shift by the restrictive government programs. They were drawn toward capital investment by the government's easy credit and easy money policies. That is not to say that some of the shift might not have occurred without the government intervention, but the fact is that it did occur within the framework of active government programs. The Federal Reserve Act passed in 1913 was specifically designed to provide easy credit. The banks authorized under it were to become engines of inflation by expanding credit.

The Federal Reserve System has been the basic fount of easy credit since its founding. It is important to emphasize, however, that farm credit is a breed all its own, or at least a large portion of it is. Much of the credit has been advanced by what is now known as the Farm Credit System. This was a government inspired, government authorized and government controlled system, financed under the auspices of the United States Government. The basic system was authorized by the Federal Farm Loan Act of 1916. The Federal Land Banks, probably the best known of the organizations, were first authorized in 1917 pursuant to the above act. The system has been expanded over the years, and the following description of it from a government manual that was published based on its provisions as of 1971:

> The Farm Credit Administration, an independent agency, supervises and coordinates activities of the cooperative Farm Credit System. The system is comprised of Federal land banks and Federal land bank associations, Federal intermediate credit banks and production credit associations, banks for cooperatives. Initially capitalized by the United States, the entire System is now owned by its users.

Some of the above information could be misleading, however. The Farm Credit Administration is "independent" in the sense that it does not fall under the authority of any regular department of the government. Otherwise, it is in effect a government agency, as are those acting under its authority, and the governing board is politically appointed: twelve members by the President of the United States and one by the Secretary of Agriculture.

The Federal Land Banks make long term (5 to 40 year) loans to farmers, which are secured by real estate. Although portions of the loans may be used for other purposes, they are made basically for the acquisition of farm land. The Intermediate Credit Banks are discount banks, serving mainly Production Credit Associations. Their main purpose is to discount intermediate term notes, such as would be needed for the purchase of farm equipment. Production Credit Associations mainly make what should be called risk capital loans to farmers. The loans may be for periods of up to seven years. Banks for Cooperatives are to provide largely capital loans to cooperatives.

None of these organizations are banks in the usual meaning of the terms. They are neither depositories of money nor issuers of currency. They might better be called loan organizations, for that is their function. In fact, they are not ordinary businesses or corporations. The financing for them came initially from the federal government, and ongoing financing (except from repayment of loans) comes from bonds sold to investors backed by notes from borrowers. (Technically, the government does not guarantee the repayment of the bonds, but in a pinch it probably would, in view of the government relationship to the organizations.) The investors neither own nor control the organizations nor their lending policies. On the contrary, the borrowers have the voting stock in the organizations, which they acquire when they take out loans. The voting stock exists primarily to enable them to elect the loan officers.

The point of this description is to show that the Farm Credit System is an easy credit system. After all, the borrowers hold the power in the organizations, subject to policies drawn either by Congress or made by political appointees. In sum, the rabbits have been put in charge of the carrot field, so to speak. The money is at least partially under the control of those who get the loans.

However, there is an even easier credit organization to back up the Farm Credit System. It is the Farmer's Home Administration (known as the FHA in rural circles). This organization was basically set up for those who could not otherwise get loans. (Applicants are usually expected to submit evidence that they have been turned down by other lending institutions.) Its authority stems from an act passed by Congress in 1921. The Farmer's Home Administration operates within the Department of Agriculture, and it is financed by proceeds from the sale of Treasury certificates. It makes loans to "pay for equipment, livestock, feed, seed, fertilizer, other farm and home operating needs; refinance chattel debts; provide operating credit for fish farmers;" for the purchase of land, houses, and other sorts of things for rural inhabitants and farmers. Terms of repayment and interest are adjusted to the financial situation of the borrowers. That is, they get low interest rates and long terms for repayment.

None of this is meant to suggest that farmers have borrowed exclusively from government agencies. They may borrow from regular banks, from insurance companies, from equipment dealers, and from other private as well as public sources. There is much evidence, however, that those who have gone deeply into debt in recent decades have borrowed mainly from government sponsored agencies.

What all of this easy money and credit for farming did was to increase the farmer's debt. Here is how a particular farmer told his story in an Associated Press release in 1983. He began farming in 1965 with 68 acres of land and $600. By 1970, he was planting 900 acres and feeding several hundred hogs. This expansion was built upon a mountain of debt; it eventually totaled nearly $400,000. Low prices for his produce, drought, and a disease that decimated his hog population, drove this farmer to the wall. The Production Credit Association, which had been supplying the risk capital for his operation, could carry him no longer. He turned to the Farmer's Home Administration, but that aid did not last him long. His farm was sold at auction, but many of the debts remain unpaid.

In retrospect, this farmer understands what happened to him this way. He believes,

...he still would be farming had he not expanded with such zeal. Had his appetite for money not been so voracious. Had that money not been dished out so readily.... "They made a feather bed for me to lie on...," [he] said of the lenders. "You know I could basically sit down at my kitchen table and write out a loan. It was just too simple."

The broader problem, however, lies primarily in government promoted and subsidized corporatism, which has so thoroughly distorted agricultural markets. The point here is *not* to deny that capital can be beneficial or that its use is somehow undesirable. On the contrary, the benefits of capital are clear and can be readily described. As noted earlier, capital—whether it be thought of as buildings for production, machinery, seeds, fertilizer, or what not—tends to have a multiplier effect in production. It makes a bounty of goods with less expense for consumers. Indeed, if the matter were looked at over the short range and only in terms of consumers, it might appear that the more capital the better and that government intervention on behalf of supplying capital would be beneficial.

A major reason that it is not is demonstrated in the hard times and bankruptcies of farmers in the 1970s and 1980s. Consumers have indeed been benefited by a bounty of farm products at much lower prices than would have prevailed without the government intervention. The fact is that farmers have been able with their huge equipment, improved seeds, fertilizers, and herbicides to produce more goods than can be sold at sufficient return to keep the farmers in business. But at some point economic reality must prevail and then the hardship of business failure becomes apparent. What led to this was easy money resulting from government programs promoting capital investment. It created an imbalance between the means of production and the effective demand for the goods. Such an imbalance would not last for long in the free market. Money is always hard to borrow there.

---

**The Benefits of Capital Do Not Justify Corporatism**
The point here is not to deny that capital can be beneficial or that its use is somehow undesirable. On the contrary, the benefits of capital are clear and can be readily described. Capital tends to have a multiplier effect in production. It makes a bounty of goods with less expense for consumers. Indeed, if the matter were looked at over the short range and only in terms of consumers, it might appear that the more capital the better and that government intervention on behalf of supplying capital would be beneficial.

But at some point economic reality must prevail and then the hardship of business failure becomes apparent. Corporatism always produces imbalances in many directions. One such imbalance is indebtedness. Another imbalance is unemployment. When government inflates to create money for investment, it takes the value of the new money from that already in circulation. Whatever the purpose behind government established preferences, the result will be unwanted economic consequences.

Corporatism always produces imbalances in many directions. One such imbalance is indebtedness. Another imbalance is unemployment. Large scale unemployment and migration from rural areas took place as a result of minimum wage laws and cheap money for buying capital goods. When government inflates to create money for investment, it takes the value of the new money from that already in circulation. Whatever the purpose behind government established preferences, the result will be unwanted economic consequences.

### 20.2.8 In Sweden

Another national example of private corporatism may be helpful. Sweden may appear to be a strange example for this, but on closer examination the appropriateness of the choice should be clear. That the choice would appear to be odd is that Sweden has had the reputation of being a socialist country since the 1930s, at least in the United States. In the strict sense, however, Sweden is not socialist. If socialism be understood to mean the public (or governmental) ownership of the means of production, then that is not generally the case in Sweden. Most of the productive enterprises in Sweden are privately owned, though there is considerable government intervention in the running of them. A London newspaper once observed, "Sweden has proportionately more private enterprise than any other country in west Europe." The usual figures cited run something like this: about 7% of the enterprises are state owned; 4% cooperatively owned; and the rest are privately owned. The state is deeply involved in iron mining, the railways, the airlines, atomic energy, and the making of alcoholic beverages. Most of the rest of manufacturing is privately owned. There is a sense in which Sweden is socialist, but it is not in the ownership of the means of production.

Sweden has indeed carried private corporatism about as far as it can go and remain private. Sweden uses both tax policies and other devices to promote capital investments. One way this is done is by the Investment Funds. These were first authorized by law in 1938, and the enactment has since been amended several times. The practice was described this way:

> The current position is that by law, every company is permitted to set aside 40 percent of its profits before taxes in any year to an investment fund. There are, however, restrictions attached to this exemption from taxation. Forty-six percent of this money must be deposited interest free in the Central Bank of Sweden and can only be spent on authorization either by the Crown or by the Labour Market Board for specific projects concerned with investment—the only exception is that after five years a company can spend up to 30 percent of the money set aside without authority from the Board provided this is on a capital project.

In short, the government uses its power over the disposal of a portion of the earnings of a company by offering the lure of tax exemption for that portion.

The other major device for promoting investment of capital is the depreciation policy of the government. All capital expenditures from the Investment Fund must be fully depreciated within twelve months of the outlay. All other capital expenditures must be depreciated fully within five years, either in equal installments or on a prearranged scale. The result: "There is pressure on the companies to maintain a steady stream of investment with a major installation at least every five years, both to obtain the depreciation tax allowance and to even after-tax profits." This is a preference for capital with a vengeance, for the encouragement to investment is clearly ingrained in government policy.

Yet the real aim of the preference is for other ends than merely production; its most appropriate name might be welfare corporatism. The program's real aim is to promote the welfare state in Sweden. As one Swede put it, "The state keeps the cow fat in order to increase the amount of milk it can get from it." It takes a great deal of production to provide the goodies the welfare state gives out, and none have seen more clearly than the Swedes that capital equipment, ever renewed and expanded, is the most effective means to that end. Even so, such government entanglement with private capital produces imbalances—such as an overbuilt shipping industry and shortage of space in private homes—in Sweden as elsewhere.

It is well to observe that the road from mercantilism to corporatism is not long, nor is the way from corporatism to welfarism, as the history of the modern world has demonstrated.

## 20.3 State Corporatism

State corporatism exists when the government (or the state or the "public") owns, controls, and directs the use of capital or where there is no significant private ownership of the means of production. Such arrangements are usually referred to as socialism or communism. There is a further incongruity, or the appearance of one, in that socialists and communists have generally been the most outspoken opponents of free enterprise. Karl Marx, the progenitor of modern communism, as well as a major influence on socialism generally, proclaimed that labor is the source of all value. By so doing, he apparently left little room for capital though to do so is to promote economic ignorance. Indeed, he denounced capitalists as exploiters of the laboring man and bloodsuckers of the productive, thus confusing the meaning of free enterprise. To deny the role of capital is not, however, to banish it from the scene. The stone rejected by the architects of socialism and communism has become the cornerstone of these systems, and the working man who was supposed to be elevated has instead been subject to the state, which controls the capital.

There is no great mystery as to why this has taken place. To banish capital from a society would be to consign them to the Stone Age, or worse, for even stones were capital in the Stone Age. It would be to return people to the most primitive means of providing goods for themselves, to the use of their limbs mainly in the production of goods, without the aid of any equipment. There is simply no way that even a small portion of the population in any country in the world could be fed, clothed, and housed without extensive capital or equipment. And this capital has to be obtained from that which is not consumed. When private ownership of the means of production is abolished, this means that the capital must be acquired by confiscation.

State corporatism is the logical culmination or completion of government instituted preferences in the market place. Government is by nature monopolistic, and when it asserts its preferences in the market it eventually displaces all other enterprises. Such a monopoly over the economy is state corporatism. State corporatism is to corporatism what feudalism was to landism, i.e., the joining of power and wealth. The affinity of

**Bolsheviks**—followers of Marx who launched a communist revolution in Russia in 1917.

**revolution**—means simply a successful revolt against those who govern or rule in a country. To Marxists, however, revolution has a much broader and all-inclusive meaning. It means a revolt against the existing order, not simply against those who rule, but against all existing institutions, arrangements, beliefs, and conditions. Socialists, more generally, see a revolution as the opportunity for redistribution of land and other wealth.

> **Vladimir I. Lenin (Nikolai) (1870–1924)**
>
> Radical revolutionary who provided the ideological justification for, led, and consolidated the Bolshevik Revolution in Russia from 1917 until his death. As soon as the Bolsheviks had consolidated their power they changed their name to Communist and formed a Communist International with headquarters in Moscow to spread communism around the world. Lenin was born in Russia, with the family name Ulyanov, which he changed, in his case, to Lenin, trained at Kazan University and passed the law examination at St. Petersburg. Soon afterward, he abandoned the practice of law to foment revolution and become, in effect, an outlaw in Czarist Russia. Lenin succeeded in taking charge of the most radical element among the revolutionaries in Russia. With that base, he seized power in the government, destroyed all other political parties, and created a one-party dictatorship. He bypassed Marxian theory to install the communists in power in Russia.

wealth and power is great in any case, and socialism is the doctrine under which that affinity has been brought toward its fruition in the contemporary world. It is a fearful combination.

Since communism will be discussed much more fully in a chapter devoted to it, only so much will be told here as is necessary to point up its corporatist features. The discussion can be largely confined to the former Soviet Union and some further references to capital hunger in the countries in the communist orbit of that time. The discussion of democratic or evolutionary socialism will be deferred to the next chapter on Welfarism, since most countries under sway of that doctrine have not usually gone all the way to state corporatism, at least not yet.

The **Bolsheviks** seized power in Russia in late 1917 and consolidated their hold on the government in early 1918, though civil war raged in Russia for the better part of the next three years or so. Shortly after they came to power, the Bolsheviks, who were a Marxist sect, took the name of communism and set up their seat of power as the center of international communism. As a part of this movement, groups of workers, often styled soviets took over the factories, mines, and mills in Russia, wherever they had power, and farmers or peasants often seized the land of the landlords, claiming it as their own. Indeed, at this stage of the Bolshevik Revolution, mobs frequently took what they wanted, whether from stores, private homes, or whatever. The former possessors were dispossessed, often driven from their premises.

Amidst the chaos of internal **revolution** and civil war, the Bolsheviks or communists took over control of as much as they could as quickly as they could. Commissars took over control and direction of the factories, mines, mills, banks, and distribution. The professed allegiance of the communist was to the industrial workers; hence, farmers were often ignored at first, except to confiscate most of their produce. The communists destroyed the currency by issuing vast quantities of paper money. These moves tended to make the populace absolutely dependent upon the will of the government. Actually, starvation, or at least hunger and deprivation became virtually the common lot as both industrial and agricultural production fell drastically. Many people fled from the largest cities, for it was difficult to find sustenance there in what amounted to a breakdown of civilization.

In 1921, **Vladimir Lenin**, who had taken over as leader of the revolution and became dictator, proclaimed a New Economic Policy (NEP). Some property rights were to be restored, especially to small merchants and the like. They could buy and sell and make modest profits. Former managers were often restored to their former positions, under the watchful eyes of commissars no doubt, and small farmers were allowed to keep possession of their land. By 1928, however, Stalin, who had now achieved dictatorial power, thrust Russia toward communism once again. The NEP men (as they were called) were cast out and persecuted; the small farmers were driven from their land; and farming was socialized as well as industry, as farmers were herded into state farms and collectives. The government had now taken over all the instruments of production, including the workers, and began trying to operate them by way of the Five-Year Plans.

The **Soviet Union** was capital hungry from the outset. Russia had lagged behind Europe in industrializing, and capital was desperately wanted for industrialization. The communists also wanted farm machinery for their state farms and collectives. Marxist–Leninist doctrine taught that communism could only be achieved in industrialized countries, and the communists were bent on using the full power of the state to press industrialization.

The capital hunger of the communists had many faces. Lenin had believed that electrical power was the key to industrialism and the future of communism. Thus, great hydroelectric dams were visualized. Engineers were drawn from other lands, including the United States, to design and work on these and other projects. Soviet rulers were ravenous for information about the design and manufacture of machinery. Thus, they sent emissaries wherever in the world they were invited to gain knowledge of techniques and equipment. The great spy network diligently carried on espionage to learn military and private production secrets. Universities focused on science and technology, and publications from around the world were eagerly obtained, translated and interpreted. To get money for foreign trade, gold mining was pressed in the Soviet Union, often carried on by slave labor from political prisoners. The great forests of Russia yielded timber, much of it was cut with slave labor. The same could be said for the mining of all sorts of minerals. The government controlled all financial institutions that were left or revived in the Soviet Union. In any case, state corporatism prevailed from the 1920s to the collapse of the Soviet system at the end of the 1980s.

While there are many differences between private corporatism and state corporatism, at least one of the main differences needs to be pointed out here. Whatever the imbalances and distortions of private corporatism, the desires of consumers are still generally served. After all, the profits of private companies are tied to the voluntary sales to consumers of goods that are generally found to be satisfactory. By contrast, state corporatism, particularly of the communist variety, gives no priority to general consumers; no profits are involved, and goods that are produced are produced for official reasons of state authorities and not because of the demand of consumers. The Soviet Union concentrated much of the effort over the years to producing capital goods rather than consumer goods. Moreover, the making of arms and munitions was generally the top priority. Consumer goods were generally inferior and had little market value. Indeed, it took the communists several decades to get production up to levels it had been in Czarist times in Russia, and agricultural production never achieved those heights, so far as can be determined.

Moscow was long the center of the movement to extend communism into other countries. In the mid-1950s, Communist China made the move to become at least a second center for the spread of communism. As a rule, the countries that have become communist have not been industrialized countries; most have been poor and relatively underdeveloped. There are a few exceptions, but all have tended to be capital hungry.

To spread communism, the Soviet Union offered a vision of rapid industrialization to other nations. What they were selling with this claim was that communism is the way for underdeveloped countries to achieve economic progress. Strange as it may seem, Communist China adopted the same line, though China has directed its pitch especially to the supposed "unaligned" countries (unaligned, that is, with the Soviet Union or the United States). In any case, both the Soviet Union and the People's Republic (i.e., communist) of China got into the business of trying to

**Soviet Union**—a confederation of communist countries formed after World War II with its seat of power in Moscow. It collapsed between 1989-91 as the nations in it broke away from Russian rule.

spread communism by a poor imitation of American foreign aid. To put it simply, they made some show of sending capital goods to some of these countries. Thus, a Soviet writer claimed the following in a piece published in the 1960s:

> The Soviet Union began to establish extensive economic ties with Afro–Asian countries in the mid-1950's. Alongside the growing volume of ordinary export-import trade, an important role was played by technical and economic cooperation based on inter-government agreements. By 1956, such agreements had been signed with Afghanistan and India alone, where today the USSR is giving economic and technical assistance to 29 Afro–Asian countries.

While much of Soviet aid was military supplies, they at least made a show of sending capital goods. In more recent years countries in Western Europe and the United States as well have provided credit and bank loans to countries that are more or less communist. The point here, however, is that wherever communism is more or less established state corporatism is on its way to being established as well.

---

**A Difference Between Private and State Corporatism**

Whatever the imbalances and distortions of private corporatism, the desires of consumers are still generally served. After all, the profits of private companies are tied to the voluntary sales to consumers of goods that are generally found to be satisfactory. By contrast, state corporatism, particularly of the communist variety, gives no priority to general consumers; no profits are involved, and goods that are produced are produced for official reasons of state authorities and not because of the demand of consumers.

---

*No one will really understand politics until they understand that politicians are not trying to solve our problems. They are trying to solve their own problems—of which getting elected and re-elected are number one and number two. Whatever is number three is far behind.*

**Thomas Sowell**

# Study Guide for:

# 20 Corporatism

## Chapter Summary

Several diverse politico-economic systems emerged during the twentieth century. The central ideology behind all of them is socialism, but that ideology has manifested itself in numerous ways. Therefore, it might be helpful to separate socialist thought into two camps: evolutionary socialism and revolutionary socialism. The first is a movement toward socialism by working through existing political structures while the latter seeks to accomplish the change via a radical overthrow of the political system.

Although the term capitalism is often treated as if it has the same meaning as free enterprise, that is not always the case. When governments grant special privilege to certain private or state interests they are practicing what is best called corporatism. The term suggests a politico-economic system in which certain capital is given preferential treatment over the other means of production. In this sense, corporatism is the forced transformation of wealth without regard to the choices of all the individuals involved. It is accomplished by government ownership or manipulation of markets.

Corporatism in this sense has taken two forms: private corporatism and state corporatism. In private corporatism, capital is technically privately owned but manipulated by government. In state capitalism, capital is both owned and controlled by the state. Economic history over the past century provides some excellent examples of both types. The history of the United States is an excellent study of a nation's move to private corporatism while the Russian experience is a study in state run corporatism.

## Points of Emphasis

1. The term capitalism can be used to describe a politico-economic system in which certain capital is given preferential treatment over the other means of production.

2. Interestingly, socialistic policies tend to be corporatist in practice.

3. There are numerous ways in which the U.S. economy has enacted corporatist policies and these can be compared to those of other countries around the world.

## Identification

1. evolutionary socialism
2. revolutionary socialism
3. capitalism
4. bourgeoisie
5. crony capitalism
6. corporatism
7. private corporatism
8. state corporatism
9. fractional reserves
10. due diligence
11. Pacific Railway Act of 1862
12. regulation
13. New Deal
14. rent seeking
15. farm problem
16. Bolsheviks
17. revolution
18. Vladimir Lenin
19. Soviet Union

## Review Questions

1. What three other names were given for the term "evolutionary socialism"?

2. List three examples of "revolutionary socialism."

3. What is the central focus of socialist ideology?

4. Who popularized the use of the term capitalism? Why is this problematic in discussions with people about free enterprise?

5. Is capitalism the same as free enterprise?

6. Contrast the view of consumers in private corporatism to that in state corporatism.

7. Why does increased government regulation and control over economic activity seem to invariably follow government grants of privilege?

## Activity

1. Develop a list of laws that provide special favors for some interests in production relative to all other interests. Explain how each law operates to redistribute wealth.

> **Chapter Content**
>
> 21.1 Socialism in Great Britain    333
>     21.1.1 The Labour Party in Power    334
>     21.1.2 The Failure of British Socialism    337
>     21.1.3 The Repercussions of the British Failure    338
> 21.2 Welfarism in the United States    339
>     21.2.1 Social Security    339
>     21.2.2 Ever-Increasing Welfarist Programs    341
>     21.2.3 The Corporatism of Welfarism    342
>     21.2.4 Negative Consequences of Welfarism    343

# 21 WELFARISM

By itself, **welfarism** is hardly a politico-economic system. At its heart, it is more of a *dis*-economic system than an economic one. So far as it deals with economy at all, its concern is primarily with the distribution or, as the case may be, the redistribution of goods and services and not with their production. Unless it is linked with corporatism in one form or another, either private or state corporatism, it has no plan for production. It is not economic in that it tends to separate production from distribution by separating the fruits of labor from their producers. Welfarism is not much better off with its political system. Its political theory has to do mainly with changing government from its role of maintaining the peace by punishing offenders to the provider or distributor of goods and services. Since welfarism is usually carried on in a democratic context, politicians are expected to gain office by promises of a better distribution of wealth. Political elites aim to reward their followers by providing them with a larger slice of the pie.

Those who view welfarism as a system of **social justice** would undoubtedly characterize it in other terms, but that is the face it wears as a politico-economic system. At any rate, welfarism has its roots in socialism. In the United States, the socialist roots are usually ignored or obfuscated, mainly because avowed socialism has been decisively rejected at the polls. In some European countries, by contrast, the socialist roots are apt to be not only admitted but often proudly claimed. The confusions of welfarism or perhaps some of its inadequacies as a politico-economic system stem from both socialism and the attempts to attain it within a democratic system of government. To see that requires some examination of socialism and its development.

**Socialism** was the offspring of a motley assortment of European intellectuals in the late eighteenth and in the nineteenth century. Most of the early socialists were French. Indeed, the French Revolution was a seminal event for socialism, both because some socialist ideas played some small part in it and because later socialists looked back to it as a kind of prototype of revolution. Some German intellectuals entered the ranks of socialists in the nineteenth century, and people from other lands followed. Socialist intellectuals were mostly outcasts during the nineteenth century. They tended to be despised by the generality of people and sometimes persecuted by the rulers. There was good reason to fear their ideas. They were generally opposed to private property and wished to see the institution abolished. They were radical reformers and/or revolutionaries, who sought to transform society. Some were revolutionists; others anarchists, or both, who sought to destroy government. They were **collectivists** who thought and wished to act by groups, societies, and nations. They conceived of humans as desperately needing transformation, and their method for doing so was through using the power of the state. They were typically anti-clerical, anti-religious, and atheistic. They were utopians, conceiving visions of the perfect society that would supposedly come about once people were transformed or socialized, hence the name, "socialism."

> **Some Common Characteristics of Socialists**
> They were generally opposed to private property and wished to see the institution abolished. They were radical reformers and/or revolutionaries, who sought to transform society. Some were revolutionists; others anarchists, or both, who sought to destroy government. They were collectivists who thought and wished to act by groups, societies, and nations. They conceived of humans as desperately needing transformation, and their method for doing so was through using the power of the state. They were typically anti-clerical, anti-religious, and atheistic. They were utopians, conceiving visions of the perfect society that would supposedly come about once people were transformed or socialized, hence the name, "socialism."

**welfarism**—the concept that governments should be the provider of economic goods and services achieved by taking the wealth of some people and giving it to others.

**social justice**—the idea that the current distribution of economic goods is unjust and must be corrected by a governmentally imposed redistribution.

**socialism**—in the broadest sense, it is any political system where governments control the economy.

**collectivists**—people who believe the individual should always be forced to submit to the will of the group for the so called common good.

**laborism**—see definition, p. 269.

**labor theory of value**—see definition, p. 193.

In economic terms, socialism is more or less equivalent to **laborism**. Indeed, it is the only doctrine we encounter in the examination of politico-economic systems that is laborist in emphasis. Not all socialists have been laborists at every stage, but laborism became the linchpin of socialism in the course of the nineteenth century. That is, laborism is to socialism what landism was to feudalism, and capitalism has been to the industrial era, or mercantilism to absolute monarchy. Laborism holds that labor, particularly manual work, is the source of economic value and hence of economic production.

Karl Marx was a highly influential exponent of the **labor theory of value**. In its simplest formulation, Marx put it this way: "The relative values of commodities are, therefore, determined by the respective quantities or amounts of labour, worked up, realized, fixed in them." In short, the value of goods is determined by the amount of labor, or as Marx refined his thought, "laboring power" that goes into it. But what is value? Marx answered, "Price taken by itself, is nothing but the monetary expression of value." And, he concluded, "the market price of a commodity coincides with its value." What about all the other things that go into producing and distributing goods? What about land and its rent? Money and its interest? Capital goods? Entrepreneurial activity? Well, if labor were the sole determinant of value, then all other costs were bogus and workmen were simply being robbed by the amount that was taken away from the price of the product to pay for them.

Hence, the socialist claim that labor was being alienated from its product and that a vast system of the exploitation existed. In other words, Marxists believe that injustice pervades all societies. There is much more in the detail of socialism, but this is the crux of the argument that the system must be changed to restore justice. The crux is, in essence, laborism.

Socialists differed with one another almost from the beginning about many particulars of their subject, but by the late nineteenth century socialism was diverging into two main strains, as noted earlier. These two strains have had the major impact in the twentieth century, and it should be emphasized that by the middle of the twentieth century virtually every country in the world was under the sway of one or the other of these strains. The two strains can be simply described as **evolutionary socialism** and **revolutionary socialism**.

evolutionary socialism—*see definition*, p. 310.

revolutionary socialism—*see definition*, p. 310.

The most spectacular development of revolutionary socialism stems from Karl Marx. Since the twentieth century, this form of socialism has usually been called communism, though fascism and Nazism were non-Marxist variations of revolutionary socialism. Revolutionary socialism is the view that socialism entails a revolution. If it does not entail an armed revolt, which it generally does, the changes that accompany it are themselves revolutionary. According to Marx, the revolution that would usher in socialism was inevitable. As soon as a country reached the stage in industrial development in which wealth had been consolidated in the hands of a few wealthy people, the proletariat would rise against them and seize all power. In Marxist–Leninist theory, the Communist Party is thought to be the active arm of the proletariat. Under the guidance of the party, the country will proceed from socialism to communism by way of the dictatorship of the proletariat. Beyond that, communism has no political theory, for when the revolution has been completed the state will wither away.

Evolutionary socialism, by contrast, proposes to move toward socialism gradually within the existing framework. It is also referred to as gradualism and democratic socialism. Evolutionary socialists were originally mostly Marxists who had abandoned revolutionary doctrine. They were as convinced as other socialists, initially anyway, that socialism would be achieved when private property in productive wealth had been abolished and the instruments of production were in the hands of the workers. Practically, however, they worked to shift the public mind toward collective control and regulation, and eventually toward collectivism. Evolutionary socialists have become, if they were not always, **statists**. That is, they proposed to use the power of the government—the existing government—to achieve their ends. Meanwhile, of course, they worked to change the character of the government.

statists—people who believe central governments should control society.

## 21.1 Socialism in Great Britain

Evolutionary socialism, or gradualism, was first shaped by the Fabians in England in the late nineteenth century. The **Fabian Society** was organized in 1884. It drew into its ranks many of the leading intellectuals, unionists, and an assortment of politicians. The purposes and methods of the Society were set forth over the years in a series of Fabian Tracts. For example, Tract #7 deals with the question of **"socializing" property**:

> It therefore aims at the re-organization of Society by the emancipation of Land and Industrial Capital from individual and class ownership, and vesting of them in the community for the general benefit....
>
> The Society accordingly works for the extinction of private property in Land and the consequent individual appropriation, in the form of Rent, of the price paid for permission to use the earth, as well as for the advantages of superior soils and sites.
>
> The Society, further, works for the transfer to the community of the administration of such Industrial Capital as can conveniently be managed socially....

Fabianism—an ideology for a gradual movement toward socialism within a country. The Fabian Society was organized in England in the late nineteenth century. It aimed to establish socialism in that country without any radical change in the political system. In contrast to the Marxists, Fabians sought to attain socialism peacefully rather than through revolution.

socializing property—expropriating or taking private property from individual owners and giving control of it to government.

That the Fabians were socialists they never left any doubt. Nor did they leave any doubt that they intended to use the power of government to achieve their end. As Tract #70 said: "The Socialism advanced by the Fabian Society is State Socialism exclusively." Moreover,

> Socialism, as understood by the Fabian Society means the organization and conduct of the necessary industries of the country and appropriation of all forms of economic rent of land and capital by the nation as a whole, through the most suitable public authorities, parochial, municipal, provincial, or central.

But the Fabians expected that this would be achieved gradually and step by step. The first step was to begin to persuade people of the desirability of using government power to change society. To that end, they published the many Fabian Tracts. They sought to influence existing organizations. Fabians were urged to join all sorts of organizations and societies, and so far as they could, influence them as levers for shifting Britain in a socialist direction. They did not expect that the state would immediately take over land and productive industry. Thus, instead of pressing for this to be done, they sought to move people toward the ultimate goal by pressing less drastic government interventions such as: setting minimum wages and maximum hours of work, adopting welfare payments to relieve the poor, having government build hospitals, having municipal bakeries, and so on and on. Once people became accustomed to such part-way measures, they would be prepared to go further.

Toward the end of World War I, the English Fabians became a significant political player. They became very influential in the **Labour Party**, which was on its way to becoming a major party in England. The Labour Party had been an almost exclusively unionist party up to this point and had not been committed to socialism. The party adopted a new constitution in 1918, mainly the work of Sidney Webb, a leading Fabian. This constitution committed the Labour Party to the socialist program. It read, in part,

> To secure for the producers by hand and brain the full fruits of their industry, and the most equitable distribution thereof that may be possible, upon the basis of the common ownership of the means of production and the best obtainable system of popular administration and control of each industry or service.

Not only did the new constitution commit the party to socialism but it also moved the party to a broad commitment that could draw in other than union members.

**Labour Party**—political party in Great Britain advocating for greater socialism in that nation.

### 21.1.1 The Labour Party in Power

The fortunes of the Labour Party were mostly up and down during the interval between World War I and World War II. The Conservative Party generally dominated, though twice Ramsay MacDonald, a Labourite became Prime Minister during this period. After his second stint, the Labourites vowed that when they came to power again it would be on a platform of socialism through **nationalization** of major industries. Their opportunity came near the end of World War II, when a general election in 1945 gave them a majority in the House of Commons.

**nationalization**—the government take over of private companies.

In one sense, the time was right for nationalization and other socialist programs in England. That is, the people were prepared for ever greater involvement of government in their lives. The necessities of war had seen to that. The British were acclimated to vast undertakings by government—to large scale evacuations, to massive mobilizations of armed forces and their deployment around the world, to collective responses to air raids and the attendant blackouts, to concentration on war production for what was understood to be the general good, and the like. As one writer said, "All this produced a revolution in British economic life, until in the end direction and control turned Great Britain into a country more fully socialist than anything achieved by the conscious planners of Soviet Russia."

From another angle, it may have been about the worst possible time to introduce drastic and revolutionary changes in the economy. The British had been drained by the war effort. Major damage had been done to such cities as London by the bombings. The British were suffering wartime shortages in every direction. Moreover, the British had come to depend on imports from other countries in order to live. About three-quarters of the food they consumed had to be imported. What made this situation especially pressing was that the British had long since ceased to balance these imports with commodities exported. The difference had been increasingly made up in recent decades by income from foreign investments, the providing of such services as shipping and insurance, and payments in gold. At the end of the war, Britain was deeply in debt abroad, most of the gold supply was depleted and many of their foreign investments were sold to defray the expenses of the war. There may be no good time to plunge into socialism; if there ever is, this was not it.

At any rate, once in power, the Labour Party rushed headlong into their version of socialism. Within a year or so they pushed along three lines toward their goal: (1) by adopting welfarist measures; (2) by taking key industries from their owners; and (3) by controlling and regulating those portions of the economy still technically privately owned.

> **Three Socialist Tactics of the Labour Party**
> Once in power, the Labour Party rushed headlong into their version of socialism. Within a year or so they pushed along three lines toward their goal: (1) by adopting welfarist measures; (2) by taking key industries from their owners; and (3) by controlling and regulating those portions of the economy still technically privately owned.

One major welfarist measure—the Education Act of 1944—had been passed before the Labourites came to power. It provided that children were to attend school until they were at least 15 years of age. In addition, "free" secondary education for all children was provided, and the act set up a system of separating at the age of eleven those pupils to go to preparatory and those to attend "terminal" schools. The two most dramatic welfarist acts were passed in 1946: National Insurance Act and National Health Service Act. The insurance act provided an assortment of protections for all who reached school leaving age and were not yet retirement age. These would be eligible for unemployment benefits, sickness benefits, maternity benefits, and so on and on. The National Health Service Act was the more controversial of the two. Many physicians opposed it, but it was passed and went into effect in 1948. The act provided for free medical and dental services for everyone, and for physicians and other providers of medical and dental services to be paid by the government.

Nationalization was undertaken with considerable vigor. The broad categories of industries nationalized were banking, power and light, transport, and iron and steel. The Bank of England Act of 1946 nationalized banking. The last major act of nationalization was the Iron and Steel Act of 1949. In between, power and light, coal, and transport were taken over by the government. Socialists favored taking over these industries because they rightly understood it would give the government a grip on the whole economy. If the government controlled light, heat, transport, financing, and structural materials, the whole economy was tied to the government operations.

Of course, the British Labourites did not content themselves with merely nationalizing the key industries. A vast network of controls, subsidies, priorities, prescriptions, proscriptions, and regulations were extended over the remainder of industry and agriculture. A few examples will at least indicate how severe and thorough the controls were.

One of the most dramatic examples of compulsion can be examined in connection with the regulation of the location of industry. The legal bases for these controls were the Distribution of Industry Act, the Town and Country Planning Act, and the procedures for locating industry adopted by the powerful Board of Trade. The main drive of these programs was to locate new industries in areas where labor was most abundantly available. The Distribution of Industry Act pushed in this direction by making loans, by giving financial assistance to companies that would open factories in desired areas, and by the use of tax money to build factories for lease. This, in itself, was largely an effort by the government to influence the location of industry. But stronger weapons were at hand. The Board of Trade could, in effect, veto a plan to build a factory in an unapproved area. This was bolstered by the powers exercised under the Town and Country Planning Act: not only were new towns planned but also building activity was directed.

Economic activity of every sort was minutely regulated. Wanted production (wanted by the government regulators, that is) was encouraged; luxury production was limited. Foreign exports were controlled, limited, and, in some cases, prohibited. A government committee had to approve new investments of capital. The aim was to subject all productive activity to those appointed by government.

As for agriculture, it was decided not to nationalize the land but to regulate and control farmers and their activities. The Ministry of Food was authorized to buy agricultural produce and it became, in effect, the sole market in which farmers were to sell. As the only buyer and seller, the ministry proceeded to set prices to the farmers, on the one hand, and to the consumers, on the other. In general, the ministry paid high prices for products that it determined were needed and sold them at a loss. The aim of this uneconomic behavior was to encourage the kind of production and consumption they wanted. The Ministry exercised such controls as allotting acreage to be planted to particular crops, to decide what crops should be grown, and the like.

Finally, a large portion of the income of Englishmen was "nationalized," i.e., taken by the government as taxes. An economic historian concluded that the government took 37.7% of the value of the gross national product from the people in 1946. The income tax on larger incomes was confiscatory. In short, the government not only nationalized key industries, controlled and regulated all others, but also redistributed the wealth with vigor.

## 21.1.2 The Failure of British Socialism

Socialism was a dismal failure in England. True, the times were not favorable for it to succeed, but, then, they never are. The basic trouble with socialism, both revolutionary and evolutionary, is that it turns the power of government upon their own people, and by so doing inhibits, restrains, and tends to prevent the people from accomplishing their productive tasks. How this power was abused at its lower reaches is illustrated by the following examples from the latter years of the 1940s:

> The Ministry of Food prosecuted a greengrocer for selling a few extra pounds of potatoes, while admitting that they were frostbitten and would be thrown away at once. The Ministry clamped down on a farmer's wife who served the Ministry snooper with Devonshire cream for his tea. A shopkeeper was fined £5 for selling home-made sweets that contained his own ration of sugar. Ludicrous penalties were imposed on farmers who had not kept strictly to the letter of licenses to slaughter pigs; in one case, the permitted building was used, the authorized butcher employed, but the job had to be done the day before it was permitted; in another case the butcher and the timing coincided, but the pig met its end in the wrong building. . . .

Very soon, the socialists were able virtually to wreck what remained of a once vigorous and healthy economy. Economy had suffered greatly from the interventions before World War I and World War II. It was hampered even more drastically by wartime restrictions. But the measures of the Labour government made economic behavior very difficult to follow.

The wreckage was wrought by nationalization, controls, regulations, high taxes, restrictions, and compulsory services. The government attempted to plan for and control virtually all economic activity in the land. The initiative for action was taken from the people and vested in a bureaucracy. Where industries were actually taken over, they were placed under the authority of boards, who were relieved of the managerial responsibility to make a profit. In short, the bureaucracy was let loose and the people were bound up. To put it another way, much of the great ability and energy of the British people was turned from productive purposes to wrestling with the bureaucracy.

> **Causes for the Failure**
> The wreckage was wrought by nationalization, controls, regulations, high taxes, restrictions, and compulsory services. The government attempted to plan for and control virtually all economic activity in the land. The initiative for action was taken from the people and vested in a bureaucracy. In short, the bureaucracy was let loose and the people were bound up. To put it another way, much of the great ability and energy of the British people was turned from productive purposes to wrestling with the bureaucracy.

Moreover, the Labour government vigorously undertook redistribution. They levied highly graduated income taxes, taxed luxury goods at high prices, controlled prices of food, clothing, and shelter, and rationed many items in particularly short supply. Not only that, but they provided free medical services, pensions, and otherwise aided those with little or no income. They distributed and they redistributed.

Yet, a strange thing—at least to them—occurred: the more they redistributed the less they had to distribute at all. Not only did such shortages as the British had known during World War continue, but others cropped up as well. Even bread, which had *not* been rationed during the war, was rationed beginning in 1946. The government had first attempted to fool the English people into buying less bread by reducing the amount in a loaf. When this did not work, they turned to rationing. All sorts of other items were rationed as well. In 1948, the weekly allowance for the average man was thirteen ounces of meat, one and half ounces of cheese, six ounces of butter and margarine, one ounce of cooking fat, eight ounces of sugar, two pints of milk, and one egg. Fuel was so low that British homes were heated far below the comfort level. Everything, it seemed, was in short supply. The government had to turn to the United States for huge loans to try to keep going.

> **Getting the Point...**
>
> Explain why shortages tend to be a logical consequence of socialism.

### 21.1.3 The Repercussions of the British Failure

The failure of British socialism had political repercussions at home, of course. The Labourites were turned out of power by the electorate in 1951, and the government began tentatively to back off from nationalization and to restore some industries to private ownership. The **Conservative Party** remained in power to the mid 1960s, but even the return of Labour did not result in any new surge of nationalization. After 1979, a Conservative government under the leadership of **Margaret Thatcher** moved more aggressively toward removing the tentacles of socialism.

The failure of nationalization in Britain had international repercussions as well. These were accentuated by the fact that Britain's decline to minor power status came swiftly after World War II, coinciding with the rule of the Labour government. Thus, British influence in the world waned as that of the United States rose. The British failure apparently convinced many evolutionary socialists that government ownership of the means of production was neither politically desirable nor necessary for the attainment of their ends. They could have welfarism without such government ownership. (The horrid failure of the even more drastic government takeover in the Soviet Union gave even better evidence of the failure of government ownership.) The influence of the United States was in the direction of welfarism. Government ownership laid responsibilities on politicians that they found inconvenient to bear, since they could be thrown out of office for their mismanagement of the economy.

**Conservative Party**—political party of Great Britain that is generally opposed to socialist efforts.

**Margaret Thatcher**—Conservative Party prime minister of England during the 1980s who worked to undo many socialist policies and programs.

Thus, the tendency in most Western countries has been to leave productive property in private hands, to foster welfare measures rather than government ownership, to control privately owned industries by a variety of devices, and to redistribute the wealth produced by workers and private farms, factories, mines, and mills. Nationalization has continued to occur, of course, but much more commonly in Third World and communist countries than in Western parliamentary and republican governments. To put it more bluntly, those governments of countries that have wealth to distribute have tended to content themselves with redistributing what is privately produced rather than taking over the means of production. The less developed countries, by contrast, which frequently have little wealth to redistribute in any case, have often followed the communist route by nationalization and other means of seizing private property.

Countries that have focused upon welfarism have not entirely abandoned the idea of a planned economy, however. Instead, they have tried to influence it through regulation, taxation, and monetary and credit manipulation. The main instruments for monetary and credit manipulation are central banks, the banking and financial system in general, and government lending institutions. The main means by which governments attempt to manage the economy are by reducing and expanding credit and the money supply. Reductions of credit and money—monetary deflation—is not popular. Therefore, monetary inflation has been the rule, and deflation the exception. In consequence, government policy has worked in the direction of destroying the value of the currency and has often resulted in huge debts.

While welfarism differs from country to country, there are many common features to the welfare programs in the industrialized countries of the West. They tend to be laborist both in origin and in those on whom many of their programs are focused. That is, many of the programs have been slanted toward the wage-worker, toward raising wages, toward shortening hours, toward reducing the years when people work for a living, and the like. They operate on the assumption that there is a surplus of labor, and that full employment during the working years is an ideal. Another common feature is that the welfare programs tend to redistribute the wealth. Underlying these programs is the equalitarian assumption that if people should not all have equal income there should at least be no hardship. The welfarist countries have tended to the view that certain goods and services are essential and that it is the business of government to see that no one is denied them.

## 21.2 Welfarism in the United States

The United States has what may well be called a Welfare State. Welfarism was so well established by the 1950s that most of those who run for election to office neither criticize nor attack the welfare premise or the main legislation by which it was established. Welfarism was established in its main lines in the 1930s during the **New Deal**. Some earlier enactments and programs have been around longer than that, and a large number have been added since the 1930s. But to understand the Welfare State in the United States, it is important to see what was done in the 1930s.

**New Deal**—*see definition, p. 317.*

### 21.2.1 Social Security

The center piece of the Welfare State in the United States was the **Social Security Act** passed in 1935. Indeed, the notion of calling the whole variation of socialism "welfare" in English may have come into being following the passage of this act. Historically, the term **welfare** had not been associated with government programs to aid the poor, the aged, unemployed, and the like. Such programs, when they existed had been referred to as "relief" or "poor relief," and the like, or in England, "the dole." Welfare means basically to fare well or a condition of well-being or in a condition of being well enough off. Such conditions as have elicited government aid have not usually been thought of as faring well.

Even so, the term was used in the preamble to the Social Security Act. It reads, in part:

> An Act to provide for the general welfare by establishing
> a system of Federal old-age benefits, and by enabling the

**Social Security Act**—The centerpiece welfare legislation of the New Deal. It established a government mandated pyramid scheme aimed at providing retirement benefits to the elderly.

**welfare**—a term that socialists have twisted to mean government provision of certain economic goods.

several States to make more adequate provision for aged persons, blind persons, dependent and crippled children, maternal and child welfare, public health, and the administration of their unemployment compensation laws....

The reference to the "general welfare" was an effort to give at least a facade of constitutionality to the law, since the Constitution specifies that taxes levied shall be for the "general welfare." County offices that administered some of these programs operated under state welfare departments and thus the programs became known as "welfare."

Although what were at that time technically called "old-age benefits" have since come to be thought of as Social Security, the Act covered a variety of programs. In addition to retirement benefits, it provided for unemployment compensation under the control of the states, for aid to dependent children, for aid to the blind and disabled, and even for public health programs. Coverage under Social Security for retirement benefits and unemployment compensation originally applied to industrial workers. This is still true in the main for unemployment compensation, but old-age benefits have now been expanded to cover virtually every employed person in the country. The tax, which, except for self-employed persons, is levied one-half on the worker and one-half on the employer has been raised steadily. The original tax was two cents for each dollar a worker earned: one cent to be deducted from the wages of the worker, and one cent to be paid by the employer. The tax has now risen to over fifteen cents, though it is still levied one-half upon the employee and one-half upon the employer. Benefits have been expanded over the years as well. The retirement age was originally set at age 65 or older. Because of ever increasing costs of the program the retirement age has increased to 67.

The Social Security program is a collectivist and redistributionist plan. It is collectivist in that neither the individual who is taxed nor his heirs will necessarily receive anything from the money taken in to pay for retirement benefits. A person might die before he reaches the retirement age, may have worked and paid in to the fund a large sum of money, and yet might never receive any benefit from it. Nor does the amount he has been taxed belong to him or his heirs in any sense whatsoever. The money is forfeited to the general Social Security fund when it is received, and any given person can only receive benefits when, according to changing laws, he has become eligible or otherwise qualified. That is collectivist, not individualist. It is redistributionist in that the money is paid out not according to whose money it was but by whatever the existing program mandates. It is redistributionist, on its face, and always has been, in that it taxes the employer to pay for benefits for his workers. Granted, the employer may in keeping his books charge such payments to labor costs, but the intent to redistribute is clearly there.

The Social Security program most nearly resembles what is called a **pyramid scheme** economically. That is, the early beneficiaries, at the top of the pyramid, get the greatest advantage from the redistribution while those at the base bear the burden and stand in danger of not getting out what they have put in, even if they should live long enough to do so. Moreover, the program has to be continually expanded to bring in more and more of the employed as well as by raising the proportion of their incomes that goes to Social Security, as has been done over the years. (A government pyramid scheme has one large advantage over a private one, for the government can force whole categories of people to pay the taxes involved, while private entrepreneurs have to sell their scheme to more and more people.) Social Security is based on an illusion, an illusion that

**pyramid scheme**—a financially fraudulent scheme whereby money taken from later participants is used to reward earlier investors in the program to give the appearance of profits where none exist.

an endless number of people can all receive more in benefits than they have paid in taxes, plus any interest the money might have drawn. Social Security is not actuarially sound. Although it was at one point called "old-age and survivor's insurance" it is, as set up, much more a redistributionist than insurance program. It is not based on reasonable expectations of longevity, nor are benefits tied in any practical way to what each individual has paid in. Hence, in recent years, the program has had several crises because of the imminent danger of running out of funds.

> **The Social Security program** is a collectivist and redistributionist plan. It is collectivist in that neither the individual who is taxed nor his heirs will necessarily receive anything from the money taken in to pay for retirement benefits. Nor does the amount he has been taxed belong to him or his heirs in any sense whatsoever.

Since the late 1970s, Congress has taken steps toward narrowing the benefits at the top. Restrictions of various kinds have been placed on Medicare benefits. The move is on to raise the retirement age, and some changes in this have been scheduled for the future. Social Security is nearing the limits, as the number of employed people who are taxed to provide the benefits has been declining. The tax on wages has already reached the point where it is a great burden on both employers and employees, to say nothing of the self-employed. The only other recourse in order to continue the program the way it is set up is to reduce benefits. Steps are being taken in that direction.

### 21.2.2 Ever-Increasing Welfarist Programs

Welfarism in the United States has been laborist in emphasis from the outset. The National Labor Relations Act was passed the same year as the Social Security Act—1935. This act threw the weight of government on the side of labor unions and, in effect, empowered them in their efforts to get higher wages, shorter hours, and other benefits from employers. In 1938, Congress passed the Fair Labor Standards Act, which prescribed minimum wages and maximum hours for workers generally, though minimum wages have been pegged well below union wages. This legislation accepted the assumptions—those of laborism—that there is a surplus of labor and that the worker does not get his fair share of the returns from his produce. In actuality, higher than market wages do tend to cause unemployment, i.e., a surplus of labor, by pricing many workers out of jobs.

There are many other types of welfare programs in the United States, of course, in addition to those that were authorized by the Social Security Act or are entailed in labor legislation. The farm programs that have abounded since the 1930s, though some go back to earlier periods, are welfarist in tendency. Government subsidy and loan programs have already been discussed. Housing is another major area of welfarism, particularly urban and town housing. Large government expenditures have been made on low income housing projects over the years. Government has also provided or subsidized low interest loans for otherwise unqualified buyers of homes. More generally, the Federal Housing Administration (FHA, it is called, except in rural areas where it could be confused with

Farmers Home Administration) guarantees low down payment loans, and tacitly subsidizes home ownership. Those who have qualified for the G.I. Bill are able to buy homes with no down payment, since the government guarantees the full repayment of the loans. These programs have cost taxpayers much less than would otherwise have been the case because of the ongoing inflation. Prices of used houses have risen over the years so that FHA does not usually lose much if it has to pay off on the guarantees. The same goes for the program under the G.I. Bill.

Another area that has been somewhat welfarist and very much redistributionist has been government support for schooling. State and local government usually pay the cost of schooling for all children through high school, with subsidies for some programs by the federal government. Most states also provide large tax money support for colleges and universities, though these institutions usually charge tuition to the students as well. The federal government has had many programs that aided colleges and universities as well, including the land grants, the G.I. Bill, loans for buildings on private campuses, student loan programs, and an assortment of grants made more directly to students, such as Pell grants. School lunch programs are subsidized by government.

Welfarism has so many aspects that only the highlights can be covered here. One of the more obvious cases is that of government food stamp programs. All sorts of welfare programs have been developed around medical care. Federal and local governments have provided funds for the building of hospitals and clinics. Medicaid pays medical bills for those who have neither insurance coverage nor the means to pay them. Public health services provide vaccinations, prenatal care, and a variety of other medical services at little or no cost to the recipient. The number of **"entitlement" programs** for this, that, or the other seem almost endless.

The United States has not only practiced welfarism at home but also abroad. Since World War II, the government has extended all sorts of aid to foreign countries. Some of it has been military and was long associated with the Cold War, but much of it has been economic aid to other countries. The economic aid, much of it, has been welfarist in tendency, encouraging foreign governments to establish public services and especially help the poor. Much of this has been to provide governments in non-industrialized countries with the means to redistribute wealth that has not even been produced in their countries.

### 21.2.3 The Corporatism of Welfarism

The basic assumption of welfarism is that it is the duty of government to look after and provide for the well-being of those within its jurisdiction. Since government is not a producer of goods, this means that it takes goods from those who produce them and redistributes them to its favorites. It may be well to emphasize that government redistribution is to the favorites of those who have the power to govern. It is often alleged by politicians and others that welfare is for the have-nots, the deprived, the poor, and the neglected. Undoubtedly, some of the benefits of the welfare programs do reach people in these categories. But there are many other beneficiaries of government welfare programs who are very far from being poor, deprived, or in dire need of help.

Governments undertake great construction projects, such as hospitals, low income housing, dormitories, or whatever. The prime beneficiaries of these are often builders, construction companies, and construction workers. The prime beneficiaries of government run and subsidized schooling are teachers, professors, administrators, and other school and

---

**entitlement programs**—also called entitlements. Once government welfare programs are established, all people who qualify for benefits are said to be entitled to them as a matter of right.

college support personnel. That is to say nothing of textbook publishers, salesmen, paper manufacturers, and the like. The medical profession has reaped quite a bonanza from government programs for building hospitals, paying medical bills, and otherwise subsidizing medical care. The same goes, more or less, for pharmacists, pharmaceutical manufacturers, medical device manufacturers, and so on.

> **Power of Political Favor**
> The basic assumption of welfarism is that it is the duty of government to look after and provide for the well-being of those within its jurisdiction. Since government is not a producer of goods, this means that it takes goods from those who produce them and redistributes them to its favorites.

Indeed, some government programs that are vaguely supposed to be for the aid of the poor may have little or nothing to do with that. Urban renewal comes most readily to mind. These were large government programs for the purpose of revitalizing inner cities. Since many of the poor did indeed live in inner cities, this might be supposed to benefit them. Actually, the poor were often driven from the inner cities where urban renewal was taking place, driven from their homes and businesses that were scheduled for demolition. In turn, these lands laid waste were often used to build luxury high rise apartments and office buildings—hardly the domain of the poor. Government loans to foreign countries to buy farm or manufactured products are sometimes identified by politicians who support them as in some measure efforts to help American farmers, manufacturers, and industrial workers. Some Federal aid for domestic programs have no clear connection with what is ordinarily thought of as welfare programs. For example, Federal aid for building airports for small planes have little or no conceivable connection with aid to the poor, who rarely own or fly airplanes. Indeed, such programs often take from the relatively "have-nots" to give to the "haves."

> **Getting the Point...**
> What are some corporatist actions that an elected legislator might take when designing welfare programs?
>
> What might motivate an elected official to act in corporatist ways in designing welfare programs?

Some of the incongruities of welfarism stem from the fact that it usually exists in countries that have popularly elected legislatures. The electorate is often ambiguous about these programs, vacillating in their support of them. So it is that politicians spread their goodies around more broadly to get support. In any case, welfarism, government redistribution, and the taking from producers to give to government favorites are deeply ingrained in many countries.

### 21.2.4 Negative Consequences of Welfarism

Welfarism turns the rules of economy upside down and wrong side out. It operates on the assumption that the problem of production has been solved and that the problem is one of distributing the wealth properly. Its premises are that there are surpluses of goods and of labor, and that society is confronted by the anomaly of abundance. It supposes that economic activity is spurred by consumer demand. In fact, scarcity remains, and it is still the productive who provide the means of economic activity. Welfarism takes from the productive and bestows at least some of the production on the unproductive or under-productive. By so doing, it reduces the incentives to work and produce. It pays people not to work, by such devices as unemployment compensation and subsidized college attendance. It prices labor out of the market and sometimes goods as well, as it did with butter and cotton, and fulfills its prophecy of surpluses.

The logical consequence of such a topsy-turvy economy would be poverty, widespread deprivation, and want. After all, redistribution only works when there is something—indeed, a great deal of something—to distribute. Welfarism turns the incentives toward consumption and away from production. The United States and Western Europe have been saved from most of the worst consequences of welfarism thus far. Most of the countries that are deeply into welfarism got a good head start on production under more or less free enterprise in the nineteenth century. Most of them still retain important remnants of that freedom. By no means have all the incentives to production been removed. Welfarism often leaves its recipients still impoverished so that the incentives to work and produce remain. Moreover, the free enterprise that remains has made great strides in providing the goods to distribute. It is the tempestuous alliance between corporatism and welfarism that has kept the system going.

The worst of the consequences have not been so much economic as moral, ethical, and societal. The currency has, of course, been debauched by welfarism. That is, its value has been progressively destroyed. Governments have not found it expedient, since they are popularly elected, to raise the money to pay for all this redistribution by direct taxation. They have, as a major supplement, turned to the hidden tax of monetary inflation, thus laying hold of the wealth of the productive, without appearing to do so. The savings, and the means of saving, by money have been taken away, stolen, as it were. The welfare state depends, too, on taking away large portions of the property, i.e., earnings, liquid wealth, and other forms of property, by more direct taxation. Above all, much of the independence of people has been given up or eroded by an increasing dependence on government and its privileged businesses and institutions. So far as government has taken over the responsibility and the means for looking after the well-being of people, the people have tended to yield up their own responsibility for doing so. The larger results can be seen in the dissolution of the family and the decline of voluntary community.

---

**The Most Devastating Consequences of Welfarism**

The worst of the consequences have not been so much economic as moral, ethical, and societal. Much of the independence of people has been given up or eroded by an increasing dependence on government and its privileged businesses and institutions. So far as government has taken over the responsibility and the means for looking after the well-being of people, the people have tended to yield up their own responsibility for doing so. The larger results can be seen in the dissolution of the family and the decline of voluntary community.

---

*The problem with socialism is that you eventually run out of other peoples' money.*

**Margaret Thatcher**

# Study Guide for:

# 21 Welfarism

## Chapter Summary

The primary concern of welfarism is the distribution of goods and services, not their production. The imposition of welfare policies in a nation is best understood in the context of socialism. As discussed in the previous chapter socialism has taken on two forms in the twentieth century: evolutionary and revolutionary. Further, although socialism is laborism in theory, in practice it tends toward corporatism. Welfarism in government policy is the tendency of the evolutionary form of socialism. That is, in an effort to eliminate property rights within a country, socialists begin by proposing gradual policies of change. The implementation of welfare programs serves as a useful beginning for they undermine property rights. These policies veil the force of government behind a mask of benevolence even though the thrust of them is the gradual erosion of property rights and the development of socialism. Often the proposals are willingly accepted because their stated end is to alleviate the suffering of the poor.

England's profound change toward socialism in the twentieth century proved disastrous. The fundamental problem with socialism is that it turns the force of government upon the people. It treats the governed as if they were putty to be remade. It restrains individual effort and prevents people from accomplishing productive tasks. As a result, the more socialists seek to redistribute income in society, the less income they find available to redistribute. In the end, socialism is oppressive.

## Points of Emphasis

1. Gradualist socialism has usually produced welfare states in practice.

2. England, more than any other country, has experienced more economic hardship stemming from evolutionary socialism.

## Identification

1. welfarism
2. social justice
3. socialism
4. collectivists
5. laborism
6. labor theory of value
7. evolutionary socialism
8. revolutionary socialism
9. statists
10. Fabianism
11. socializing property
12. Labour Party
13. nationalization
14. Conservative Party
15. Margaret Thatcher
16. New Deal
17. Social Security Act
18. welfare
19. pyramid scheme
20. entitlement programs

# Review Questions

1. During the twentieth century England moved substantially away from its free market economy to a more socialist system. What form did socialism take and how did it develop in England?

2. What were the consequences that followed from this change?

3. Contrast the tactics used by communists with those used in Western parliamentary and republican governments.

4. What policies in the United States have served the purpose of democratic socialists?

5. What consequences are currently being borne in the U.S. for these policies?

# Activity

1. Find a news article about a policy proposal currently being discussed in the United States. Point out any socialist aspects being proposed. Point out any natural law/free enterprise aspects. Describe any ways the problem could be approached from more of a natural law/free enterprise perspective. List some pros and cons of each perspective.

# For Further Study

1. Clarence Carson, Paul Cleveland, and Dewayne Barney, *The Great Utopian Delusion*, Boundary Stone: Birmingham, AL, 2015.

**CHAPTER CONTENT**

22.1 Communist Ideology and Practice 348
22.2 The Centrally Planned Economy 351
22.3 The Production of Goods 353
22.4 The Distribution of Goods 357

# 22 COMMUNISM

The reason for discussing communism last is neither chronological nor any concession to its future prospects. In a strictly chronological treatment welfarism most likely would be dealt with last. It is of more recent vintage than communism, emerging as a system only in the 1930s. Whereas, Marxism goes well back into the nineteenth century, and communism of one sort or another is a much older idea. Moreover, Soviet communism antedated welfarism. Nor is communism necessarily the wave of the future, as evidenced by the collapse of the Soviet Union and by the fundamental economic changes occurring in China. Communism's ideology has been about as thoroughly disproved in theory as an ideology can be, and in practice it has discredited itself.

Rather than any of the above reasons, communism is discussed last because it is the logical end toward which socialism tends. It is the logical extension of an ingrained opposition to private property. It is the logical extension of the belief that man should be transformed by the exercise of the power of the state. It is the logical culmination of the doctrine that the means of production and the distribution of goods should be commonly owned. It is the logical result of utopianism, of both the revolutionary and evolutionary use of government power to bring heaven on earth. To argue that communism in power is different from what Marx taught, as some intellectuals have done, is both right and more than a little irrelevant. Marx taught much that has not and probably cannot happen. But what has happened is nonetheless an extension of his errant claims into the real world of actual people living in actual countries.

Strictly speaking, communism does not have an economic system. Granted, in countries that are communist there is some production and distribution of goods, but the system is hardly economic. Nor does it do full justice to it to describe it as dis-economic. So far as any communist system is communist in origin and practice it is anti-economic. Economics as a system of thought is built around the market. Communism is profoundly anti-market in concept and, so far as the concept is followed, in practice. Large efforts have been made to deactivate or destroy the determinative role of the market in communist countries. Prices are determined by decree, not by supply and demand. What will be produced in what quantities and where it will be offered for sale is determined by political authority. The buying and selling of goods outside the government stores has often been prohibited (though sale of vegetables and the like is sometimes allowed) and punished by severe penalties. In short, the market is nullified, and without it there can be no economics.

The attitude toward the market follows quite naturally from the attitude toward private property under communism. Without private property there can be no valid market. Nor can there be a social economy. If people cannot trade their labor and the goods that they produce freely, they are quite limited in the extent that they can behave economically. Economy such as it is becomes something that can only be practiced in private; it goes underground, so to speak.

## 22.1 Communist Ideology and Practice

Before proceeding to what can be done to describe such economic arrangements as exist under communism, some more general remarks need to be made about communist ideology and practice. It must be understood that communism is an attempt to overturn the norms and practices that have existed before and do exist elsewhere. It is profoundly revolutionary, and the full meaning of that needs to be grasped. Futile attempts have been made to describe communist economies as if they could be described in Western terms that embrace the rule of natural law. Futile attempts have been made to describe the governments of communist countries as if they were like all governments. For example, many writers attempted to speak of the former Soviet constitutions as if they could in some way be equated with Western constitutions. Communism, it must be understood, is new wine, however sour, and to pour it into old bottles is a profound mistake.

Westerners are often troubled by this thesis, and they often focus on the similarities of things rather than on the stark differences. They have even been encouraged to do so by communists, who have spent much energy in attempting to wash over differences in the general conception of life and the nature of the rule of law. For instance, in the former Soviet Union they set up model farms, model factories, and other models to display what they had done in a favorable light. It pleased many to believe that things were not very different there. There was a man who was a college president who liked to tell the story of meeting several Russian soldiers in Europe after World War II. He assured his listeners that the Russians were not very different, that they had the same yearnings as we do, and that they no more liked or wanted war than we do. So far as it goes, his point might be well taken. It is nonetheless irrelevant to the larger point about communist revolution. If it proves anything, it proves that human nature is much the same throughout the human race. But this is the point that communists have been busily trying to disprove for quite some time.

Marxist ideology, which is basically communist ideology, holds that in the process of revolution everything will be overturned, changed, and transformed. Marx taught **dialectical materialism**, which he further specialized as **economic determinism**. Matter alone is real, and change takes place in the contest of those who control material forces for domination. The basic contest is over control of the means of production. He held that ideas were a result of this material quest and that the dominant forces had an ideology that supported, buttressed and followed from their control. Every social, cultural, and religious institution buttressed this control. Politics, or government, and law were simply a reflex of this control. In the modern era, Marx held, **bourgeoisie** society had come to dominate, and the capitalists were consolidating their hold over the instruments of production. He predicted that the **proletariat** (the workers) would eventually revolt in the land where this was furthest advanced, seize the instruments of production, and begin to overturn all that had been the result of the old ideology. Marx was anti-market, anti-economics, anti-political, anti-social, anti-Christian, indeed, anti-religion, and anti-the whole civilization or culture that prevailed. All this must be swept away. All conflict would end; the state would wither away, religion would die out, and a new man in a new

**dialectical materialism**—a Marxist term denoting the process by which change has occurred in the course of history. Dialectic refers to a contest, conflict, discussion or argument. Materialism is a belief in the primacy of matter. Marx used it to describe the conflict of classes over control of the means of production of material goods.

**economic determinism**—the doctrine that people's beliefs and practices are determined by the economic class or position in which they find themselves. Karl Marx formulated the most uncompromising position of economic determinism, but, in a less rigorous sense, modern intellectuals, indeed, most of us, have been greatly influenced by this notion.

**bourgeoisie**—see definition, p. 310.

**proletariat**—blue collar workers, those who provide manual labor.

society would emerge. The main point here, however, is that all the old beliefs and practices would be wiped out. The contest for control over the instruments of production would end, for they would all be held in common.

> **The Old Culture Must Be Destroyed**
> Marx was anti-market, anti-economics, anti-political, anti-social, anti-Christian, indeed, anti-religion, and anti-the whole civilization or culture that prevailed. All this must be swept away. All conflict would end; the state would wither away, religion would die out, and a new man in a new society would emerge. The main point here, however, is that all the old beliefs and practices would be wiped out. The contest for control over the instruments of production would end, for they would all be held in common.

That Marx's analysis was largely hogwash can now be stated with considerable assurance. Granted, there are enough half- or quarter-truths in his historical analysis to give it at least an appearance of plausibility. The same could probably be said for his claims about a bourgeoisie ideology. But as for his vision for the future following the revolution, it was nothing more than hokum. He had no political theory, for in his view the state would wither away. He had nothing more than a truncated economic theory, and that was of no use in the production or distribution of goods. Nor did he give any good reason for supposing that all conflict would end when and if the proletariat should come to power. He denied the reality of the spiritual, thus, leaving nothing to restrain man's base instincts and inclinations. Revolution was to be a universal solvent from which man would emerge purified, so to speak. The history of revolutions provides no substantial grounds for such an unabashed faith. Revolutions typically loose the destructive side of people, which must be brought to heel by some strong man in power. Marxist revolution in practice has been no different; indeed, it has exaggerated the worst features of revolution.

Communism in power has been remote from the Marxist vision. Yet a good case can be made that it follows both from the analysis and prescriptions of Marx. Karl Marx had what may best be described as a criminal mind. Not the mind of a petty criminal, of course. Not even the mind of those who are ordinarily thought of as directing organized crime. He had a cosmic criminal mind.

The crime that Marx contemplated was theft, the theft of all property used in the production and distribution of goods, in effect, all property. The method by which the property was to be taken he called Revolution. The cohorts who would assist in this enterprise—the proletariat—would be rewarded by receiving the fruits of production. Marx attempted to justify this universal robbery by wrapping it in a theory of **historical inevitability**, claiming that the proletariat were only reclaiming what was rightfully theirs. But in the eyes of man and of God it was no less than thievery on a grand scale.

Communism in practice has been **totalitarian**. That, too, followed from the Marxian prescription. Marx called for rule during a period of transition from the old system to the new (communism) by a "dictatorship of the proletariat." What he got was one man rule, in the name of the proletariat, of course, but in fact by the leader of the gangsters who seized power. The totalitarianism was the logical consequence of prescribing the

**historical inevitability**—the view that future historical developments will inevitably—unavoidably—unfold. This doctrine was propounded by Marx. What is supposed to be particularly inevitable is the eventual communist revolution in every country in the world.

**totalitarian**—*see definition*, p. 6.

**Vladimir I. Lenin**—*see biographical sketch, p. 326.*

**Bolshevik Revolution**—communist revolution launched by the Bolsheviks in Russia in 1917.

destruction of all the old ways and the confiscation of all wealth. Only total power in the government could even have an opportunity to root out all the old ways and lay hold of all property. And, in power, communists have ruled by terror.

These things happened first in Russia; they have since happened in other lands that have become communist. The consolidation of power did not come instantly, but it came as if it were inevitable. When people have lost all claims to or control over their property, there are no means to resist the power over them. **Vladimir I. Lenin** who led the **Bolshevik Revolution** in Russia in 1917 and headed the government as it consolidated power in the ensuing years was an outlaw. So were the others who gathered around him to assist in the undertaking. To say that they were outlaws is not to use the language loosely; many of them, including Lenin, were literally outlaws. They led a small party that seized or claimed control over the Russian Empire. Eventually, they made good most of their claim. They were nonetheless outlaws, gangsters in power, and so were their successors. They ruled by the most brutal exertion of power. The terror, by which Soviet rulers subdued the peoples under them, reached its peak under the one-man rule of **Joseph Stalin** in the 1930s, 1940s, and into the 1950s. Millions of political prisoners were rounded up, forced to make confessions by brutal torture, and, if they were not shot they were shipped off to slave labor camps, often to the forbidding climate of Siberia. Communism may well be the most tyrannical rule that has ever been exercised over any extensive area.

These general observations about communist systems needed to be made to place the economy in context. To discuss the economy outside the context of the general tyranny might be to give a false impression, the impression that Marxian Communism (or Marxism–Leninism) provides an alternative economic system without regard to the general tyranny. Instead, the economic system is part and parcel of the tyranny. Not only does it pervade the economy, but it could be in no way so completely tyrannical if it did not. Only a people without property could be so exposed to the power of the state. And, the communist economy is based on state control of the instruments of production, which is to say at root, the wealth of the people.

There should be no doubt, however, that the economy and economic arrangements were central to communism. After all, communists are materialists, and the economy brooked large to communists. Communists are also collectivists. They are dead set against individualism. Everything is supposed to be subordinate to the common good. In theory, communists are also egalitarians, though that has generally been given a collectivist twist. The equality advanced, or proclaimed, has been not so much that each individual should have equal income, though some have believed that. Rather, as a general rule, equality meant that each should contribute as much as he is able to the common good. As the formula has it, "From each according to his ability, to each according to his need."

---

### Joseph Stalin (1879–1953)

Stalin (born Dzhugashvili) was a Bolshevik agitator and organizer, party leader, and dictator of the Soviet Union from the late 1920s to 1953. He initiated the Five-Year Plans for forced collectivization, ordered the infamous purge trials of the 1930s, developed a vast slave labor camp system (the Gulag Archipelago), and peopled it with millions of his countrymen. He was born in the province of Georgia in the Russian Empire, attended a theological seminary, and was headed toward becoming a priest. However, he became involved with socialist groups and Marxist ideology and was expelled from seminary shortly before he would have graduated. Thereafter, he pursued the peculiar gangster-like life of so many revolutionaries in the years before World War I: in and out of jail, being deported and escaping from exile, organizing revolutionary groups, publishing ideological materials, and the like. Stalin became a follower of Lenin, and after the Bolshevik Revolution became a commissar. In the 1920s, he was secretary general of the Communist Party, and from this power position, he propelled himself to the head of the government after Lenin's death.

Just what "each" needed has not apparently ever been explained by the theoreticians, at least with any clarity.

Communism should have been, following Marxist lines, the very embodiment of laborism. However, as noted in an earlier chapter, it has in practice been more nearly the embodiment of state corporatism. Almost everything has been subordinated to the acquisition of capital goods, including especially the subordination of labor. Communist theorists may well argue that this has been the result of the fact that communism has come to power in industrially backward countries, rather than, as Marx predicted, in the most industrially advanced countries. If the technology and industries were already developed and in operation, it would no doubt be easier, at least at the beginning, for the workers to benefit. In any case, it is capital that has occupied communist practice, and there is reason enough to suppose this would have been so in any case, for capital represents material advance in their outlook.

Now we turn to illustrate the above and other aspects of communism by a more detailed discussion of how it was practiced in the former Soviet Union, which had by far the longest experience with it. As explained in an earlier chapter, Lenin backed off from thoroughgoing socialism in 1921 by introducing his New Economic Policy (NEP). He restored private trade to some extent and allowed private production widely in farming. The NEP was proclaimed as temporary, however, and by 1928, Stalin had sufficiently consolidated his power to make a bold thrust toward collectivization.

> **Getting the Point...**
>
> Explain the statement:
>
> Communism should have been, following Marxist lines, the very embodiment of laborism. However, it has in practice been more nearly the embodiment of state corporatism.
>
> Compare and contrast laborism and state corporatism.

## 22.2 The Centrally Planned Economy

What Stalin and his cohorts had in mind was to have a **centrally planned and directed economy**. In the minds of the Soviet economists, the old individualistic economy was unplanned, inefficient, and wasteful. Competition had long been pictured by socialists as wasteful. There was far too much duplication of services, overproduction of goods, production of what was not really needed, and so on. It was haphazard, in their view, and uncoordinated. How much more effective, or so they claimed, to have everything planned in advance; production allotted, distribution taken into account, and everything coordinated according to a general plan. It never occurred to the planners that they were giving up the vast plans and efforts of millions of people.

At any rate, Stalin initiated his Five-Year Plan in 1928. It was supposed to take until 1933 to complete. As it turned out, it was only the first of a succession of such plans. A second Five-Year Plan was inaugurated in 1933, and a third one in the late 1930s. The broad purpose of these plans was to achieve the rapid industrialization of the Soviet Union, to catch up with and surpass the advanced industrialized nations of the world. As Stalin boasted at one point:

> We are becoming a country of metal, a country of automobiles, a country of tractors. And when we have put the U.S.S.R. on an automobile, and the muzhik [peasant] on a tractor, let the esteemed capitalists who boast so loudly of their 'civilization,' try to overtake us! We shall see which countries may then be 'classified' as backward and which as advanced.

But the Five-Year Plans were not only aimed at a vast expansion of manufacturing, they sought to "industrialize" agriculture as well. Earlier, Soviet Communists had in mind mainly to push state farms. These would

**centrally planned and directed economy**—an idea associated with overall government planning and control over an economy. Probably, the best (or worst) examples of this were Stalin's Five-Year Plans. The idea is somewhat misleading, however, for it implies that anything less than an overall planned economy is unplanned.

be organized as if they were factories, using hired workers. The emphasis with the Five-Year Plans shifted somewhat toward collective farms, on which the farmers kept a share of the produce. The idea of organizing these as a factory, or making them factory-like with much greater use of machinery than before no doubt persisted. In any case, the idea was to replace individual farms with collective farms.

Stalin described the process of collectivization as he envisioned it. He said that if industry and agriculture were not both organized along collectivist lines there would be a rift between them. He said:

> And so in order to avoid the danger of a rift, we must begin thoroughly to re-equip agriculture on the basis of modern technique. But in order to re-equip it we must gradually amalgamate the scattered peasant farms into large farms, into collective farms; we must build up agriculture on the basis of collective labor, we must enlarge the collective farms, we must develop the old and new state farms, we must systematically employ the contract system on a mass scale in all the principal branches of agriculture, we must develop the system of machine and tractor stations which help the peasantry to assimilate the new technique and to collectivize labor—in a word, we must gradually transfer the small peasant farms to the basis of large-scale collective production.

Both agriculture and industry were to develop and operate according to a master plan that had been drawn in advance. The plan had been drawn up by a commission between 1926 and 1928. It consisted of three volumes with a total of 1600 printed pages. Later plans were not quite so long winded, but all of them proposed rapid development of industry and the introduction of collective practices in both agriculture and industry. The plan contained extensive details about how the whole economy should be developed. It specified where new factories should be built, how many workers each factory would employ, what costs of production should be, and what prices should be charged. The principles of organization and the goals were to remain unchanged, but specific details could be altered. For example, in construction and operation it might require more persons than were originally allotted to do the work on time. These were details that could be altered along the way. Collective farms were assigned what to plant and where, if not originally, in the course of time.

The fulfillment of the plans was pushed with great vigor. The goals appeared to be impossible to attain in the times allotted and with the materials available. For example, tens of thousands of engineers, technicians, and experts had to be trained or obtained somehow. Universities and technical schools had to be built or greatly expanded. Whole cities were to be brought into being in places where there were only villages, if even that. But the whole coercive power of the state was behind the effort, power backed by secret police who had no qualms about using it. Besides, there were many communists convinced and eager to prove what state planning could do. (That species of enthusiasm later disappeared from the Soviet Union, but it was no doubt there in the first decade or so.) These were often joined by foreigners, especially engineers, some of whom shared in the enthusiasm both for communism and central planning. But enthusiastic or not, large numbers of people took part in these vast building projects. Among them, though often out of sight of the others, were millions of political prisoners. There is no proof that they performed the work with

---

**Getting the Point...**

What are some of the basic differences between the organization of industry under free enterprise and industry that is collectivized?

enthusiasm, but they did do a lot of hard labor. At any rate, these massive construction projects laid a foundation, of sorts, for industrialization.

Collectivization of agriculture did not go well in the early years. There were many who held out and avoided as best they could collectivization. They were mostly independent farmers who had done well during the period of the New Economic Policy and did not wish to give up what they had acquired individually. The government identified them as Kulaks, a supposedly well off farmer, though in fact many of those so identified were small farmers and far from being wealthy. Rather than giving up what they had, many of them killed and ate or otherwise disposed of their animals. The government launched a brutal campaign against them in the early 1930s. Some of them were gunned down; others were driven from their farms, and millions starved. Ultimately, most of the remaining farmers were on some sort of collective farm by the late 1930s.

> **Collectivization of agriculture** did not go well in the early years. There were many who held out and avoided as best they could collectivization. They were mostly independent farmers who had done well during the period of the New Economic Policy and did not wish to give up what they had acquired individually. The government launched a brutal campaign against them in the early 1930s. Some of them were gunned down; others were driven from their farms, and millions starved. Ultimately, most of the remaining farmers were on some sort of collective farm by the late 1930s.

## 22.3 The Production of Goods

The production of goods that were wanted was an intractable problem for Soviet Communists, as well as communists in power elsewhere. It is an old socialist cliché that the **"problem of production** has been solved." Indeed, Karl Marx had written in the middle of the nineteenth century that the great problem was overproduction and mal-distribution of goods. Once in power, however, the Soviet Communists discovered that they were confronted with a very large problem of producing enough to supply the minimal needs of the population. Stalin's frantic Five-Year Plans entailed huge efforts to solve these problems along collectivist lines.

**problem of production**—see *definition*, p. 69.

The problem of production was and is inherent in the communist approach. First and foremost was centralized planning. The task of planning a whole economy is insurmountable. Imagine, if you will, trying to conceive of all the goods that will be wanted in advance, planning how, where, with what materials, what quantity and quality of goods may be wanted. No one person can begin to have the knowledge or foresight for the job. Nor can any committee, however large, do it much better. Complicated machines, such as an automobile or airplane, have hundreds and thousands of parts. The late Leonard Read's observation is very much in order here. He said that no one knows how to make a pencil, which to all appearances is the simplest of devices. Yet its making is a cooperative undertaking utilizing the skills, abilities, and knowledge of many persons. Granted, a central planner does not have to know all these skills, but he has to know what is involved so as to provide for everything. The Soviet Union was plagued throughout its seventy-year history with shortages, with some goods simply not being generally available, or, if so at all, very infrequently. The problem is illustrated in this Russian joke related by John Gunther:

> One Russian tells another that the Soviet authorities have perfected an intricate atomic bomb that will fit into a suitcase, and that this will one day be delivered to a target like New York. The second Russian replies, "Impossible. Where would anybody get a suitcase?"

A true story may illustrate the point even better. For some reason, or unreason, replacement windshield wipers were very nearly impossible to find, so that those fortunate enough to have a car would take their windshield wipers inside with them at night to prevent their being stolen.

The problem of centralized planning may be best understood in terms of its solution. In a relatively free economy, such as that of the United States, hundreds of thousands, indeed millions, of people deal with decisions about producing different goods, while under centralized planning only a few people attempt to deal with it. In a free society, market prices serve as signals to people. As each person seeks to personally gain from his efforts he responds to those prices in order to make a profit. If windshield wipers were in short supply in the United States, the rising price would signal the fact, and producers would come forth to produce and offer them for sale. Shortages offer an opportunity in a free economy; they were a constant problem in the Soviet economy.

> **The problem of centralized planning** may be best understood in terms of its solution. In a relatively free economy, such as that of the United States, hundreds of thousands, indeed millions, of people deal with decisions about producing different goods, while under centralized planning only a few people attempt to deal with it. In a free society, market prices serve as signals to people. As each person seeks to personally gain from his efforts he responds to those prices in order to make a profit.

**command economy**—an economy centrally planned and controlled by the government.

The Soviet Union had what economists call a "**command economy**." A command economy is one in which the government commands the production of goods, determines what will be paid to producers for them, and for what price they will sell to consumers. A command economy is based upon the use of force to greater or lesser extent in getting goods produced. Force is not very effective in production. Production requires constructive effort, quite often the best effort an individual can give. Force can be used quite effectively either destructively or to prevent destruction. In the delicate operations and decisions of production, force tends to interfere with rather than advance production. That is especially so when the force is exerted by remote central planners.

**bureaucracy**—a system of government agencies assigned with the tasks of putting into action and enforcing the various mandates of legislation.

When government undertakes to plan and direct an economy it necessarily bureaucratizes production. That is how governments operate in everything they control. They proceed to impose extensive rules and set up procedures. **Bureaucracies** are notoriously slow to act, timid, and unproductive. An innovative bureaucrat is a contradiction in terms. The great virtue for the bureaucrat is to follow to the letter procedures and specifications. This becomes even more imperative when he is a bureaucrat in a totalitarian dictatorship, for in this case he may not only lose his job by failing to do exactly what he is supposed to do but also his liberty and even possibly his life. These are hardly prime conditions for those who are trying to direct the production of goods. In a free market, the main business is to get the job done in whatever way it requires, without slavishly following some procedures from on high. Corporate procedures are often bureaucratic as well, especially in large businesses, but they are nothing to compare with government planning, where one may be charged with a crime for some failure to comply.

Two examples may help to show how these things interfere with production. A Soviet inspector told this story:

> As inspector I once arrived at a plant which was supposed to have delivered mining machines, but did not do it. When I entered the plant premises, I saw that the machines were piled up all over the place, but they were all unfinished. I asked what was going on. The director gave evasive answers. Finally, when the big crowd surrounding us had disappeared, he called me to his office.

There, the story came out. It seems that the specifications called for red oil-resistant varnish. But the only red varnish that he had was not oil-resistant. He had green oil-resistant varnish, but was afraid that if he used this in violation of instructions he would get eight years in prison. The inspector knew the machines were badly needed, was certain that whether they were painted red or green could make little difference, if any, but he too feared a prison sentence should he authorize a change. He did cable the ministry hoping for a quick decision in favor of using the green varnish:

> But it took unusually long. Apparently they did not want to take any chances at the ministry either, and they wanted to cover themselves. Finally, I received permission. I put this cablegram from the ministry in my pocket and kept it . . . , and signed the note allowing the use of the green paint. . . .

Victor Kravchenko, who later left Russia and wrote a book entitled *I Chose Freedom*, describes here in more general terms the bureaucratic problems he encountered in a large construction project:

> Under our Soviet system every step required formal decisions by endless bureaus, each of them jealous of its rights and in mortal dread of taking initiative. Repeatedly petty difficulties tied us into knots which no one dared untie without instructions from Moscow. We lived and labored in a jungle of questionnaires, paper forms and reports in seven copies.

It was not that Soviet authorities were not aware of the need for positive incentives to worker productivity. Over the years they introduced a variety of incentives in their programs. Soviet Communists were reluctant to introduce individual incentive in their economy or those that smacked of what they called "capitalism." They tried to use collective incentives instead. Early on, they tried what they called collective competition, to pit the output of one factory in an industry against that of another. No amount of such cheerleading, so to speak, ever achieved much in this undertaking. They then began to introduce differentiation in wages based on productivity and turned to payment for piecework rather than for hours of work. These things undoubtedly had some effect on production, and they also succeeded into turning factories into "sweat shops," as communists and labourites had called them under "capitalism." Toward the end, there was much talk about organizing in such a way as to get more local responsibility in production. The basic problem, of course, was communism itself, the confinements of which do not allow for effective production.

All this is a way of saying that the Soviet Union was, as noted earlier, plagued with shortages throughout its history and this eventually brought the whole economy down. The point can well be reiterated. The inevitable shortages arising in communism are well illustrated by Leopold Tyrmand (in *The Rosa Luxemburg Contraceptive Cooperative*). Tyrmand was a Pole who lived under communist rule until he migrated to the United States, where he denounced it, often with biting humor. Tyrmand said:

> The line is just as much a symbol of communism as the hammer and sickle. But unlike the hammer and sickle, it, is also its most inherent characteristic, defining human existence within it. Under communism men spend their lives on line. We can analyze the tragicality of the line by taking the example of ham. Someone—let's say the Communist Everyman—is wandering through a food store one day when he sees that ham is being sold at one of the counters—lovely ham, lean and pink, the kind of ham people in Communist countries dream of at nights. Everyman sighs deeply, for he knows that such a ham implies a line, which will mean a long wait. But the ham smells, calls, tempts, beckons. Everyman's family has not known the taste of ham for many weeks, perhaps months.... Thus Everyman gets on line and slowly, very slowly moved forward....

Usually, he would have been concerned lest the ham run out before he was served, but as Everyman drew closer he began to hope that it would. There was another ham not yet touched beside it, and the quality of the one being cut up was worse as it got nearer the bone. But alas, Everyman got no ham. When the other one was used up, the clerk refused to cut the new one, saying it must be saved for tomorrow. Darkly, Everyman suspected the clerk of wanting to keep it to get some choice slices for herself, other store personnel, her boss, and perhaps to sell on the black market. Tyrmand's example was imaginary, but the actuality of life under communism to which it points has been all too real to whole populations.

As the above example points up, farm products as well as manufactured products were in short supply over the years in the Soviet Union. Most of this can be attributed directly to the communist collectivizing efforts. Before the Bolshevik Revolution, Russia had long been an exporting region for farm products, especially of grain. After the government takeover of most of the land, it had to import grain. The situation would have been much worse had not the government allowed farmers to keep small plots on which they grew and sold goods in the market. A number of years ago, Eugene Lyons described the difference between the produce of these tiny plots and that on the giant farms this way:

> According to the government's own figures..., private plots with a mere 3 percent of the nation's sown land account for 30 percent of the gross harvest, other than grains; 40 percent of all cattle-breeding; 60 percent of

the country's potato crops; 40 percent of all vegetables and milk; 68 percent of all meat products. Their fruit yields ... are double those of state orchards for equivalent areas, its potato harvest per hectare two-thirds higher than on collective farms. Even in grain, which is a very minor element in the private sector, it produces one-third more per sown unit than an average socialized farm.

## 22.4 The Distribution of Goods

The major distribution, or redistribution, occurred with the onset of the Revolution and was completed during the early years of Stalin. Virtually all land, and with it all real property, came under the control, in effect the ownership, of the state (i.e., the government). Virtually all capital, i.e., the instruments of production, was confiscated and thereafter was owned by the government. This involved not only what was ordinarily thought of as private property but also institutional property, such as churches, seminaries, and colleges. There were no private schools, colleges, or churches. In fact, there were no private banks, insurance companies, publishers or printers, importers or exporters, television or radio stations, department stores, or what have you. In sum, two of the three means of production—land and capital—were taken over lock, stock, and barrel by the state. In like manner, the power over distribution was taken over entirely by the state, a point that requires some elaboration.

What that meant was that persons in their private capacity as individual owners no longer received or collected rents. Rents were collected by government whether they were rents on houses, land, apartments, or machines. These rents were not determined in the market. Neither land nor dwellings nor equipment was rented to the highest bidder. All these were assigned by government, and such rents as applied were paid to government. Nor did individuals in their private capacity draw dividends on investments, since technically they did not make investments. There was neither a stock market nor stock exchange in the Soviet Union. In sum, there was no distribution even to take into account in the Soviet Union of two of the three means of production.

In theory, then, all the distribution of goods and services would be to labor. In fact, that gives a wrong impression of the situation. Granted, there was some distribution to labor, but even that was not a market distribution. There was only one employer in the Soviet Union—the state. People had no choice for whom they worked, or even whether they worked or not, though people frequently joked that they pretended to work even as the authorities pretended to pay them. Just the same, all decisions belonged to the monolithic state. Nor was there necessarily much choice as to what a person did for a living for most people. Work, too, was more or less assigned. Payment consisted of what the state paid and what prerequisites went with the job. Those reckoned to be more important by the state undoubtedly were paid better, had the choicest apartments, and were permitted to shop in special exclusive stores.

In sum, the state distributed the wealth in the Soviet Union. That is something quite different from market distribution. So far as labor is concerned, there were no independent labor unions in the Soviet Union. Communists have often been prime movers in the organization and control over labor unions in countries not under Communist Party rule. But once they take over the government, the unions lose their independence.

They become instruments of the state. There are all sorts of organizations in the Soviet Union, but they are instruments of the Party, which is to say the state, not independently of their members.

At any rate, the state allocated or distributed the wealth in the Soviet Union according to the priorities of the rulers. Consumers were never even near the top in priority under communism. Capital expenditures had a high priority in the former Soviet Union. Indeed, as noted earlier, far from being laborist, it would be much more accurate to describe the government as corporatist, albeit state corporatism. Military expenditures were a top priority. In fact, the most impressive achievements made were in that field. The quality of the military output was, so far as can be told, vastly superior to the consumer goods that were produced. They were even able to export some of their military equipment to other countries. On the other hand, there was hardly a country in the world so poor that its people would have wanted to buy the consumer goods they produced, even if they had a surplus to sell.

Other priorities of the Soviets included the building of showplaces that were shown to visitors. These were apt to get the best equipment and materials available in the Soviet Union. The consumer goods were much more readily available in and around such great cities as Moscow and Leningrad, much scarcer in out of the way places. (These cities were, after all, places where the rulers and foreign visitors were likely to go.) Hedrick Smith, in his book on *The Russians*, quoted a description by a Russian on this difference:

> On the stronger, larger state farms not far from Moscow or Leningrad, or those built for show..., conditions are better in every way—stone buildings, separate apartments for each working family, a sewage system, running water. This was the way it was on the first two state farms where I worked. They were each about an hour from Leningrad. But the third state farm was further out—about two hours. It was a weak farm. Wooden buildings. It lacked all conveniences. No central heating system. No sewage system. No running water. The greatest problem on all three was the lack of meat. There was almost none. As far as other food goes, the closer to Leningrad the more the stores were selling. That was the rule. Apples you could get. But oranges, tangerines—only in Leningrad.

Communists had supposed before they came to power that they could dispense with money entirely. In power, however, they found it invaluable as a means of distributing goods. Thus, most goods and services were sold in the Soviet Union. Money was used in the allocation of consumer goods, at least. It was very much a truncated market, however. Both in quantity and quality consumer goods were limited. Nor were they produced in any order having to do with the demand as reflected in the money. The money served only as a minimal reward for labor generally and a partial means of allocating the goods that were always in short supply. The unavailability of goods was even more pressing than the short supply of money.

Since government basically distributed the goods and the supply of quality goods was quite limited, those classes favored by government got the best and the most. Communism was supposed to usher in the classless society, but in the Soviet Union a whole new class system emerged. They ranged all the way from the slightly favored to the pampered, so to speak.

Among the slightly favored, the largest category historically was the industrial worker. Of much more significance were Communist Party members, for in theory all power was concentrated there. Beyond the members were party leaders, ranging all the way to Party Secretary, who sometimes ruled the Soviet Union. The secret police, the **KGB**, were favored with special powers and privileges, as were, in even greater degree, those at the very pinnacle of power. There were special stores to which those belonging to a particular class alone were admitted. These were stocked with goods not available to the general public. Loyalty to the Party, to the regime, was rewarded with perks.

In general, the economic performance of the Soviet Union, as reflected in the lot of most people, was especially poor. This fact might seem astonishing since communism is based upon materialism, upon the supremacy of matter, and does not accord reality to the metaphysical or spiritual realms. It might be supposed then that by focusing upon the material, of which the economic is a major part, they would have been highly successful. Yet, we are reminded on very high authority that this is not the order for accomplishment, even in the realm of things. Jesus said (Matthew 6:31–33):

> **KGB**—the name under which the secret police in the Soviet Union operated.

---

**Goods Distributed Based on Political Connections**
Since government basically distributed the goods and the supply of quality goods was quite limited, those classes favored by government got the best and the most. Communism was supposed to usher in the classless society, but in the Soviet Union a whole new class system emerged. There were special stores to which those belonging to a particular class alone were admitted. These were stocked with goods not available to the general public. Loyalty to the Party, to the regime, was rewarded with perks.

---

> Therefore do not be anxious, saying, "What shall we eat?" or "What shall we drink?" or "What shall we wear?" For the Gentiles seek after all these things, and your heavenly Father knows that you need them all. But seek first the kingdom of God and his righteousness and all these things will be added to you.

It seems somehow appropriate that those who deny the realm of the spiritual and of God, believing in and seeking material things above all, should be denied these as well.

*Mr. Gorbachev, tear down this wall!*

**Ronald Reagan**


*Communist regimes were not some unfortunate aberration, some historical deviation from a socialist ideal. They were the ultimate expression, unconstrained by democratic and electoral pressures, of what socialism is all about. . . . In short, the state [is] everything and the individual nothing.*

**Margaret Thatcher**


*How do you tell a communist? Well, it's someone who reads Marx and Lenin. And how do you tell an anti-Communist? It's someone who understands Marx and Lenin.*

**Ronald Reagan**


*Freedom is never more than one generation away from extinction.*

**Ronald Reagan**

# Study Guide for:

# 22 Communism

## Chapter Summary

Communism is the logical end of all socialism and of all human effort to bring heaven on earth. The heart of communism is the elimination of private property and the market. In a word, communism is anti-economic. It emerges from philosophical materialism, which presumes that reality is entirely made up of matter and rejects the view that man has a threefold nature: spirit, mind, and matter. As a result, power resides in the hands of those who control matter. Karl Marx, who has been credited with founding modern communism, was himself anti-market, anti-political, anti-social, and anti-religious.

For Marx and his followers the overthrow of the political system is the aim. Marx naively believed that out of the ashes of such a revolution, utopia would arise. Unfortunately, having denied the spiritual nature of mankind, hence the validity of religion, the reality is that there is nothing left to restrain the base inclinations of man in practice. As a result, in practice communism is a living hell rather than a fruitful paradise. Totalitarian rulers who are able to gain political control exercise their control over people ruthlessly and have proven that they are quite willing to kill anyone who might object.

The Russian experience and the other communist experiments of the last century illustrate this reality well. In addition to the oppressive control exercised by the rulers, communism is also plagued by inadequate production, which arises from central planning. Without price signals from the market to allocate resources and serve to coordinate resource flows from production of one type to another, communist nations are forever in a maze. Ultimately the dictates of the ruling tyrant direct all productive efforts such as they are. As a result, communism tends toward state corporatism.

## Points of Emphasis

1. Communism is the logical end of socialism.

2. Communism is based on philosophical materialism and denies the spiritual nature of man.

3. Though socialists visualize paradise as the outgrowth of communism, the practical result is invariably an oppressive hell where the force of government is used by tyrants in a heavy handed fashion upon the populace of the nation.

## Identification

1. dialectical materialism
2. economic determinism
3. bourgeoisie
4. proletariat
5. historical inevitability
6. totalitarian
7. Vladimir I. Lenin
8. Bolshevik Revolution
9. Joseph Stalin
10. centrally planned and directed economy
11. problem of production
12. command economy
13. bureaucracy
14. KGB

## Review Questions

1. Why is the denial of the spiritual nature of man fundamental to socialism?

2. Why does central economic planning result in economic chaos whereas shortages are short lived in the absence of government planning?

3. What is the difference between "state farms" and "collective farms"?

4. Why were workers less motivated to take initiative in their work under socialism than under free enterprise?

5. Was the former Soviet Union able to export any products? Explain.

## Activity

1. Prepare a case either to support or oppose the following position: "The test of virtue is the sincerity with which the individual holds his beliefs and acts upon them."

## For Further Study

1. Leonard Read, "I Pencil", https://fee.org/resources/i-pencil/.

# Glossary

## A

**abstractions**—an attempt to model or simplify some real world phenomenon to a general quality or characteristic, apart from concrete realities, specific objects, or actual instances in order to promote a better understanding.   p. 8

**advertising**—promoting a product or service to the public.   p. 176

**anarchists**—people who believe that there is no need for government.   p. 6

**apprentice**—a workman who is learning a trade, such as carpentry or plumbing. In feudal times, apprentices often were required to work under a master for seven years before they could hire out to others in practicing their trade.   p. 268

**assets**—what someone owns.   p. 91

**auction**—type of trade where would-be buyers bid on items and the sale goes to the highest bidder.   p. 77

## B

**balance of trade**—a concept developed in connection with mercantilism, in which nations sought to have a favorable balance of trade. This meant to them that the nation in the favored position was one that exported more goods than it imported. An unfavorable balance of trade, then, was for a nation to import more than it exported.   p. 275

**bank of issue**—bank that issues bank notes intended to serve as a currency. By law in the United States today Federal Reserve banks are the only banks of issue, but in earlier times banks generally issued such bank notes, especially in the first half of the nineteenth century.   p. 101

**barter**—direct trade with someone else where goods are traded for other goods.   p. 79

**bear market**—the situation where the prices of common stock are generally falling.   p. 213

**bill of exchange**—paper on which the buyer of something of value promises to pay a certain sum of money either on demand or on some specified maturity date.   p. 100

**bimetallic**—system where both gold and silver are used as money in trade.   p. 94

**black market**—when economic goods are bought and sold in illegal markets.   p. 159

**Bolshevik Revolution**—communist revolution launched by the Bolsheviks in Russia in 1917.   p. 350

**Bolsheviks**—followers of Marx who launched a communist revolution in Russia in 1917.   p. 326

**boom–bust cycle**—cycle started by government interference in the money supply that continues as long as government continues its interference.   p. 121

**bourgeoisie**—a French word that means, literally, townsmen or burgers. The word has come to be used to refer to members of the middle class. In Europe, that means the class between the aristocrats at the top and the peasants or proletariat at the bottom. Marx used the term specifically to refer to the capitalistic class, i.e., those who owned the instruments of production.   p. 310

**bullionism**—a system in which the government focuses upon getting and keeping precious metals within the realm. Thus, the government may attempt to get a favorable balance of trade in order to collect the difference in precious metals while it prohibits the export of gold. Thereby, the nation heaps up unto itself gold and silver, so to speak.   p. 275

**bullionist**—someone who believed that increasing one's personal holdings of gold and silver money necessarily made one wealthy.   p. 146

**bull market**—the situation where the prices of common stock are generally rising.   p. 213

**bureaucracy**—a system of government agencies assigned with the tasks of putting into action and enforcing the various mandates of legislation.   p. 354

**busybody**—someone who mettles in the private affairs of another person.   p. 291

## C

**capital**—most broadly defined as wealth used in the production of further wealth. Equally broadly, capital is sometimes identified with money invested in productive enterprises. More narrowly, when capital is considered as one of the three means of production, it refers to tools, equipment, or technology used in production.   p. 66

**capitalism**—an imprecise word coined by Karl Marx aimed at deriding the free market as a system of exploitation. Many mistakenly use the term interchangeably with free enterprise.   p. 310

**cartel**—an association of manufacturers or suppliers with the purpose of maintaining prices at a high level and restricting competition.   p. 172

**centrally planned and directed economy**—an idea associated with overall government planning and control over an economy. Probably, the best (or worst) examples of this were Stalin's Five-Year Plans. The idea is somewhat misleading, however, for it implies that anything less than an overall planned economy is unplanned.   p. 351

**certification**—occurs when government recognizes the expertise of an individual by issuing a certificate, but does not restrict the practice to only those holding a certificate.   p. 168

***ceteris paribus***—this Latin term will be used often in this book. It simply means that while examining the effects of one factor of an issue holding that all other factors are held equal or constant.   p. 133

**charity**—the voluntary act of giving to someone without expecting anything in return.   p. 74

**Clayton Antitrust Act**—antitrust legislation that provided special legal privileges to labor unions.   p. 141

**clipped coins**—coins that have had some portion shaved off in order to make more coins with the scraps. Many coins have ridged edges to make it more difficult to hide clipping.   p. 108

**coins**—originally instituted as certain weights of precious metals. Today's coinage is made mostly of base metals and are thus cheap imitations with no inherent value other than what the issuing government declares.   p. 94

**collective bargaining**—when an employer bargains on working conditions and wages with a labor union that represents a group of its employees.   p. 153

**collectivists**—people who believe the individual should always be forced to submit to the will of the group for the so called common good.   p. 332

**collusion**—when multiple firms come together and decide to manipulate their prices in the market.   p. 171

**command economy**—an economy centrally planned and controlled by the government.   p. 354

**commercial bank**—bank that takes deposits, cashes checks, and makes loans.   p. 102

**commercial banking**—a system of financial institutions that accept deposits and process checks.   p. 118

**commodity**—an economic good.   p. 88

**common law**—the law that the King's courts began to develop in the twelfth century—a law common to all England. It replaced many local customs that frequently had the force of law and tended to bring all those in England under the same legal rules.   p. 209

**common ownership**—true ownership of property would mean that you have the right to determine how it is used or consumed. Ownership of anything cannot be completely common. Common property is generally a public place such as a park—it is open to the public and for the public to use, but the public does not have the right to use it in any way they want. Somebody (typically a government body) oversees the place and makes rules about how it may be used..   p. 50

**common stock**—shares in the ownership, control, and residue of the profits of a corporation. The liability of such owners is generally limited to the amount of their investment.   p. 210

**comparative advantage**—advantage that exists when someone has a lower opportunity cost of production than someone else.   p. 81

**competition**—occurs when there are two or more sellers or buyers of similar goods or services in a market. Substitutes should also be taken into account when deciding whether competition exists in a market or not. It is well, too, to keep in mind that so long as anyone who wishes may offer the good or service, and so long as there are no prohibitions against offering the goods, the market is at least open to competition.   p. 139

**compound interest**—when some principal amount of money is deposited in a financial account at interest and left there over many years, the interest earned in the first year will itself earn interest in future years, thus compounding annually.   p. 93

**Conservative Party**—political party of Great Britain that is generally opposed to socialist efforts.   p. 338

**consumer economics**—attempting to approach economics from the mistaken view that abundance has replaced scarcity. The problem is viewed as one of getting consumers to spend, to expand credit to spur on consumer spending, and to consume more and more so that businesses can prosper and more jobs can be created to put people to work.   p. 68

**consumers**—those who purchase goods and services in the market economy.   p. 293

**contracts**—legal agreements, whether written, spoken, or implied, between two or more people to do something.   p. 25

**corporate drag**—large businesses develop rules and regulations to govern those acting in it. These typically become bureaucratic and tend to impede entrepreneurial human action.   p. 211

**corporate income tax**—tax imposed on taxable income earned by corporations. The definition of taxable income is arbitrarily defined and it is usually subject to progressive taxation.   p. 32

**corporatism**—the advancement of the special interests of some by governmental means.   p. 311

**counterfeit**—creating fake money with the intention of passing it off as real.   p. 94

**craft guilds**—a guild organized around a specific craft or product.   p. 269

**credit expansion**—the increasing of the money supply by increasing credit. Most of monetary inflation occurs by expanding credit, not by increasing the currency, though both may be going on at the same time. Both fractional reserve banks and the Federal Reserve can expand credit.   p. 121

**crony capitalism**—the ongoing result of evolutionary socialism whereby political privileges are bestowed on a few while restricting people generally.   p. 310

**currency**—that which circulates as money in a country usually consisting of paper bills and base metals. But it can be said that any medium of exchange is currency, whatever it happens to be.   p. 88

**cutthroat competition**—competition that is excessive or mean spirited in nature. It is difficult to distinguish between "cutthroat competition" and regular competition.   p. 164

# D

**debasing the currency**—reducing the worth or value of the currency. When currency consisted primarily of coins made from precious metals, the coins were literally debased when they were melted down and recast with an addition of base metals. Also, when cupronickel coins were substituted for those with silver content, they were literally debased. Today, the currency is often figuratively debased by increasing the amount of paper money and by credit expansions.   p. 124

**debt money**—money issued on the basis of debt. There are two basic types. One promises to pay in an actual commodity on demand. The other has no inherent value, but can be traded for something of value. Federal Reserve notes in the United States today are the second type.   p. 98

**deductive reasoning**—discovering truth by reasoning from established facts to reach inevitable conclusions. This type of reasoning is used in geometry proofs.　p. 14

**demand**—the relationship of prices and the various quantities that people would desire to purchase in the market per unit of time, *ceteris paribus*.　p. 134

**deregulation**—the act of removing the controls government has previously put into effect restraining businesses.　p. 178

**dialectical materialism**—a Marxist term denoting the process by which change has occurred in the course of history. Dialectic refers to a contest, conflict, discussion or argument. Materialism is a belief in the primacy of matter. Marx used it to describe the conflict of classes over control of the means of production of material goods.　p. 348

**direct exchange**—occurs when goods are traded for other goods.　p. 79

**discount rate**—interest rate that the Federal Reserve charges to lend money to a bank that it needs to meet their reserve requirements when they for any reason fail to do so.　p. 119

**distribution of wealth**—the result of economic action in determining who gets what. It also answers the questions of when and why he receives it.　p. 226

**division of labor**—the dividing up of the tasks of producing goods among those who operate most efficiently. It involves specialization, cooperation, and, in the broadest sense, widespread trade.　p. 80

**doctrine of limits**—because all humans are fallible, all the organizations, institutions, and structures that we create will also be flawed.　p. 6

**domestic**—situated inside one's own country.　p. 243

**Dominion Mandate**—as recorded in Genesis 1:28, after God created Adam and Eve and placed them in the Garden of Eden, he commanded them and their descendants to take dominion of the whole earth.　p. 4

**Dow Jones Industrial Average**—a market measure of the prices of thirty of the largest corporations.　p. 211

**due diligence**—the practice of engaging in the thorough, prudent investigation of a matter before making a decision to act in a certain way.　p. 314

# E

**economic determinism**—the doctrine that people's beliefs and practices are determined by the economic class or position in which they find themselves. Karl Marx formulated the most uncompromising position of economic determinism, but, in a less rigorous sense, modern intellectuals, indeed, most of us, have been greatly influenced by this notion.　p. 348

**economic freedom**—being at liberty to produce and trade goods and services on mutually agreeable terms.　p. 291

**economic goods**—those things that are wanted that are scarce. *See a more detailed definition of goods*, p. 4.　p. 66

**economicism**—an ideology or economic theory that makes economics the centerpiece in thought and gives it priority over moral, ethical, or other philosophical or religious considerations in the making of decisions.　p. 242

**economic principles**—God's built-in features of well-functioning human interaction in the material world.　p. 4

**economics**—the systematic study of the effective production of those goods that are most wanted with the least use of the scarce resources available.　p. 4

**economic system**—the political structure under which an economy exists. Examples include: communism, feudalism, capitalism, etc.　p. 64

**economy of scale**—refers to the reduced cost of production for each additional unit produced. In the broadest terms, it refers to the economy of producing larger rather than smaller amounts of something.　p. 220

**elasticity**—the responsiveness of buyers and sellers to price changes.　p. 137

**eminent domain**—provision in the United States Constitution for government to take private property for public use, provided the owner is awarded just compensation.　p. 165

**enlightened self-interest**—reason teaches us that it is in our highest self-interest to behave in accordance with the objective moral boundaries established by God. As enlightened self-interest gains sway in someone's life he becomes more self-controlled.　p. 24

**entitlement programs**—also called entitlements. Once government welfare programs are established, all people who qualify for benefits are said to be entitled to them as a matter of right.　p. 342

**entrepreneur**—an individual who undertakes to organize the production of a particular good at his own personal risk of economic loss.　p. 206

**equilibrium price**—the price of an economic good such that the amount of it that consumers desire to buy in a time period is equal to what sellers wish to sell.　p. 130

**equilibrium price theory**—modern day price theory attempts to enact utilitarianism by way of cost/benefit studies. The problem is that costs and benefits are always subjective and based on assumptions.　p. 46

**escheat**—the reversion of property to the state. This usually occurs when there are no surviving heirs or none who lay claim to an estate.　p. 303

**estates (feudal)**—the three classes of people in feudal times, which included the nobility, the clergy, and the serfs.　p. 262

**European Common Market**—the European Union was formed to allow for the smooth, less hindered trade of goods among the European nations that have joined it and this is their trade agreement.　p. 252

**evolutionary ideas**—view that everything is always undergoing change. Some changes take longer than others, but everything changes. These ideas undercut any fixed principles or absolutes because those principles would also be subject to change.　p. 12

**evolutionary socialism**—a political movement whereby socialism is imposed gradually upon a nation by implementing new rules and regulations legislatively.　p. 310

**excise tax**—a tax levied on specific items. Some of these are referred to as "sin taxes." This tax is often designed to limit the consumption of these products, as well as collect revenue from "sinners" who use them.　p. 31

# F

**Fabianism**—an ideology for a gradual movement toward socialism within a country. The Fabian Society was organized in England in the late nineteenth century. It aimed to establish socialism in that country without any radical change in the political system. In contrast to the Marxists, Fabians sought to attain socialism peacefully rather than through revolution.   p. 333

**factory system**—a process of production where goods are produced in a large volume in a factory thus consolidating the use of labor.   p. 214

**Fair Labor Standards Act**—federal law aimed at controlling and restricting voluntary exchange in labor markets.   p. 155

**fair (medieval)**—an event organized by merchants to draw people together to promote merchant trade.   p. 267

**fallacy of composition**—believing that what is good for the individual, or one particular case, is always good for everyone, or all cases generally. This is logically inconsistent. It may or may not be true.   p. 147

**farm problem**—farmers work in a highly competitive industry that keeps profit margins low. As a result, it is difficult to succeed in the farming business.   p. 320

**fealty**—the obligation of a vassal to be faithful—maintain fidelity—to his lord. Most often this required military service.   p. 262

**Federal Reserve Act**—law passed in 1913 to set up the Federal Reserve System.   p. 119

**Federal Reserve System**—system of banks put into place in order to create a flexible money supply. This system can increase or decrease the money supply as they see fit.   p. 116

**fee simple**—a term that arose from English Common Law where the lands belong to the owner and his heirs absolutely, without any end or limit put to his estate. Land held in fee simple can be conveyed to whomsoever its owner pleases; it can also be mortgaged or put up as security.   p. 56

**feud**—a dispute as to who holds the rightful claim to a parcel of land, which was usually settled by force.   p. 263

**feudal system (feudalism)**—a system of political and economic control that prevailed for much of the Middle Ages in Europe. Economic control of the land was linked to political control over the people and vested in the feudal nobility, who were primarily warriors.   p. 262

**fiat money**—money that has no commodity backing it, and only has value because a government entity has declared it so.   p. 98

**fiduciary**—individual who has been placed in a position of trust to manage money or property. A fiduciary is permitted to treat people's money in many respects as their own. However, they must still be able to meet any demands the original owner might make to withdraw the money or else be subject to bankruptcy.   p. 102

**first rule of taxation**—as much as possible taxes should be justly levied, that people should pay an amount of tax that equals the benefits received.   p. 29

**fixed costs**—costs that precede the performing of the service. Example: purchasing a building.   p. 173

**foreign**—situated outside one's own country.   p. 243

**fractional reserve banking**—a system in which banks keep only a small portion—a fraction—of deposits on hand to meet the demands of the depositors. The system is vulnerable before the depositors, because if large numbers, or most of them, demand their money, the bank cannot do what it promised.   p. 101

**fractional reserves**—the fraction of deposits that a bank keeps on deposit and does not loan out. See *definition of fractional reserve banking,*  p. 101.   p. 314

**free enterprise**—*see* economic freedom,   p. 291

**frugality**—being thrifty.   p. 64

# G

**going price**—that range of prices at which sellers can dispose of most of their goods and at which buyers with some intensity of demand for the good can be satisfied.   p. 132

**good (n.)**—a commodity or service that can be utilized to satisfy human wants and that has exchange value; in other words, the means that we use to achieve our ends.   p. 4

There are four necessary conditions for something to be considered an economic good:   p. 4

- the existence of a human desire   p. 4
- the commodity or service must be useful to the satisfaction of that desire   p. 4
- the causal connection (that it is useful to satisfy a desire) must be known   p. 4
- humans must have command over the commodity or service to direct it to productive use.   p. 4

Example: crude oil was not always thought of as a good, but was once thought of as merely a pollutant.   p. 4

**government bonds**—a debt security issued by a government to pay for its expenses. It is sold with a guarantee of interest to be paid when redeemed.   p. 117

**government intervention to control prices**—legal mandates by government to set prices. See *price fixing,* p. 130.   p. 146

**graduated income tax**—a progressive income tax imposed upon an individual's earned income such that the more taxable income that is made the greater the proportion of it is taken as tax.   p. 32

**Great Khan**—ruler in China who was first recorded as using paper money, and required its acceptance by threat of death.   p. 98

**Greco-Roman tradition**—Western Civilization draws its roots from Greece and Rome. Specifically, Greek and Roman philosophers used reason and observation to find universal principles, from which, they attempted to build their philosophy.   p. 6

# H

**head tax**—uniform tax where amount due is determined by the number of people in a household. It might have a different rate for adults than for dependents.   p. 29

**hedonistic calculus**—the idea that any law or government program should be evaluated by adding up all the pleasure it would create and subtracting out any pain it might cause. If the sum is positive, proponents argue that the law or program is good.   p. 45

**historical inevitability**—the view that future historical developments will inevitably—unavoidably—unfold. This doctrine was propounded by Marx. What is supposed to be particularly

**historical inevitability**—the view that future historical developments will inevitably—unavoidably—unfold. This doctrine was propounded by Marx. What is supposed to be particularly inevitable is the eventual communist revolution in every country in the world.   p. 349

**homage**—a ceremony in which a vassal pledged his loyalty and service to his overlord. It might also involve some symbolic transfer to him of his fief or feudal estate.   p. 262

**homestead exemption**—a reduction in property tax rate due for the primary residence of the household.   p. 31

**human action**—people are created with a mind to know. In addition, all people possess a body and can act. Thus, human action is the purposeful pursuit of a defined end by using the ordinary means at hand.   p. 18

**human nature**—the traits that all humans have in common, especially those that separate them from the other animals.   p. 15

# I

**indirect exchange**—occurs when the exchange is made through some kind of medium (money).   p. 79

**inductive reasoning**—discovering truth by hypothesis and experimentation using the scientific method. This type of reasoning is used in the hard sciences.   p. 14

**inflation**—has historically meant an increase of the money supply. However, for the past 50 years there has been a politically inspired effort to have inflation mean the general rise in prices that follows upon a monetary inflation. This change in terminology helps to obscure the cause of the rise of prices.   p. 108

**inheritance**—the gift of one's property to one's heirs.   p. 237

**intangible property**—property that is not tangible—touchable or reachable by the sense of touch—but is usually represented by paper only, such as a share in a corporation (no particular piece of property involved) or the good will of a business.   p. 30

**interest**—usually expressed as a percentage, it is a fee paid for use of someone else's money for a time period.   p. 121

**International Monetary Fund (IMF)**—an international organization created in the Bretton Woods treaty to provide for currency exchange in a world of fiat money.   p. 248

**invisible hand theory**—Adam Smith's theory that there is a natural harmony between the self-interest of the individual seeking his own gain and the general well-being of societies. By pursuing his own advantage in his production, he produces the most of what he can that is most wanted by others. In doing so he increases not only his own supply but that available to others as well.   p. 17

# J

**journeyman**—a person who has completed his apprenticeship in some trade. At that point, he can work for hire, usually under a master craftsman.   p. 268

**Judeo-Christian tradition**—tradition pertaining to Jewish and Christian heritage. Specifically, that all humans are fallen, guilty of sin, and desperately in need of a Savior.   p. 6

**justice**—giving every person his due. In economic terms, justice is concerned that each person gets what he has earned or has by right.   p. 26

**just price**—the concept of the pricing of something such that justice is served.   p. 130

# K

**KGB**—the name under which the secret police in the Soviet Union operated.   p. 359

# L

**labor**—the work that goes into production. This includes manual labor, but also includes the application of your time, energy, and talents in any way.   p. 65

**labor (as property**—all people possess themselves and are aware of themselves. Since a person achieves his desired ends through human action, his efforts or labor is his very first and most valuable property. Labor will be discussed and defined more specifically in the next chapter. *See definition*, p. 65.   p. 51

**labor intensive**—an undertaking that uses labor much more than land or capital in producing a good or service. For example, the writing of a book is by its nature labor intensive. By contrast, the transport of coal by railroad is capital intensive. The growing of cattle is land intensive.   p. 193

**laborism**—an established preference for labor over land and capital. The preference must be supported by government policy to prevail. Marx provided an ideology in support of laborism, but communist practice favors state capitalism.   p. 269

**labor theory of value**—says that value is entirely determined by the amount of labor that goes into the production of the good. Or as Marx himself thought, the value of anything was the value of laboring power used in the production of it. Exactly what the value of laboring power is, is not known.   p. 193

**labor union**—an organization of employees aimed at bargaining with employers for the collective.   p. 149

**Labour Party**—political party in Great Britain advocating for greater socialism in that nation.   p. 334

*laissez-faire*—French phrase conveying the idea that government should not interfere in the economy of men. This belief was justified by the concept of human nature and natural law, which would hold sway in economic activity in the absence of government interference.   p. 17

**landism**—an established preference for land over capital and labor. The preference must be supported by government policy to prevail. Such a preference for land and those who controlled it was established by the feudal system.   p. 262

**land**—land and all the material on or under it.   p. 65

**legal tender**—money that is legally enforced as having a certain value by law, regardless of if a commodity backs it up.   p. 95

**liabilities**—what someone owes.   p. 91

**licensing**—restricts entry to the field and tends to give at least some of the conditions of monopoly to those who are licensed.   p. 168

**limited liability corporation**—a form of business organization whereby a legal entity is formed. The resulting firm's financial liability is limited to the funds invested in it.   p. 209

the cause of the crisis is usually fractional reserve banking or the holding by some institution of only a fraction of reserves against the potential demand.   p. 126

**liquidity preference**—the preference for having access to money quickly over access to other goods, which might take time to sell for money, might be perishable, or subject to rapid deterioration. When liquidity preference is widespread, people generally avoid long-term or risky investments.   p. 91

**loss leader**—offering a product at a price where the seller is actually losing money to draw people into the store in hope they will purchase enough other products while there to more than make up for the loss.   p. 132

# M

**manor**—an estate of a size and wealth reckoned to be sufficient to maintain a mounted warrior and his household. A manor consisted of the land, the manor house, the mills and shops, and the huts of the peasants. The serfs themselves could also be said to belong to the manor, since they were bound to the land.   p. 264

**marginal theory**—as it applies to the degree of taxation—any level of taxation will make some undertakings unprofitable or sub-marginal. Basically, any level of taxes will make certain undertakings not worth it and will push certain people and businesses into harder financial situations, debt, or bankruptcy.   p. 28

**marginal utility**—the additional utility derived from consuming an additional unit of some good.   p. 220

**market**—all the places and institutional arrangements providing for the exchange of an economic good.   p. 77

**master craftsman**—one who had mastered his trade, could go into business for himself, train apprentices, and hire journeymen to work under him.   p. 268

*McCulloch vs. Maryland*—landmark Supreme Court decision that effectively blocked states from taxing the federal government. Chief Justice John Marshall said in his opinion, "That the power to tax involves the power to destroy; that the power to destroy may defeat and render useless the power to create. . . ."   p. 27

**means of production**—the factors or elements that go into the production of any economic good. Producing anything takes some combination of the three means: land, labor, and capital.   p. 65

**medium of exchange**—money or currency that allows trades to take place indirectly.   p. 79

**mercantilism**—a politico-economic system that is nationalistic, usually involves an alliance, in effect, between the rulers and the merchants, seeks a favorable balance of trade, and tends to operate on the principle that a nation's wealth consists of its holdings in precious metals.   p. 275

**merchant guilds**—associations of people engaged in selling goods to promote the interests of the guild members.   p. 266

**metaphysical**—metaphysical reality is discovered by reason and empirical observation. It is enduring, meaning it lasts over time. Metaphysical realities exist between the physical world that changes and the spiritual world that is eternal. This reality is where we find natural law, which gives an underlying order to the way things work.   p. 12

**minimum wage**—a governmentally mandated lowest wage rate that can be paid to an employee. When set above the market wage it results in unemployment and a surplus of labor.   p. 153

**money**—a commodity or the promise to pay in some specified amount of one or more commodities.   p. 88

**money multiplier**—the multiplier effect on money in the marketplace in a fractional reserve banking system. (When someone borrows from a bank, that money normally ends up back in a bank, a portion of which can be loaned out again.)   p. 120

**monopoly**—the absence of competition of a supplier of particular goods or services in a market. Historically, it has consisted of an exclusive right to sell some good or class of goods in particular markets, a right, or privilege that could only be granted by the ruling powers.   p. 164

**morality**—occurs when someone acts or behaves in accord with the principles or standards of right conduct.   p. 40

**moral positivism**—a rejection of a natural moral order and of God-given individual rights in favor of a naturalist view of mankind. In the naturalist view, what is right becomes simply what legislatures declare is right.   p. 44

**motor vehicles**—property that is used to transport people and/or goods, which at times will be left unattended away from the real property of the owner.   p. 51

**multiplier effect of capital**—when it is used, capital multiplies the output that is possible by labor. The effect is typically greater for capital that is more roundabout. For example, using a chainsaw greatly increases the number of trees a lumberjack can fell as compared to an ax.   p. 199

# N

**nationalization**—the government take over of private companies.   p. 334

**National Labor Relations Board (NLRB)**—established in 1935 by the National Labor Relations Act (also known as the Wagner Act), it is a government institution empowered to enforce the provisions of the legislation.   p. 153

**natural advantage**—an advantage owed to something unique to a particular location.   p. 244

**naturalism**—the worldview that asserts that nature is all there is and, hence, embraces atheism.   p. 45

**natural law**—the natural law exists on the metaphysical level of reality that is mainly understood by reason. It gives form and order to actual classes of physical beings and is the structural part of reality.   p. 13

**natural liberty**—the idea that God created people to be free to choose their way in this world as long as they did not violate the rights of others.   p. 290

**natural monopoly**—a natural monopoly provides a service that, in the nature of things, would be impractical to have multiple companies provide. Examples include electricity, streetcars, or anything that involves laying down wires, tracks, or pipelines.   p. 167

**natural order**—the idea that God had established natural principles of conduct that comprise a moral code to be acknowledged and followed.   p. 290

**natural price**—the idea that any economic good has some inherent price. Some think this price is its cost of production.   p. 130

**natural resources**—materials that exist in nature, such as coal or oil, for which valuable uses have been found. It should be pointed out, however, that whether a material is a resource or

**natural resources**—materials that exist in nature, such as coal or oil, for which valuable uses have been found. It should be pointed out, however, that whether a material is a resource or not generally depends upon some use having been discovered or made of it.   p. 190

**net worth**—total assets minus total liabilities.   p. 90

**New Deal**—political program of the Roosevelt administration of the 1930's supposedly aimed at addressing the economic issues of the Great Depression.   p. 317

**New York Stock Exchange**—a private stock exchange located in New York City.   p. 211

# O

**oligopoly**—a condition in which two or more producers or distributors dominate the market in providing some particular good or class of goods and are thus able to control prices. While the claims have doubtful validity, and even the use of the term is suspect, the idea has nonetheless caught on.   p. 171

**open market operations**—buying debt securities such as bonds, Treasury bills, or others, from securities dealers or large banks. When the Federal Reserve issues new currency, it uses it to buy these securities, and transfers money to a bank, which increases that bank's total deposits.   p. 119

**opportunity cost**—the highest valued alternative given up to do or get something.   p. 81

# P

**Pacific Railway Act of 1862**—federal legislation that authorized two corporations to build and operate a transcontinental railroad.   p. 315

**paper money**—paper used to represent money in exchanges.   p. 98

**partnership**—a form of business organization where two or more people partner in an enterprise together.   p. 208

**personal property**—anything you own for personal use: your toothbrush, your cat, your books, all the stuff in your home.   p. 51

**philosophy**—the study of God's creation..   p. 6

**Physiocrats**—eighteenth century French thinkers who opposed government intervention in the economy and, more broadly, mercantilism. They believed in laissez-faire, that government should keep hands off the economy and allow natural law to prevail in these matters. In a sense, they were landists, for they usually believed that land is the source of all wealth.   p. 17

**planned economy**—an idea associated with overall government planning for and control over an economy. Probably, the best (or worst) examples of this were Stalin's Five-Year Plans. The idea is somewhat misleading, however, for it implies that anything less than an overall planned economy is unplanned. Actually, all economic activity is planned, whether by individual owners or by the state.   p. 276

**political economy**—the conditions under which an economy exists in a country. It includes laws and government regulations, customs, traditions, and morality. The early study of economics was pursued in terms of the political context in which the economy operated. All economies have some political context and it is important to understand that framework to appropriately analyze the economy.   p. 42

**preferred stock**—shares in the first claim to receive a dividend out of the profits of a corporation according to the terms of the contract. Preferred stockholders, as such, do not own or take part in control of the corporation.   p. 210

**price**—in a free market is the amount that a willing seller will take and a willing buyer will pay.   p. 131

**price ceiling**—the maximum legal price that can be charged as mandated by the government.   p. 156

**price fixing**—when governments mandate the price of something.   p. 130

**price floor**—setting a government mandated lowest price that can be charged for an economic good. The minimum wage is an example.   p. 153

**pricing function of money**—the comparison of money to other goods via trade gives us a relative standard to compare goods with other goods.   p. 90

**private corporatism**—occurs when the special privileges are granted to certain private interests.   p. 311

**private property**—the acknowledgment that property is the result of human action and that the individual has a right to acquire it through production and voluntary trade.   p. 292

**problem of production**—to allocate resources and manpower so as to produce what is most wanted from the scarce materials available.   p. 69

**producers**—those who produce goods and services for sale in the market.   p. 293

**productivity**—the rate at which a worker can accomplish a particular task. The more productive, the greater the output in a given time frame.   p. 152

**profit**—the residual funds left from producing and selling an economic good in the market after all other costs are met.   p. 234

**proletariat**—blue collar workers, those who provide manual labor.   p. 348

**property**—anything that belongs to someone. There are different kinds: labor, money, real property (land, buildings), personal property (clothes, books, furniture, etc.), tangible property, and intangible property (stocks, bonds, etc.).   p. 50

**property rights**—the right to make decisions about the things you own. A person's rights to his or her own property and the right to protect it.   p. 52

**protective tariff**—a tax levied by a government, usually on imports, aimed at reducing the amount being imported to protect domestic production from foreign goods. As a result, consumers usually pay a higher price for protected goods, whether they buy domestic goods or foreign imports.   p. 31

**public policy**—programs of action that proceed from legislation. Policy is set by government action; first by the legislature that passes laws, then by the executive branch that executes laws, and finally by the judicial branch that judges whether the law is upheld. The limits of what the government could do were explicitly restricted by the U.S. Constitution. The basic underlying assumptions about human nature and economic principles will determine the results of policy.   p. 4

**public property**—public ownership is an illusion—it may be open to the public and for the public to use, but the public does not have the right to use it in any way they want. Some government body oversees the place and makes rules about how it may be used.   p. 50

**public theft**—theft that is carried out by the government; money is taken by force through taxes from some and given to others through welfare programs.   p. 83

**pyramid scheme**—a financially fraudulent scheme whereby money taken from later participants is used to reward earlier investors in the program to give the appearance of profits where none exist.   p. 340

# Q

**quid pro quo**—literally, "this for that." When something is given or done in exchange for something else.   p. 125

# R

**rate fixing**—the effort of the government to regulate prices of some product or service.   p. 180

**real property**—land and the permanent structures on it. It is distinct from chattels(movable property), personal property, and intangible property.   p. 30

**redistribution of wealth**—a governmental forced effort to take wealth from some people and give it to other people.   p. 236

**registration**—buying a license to permit operation of a certain business.   p. 168

**regulation**—government controls set by legislation or agencies of the executive branch of government. They are put into place to restrain certain activities of businesses.   p. 178

**rent**—the payment to someone to use his property for a specified period of time.   p. 228

**rent controls**—when property rental rates are mandated by government below market rates. This is an example of a price ceiling.   p. 159

**rent seeking**—when private individuals and businesses use their resources to lobby Congress for special legislative privileges.   p. 318

**reserve ratio**—the mandated fraction of deposits that commercial banks must hold in reserve. Remember that because of fractional reserve banking practices, they are permitted to loan out all money they have deposited by customers except this percentage, which is determined by the Federal Reserve..   p. 119

**revolution**—means simply a successful revolt against those who govern or rule in a country. To Marxists, however, revolution has a much broader and all-inclusive meaning. It means a revolt against the existing order, not simply against those who rule, but against all existing institutions, arrangements, beliefs, and conditions. Socialists, more generally, see a revolution as the opportunity for redistribution of land and other wealth.   p. 326

**revolutionary socialism**—a political movement whereby socialism is imposed all at once in a revolution that overthrows the existing political structures.   p. 310

**roundabout**—in economics, roundabout refers to how much labor went into producing capital needed to produce some good. When a great deal more labor is required to produce the capital needed, the method is more roundabout.   p. 197

# S

**sales tax**—a tax levied on sales of goods and services at the point of sale in the market.   p. 31

**saving**—the act of postponing consumption.   p. 198

**Say's Law**—no one would ever produce more of whatever they are producing than they could use unless they intended to trade the surplus for something else.   p. 89

**scarcity**—the first principle of economics: that although human wants are unlimited, our means for satisfying them are limited. We must make choices as to how to use our scarce means to accomplish the ends we desire most.   p. 64

**schooling**—instruction or education received inside a school.   p. 184

**"schools" of economic thought**—general categories of ideas related to the application of economic principles. This book is based in the Austrian school of thought because it is based on the natural law premise. Other schools you may hear of during the course are Keynesian, monetarist, and Marxian.   p. 5

**self-evident**—truths that are self-evident need no proof since any attempt to deny one must affirm it. For example, a person need not prove his awareness of himself. It is an immediately obvious fact. Also, self-evident truths can be driven by logic as in the case of the natural rights of people—the right to life, liberty, and property.   p. 14

**self-sufficient farms**—farm that produces most everything it needed to survive without trading with others.   p. 76

**serf**—a person bound to the land on which he lives, owing work to the lord of the manor, and generally entitled to the land that he works and the hut in which he lives.   p. 262

**Sherman Antitrust Act**—The first major anti-monopoly act passed by the U.S. government. It was vague, ambiguous, and poorly defined.   p. 179

**shortage**—when the price of something is legally held below the market clearing price, then people desire more of the good than sellers are willing and able to sell. The result is called a shortage.   p. 156

**shortage of money**—the illusion that there is less money in the market than there needs to be, and that if we increase the money supply, we will reach a better equilibrium point where more people can afford to live.   p. 90

**socialism**—in the broadest sense, it is any political system where governments control the economy.   p. 332

**socializing property**—expropriating or taking private property from individual owners and giving control of it to government.   p. 333

**social justice**—the idea that the current distribution of economic goods is unjust and must be corrected by a governmentally imposed redistribution.   p. 332

**Social Security Act**—The centerpiece welfare legislation of the New Deal. It established a government mandated pyramid scheme aimed at providing retirement benefits to the elderly.   p. 339

**sovereignty of owners**—the right of property owners to treat their property however they wish. In other words, they have a monopoly over their property.   p. 165

**Soviet Union**—a confederation of communist countries formed after World War II with its seat of power in Moscow. It collapsed between 1989-91 as the nations in it broke away from Russian rule.   p. 327

**specialization**—the focus of a person's work on some particular operation, skill, or practice. When such specialization is widespread it could be said that a division of labor exists.   p. 80

**specie**—precious metals used as money.   p. 111

**speculators**—people who buy or sell shares of stock based on expectations about their future prices.   p. 213

**Standard Oil Trust**—nationwide oil distributing business started by John D. Rockefeller in the 1880s. It was the first of its kind and controlled between 80–90% of the market.   p. 169

**state corporatism**—occurs when the productive property is owned by the government and special privileges are granted to government entities.   p. 311

**statists**—people who believe central governments should control society.   p. 333

**stock exchange**—a physical location where individuals meet together to buy and sell stock.   p. 211

**stock market**—the broad array of institutional arrangements that allow for the trade of existing shares of stock issued by corporations.   p. 211

**store credit**—allowing customers to buy now and pay later. Some stores issue a credit card that can only be used in their store.   p. 176

**subinfeudination**—process by which a vassal might extend his holdings by obligating himself to two or more overlords. This was only possible legally when the vassal limited his loyalty to particular overlords.   p. 262

**supply**—the various amounts of the good that would be offered for sale in the market at various prices, other things being equal.   p. 133

**surplus of labor**—when there are more people willing to work for a particular wage rate than there are employers willing to hire them.   p. 152

# T

**tangible property**—the personal property that someone owns that you can literally touch.   p. 30

**tariff**—any list of fixed charges. In economics, it usually refers to a tax levied on exports or imports.   p. 31

**tariff for revenue**—a tax levied on exports or imports for the primary purpose of raising revenue. It is distinguished from a protective tariff in that it is generally low enough so as not to actually keep foreign goods out.   p. 31

**technological unemployment**—idea that people can be put out of work with the increase of technology and the use of machines.   p. 201

**thaler**—sixteenth–nineteenth century German word for a coin consisting of an ounce of silver.   p. 97

**Thatcher, Margaret**—Conservative Party prime minister of England during the 1980s who worked to undo many socialist policies and programs.   p. 338

*The Communist Manifesto*—one of the earliest works to attempt to make the false claim that abundance has replaced scarcity as the problem to be solved..   p. 67

**theft**—taking property from someone else using force or fraud.   p. 74

**the market**—a market is any place or arrangement where trading takes place. When economists refer to "the market" they are referring to the general nature of the market as a whole, or the process by which people generally achieve their economic ends.   p. 130

**theology**—the study of God.   p. 6

*The Wealth of Nations*—book written by Adam Smith in 1776 where he set forth the idea that there is a natural order for the economy, which involves a natural harmony between the self-interest of the individual seeking his own gain and the general well-being of societies.   p. 17

**thrifty**—avoiding waste or extravagance; being economical.   p. 64

**time preference**—the preference for present goods over future ones. The degree of the preference is said to be the prime ingredient in the interest rate. At least, it is a major factor in the determination of whether or not to lend goods or what they would accept as payment for doing so.   p. 121

**totalitarian**—state where government uses force to control any aspect of life that the leader might decree. In an economic sense, central planning would be used to determine the production and distribution of goods and would displace the market.   p. 6

**trust**—a business holding company. It can be a combination of businesses of similar products, or in the same stream of a production process, or a combination of diverse business enterprises.   p. 164

# U

**unit of account**—the standard monetary unit that is widely accepted and used for calculations of accounts.   p. 97

**universal principles**—principles that apply to all people, in all places, at all times.   p. 4

**user fee**—a tax or fee paid for a government function or service that goes directly to financing that service.   p. 29

**usury**—the charging of interest on a loan. In today's use it has come to mean the charging of excessive interest on a loan.   p. 232

**utilitarianism**—a form of legal positivism that argues that laws should be based on a hedonistic calculus.   p. 45

# V

**variable costs**—the change in the cost of producing an additional unit of some good. When costs are highly variable, it means each additional unit can be produced at a significantly lower cost than the one that preceded it.   p. 174

**vassal**—a Medieval term referring to the fact that a person owed loyalty and military service to some overlord. It does not signify any rank that the vassal might hold, since kings might be vassals as well as knights. Indeed, it was sometimes held in the Middle Ages that every man should have an overlord.   p. 262

## W

**wages**—payment to an employee for his or her labor services. p. 141

**want**—all people aim to achieve some purpose or end. To do so they need the means necessary to realize the end. The desire to obtain the means constitute wants. p. 79

**warehouse receipt**—receipt detailing an amount of some commodity stored in a warehouse or bank. p. 100

**welfare**—a term that socialists have twisted to mean government provision of certain economic goods. p. 339

**welfarism**—the concept that governments should be the provider of economic goods and services achieved by taking the wealth of some people and giving it to others. p. 332

**withholding**—a method of collecting taxes where tax is deducted before the workman receives his paycheck. It has the effect of taking away from the workman any choice as to whether or when he will pay the tax. p. 32

## Z

**zoning laws**—local laws that restrict the uses of land within particular zones of the city. p. 218

# Index

## A

abstraction **8**, 243
Adams, Henry 300
Adams, John 112, 300
advertisers 64
advertising **176**, 178, 236
Afghanistan 241, 328
*Age of Faith* 261
American Medical Association 169
American Stock Exchange 211
anarchist **6**, 331
*An Introduction to Medieval Europe* 268
apprentice **268**
Aquinas, Thomas 130
Aristotle 13
Ashton, T. S. 299
assets 90, **91**, 101, 102, 104, 122, 126, 196, 200, 210, 211, 212
*A Treatise on Political Economy* 88
auction **77**, 77–79, 96, 322
Australia 241
Austrian 5, 6, 49, 51, 197, 201, 310. *See also* schools of economic thought

## B

balance of trade **275**, 276, 278, 285
bank of issue **101**
barter **79**, 87–88, 93, 112, 129, 244, 284, 285
**Bastiat, Frédéric** 49, 52, **53**, 146, 147
bear market **213**
**Bentham, Jeremy** 6, **45**
bill of exchange 96, **100**, 273
bill of sale 51
bills of credit 36, 96, 111, 115, 125, 248
bimetallic **94**
black market **159**, 356
**Böhm-Bawerk, Eugen von 197**
Bolshevik Revolution 326, **350**, 356
Bolsheviks **326**, 350
boom-bust cycle **121**
Boston Tea Party 167
bourgeoisie 309, **310**, 348, 349
Bowman Transportation 150
Brindley, James 295

British Civil War 278
Budget Project 20
bullionism **275**, 276
bullionist **146**, 284, 285
bull market **213**
bureaucracy 30, 192, 337, **354**
busybody **291**

## C

Canada 68, 207, 241
capital 17, 65, **66**, 83, 93, 109, 115, 119, 121, 122, 126, 150, 152, 171, 179, 189, 193–202, 206, 215, 217, 218, 222, 227, 228, 231, 234, 235, 236, 237, 261, 262, 265, 266, 269, 277, 278, 284, 286, 289, 294, 297, 302, 305, 306, 309–328, 311, 334, 336, 351, 357
   multiplier effect **199**
*Capital and Interest* 197
capitalism 63, 64, 269, 309, **310**, 311, 317, 332, 355, 356
cartel **172**, 173
Cecil, William 276
centrally planned and directed economy **351**
Central Pacific Railroad 315
certification **168**, 183, 292, 293, 303
*ceteris paribus* **133**, 134
Chamberlain, John 235
charity **74**, 81, 84
Chartism 298
Chase, Stuart 67
China 98, 328, 347
   Communist 328
Churchill, Winston 246
Civil War 96, 116, 117, 118, 137, 169, 303, 312, 314, 315
classical economics 7
classical economists 42, 228, 231
classicist 5
Clayton Antitrust Act **141**, 181
clipped coins 97, 107, **108**
coinage 94, 97, 117, 245
coins 36, 52, **94**, 95, 101, 107, 108, 110, 113, 116, 123–125, 245, 261, 266, 279, 284
Cokayne, Sir William 277, 278
Colbertism 280, 282
**Colbert, Jean Baptiste 280**, 282, 283
Cold War 342
collective bargaining **153**, 154
collective farms 352, 357
collectivists 331, **332**, 350
collusion **171**
colonization 283
Columbus, Christopher 274
Commager, Henry Steele 179
command economy **354**
commercial bank **102**
commercial banking 102, **118**
commodity 4, 52, **88**, 90, 93, 94, 95, 96, 98, 100, 123–126, 130, 141, 165, 172, 181, 193, 194, 212, 243, 245, 247, 285, 314, 332, 335
common law **209**, 264
common ownership **50**, 192, 334
Commons, John R. 67
common stock 52, **210**, 213
communism 44, 50, 51, 52, 63, 64, 67, 193, 246, 257, 259, 309, 325–328, 333, 347–352, 356, 358, 359
Communist Party 333, 350, 357, 359
comparative advantage 76, **81**
competition 31, 136, **139**, 140, 142, 145, 146, 147, 150, 153, 154, 159, 163–185, 206, 227, 230, 236, 237, 250, 251, 269, 279, 285, 289, 293, 303, 314, 355
   cutthroat 163, **164**

compound interest **93**
compulsory 74, 154, 185, 186, 304, 337
conscience 24, 41
Conservative Party 334, **338**
Constitutional Amendments
    Fifth 36
    First 33
    Fourth 36
    Ninth 34
    Seventeenth 35
    Seventh 36
    Sixteenth 32, 36
    Tenth 34
Constitutional Convention 33
Constitution U.S. 4, 7, 11, 31–36, 55, 76, 83, 95, 115, 116, 165, 290, 292, 302, 303, 313, 314, 340
consumer economics **68**
consumers 31, 32, 64, 68, 78, 90, 123, 130, 135, 136, 137, 139, 140, 147, 148, 158, 160, 165, 173, 178, 197, 200, 205, 213, 216, 237, 277, 290, **293**, 313, 319, 323, 324, 327, 328, 336, 343, 354
contract **25**, 39, 52, 132, 165, 274
Corn Laws 296
corporate drag **211**, 217, 221, 251
corporate tax **32**, 252, 317
corporatism 5, **311**, 312, 315, 316, 317, 318, 319, 323, 324, 325, 326, 327, 328, 331, 344, 351, 358
Costa Rica 243
counterfeit **94**
courts 28, 29, 35, 39, 40, 56, 83, 149, 151, 180, 181, 209, 262, 264, 267, 289, 290, 298, 303
craft guilds 268, **269**
credit contraction 123
credit expansion 119, **121**, 122, 123, 124, 125, 126
crony capitalism **310**
currency 27, 36, 45, **52**, 79, 82, 87, **88**, 94, 95, 101, 103, 104, 107, 109–119, 121, 123–126, 165, 234, 243, 244, 246–249, 303, 314, 315, 316, 317, 320, 322, 326, 339, 344
cutthroat competition 163, **164**

# D

da Gama, Vasco 274
Darby, Abraham 295
Darwin, Charles 11
debasing the currency 97, **124**, 316, 317
debt money **98**, 100, 101, 111, 121
deductive reasoning **14**
deed 50
de la Gomberdière, The Marquis 281
demand **134**
    graph **135**
democratic socialist. *See* socialist
deregulation **178**
dialectical materialism **348**
Dickinson, John 32
Dietze, Gottfried 23
direct exchange **79**
discount rate **119**
distribution of wealth 42, 82, 194, 225, **226**, 227, 232, 235, 237, 238, 331
division of labor **80**, 147, 155, 226, 244, 265
doctrine of limits **6**
*Documents of American History* 179
domestic 17, 25, 26, 31, 34, 146, 147, 148, 159, 210, **243**, 244, 250, 251, 252, 275, 277, 286, 313, 343
Dominion Mandate **3–4**
Dow Jones Industrial Average **211**
Drake, Sir Francis 276

due diligence **314**
Durant, Will 261

# E

economical 63, 64, 84
economic determinism **348**
economic freedom 6, 46, 201, **291**, 310, 311
economic goods **66**, 73, 159, 311
economicism **242**, 260
economic principles **4**, 5, 11, 14, 15, 18, 131, 241, 258
economics 3–10, **4**, 63, 64, 73, 163, 173, 174, 205, 215, 225, 235, 242, 250, 259, 260, 284, 286, 347
    Christian 5, 7
*Economic Sophisms* 53, 146
economic system **64**
economy 26, 36, 42, 46, 50, 61, 63, 71, 88, 189, 201, 337, 348, 351
economy of scale 211, **220**, 221
elasticity **137**
Eliot, John 112
Elkins Act 180
Elsworth, Oliver 116
eminent domain **165**
enforcement 25, 165
**Engels, Friedrich 67**
England 7, 67, 88, 97, 108, 170, 209, 215, 218, 243, 246, 264, 268, 270, 274, 276, 277, 278, 279, 280, 284, 286, 294, 296, 297, 299–302, 333–339
*England in the Nineteenth Century* 299
*English History, 1914–1945* 243
enlightened self-interest **24**
Enlightenment (the) 45
entitlement programs **342**
entrepreneur **206**, 207, 208, 215, 235, 236
Eon, Jean 280
equilibrium price 46, **130**, 136
equilibrium price theory **46**
escheat **303**
estates (feudal) **262**
European Common Market **252**
European Union 252
evolutionary ideas **11–12**
evolutionary socialism 309, **310**, 326, 333
exchange 79
excise tax **31**, 138
*Extraordinary Popular Delusions and the Madness of the Crowd* 109

# F

Fabian 5, 333, 334
Fabianism **333**
factory system **214**, 215–216
Fair Labor Standards Act **155**, 183, 341
fair (medieval) **267**
fallacy of abundance 69. *See also* surpluses
fallacy of composition **147**
fallen 6, 24, 289
fallible 6, 18, 24
family businesses 209
Farewell Address, George Washington 27, 148, 241
Farm Credit Administration 321
Farmer's Home Administration 322
farm problem **320**
fealty **262**
Federal Deposit Insurance Corporation 317
Federal Farm Loan Act of 1916 321

Federal Housing Administration (FHA)  322, 341, 342
Federal Land Banks  321
Federal Reserve  98, 101, 102, 108, 116–126, 213, 232, 248, 317, 321
Federal Reserve Act  116, 117, **119**, 321
Federal Reserve Banks  119
Federal Reserve System  108, **116**, 119, 120, 122, 317, 321
fee simple  **56**, 57, 262, 302
feud  **263**
feudalism  63, 64, 262, 264, 265, 269, 311, 326, 332
feudal system  **262**, 263, 266, 267, 269
fiat money  52, **98**, 99, 103, 104, 116, 117, 125, 126, 246, 247, 248
*Fiat Money Inflation in France*  114
fiduciary  **102**
Fink, Henry  174
first rule of taxation  **29**
Five-Year Plan  327, 351
Five-Year Plans  276, 327, 350, 351, 352, 353
fixed costs  **173**, 174, 175
force  24–27, 29, 73–74, 81, 83, 96, 113, 145, 149, 153, 159, 169, 192, 263, 311–312, 340, 354
   legal  26
   use of  7, 25, 26, 35, 55, 81, 82, 166, 169, 178, 179, 354
foreign  17, 18, 25, 26, 31, 36, 82, 100, 109, 146, 147, 148, 159, 173, 179, 219, 241, **243**, 247–253, 267, 268, 275, 277, 279, 280, 282, 283, 303, 304, 313, 319, 327, 328, 335, 342, 343, 358
Founders  35–37, 165
four ways to get what you want  **74**
fractional reserve banking  100, **101**, 102, 103, 117, 119, 120, 123, 126, 314, 316
fractional reserves  102, 121, **314**
France  108–115, 264, 273, 274, 279–286, 296, 297
free enterprise  7, 18, 43, 46, 53, 77, 165, 207, 258, 290, **291**, 292–306, 309, 310, 312, 314, 317, 318, 320, 325, 344, 352
free market  6, 18, 43, 93, 96, 102, 118, 121, 131, 132, 140, 141, 145, 149, 178, 201, 227, 230, 241, 245, 258, 292, 293, 296, 310, 314, 323, 355
French and Indian War  285, 286
French National Assembly  115, 146
French Revolution  113, 279, 286, 296, 331
frugality, frugal, or frugally  50, 63, **64**, 235, 258

# G

**Galbraith, John Kenneth**  67, **68**, 177
Galileo  13, 16
Gellhorn, Walter  168
Germany  34, 52, 67, 97, 246, 274, 297
G.I. Bill  342
going price  **132**, 133, 136, 153, 156, 158
going wage  142, 153
gold  36, 52, 88, 93–101, 103, 110, 111, 116, 118, 120, 123, 125, 146, 173, 244–249, 274–278, 280, 285, 297, 303, 314, 316, 317, 327, 335
gold standard  120, 123, 245, 246, 317
good (n.)  **4**, 6, 8, 17, 24–27, 31, 32, 42, 52
   distribution of  4, 6, 8, 39, 40, 63, 68, 251, 252, 313, 347, 349, 353, 357
government  6–7, 23–36, 40
   function of  82, 84, 185
   functions useful to economy  25
   impact on the economy  26–27
   nature of  25
   necessity for  24
   purposes of  82
*Government and Collective Bargaining*  154
government bonds  **117**, 315, 316
government intervention to control prices  145, **146**
graduated income tax  **32**, 82, 337
Great Britain  34, 241, 274, 291, 293, 294, 296, 297, 300, 333, 335

Great Depression  246
Great Khan  **98**
Greco-Roman tradition  **6**
Greenback-Labor Party  117
**Gresham, Sir Thomas**  **95**, 96, 124
Gresham's Law  95, 96, 124
Groseclose, Elgin  100, 118, 122
guild  282
Gunther, John  354

# H

Haggard, Thomas R.  151
Hamilton, Alexander  146, 312, 313, 315
Hat Act of 1732  279
head tax  **29**, 30, 31, 36
hedonistic calculus  **45**
Heilbroner, Robert  170
Hepburn Act  180
*Hidden Persuaders*  176
Hill, Christopher  277
**Hill, James J.**  **207**, 208
historical inevitability  **349**
homage  **262**
home school  185, 186
homestead exemption  **31**
Hong Kong  191
House of Commons  334
House of J.P. Morgan  170
human action  **18**, 19, 51, 211, 292, 311, 317
*Human Action*  51
human nature  4, 11, **15**, 24, 36, 348
   fallen  24, 289
human rights  56, 57
human wants  4, 64, 77, 88, 175
Hume, David  18, 192
Hundred Year's War  273

# I

*I Chose Freedom*  355
India  46, 98, 167, 274, 277, 328
indirect exchange  **79**, 88
*Individual Freedom and Governmental Restraints*  168
individual liberty  18, 293, 294
inductive reasoning  **14**
inflation  27, 32, 107–118, **108**, 121, 123–126, 138–140, 171, 234, 246, 248, 304, 316–317, 320–321, 339, 342, 344
inheritance  192, 225, **237**, 302
injustice  23, 32, 42, 82, 112, 332
institutionalist  5
intangible property  **30**, 52
interest  **121**, 231–234
interest rate  119, 121, 122, 232, 233, 234, 282
Intermediate Credit Banks  322
International Monetary Fund (IMF)  **248**
Interstate Commerce Act  173, 174, 180, 316
Interstate Commerce Commission  180, 182, 183
intervention  17, 40, 42, 44, 70, 84, 94, 97, 145, 146, 152, 153, 234, 291, 305, 306, 314, 320, 321, 323, 324
invisible hand theory  **17**
I, Pencil  80
Iron Act of 1750  279
Iron Curtain  246

# J

Jackson, Andrew 314, 315
Jacksonians 305
Jefferson, Thomas 14, 32, 33, 314
Johnson, Edgar N. 268
journeyman **268**
Judeo-Christian **6**, 44, 289
justice 24, 25, **26**, 29, 30, 31, 39, 54, 55, 130, 225, 226, 227, 228, 237, 289, 332
  distributive 82
just price **130**
just taxes 31

# K

Kepler, Johann 16
Keynesian 5
**Keynes, John Maynard** 67, **246**
KGB 359
King Charles I 277
King Charles II 279
King Henry II 264
King Henry VII 274
King Henry VIII 274
King James I 277, 278
King Louis XIV 108, 274, 280, 281, 282, 299
King Louis XV 108
King's Courts 264
King William's War 285
Kitto, H. D. F. 16
Kravchenko, Victor 355
Kulaks 353

# L

labor 4, 39, 51, 54, 56, **65**, 70, 73–83, 89, 109, 125, 130, 134, 141–142, 145, 149–159, 164, 169, 179, 181, 189–201, 192, 206, 215, 218, 222, 234, 235, 244, 247, 265, 269, 284, 303, 305, 310, 313, 320, 321, 325, 331, 332, 336, 340, 343, 348, 351
  as property **51**
    child 216
    price of 231, 232, 253
labor intensive **193**
laborism 193, **269**, 310, 332, 341, 351
labor theory of value **193**, 197, 332
labor union 56, 82, 141, 142, 148, **149**, 150, 152, 153, 154, 156, 169, 183, 216, 252, 253, 303, 304, 341, 357
Labourites **334**, 335, 336, 338
Labour Party **334**, 335
*laissez-faire* **17**, 289, 290
land 50, 54, 55, **65**, 66, 77, 78, 83, 114, 164, 189–193, 199–202, 215, 219, 226, 228–234, 229, 247, 259, 262–265, 273, 294, 305, 311, 315, 321, 332, 357
  as property 55
landism **262**, 269, 310, 326, 332
Law, John 108, 110, 113, 115
Lee, Richard Henry 32, 34
legal force 26
legal tender 36, **95**, 99, 102, 103, 111, 112, 115, 116, 125, 246, 249, 303, 315, 316
Leibniz 16
**Lenin, Vladimir 326**, 327, 350, 351
Lewis, John L. 150
liabilities 90, **91**, 118, 209

liberty 4, 23, 26, 32, 160, 283, 289, 290, 355
licensing **168**, 169, 292, 293
life, liberty, and property 7, 14, 26, 36, 41, 42, 83
limited liability corporation **209**
Link, Arthur S. 183
liquidity crisis **126**
liquidity preference **91**, 93, 122, 126
Lloyd's of London 297
**Locke, John 7**, 32
logic 14, 41, 149, 175, 285, 292, 316
loss leader **132**
Lyon, Eugene 356

# M

Mackay, Charles 109
Madison, James 33
Magellan, Ferdinand 274
Magna Carta 32
Mann–Elkins Act 180
manor 262, **264**, 265, 267, 269, 270
marginal theory **28**, 156
marginal utility 220
markets 4, 18, 23, 24, 40, **77**, 91, 92, 93, 102, 121, 129, 140, 142, 159, 171, 174, 199, 267, 296
  financial 91, 92, 93, 121, 199, 233
market, (the) 6, 8, 18, 25, 27, 29, 31, 42, 46, 49, 50, 52, 57, 63, 65, 69, 70, 76, 77, 79, 80, 81, 87, 89, 129, **130**
Marshall, John 27
Martin, Albro 207
Marxist 5, 6, 150, 192, 194, 326, 327, 332, 333, 348, 349, 350, 351
Marxists 5, 6, 192, 194, 326, 332, 333
**Marx, Karl** 51, **52**, 56, **67**, 82, 193, 197, 227, 269, 309, 310, 325, 332, 333, 348, 349, 353
  Father of Communism 51
master craftsman **268**
*McCulloch vs. Maryland* **27**
means of production 49–52, 56, **65**, 66, 139, 140, 167, 189, 190, 191, 193, 194, 195, 200, 201, 202, 205, 206, 228, 261, 262, 269, 284, 305, 310, 311, 312, 323, 324, 325, 326, 334, 338, 347, 348, 357
Medieval 262, 263, 265, 267, 268, 269, 270, 276
medium of exchange 3, **79**, 87–96, 100, 101, 107, 114, 125, 129, 195, 226, 244, 245, 246, 266, 275, 320
mercantilism 17, 18, 146, 148, 260, 273–287, **275**, 290, 294, 295, 296, 300, 311, 319, 325, 332
mercantilist 5, 146, 275, 276, 280, 284, 289, 294, 313
mercantilistic 167
merchant guilds **266**, 267–269
metaphysical **12**, 13, 14, 15, 359
metaphysics 13, 14
Mexico 275
Middle Ages 100, 130, 185, 189, 231, 259, 261–270, 273, 274, 279, 283
**Mill, John Stuart** 6, **46**
minimum wage 20, 70, 153, 155, 156, 157, 303, 317, 323
**Mises, Ludwig von** 6, 49–51, **51**, 201, 310
Molasses Act of 1733 279
monetarist 5
money 3, 36, 52, 64, 79, **88**
  supply 81, 90, 96, 97, 101, 103, 107, 108, 112, 113, 116, 118, 119, 120, 121, 124, 126, 138, 213, 246, 316, 339
money multiplier **120**
monopoly 7, 25, 102, 118, 119, 163–175, **164**, 178, 179, 180, 181, 182, 184, 186, 210, 265, 266, 268, 277, 278, 279, 282, 284, 326
  dangers of 175
  on the use of major force 25
  private 169
morality 24, 39, 39–44, **40**, 63, 319

moral positivism **44**
Morgan, J.P. 170
Morrill Land Grant Act 315
Motor Carriers Act 183
motor vehicles **51**
multiplier effect of capital **199**, 200

# N

Napoleonic Wars 285, 296
National Bank Act 315
national debt 120, 123, 124
National Health Service Act 335
National Industrial Recovery Act 182, 183
National Insurance Act 335
nationalization 251, 252, **334**, 335, 336, 337, 338
National Labor Relations Act **153**, 183, 341
National Labor Relations Board 153, 154
National Reconstruction Administration 317
natural advantage **244**
naturalism **45**
natural law 5, 7, **13**, 14, 17, 32, 44, 45, 53, 55, 115, 289, 348
natural liberty 23, 289, **290**
natural monopoly 164, **167**
natural order 8, 12, 15, 16, 17, 18, 289, **290**
  of economy 18
natural price **130**
natural resources **190**, 191, 200
natural rights 44
nature of things 3, 4, 11, 13, 14, 15, 24, 27, 36, 52, 64, 65, 66, 73, 79, 83, 148, 167, 192, 206, 220, 225, 229, 234, 242, 269, 289
Navigation Acts 278, 284
Nazism 309, 333
neoclassicist 5
net worth **90**
New Deal 68, 158, 163, 166, 182, 183, **317**, 318, 320, 339
New Economic Policy 327, 351, 353
Newton, Sir Isaac 13, 16, 18
New World 274, 275, 276, 278
New York Stock Exchange 77, **211**, 212

# O

oligopoly **171**, 173
OPEC 170, 172, 173
open market operations **119**
opportunity cost **81**, 92, 93, 228
order in the universe 12, 14–19, 16, 44
overproduction 67, 70
over-the-counter 211
Owen, Robert 298

# P

Pacific Railway Act of 1862 **315**
Packard, Vance 68, 176
paper money 36, 93, 95, 96, 97, **98**, 99, 100, 101, 103, 108, 110, 111, 112, 113, 114, 115, 116, 117, 124, 126, 303, 326
Parliament 280, 286, 294
partners 208, 209, 220
partnership **208**, 209, 214
Peru 275
Petro, Sylvester 151
philosophy **6**, 12
  Bentham's 46
  natural law 7, 14, 32

Western 11
Physiocrats **17**, 18, 289, 290
planned economy **276**, 339, 351
political economy **42**, 45, 51, 63, 64, 88
Polo, Marco 98, 99, 274
Pope Innocent III 262
Pope Leo XIII 49, 54
Populist Party 117
Portugal 274
power 28, 32
precious metals 52, 88, 94, 95, 96, 97, 99, 100, 101, 103, 110, 111, 116, 117, 124, 146, 244, 245, 246, 247, 274, 275, 276, 284, 285
preferred stock **210**, 213
price **131**, 332
price ceiling **156**, 159
price fixing **130**, 140, 146, 183
price floor **153**
pricing function of money **90**, 93
principles of economics. *See* economic principles
private corporatism **311**, 312, 324, 327, 328
private property 36, 46, 49, 50, 54, 56, 57, 73, 82, 84, 164, 165, 228, 229, 234, 243, 251, 252, **292**, 293, 294, 310, 318, 331, 332, 333, 338, 347, 357
problem of production **69**, **70**, 343, 353
producer 69, 70, 77, 82, 139, 140, 165, 170, 174, 177, 193, 234, 235, 236, 250, 277, 297, 301, 342, 343
producers 27, 31, 69, 90, 107, 137, 139, 140, 146, 158, 159, 160, 165, 171, 174, 175, 176, 177, 178, 183, 194, 205, 227, 250, 269, **293**, 331, 334, 343, 354
Production Credit Association 322
Production Credit Associations 322
productivity 84, 93, **152**, 153, 199, 200, 253, 295, 296, 298, 299, 304, 355, 356
profit 70, 90, 92, 100, 132, 137, 138, 166, 167, 186, 198, 199, 210, 230, 231, **234**, 235, 236, 237, 298, 316, 320, 337, 354
proletariat 310, 333, **348**, 349
property 24, 36, 43, **50**
  personal 30, 50, **51**, 52, 170
  public **50**
  real **30**, 31, 50, 51, 56, 57, 232, 302, 357
property rights **52**, 53, 55, 56, 57, 319, 327
public policy **4**, 45, 280
public theft 83
pyramid scheme 339, **340**

# Q

Queen Elizabeth I 276
Queen Isabella of Spain 274
*quid pro quo* **125**, 312

# R

railroads 171, 173, 174, 175, 180, 181, 182, 301, 315, 316, 319
Raleigh, Sir Walter 276
rate fixing **180**
Read, Leonard 353
reason 6, 8, 12, 13, **14**, 15, 24, 29, 39, 41, 53
redistribution 82
  of wealth 112, 113, **236**, 237, 248
redistributionist 5, 82, 226, 237, 252, 253, 340, 341, 342
Reed, Leonard 80
Reformation 273, 274
registration **168**
regulation 36, 42, 46, 56, 163, 166, 173, **178**, 181, 183, 232, 279, 312, 316, 317, 318, 319, 333, 336, 339

religion  7, 8, 33, 39, 43, 155, 294, 348, 349
Renaissance  232, 269, 273, 274
rent  130, 159, 193, **228**, 229, 230, 231, 232, 234, 235, 236, 265, 303, 318, 319, 332, 334
rent controls  **159**, 303
rent seeking  **318**
reserve ratio  **119**, 120
revolution  56, 217, 218, 310, **326**, 327, 331, 333, 335, 348, 349, 350
revolutionary socialism  309, **310**, 333
**Ricardo, David**  7, 8
Robinson–Patman Act  184
Rockefeller, John D.  169
Roman Catholic Church  263, 266, 274
roundabout  **197**, 198, 199, 202, 244
Russia  266, 326, 327, 335, 350, 355, 356

# S

sales tax  **31**, 219
saving  63, 77, 91, 92, 93, 102, 112, 113, 126, 174, 196, **198**, 199, 201, 208, 225, 235, 344
**Say, Jean-Baptiste**  88
Say's Law  88, **89**, 243
scarce resources  4, 50, 63, 64, 318
scarcity  **64**, 64–70, 83, 158, 160, 168, 169, 189, 190, 201, 258, 343
schooling  **184**, 185, 186, 216, 293, 304, 342
    government monopoly of  184
schools of economic thought  **5**
    Austrian  5, 310
    British  46
    classical  5
    institutionalist  5
    Keynesian  5
    neoclassical  5
science  6, 12, 14, 18, 44, 63, 327
Scripture
    Deuteronomy 27:17  291
    Exodus 20:15, 17  49
    Exodus 20:17  225
    Genesis 1:28  3
    Matthew 6:31–33  359
    Matthew 6:33  39
    Matthew 22:21  29
    Romans 13:1–4  23
self-defense  25
self-evident  **14**
self-interest  17, 18, 40, 250, 258
    enlightened  24
self-sufficient farms  **76**
serf  261, **262**, 263, 264, 265, 266, 267, 268, 270
serfdom  4, 229, 264, 268
Seven Year's War  285
Sherman Antitrust Act  **179**, 180
shortage  90, 122, 136, **156**, 157, 158, 159, 160, 320, 325
shortage of money  **90**, 320
slavery  164, 195, 229, 259, 264, 302
smart ape  44, 45
**Smith, Adam**  7, 8, **17–18**, 23, 80, 130, 147, 148, 192, 193, 228, 275, 289, 290, 295
Smith, Hedrick  358
socialism  44, 46, 51, 53, 56, 167, 245, 246, 251, 252, 270, 309, 310, 324, 325, 326, 331, **332**, 333–339, 347, 351
    democratic  309, 333
*Socialism*  51
socialist  5, 6, 52, 56, 197, 228, 233, 237, 243, 246, 251, 252, 276, 311, 316, 324, 325, 331–339, 351, 353
    democratic  6
    radical  56

revolutionary  309
socialistic  167, 251, 252, 276, 309
socializing property  **333**
social justice  82, **332**
social science  5, 45, 176
Social Security  32, 82, 83, 154, 155, 156, 219, 253, 339, 340, 341
Social Security Act  **339**, 341
society  40
sovereignty of owners  **165**
Soviet  191, 246, 326, 327, 328, 335, 338, 347, 348, 350–359
Soviet Union  191, 246, 326, **327**, 328, 338, 347, 348, 350, 351, 352, 353, 354, 356, 357, 358, 359
Spain  34, 273, 274, 275, 281
Spanish Armada  276
specialization  **80**, 81, 199, 215, 216, 220, 221, 244
specie  **111**, 114
speculators  **213**
Spencer, Herbert  11
**Stalin, Joseph**  246, 276, 327, **350**, 351–353, 357
Standard Oil  171
Standard Oil Trust  **169**, 170
state corporatism  **311**, 326, 327, 328, 331, 351, 358
statists  **333**
stock exchange  8, **211**, 212, 213, 357
stock market  77, 121, 122, 139, **211**, 212, 213, 317, 357
store credit  **176**
Stover, John F.  180
subinfeudination  **262**
supply  **133**, 134
supply and demand  87, 110, 125, 129, 130, 133, 135–142, 149, 157, 159, 190, 227, 230, 232, 233, 241, 347
    graphs  **134–135**
surpluses  67, 70
    allegations about  67
surplus of labor  **152**, 153, 154, 339, 341
Sweden  274, 282, 324, 325
syndicalist  5

# T

tangible property  **30**, 52
tariff  **31**, 174, 279, 284, 296, 303, 315
    for revenue  **31**
    protective  **31**, 146–147, 249, 250, 253, 260, 282, 283, 304, 313, 314, 315, 319
taxes
    corporate income  32, 252, 317
    excise. *See* excise tax
    graduated income. *See* graduated income tax
    head. *See also* head tax
    necessity for  29
    sales tax. *See* sales tax
    tariff. *See* tariff
Taylor, A. J. P.  243
Teamster  150, 151
technological unemployment  201
technology  51, 66, 69, 99, 126, 134, 172, 175, 190, 196, 199, 200, 201, 206, 214, 215, 217, 218, 219, 228, 236, 242, 244, 250, 251, 253, 265, 269, 273, 327, 351
Tennessee Valley Authority  166, 167
thaler  **97**
Thatcher, Margaret  **338**
*The Affluent Society*  68, 177
*The Age of Reform*  300
*The American Epoch*  183
*The American Spectator*  159
The Bank of England Act of 1946  336
"The Candlemakers' Petition"  146

*The Century of Revolution* 277
*The Communist Manifesto* **67**
*The Economic Problem* 170
The Foundation for Economic Education 80
*The Freeman* 310
theft 24, 55, **73–74**, 96, 228, 237, 349
    by government 81, 82, 83, 84
*The Greeks* 16
*The Harmony of the World* 16
*The Life and Decline of the American Railroad* 181
The National Labor Relations Act 183, 341
the Netherlands 274
theology **6**, 8
*The Rosa Luxemburg Contraceptive Cooperative* 356
*The Russians* 358
*The Travels of Marco Polo* 99
*The Ultimate Foundations of Economic Science* 51
*The United States in 1800* 300
*The War on the Poor* 84
*The Wealth of Nations* **17**, 23, 80
*The Workshop of the World* 296, 297
Thieblot, Jr., Armand J. 151
Thompson, David 299
Thompson, James W. 267
thrifty 4, 63, **64**
*Time* 150, 233
time preference **121**, 122, 233, 234
tithe 265
totalitarian **6**, 40, 172, 246, 259, 286, 291, 309, 349, 354
    socialism 246
trade
    international 241, 243, 244, 245, 247, 248, 249, 251, 252, 297
Transportation Act of 1920 182, 316
trust **164**
Tucker, William 159
Tugwell, Rexford G. 67, 68
Tyrmand, Leopold 356

# U

unconstitutional 84, 183, 317
unemployment 65, 67, 70, 83
Union Pacific Railroad 315
*Union Violence* 151
United Kingdom (England, Scotland, and Wales) 243
United States Postal Service 165, 166, 172
unit of account 94, **97**
universal evolution 11
universal principles **4**, 5–7
user fee **29**
USSR 328. *See also* Soviet Union
usury 232, 233
util 45
utilitarianism **45**, 46

# V

variable costs **174**, 175
vassal 262, 263, 266
Veblen, Thorstein 67
Voltaire 294
voluntary 23, 25, 73, 74, 75, 77, 81, 94, 155, 165, 166, 306, 327, 328, 344

# W

wages 27, 51, 82, 107, 108, 109, 130, 131, 132, **141**, 142, 145, 146, 149, 151–159, 172, 183, 193, 201, 215, 227, 230, 231, 232, 234, 235, 236, 244, 252, 253, 269, 286, 299, 300, 304, 334, 339, 340, 341, 355
want **79**
warehouse receipt **100**
War for Independence 111, 115
War of the Austrian Succession 285
War of the Roses 273
War of the Spanish Succession 285
Washington, George 27, 39, 112, 148, 241
Watt, James 295
wealth 8, 17, 30, 32, 42, 43, 56, 66, 68, 82, 83, 84
Webb, Sidney 334
**Webster, Pelatiah 7**
welfare 18, 40, 74, 82, 83, 84, 147, 182, 246, 252, 315, 325, 334, 338, **339**, 340, 341, 342, 343, 344
welfarism 251, 252, 325, 331, **332**, 338, 339, 341, 342, 343, 344, 347
White, Andrew Dickson 114, 115
Whitney, Eli 199
Wilson, James 116
Wilson, Woodrow 117, 170
withholding **32**, 149
Witney, Fred 154
Woodward, Llewellyn 300
Woolens Act 279
work 3, 44, 56, 65, 66, 74, 76–77, 81, 83, 91, 132–133, 141, 149–150, 153, 155–158, 190, 194, 196–197, 207, 215–222, 226–227, 230–231
    nature of 4
workshop of the world 296, 297, 300
World War I 153, 180, 181, 245, 246, 296, 303, 315, 334, 337, 350
World War II 43, 116, 159, 245–248, 334, 337, 338, 342, 348

# Z

zoning laws **218**

## About the Authors:

**The Late Clarence B. Carson** held a Ph.D. in history from Vanderbilt. During his career he published fifteen books and more than 500 articles and reviews. He was the consummate gentleman scholar.

**Paul A. Cleveland** is a Professor of Economics and Finance at Birmingham-Southern College. He is the author of several books and numerous articles. He has traveled internationally and lectured widely on economic and political freedom.

We at Boundary Stone would love to hear from you.
Please send your comments or questions to us:

P.O. Box 19515
Birmingham, AL 35219
www.boundarystone.org